Lecture Notes in Computer Science 2986

Edited by G. Goos, J. Hartmanis, and J. van Leeuwen

Springer
Berlin
Heidelberg
New York
Hong Kong
London
Milan
Paris
Tokyo

David Schmidt (Ed.)

Programming Languages and Systems

13th European Symposium on Programming, ESOP 2004
Held as Part of the Joint European Conferences
on Theory and Practice of Software, ETAPS 2004
Barcelona, Spain, March 29 – April 2, 2004
Proceedings

Springer

Series Editors

Gerhard Goos, Karlsruhe University, Germany
Juris Hartmanis, Cornell University, NY, USA
Jan van Leeuwen, Utrecht University, The Netherlands

Volume Editor

David Schmidt
Kansas State University, Department of Computing and Information Sciences
234 Nichols Hall, Manhattan, KS 66506, USA
E-mail: schmidt@cis.ksu.edu

Library of Congress Control Number: 2004102322

CR Subject Classification (1998): D.3, D.1, D.2, F.3, F.4, E.1

ISSN 0302-9743
ISBN 3-540-21313-9 Springer-Verlag Berlin Heidelberg New York

Springer-Verlag is a part of Springer Science+Business Media

springeronline.com

Printed in Germany

Typesetting: Camera-ready by author, data conversion by PTP-Berlin, Protago-TeX-Production GmbH
Printed on acid-free paper SPIN: 10994481 06/3142 5 4 3 2 1 0

Foreword

ETAPS 2004 was the seventh instance of the European Joint Conferences on Theory and Practice of Software. ETAPS is an annual federated conference that was established in 1998 by combining a number of existing and new conferences. This year it comprised five conferences (FOSSACS, FASE, ESOP, CC, TACAS), 23 satellite workshops, 1 tutorial, and 7 invited lectures (not including those that are specific to the satellite events).

The events that comprise ETAPS address various aspects of the system development process, including specification, design, implementation analysis and improvement. The languages, methodologies and tools that support these activities are all well within its scope. Different blends of theory and practice are represented, with an inclination towards theory with a practical motivation on the one hand and soundly based practice on the other. Many of the issues involved in software design apply to systems in general, including hardware systems, and the emphasis on software is not intended to be exclusive.

ETAPS is a loose confederation in which each event retains its own identity, with a separate program committee and independent proceedings. Its format is open-ended, allowing it to grow and evolve as time goes by. Contributed talks and system demonstrations are in synchronized parallel sessions, with invited lectures in plenary sessions. Two of the invited lectures are reserved for "unifying" talks on topics of interest to the whole range of ETAPS attendees. The aim of cramming all this activity into a single one-week meeting is to create a strong magnet for academic and industrial researchers working on topics within its scope, giving them the opportunity to learn about research in related areas, and thereby to foster new and existing links between work in areas that were formerly addressed in separate meetings.

ETAPS 2004 was organized by the LSI Department of the Catalonia Technical University (UPC), in cooperation with:

European Association for Theoretical Computer Science (EATCS)
European Association for Programming Languages and Systems (EAPLS)
European Association of Software Science and Technology (EASST)
ACM SIGACT, SIGSOFT and SIGPLAN

The organizing team comprised

Jordi Cortadella (Satellite Events), Nikos Mylonakis, Robert Nieuwenhuis, Fernando Orejas (Chair), Edelmira Pasarella, Sonia Perez, Elvira Pino, Albert Rubio

and had the assistance of TILESA OPC.
ETAPS 2004 received generous sponsorship from:

UPC, Spanish Ministry of Science and Technology (MCYT), Catalan Department for Universities, Research and Information Society (DURSI), IBM, Intel.

Overall planning for ETAPS conferences is the responsibility of its Steering Committee, whose current membership is:

Ratislav Bodik (Berkeley), Maura Cerioli (Genoa), Evelyn Duesterwald (IBM, Yorktown Heights), Hartmut Ehrig (Berlin), José Fiadeiro (Leicester), Marie-Claude Gaudel (Paris), Andy Gordon (Microsoft Research, Cambridge), Roberto Gorrieri (Bologna), Nicolas Halbwachs (Grenoble), Gûrel Hedin (Lund), Kurt Jensen (Aarhus), Paul Klint (Amsterdam), Tiziana Margaria (Dortmund), Ugo Montanari (Pisa), Hanne Riis Nielson (Copenhagen), Fernando Orejas (Barcelona), Mauro Pezzè (Milan), Andreas Podelski (Saarbrücken), Mooly Sagiv (Tel Aviv), Don Sannella (Edinburgh), Vladimiro Sassone (Sussex), David Schmidt (Kansas), Bernhard Steffen (Dortmund), Perdita Stevens (Edinburgh), Andrzej Tarlecki (Warsaw), Igor Walukiewicz (Bordeaux), Michel Wermelinger (Lisbon)

I would like to express my sincere gratitude to all of these people and organizations, the program committee chairs and PC members of the ETAPS conferences, the organizers of the satellite events, the speakers themselves, and finally Springer-Verlag for agreeing to publish the ETAPS proceedings. This year, the number of submissions approached 600, making acceptance rates fall to 25%. I congratulate the authors who made it into the final program! I hope that all the other authors still found a way of participating in this exciting event and I hope you will continue submitting.

In 2005, ETAPS will be organized by Don Sannella in Edinburgh. You will be welcomed by another "local": my successor as ETAPS Steering Committee Chair – Perdita Stevens. My wish is that she will enjoy coordinating the next three editions of ETAPS as much as I have. It is not an easy job, in spite of what Don assured me when I succeeded him! But it is definitely a very rewarding one. One cannot help but feel proud of seeing submission and participation records being broken one year after the other, and that the technical program reached the levels of quality that we have been witnessing. At the same time, interacting with the organizers has been a particularly rich experience. Having organized the very first edition of ETAPS in Lisbon in 1998, I knew what they were going through, and I can tell you that each of them put his/her heart, soul, and an incredible amount of effort into the organization. The result, as we all know, was brilliant on all counts! Therefore, my last words are to thank Susanne Graf (2002), Andrzej Tarlecki and Paweł Urzyczyn (2003), and Fernando Orejas (2004) for the privilege of having worked with them.

Leicester, January 2004

José Luiz Fiadeiro
ETAPS Steering Committee Chairman

Preface

This volume contains the 28 papers presented at ESOP 2004, the 13th European Symposium on Programming, which took place in Barcelona, Spain, March 29–31, 2004. The ESOP series began in 1986 with the goal of bridging the gap between theory and practice, and the conferences continue to be devoted to explaining fundamental issues in the specification, analysis, and implementation of programming languages and systems.

The volume begins with a summary of an invited contribution by Peter O'Hearn, titled *Resources, Concurrency and Local Reasoning*, and continues with the 27 papers selected by the Program Committee from 118 submissions.

Each submission was reviewed by at least three referees, and papers were selected during a ten-day electronic discussion phase. I would like to sincerely thank the members of the Program Committee, as well as their subreferees, for their diligent work; Torben Amtoft, for helping me collect the papers for the proceedings; and Tiziana Margaria, Bernhard Steffen, and their colleagues at METAFrame, for the use of their conference management software.

David Schmidt
Program Chair
ESOP 2004

Organization

Program Committee

Torben Amtoft	Kansas State University (USA)
Henri Bal	Vrije Universiteit (Netherlands)
Radhia Cousot	École Polytechnique (France)
Pierpaolo Degano	Università di Pisa (Italy)
Mariangiola Dezani-Ciancaglini	Università di Torino (Italy)
Pascal Fradet	INRIA Rhône-Alpes (France)
Michael Gordon	University of Cambridge (UK)
Eric Goubault	CEA/Saclay (France)
Joshua Guttman	MITRE (USA)
Fritz Henglein	University of Copenhagen (Denmark)
Matthew Hennessy	University of Sussex (UK)
Markus Müller-Olm	Universität Hagen (Germany)
Martin Odersky	École Polytechnique Fédérale de Lausanne (Switzerland)
German Puebla	Technical University of Madrid (Spain)
David Schmidt	Kansas State University (USA)
Michael Schwartzbach	University of Aarhus (Denmark)
Harald Søndergaard	University of Melbourne (Australia)
Peter Thiemann	Universität Freiburg (Germany)
Mitchell Wand	Northeastern University (USA)
Kwangkeun Yi	Seoul National University (Korea)

Referees

Mads Sig Ager, Elvira Albert, Thomas Ambus, Ki-yung Ahn, Ricardo Baeza-Yates, Roberto Bagnara, Harald James Bailey, Steffen Bakel, Massimo Bartoletti, Josh Berdine, Martin Berger, Frederic Besson, Massimo Bartoletti, Lorenzo Bettini, Bruno Blanchet, Chiara Bodei, Viviana Bono, Mikael Buchholtz, Michele Bugliesi, Emir Burak, Lilian Burdy, Marzia Buscemi, Daniel Cabeza, Luis Caires, Manuel Carro, Rohit Chadha, Manuel Chakravarty, Byeong-Mo Chang, Aske Simon Chistensen, Woongsik Choi, Damien Ciabrini, Ana Cristina Vieira de Melo, Mario Coppo, Andrea Corradini, Patrick Cousot, Silvia Crafa, Vincent Cremet, Michele Curti, Vincent Danos, Kyung-Goo Doh, Guillaume Dufay, Hyunjun Eo, Francois Fages, Manuel Fähndrich, Matthias Felleisen, Jérôme Feret, Mary Fernandez, GianLuigi Ferrari, Kathleen Fisher, Matthew Flatt, Riccardo Focardi, Cedric Fournet, Alain Frisch, Carsten Führmann, Fabio Gadducci, Vladimir Gapeyev, Martin Gasbichler, Thomas Genet, Roberto Giacobazzi, Paola Giannini, Mariangiola Elio Giovannetti, Alain Girault, Roberto Gorrieri, Jean Goubault-Larrecq, Dick Grune, Stefano Guerrini, John Hatcliff, Simon Helsen, Fergus Henderson, Angel Herranz, Christoph Herrmann, Jonathan Herzog, Michael Thomas Hildebrandt, Ralf Hinze, Daniel Hirschkoff, Tom Hirschowitz, Frank Huch, Paul Hudak, Sebastian Hunt, Charles Hymans, Ceriel Jacobs, Alan Jeffrey, Johan Jeuring, Neil Jones, Hyun-Goo Kang, Jeroen Ketema, Iksoon Kim, Andy King, Christian Kirkegaard, Oleg Kiselyov, Dexter Kozen, Karl Krukow, Ralf Laemmel, Cosimo Laneve, Oukseh Lee, Ugo de' Liguoro, Jim Lipton, Francesco Logozzo, Michele Loreti, Henning Makholm, Julio Mariño, Matthieu Martel, Damien Massé, Laurent Mauborgne, Richard Mayr, Edison Mera, Nikolay Mihaylov, Dale Miller, Antoine Miné, Alberto Momiglliano, Benjamin Monate, David Monniaux, Anders Møller, Jose F. Morales, Peter Müller, Harald Lee Naish, George Necula, Matthias Neubauer, Oliver Niese, Henrik Nilsson, Henning Niss, Thomas Noll, Peter O'Hearn, Peter Padawitz, Benjamin Pierce, Adolfo Piperno, Marco Pistore, Enrico Pontelli, Bernard Pope, Rosario Pugliese, John Ramsdell, Femke Raamsdonk, Olivier Ridoux, Xavier Rival, Simona Ronchi Della Rocca, Andreas Rossberg, Oliver Rüthing, Eric Rutten, Luca Roversi, Jean-Claude Royer, Sukyoung Ryu, Jaime Sanchez-Hernandez, Dave Sands, Vladimiro Sassone, Helmut Seidl, Harald R. Sekar, Sunae Seo, Alexander Serebrenik, Manuel Serrano, Wendelin Serwe, Peter Sestoft, Peter Sewell, Nikolay Shilov, Seung-Cheol Shin, Detlef Sieling, Axel Simon, Élodie-Jane Sims, Jan-Georg Smaus, Christian Stefansen, Erik Stenman, Peter Stuckey, Josef Svenningsson, Vipin Swarup, Nik Swoboda, Lucy Mari Tabuti, Javier Thayer, Simone Tini, Franklyn Turbak, Pawel Urzyczyn, Frank D. Valencia, Vasco Vasconcelos, Roel de Vrijer, Joe Wells, Hongseok Yang, Nobuko Yoshida, Matthias Zenger, Roberto Zunino

Table of Contents

Resources, Concurrency, and Local Reasoning
(Abstract)

Peter W. O'Hearn

Queen Mary, University of London

In the 1960s Dijkstra suggested that, in order to limit the complexity of potential process interactions, concurrent programs should be designed so that different processes behave independently, except at rare moments of synchronization [3]. Then, in the 1970s Hoare and Brinch Hansen argued that debugging and reasoning about concurrent programs could be considerably simplified using compiler-enforceable syntactic constraints that preclude interference [4,1]; scope restrictions were described which had the effect that all process interaction was mediated by a critical region or monitor. Based on such restrictions Hoare described proof rules for shared-variable concurrency that were beautifully modular [4]: one could reason locally about a process, and simple syntactic checks ensured that no other process could tamper with its state in a way that invalidated the local reasoning.

The major problem with Hoare and Brinch Hansen's proposal is that its scope-based approach to resource separation is too restrictive for many realistic programs. It does not apply to flexible but unstructured constructs such as semaphores, and the syntactic checks it relies on are insufficient to rule out interference in the presence of pointers and aliasing. Proof methods were subsequently developed which allow reasoning in the presence of interference [9,10,5], and the reasoning that they support is much more powerful that that of [4], but also much less modular.

There is thus a mismatch, between the intuitive basis of concurrent programming with resources, where separation remains a vital design idea, and formal techniques for reasoning about such programs, where methods based on separation are severely limited. The purpose of this work is to revisit these issues, using the recent formalism of separation logic [11]. The general point is that by using a logic of resources [7] rather than syntactic constraints we can overcome the limitations of scope-based approaches, while retaining their modular character. We describe a variation on the proof rules of Hoare for contitional critical regions, using the "separating conjunction" connective to preclude pointer-based interference. With the modified rules we can at once handle many examples where a linked data structure rather than, say, an array is used within a process, or within a data abstraction that mediates interprocess interaction.

The rules have a further interesting effect when a data abstraction keeps track of pointers as part of its data, rather than just as part of its implementation. The separating conjunction allows us to partition memory in a dynamically reconfigurable way, extending the static partioning done by critical regions or monitors when there is no heap. This enables us to handle a number of subtler

D.A. Schmidt (Ed.): ESOP 2004, LNCS 2986, pp. 1–2, 2004.

programs, where a pointer is transferred from one process to another, or between a process and a monitor, and the ownership of the storage pointed to transfers with it. Ownership transfer is common in systems programs. For example, interaction with a memory manager results in pieces of storage transferring between the manager and its clients as allocation and deallocation operations are performed [8]. Another typical example is efficient message passing, where a pointer is transferred from one process to another in order to avoid copying large pieces of data.

Dynamic partitioning turns out also to be the key to treating lower level, unstructured constructs which do not use explicit critical regions. In particular, our formalism supports a view of semaphores as ownership transformers, that (logically) release and seize portions of storage in addition to their (operational) behaviour as counting-based synchronizers. Local reasoning [6] is possible in such a situation because dynamic, non scope-based, uses of semaphores to protect resources are matched by the dynamic, non scope-based, approach to resource separation provided by separation logic.

A special role in this work is played by "precise" assertions, which are ones that unambiguously specify a portion of storage (an assertion is precise if, for any given heap, there is at most one subheap that satisfies it). Precision is essential for the soundness of the proof rules, which work by decomposing the state in a system into that owned by various processes and resources (or monitors). Precise assertions fulfill a similar role in recent work on information hiding [8], and are used by Brookes in his semantic analysis of our concurrency proof rules [2].

References

[1] P. Brinch Hansen. *Operating System Principles.* Prentice Hall, 1973.

[2] S. D. Brookes. A semantics for concurrent separation logic. Draft of 7/25/03, 2003.

[3] E. W. Dijkstra. Cooperating sequential processes. In F. Genuys, editor, *Programming Languages*, pages 43–112. Academic Press, 1968.

[4] C. A. R. Hoare. Towards a theory of parallel programming. In Hoare and Perrot, editors, *Operating Systems Techniques.* Academic Press, 1972.

[5] C. B. Jones. Specification and design of (parallel) programs. *IFIP Conference*, 1983.

[6] P. O'Hearn, J. Reynolds, and H. Yang. Local reasoning about programs that alter data structures. In *Proceedings of 15th Annual Conference of the European Association for Computer Science Logic*, LNCS, pages 1–19. Springer-Verlag, 2001.

[7] P. W. O'Hearn and D. J. Pym. The logic of bunched implications. *Bulletin of Symbolic Logic*, 5(2):215–244, June 99.

[8] P. W. O'Hearn, H. Yang, and J. C. Reynolds. Separation and information hiding. In *31st POPL*, pages 268–280, Venice, January 2004.

[9] S. Owicki and D. Gries. An axiomatic proof technique for parallel programs. *Acta Informatica*, (19):319–340, 1976.

[10] A. Pnueli. The temporal semantics of concurrent programs. Theoretical Computer Science, 13(1), 45–60, 1981.

[11] J. C. Reynolds. Separation logic: a logic for shared mutable data structures. Invited Paper, LICS'02, 2002.

Relational Abstract Domains for the Detection of Floating-Point Run-Time Errors*

Antoine Miné

DI-École Normale Supérieure de Paris, France,
mine@di.ens.fr

Abstract. We present a new idea to adapt relational abstract domains to the analysis of IEEE 754-compliant floating-point numbers in order to statically detect, through Abstract Interpretation-based static analyses, potential floating-point run-time exceptions such as overflows or invalid operations. In order to take the non-linearity of rounding into account, expressions are modeled as linear forms with interval coefficients. We show how to extend already existing numerical abstract domains, such as the octagon abstract domain, to efficiently abstract transfer functions based on interval linear forms. We discuss specific fixpoint stabilization techniques and give some experimental results.

1 Introduction

It is a well-established fact, since the failure of the Ariane 5 launcher in 1996, that run-time errors in critical embedded software can cause great financial—and human—losses. Nowadays, embedded software is becoming more and more complex. One particular trend is to abandon fixed-point arithmetics in favor of floating-point computations. Unfortunately, floating-point models are quite complex and features such as rounding and special numbers (infinities, *NaN*, etc.) are not always understood by programmers. This has already led to catastrophic behaviors, such as the Patriot missile story told in [16].

Much work is concerned about the *precision* of the computations, that is to say, characterizing the amount and cause of drift between a computation on perfect reals and the corresponding floating-point implementation. Ours is *not*. We seek to prove that an exceptional behavior (such as division by zero or overflow) will not occur in any execution of the analyzed program. While this is a simpler problem, our goal is to scale up to programs of hundreds of thousands of lines with full data coverage and very few (even none) false alarms.

Our framework is that of Abstract Interpretation, a generic framework for designing sound static analyses that already features many instances [6,7]. We adapt existing relational numerical abstract domains (generally designed for the analysis of integer arithmetics) to cope with floating-point arithmetics. The need for such domains appeared during the successful design of a commissioned special-purpose prototype analyzer for a critical embedded avionics

* This work was partially supported by the ASTRÉE RNTL project.

D.A. Schmidt (Ed.): ESOP 2004, LNCS 2986, pp. 3–17, 2004.

system. Interval analysis, used in a first prototype [3], proved too coarse because error-freeness of the analyzed code depends on tests that are inherently poorly abstracted in non-relational abstract domains. We also had to design special-purpose widenings and narrowings to compensate for the pervasive rounding errors, not only in the analyzed program, but also introduced by our efficient abstractions. These techniques were implemented in our second prototype whose overall design was presented in [4]. The present paper focuses on improvements and novel unpublished ideas; it is also more generic.

2 Related Work

Abstract Domains. A key component in Abstract-Interpretation-based analyses is the abstract domain which is a computer-representable class of program invariants together with some operators to manipulate them: transfer functions for guards and assignments, a control-flow join operator, and fixpoint acceleration operators (such as widenings $\triangledown$ and narrowings $\vartriangle$) aiming at the correct and efficient analysis of loops. One of the simplest yet useful abstract domain is the widespread interval domain [6]. Relational domains, which are more precise, include Cousot and Halbwachs's polyhedron domain [8] (corresponding to invariants of the form $\sum c_i v_i \leq c$), Miné's octagon domain [14] ($\pm v_i \pm v_j \leq c$), and Simon's two variables per inequality domain [15] ($\alpha v_i + \beta v_j \leq c$). Even though the underlying algorithms for these relational domains allow them to abstract sets of reals as well as sets of integers, their efficient implementation—in a maybe approximate but sound way—using floating-point numbers remains a challenge. Moreover, these relational domains do not support abstracting floating-point expressions, but only expressions on perfect integers, rationals, or reals.

Floating-Point Analyses. Much work on floating-point is dedicated to the analysis of the precision of the computations and the origins of the rounding errors. The CESTAC method [17] is widely used, but also much debated as it is based on a probabilistic model of error distribution and thus cannot give sound answers. An interval-based Abstract Interpretation for error terms is proposed in [1]. Some authors [11,13] go one step further by allowing error terms to be related in relational, even non-linear, domains. Unfortunately, this extra precision does not help when analyzing programs whose correctness also depends upon relations between variables and not only error terms (such as programs with inequality tests, as in Fig. 3).

Our Work. We first present our IEEE 754-based computation model (Sect. 3) and recall the classical interval analysis adapted to floating-point numbers (Sect. 4). We present, in Sect. 5, an abstraction of floating-point expressions in terms of interval linear forms over the real field and use it to refine the interval domain. Sect. 6 shows how some relational abstract domains can be efficiently adapted to work on these linear forms. Sect. 7 presents adapted widening and narrowing techniques. Finally, some experimental results are shown in Sect. 8.

3 IEEE 754-Based Floating-Point Model

We present in this section the concrete floating-point arithmetics model that we wish to analyze and which is based on the widespread IEEE 754-1985 [5] norm.

3.1 IEEE 754 Floating-Point Numbers

The binary representation of a IEEE 754 number is composed of three fields:

- a 1-bit sign s;
- an exponent $e - \mathbf{bias}$, represented by a biased $\mathbf{e}$-bit unsigned integer e;
- a fraction $f = .b_1 \dots b_\mathbf{p}$, represented by a $\mathbf{p}$-bit unsigned integer.

The values $\mathbf{e}$, $\mathbf{bias}$, and $\mathbf{p}$ are format-specific. We will denote by $\mathbf{F}$ the set of all available formats and by $\mathbf{f} = \mathbf{32}$ the 32-bit *single* format ($\mathbf{e} = 8$, $\mathbf{bias} = 127$, and $\mathbf{p} = 23$). Floating-point numbers belong to one of the following categories:

- *normalized* numbers $(-1)^s \times 2^{2-\mathbf{bias}} \times 1.f$, when $1 \leq e \leq 2^\mathbf{e} - 2$;
- *denormalized* numbers $(-1)^s \times 2^{1-\mathbf{bias}} \times 0.f$, when $e = 0$ and $f \neq 0$;
- $+0$ or -0 (depending on s), when $e = 0$ and $f = 0$;
- $+\infty$ or $-\infty$ (depending on s), when $e = 2^\mathbf{e} - 1$ and $f = 0$;
- error codes (so-called *NaN*), when $e = 2^\mathbf{e} - 1$ and $f \neq 0$.

For each format $\mathbf{f} \in \mathbf{F}$ we define in particular:

- $mf_\mathbf{f} = 2^{1-\mathbf{bias}-\mathbf{p}}$ the smallest non-zero positive number;
- $Mf_\mathbf{f} = (2 - 2^{-\mathbf{p}})2^{2^\mathbf{e}-\mathbf{bias}-2}$, the largest non-infinity number.

The special values $+\infty$ and $-\infty$ may be generated as a result of operations undefined on $\mathbb{R}$ (such as $1/{+0}$), or when a result's absolute value overflows $Mf_\mathbf{f}$. Other undefined operations (such as $+0/{+0}$) result in a *NaN* (that stands for *Not A Number*). The sign of 0 serves only to distinguish between $1/{+0} = +\infty$ and $1/{-0} = -\infty$; $+0$ and -0 are indistinguishable in all other contexts (even comparison).

Due to the limited number of digits, the result of a floating-point operation needs to be rounded. IEEE 754 provides four rounding modes: towards 0, towards $+\infty$, towards $-\infty$, and to nearest. Depending on this mode, either the floating-point number directly smaller or directly larger than the exact real result is chosen (possibly $+\infty$ or $-\infty$). Rounding can build infinities from non-infinities operands (this is called *overflow*), and it may return zero when the absolute value of the result is too small (this is called *underflow*). Because of this rounding phase, most algebraic properties of $\mathbb{R}$, such as associativity and distributivity, are lost. However, the opposite of a number is always exactly represented (unlike what happens in two-complement integer arithmetics), and comparison operators are also exact. See [10] for a description of the classical properties and pitfalls of the floating-point arithmetics.

3.2 Custom Floating-Point Computation Model

We focus our analysis on the large class of programs that treat floating-point arithmetics as a practical approximation to the mathematical reals $\mathbb{R}$: roundings and underflows are tolerated, but not overflows, divisions by zero or invalid operations, which are considered run-time errors and halt the program. Our goal is to detect such behaviors. In this context, $+\infty$, $-\infty$, and *NaN*s can never

$$R_{\mathbf{f},+\infty}(x) = \begin{cases} \Omega & \text{if } x > Mf_{\mathbf{f}} \\ \min\{y \in \mathbb{F}_{\mathbf{f}} \mid y \geq x\} & \text{otherwise} \end{cases}$$

$$R_{\mathbf{f},-\infty}(x) = \begin{cases} \Omega & \text{if } x < -Mf_{\mathbf{f}} \\ \max\{y \in \mathbb{F}_{\mathbf{f}} \mid y \leq x\} & \text{otherwise} \end{cases}$$

$$R_{\mathbf{f},0}(x) = \begin{cases} \min\{y \in \mathbb{F}_{\mathbf{f}} \mid y \geq x\} & \text{if } x \leq 0 \\ \max\{y \in \mathbb{F}_{\mathbf{f}} \mid y \leq x\} & \text{if } x \geq 0 \end{cases}$$

$$R_{\mathbf{f},n}(x) = \begin{cases} \Omega & \text{if } |x| \geq (2 - 2^{-\mathbf{p}-1})2^{2^{\mathbf{e}}-\mathbf{bias}-2} \\ Mf_{\mathbf{f}} & \text{else if } x \geq Mf_{\mathbf{f}} \\ -Mf_{\mathbf{f}} & \text{else if } x \leq -Mf_{\mathbf{f}} \\ R_{\mathbf{f},-\infty}(x) & \text{else if } |R_{\mathbf{f},-\infty}(x) - x| < |R_{\mathbf{f},+\infty}(x) - x| \\ R_{\mathbf{f},+\infty}(x) & \text{else if } |R_{\mathbf{f},+\infty}(x) - x| < |R_{\mathbf{f},-\infty}(x) - x| \\ R_{\mathbf{f},-\infty}(x) & \text{else if } R_{\mathbf{f},-\infty}(x)\text{'s least significant bit is 0} \\ R_{\mathbf{f},+\infty}(x) & \text{else if } R_{\mathbf{f},+\infty}(x)\text{'s least significant bit is 0} \end{cases}$$

Fig. 1. Rounding functions, extracted from [5].

$$\begin{array}{lll}
[\![const_{\mathbf{f},\mathbf{r}}(c)]\!]\rho = R_{\mathbf{f},\mathbf{r}}(c) & & \\
[\![v]\!]\rho & = \rho(v) & \\
[\![cast_{\mathbf{f},\mathbf{r}}(e)]\!]\rho & = R_{\mathbf{f},\mathbf{r}}([\![e]\!]\rho) & \text{if } [\![e]\!]\rho \neq \Omega \\
[\![e_1 \odot_{\mathbf{f},\mathbf{r}} e_2]\!]\rho & = R_{\mathbf{f},\mathbf{r}}(([\![e_1]\!]\rho) \cdot ([\![e_2]\!]\rho)) & \text{if } [\![e_1]\!]\rho, [\![e_2]\!]\rho \neq \Omega,\ \cdot \in \{+,-,\times\} \\
[\![e_1 \oslash_{\mathbf{f},\mathbf{r}} e_2]\!]\rho & = R_{\mathbf{f},\mathbf{r}}(([\![e_1]\!]\rho)/([\![e_2]\!]\rho)) & \text{if } [\![e_1]\!]\rho \neq \Omega,\ [\![e_2]\!]\rho \notin \{0, \Omega\} \\
[\![\ominus e]\!]\rho & = -([\![e]\!]\rho) & \text{if } [\![e]\!]\rho \neq \Omega \\
[\![expr_{\mathbf{f}}]\!]\rho & = \Omega & \text{in all other cases}
\end{array}$$

Fig. 2. Expression concrete semantics, extracted from [5].

be created and, as a consequence, the difference between $+0$ and -0 becomes irrelevant. For every format $\mathbf{f} \in \mathbf{F}$, the set of floating-point numbers will be assimilated to a finite subset of $\mathbb{R}$ denoted by $\mathbb{F}_{\mathbf{f}}$. The grammar of floating-point expressions of format $\mathbf{f}$ includes constants, variables $v \in \mathcal{V}_{\mathbf{f}}$ of format $\mathbf{f}$, casts (conversion from another format), binary and unary arithmetic operators (circled in order to distinguish them from the corresponding operators on reals):

$$\begin{array}{rcll}
expr_{\mathbf{f}} & :== & const_{\mathbf{f},\mathbf{r}}(c) & c \in \mathbb{R} \\
& | & v & v \in \mathcal{V}_{\mathbf{f}} \\
& | & cast_{\mathbf{f},\mathbf{r}}(expr_{\mathbf{f}'}) & \\
& | & expr_{\mathbf{f}} \odot_{\mathbf{f},\mathbf{r}} expr_{\mathbf{f}} & \odot \in \{\oplus, \ominus, \otimes, \oslash\} \\
& | & \ominus expr_{\mathbf{f}} &
\end{array}$$

Some constructs are tagged with a floating-point format $\mathbf{f} \in \mathbf{F}$ and a rounding mode $\mathbf{r} \in \{n, 0, +\infty, -\infty\}$ (n representing rounding to nearest). A notable exception is the unary minus $\ominus$ which does not incur rounding and never results in a run-time error as all the $\mathbb{F}_{\mathbf{f}}$s are perfectly symmetric.

An environment $\rho \in \prod_{\mathbf{f} \in \mathbf{F}} (\mathcal{V}_{\mathbf{f}} \to \mathbb{F}_{\mathbf{f}})$ is a function that associates to each variable a floating-point value of the corresponding format. Fig. 2 gives the concrete semantics $[\![expr_{\mathbf{f}}]\!]\rho \in \mathbb{F}_{\mathbf{f}} \cup \{\Omega\}$ of the expression $expr_{\mathbf{f}}$ in the environment ρ: it can be a number or the run-time error Ω. This semantics uses solely the regular operators $+,-,\times,/$ on real numbers and the rounding function $R_{\mathbf{f},\mathbf{r}} : \mathbb{R} \rightarrow \mathbb{F}_{\mathbf{f}} \cup \{\Omega\}$ defined in Fig. 1. It corresponds exactly to the IEEE 754 norm [5] where the overflow, division by zero, and invalid operation exception traps abort the system with a run-time error.

4 Floating-Point Interval Analysis

Floating-Point Interval Arithmetics. The idea of interval arithmetics is to over-approximate a set of numbers by an interval represented by its lower and upper bounds. For each format $\mathbf{f}$, we will denote by $\mathbb{I}_{\mathbf{f}}$ the set of real intervals with bounds in $\mathbb{F}_{\mathbf{f}}$. As $\mathbb{F}_{\mathbf{f}}$ is totally ordered and bounded, any subset of $\mathbb{F}_{\mathbf{f}}$ can be abstracted by an element of $\mathbb{I}_{\mathbf{f}}$. Moreover, as *all rounding functions* $R_{\mathbf{f},\mathbf{r}}$ *are monotonic*, we can compute the bounds of any expression using pointing-point operations only, ensuring efficient implementation within an analyzer. A first idea is to use the very same format and rounding mode in the abstract as in the concrete, which would give, for instance, the following addition (Ω denoting a run-time error):

$$[a^-;a^+] \oplus^\sharp_{\mathbf{f},\mathbf{r}} [b^-;b^+] = \begin{cases} \Omega & \text{if } a^- \oplus_{\mathbf{f},\mathbf{r}} b^- = \Omega \text{ or } a^+ \oplus_{\mathbf{f},\mathbf{r}} b^+ = \Omega \\ [a^- \oplus_{\mathbf{f},\mathbf{r}} b^-; a^+ \oplus_{\mathbf{f},\mathbf{r}} b^+] & \text{otherwise} \end{cases}$$

A drawback of this semantics is that it requires the analyzer to determine, for each instruction, which rounding mode $\mathbf{r}$ and which format $\mathbf{f}$ are used. This may be difficult as the rounding mode can be changed at run-time by a system call, and compilers are authorized to perform parts of computations using a more precise IEEE format that what is required by the programmer (on Intel x86, all floating-point registers are 80-bit wide and rounding to the user-specified format occurs only when the results are stored into memory). Unfortunately, using in the abstract a floating-point format different from the one used in the concrete computation is not sound.

The following semantics, inspired from the one presented in [11], solves these problems by providing an approximation that is independent from the concrete rounding mode (assuming always the worst: towards $-\infty$ for the lower bound and towards $+\infty$ for the upper bound):

- $const^\sharp_{\mathbf{f}}(c) = [const_{\mathbf{f},-\infty}(c); const_{\mathbf{f},+\infty}(c)]$
- $cast^\sharp_{\mathbf{f}}(c) = [cast_{\mathbf{f},-\infty}(c); cast_{\mathbf{f},+\infty}(c)]$
- $[a^-;a^+] \oplus^\sharp_{\mathbf{f}} [b^-;b^+] = [a^- \oplus_{\mathbf{f},-\infty} b^-; a^+ \oplus_{\mathbf{f},+\infty} b^+]$
- $[a^-;a^+] \ominus^\sharp_{\mathbf{f}} [b^-;b^+] = [a^- \ominus_{\mathbf{f},-\infty} b^+; a^+ \ominus_{\mathbf{f},+\infty} b^-]$
- $[a^-;a^+] \otimes^\sharp_{\mathbf{f}} [b^-;b^+] =$
  $[\min((a^+ \otimes_{\mathbf{f},-\infty} b^+), (a^- \otimes_{\mathbf{f},-\infty} b^+), (a^+ \otimes_{\mathbf{f},-\infty} b^-), (a^- \otimes_{\mathbf{f},-\infty} b^-));$
  $\max((a^+ \otimes_{\mathbf{f},+\infty} b^+), (a^- \otimes_{\mathbf{f},+\infty} b^+), (a^+ \otimes_{\mathbf{f},+\infty} b^-), (a^- \otimes_{\mathbf{f},+\infty} b^-))]$
- $[a^-;a^+] \oslash^\sharp_{\mathbf{f}} [b^-;b^+] =$
  - Ω if $b^- \leq 0 \leq b^+$
  - $[\min((a^+ \oslash_{\mathbf{f},-\infty} b^+), (a^- \oslash_{\mathbf{f},-\infty} b^+), (a^+ \oslash_{\mathbf{f},-\infty} b^-), (a^- \oslash_{\mathbf{f},-\infty} b^-));$

```
for (n=0;n¡N;n++) {
  // fetch X in [−128; 128] and D in [0; 16]
  S = Y;   R = X ⊖32,n S;   Y = X;
  if (R ≤ ⊖D) Y = S ⊖32,n D;
  if (R ≥ D) Y = S ⊕32,n D;
}
```

Fig. 3. Simple rate limiter function with input X, output Y, and maximal rate variation D.

$\max((a^+ \oslash_{\mathbf{f},+\infty} b^+), (a^- \oslash_{\mathbf{f},+\infty} b^+), (a^+ \oslash_{\mathbf{f},+\infty} b^-), (a^- \oslash_{\mathbf{f},+\infty} b^-))]$
otherwise

- $\ominus^\sharp[a^-; a^+] = [\ominus a^+; \ominus a^-]$
- return Ω if one interval bound evaluates to Ω

This semantics frees the analyzer from the job of statically determining the rounding mode of the expressions and allows the analyzer to use, in the abstract, less precise formats that those used in the concrete (however, using a more precise format in the abstract remains unsound).

Floating-Point Interval Analysis. Interval analysis is a non-relational Abstract Interpretation-based analysis where, at each program point and for each variable, the set of its possible values during all executions reaching this point is over-approximated by an interval. An abstract environment $\rho^\sharp$ is a function mapping each variable $v \in \mathcal{V}_\mathbf{f}$ to an element of $\mathbb{I}_\mathbf{f}$. The abstract value $[\![expr_\mathbf{f}]\!]^\sharp \rho^\sharp \in \mathbb{I}_\mathbf{f} \cup \{\Omega\}$ of an expression $expr_\mathbf{f}$ in an abstract environment $\rho^\sharp$ can be derived by induction using the interval operators defined in the preceding paragraph.

An assignment $v \leftarrow expr_\mathbf{f}$ performed in an environment $\rho^\sharp$ returns $\rho^\sharp$ where v's value has been replaced by $[\![expr_\mathbf{f}]\!]^\sharp \rho^\sharp$ if it does not evaluate to Ω, and otherwise by $\mathbb{F}_\mathbf{f}$ (the *top* value) and reports an error. Most tests can only be abstracted by ignoring them (which is sound). Even though for simple tests such as, for instance, $X \leq Y \oplus_{\mathbf{f},\mathbf{r}} c$, the interval domain is able to refine the bounds for X and Y, it cannot remember the relationship between these variables. Consider the more complete example of Fig. 4. It is a rate limiter that given random input flows X and D, bounded respectively by $[-128; 128]$ and $[0; 16]$, computes an output flow Y that tries to follow X while having a change rate limited by D. Due to the imprecise abstraction of tests, the interval domain will bound Y by $[-128 - 16n; 128 + 16n]$ after n loop iterations while in fact it is bounded by $[-128; 128]$ independently from n. If N is too big, the interval analysis will conclude that the limiter may overflow while it is in fact always perfectly safe.

5 Linearization of Floating-Point Expressions

Unlike the interval domain, relational abstract domains rely on algebraic properties of operators, such as associativity and distributivity, that are not true in the floating-point world. Our solution is to approximate floating-point expressions by *linear expressions* in the *real* field with *interval coefficients* and free variables in $\mathcal{V} = \cup_{\mathbf{f} \in \mathbf{F}} \mathcal{V}_\mathbf{f}$. Let $i + \sum_{v \in \mathcal{V}} i_v v$ be such a linear form; it can be viewed as a function from $\mathbb{R}^{\mathcal{V}}$ to the set of real intervals. For the sake of efficiency, interval coefficient bounds will be represented by floating-point numbers in a format **fa** that is efficient on the analyzer's platform: $i, i_v \in \mathbb{I}_{\mathbf{fa}}$. Because, for all $\mathbf{f}$ and $\cdot \in \{+,-,\times,/\}$, $\odot^\sharp_{\mathbf{f}}$ is a valid over-approximation of the corresponding real interval arithmetics operation, we can define the following sound operators $\boxplus^\sharp$, $\boxminus^\sharp$, $\boxtimes^\sharp$, $\boxslash^\sharp$ on linear forms:

- $(i + \sum_{v\in\mathcal{V}} i_v v) \boxplus^\sharp (i' + \sum_{v\in\mathcal{V}} i'_v v) = (i \oplus^\sharp_{\mathbf{fa}} i') + \sum_{v\in\mathcal{V}} (i_v \oplus^\sharp_{\mathbf{fa}} i'_v) v$
- $(i + \sum_{v\in\mathcal{V}} i_v v) \boxminus^\sharp (i' + \sum_{v\in\mathcal{V}} i'_v v) = (i \ominus^\sharp_{\mathbf{fa}} i') + \sum_{v\in\mathcal{V}} (i_v \ominus^\sharp_{\mathbf{fa}} i'_v) v$
- $i \boxtimes^\sharp (i' + \sum_{v\in\mathcal{V}} i'_v v) = (i \otimes^\sharp_{\mathbf{fa}} i') + \sum_{v\in\mathcal{V}} (i \otimes^\sharp_{\mathbf{fa}} i'_v) v$
- $(i + \sum_{v\in\mathcal{V}} i_v v) \boxslash^\sharp i' = (i \oslash^\sharp_{\mathbf{fa}} i') + \sum_{v\in\mathcal{V}} (i_v \oslash^\sharp_{\mathbf{fa}} i') v$

Given an expression $expr_{\mathbf{f}}$ and an interval abstract environment $\rho^\sharp$ as in Sect. 4, we construct the interval linear form $(\!| expr_{\mathbf{f}} |\!)\rho^\sharp$ on $\mathcal{V}$ as follows:

- $(\!| const_{\mathbf{f},\mathbf{r}}(c) |\!)\rho^\sharp = [const_{\mathbf{f},-\infty}(c); const_{\mathbf{f},+\infty}(c)]$
- $(\!| v_{\mathbf{f}} |\!)\rho^\sharp = [1;1]v_{\mathbf{f}}$
- $(\!| cast_{\mathbf{f},\mathbf{r}}(e) |\!)\rho^\sharp = (\!| e |\!)\rho^\sharp \boxplus^\sharp \varepsilon_{\mathbf{f}}((\!| e |\!)\rho^\sharp) \boxplus^\sharp mf_{\mathbf{f}}[-1;1]$
- $(\!| e_1 \oplus_{\mathbf{f},\mathbf{r}} e_2 |\!)\rho^\sharp =$
  $(\!| e_1 |\!)\rho^\sharp \boxplus^\sharp (\!| e_2 |\!)\rho^\sharp \boxplus^\sharp \varepsilon_{\mathbf{f}}((\!| e_1 |\!)\rho^\sharp) \boxplus^\sharp \varepsilon_{\mathbf{f}}((\!| e_2 |\!)\rho^\sharp) \boxplus^\sharp mf_{\mathbf{f}}[-1;1]$
- $(\!| e_1 \ominus_{\mathbf{f},\mathbf{r}} e_2 |\!)\rho^\sharp =$
  $(\!| e_1 |\!)\rho^\sharp \boxminus^\sharp (\!| e_2 |\!)\rho^\sharp \boxplus^\sharp \varepsilon_{\mathbf{f}}((\!| e_1 |\!)\rho^\sharp) \boxplus^\sharp \varepsilon_{\mathbf{f}}((\!| e_2 |\!)\rho^\sharp) \boxplus^\sharp mf_{\mathbf{f}}[-1;1]$
- $(\!| [a;b] \otimes_{\mathbf{f},\mathbf{r}} e_2 |\!)\rho^\sharp =$
  $([a;b] \boxtimes^\sharp (\!| e_2 |\!)\rho^\sharp) \boxplus^\sharp ([a;b] \boxtimes^\sharp \varepsilon_{\mathbf{f}}((\!| e_2 |\!)\rho^\sharp)) \boxplus^\sharp mf_{\mathbf{f}}[-1;1]$
- $(\!| e_1 \otimes_{\mathbf{f},\mathbf{r}} [a;b] |\!)\rho^\sharp = (\!| [a;b] \otimes_{\mathbf{f},\mathbf{r}} e_1 |\!)\rho^\sharp$
- $(\!| e_1 \otimes_{\mathbf{f},\mathbf{r}} e_2 |\!)\rho^\sharp = (\!| \iota((\!| e_1 |\!)\rho^\sharp)\rho^\sharp \otimes_{\mathbf{f},\mathbf{r}} e_2 |\!)\rho^\sharp$
- $(\!| e_1 \oslash_{\mathbf{f},\mathbf{r}} [a;b] |\!)\rho^\sharp =$
  $((\!| e_1 |\!)\rho^\sharp \boxslash^\sharp [a;b]) \boxplus^\sharp (\varepsilon_{\mathbf{f}}((\!| e_1 |\!)\rho^\sharp) \boxslash^\sharp [a;b]) \boxplus^\sharp mf_{\mathbf{f}}[-1;1]$
- $(\!| e_1 \oslash_{\mathbf{f},\mathbf{r}} e_2 |\!)\rho^\sharp = (\!| e_1 \oslash_{\mathbf{f},\mathbf{r}} \iota((\!| e_2 |\!)\rho^\sharp)\rho^\sharp |\!)$

where the "error" $\varepsilon_{\mathbf{f}}(l)$ of the linear form l is the following linear form:

$$\varepsilon_{\mathbf{f}}\left([a;b] + \sum_{v\in\mathcal{V}} [a_v;b_v]v\right) = (\max(|a|,|b|) \otimes^\sharp_{\mathbf{fa}} [-2^{-\mathbf{p}};2^{-\mathbf{p}}]) + \sum_{v\in\mathcal{V}} (\max(|a_v|,|b_v|) \otimes^\sharp_{\mathbf{fa}} [-2^{-\mathbf{p}};2^{-\mathbf{p}}])v$$

(**p** *is the fraction size in bits for the format* **f**, *see Sect. 3.1)*

and the "intervalization" $\iota(l)\rho^\sharp$ function over-approximates the range of the linear form l in the abstract environment $\rho^\sharp$ as the following interval of $\mathbb{I}_{\mathbf{fa}}$:

$$\iota\left(i + \sum_{v\in\mathcal{V}} i_v v\right)\rho^\sharp = i \oplus^\sharp_{\mathbf{fa}} \left(\bigoplus^\sharp_{\mathbf{fa}\; v\in\mathcal{V}} i_v \otimes^\sharp_{\mathbf{fa}} \rho^\sharp(v)\right)$$

(any summation order for $\oplus^\sharp_{\mathbf{fa}}$ is sound)

Note that this semantics is very different from the one proposed by Goubault in [11] and subsequently used in [13]. In [11], each operation introduces a new variable representing an error term, and there is no need for interval coefficients.

About ι. Dividing a linear form by another linear form which is not reduced to an interval does not yield a linear form. In this case, the ι operator is used to over-approximate the divisor by a single interval before performing the division. The same holds when multiplying two linear forms not reduced to an interval, but we can choose to apply ι to either argument. For the sake of simplicity, we chose here to "intervalize" the left argument. Moreover, any non-linear operator (such as, e.g., square root or sine) could be dealt with by performing the corresponding operator on intervals after "intervalizing" its argument(s).

About $\varepsilon_{\mathbf{f}}$. To account for rounding errors, an upper bound of $|R_{\mathbf{f},\mathbf{r}}(x \cdot y) - (x \cdot y)|$ (where $\cdot \in \{+, -, \times, /\}$) is included in $(\!|\, expr_{\mathbf{f}} \,|\!)\rho^\sharp$. It is the sum an error relative to the arguments x and y, expressed using $\varepsilon_{\mathbf{f}}$, and an absolute error $mf_{\mathbf{f}}$ due to a possible underflow. Unlike what happened with interval arithmetics, correct error computation does not require the abstract operators to use floating-point formats that are no more precise than the concrete ones: the choice of **fa** is completely free.

About Ω. It is quite possible that, during the computation of $(\!|\, expr_{\mathbf{f}} \,|\!)\rho^\sharp$, a floating-point run-time error Ω occurs. In that case, we will say that the linearization "failed". It does not mean that the program has a run-time error, but only that we cannot compute a linearized expression and must revert to the classical interval arithmetics.

Main Result. When we evaluate in $\mathbb{R}$ the linear form $(\!|\, expr_{\mathbf{f}} \,|\!)\rho^\sharp$ in a concrete environment ρ included in $\rho^\sharp$ we get a real interval that over-approximates the concrete value of the expression:

Theorem 1.
If $[\![expr_{\mathbf{f}}]\!]^\sharp \rho^\sharp \neq \Omega$ and the linearization does not fail and $\forall v \in \mathcal{V},\ \rho(v) \in \rho^\sharp(v)$, then $[\![expr_{\mathbf{f}}]\!]\rho \in (\!|\, expr_{\mathbf{f}} \,|\!)\rho^\sharp\ (\rho)$.

Linear Form Propagation. As the linearization manipulates expressions symbolically, it is able to perform simplifications when the same variable appears several times. For instance $Z \leftarrow X \ominus_{\mathbf{32},n} (0.25 \otimes_{\mathbf{32},n} X)$ will be interpreted as $Z \leftarrow [0.749 \cdots ; 0.750 \cdots]X + 2.35 \cdots 10^{-38}[-1;1]$. Unfortunately, no simplification can be done if the expression is broken into several statements, such as in $Y \leftarrow 0.25 \otimes_{\mathbf{32},n} X; Z \leftarrow X \ominus_{\mathbf{32},n} Y$. Our solution is to remember, in an extra environment $\rho_l^\sharp$, the linear form assigned to each variable and use this information while linearizing: we set $(\!|\, v_{\mathbf{f}} \,|\!)(\rho^\sharp, \rho_l^\sharp) = \rho_l^\sharp(v)$ instead of $[-1;1]v_{\mathbf{f}}$. Care must be taken, when a variable v is modified, to discard all occurrences of v in $\rho_l^\sharp$. Effects of tests on $\rho_l^\sharp$ are ignored. Our partial order on linear forms is flat, so, at control-flow joins, only variables that are associated with the same linear form in both environments are kept; moreover, we do not need any widening. This technique is reminiscent of Kildall's constant propagation [12].

Applications. A first application of linearization is to improve the precision of the interval analysis. We simply replace $[\![expr_{\mathbf{f}}]\!]^\sharp \rho^\sharp$ by $[\![expr_{\mathbf{f}}]\!]^\sharp \rho^\sharp \ \cap\ \iota((\!|\, expr_{\mathbf{f}} \,|\!)\rho^\sharp)\rho^\sharp$ whenever the hypotheses of Thm. 1 hold.

While improving the assignment transfer function (trough expression simplification), this is not sufficient to treat tests precisely. For this, we need relational domains. Fortunately, Thm. 1 also means that if we have a relational domain that manipulates sets of points with real coordinates $\mathbb{R}^{\mathcal{V}}$ and that is able to perform assignments and tests of linear expressions with interval coefficients, we can use it to perform relational analyses on floating-point variables. Consider, for instance, the following algorithm to handle an assignment $v \leftarrow expr_{\mathbf{f}}$ in such a relational domain (the procedure would be equivalent for tests):

- If $[\![expr_{\mathbf{f}}]\!]^\sharp \rho^\sharp = \Omega$, then we report a run-time error and apply the transfer function for $v \leftarrow \mathbb{F}_{\mathbf{f}}$.
- Else, if the linearization of $expr_{\mathbf{f}}$ fails, then we do not report an error but apply the transfer function for $v \leftarrow [\![expr_{\mathbf{f}}]\!]^\sharp \rho^\sharp$.
- Otherwise, we do not report an error but apply the transfer function for $v \leftarrow (\!|\, expr_{\mathbf{f}} \,|\!) \rho^\sharp$.

Remark how we use the interval arithmetics to perform the actual detection of run-time errors and as a fallback when the linearization cannot be used.

6 Adapting Relational Abstract Domains

We first present in details the adaptation of the octagon abstract domain [14] to use floating-point arithmetics and interval linear forms, which was implemented in our second prototype analyzer [4]. We then present in less details some ideas to adapt other domains.

6.1 The Octagon Abstract Domain

The octagon abstract domain [14] can manipulate sets of constraints of the form $\pm x \pm y \leq c$, $x, y \in \mathcal{V}$, $c \in \mathbb{E}$ where $\mathbb{E}$ can be $\mathbb{Z}$, $\mathbb{Q}$, or $\mathbb{R}$. An abstract element $\mathbf{o}$ is represented by a half-square constraint matrix of size $|\mathcal{V}|$. Each element at line i, column j with $i \leq j$ contains four constraints: $v_i + v_j \leq c$, $v_i - v_j \leq c$, $-v_i + v_j \leq c$, and $-v_i - v_j \leq c$, with $c \in \overline{\mathbb{E}} = \mathbb{E} \cup \{+\infty\}$. Remark that diagonal elements represent interval constraints as $2v_i \leq c$ and $-2v_i \leq c$. In the following, we will use notations such as $\max_{\mathbf{o}}(v_i + v_j)$ to access the upper bound, in $\overline{\mathbb{E}}$, of constraints embedded in the octagon $\mathbf{o}$.

Because constraints in the matrix can be combined to obtain implied constraints that may not be in the matrix (e.g., from $x - y \leq c$ and $y + z \leq d$, we can deduce $x + z \leq c + d$), two matrices can represent the same set of points. We introduced in [14] a Floyd-Warshall-based closure operator that provides a normal form by combining and propagating, in $\mathcal{O}(|\mathcal{V}|^3)$ time, all constraints. The optimality of the abstract operators requires to work on closed matrices.

Floating-Point Octagons. In order to represent and manipulate efficiently constraints on real numbers, we choose to use floating-point matrices: $\mathbb{F}_{\mathbf{fa}}$ replaces $\mathbb{E}$ (where **fa** is, as before, an efficient floating-point format chosen by the analyzer implementation). As the algorithms presented in [14] make solely use of the $+$ and $\leq$ operators on $\overline{\mathbb{E}}$, it is sufficient to replace $+$ by $\oplus_{\mathbf{fa},+\infty}$ and map Ω to $+\infty$ in these algorithms to provide a sound approximation of all the transfer functions and operators on reals using only $\overline{\mathbb{F}}_{\mathbf{fa}} = \mathbb{F}_{\mathbf{fa}} \cup \{+\infty\}$. As all the nice properties of $\mathbb{E}$ are no longer true in $\mathbb{F}_{\mathbf{fa}}$, the closure is no longer a normal form. Even though working on closed matrices will no longer guaranty the optimality of the transfer functions, it still greatly improves their precision.

Assignments. Given an assignment of the form $v_k \leftarrow l$, where l is a interval linear form, on an octagon $\mathbf{o}$, the resulting set is no always an octagon. We can choose between several levels of approximation. Optimality could be achieved at great cost by performing the assignment in a polyhedron domain and then computing the smallest enclosing octagon. We propose, as a less precise but much faster alternative ($\mathcal{O}(|\mathcal{V}|$ time cost), to replace all constraints concerning the variable v_k by the following ones:

$$\begin{array}{lll} v_k + v_i & \leq u(\mathbf{o}, l \boxplus^\sharp v_i) & \forall i \neq k \\ v_k - v_i & \leq u(\mathbf{o}, l \boxminus^\sharp v_i) & \forall i \neq k \\ -v_k + v_i & \leq u(\mathbf{o}, v_i \boxminus^\sharp l) & \forall i \neq k \\ -v_k - v_i & \leq u(\mathbf{o}, \boxminus^\sharp (l \boxplus^\sharp v_i)) & \forall i \neq k \\ v_k & \leq u(\mathbf{o}, l) & \\ -v_k & \leq u(\mathbf{o}, \boxminus^\sharp l) & \end{array}$$

where the upper bound of a linear form l on an octagon $\mathbf{o}$ is approximated by $u(\mathbf{o}, l) \in \overline{\mathbb{F}}_{\mathbf{fa}}$ as follows:

$$u\left(\mathbf{o},\ [a^-; a^+] + \sum_{v \in \mathcal{V}} [a_v^-; a_v^+] v\right) = a^+ \oplus_{\mathbf{fa},+\infty}$$
$$\left(\bigoplus_{v \in \mathcal{V}}{}_{\mathbf{fa},+\infty} \begin{array}{l} \max(\, \max_{\mathbf{o}}(v) \otimes_{\mathbf{fa},+\infty} a_v^+ ,\ \ominus(\max_{\mathbf{o}}(-v) \otimes_{\mathbf{fa},-\infty} a_v^+), \\ \qquad \max_{\mathbf{o}}(v) \otimes_{\mathbf{fa},+\infty} a_v^- ,\ \ominus(\max_{\mathbf{o}}(-v) \otimes_{\mathbf{fa},-\infty} a_v^-)) \end{array} \right)$$

(any summation order for $\oplus_{\mathbf{fa},+\infty}$ is sound)

and $\oplus_{\mathbf{fa},+\infty}$ and $\otimes_{\mathbf{fa},+\infty}$ are extended to $\overline{\mathbb{F}}_{\mathbf{fa}}$ as follows:

$$+\infty \oplus_{\mathbf{fa},+\infty} x = x \oplus_{\mathbf{fa},+\infty} +\infty = +\infty$$
$$+\infty \otimes_{\mathbf{fa},+\infty} x = x \otimes_{\mathbf{fa},+\infty} +\infty = \begin{cases} 0 & \text{if } x = 0 \\ +\infty & \text{otherwise} \end{cases}$$

Example 1. Consider the assignment $X = Y \oplus_{\mathbf{32},n} Z$ with $Y, Z \in [0; 1]$. It is linearized as $X = [1 - 2^{-23}; 1 + 2^{-23}](Y + Z) + mf_{\mathbf{32}}[-1; 1]$, so our abstract transfer function will infer relational constraints such as $X - Y \leq 1 + 2^{-22} + mf_{\mathbf{32}}$.

Tests. Given a test of the form $l_1 \leq l_2$, where l_1 and l_2 are linear forms, for all variable $v_i \neq v_j$, appearing in l_1 or l_2, the constraints in the octagon $\mathbf{o}$ can be tightened by adding the following extra constraints:

$$\begin{array}{ll} v_j - v_i & \leq u(\mathbf{o},\ l_2 \boxminus^\sharp l_1 \boxminus^\sharp v_i \boxplus^\sharp v_j) \\ v_j + v_i & \leq u(\mathbf{o},\ l_2 \boxminus^\sharp l_1 \boxplus^\sharp v_i \boxplus^\sharp v_j) \\ -v_j - v_i & \leq u(\mathbf{o},\ l_2 \boxminus^\sharp l_1 \boxminus^\sharp v_i \boxminus^\sharp v_j) \\ -v_j + v_i & \leq u(\mathbf{o},\ l_2 \boxminus^\sharp l_1 \boxplus^\sharp v_i \boxminus^\sharp v_j) \\ v_i & \leq u(\mathbf{o},\ l_2 \boxminus^\sharp l_1 \boxplus^\sharp v_i) \end{array}$$

$$-v_i \leq u(\mathbf{o},\ l_2 \boxminus^\sharp l_1 \boxminus^\sharp v_i)$$

Example 2. Consider the test $Y \oplus_{\mathbf{32},n} Z \leq 1$ with $Y, Z \in [0;1]$. It is linearized as $[1-2^{-23}; 1+2^{-23}](Y+Z) + mf_{\mathbf{32}}[-1;1] \leq [1;1]$. Our abstract transfer function will be able to infer the constraint: $Y + Z \leq 1 + 2^{-22} + mf_{\mathbf{32}}$.

Example 3. The optimal analysis of the rate limiter function of Fig. 3 would require representing interval linear invariants on *three* variables. Nevertheless, the octagon domain with our approximated transfer functions can prove that the output Y is bounded by $[-136;136]$ independently from n (the optimal bound being $[-128;128]$), which is sufficient to prove that Y does not overflow.

Reduction with Intervals. The interval environment $\rho^\sharp$ is important as we use it to perform run-time error checking and to compute the linear form associated to an expression. So, we suppose that transfer functions are performed in parallel in the interval domain and in the octagon domain, and then, information from the octagon result $\mathbf{o}$ is used to refine the interval result $\rho^\sharp$ as follows: for each variable $v \in \mathcal{V}$, the upper bound of $\rho^\sharp(v)$ is replaced by $\min(\max \rho^\sharp(v), \max_{\mathbf{o}}(v))$ and the same is done for its lower bound.

6.2 Polyhedron Domain

The polyhedron domain is much more precise than the octagon domain as it allows manipulating sets of invariants of the form $\sum_v c_v v \leq c$, but it is also much more costly. Implementations, such as the New Polka or the Parma Polyhedra libraries [2], are targeted at representing sets of points with integer or rational coordinates. They internally use rational coefficients and, as the coefficients usually become fairly large, arbitrary precision integer libraries.

Representing Reals. These implementations could be used as-is to abstract sets of points with real coordinates, but the rational coefficients may get out of control, as well as the time cost. Unlike what happened for octagons, it is not so easy to adapt the algorithms to floating-point coefficients while retaining soundness as they are much much more complex. We are not aware, at the time of writing, of any such floating-point implementation.

Assignments and Tests. Assignments of the form $v \leftarrow l$ and tests of the form $l \leq 0$ where $l = [a^-;a^+] + \sum_{v\in\mathcal{V}}[a_v^-;a_v^+]v$ seem difficult to abstract in general. However, the case where all coefficients in l are scalar except maybe the constant one is much easier. To cope with the general case, an idea (yet untested) is to use the following transformation that abstracts l into an over-approximated linear form l' where $\forall v,\ a_v^- = a_v^+$ by transforming all relative errors into absolute ones:

$$l' = \left([a^-;a^+] \oplus^\sharp_{\mathbf{fa}} \bigoplus^\sharp_{\mathbf{fa}\ v\in\mathcal{V}} (a_v^+ \ominus_{\mathbf{fa},+\infty} a_v^-) \otimes^\sharp_{\mathbf{fa}} [0.5;0.5] \otimes^\sharp_{\mathbf{fa}} \rho^\sharp(v) \right) + \sum_{v\in\mathcal{V}} ((a_v^- \oplus_{\mathbf{fa},+\infty} a_v^+) \otimes^\sharp_{\mathbf{fa}} [0.5;0.5])v$$

(any summation order for $\oplus^\sharp_{\mathbf{fa}}$ is sound)

6.3 Two Variables per Linear Inequalities Domain

Simon's domain [15] can manipulate constraints of the form $\alpha v_i + \beta v_j \leq c$, $\alpha, \beta, c \in \mathbb{Q}$. An abstract invariant is represented using a planar convex polyhedron for each pair of variables. As for octagons, most computations are done point-wise on variable pairs and a closure provides the normal form by propagating and combining constraints. Because the underlying algorithms are simpler than for generic polyhedra, adapting this domain to handle floating-point computations efficiently may prove easier while greatly improving the precision over octagons. This still remains an open issue.

6.4 Ellipsoid and Digital Filter Domains

During the design of our prototype analyzer [4], we encountered code for computing recursive sequences such as $X_i = ((\alpha \otimes_{\mathbf{32},n} X_{i-1}) \oplus_{\mathbf{32},n} (\beta \otimes_{\mathbf{32},n} X_{i-2})) \oplus_{\mathbf{32},n} \gamma$ (1), or $X_i = (\alpha \otimes_{\mathbf{32},n} X_{i-1}) \oplus_{\mathbf{32},n} (Y_i \ominus_{\mathbf{32},n} Y_{i-1})$ (2). In order to find precise bounds for the variable X, one has to consider invariants out of the scope of classical relational abstract domains. Case (1) can be solved by using the ellipsoid abstract domain of [4] that can represent non-linear real invariants of the form $aX_i^2 + bX_{i-1}^2 + cX_iX_{i-1} \leq d$, while case (2) is precisely analyzed using Feret's filter domains [9] by inferring temporal invariants of the form $|X_i| \leq a \max_{j \leq i} |Y_j| + b$. It is not our purpose here to present these new abstract domains but we stress the fact that such domains, as the ones discussed in the preceding paragraphs, are naturally designed to work with perfect reals, but used to analyze imperfect floating-point computations.

A solution is, as before, to design these domains to analyze interval linear assignments and tests on reals, and feed them with the result of the linearization of floating-point expressions defined in Sect. 5. This solution has been successfully applied (see [9] and Sect. 8).

7 Convergence Acceleration

In the Abstract Interpretation framework, loop invariants are described as fixpoints and are over-approximated by iterating, in the abstract, the body transfer function $F^\sharp$ until a post-fixpoint is reached.

Widening. The widening ∇ is a convergence acceleration operator introduced in [6] in order to reduce the number of abstract iterations: $\lim_i (F^\sharp)^i$ is replaced by $\lim_i E_i^\sharp$ where $E_{i+1}^\sharp = E_i^\sharp \nabla F^\sharp(E_i^\sharp)$. A straightforward widening on intervals and octagons is to simply discard unstable constraints. However, this strategy is too aggressive and fails to discover sequences that are stable after a certain bound, such as, e.g., $X = (\alpha \otimes_{\mathbf{32},n} X) \oplus_{\mathbf{32},n} \beta$. To give these computations a chance to stabilize, we use a staged widening that tries a user-supplied set of bounds in increasing order. As we do not know in advance which bounds will be stable, we use, as set $\mathbb{T}$ of thresholds, a simple exponential ramp: $\mathbb{T} = \{\pm 2^i\} \cap \mathbb{F}_{\mathbf{fa}}$. Given two octagons $\mathbf{o}$ and $\mathbf{o}'$, the widening with thresholds $\mathbf{o} \nabla \mathbf{o}'$ is obtained by setting, for each binary unit expression $\pm v_i \pm v_j$:

$$\max_{\mathbf{o} \nabla \mathbf{o}'}(C) = \begin{cases} \max_{\mathbf{o}}(C) & \text{if } \max_{\mathbf{o}'}(C) \leq \max_{\mathbf{o}}(C) \\ \min\{t \in \mathbb{T} \cup \{+\infty\} \mid t \geq \max_{\mathbf{o}'}(C)\} & \text{otherwise} \end{cases}$$

Decreasing Iterations. We now suppose that we have iterated the widening with thresholds up to an abstract post-fixpoint $X^\sharp$: $F^\sharp(X^\sharp) \sqsubseteq X^\sharp$. The bound of a stable variable is generally over-approximated by the threshold immediately above. One solution to improve such a bound is to perform some decreasing iterations $X^\sharp_{i+1} = X^\sharp_i \sqcap F(X^\sharp_i)$ from $X^\sharp_0 = X^\sharp$. We can stop whenever we wish, the result will always be, by construction, an abstraction of the concrete fixpoint; however, it may no longer be a post-fixpoint for $F^\sharp$. It is desirable for invariants to be abstract post-fixpoint so that the analyzer can check them independently from the way they were generated instead of relying solely on the maybe buggy fixpoint engine.

Iteration Perturbation. Careful examination of the iterates on our benchmarks showed that the reason we do not get an abstract post-fixpoint is that the *abstract* computations are done in floating-point which incurs a somewhat non-deterministic extra rounding. There exists, between $F^\sharp$'s definitive pre-fixpoints and $F^\sharp$'s definitive post-fixpoints, a chaotic region. To ensure that the $X^\sharp_i$ stay above this region, we replace the intersection $\sqcap$ used in the decreasing iterations by the following narrowing $\triangle$: $\mathbf{o} \triangle \mathbf{o}' = \epsilon(\mathbf{o} \sqcap \mathbf{o}')$ where $\epsilon(\mathbf{o})$ returns an octagon where the bound of each unstable constraint is enlarged by $\epsilon \times d$, where d is the maximum of all non $+\infty$ constraint bounds in $\mathbf{o}$. Moreover, replacing $\mathbf{o} \triangledown \mathbf{o}'$ by $\epsilon(\mathbf{o} \triangledown \mathbf{o}')$ allows the analyzer to skip above $F^\sharp$'s chaotic regions and effectively reduces the required number of increasing iterations, and so, the analysis time.

Theoretically, a good ϵ can be estimated by the relative amount of rounding errors performed in the abstract computation of one loop iteration, and so, is a function of the complexity of the analyzed loop body, the floating-point format **fa** used in the analyzer and the implementation of the abstract domains. We chose to fix ϵ experimentally by enlarging a small value until the analyzer reported it found an abstract post-fixpoint for our program. Then, as we improved our abstract domains and modified the analyzed program, we seldom had to adjust this ϵ value.

8 Experimental Results

We now show how the presented abstract domains perform in practice. Our only real-life example is the critical embedded avionics software of [4]. It is a 132,000 lines reactive C program (75 KLoc after preprocessing) containing approximately 10,000 global variables, 5,000 of which are floating-point variables, single precision. The program consists mostly of one very large loop executed $3.6 \cdot 10^6$ times. Because relating several thousands variables in a relational domain is too costly, we use the "packing" technique described in [4] to statically determine sets of variables that should be related together and we end up with approximately 2,400 octagons of size 2 to 42 instead of one octagon of size 10,000.

Fig. 4 shows how the choice of the abstract domains influence the precision and the cost of the analysis presented in [4] on our 2.8 GHz Intel Xeon. Together with the computation time, we also give the number of abstract executions of the big loop needed to find an invariant; thanks to our widenings and narrowings, it is much much less than the concrete number of iterations. All cases use the

	domains			time	nb. of	memory	nb. of
	linearize	octagons	filters		iterations		alarms
(1)	×	×	×	1623 s	150	115 MB	922
(2)	√	×	×	4001 s	176	119 MB	825
(3)	√	√	×	3227 s	69	175 MB	639
(4)	√	×	√	8939 s	211	207 MB	363
(5)	√	√	√	4541 s	72	263 MB	6

Fig. 4. Experimental results.

interval domain with the symbolic simplification automatically provided by the linearization, except (1) that uses plain interval analysis. Other lines show the influence of the octagon (Sect. 6.1) and the specialized digital filter domains ([9] and Sect. 6.4): when both are activated, we only get six potential run-time errors for a reasonable time and memory cost. This is a sufficiently small number of alarms to allow manual inspection, and we discovered they could be eliminated without altering the functionality of the application by changing only three lines of code. Remark that as we add more complex domains, the time cost per iteration grows but the number of iterations needed to find an invariant decreases so that a better precision may reduce the overall time cost.

9 Conclusion

We presented, in this paper, an adaptation of the octagon abstract domain in order to analyze programs containing IEEE 754-compliant floating-point operations. Our methodology is somewhat generic and we proposed some ideas to adapt other relational numerical abstract domains as well. The adapted octagon domain was implemented in our prototype static analyzer for run-time error checking of critical C code [4] and tested on a real-life embedded avionic application. Practical results show that the proposed method scales up well and does greatly improve the precision of the analysis when compared to the classical interval abstract domain while maintaining a reasonable cost. To our knowledge, this is the first time relational numerical domains are used to represent relations between floating-point variables.

Acknowledgments. We would like to thank all the members of the "magic" team: Bruno Blanchet, Patrick Cousot, Radhia Cousot, Jérôme Feret, Laurent Mauborgne, David Monniaux, Xavier Rival, as well as the anonymous referees.

References

1. Y. Aït Ameur, G. Bel, F. Boniol, S. Pairault, and V. Wiels. Robustness analysis of avionics embedded systems. In *LCTES'03*, pages 123–132. ACM Press, 2003.
2. R. Bagnara, E. Ricci, E. Zaffanella, and P. M. Hill. Possibly not closed convex polyhedra and the Parma Polyhedra Library. In *SAS'02*, volume 2477 of *LNCS*, pages 213–229. Springer, 2002.

3. B. Blanchet, P. Cousot, R. Cousot, J. Feret, L. Mauborgne, A. Miné, D. Monniaux, and X. Rival. Design and implementation of a special-purpose static program analyzer for safety-critical real-time embedded software, invited chapter. In *The Essence of Computation: Complexity, Analysis, Transformation. Essays Dedicated to Neil D. Jones*, LNCS, pages 85–108. Springer, 2002.
4. B. Blanchet, P. Cousot, R. Cousot, J. Feret, L. Mauborgne, A. Miné, D. Monniaux, and X. Rival. A static analyzer for large safety-critical software. In *ACM PLDI'03*, volume 548030, pages 196–207. ACM Press, 2003.
5. IEEE Computer Society. IEEE standard for binary floating-point arithmetic. Technical report, ANSI/IEEE Std 745-1985, 1985.
6. P. Cousot and R. Cousot. Abstract interpretation: a unified lattice model for static analysis of programs by construction or approximation of fixpoints. In *ACM POPL'77*, pages 238–252. ACM Press, 1977.
7. P. Cousot and R. Cousot. Abstract interpretation frameworks. *Journal of Logic and Computation*, 2(4):511–547, August 1992.
8. P. Cousot and N. Halbwachs. Automatic discovery of linear restraints among variables of a program. In *ACM POPL'78*, pages 84–97. ACM Press, 1978.
9. J. Feret. Static analysis of digital filters. In *ESOP'04*. LNCS, 2004.
10. D. Goldberg. What every computer scientist should know about floating-point arithmetic. *ACM Computing Surveys (CSUR)*, 23(1):5–48, 1991.
11. É. Goubault. Static analyses of floating-point operations. In *SAS'01*, volume 2126 of *LNCS*, pages 234–259. Springer, 2001.
12. G. Kildall. A unified approach to global program optimization. In *POPL'73*, pages 194–206. ACM Press, 1973.
13. M. Martel. Static analysis of the numerical stability of loops. In *SAS'02*, volume 2477 of *LNCS*, pages 133–150. Springer, 2002.
14. A. Miné. The octagon abstract domain. In *AST 2001 in WCRE 2001*, IEEE, pages 310–319. IEEE CS Press, 2001.
15. A. Simon, A. King, and J. Howe. Two variables per linear inequality as an abstract domain. In *LOPSTR'02*, volume 2664 of *LNCS*, pages 71–89. Springer, 2002.
16. R. Skeel. Roundoff error and the Patriot missile. *SIAM News*, 25(4):11, July 1992.
17. J. Vignes. A survey of the CESTAC method. In J-C. Bajard, editor, *Proc. of Real Numbers and Computer Conference*, 1996.

Strong Preservation as Completeness in Abstract Interpretation

Francesco Ranzato and Francesco Tapparo

Dipartimento di Matematica Pura ed Applicata, Università di Padova
Via Belzoni 7, 35131 Padova, Italy
{franz,tapparo}@math.unipd.it

Abstract. Many algorithms have been proposed to minimally refine abstract transition systems in order to get strong preservation relatively to a given temporal specification language. These algorithms compute a state equivalence, namely they work on abstractions which are partitions of system states. This is restrictive because, in a generic abstract interpretation-based view, state partitions are just one particular type of abstraction, and therefore it could well happen that the refined partition constructed by the algorithm is not the optimal generic abstraction. On the other hand, it has been already noted that the well-known concept of complete abstract interpretation is related to strong preservation of abstract model checking. This paper establishes a precise correspondence between complete abstract interpretation and strongly preserving abstract model checking, by showing that the problem of minimally refining an abstract model checking in order to get strong preservation can be formulated as a complete domain refinement in abstract interpretation, which always admits a fixpoint solution. As a consequence of these results, we show that some well-known behavioural equivalences used in process algebra like simulation and bisimulation can be elegantly characterized in pure abstract interpretation as completeness properties.

1 Introduction

The design of any abstract model checking framework and/or tool comes always together with a preservation result, roughly stating that for a formula φ specified in some temporal language $\mathcal{L}$, the validity of φ on the abstract model implies the validity of φ on the concrete model. On the other hand, *strong preservation* means that any formula of $\mathcal{L}$ is valid in the abstract model if and only if it is valid in the concrete model. Strong preservation is highly desirable since it allows to draw consequences from negative answers on the abstract side.

This paper follows a standard abstract interpretation approach to abstract model checking, as applied for instance in temporal abstract interpretation [9]. The concrete state semantics of a temporal specification language $\mathcal{L}$ is given by a function $[\![\cdot]\!]$ mapping a formula $\varphi \in \mathcal{L}$ to the set of states $s \in \mathit{State}$ satisfying φ, that is $[\![\varphi]\!] = \{s \in \mathit{State} \mid s \models \varphi\}$. This concrete state semantics is approximated by the abstract semantics induced by any abstract interpretation of $\wp(\mathit{State})$,

D.A. Schmidt (Ed.): ESOP 2004, LNCS 2986, pp. 18–32, 2004.

namely a Galois connection (or, equivalently, a closure operator). This approach is more general than classical abstract model checking [5,6] where the abstract model is, analogously to the concrete model, a transition system or a Kripke structure. In our framework, this classical approach corresponds to a particular case of abstraction, namely an abstract domain encoding a partition of the system states. In a general abstract interpretation setting, an abstract model checking is associated to *any abstraction* of the powerset of system states, and this obviously enables a finer-grain taxonomy of abstract model checkers. The concept of *complete* abstract interpretation is well known [8,15]: this encodes an ideal situation where the abstract semantics coincides with the abstraction of the concrete semantics. It should be quite clear that completeness of an abstract interpretation with respect to some semantic functions and strong preservation of an abstract model checker with respect to a temporal language are, somehow, related concepts: this was first formalized by Giacobazzi and Quintarelli [13], who put forward a method for systematically refining abstract model checking in order to eliminate Clarke et al.'s [4] spurious counterexamples. The relationship between completeness and spurious counterexamples was further studied in [10], where it is also shown that stability *à la* Paige and Tarjan [20] for a state partition can be formulated through complete abstract interpretations.

We first generalize the notion of classical strong preservation to our abstract interpretation framework. Namely, the classical concept of strong preservation for an abstract model specified as an abstract transition system, viz. a state partition, is here generalized to an abstract model specified by any generic abstract domain. It turns out that any generic abstract model induces a classical partition-based abstract model checking, but this could give rise to a loss of information. Our results rely on the notion of *forward complete* abstract domain. An abstract domain μ, viewed as a closure operator (closure operators are particularly useful here since they allow us to be independent from the representation of abstract objects), is forward complete for a concrete semantic function $f : \mathit{Concrete} \rightarrow \mathit{Concrete}$ when $\mu \circ f \circ \mu = f \circ \mu$. Forward completeness is dual to the aforementioned standard completeness, i.e. $\mu \circ f \circ \mu = \mu \circ f$ — called backward completeness — and intuitively states that when the concrete function f is restricted to abstract objects then it coincides with the abstract function $\mu \circ f$, i.e., the best correct approximation of f in the abstract domain μ. Giacobazzi et al. [15] showed how to systematically and constructively derive backward complete abstract domains from non-complete ones by minimal refinements. This can be done for forward completeness as well: Given any domain μ, the most abstract domain which refines μ and is forward complete for f does exist and it can be characterized as a greatest fixpoint. We call such a domain the (forward) *complete shell* of μ for f.

Let us turn to strong preservation. We consider generic inductively defined languages $\mathcal{L}$, generated from atomic propositions and a set of logical operators $op_1, ..., op_k$ whose interpretations are $\mathbf{op_i} : \wp(\mathit{State})^n \rightarrow \wp(\mathit{State})$, where n is the arity of the operator. In our framework any abstraction μ of $\wp(\mathit{States})$ induces an abstract semantics $[\![\cdot]\!]^\mu : \mathcal{L} \rightarrow \mu$ for the language $\mathcal{L}$. Given any abstraction μ, we show that the most abstract semantics which refines μ and is strongly preserving for $\mathcal{L}$ is precisely the complete shell of μ for all the language operators $\mathbf{op_1}, ..., \mathbf{op_n}$. This result can be also read as follows. A number of algorithms have been proposed to minimally refine classical abstract models, i.e. state partitions, in order to get strong preservation relatively to some relevant temporal specification languages. Typically, these are coarsest partition refinement algorithms which compute the state equivalence induced by some *behavioural state equivalence*, e.g., bisimulation, stuttering equivalence (or branching bisimulation) or simulation equivalence, since they exploit the fact that this behavioural equivalence coincides with the state equivalence $\equiv_{\mathcal{L}}$ induced by a temporal language $\mathcal{L}$, namely, $s \equiv_{\mathcal{L}} s'$ iff s and s' agree on each formula of $\mathcal{L}$. This is the case of Paige and Tarjan algorithm [20] for strong preservation of CTL* [2] and of Groote and Vaandrager algorithm [16] for strong preservation of CTL*-X. Our results allow us to provide a clean and elegant generalization of these coarsest partition refinement algorithms in our abstract interpretation framework. Due to lack of space we do not consider stuttering equivalence here (we refer to the full version of the paper).

2 Basic Notions

Notation. Let X be any set. When writing a set $S \in \wp(\wp(X))$, we often write the sets in S in a compact form like in $\{1, 12, 123\} \in \wp(\wp(\{1,2,3\}))$. $\complement$ denotes the complement operator. Fun(X) denotes the set of all the functions $f : X^n \to X$, for some $n \geq 0$. When $n = 0$, f is just a specific object of X. We will denote by Part(X) the set of partitions on X. The sets in a partition are called blocks. If $\equiv \subseteq X \times X$ is an equivalence relation then we will denote by $P_{\equiv} \in \text{Part}(X)$ the corresponding partition of X. Vice versa, if $P \in \text{Part}(X)$ then we will denote by $\equiv_P \subseteq X \times X$ the corresponding equivalence relation on X. Part(X) is endowed with the following standard partial order $\preccurlyeq$: given $P_1, P_2 \in \text{Part}(X)$, $P_1 \preccurlyeq P_2$, i.e. P_2 is coarser than P_1 (or P_1 refines P_2) iff $\forall B \in P_1. \exists B' \in P_2. B \subseteq B'$.

We consider transition systems (Q, R) where the relation $R \subseteq Q \times Q$ (also denoted by $\xrightarrow{R}$) is total, i.e., for any $s \in Q$ there exists some $t \in Q$ such that sRt. A Kripke structure (Q, R, AP, ℓ) consists of a transition system (Q, R) together with a (typically finite) set AP of atomic propositions and a labelling function $\ell : Q \to \wp(AP)$. A transition relation $R \subseteq Q \times Q$ defines the usual pre/post transformers on $\wp(Q)$: $\text{pre}[R]$, $\widetilde{\text{pre}}[R]$, $\text{post}[R]$, $\widetilde{\text{post}}[R]$.

Abstract interpretation and completeness. In standard Cousot and Cousot's abstract interpretation theory, abstract domains can be equivalently specified either by Galois connections or by (upper) closure operators (uco's) [8]. These two approaches are equivalent, modulo isomorphic representations of domain's objects. The closure operator approach has the advantage of being independent from the representation of domain's objects and is therefore appropriate for reasoning on abstract domains independently from their representation. Given a complete lattice C, it is well known that the set uco(C) of all uco's on C, endowed with the pointwise ordering $\sqsubseteq$, gives rise to the complete lattice $\langle \mathrm{uco}(C), \sqsubseteq, \sqcup, \sqcap, \lambda x.\top_C, id\rangle$. Let us recall that each $\mu \in \mathrm{uco}(C)$ is uniquely determined by the set of its fixpoints, which is its image. Moreover, a subset $X \subseteq C$ is the set of fixpoints of a uco on C iff X is meet-closed, i.e. $X = \mathcal{M}(X) \stackrel{\text{def}}{=} \{\wedge Y \mid Y \subseteq X\}$ (where $\top_C = \wedge_C \varnothing \in \mathcal{M}(X)$). $\mathcal{M}(X)$ is called the Moore-closure of X. Also, $\mu \sqsubseteq \rho$ iff $\rho(C) \subseteq \mu(C)$; in this case, we say that μ is a refinement of ρ. Often, we will identify closures with their sets of fixpoints since this does not give rise to ambiguity. In view of the equivalence above, throughout the paper, $\langle \mathrm{uco}(C), \sqsubseteq\rangle$ will play the role of the lattice of abstract interpretations of C [7,8], i.e. the complete lattice of all the abstract domains of the concrete domain C. The ordering on $\mathrm{uco}(C)$ corresponds to the standard order used to compare abstract domains with regard to their precision: A_1 is more precise than A_2 (or A_2 is more abstract than A_1) iff $A_1 \sqsubseteq A_2$ in $\mathrm{uco}(C)$.

Let $f : C \to C$ be a concrete semantic function and let $f^\sharp : A \to A$ be a corresponding abstract function, where $A = \mu(C)$ for some closure $\mu \in \mathrm{uco}(C)$. Then, $\langle A, f^\sharp\rangle$ is a sound abstract interpretation when $\mu \circ f \sqsubseteq f^\sharp \circ \mu$. The abstract function $\mu \circ f : A \to A$ is called the best correct approximation of f in A. Completeness in abstract interpretation corresponds to require that, in addition to soundness, no loss of precision is introduced by the approximated function $f^\sharp \circ \mu$ on a concrete object $c \in C$ with respect to approximating by μ the concrete computation $f(c)$, namely the equation $\mu \circ f = f^\sharp \circ \mu$ holds. The following dual form of completeness may be considered. The soundness equation $\mu \circ f \sqsubseteq f^\sharp \circ \mu$ is also equivalent to the equation $f \circ \mu \sqsubseteq f^\sharp \circ \mu$. Then, *forward completeness* for $f^\sharp$ corresponds to the equation $f \circ \mu = f^\sharp \circ \mu$, and therefore means that no loss of precision occurs by approximating a concrete computation of f on an abstract object $a \in A$ with the abstract computation of $f^\sharp$ on the same a.

Giacobazzi et al. [15] observed that completeness uniquely depends upon the abstraction map, namely, one may define a complete abstract semantic operation $f^\sharp : A \to A$ over A if and only if $\mu \circ f : A \to A$ is complete. Hence, an abstract domain $\mu \in \mathrm{uco}(C)$ is defined to be complete for f iff $\mu \circ f = \mu \circ f \circ \mu$ holds. This simple observation makes completeness an abstract domain property. The same observations are also true for forward completeness, which is therefore a domain property as well: μ is forward complete iff $f \circ \mu = \mu \circ f \circ \mu$. This justifies the terminology forward completeness and, dually, backward completeness for the first standard form of completeness. A constructive characterization of backward complete abstract domains is given in [15], under the assumption of dealing with Scott-continuous concrete functions. This result allows to systematically and constructively derive complete abstract domains from non-complete ones by minimal refinements: this complete minimal refinement of a domain A for a function f is called *backward complete shell* of A for f.

3 Partitions as Abstractions

Let Q be any (possibly infinite) set of states. We associate to a closure $\mu \in \mathrm{uco}(\wp(Q)_\subseteq)$ a state equivalence $\equiv_\mu$ on Q, i.e. a partition of Q, by identifying those states that cannot be distinguished by the closure μ, namely those states belonging to the same set of fixpoints of the closure μ:

$$s \equiv_\mu s' \Leftrightarrow \forall S \in \mu. (s \in S \Leftrightarrow s' \in S).$$

It is easy to show that $s \equiv_\mu s'$ iff $\mu(\{s\}) = \mu(\{s'\})$. Hence, this allows us to view partitions as particular abstractions of $\wp(Q)$. We will denote by $\mathrm{par}(\mu) \in \mathrm{Part}(Q)$ the partition associated to the abstract domain $\mu \in \mathrm{uco}(\wp(Q))$. For example, for $Q = \{1, 2, 3\}$, the closures $\mu_1 = \{1, 12, 13, 123\}$, $\mu_2 = \{\varnothing, 1, 2, 3, 123\}$ and $\mu_3 = \wp(\{1, 2, 3\})$ all induce the same partition $\mathrm{par}(\mu) = \{\{1\}, \{2\}, \{3\}\}$. However, these closures carry additional information other than the underlying state partition, and this additional information allows us to distinguish them. It is then natural to say that a closure μ represents exactly a state partition when μ carries all this possible additional information, or, otherwise stated, when μ is the most precise among the closures inducing a given partition.

Definition 3.1. μ is *partitioning* if $\mu = \mathbb{P}(\mu) \stackrel{\text{def}}{=} \sqcap \{\eta \in \mathrm{uco}(\wp(Q)) \mid \equiv_\eta = \equiv_\mu\}$. $\mathrm{uco}^{\mathrm{P}}(\wp(Q))$ will denote the set of partitioning closures. □

The operator $\mathbb{P}$ is a refinement of abstract domains in the sense of [14], i.e., it can be proved that $\mathbb{P}$ is a lower closure operator on $\mathrm{uco}(\wp(Q))$. Accordingly, $\mathbb{P}$ will be called the *partitioning shell* operator. It turns out that partitioning closures can be characterized as follows.

Lemma 3.2. *Let* $\mu \in \mathrm{uco}(\wp(Q))$. *Then,* $\mu \in \mathrm{uco}^{\mathrm{P}}(\wp(Q))$ *iff* μ *is additive and* $\{\mu(\{q\})\}_{q \in Q}$ *is a partition of* Q. *Moreover, in this case,* $\mathrm{par}(\mu) = \{\mu(\{q\})\}_{q \in Q}$.

For instance, for all the above closures we have that $\mathbb{P}(\mu_i) = \wp(\{1, 2, 3\})$, and hence μ_1 and μ_2 are not partitioning. Also, the closure $\{\varnothing, 3, 12, 123\}$ is partitioning and represents the partition $\{12, 3\}$.

Lemma 3.2 allows us to see classical partition-based abstractions — i.e., partitions induced by a surjective abstraction map "h" in the style of Clarke et al. [5] — as a particular case of generic abstract domain through the following isomorphism between partitions and partitioning closures:

- par : $\mathrm{uco}^{\mathrm{P}}(\wp(Q)) \to \mathrm{Part}(Q)$ is the restriction of the above operator par to partitioning closures, i.e. $\mathrm{par}(\mu) = \{\mu(\{q\}) \mid q \in Q\}$;
- pcl : $\mathrm{Part}(Q) \to \mathrm{uco}^{\mathrm{P}}(\wp(Q))$ is defined as follows: $\mathrm{pcl}(P) \stackrel{\text{def}}{=} \mathbb{P}(\mathcal{M}(P)) = \lambda X \in \wp(Q). \cup \{B \in P \mid X \cap B \neq \varnothing\}$.

Theorem 3.3. *The mappings* par *and* pcl *are well defined and give rise to an order isomorphism between* $\langle \mathrm{Part}(Q), \preccurlyeq \rangle$ *and* $\langle \mathrm{uco}^{\mathrm{P}}(\wp(Q)), \sqsubseteq \rangle$.

4 Strongly Preserving Abstract Model Checking

We deal with specification languages $\mathcal{L}$ whose syntactic (state) formulae φ are inductively defined by a grammar:

$$\varphi ::= p \mid f(\varphi_1, \ldots, \varphi_n)$$

where $p \in AP$ ranges over a finite set of atomic propositions and $f \in Op$ ranges over a finite set of operators. Each operator $f \in Op$ will have an arity[1] $\sharp(f) > 0$.

The concrete semantic domain for interpreting formulae is the boolean algebra $\langle \wp(Q), \subseteq \rangle$, where Q is any (possibly infinite) set of states. The state semantics of formulae in $\mathcal{L}$ is determined by an interpretation function I such that for any $p \in AP$, $I(p) \in \wp(Q)$ and for any $f \in Op$, $I(f) : \wp(Q)^{\sharp(f)} \to \wp(Q)$. We will also use the notations $\mathbf{p}$ and $\mathbf{f}$ to denote, respectively, $I(p)$ and $I(f)$. As usual, the interpretation I on AP can be equivalently specified by a labelling function $\ell : Q \to \wp(AP)$ provided that $\ell(s) = \{p \in AP \mid s \in I(p)\}$ holds for any s. The *concrete state semantic function* $[\![\cdot]\!]_I : \mathcal{L} \to \wp(Q)$ is inductively defined as follows:

$$[\![p]\!]_I = \mathbf{p} \quad \text{and} \quad [\![f(\varphi_1, ..., \varphi_n)]\!]_I = \mathbf{f}([\![\varphi_1]\!]_I, ..., [\![\varphi_n]\!]_I).$$

We will freely use standard logical and temporal operators together with their usual interpretations: for example, $\wedge/\cap$, $\vee/\cup$, $\neg/\complement$, EX/ pre$[R]$, etc.

If g is any synctatic operator with arity $\sharp(g) = n$ whose semantics is given by $\mathbf{g} : \wp(Q)^n \to \wp(Q)$ then we say that the language $\mathcal{L}$ is *closed under* g when for any $\varphi_1, ..., \varphi_n \in \mathcal{L}$, there exists some $\psi \in \mathcal{L}$ such that $\mathbf{g}([\![\varphi_1]\!]_I, ..., [\![\varphi_n]\!]_I) = [\![\psi]\!]_I$.

Let us now apply the standard abstract interpretation approach for defining abstract semantics. Consider any abstract domain $\mu \in \mathrm{uco}(\wp(Q))$. The *abstract semantic function* $[\![\cdot]\!]_I^\mu : \mathcal{L} \to \mu$ induced by the abstract domain μ evaluates any formula $\varphi \in \mathcal{L}$ to an abstract value $[\![\varphi]\!]_I^\mu$ belonging to μ. $[\![\cdot]\!]_I^\mu$ is induced by the abstraction μ (and the interpretation I) and is inductively defined as best correct approximation of the concrete semantics as follows:

$$[\![p]\!]_I^\mu = \mu(\mathbf{p}) \quad \text{and} \quad [\![f(\varphi_1, ..., \varphi_n)]\!]_I^\mu = \mu(\mathbf{f}([\![\varphi_1]\!]_I^\mu, ..., [\![\varphi_n]\!]_I^\mu)).$$

Generalizing strong preservation. Classical abstract model checking [5,6] is state-based, namely it relies on an abstract model which, like the concrete model, is a transition system. If $\mathcal{T} = (Q, R)$ is the concrete transition system then this classical approach is based on a surjective abstraction $h : Q \to A$ mapping concrete states into abstract states, namely a state partition $P_h \in \mathrm{Part}(Q)$ is required. This gives rise to an abstract model $\mathcal{A} = (A, R^\sharp)$ which is a transition system, where, typically, the abstract transition relation $R^\sharp$ is existentially defined as the following $R^{\exists\exists}$:

$$h(s_1)\, R^{\exists\exists}\, h(s_2) \;\Leftrightarrow\; \exists s_1', s_2'. h(s_1') = h(s_1) \;\&\; h(s_2') = h(s_2) \;\&\; s_1' R s_2'.$$

Abstract model checking then consists in checking a temporal formula φ specified in some language $\mathcal{L}$ in the abstract model $\mathcal{A}$: a *preservation theorem* ensures that if $a \models^{\mathcal{A}} \varphi$ and $h(s) = a$ then $s \models^{\mathcal{T}} \varphi$. In this classical state-based framework, strong preservation (s.p. for short) for $\mathcal{L}$ means that for any $\varphi \in \mathcal{L}$, if $h(s) = a$ then $a \models^{\mathcal{A}} \varphi \;\Leftrightarrow\; s \models^{\mathcal{T}} \varphi$. Loiseaux et al. [19] generalized this approach to more general abstract models where an abstraction relation $\sigma \subseteq Q \times A$ is used instead of the surjection $h : Q \to A$. However, the strong preservation results given there (cf. [19, Theorems 3 and 4]) require the hypothesis that the relation

[1] It is possible to consider generic operators whose arity is any possibly infinite ordinal, thus allowing, for example, infinite conjunctions or disjunctions.

σ is difunctional: as a consequence, the class of abstract models allowed by this framework is not really larger than the class of classical partition-based abstract models (see the detailed discussion by Dams et al. [12, Sect. 8.1]).

Following Dams [11, Sect. 6.1], the above classical state-based notion of strong preservation can be equivalently given through state equivalences as follows. The language $\mathcal{L}$ and the semantic function $[\![\cdot]\!]_I$ induce the following state logical equivalence $\equiv_{\mathcal{L}} \subseteq Q \times Q$: $s \equiv_{\mathcal{L}} s'$ iff $\forall \varphi \in \mathcal{L}. s \in [\![\varphi]\!]_I \Leftrightarrow s' \in [\![\varphi]\!]_I$. Let $P_{\mathcal{L}} \in \mathrm{Part}(Q)$ be the corresponding partition of Q. Then, a partition $P \in \mathrm{Part}(Q)$ is strongly preserving for $\mathcal{L}$ (and interpretation I) if $P \preccurlyeq P_{\mathcal{L}}$, while P is fully abstract[2] for $\mathcal{L}$ if $P = P_{\mathcal{L}}$. For most known temporal languages (e.g., CTL*, CTL-X, ∀CTL*, see [11]), if the partition P is s.p. for $\mathcal{L}$ then it turns out that the quotient transition system $(Q/_{\equiv_P}, R^{\exists\exists})$ is s.p. for $\mathcal{L}$. Moreover, if P is fully abstract then the quotient $(Q/_{\equiv_P}, R^{\exists\exists})$ is the smallest transition system (smallest in the number of states) that strongly preserves $\mathcal{L}$.

We consider now an equivalent formulation of strong preservation for partitions that will allow us to generalize the notion of strong preservation to generic abstract domains. We showed above how any partition $P \in \mathrm{Part}(Q)$ can be viewed as a partitioning closure $\mathrm{pcl}(P) \in \mathrm{uco}^{\mathrm{p}}(\wp(Q))$. Thus, any partition P induces the abstract semantics $[\![\cdot]\!]_I^P = [\![\cdot]\!]_I^{\mathrm{pcl}(P)} : \mathcal{L} \to \mathrm{pcl}(P)$. The following result characterizes strong preservation for P in terms of the associated closure $\mathrm{pcl}(P)$.

Lemma 4.1. *$P \in \mathrm{Part}(Q)$ is s.p. for $\mathcal{L}$ and I iff $\forall \varphi \in \mathcal{L}$ and $s \in Q$, $s \in [\![\varphi]\!]_I \Leftrightarrow \mathrm{pcl}(P)(\{s\}) \subseteq [\![\varphi]\!]_I^P$.*

Let us stress the paradigm shift stated by Lemma 4.1. This tells us that a partition $P \in \mathrm{Part}(Q)$ is s.p. for $\mathcal{L}$ and I if and only if to check that some system state $s \in Q$ satisfies some formula $\varphi \in \mathcal{L}$, i.e. $s \in [\![\varphi]\!]_I$, is equivalent to checking whether the abstract state associated to s, i.e. the block $\mathrm{pcl}(P)(\{s\})$ of P containing s, is less than or equal to, namely is contained in, the abstract semantics $[\![\varphi]\!]_I^P$ of φ, which is an element of the abstract domain $\mathrm{pcl}(P)$. Here, the key observation is that in our abstract interpretation-based framework partitions are just particular abstract domains. Thus, the above characterization leads to generalize the notion of strong preservation from partitions to generic abstract semantic functions as follows.

Definition 4.2. Let I be an interpretation for a language $\mathcal{L}$ (inducing the concrete semantic function $[\![\cdot]\!]_I$). Let $\mu \in \mathrm{uco}(\wp(Q))$ and let $[\![\cdot]\!]^\sharp : \mathcal{L} \to \mu$ be an abstract semantic function for $\mathcal{L}$. We say that $[\![\cdot]\!]^\sharp$ is *strongly preserving* for $\mathcal{L}$ and I if for any $S \subseteq Q$ and $\varphi \in \mathcal{L}$, $\mu(S) \subseteq [\![\varphi]\!]^\sharp \Leftrightarrow S \subseteq [\![\varphi]\!]_I$. □

Definition 4.2 generalizes classical state-based strong preservation, as characterized by Lemma 4.1, both to an arbitrary abstract domain $\mu \in \mathrm{uco}(\wp(Q))$ and to an arbitrary semantic function $[\![\cdot]\!]^\sharp : \mathcal{L} \to \mu$ evaluating formulae on μ. Hence, $[\![\cdot]\!]^\sharp$ may be different from the abstract semantics $[\![\cdot]\!]_I^\mu$ induced by the abstract domain μ. It turns out that indeed this notion of *strong preservation*

[2] Dams [11] uses the term "adequate".

is an abstract domain property, namely if a s.p. abstract semantics $[\![\cdot]\!]^\sharp$ may be defined on some abstract domain μ then the induced abstract semantics $[\![\cdot]\!]_I^\mu$ is s.p. as well, as stated by the following result.

Lemma 4.3. *If $[\![\cdot]\!]^\sharp : \mathcal{L} \to \mu$ is strongly preserving for $\mathcal{L}$ and I then $[\![\cdot]\!]_I^\mu$ is strongly preserving for $\mathcal{L}$ and I.*

This result allows us to define without loss of generality strong preservation for abstract domains as follows: a closure $\mu \in \mathrm{uco}(\wp(Q))$ is strongly preserving for $\mathcal{L}$ and I when $[\![\cdot]\!]_I^\mu$ is s.p. for $\mathcal{L}$ and I.

As recalled above, the concrete semantic function $[\![\cdot]\!]_I$ induces a state partition $P_\mathcal{L}$, which is the fully abstract partition according to our definition, since $P_\mathcal{L}$ encodes the "best" strongly preserving partition, where "best" means coarsest (i.e. the greatest w.r.t. the ordering $\preceq$). In other terms, $P_\mathcal{L}$ is the coarsest partition such that the states in any block cannot be distinguished by the language $\mathcal{L}$. We aim at defining an analogous of $P_\mathcal{L}$ for closure-based abstractions, namely the "best" strongly preserving closure. Given a partition $P \in \mathrm{Part}(Q)$, the associated partitioning closure $\mathrm{pcl}(P) \in \mathrm{uco}^{\mathrm{P}}(\wp(Q))$ is completely determined by its behaviour on states $q \in Q$, namely on singletons $\{q\} \in \wp(Q)$, since $\mathrm{pcl}(P)$ is additive (cf. Lemma 3.2). Of course, this does not happen for a generic closure $\mu \in \mathrm{uco}(\wp(Q))$. This means that a generalization of $P_\mathcal{L}$ to closures must take into account the behaviour of the closure on all the subsets of Q. Thus, if we define, for $S \subseteq Q$, $S \models \varphi$ iff $\forall s \in S. s \models \varphi$, one might try the following definition: the "best" s.p. closure $\mu_\mathcal{L}$ for $\mathcal{L}$ is given by

$$\mu_\mathcal{L}(S) = \cup\{T \in \wp(Q) \mid \forall \varphi \in \mathcal{L}.\, S \models \varphi \Leftrightarrow T \models \varphi\}.$$

However, this does not work, as shown by the following example.

Example 4.4. Let us consider the simple transition system (Q, R) depicted in the figure and the language $\mathcal{L}$ generated by the grammar $\varphi ::= p \mid \mathrm{EX}\varphi$, where the set of the atomic propositions is $AP = \{p_1, p_2\}$ with interpretation $I(p_1) = \{a, b\}$ and $I(p_2) = \{c\}$ (and $I(\mathrm{EX}) = \mathrm{pre}[R]$). Note that $b \models \mathrm{EX}p_1$ while $a \not\models \mathrm{EX}p_1$. In this case, we have that $P_\mathcal{L} = \{a, b, c\} \in \mathrm{Part}(Q)$. By using the above definition of $\mu_\mathcal{L}$, it turns out that $\mu_\mathcal{L} = \lambda x.x \in \mathrm{uco}(\wp(Q))$. However, the closure $\mu = \{\varnothing, b, c, ab, abc\}$ is more abstract than $\mu_\mathcal{L}$ and still strongly preserving. In fact, it is not difficult to check that for any $\varphi \in \mathcal{L}$, $[\![\varphi]\!]_I^\mu = [\![\varphi]\!]_I$, and therefore, according to Definition 4.2, μ is strongly preserving for $\mathcal{L}$. □

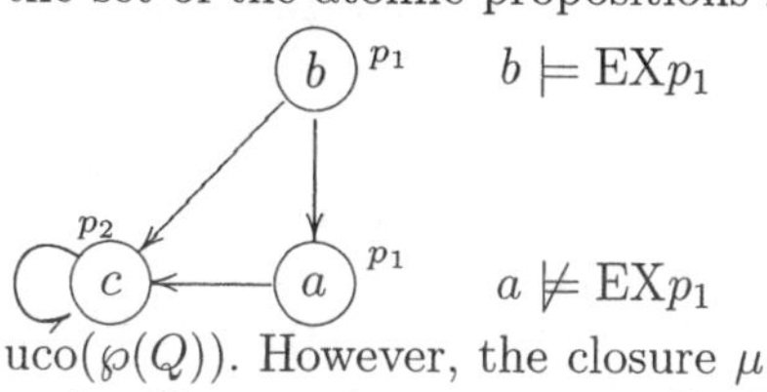

Instead, we may note that if $\mu \in \mathrm{uco}(\wp(Q))$ is s.p. for $\mathcal{L}$ then the following property holds: for any $S \in \wp(Q)$ and $\varphi \in \mathcal{L}$, $S \models \varphi \Rightarrow \mu(S) \models \varphi$. In fact, if $S \models \varphi$ and $x \in \mu(S)$ then $\mu(\{x\}) \subseteq \mu(S)$ and therefore, since $\mu(S) \subseteq [\![\varphi]\!]_I^\mu \Leftrightarrow S \models \varphi$, we have that $\mu(\{x\}) \subseteq [\![\varphi]\!]_I^\mu$, and thus, again by strong preservation, $x \models \varphi$. Actually, it turns out that this weaker property characterizes the best s.p. closure for $\mathcal{L}$.

Definition 4.5. Let $[\![\cdot]\!]_I : \mathcal{L} \to \wp(Q)$ be the concrete semantic function. Then, we define $\mu_{\mathcal{L}} : \wp(Q) \to \wp(Q)$ as follows: for any $S \in \wp(Q)$,

$$\mu_{\mathcal{L}}(S) \stackrel{\text{def}}{=} \bigcup\{T \in \wp(Q) \mid \forall \varphi \in \mathcal{L} \,.\, S \models \varphi \Rightarrow T \models \varphi\}. \qquad \square$$

It is not hard to check that $\mu_{\mathcal{L}}$ is indeed a closure. It turns out that $\mu_{\mathcal{L}}$ actually is the right candidate for the best s.p. abstract domain.

Theorem 4.6. *Let $\mu \in \text{uco}(\wp(Q))$. Then, μ is s.p. for $\mathcal{L}$ and I iff $\mu \sqsubseteq \mu_{\mathcal{L}}$.*

Thus, $\mu_{\mathcal{L}}$ actually is the "best" s.p. abstract domain, i.e., it is the most abstract s.p. closure: $\mu_{\mathcal{L}} = \sqcup\{\mu \in \text{uco}(\wp(Q)) \mid \mu \text{ is s.p. for } \mathcal{L} \text{ and } I\}$. Moreover, it turns out that $\mu_{\mathcal{L}}$ is exactly the closure meet-generated by the set of concrete semantics of all the formulae in $\mathcal{L}$.

Proposition 4.7. $\mu_{\mathcal{L}} = \mathcal{M}(\{[\![\varphi]\!]_I \mid \varphi \in \mathcal{L}\})$.

As a consequence, we have that μ is s.p. for $\mathcal{L}$ and I iff $\forall \varphi \in \mathcal{L}.\ [\![\varphi]\!]_I \in \mu$ iff $\forall \varphi \in \mathcal{L}. [\![\varphi]\!]_I = [\![\varphi]\!]_I^{\mu}$. Let us remark that as strong preservation for a partition P w.r.t. $\mathcal{L}$ means that P is a refinement of the state partition $P_{\mathcal{L}}$ induced by $\mathcal{L}$ likewise strong preservation for a closure μ means that μ is a refinement of the closure $\mu_{\mathcal{L}}$ of Definition 4.5 induced by $\mathcal{L}$. Strong preservation and full abstraction for partitions become particular instances, through the isomorphism of Theorem 3.3, of the corresponding notions for closures, as stated by the following result.

Proposition 4.8. *Let $P \in \text{Part}(Q)$.*
(1) $P_{\mathcal{L}} = \text{par}(\mu_{\mathcal{L}})$ and $\text{pcl}(P_{\mathcal{L}}) = \mathbb{P}(\mu_{\mathcal{L}})$.
(2) P is s.p. for $\mathcal{L}$ and I iff $P \preccurlyeq \text{par}(\mu_{\mathcal{L}})$ iff $\text{pcl}(P) \sqsubseteq \mathbb{P}(\mu_{\mathcal{L}})$.

Finally, it is natural to ask when the closure $\mu_{\mathcal{L}}$ induced by a language $\mathcal{L}$ is partitioning.

Proposition 4.9. *Let $\mathcal{L}$ be closed under possibly infinite logical conjunction. Then, $\mu_{\mathcal{L}}$ is partitioning iff $\mathcal{L}$ is closed under logical negation.*

Example 4.10. Consider the transition system (Q, R) depicted in the figure and the temporal language CTL with atomic propositions p and q where $I(p) = \{1, 2, 4\}$ and $I(q) = \{3\}$. Consider the partition $P = \{124, 3\} \in \text{Part}(Q)$ induced by the interpretation I. It is well known [2] that the state partition $P_{\text{CTL}} \in \text{Part}(Q)$ induced by CTL can be obtained by refining P using the Paige-Tarjan [20] partition refinement algorithm. It is easy to check that $P_{\text{CTL}} = \{14, 2, 3\}$. However, the partition P_{CTL} does not carry all the semantic information. By Proposition 4.8 (1), P_{CTL} is the state equivalence induced by μ_{CTL}. Also, by Proposition 4.7, μ_{CTL} is the Moore-closure of $\{[\![\varphi]\!]_I \mid \varphi \in \text{CTL}\}$. In this very simple case, it is easy to check that $\mu_{\text{CTL}} = \{\varnothing, 2, 3, 14, 23, 124, 134, 1234\}$. Thus, as expected from Proposition 4.8 (1), $P_{\text{CTL}} = \text{par}(\mu_{\text{CTL}})$. Since CTL is closed under logical negation, by

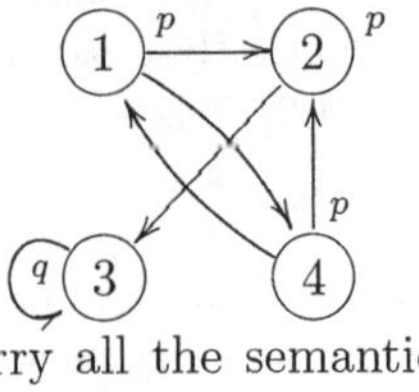

Proposition 4.9, it turns out that μ_{CTL} is partitioning and $\mu_{\mathrm{CTL}} = \mathrm{pcl}(P_{\mathrm{CTL}})$. Of course, this is not always the case. As an example, consider the following sublanguage $\mathcal{L}$ of CTL: $\varphi ::= p \mid q \mid \varphi_1 \wedge \varphi_2 \mid \mathrm{EX}\varphi$. Then, $\{1,3,4\} \notin \mu_{\mathcal{L}}$: in fact, $\{1,3,4\}$ can be obtained as the semantics of the CTL formula $q \vee \mathrm{EX}p$, i.e. $[\![q \vee \mathrm{EX}p]\!]_I = \{1,3,4\}$, while it is easy to observe that it cannot be obtained from a formula in $\mathcal{L}$. In this case, $\mu_{\mathcal{L}} = \{\varnothing, 2, 3, 14, 23, 124, 1234\}$ and $P_{\mathcal{L}} = \{14, 2, 3\}$. Here, it turns out that $\mu_{\mathcal{L}}$ is not a partitioning closure, namely a loss of precision occurs in abstracting $\mu_{\mathcal{L}}$, through the mapping par, to the partition $P_{\mathcal{L}}$. □

5 Completeness and Strong Preservation

We need to consider forward completeness of abstract domains for generic n-ary semantic functions. Let C be any complete lattice, $f : C^n \to C$, with $n \geq 0$, and $\mu \in \mathrm{uco}(\wp(Q))$. Thus, μ is forward f-complete, or simply f-complete, when $f \circ \langle \mu, ..., \mu \rangle = \mu \circ f \circ \langle \mu, ..., \mu \rangle$, i.e., for any $\vec{x} \in \mu^n$, $f(\vec{x}) \in \mu$. If $F \subseteq \mathrm{Fun}(C)$, μ is F-complete when μ is f-complete for each $f \in F$. Note that when $f : C^0 \to C$, i.e. $f \in C$, μ is forward f-complete iff $f \in \mu$. Moreover, note that any $\mu \in \mathrm{uco}(C)$ is always forward meet-complete, because any closure operator is Moore-closed.

We first note that the *forward F-complete shell* refinement always exists.

Lemma 5.1. *Let $F \subseteq \mathrm{Fun}(\wp(Q))$ and $\mu \in \mathrm{uco}(C)$. Then, $\mathcal{S}_F(\mu) \stackrel{\mathrm{def}}{=} \sqcup \{\rho \in \mathrm{uco}(C) \mid \rho \sqsubseteq \mu, \rho$ is F-complete$\}$ is F-complete.*

We call $\mathcal{S}_F : \mathrm{uco}(C) \to \mathrm{uco}(C)$ the *F-complete shell* (or complete shell, when F is clear from the context) refinement, since $\mathcal{S}_F(\mu)$ is the most abstract F-complete domain which refines μ. As a straight consequence, the complete shell of a closure admits the following constructive fixpoint characterization.

Lemma 5.2. *Let $R_F : \mathrm{uco}(C) \to \wp(C)$ be defined as follows: $R_F(\mu) \stackrel{\mathrm{def}}{=} \{f(\vec{x}) \in C \mid f \in F, \vec{x} \in \mu^{\sharp(f)}\}$. Then, $\mathcal{S}_F(\mu) = \mathrm{gfp}(\lambda\rho.\mu \sqcap \mathcal{M}(R_F(\rho)))$.*

For finite state systems, for any $\mu \in \mathrm{uco}(C)$, the operator $\lambda\rho.\mu \sqcap \mathcal{M}(R_F(\rho)) : \mathrm{uco}(C) \to \mathrm{uco}(C)$ is trivially co-continuous and therefore its greatest fixpoint can be computed through the Kleene's iteration sequence. Moreover, for unary operators, the iterative computation of the fixpoint $\mathcal{S}_F(\mu)$ can be simplified by applying R_F just to the new sets added in the previous iteration step, as follows.

Lemma 5.3. *Let C be finite, $F \subseteq C \to C$ and $\mu \in \mathrm{uco}(C)$. Define inductively $\mu_0 \stackrel{\mathrm{def}}{=} \mu$, $\mu_1 \stackrel{\mathrm{def}}{=} \mathcal{M}(\mu_0 \cup R_F(\mu_0))$, and, for $i \in \mathbb{N}$, $\mu_{i+2} \stackrel{\mathrm{def}}{=} \mathcal{M}(\mu_{i+1} \cup R_F(\mu_{i+1} \smallsetminus \mu_i))$. Then, there exists $n \in \mathbb{N}$ such that $\mathcal{S}_F(\mu) = \mu_n$.*

Let us now turn to strong preservation. Given a language $\mathcal{L}$, our goal is to single out a set of operators F such that refining a closure η for F-completeness is equivalent to refining η in order to get strong preservation for $\mathcal{L}$. The semantics of $\mathcal{L}$ is determined by the interpretations **AP** and **Op** of, respectively, the set of atomic propositions AP and the set of operators Op. Thus, **Op** is the obvious candidate for F. Moreover, we know (cf. Theorem 4.6) that an atomic proposition p is strongly preserved by a domain η if and only if $\mathbf{p} \in \eta$. Also, recall that in partition refinement algorithms like Paige-Tarjan [20] for CTL and Groote-Vaandrager [16] for CTL-X, the interpretation of the atomic propositions determine the blocks of the initial partition, or, otherwise stated, the blocks of the partition to refine give the atomic propositions of the language. Likewise, here the fixpoints of the initial closure η provide the interpretation of the atomic propositions of $\mathcal{L}$. This is more general, since η need not to be a partition of system states. This can be formalized by associating to any set of sets $S \subseteq \wp(Q)$ a set of atomic propositions $AP_S = \{p_T \mid T \in S\}$ that are interpreted by the interpretation function I_S defined by $I_S(p_T) = T$. Also, given a closure $\eta \in \mathrm{uco}(\wp(Q))$ and a language $\mathcal{L}$ with operators ranging in Op, we consider the language $\mathcal{L}_\eta$ where AP_η is the set of atomic propositions while the operators still are in Op. The interpretation for $\mathcal{L}_\eta$ therefore is $I_\eta = \eta \cup \mathbf{Op}$. Then, the following key result shows the announced relationship between forward complete shells and strong preservation.

Theorem 5.4. *Let $\eta \in \mathrm{uco}(\wp(Q))$ and $\mathcal{L}$ be a language with operators in Op closed under logical conjunction. Then, $\mathcal{S}_{\mathbf{Op}}(\eta)$ is the most abstract closure which refines η and is s.p. for $\mathcal{L}_\eta$. In particular, $\mathcal{S}_{\mathbf{Op}}(\eta) = \mu_{\mathcal{L}_\eta}$.*

The opposite direction is also interesting: given a language $\mathcal{L}$, the following result characterizes the "best" s.p. closure $\mu_\mathcal{L}$ for $\mathcal{L}$ as a forward complete shell of a closure associated to $\mathcal{L}$. This comes as a straight consequence of Theorem 5.4.

Corollary 5.5. *Let $\mathcal{L}$ be given by AP and Op, let I be the interpretation and let $\mathcal{L}$ be closed under logical conjunction. Let $\mu_{AP} \stackrel{\text{def}}{=} \mathcal{M}(\{I(p) \mid p \in AP\})$. Then, $\mu_\mathcal{L} = \mathcal{S}_{\mathbf{Op}}(\mu_{AP})$.*

It is also worth remarking that, as a consequence of Proposition 4.8 (1), the state equivalence induced by the language $\mathcal{L}_\mu$ can be retrieved from the closure $\mathcal{S}_{\mathbf{Op}}(\mu)$: $\equiv_{\mathcal{S}_{\mathbf{Op}}(\mu)} = \equiv_{\mathcal{L}_\mu}$.

Theorem 5.4 provides a clean and precise generalization of the many existing coarsest partition refinement algorithms from an abstract interpretation perspective. Indeed, the coarsest refinement of a given partition which is strongly preserving for a given language can be characterized using our abstract domain-based approach as follows.

Corollary 5.6. *Let $\mathcal{L}$ be closed under logical conjunction and $P \in \mathrm{Part}(Q)$.*
(1) Let P^r be the coarsest partition refinement of P which is strongly preserving for $\mathcal{L}$ and I_P. Then, $P^r = \mathrm{par}(\mathcal{S}_{\mathbf{Op}}(\mathcal{M}(P)))$.
(2) Let $\mathcal{L}$ be closed under logical negation and let P^r be the coarsest partition refinement of P which is strongly preserving for $\mathcal{L}$ and I_P. Then, $\mathrm{pcl}(P^r) = \mathcal{S}_{\mathbf{Op}}(\mathrm{pcl}(P))$.

Note that, by the corollary above, in general the closure-based complete refinement of a partitioning closure $\mathrm{pcl}(P)$ associated to a partition P does not provide the closure associated to the corresponding partition-based refinement, but a more abstract closure. The following result shows that a closure is partitioning iff it is forward complete for the complement $\complement$. As a consequence, when the language is closed under logical negation the two refinement techniques agree.

Lemma 5.7. *If $\mu \in \mathrm{uco}(\wp(Q))$ then, μ is partitioning iff μ is forward $\complement$-complete.*

We can draw the following consequence. Let $\mathcal{L}$ be closed under logical conjunction. Then, by Theorem 5.4 and Lemma 5.7, $\mathcal{L}$ is closed under logical negation iff for any $\mu \in \mathrm{uco}(\wp(Q))$, $\mathcal{S}_{\mathbf{Op}}(\mu)$ is partitioning. Hence, for languages which are not closed under logical negation, the output partition of any partition refinement algorithm for achieving strong preservation for $\mathcal{L}$ is not the optimal, i.e. "best", abstraction refinement.

6 Application to Behavioural State Equivalences

We apply the above results to a number of standard temporal languages. It is well known that some of these languages like CTL and CTL-X induce state equivalences which coincide with standard behavioural equivalences used in process algebra like bisimulation and stuttering equivalence. We obtain as consequences a new characterization of these behavioural equivalences in terms of forward complete abstract interpretations which shows the following remarkable fact: these behavioural properties for a state equivalence $\sim$ can be interpreted as suitable completeness properties of $\sim$ viewed as an abstract interpretation. Due to lack of space we do not consider here the case of CTL-X and stuttering equivalence.

Bisimulation. Let $\mathcal{T} = (Q, R, AP, \ell)$ be a Kripke structure (R is assumed to be total). Let us recall the well known notion of bisimulation. A symmetric relation $\sim \subseteq Q \times Q$ is a bisimulation on the Kripke structure $\mathcal{T}$ if for any $s, s' \in Q$ such that $s \sim s'$: (1) $\ell(s) = \ell(s')$; (2) for any $t \in Q$ such that $s \xrightarrow{R} t$, there exists $t' \in Q$ such that $s' \xrightarrow{R} t'$ and $t \sim t'$. In particular, a partition $P \in \mathrm{Part}(Q)$ is called a bisimulation on $\mathcal{T}$ when the relation $\equiv_P$ is a bisimulation on $\mathcal{T}$. The (set-theoretically) largest bisimulation relation exists and will be denoted by $\sim_{\mathrm{bis}}$. It is well known [2] that $\sim_{\mathrm{bis}}$ is an equivalence relation, called *bisimulation equivalence*, which coincides with the state logical equivalence induced by the language CTL, i.e., $\sim_{\mathrm{bis}} = \equiv_{\mathrm{CTL}}$ (the same holds for CTL*). On the other hand, it is also known that it is enough to consider Hennessy-Milner logic [17], i.e. a language $\mathcal{L}_1$ allowing full propositional logic, i.e. conjunction plus negation, and the temporal connective EX, in order to have a state equivalence $\equiv_{\mathcal{L}_1}$ which coincides with $\equiv_{\mathrm{CTL}}$. The language $\mathcal{L}_1$ is then defined by the following grammar:

$$\varphi ::= p \mid \varphi_1 \wedge \varphi_2 \mid \neg\varphi \mid \mathrm{EX}\varphi$$

where $p \in AP$ and the interpretation I for the connectives is standard.

It is also well known that the bisimulation equivalence $\sim_{\mathrm{bis}}$ can be obtained through the Paige-Tarjan [20] partition refinement algorithm on the input partition determined by the interpretation of atomic propositions, i.e., the partition $\mathrm{par}(\mu_{AP})$ where $\mu_{AP} = \mathcal{M}(\{\mathbf{p} \mid p \in AP\})$. Here, exploiting Theorem 5.4, we get the characterization of bisimulation equivalence in terms of forward completeness (points (1) and (3) below) and of the Paige-Tarjan partition refinement algorithm as a complete shell refinement (points (2) and (4) below).

Corollary 6.1. *Let $\mathcal{T}$ be finite and $P \in \text{Part}(Q)$.*
(1) *P is a bisimulation on $\mathcal{T}$ iff pcl(P) is forward complete for* $\{\mathbf{p} \mid p \in AP\} \cup \{\text{pre}[R]\}$.
(2) *Let P^r be the output partition of the Paige-Tarjan algorithm on input P. Then,* $\text{pcl}(P^r) = \mathcal{S}_{\{\mathtt{C},\text{pre}[R]\}}(\mathcal{M}(P))$.
(3) $\sim_{\text{bis}} = \equiv_{\mathcal{S}_{\{\mathtt{C},\text{pre}[R]\}}(\mu_{AP})}$.
(4) *For any* $\mu \in \text{uco}(\wp(Q))$, $\mathcal{S}_{\{\mathtt{C},\text{pre}[R]\}}(\mu) = \text{pcl}(P^r_\mu)$, *where P^r_μ is the output partition of the Paige-Tarjan algorithm on input* $\text{par}(\mu)$.

In our abstract interpretation-based terminology, given a generic closure $\mu \in \text{uco}(\wp(Q))$, $\mathcal{S}_{\{\mathtt{C},\text{pre}[R]\}}(\mu)$ is the most abstract refinement of μ which is s.p. for $\mathcal{L}_1$ (where the atomic propositions are determined by μ). Since the operators of $\mathcal{L}_1$ include both logical conjunction and negation, by Lemma 5.7, this complete shell is always partitioning, i.e. it is a representation of a partition by a closure.

Example 6.2. Let us consider the transition system in the figure, taken from [11, Sect. 6.6]. Also, consider the partition $P = \{1, 4, 2356\}$ which induces the atomic propositions $AP = \{p, q, r\}$, where $\mathbf{p} = \{2356\}$, $\mathbf{q} = \{4\}$ and $\mathbf{r} = \{1\}$.

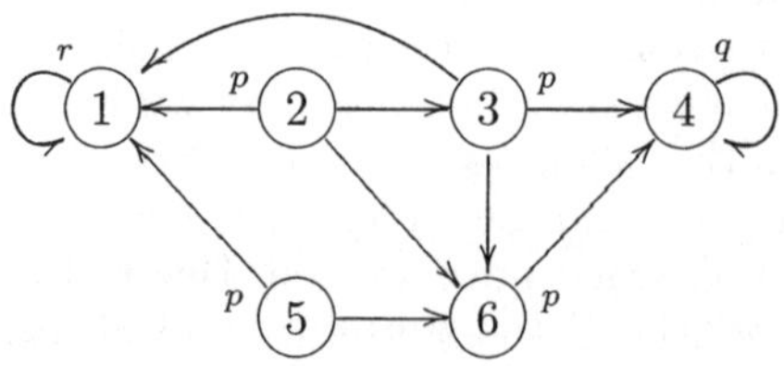

It turns out that P is not a bisimulation. This can be checked on the abstract interpretation side by Corollary 6.1 (1): in fact, $\mu = \text{pcl}(P) = \{\varnothing, 1, 4, 2356, 14, 12356, 23456, 123456\}$ is not pre$[R]$-complete, because, for instance, $\text{pre}[R](\{1\}) = \{1235\} \notin \text{pcl}(P)$. Obviously, this logically corresponds to the fact that for $\text{EX}\, r \in \mathcal{L}_1$, $[\![\text{EX}r]\!] = \{1, 2, 3, 5\}$ while $[\![\text{EX}r]\!]^\mu = \mu(\{1235\}) = \{12356\}$. Using Definition 4.2 of strongly preserving closure, this corresponds to the fact that $\mu(\{6\}) = \{2356\} \subseteq [\![\text{EX}r]\!]^\mu$ while $6 \notin [\![\text{EX}r]\!]$. It is easy to check that the Paige-Tarjan algorithm on the input partition P yields the partition $P^r = \{1, 2, 3, 4, 5, 6\}$. Thus, by Corollary 6.1 (4), we have that $\mathcal{S}_{\{\mathtt{C},\text{pre}[R]\}}(\mu) = \text{pcl}(P^r) = \wp(Q)$. Thus, for any $S \subseteq Q$ there exists a formula $\varphi \in \mathcal{L}_1$ such that $[\![\varphi]\!] = S$. □

Simulation equivalence. Consider the language $\mathcal{L}_2$ obtained from $\mathcal{L}_1$ by dropping logical negation, namely $\mathcal{L}_2$ is defined by the following grammar:

$$\varphi ::= p \mid \varphi_1 \wedge \varphi_2 \mid \text{EX}\varphi$$

It is known — see for example the handbook chapter by van Glabbeek [22, Sect. 8] — that the state equivalence $\equiv_{\mathcal{L}_2}$ induced by $\mathcal{L}_2$ coincides with simulation equivalence. Let us briefly recall the notion of simulation relation. Let $\mathcal{T} = (Q, R, AP, \ell)$ be a Kripke structure. A relation $\sigma \subseteq Q \times Q$ is a simulation if for any $s, s' \in Q$ such that $s\sigma s'$: (1) $\ell(s) = \ell(s')$; (2) if, for some $t \in Q$, $s \xrightarrow{R} t$ then there exists some $t' \in Q$ such that $s' \xrightarrow{R} t'$. Then, *simulation equivalence* $\sim_{\text{sim}} \subseteq Q \times Q$ is defined as follows: $s \sim_{\text{sim}} s'$ iff there exist two simulation relations $\sigma, \tau \subseteq Q \times Q$ such that $s\sigma s'$ and $s'\tau s$. A number of algorithms for computing the partition $\sim_{\text{sim}}$, which coincides with $P_{\mathcal{L}_2}$, have been designed (e.g. [1,3,18]). Here, as a consequence of Theorem 5.4, we get the following characterization of simulation equivalence in terms of forward completeness (recall that μ_{AP} is the closure determined by the interpretation of atomic propositions AP):

Corollary 6.3. $\sim_{\rm sim} = \equiv_{\mathcal{S}_{{\rm pre}[R]}(\mu_{AP})}$.

Moreover, as argued after Lemma 5.7, since $\mathcal{L}_2$ is not closed under logical negation, we have that the output partition P^r of simulation equivalence computed by the aforementioned algorithms is not optimal for the strong preservation of $\mathcal{L}_2$, in the sense that the partitioning closure $\mathrm{pcl}(P^r)$ does not coincide with the set of formula semantics $\{[\![\varphi]\!]_\ell \mid \varphi \in \mathcal{L}_2\}$.

Example 6.4. Consider the transition system of Example 6.2. Let us compute the simulation equivalence $\sim_{\rm sim}$ by resorting to Corollary 6.3 and to the iterative method of Lemma 5.3. Let $\mu_{AP} = \mathcal{M}(\{1,4,2356\}) = \{\varnothing,1,4,2356,123456\}$.

$$\mu_0 = \mu_{AP}$$

$$\begin{aligned}\mu_1 &= \mathcal{M}(\mu_0 \cup R_{{\rm pre}[R]}(\mu_0))\\ &= \mathcal{M}(\mu_0 \cup \{1235 = {\rm pre}[R](\{1\}), 346 = {\rm pre}[R](\{4\}), 235 = {\rm pre}[R](\{2356\})\})\\ &= \{\varnothing,1,1235,235,2356,3,346,36,4,123456\}\end{aligned}$$

$$\begin{aligned}\mu_2 &= \mathcal{M}(\mu_1 \cup R_{{\rm pre}[R]}(\mu_1 \smallsetminus \mu_0)) = \mathcal{M}(\mu_1 \cup \{23456 = {\rm pre}[R](\{346\})\}\\ &= \{\varnothing,1,1235,2,235,2356,23456,3,346,36,4,123456\} \qquad \text{(fixpoint)}\end{aligned}$$

Thus, $\mu_{\mathcal{L}_2} = \mu_2 = \mathcal{S}_{{\rm pre}[R]}(\mu_{AP})$ and $\equiv_{\mu_2} = \sim_{\rm sim}$, i.e., the partition associated to the simulation equivalence is $P_{\mathcal{L}_2} = \{1,2,3,4,5,6\}$. As expected, note that $\mathrm{pcl}(P_{\mathcal{L}_2}) \sqsubset \mathcal{S}_{{\rm pre}[R]}(\mu_{AP})$. Also note that $P_{\mathcal{L}_2}$ is the same partition obtained for bisimulation in Example 6.2, although the closures $\mu_{\mathcal{L}_1}$ and $\mu_{\mathcal{L}_2}$ are well different. □

7 Conclusion

We designed an abstract interpretation-based framework to study the properties of strong preservation of abstract model checking, where classical abstract model checking systems based on state partitions are embedded as particular abstract interpretations. Our main result showed that the minimal refinement of an abstract domain for achieving the completeness property w.r.t. the semantic operators of some language $\mathcal{L}$ is exactly equivalent to the minimal refinement of the corresponding abstract model checking in order to get strong preservation for $\mathcal{L}$. It is worth mentioning that we exploited the results in this paper to devise a generalized abstract interpretation-based Paige-Tarjan partition refinement algorithm which is able to compute the minimal refinements of abstract models which are strongly preserving for a generic inductively defined language [21].

Acknowledgements. We wish to thank Mila Dalla Preda and Roberto Giacobazzi who contributed to the early stage of this work. This work was partially supported by the FIRB Project "Abstract interpretation and model checking for the verification of embedded systems" and by the COFIN2002 Project "CoVer".

References

1. B. Bloom and R. Paige. Transformational design and implementation of a new efficient solution to the ready simulation problem. *Sci. Comp. Program.*, 24(3):189–20, 1995.
2. M.C. Browne, E.M. Clarke and O. Grumberg. Characterizing finite Kripke structures in propositional temporal logic. *TCS*, 59:115–131, 1988.
3. D. Bustan and O. Grumberg. Simulation-based minimization. *ACM TOCL*, 4(2):181–204, 2003.
4. E.M. Clarke, O. Grumberg, S. Jha, Y. Lu, and H. Veith. Counterexample-guided abstraction refinement. In *Proc. CAV'00.* LNCS 1855:154–169, 2000.
5. E.M. Clarke, O. Grumberg and D. Long. Model checking and abstraction. *ACM TOPLAS*, 16(5):1512–1542, 1994.
6. E.M. Clarke, O. Grumberg and D.A. Peled. *Model checking.* The MIT Press, 1999.
7. P. Cousot and R. Cousot. Abstract interpretation: a unified lattice model for static analysis of programs by construction or approximation of fixpoints. In *Proc. 4th ACM POPL*, pp. 238–252, 1977.
8. P. Cousot and R. Cousot. Systematic design of program analysis frameworks. In *Proc. 6th ACM POPL*, pp. 269–282, 1979.
9. P. Cousot and R. Cousot. Temporal abstract interpretation. In *Proc. 27th ACM POPL*, pp. 12–25, 2000.
10. M. Dalla Preda. *Completeness and stability in abstract model checking.* Master Thesis, Univ. of Verona, 2003.
11. D. Dams. *Abstract interpretation and partition refinement for model checking.* Ph.D. Thesis, Eindhoven Univ., 1996.
12. D. Dams, O. Grumberg, and R. Gerth. Abstract interpretation of reactive systems. *ACM TOPLAS*, 16(5):1512–1542, 1997.
13. R. Giacobazzi and E. Quintarelli. Incompleteness, counterexamples and refinements in abstract model checking. In *Proc. SAS '01*, LNCS 2126:356–373, 2001.
14. R. Giacobazzi and F. Ranzato. Refining and compressing abstract domains. In *Proc. 24th ICALP*, LNCS 1256:771–781, 1997.
15. R. Giacobazzi, F. Ranzato, and F. Scozzari. Making abstract interpretations complete. *J. ACM*, 47(2):361–416, 2000.
16. J.F. Groote and F. Vaandrager. An efficient algorithm for branching bisimulation and stuttering equivalence. In *Proc. ICALP '90*, LNCS 443:626–638, 1990.
17. M. Hennessy and R. Milner. Algebraic laws for nondeterminism and concurrency. *J. ACM*, 32(1):137–161, 1985.
18. M.R. Henzinger, T.A. Henzinger and P.W. Kopke. Computing simulations on finite and infinite graphs. In *Proc. 36th FOCS*, pp. 453–462, 1995.
19. C. Loiseaux, S. Graf, J. Sifakis, A. Bouajjani, and S. Bensalem. Property preserving abstractions for the verification of concurrent systems. *Formal Methods in System Design*, 6:1–36, 1995.
20. R. Paige and R.E. Tarjan. Three partition refinement algorithms. *SIAM J. Comput.*, 16(6):973–989, 1987
21. F. Ranzato and F. Tapparo. Generalizing the Paige-Tarjan partition refinement algorithm through abstract interpretation. Manuscript, Univ. of Padova, 2004.
22. R.J. van Glabbeek. The linear time - branching time spectrum. In *Handbook of Process Algebra*, pp. 3–99, 2001.

Static Analysis of Digital Filters*

Jérôme Feret

DI, École Normale Supérieure, Paris, FRANCE
jerome.feret@ens.fr

Abstract. We present an Abstract Interpretation-based framework for automatically analyzing programs containing digital filters. Our framework allows refining existing analyses so that they can handle given classes of digital filters. We only have to design a class of symbolic properties that describe the invariants throughout filter iterations, and to describe how these properties are transformed by filter iterations. Then, the analysis allows both inference and proofs of the properties about the program variables that are tied to any such filter.

1 Introduction

Digital filters are widely used in real-time embedded systems (as found in automotive, aeronautic, and aerospace applications) since they allow modeling into software behaviors previously ensured by analogical filters. A filter transforms an input stream of floating-point values into an output stream. Existing analyses are very imprecise in bounding the range of the output stream, because of the lack of precise linear properties that would entail that the output is bounded. The lack of precise domains when analyzing digital filters was indeed the cause of almost all the remaining warnings (potential floating-point overflows) in the certification of a critical software family with the analyzer described in [1,2].

In this paper, we propose an Abstract Interpretation-based framework for designing new abstract domains which handle filter classes. Human intervention is required for discovering the general shape of the properties that are required in proving the stability of such a filter. Roughly speaking, filter properties are mainly an abstraction of the input stream, from which we deduce bounds on the output stream. Our framework can then be used to build the corresponding abstract domain. This domain propagates all these properties throughout the abstract computations of programs. Our approach is not syntactic, so that loop unrolling, filter reset, boolean control, and trace (or state) partitioning are dealt with for free and any filter of the class (for any setting) is analyzed precisely.

Moreover, in case of linear filters, we propose a general approach to build the corresponding class of properties. We first design a rough abstraction, in which at each filter iteration, we do not distinguish between the contributions of each input. Then, we design a precise abstraction: using linearity, we split the output between the global contribution of floating-point errors, and the contribution of

* This work was partially supported by the ASTRÉE RNTL project.

D.A. Schmidt (Ed.): ESOP 2004, LNCS 2986, pp. 33–48, 2004.

the ideal filter behavior. Global floating-point error contribution is then bounded using the rough abstraction, while ideal filter output is precisely described by formally expanding it, so that the contribution of each input is exactly described in the real field, and then approximated in floating-point arithmetics.

We have instantiated our framework for two kinds of widely used linear filters: the *high bandpass* and *second order* filters. The framework was fully implemented in OCaml [8] and plugged into an existing analyzer. We have obtained bounds that are very close to sample experimental results, which has allowed solving nearly all of our remaining warnings [2].

Previous works. To our knowledge, this is the first analysis that abstracts filter output invariants. Nevertheless, some work has been done in filter optimization. In [7], affine equality relationships [6] among variables at the beginning and at the end of loop iterations are used to factorize filters at compile time. In our case, because of floating-point rounding errors, there are no such affine equality relationships, so a more complex domain such as polyhedra [5] is required to perform the same task. Moreover, our programs involve complex boolean control flows. Thus, filter factorization cannot be performed without a highly expensive partitioning. Furthermore, our goal is just to prove the absence of error at runtime, and not to describe precisely the global behavior of filters.

Outline. In Sect. 2, we present the syntax and semantics of our language. In Sect. 3, we describe a generic abstraction for this language. In Sect. 4, we define a generic extension for refining existing abstractions. In Sect. 5, we give numerical abstract domains for describing sets of real numbers. In Sect. 6, we describe, on our examples, the general approach to building such generic extensions. In Sect. 7, we describe the impact of these extensions on the analysis results.

2 Language

We analyze a subset of C without dynamic memory allocation nor side-effect. Moreover, the use of pointer operations is restricted to call-by reference. For the sake of simplicity, we introduce an intermediate language to describe programs interpreted, between the concrete and an abstract level. We suppose that *lvalue* resolution has been partially solved (see [2, Sect. 6.1.3]). Furthermore, assignments (which use floating-point arithmetics at the concrete level) have been conservatively abstracted into non-deterministic assignments in the real field, i.e., floating-point expressions have been approximated by linear forms with real interval coefficients. These linear forms include both the rounding errors and some expression approximations (see [10]). We also suppose that runtime errors (such as floating-point overflows) can be described by interval constraints on the memory state after program computations.

Let $\mathcal{V}$ be a finite set of variables. We denote by $\mathcal{I}$ the set of all real number intervals (including $\mathbb{R}$ itself). We define inductively the syntax of programs in Fig. 1. We denote by $\mathcal{E}$ the set of expressions E. We describe the semantics of these programs in a denotational way. An *environment* ($\rho \in \mathcal{V} \rightarrow \mathbb{R}$) denotes a memory state. It maps each variable to a real number. We denote by *Env* the set

$V \in \mathcal{V}, I \in \mathcal{I}$
$E := I \mid V \mid (-V) + E \mid V + E \mid I \times V + E$
$P := V = E \mid \text{skip} \mid \text{if } (V \geq 0)\ \{P\} \text{ else } \{P\} \mid \text{while } (V \geq 0)\ \{P\} \mid P; P$

Fig. 1. Syntax.

$$\begin{array}{l}
[\![I]\!]_E(\rho) = I,\ [\![V]\!]_E(\rho) = \{\rho(V)\} \\
[\![(-V) + E]\!]_E(\rho) = \{a - \rho(V) \mid a \in [\![E]\!]_E(\rho)\},\ [\![V + E]\!]_E(\rho) = \{\rho(V) + a \mid a \in [\![E]\!]_E(\rho)\} \\
[\![I \times V + E]\!]_E(\rho) = \{b \times \rho(V) + a \mid a \in [\![E]\!]_E(\rho), b \in I\} \\
[\![V = E]\!]_P(\rho) = \{\rho[V \mapsto x] \mid x \in [\![E]\!]_E(\rho)\} \\
[\![\text{skip}]\!]_P(\rho) = \{\rho\} \\
[\![\text{if } (V \geq 0)\ \{P_1\} \text{ else } \{P_2\}]\!]_P(\rho) = \begin{cases} [\![P_1]\!]_P(\rho) & \text{if } \rho(V) \geq 0 \\ [\![P_2]\!]_P(\rho) & \text{otherwise} \end{cases} \\
[\![\text{while } (V \geq 0)\ \{P\}]\!]_P(\rho) = \{\rho' \in \mathit{Inv} \mid \rho'(V) < 0\} \\
\text{where } \mathit{Inv} = \text{lfp}\left(X \mapsto \{\rho\} \cup \left(\bigcup\{[\![P]\!]_P(\rho') \mid \rho' \in X, \rho'(V) \geq 0\}\right)\right) \\
[\![P_1; P_2]\!]_P(\rho) = \bigcup\{[\![P_2]\!]_P(\rho') \mid \rho' \in [\![P_1]\!]_P(\rho)\}
\end{array}$$

Fig. 2. Concrete semantics.

of all environments. The semantics of a program P is a function ($[\![P]\!]_P \in \mathit{Env} \to \wp(\mathit{Env})$) mapping each environment ρ to the set of the environments that can be reached when applying the program P starting from the environment ρ. The function $[\![\_]\!]_P$ is defined by induction on the syntax of programs in Fig. 2. Loop semantics requires the computation of a *loop invariant*, which is the set of all environments that can be reached just before the guard of this loop is tested. This invariant is well-defined as the least fixpoint of a $\cup$-complete endomorphism in the powerset $\wp(\mathit{Env})$. Nevertheless, such a fixpoint is usually not computable, so we give a decidable approximate semantics in the next section.

We describe two filter examples, that we will use throughout the paper.

Example 1. A *high bandpass* filter can be encoded by the following program:

$$\begin{array}{l}
V = \mathbb{R};\ E_1 = [0; 0]; \\
\text{while } (V \geq 0)\ \{ \\
\quad V = \mathbb{R};\ T = \mathbb{R};\ E_0 = I; \\
\quad \text{if } (T \geq 0)\ \{S = 0\} \\
\quad \text{else } \{S = A \times S + E_0 + (-E_1) + F\}; \\
\quad E_1 = E_0; \\
\}
\end{array}$$

Roughly speaking, the interval I denotes the range of filter entries. Floating-point rounding errors are captured by the range of both intervals A and F. The interval A describes the filter coefficient and satisfies $A \subseteq [\frac{1}{2}; 1[$. Variables V and T allow control flow enforcement. At each loop iteration, the variable S denotes the value of the current filter output, the variable E_0 denotes the value of the current filter input, and the variable E_1 denotes the value of the previous filter input. Depending on the value of T, the filter is either reset (i.e., the output is set to 0), or iterated (i.e., the value of the next output is calculated from the last output value and the two last input values). The analysis described in [2] only discovers inaccurate bounds for the variable S. It works as if the expression $A \times S + E_0 - E_1 + F$ were approximated by $A \times S + (2 \times I + F)$. The analysis discovers the first widening threshold l (see [1, Sect. 2.1.2]) such that l is greater than $\frac{2 \times i + f}{1-a}$, for any $(i, f, a) \in I \times F \times A$. It proves that l is stable, and then successive narrowing iterations refine the value l. □

Example 2. A *second order* digital filter can be encoded as follows:

$V = \mathbb{R};\ E_1 = [0; 0];\ E_2 = [0; 0];$
while $(V \geq 0)$ {
  $V = \mathbb{R};\ T = \mathbb{R};\ E_0 = I;$
  if $(T \geq 0)$ $\{S_0 = E_0;\ S_1 = E_0\}$
  else $\{S_0 = A \times S_1 + B \times S_2 + C \times E_0 + D \times E_1 + E \times E_2 + F\};$
  $E_2 = E_1;\ E_1 = E_0;\ S_2 = S_1;\ S_1 = S_0$
}

Roughly speaking, the interval I denotes the range of filter entries. Intervals A, B, C, D and E denote filter coefficients and satisfy $A \subseteq [0; \infty[$, $B \subseteq]-1; 0[$ and $\forall (a, b) \in A \times B,\ a^2 + 4 \times b < 0$. Floating-point rounding errors are captured by the range of intervals A, B, C, D, E and F. Variables V and T allow control flow enforcement. At each loop iteration, the variable S_0 denotes the value of current filter output, variables S_1 and S_2 denote the last two values of filter output, the variable E_0 denotes the value of the current filter input, and variables E_1 and E_2 denote the last two values of filter input. Depending on the value of T, either the filter is reset (i.e., both the current and the previous outputs are set to the same value), or iterated (i.e., the value of the next output is calculated from the last two output values and the last three input values). The analysis described in [2] fails to discover any bound for the variables S_0, S_1, S_2. □

3 Underlying Domain

We use the Abstract Interpretation framework [3,4] to derive a generic approximate semantics. An abstract domain $Env^\sharp$ is a set of properties about memory states. Each abstract property is related to the set of the environments which satisfy it via a concretization map γ. An operator $\sqcup$ allows the gathering of information about different control flow paths. Some primitives ASSIGN and GUARD are sound counterparts to concrete assignments and guards. To effectively compute an approximation of concrete fixpoints, we introduce an iteration basis $\bot$, a widening operator ∇ and a narrowing operator Δ. Several abstract domains collaborate, and refine each others using very simple constraints: variable ranges and equality relations. These constraints are related to the concrete domains via two concretization functions $\gamma_{\mathcal{I}}$ and $\gamma_{=}$ that respectively map each function $\rho^\sharp \in \mathcal{V} \to \mathcal{I}$ to the set of the environments ρ such that $\forall X \in \mathcal{V},\ \rho(X) \in \rho^\sharp(X)$, and each relation $\mathcal{R} \subseteq \mathcal{V}^2$ to the set of environments ρ such that for any variables X and Y, $(X, Y) \in \mathcal{R}$ implies that $\rho(X) = \rho(Y)$. The primitives RANGE and EQU capture simple constraints about the filter input stream, and about

$$
\begin{aligned}
&[\![V = E]\!]^\sharp(a) = \textsc{assign}(V = E, a)\\
&[\![\text{skip}]\!]^\sharp(a) = a\\
&[\![\text{if } (V \geq 0)\ \{P_1\} \text{ else } \{P_2\}]\!]^\sharp(a) = a_1 \sqcup a_2, \text{ with } \begin{cases} a_1 = [\![P_1]\!]^\sharp(\textsc{guard}(V, [0; +\infty[, a))\\ a_2 = [\![P_2]\!]^\sharp(\textsc{guard}(V,]-\infty; 0[, a))\end{cases}\\
&[\![\text{while } (V \geq 0)\ \{P\}]\!]^\sharp(a) = \textsc{guard}(V,]-\infty; 0[, Inv^\sharp)\\
&\text{where } Inv^\sharp = \text{lfp}^\sharp\left(X \mapsto a \sqcup [\![P]\!]^\sharp(\textsc{guard}(V, [0; +\infty[, X))\right)\\
&[\![P_1; P_2]\!]^\sharp(\rho^\sharp) = [\![P_2]\!]^\sharp([\![P_1]\!]^\sharp(\rho^\sharp))
\end{aligned}
$$

Fig. 3. Abstract semantics.

the initialization state, to be passed to the filter domains. Conversely, a primitive REDUCE receives the constraints about the filter output range to refine the underlying domain.

Definition 1 (Generic abstraction). *An abstraction is defined by a tuple* $(Env^\sharp, \gamma, \sqcup, \textsc{assign}, \textsc{guard}, \bot, \nabla, \Delta, \textsc{range}, \textsc{equ}, \textsc{reduce})$ *such that:*

1. $Env^\sharp$ *is a set of properties;*
2. $\gamma \in Env^\sharp \to \wp(Env)$ *is a concretization map;*
3. $\forall a, b \in Env^\sharp, \gamma(a) \cup \gamma(b) \subseteq \gamma(a \sqcup b)$*;*
4. $\forall a \in Env^\sharp, \rho^\sharp \in (\mathcal{V} \to \mathcal{I}),\ \gamma(a) \cap \gamma_{\mathcal{I}}(\rho^\sharp) \subseteq \gamma(\textsc{reduce}(\rho^\sharp, a))$*, moreover* $\textsc{reduce}([X \mapsto \mathbb{R}], a) = a$*;*
5. ∇ *is a widening operator such that:* $\forall a, b \in Env^\sharp,\ \gamma(a) \cup \gamma(b) \subseteq \gamma(a \nabla b)$*; and* $\forall \rho^\sharp \in (\mathcal{V} \to \mathcal{I}),\ (a_i) \in (Env^\sharp)^{\mathbb{N}}$*, the sequence* (a_i^∇) *defined by* $a_0^\nabla = \textsc{reduce}(\rho^\sharp, a_0)$ *and* $a_{n+1}^\nabla = \textsc{reduce}(\rho^\sharp, a_n^\nabla \nabla a_{n+1})$ *is ultimately stationary;*
6. Δ *is a narrowing operator such that:* $\forall a, b \in Env^\sharp,\ \gamma(a) \cap \gamma(b) \subseteq \gamma(a \Delta b)$*; and* $\forall \rho^\sharp \in (\mathcal{V} \to \mathcal{I}),\ (a_i) \in (Env^\sharp)^{\mathbb{N}}$*, the sequence* (a_i^Δ) *defined by* $a_0^\Delta = \textsc{reduce}(\rho^\sharp, a_0)$ *and* $a_{n+1}^\Delta = \textsc{reduce}(\rho^\sharp, a_n^\Delta \Delta a_{n+1})$*, is ultimately stationary;*
7. $\forall a \in Env^\sharp, X \in \mathcal{V}, E \in \mathcal{E}, \rho \in \gamma(a),\ [\![X = E]\!]_{\mathcal{P}}(\rho) \subseteq \gamma(\textsc{assign}(X = E, a))$*;*
8. $\forall a \in Env^\sharp, X \in \mathcal{V}, I \in \mathcal{I},\ \{\rho \in \gamma(a) \mid \rho(X) \in I\} \subseteq \gamma(\textsc{guard}(X, I, a))$*;*
9. $\forall a \in Env^\sharp,\ \gamma(a) \subseteq \gamma_{\mathcal{I}}(\textsc{range}(a))$ *and* $\gamma(a) \subseteq \gamma_{=}(\textsc{equ}(a))$*.*

Least fixpoint approximation is performed in two steps [3]: we first compute an approximation using the widening operator; then we refine it using the narrowing operator. More formally, let f be a $\cup$-complete endomorphism of $\wp(Env)$, and $(f^\sharp \in Env^\sharp \to Env^\sharp)$ be an abstract counterpart of f satisfying $\forall a \in Env^\sharp,\ (f \circ \gamma)(a) \subseteq (\gamma \circ f^\sharp)(a)$. The abstract upward iteration (C_n^∇) of $f^\sharp$ is defined by $C_0^\nabla = \bot$ and $C_{n+1}^\nabla = C_n^\nabla \nabla f^\sharp(C_n^\nabla)$. The sequence (C_n^∇) is ultimately stationary and its limit C_ω^∇ satisfies $\text{lfp}(f) \subseteq \gamma(C_\omega^\nabla)$. Then the abstract downward iteration (D_n^Δ) of $f^\sharp$ is defined by $D_0^\Delta = C_\omega^\nabla$ and $D_{n+1}^\Delta = D_n^\Delta \Delta f^\sharp(D_n^\Delta)$. The sequence (D_n^Δ) is ultimately stationary and its limit D_ω^Δ satisfies $\text{lfp}(f) \subseteq \gamma(D_\omega^\Delta)$. So we define $\text{lfp}^\sharp(f^\sharp)$ by the limit of the abstract downward iteration of $f^\sharp$.

The abstract semantics of a program is given by a function $([\![\_]\!]^\sharp \in Env^\sharp \to Env^\sharp)$ in Fig. 3. Its soundness can be proved by induction on the syntax:

Theorem 1. *For any program* P*, environment* ρ*, abstract element* a*, we have:*

$$\rho \in \gamma(a) \implies [\![P]\!]_{\mathcal{P}}(\rho) \subseteq \gamma\left([\![P]\!]^\sharp(a)\right). \qquad \square$$

4 Generic Extension

We now show how an analysis can be extended to take into account a given class of digital filters. We first introduce all the primitives that we need to build such a domain. Then we define a single domain. At last, we build an approximate reduced product between such a domain and an underlying domain.

4.1 Primitives

A filter domain collects constraints that relate some variables that will be used again at the next filter iteration with some filter parameters and a dynamic information. This provides approximation of both filter input and output. For instance, the variables may be the last outputs, the parameters some directing coefficients, and the dynamic information a radius inferred during the analysis. Let m be the numbers of variables to be used and n that of the filter parameters. The abstract domain maps tuples in $\mathcal{T} = \mathcal{V}^m \times \mathbb{R}^n$ to elements of the set $\mathcal{B}$ of dynamic information. The set of the environments that satisfies a constraint $c \in \mathcal{T} \times \mathcal{B}$ is given by its concretization $\gamma_{\mathcal{B}}(c)$. An operator $\sqcup_{\mathcal{B}}$ is used to merge constraints related to the same tuple, but coming from distinct flows. For each assignment $X = E$ interpreted in an environment satisfying the range constraints described by $\rho^\sharp \in \mathcal{V} \to \mathcal{I}$, the set $\text{RLVT}(X = E)$ denotes the set of tuples corresponding to the constraints that are modified by this assignment (usually the tuples containing some variables that occurs in the expression E). For each of these tuples t associated with the dynamic information a, the pair $\text{PT}(X = E, t, \rho^\sharp) = (t', \mathit{info})$ is such that t' is the tuple that is tied, after the assignment (obtained by shifting the variables), by the new constraint[1], and *info* contains all the parameters about both the filter and the input stream that are required to infer the dynamical information. This information is itself updated by $\delta(\mathit{info}, a)$. The element $\bot_{\mathcal{B}}$ provides the basis of iterations. Extrapolation operators $\nabla_{\mathcal{B}}$ and $\Delta_{\mathcal{B}}$ allow the concrete post-fixpoint approximation. A primitive BUILD receives some range and equality constraints from the underlying domain to build filter constraints when the filter is reset. Conversely, the function TO extracts information about the range of the output stream to be passed to the underlying domain.

Definition 2 (Generic extension). *An abstract extension is given by a tuple* $(\mathcal{T}, \mathcal{B}, \gamma_{\mathcal{B}}, \sqcup_{\mathcal{B}}, \text{RLVT}, \text{INFO}, \text{PT}, \delta, \bot_{\mathcal{B}}, \nabla_{\mathcal{B}}, \Delta_{\mathcal{B}}, \text{BUILD}, \text{TO})$ *which satisfies:*

1. $\mathcal{T} = \mathcal{V}^m \times \mathbb{R}^n$, *where* $m, n \in \mathbb{N}$; $\mathcal{B}$ *is a set of dynamical information;*
2. $\gamma_{\mathcal{B}} \in \mathcal{T} \times \mathcal{B} \to \wp(\mathit{Env})$ *is a concretization map;*
3. $\forall a, b \in \mathcal{B}, t \in \mathcal{T}, \gamma_{\mathcal{B}}(t, a) \cup \gamma_{\mathcal{B}}(t, b) \subseteq \gamma_{\mathcal{B}}(t, a \sqcup_{\mathcal{B}} b)$;
4. ***assignments:*** RLVT *maps an expression* $E \in \mathcal{E}$ *to a subset* T *of* $\mathcal{T}$; INFO *is a set of filter parameters;* $\forall X \in \mathcal{V}, E \in \mathcal{E}, \rho^\sharp \in \mathcal{V} \to \mathcal{I}$, *we have* $\text{PT}(X = E, t, \rho^\sharp) \in \mathcal{T} \times \text{INFO}$, *the map* $[t \mapsto \mathit{fst}(\text{PT}(X = E, t, \rho^\sharp))]$ *is injective, and*

[1] $\rho^\sharp$ may be used to interpret some variables that occur in E. It also infers a bound to the filter input.

$\forall t \in$ RLVT$(E), a \in \mathcal{B}$, such that $\rho \in \gamma_{\mathcal{B}}(t,a) \cap \gamma_{\mathcal{I}}(\rho^\sharp)$, we have $[\![X = E]\!]_{\mathcal{P}}(\rho) \subseteq \gamma_{\mathcal{B}}(t', \delta(info, a))$, with $(t', info) = \text{PT}(X = E, t, \rho^\sharp)$;

5. *$\nabla_{\mathcal{B}}$ is a widening operator such that: $\forall a, b \in \mathcal{B}$, $\forall t \in \mathcal{T}$, $\gamma_{\mathcal{B}}(t,a) \cup \gamma_{\mathcal{B}}(t,b) \subseteq \gamma_{\mathcal{B}}(t, (a \nabla_{\mathcal{B}} b))$; and $\forall (a_i) \in \mathcal{B}^{\mathbb{N}}$, the sequence (a_i^{∇}) defined by $a_0^{\nabla} = a_0$ and $a_{n+1}^{\nabla} = a_n^{\nabla} \nabla_{\mathcal{B}} a_{n+1}$ is ultimately stationary;*
6. *$\Delta_{\mathcal{B}}$ is a narrowing operator such that: $\forall a, b \in \mathcal{B}$, $\forall t \in \mathcal{T}, \gamma_{\mathcal{B}}(t,a) \cap \gamma_{\mathcal{B}}(t,b) \subseteq \gamma_{\mathcal{B}}(t, a \Delta_{\mathcal{B}} b)$; $\forall (a_i) \in \mathcal{B}^{\mathbb{N}}$, the sequence (a_i^{Δ}) defined by $a_0^{\Delta} = a_0$ and $a_{n+1}^{\Delta} = a_n^{\Delta} \Delta_{\mathcal{B}} a_{n+1}$, is ultimately stationary;*
7. ***filter constraint synthesis** from the underlying domain:*
   $\forall \rho^\sharp \in \mathcal{V} \to \mathcal{I}, \mathcal{R} \in \wp(\mathcal{V}^2), t \in \mathcal{T}$, $\gamma_{\mathcal{I}}(\rho^\sharp) \cap \gamma_{=}(\mathcal{R}) \subseteq \gamma_{\mathcal{B}}(t, \text{BUILD}(t, \rho^\sharp, \mathcal{R}))$;
8. ***interval constraint synthesis:***
   $\text{TO} \in (\mathcal{T} \times \mathcal{B}) \to (\mathcal{V} \to \mathcal{I})$ *and* $\forall t \in \mathcal{T}, a \in \mathcal{B}$, $\gamma_{\mathcal{B}}(t,a) \subseteq \gamma_{\mathcal{I}}(\text{TO}(t,a))$.

4.2 Abstract Domain

We now build an abstraction from a generic extension. We first enrich the set $\mathcal{B}$ with an extra element $\top_{\mathcal{B}} \notin \mathcal{B}$. That element will denote the fact that a tuple is tied to no constraint. We set $\gamma_{\mathcal{B}}(t, \top_{\mathcal{B}}) = Env^\sharp$ and $\text{TO}(t, \top_{\mathcal{B}}) = Env^\sharp$. We also lift other primitives of the domain so that they return $\top_{\mathcal{B}}$ as soon as one of their arguments is $\top_{\mathcal{B}}$. The abstract domain $Env_F^\sharp = (\mathcal{T} \to \mathcal{B})$ is related to $\wp(Env)$ by the concretization function γ_F which maps $f \in Env_F^\sharp$ to the set of environments $\left(\bigcap_{t \in \mathcal{T}} \gamma_{\mathcal{B}}(t, f(t))\right)$ that satisfy all the constraints encoded by f. The operator $\sqcup_F$ applies componentwise the operator $\sqcup_{\mathcal{B}}$. The abstract assignment may require information about variable ranges in order to extract filter parameters (in particular the input values). The abstract assignment $\text{ASSIGN}_F^{\rho^\sharp}(X = E, f)$ of an abstract element f under the interval constraints $\rho^\sharp \in \mathcal{V} \to \mathcal{I}$, is given by the abstract element f' where:

1. if E is a variable Y, each constraint containing Y gives a constraint for X: we take $f'(t) = f(\sigma t)$, where σ substitutes each occurrence of X by Y;
2. otherwise, we remove each constraint involving X, and add each constraint corresponding to some filter iteration, $f'(t)$ is given by:

$$\begin{cases} \delta(info, f(t_{-1})) & \text{if } \exists t_{-1} \in \text{RLVT}(E), (t, info) = \text{PT}(X = E, t_{-1}, \rho^\sharp), \\ f(t) & \text{if } t \in (\mathcal{V} \setminus \{X\})^m \times \mathbb{R}^n, \\ \top_{\mathcal{B}} & \text{otherwise;} \end{cases}$$

We also set $\text{ASSIGN}_F(X = E, f) = \text{ASSIGN}_F^{\text{RANGE}_F(f)}(X = E, f)$. Since filter invariants do not rely on guards, we set $\text{GUARD}_F(X, I, f) = f$. The function $\text{RANGE}_F(f)$ maps each variable X to the interval $\left(\bigcap_{t \in \mathcal{T}} \text{TO}_F(t, f(t))(X)\right)$; since filters do not generate syntactic equality constraints, we take $\text{EQU}_F = \emptyset$. We also ignore the constraints that are passed by the other domains, this way we take $\text{REDUCE}_F(\rho^\sharp, a) = a$. The $\perp_F$ element maps each tuple to the element $\top_{\mathcal{B}}$. The operators (∇_F, Δ_F) are defined componentwise. We define the tuple $\mathcal{A}_F$ by $(Env_F^\sharp, \gamma_F, \sqcup_F, \text{ASSIGN}_F, \text{GUARD}_F, \perp_F, \nabla_F, \Delta_F, \text{RANGE}_F, \text{EQU}_F, \text{REDUCE}_F)$.

Theorem 2. *The tuple $\mathcal{A}_F$ is an abstraction.* □

4.3 Product and Approximate Reduced Product

Unfortunately the abstraction $\mathcal{A}_F$ cannot compute any constraint, mainly because of inaccurate assignments and guards, and abstract iterations always return the top element. Hence we use a reduced product between this abstraction and an existing underlying abstraction to refine and improve the analysis.
Let $\mathcal{A}_0 = (Env_0^\sharp, \gamma_0, \sqcup_0, \text{ASSIGN}_0, \text{GUARD}_0, \perp_0, \nabla_0, \Delta_0, \text{RANGE}_0, \text{EQU}_0, \text{REDUCE}_0)$ be an abstraction. We first introduce the product of the two abstractions. The abstract domain $Env^\sharp$ is the Cartesian product $Env_0^\sharp \times Env_F^\sharp$. The operator $\sqcup$, the transfer functions (ASSIGN, GUARD), the function REDUCE and the extrapolation operators $(\perp, \nabla, \Delta)$ are all defined pairwise. The concretization and the remaining refinement primitives are defined as follows:

$$\begin{cases} \gamma(a,f) = \gamma_0(a) \cap \gamma_F(f), \\ \text{EQU}(a,f)(X,Y) \iff \text{EQU}_0(a)(X,Y) \text{ or } \text{EQU}_F(f)(X,Y), \\ \text{RANGE}(X)(a,f) = \text{RANGE}_0(X)(a) \cap \text{RANGE}_F(X)(f), \end{cases}$$

which corresponds to taking the meet of collected information.

We refine abstract assignments and binary operators:

- before assignments, we synthesize the filter constraints that are relevant for the assignment; during assignments, we use the underlying constraints to interpret the expression; and after assignments, we use the filter constraints to refine the properties in the underlying domain. That is to say, we define $\text{ASSIGN}'(X = E, (a, f))$ by $(\text{REDUCE}_0(\text{RANGE}_F(f''), a''), f'')$ where:
  - $(a'', f'') = (\text{ASSIGN}_0(X = E, a), \text{ASSIGN}_F^{\text{RANGE}_0(a)}(X = E, f'))$
  - $f'(t) = \begin{cases} \text{BUILD}(t, \text{RANGE}_0(a), \text{EQU}_0(a)) & \text{if } t \in \text{RLVT}(E) \text{ and } f(t) = \top_{\mathcal{B}}, \\ f(t) & \text{otherwise.} \end{cases}$
- before applying a binary operator, we refine the filter constraints so that both arguments constrain the same set of tuples; after applying a binary operator, we use the filter constraints to refine the underlying domain properties. That is to say, for any operator $\circledast \in \{\sqcup, \Delta, \nabla\}$, we define $(a_1, f_1) \circledast' (a_2, f_2)$ by $(\text{REDUCE}_0(\text{RANGE}_F(f''), a''), f'')$ where:
  - $(a'', f'') = (a_1 \circledast_0 a_2, f_1' \circledast_F f_2')$,
  - $f_i'(t) = \begin{cases} \text{BUILD}(t, \text{RANGE}_0(a_i), \text{EQU}_0(a_i)) & \text{if } f_i(t) = \top_{\mathcal{B}} \text{ and } f_{2-i}(t) \neq \top_{\mathcal{B}}, \\ f_i(t) & \text{otherwise.} \end{cases}$

We set $\mathcal{A} = (Env^\sharp, \gamma, \sqcup', \text{ASSIGN}', \text{GUARD}, \perp, \nabla', \Delta', \text{RANGE}, \text{EQU}, \text{REDUCE})$.

Theorem 3. *The tuple $\mathcal{A}$ is an abstraction.* □

5 Numerical Abstract Domains

Until now, we have only used real numbers. In order to implement numerical abstract domains, we use a finite subset $\mathbb{F}$ of real numbers (such as the floating-point numbers), that is closed under negation. The set $\overline{\mathbb{F}}$ is obtained by enriching the set $\mathbb{F}$ with two extra elements $+\infty$ and $-\infty$ that respectively describe the reals that are greater (resp. smaller) than the greatest (resp. smallest) element of $\mathbb{F}$. Since the result of a computation on elements of $\overline{\mathbb{F}}$ may be not in $\overline{\mathbb{F}}$, we suppose we are given a function $\lceil \_ \rceil$, that provides an upper bound in $\overline{\mathbb{F}}$ to real numbers. The set $\overline{\mathbb{F}}$ is also endowed with a finite widening ramp L [2, Sect. 7.1.2]. For any two elements a and b in $\overline{\mathbb{F}}$ we set $a \nabla_{\overline{\mathbb{F}}} b = min\{l \in L \cup \{a; +\infty\} \mid max(a,b) \leq l\}$. We now design two families of abstract domains parametrized by the integers q and r that allow tuning the extrapolation strategy.

- The domain $\mathcal{F}_{q,r}$ is the set $\overline{\mathbb{F}} \times \mathbb{Z}$. It is related to $\wp(\mathbb{R})$ via the concretization $\gamma_{\mathcal{F}_{q,r}}$ that maps any pair (e,k) into the set of the reals r such that $|r| \leq e$. The bottom element $\bot_{\mathcal{F}_{q,r}}$ is $(-\infty, 0)$. The binary operators $\sqcup_{\mathcal{F}_{q,r}}$, $\nabla_{\mathcal{F}_{q,r}}$, and $\Delta_{\mathcal{F}_{q,r}}$ are defined as follows:
  - $(a_1,k_1) \sqcup_{\mathcal{F}_{q,r}} (a_2,k_2) = (max(a_1,a_2), 0)$;
  - $(a_1,k_1) \nabla_{\mathcal{F}_{q,r}} (a_2,k_2) = \begin{cases} (a_1,k_1) & \text{if } a_1 \geq a_2 \\ (a_2, k_1+1) & \text{if } a_2 > a_1 \text{ and } k_1 < q \\ (a_1 \nabla_{\overline{\mathbb{F}}} a_2, 0) & \text{otherwise;} \end{cases}$
  - $(a_1,k_1) \Delta_{\mathcal{F}_{q,r}} (a_2,k_2) = \begin{cases} (a_1,k_1) & \text{if } a_1 \leq a_2 \text{ or } k_1 \leq (-r) \\ (a_2, min(k_1,0)-1) & \text{if } a_2 < a_1 \text{ and } k_1 > (-r); \end{cases}$

  A constraint is only widened if it has been unstable q times since its last widening. On the other side, narrowing stops after r iterations.
- The domain $\mathcal{F}^2_{q,r}$ is the Cartesian product between $\mathcal{F}_{0,r}$ and $\mathcal{F}_{q,0}$. It is related to $\wp(\mathbb{R})$ via a concretization map $\gamma_{\mathcal{F}^2_{q,r}}$ that maps elements (a,b) to $\gamma_{\mathcal{F}_{0,r}}(a) \cap \gamma_{\mathcal{F}_{q,0}}(b)$. The element $\bot_{\mathcal{F}^2_{q,r}}$ is the pair $(\bot_{\mathcal{F}_{0,r}}, \bot_{\mathcal{F}_{q,0}})$. Binary operators are defined pairwise, except the widening, that is defined as follows:
  $$((a_1,k_1),(b_1,l_1)) \nabla_{\mathcal{F}^2_{q,r}} ((a_2,k_2),(b_2,l_2)) = ((min(a_3,b_3),0),(b_3,l_3)),$$
  where $(a_3,k_3) = (a_1,k_1) \nabla_{\mathcal{F}_{0,r}} (a_2,k_2)$ and $(b_3,l_3) = (b_1,l_1) \nabla_{\mathcal{F}_{q,0}} (b_2,l_2)$.

  The elements a and b in the pair (a,b) are intended to describe the same set of reals. Nevertheless, they will be iterated using distinct extrapolation strategies and distinct transfer functions. The element a will be computed via a transfer function $f \in \overline{\mathbb{F}} \to \overline{\mathbb{F}}$, whereas b will be computed via a relaxed transfer function that try to guess the fixpoint of f. The element b is used to refine the element a after widening, in case it becomes more precise. This allows computing arbitrary thresholds during iterations. To ensure termination, it is necessary also to widen b, but this is not done at each iteration.

6 Applications

We propose a general approach to build accurate instantiations for generic extensions in case of linear filtering. We first design a rough abstraction ignoring the historical properties of the input. That way, filters will be considered as if the output only depends on the previous outputs and on only the last global contributions of the last inputs. Then, we formally expand filter equations, so that the overall contribution of each input is exactly described. We use the rough abstraction to approximate the contribution of the floating-point rounding errors during filter iterations. In the whole section, we use a function $\text{EVAL}^\sharp$ that maps each pair $(E, \rho^\sharp)$, where E is an expression and $\rho^\sharp$ is an abstract environment in $\mathcal{V} \to \mathcal{I}$, to $m \in \overline{\mathbb{F}}$ such that $\forall \rho \in \gamma_{\mathcal{I}}(\rho^\sharp)$, $[\![E]\!]_E(\rho) \subseteq [-m; m]$. We also use two natural number parameters q and r, and a real number parameter $\epsilon > 0$.

6.1 Rough Abstraction

To get the rough abstraction, we forget any historical information about the inputs during the filter iterations, so that each output is computed as an affine combination of the previous outputs. The constant term is an approximation of the contributions of both the previous inputs and the floating-point rounding errors. Human intervention is only required during the design of the domain to discover the form of the properties that are relevant, and the way these properties are propagated throughout a filter iteration.

Simplified High Passband Filter. A simplified high passband filter relates an input stream E_n to an output stream defined by $S_{n+1} = aS_n + E_n$.

Theorem 4. *Let $\varepsilon_a \geq 0$, $D \geq 0$, $m \geq 0$, a, X and Z be real numbers such that $|X| \leq D$ and $aX - (m + \varepsilon_a|X|) \leq Z \leq aX + (m + \varepsilon_a|X|)$.*
Then we have:

- $|Z| \leq (|a| + \varepsilon_a)D + m$;
- $\left[|a| + \varepsilon_a < 1 \text{ and } D \geq \frac{m}{1-(|a|+\varepsilon_a)}\right] \implies |Z| \leq D.$ □

We define two maps $\phi_1 \in \mathbb{F}^2 \times \overline{\mathbb{F}}^2 \to \overline{\mathbb{F}}$ and $\phi_2 \in \mathbb{F}^2 \times \overline{\mathbb{F}} \to \overline{\mathbb{F}}$ by:

$$\begin{cases} \phi_1(a, \varepsilon_a, m, D) = \lceil (|a| + |\varepsilon_a|)D + m \rceil, \\ \phi_2(a, \varepsilon_a, m) = \begin{cases} \left\lceil \frac{m(1+\epsilon)}{1-(|a|+|\varepsilon_a|)} \right\rceil & \text{if } |a| + |\varepsilon_a| < 1 \\ +\infty & \text{otherwise.} \end{cases} \end{cases}$$

We derive the following extension:

- $\mathcal{T}_{r_1} = (\mathcal{V} \times \mathbb{F}^2)$ and $info = \mathbb{F}^2 \times \overline{\mathbb{F}}$;
- $(\mathcal{B}_{r_1}, \bot_{r_1}, \sqcup_{\mathcal{B}_{r_1}}, \nabla_{\mathcal{B}_{r_1}}, \Delta_{\mathcal{B}_{r_1}}) = (\mathcal{F}^2_{q,r}, \bot_{\mathcal{F}^2_{q,r}}, \sqcup_{\mathcal{F}^2_{q,r}}, \nabla_{\mathcal{F}^2_{q,r}}, \Delta_{\mathcal{F}^2_{q,r}})$;
- $\gamma_{\mathcal{B}_{r_1}}((X, a, \varepsilon_a), e) = \{\rho \in Env \mid \rho(X) \in \gamma_{\mathcal{F}^2_{q,r}}(e)\}$;
- RLVT_{r_1} maps each expression E to the set of the tuples (X, a, ε_a), such that E matches $I \times X + E'$ with $I \subseteq [\frac{1}{2}; 1[$ and $I = [a - \varepsilon_a; a + \varepsilon_a]$;
- $\text{PT}_{r_1}(Z = I \times X + E', (X, a, \varepsilon_a), \rho^\sharp) = ((Z, a, \varepsilon_a), (a, \varepsilon_a, m))$ where $m = \text{EVAL}^\sharp(E', \rho^\sharp)$;[2]
- $\delta_{r_1}((a, \varepsilon_a, m), ((D_1, k_1), (D_2, k_2))) = ((r_1, 0), (r_2, 0))$ where $r_1 = \phi_1(a, \varepsilon_a, m, D_1)$ and $r_2 = max(\phi_1(a, \varepsilon_a, m, D_2), \phi_2(a, \varepsilon_a, m))$;
- $\text{BUILD}_{r_1}((X, a, \varepsilon_a), \rho^\sharp, \mathcal{R}) = ((m, 0), (m, 0))$, with $m = \text{EVAL}^\sharp(X, \rho^\sharp)$;
- $\text{TO}_{r_1}((X, a, \varepsilon_a), e) = \begin{cases} Y \mapsto \gamma_{\mathcal{F}^2_{q,r}}(e) & \text{if } X = Y \\ Y \mapsto \mathbb{R} & \text{otherwise.} \end{cases}$

A simplified second order filter relates an input stream E_n to an output stream defined by:

$$S_{n+2} = aS_{n+1} + bS_n + E_{n+2}.$$

Thus we experimentally observe, in Fig. 4, that starting with $S_0 = S_1 = 0$ and provided that the input stream is bounded, the pair (S_{n+2}, S_{n+1}) lies in an ellipsoid. Moreover, this ellipsoid is attractive, which means that an orbit starting out of this ellipsoid, will get closer of it. This behavior is explained by Thm. 5.

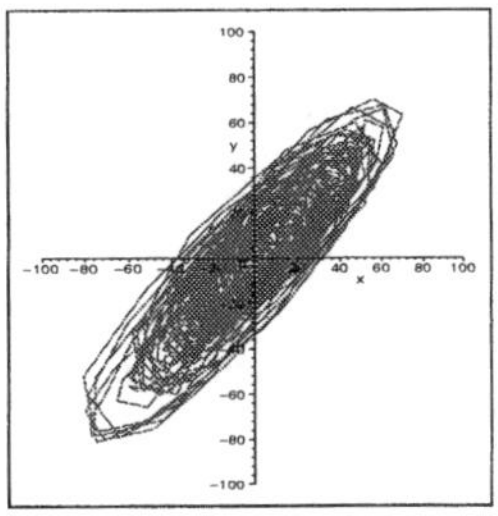

Fig. 4. Orbit.

Simplified Second Order Filter.

Theorem 5. *Let a, b, $\varepsilon_a \geq 0$, $\varepsilon_b \geq 0$, $K \geq 0$, $m > 0$, X, Y be real numbers, such that $a^2 + 4b < 0$, and $X^2 - aXY - bY^2 \leq K$. Let Z be a real number such that: $aX + bY - (m + \varepsilon_a|X| + \varepsilon_b|Y|) \leq Z \leq aX + bY + (m + \varepsilon_a|X| + \varepsilon_b|Y|)$. Let δ be $2\frac{\varepsilon_b + \varepsilon_a\sqrt{-b}}{\sqrt{-(a^2+4b)}}$, we have:*

1. $|X| \leq 2\sqrt{\frac{bK}{a^2+4b}}$ *and* $|Y| \leq 2\sqrt{\frac{-K}{a^2+4b}}$;
2. $Z^2 - aZX - bX^2 \leq \left((\sqrt{-b} + \delta)\sqrt{K} + m\right)^2$;
3. $\begin{cases} \sqrt{-b} + \delta < 1 \\ K \geq \left(\frac{m}{1-\sqrt{-b}-\delta}\right)^2 \end{cases} \implies Z^2 - aZX - bX^2 \leq K.$

□

We define two maps $\psi_1 \in \mathbb{F}^4 \times \overline{\mathbb{F}}^2 \to \overline{\mathbb{F}}$ and $\psi_2 \in \mathbb{F}^4 \times \overline{\mathbb{F}} \to \overline{\mathbb{F}}$ by:

$$\begin{cases} \psi_1(a, \varepsilon_a, b, \varepsilon_b, m, D) = \begin{cases} \left\lceil \left(\left(\sqrt{-b} + \delta(a, \varepsilon_a, b, \varepsilon_b)\right)\sqrt{D} + m\right)^2 \right\rceil & \text{if } a^2 + 4b < 0 \\ +\infty & \text{otherwise} \end{cases} \\ \psi_2(a, \varepsilon_a, b, \varepsilon_b, m) = \begin{cases} \left\lceil \left(\frac{(1+\epsilon)m}{1-\sqrt{-b}-\delta(a,\varepsilon_a,b,\varepsilon_b)}\right)^2 \right\rceil & \text{if } \begin{cases} a^2 + 4b < 0 \\ \sqrt{-b} + \delta(a, \varepsilon_a, b, \varepsilon_b) < 1 \end{cases} \\ +\infty & \text{otherwise.} \end{cases} \\ \text{where } \delta(a, \varepsilon_a, b, \varepsilon_b) = 2\frac{|\varepsilon_b| + |\varepsilon_a|\sqrt{-b}}{\sqrt{-(a^2+4b)}} \end{cases}$$

We derive the following abstract extension:

- $\mathcal{T}_{r_2} = (\mathcal{V}^2 \times \mathbb{F}^4)$ and $info = \mathbb{F}^4 \times \overline{\mathbb{F}}$;
- $(\mathcal{B}_{r_2}, \bot_{r_2}, \sqcup_{\mathcal{B}_{r_2}}, \nabla_{\mathcal{B}_{r_2}}, \Delta_{\mathcal{B}_{r_2}}) = (\mathcal{F}^2_{q,r}, \bot_{\mathcal{F}^2_{q,r}}, \sqcup_{\mathcal{F}^2_{q,r}}, \nabla_{\mathcal{F}^2_{q,r}}, \Delta_{\mathcal{F}^2_{q,r}})$;
- $\gamma_{\mathcal{B}_{r_2}}((X, Y, a, \varepsilon_a, b, \varepsilon_b), e)$ is given by the set of environments ρ that satisfies:
$$(\rho(X))^2 - a\rho(X)\rho(Y) - b(\rho(Y))^2 \leq max(\gamma_{\mathcal{F}^2_{q,r}}(e));$$
- RLVT_{r_2} maps each expression E to the set of tuples $(X, Y, a, \varepsilon_a, b, \varepsilon_b)$, such that E matches $[a - \varepsilon_a; a + \varepsilon_a] \times X + [b - \varepsilon_b; b + \varepsilon_b] \times Y + E'$ with $a^2 + 4b < 0$;

- $\text{PT}_{r_2}(Z = [a-\varepsilon_a; a+\varepsilon_a] \times X + [b-\varepsilon_b; b+\varepsilon_b] \times Y + E', (X, Y, a, \varepsilon_a, b, \varepsilon_b), \rho^\sharp))$ is given[2] by $((Z, X, a, \varepsilon_a, b, \varepsilon_b), (a, \varepsilon_a, b, \varepsilon_b, m))$, where $m = \text{EVAL}^\sharp(E', \rho^\sharp)$;
- $\delta_{r_2}((a, \varepsilon_a, b, \varepsilon_b, m), ((D_1, k_1), (D_2, k_2))) = ((r_1, 0), (r_2, 0))$ where $r_1 = \psi_1(a, \varepsilon_a, b, \varepsilon_b, m, D_1)$ and $r_2 = max(\psi_1(a, \varepsilon_a, b, m, D_2), \psi_2(a, \varepsilon_a, b, \varepsilon_b, m))$;
- $\text{BUILD}_{r_2}((X, Y, a, \varepsilon_a, b, \varepsilon_b), \rho^\sharp, \mathcal{R})(X) = ((m, 0), (m, 0))$
  where $m = \begin{cases} \lceil |1-a-b|x^2 \rceil & \text{if } (X,Y) \in \mathcal{R} \\ \lceil x^2 + |a|xy + |b|y^2 \rceil & \text{otherwise} \\ \text{with } x = \text{EVAL}^\sharp(X, \rho^\sharp) \text{ and } y = \text{EVAL}^\sharp(Y, \rho^\sharp); \end{cases}$
- $\text{TO}_{r_2}(X, Y, a, \varepsilon_a, b, \varepsilon_b)(e) = \begin{cases} V \mapsto [-m; m] & \text{if } X = V \text{ and } a^2 + 4b < 0 \\ V \mapsto \mathbb{R} & \text{otherwise} \end{cases}$
  where $m = \left\lceil 2\sqrt{\frac{max(\gamma_{\mathcal{F}^2_{q,r}}(e)) \times b}{a^2+4b}} \right\rceil$.

6.2 Formal Expansion

We design a more accurate abstraction by formally expanding the definition of the output in the real field. The overall contribution of rounding errors is then over-approximated using the rough abstraction, while the contribution of each input is exactly described. The obtained domain is history-aware: concretization uses an existential quantification over past inputs, which forbids precise abstract intersection and narrowing.

High Passband Filter

Theorem 6. *Let $\alpha \in [\frac{1}{2}; 1[$, i and $m > 0$ be real numbers. Let E_n be a real number sequence, such that $\forall k \in \mathbb{N}$, $E_k \in [-m; m]$. Let S_n be the following sequence:*

$$\begin{cases} S_0 = i \\ S_{n+1} = \alpha S_n + E_{n+1} - E_n. \end{cases}$$

We have:

1. $S_n = \alpha^n i + E_n - \alpha^n E_0 + \Sigma_{l=1}^{n-1} (\alpha - 1)\alpha^{l-1} E_{n-l}$
2. $|S_n| \le |\alpha|^n |i| + (1 + |\alpha|^n + |1 - \alpha^{n-1}|)m;$
3. $|S_n| \le 2m + |i|.$ □

We derive the following abstract extension:

- $\mathcal{T}_{d_1} = \mathcal{V}^2 \times \mathbb{F}$, $\mathcal{B}_{d_1} = \mathcal{F}_{q,r} \times \mathcal{F}_{q,r} \times \mathcal{F}^2_{q,r}$, and $\text{INFO}_{d_1} = \mathbb{F} \times \overline{\mathbb{F}} \times \overline{\mathbb{F}}$;
- $(\bot_{d_1}, \sqcup_{\mathcal{B}_{d_1}}, \nabla_{\mathcal{B}_{d_1}})$ are defined componentwise;

---

[2] If $[t \to fst(\text{PT}_{r_i}(Z = E, t, \rho^\sharp))]$ is not injective, we take a subset of $\text{RLVT}_{r_i}(E)$.

– $\gamma_{\mathcal{B}_{d_1}}((S', E', \alpha), (a, b, c))$ is given by

$$\left\{ \rho \in Env \;\middle|\; \begin{array}{l} \exists \varepsilon \in \gamma_{\mathcal{F}^2_{q,r}}(c),\ \exists S_0 \in \gamma_{\mathcal{F}_{q,r}}(a), \\ \exists n \in \mathbb{N}, \exists (E_i)_{0 \leq i \leq n} \in (\gamma_{\mathcal{F}_{q,r}}(b))^{n+1} \text{ such that} \\ \rho(E') = E_n \text{ and} \\ \rho(S') = \varepsilon + \alpha^n S_0 + E_n - \alpha^n E_0 + \Sigma_{l=1}^{n-1}(\alpha - 1)\alpha^{l-1} E_{n-l} \end{array} \right\};$$

– RLVT_{d_1} maps each expression E to the set of the tuples (X_α, X_-, α), such that E matches $[\alpha - \varepsilon_\alpha; \alpha + \varepsilon_\alpha] \times X_\alpha + [1 - \varepsilon_+; 1 + \varepsilon_+] \times X_+ + [-1 + \varepsilon_-; \varepsilon_- - 1] \times X_- + [-\varepsilon, \varepsilon]$ where $\varepsilon_\alpha \geq 0$, $\varepsilon_+ \geq 0$, $\varepsilon_- \geq 0$, $\varepsilon \geq 0$ and $[\alpha - \varepsilon_\alpha; \alpha + \varepsilon_\alpha] \subseteq [\frac{1}{2}; 1[$; the pair $\text{PT}_{r_1}(Z = E, (X_\alpha, X_-, \alpha), \rho^\sharp)$ is given by $((Z, X_+, \alpha), (\alpha, m_+, m'))$, where $m_+ = \text{EVAL}^\sharp(X_+, \rho^\sharp)$ and $m' = \text{EVAL}^\sharp(E + \{-\alpha\} \times X_\alpha + (-X_+) + X_-, \rho^\sharp)$;
– $\delta_{d_1}((\alpha, m, \varepsilon), (a, b, c)) = (a, b \sqcup_{\mathcal{F}_{q,r}} (m, 0), \delta_{r_1}((\alpha, 0, \varepsilon), c))$;
– $\text{BUILD}_{d_1}((X_\alpha, X_+, \alpha), \rho^\sharp, \mathcal{R}) = ((m_\alpha, 0), (m_+, 0), ((0,0), (0,0)))$ where $m_\alpha = \text{EVAL}^\sharp(X_\alpha, \rho^\sharp)$ and $m_+ = \text{EVAL}^\sharp(X_+, \rho^\sharp)$;
– $\text{TO}_{d_1}((X_\alpha, X_+, \alpha), (a, b, c)) = \begin{cases} Y \mapsto [-m; m] & \text{if } X = Y \text{ and } \alpha \in [\frac{1}{2}; 1[\\ Y \mapsto \mathbb{R} & \text{otherwise,} \end{cases}$

where $m = \left\lceil max(\gamma_{\mathcal{F}_{q,r}}(a)) + 2max(\gamma_{\mathcal{F}_{q,r}}(b)) + max(\gamma_{\mathcal{F}^2_{q,r}}(c)) \right\rceil$;
– $\forall a, b \in \mathcal{B}_{d_1},\ a \Delta_{\mathcal{B}_{d_1}} b = a$.

Second Order Filter

Theorem 7. *Let a, b, c, d, e, i_0, and i_1 be real numbers, such that $-1 < b < 0$ and $a^2 + 4b < 0$. Let (E_n) be a sequence of real numbers. We assume there exists $m \in \mathbb{F}$ such that $\forall k \in \mathbb{N}$, we have $E_k \in [-m; m]$, and $\forall k \in \{1; 2\}$, we have $i_k \in [-m; m]$. We define the sequence (C_n) as follows:*

$$\begin{cases} S_0 = i_0,\ S_1 = i_1, \\ S_{n+2} = aS_{n+1} + bS_n + cE_{n+2} + dE_{n+1} + eE_n \end{cases}$$

Let $(A_i)_{i \in \mathbb{N}}$, $(B_i)_{i \in \mathbb{N}}$, and $(C_i^j)_{i,j \in \mathbb{N}}$ be real coefficient families such that[3]*:*

$$\forall n \in \mathbb{N},\ S_n = A_n i_0 + B_n i_1 + \Sigma_{i=0}^n C_i^n E_i.$$

For any pair $(n, N) \in \mathbb{N}$ such that $N > 3$ and $n \geq N$, we define the residue R_n^N by $S_n - \Sigma_{i=n-N+1}^n C_i^n E_i$. We have:

1. $\forall N > 3, n \geq N + 2,\ R_n^N = aR_{n-1}^N + bR_{n-2}^N + \varepsilon_n^N$ where $\varepsilon_n^N = aC_{n-N}^{n-1} E_{n-N} + bC_{n-1-N}^{n-2} E_{n-1-N} + bC_{n-N}^{n-2} E_{n-N}$;
2. $\forall N > 3, n \in \mathbb{N},\ |S_n| \leq (max(S_\leq^N(i_1 = i_2), S_\infty^N(i_1 = i_2))).m$ where
   – $S_\leq^N(\text{B}) = max\{(\Sigma_{k=0}^p |C_k^p|) + init(p, \text{B}) \mid p \in [\![0; N+2]\!]\}$
   – $S_\infty^N(\text{B}) = \left(\Sigma_{i=0}^{N-1} |C_2^{i+2}| + 2\sqrt{\frac{-bmax(K_\infty^N, K_0^N(\text{B}))}{a^2+4b}} \right)$

[3] We omit the explicit recursive definition of these coefficients, for conciseness.

– $\forall n \geq 2,\ init(n, \text{B}) = \begin{cases} |A_n| + |B_n| & if\ (not(\text{B})) \\ |A_n + B_n| & otherwise, \end{cases}$

– $K_\infty^N = \left(\frac{|aC_2^{1+N} + bC_2^N| + |bC_2^{1+N}|}{1-\sqrt{-b}}\right)^2$ *and* $K_0^N(\text{B}) = X^2 + |a|XY - bY^2$,

where $\begin{cases} X = (init(N+2, \text{B})) + \Sigma_{i=0}^{N+2} |C_i^{N+2}| \\ Y = (init(N+1, \text{B})) + \Sigma_{i=0}^{N+1} |C_i^{N+1}|. \end{cases}$ □

We set $N \in \mathbb{N}$ and define the map ψ_∞ that maps each tuple $(\text{B}, a, b, c, d, e) \in \mathcal{B} \times \mathbb{F}^5$ into $\lceil max(S_{\leq}^N, S_\infty^N(\text{B}))\rceil$ where $S_{\leq}^N$ and S_∞^N are defined as in Thm. 7.

We derive the following abstract extension:

- $\mathcal{T}_{d_2} = \mathcal{V}^4 \times \mathbb{F}$, $\mathcal{B}_{d_2} = \mathcal{B} \times \mathcal{F}_{q,r} \times \mathcal{F}_{q,r}^2$, and $\text{INFO}_{d_2} = \overline{\mathbb{F}} \times \overline{\mathbb{F}}$;
- $(\bot_{d_2}, \sqcup_{\mathcal{B}_{d_2}}, \nabla_{\mathcal{B}_{d_2}})$ are defined componentwise.
- $\gamma_{\mathcal{B}_{d_2}}((S'', S', E'', E', a, b, c, d, e), (\text{B}, m, K_\varepsilon))$ is given by:

$$\left\{ \rho \in Env \;\middle|\; \begin{array}{l} \exists \varepsilon_X, \varepsilon_Y, \text{ such that } \varepsilon_X^2 - a\varepsilon_X\varepsilon_Y - b\varepsilon_Y^2 \leq max(\gamma_{\mathcal{F}_{q,r}^2}(K_\varepsilon)) \\ \exists n \in \mathbb{N}, \exists (E_i)_{-2 \leq i \leq n+1} \in (\gamma_{\mathcal{F}_{q,r}}(m))^{n+4} \text{ such that} \\ \rho(S'') = \varepsilon_X + A_{n+1}E_{-2} + B_{n+1}E_{-1} + \Sigma_{i=0}^{n+1} C_i^{n+1} E_i \\ \rho(S') = \varepsilon_Y + A_n E_{-2} + B_n E_{-1} + \Sigma_{i=0}^{n} C_i^n E_i \\ \rho(E'') = E_{n+1},\ \rho(E') = E_n,\ [\text{B} \implies E_{-1} = E_{-2}] \end{array} \right\}$$

- $\text{RLVT}_{d_2}(E)$ is the set of tuples $t = (X_a, X_b, X_d, X_e, a, b, c, d, e)$, such that there exists $X_c \in \mathcal{V}$ such that E matches $\Sigma_{i \in \{a;b;c;d;e\}}[i - \varepsilon_i; i + \varepsilon_i] \times X_i + [-\varepsilon, \varepsilon]$ where $\forall i \in \{a; b; c; d; e\}, \varepsilon_i \geq 0$, $\varepsilon > 0$, $a^2 + 4b < 0$, and $-1 < b < 0$, then the pair $\text{PT}_{r_1}(Z = E, t, \rho^\sharp)$ is given by $(t', (\text{EVAL}^\sharp(X_c, \rho^\sharp), \text{EVAL}^\sharp(E', \rho^\sharp)))$ where $t' = (Z, X_a, X_c, X_d, a, b, c, d, e)$ and $E' = E + \Sigma_{i \in \{a;b;c;d;e\}}\{-i\} \times X_i$;
- $\delta_{d_2}((m, \varepsilon), (\text{A}, i_E, i_\varepsilon)) = (\text{A}, i_E \sqcup_{\mathcal{F}_{q,r}} (m, 0), \delta_{r_2}((a, 0, b, 0, \varepsilon), i_\varepsilon))$;
- $\text{BUILD}_{d_2}((X_a, X_b, X_d, X_e, a, b, c, d, e), \rho^\sharp, \mathcal{R}) = (\text{B}, (m, 0), ((0, 0), (0, 0)))$ with $\text{B} = ((X_a, X_b) \in \mathcal{R})$ and $m = max\{\text{EVAL}^\sharp(X, \rho^\sharp) \mid \forall X \in \{X_a, X_b, X_d, X_e\}\}$;
- $\text{TO}_{d_2}((X_a, X_b, X_d, X_e, a, b, c, d, e), (\text{A}, i_E, i_\varepsilon)) = \begin{cases} Y \mapsto [-m; m] \text{ if } \begin{cases} X = Y \\ \frac{a^2}{4} < -b \end{cases} \\ Y \mapsto \mathbb{R} \qquad \text{otherwise} \end{cases}$

  where $m = \left\lceil max(\gamma_{\mathcal{F}_{q,r}}(i_E))\psi_\infty(\text{A}, a, b, c, d, e) + 2\sqrt{\frac{max(\gamma_{\mathcal{F}_{q,r}^2}(i_\varepsilon))b}{a^2+4b}} \right\rceil$
- $\forall a, b \in \mathcal{B}_{d_2}$, $a \Delta_{\mathcal{B}_{d_2}} b = a$.

7 Benchmarks

We tested our framework with the same program as in [2]. This program is 132,000 lines of C long with macros (75 kLOC after preprocessing) and has about 10,000 global variables. The underlying domain is the same as in [2] (i.e., we use intervals [3], octagons [9], decision trees, except the ellipsoid domain which corresponds to the rough abstraction of second order digital filters). We perform three analyses with several levels of accuracy for filter abstraction. First, we use no filter abstraction; then we only use the rough abstraction; finally we

	no filter abstraction	rough filter abstraction	accurate filter abstraction
iteration number	69	120	72
average time by iteration	48.0 s.	58.4 s.	61.7 s.
analysis time	3313 s.	7002 s.	4444 s.
warnings	639	10	6

Fig. 5. Some statistics.

use the most accurate abstraction. For each of these analyses, we report in Fig. 5 the analysis time, the number of iterations for the main loop, and the number of warnings (in polyvariant function calls). These results have been obtained on a 2.8 GHz, 4 Gb RAM PC.

8 Conclusion

We have proposed a highly generic framework to analyze programs with digital filtering. We have also given a general approach to instantiate this framework in the case of linear filtering. We have enriched an existing analyzer, and obtained results that were far beyond our expectations. As a result, we solved nearly all remaining warnings when analyzing an industrial program of 132, 000 lines of C: we obtain a sufficiently small number of warnings to allow manual inspection, and we discovered they could be eliminated without altering the functionality of the application by changing only three lines of code.

Linear filtering is widely used in the context of critical embedded software, so we believe that this framework is crucial to achieve full certification of the absence of runtime error in such programs.

Acknowledgments. We deeply thank the anonymous referees. We also thank Charles Hymans, Francesco Logozzo and each member of the magic team: Bruno Blanchet, Patrick Cousot, Radhia Cousot, Laurent Mauborgne, Antoine Miné, David Monniaux, and Xavier Rival.

References

1. B. Blanchet, P. Cousot, R. Cousot, J. Feret, L. Mauborgne, A. Miné, D. Monniaux, and X. Rival. Design and implementation of a special-purpose static program analyzer for safety-critical real-time embedded software, invited chapter. In *The Essence of Computation: Complexity, Analysis, Transformation. Essays Dedicated to Neil D. Jones*, LNCS 2566. Springer-Verlag, 2002.
2. B. Blanchet, P. Cousot, R. Cousot, J. Feret, L. Mauborgne, A. Miné, D. Monniaux, and X. Rival. A static analyzer for large safety-critical software. In *Proc. PLDI'03*. ACM Press, 2003.
3. P. Cousot and R. Cousot. Abstract interpretation: a unified lattice model for static analysis of programs by construction or approximation of fixpoints. In *Proc. POPL'77*. ACM Press, 1977.

4. P. Cousot and R. Cousot. Abstract interpretation frameworks. *Journal of logic and computation*, 2(4), August 1992.
5. P. Cousot and N. Halbwachs. Automatic discovery of linear restraints among variables of a program. In *Proc. POPL'78*. ACM Press, 1978.
6. M. Karr. Affine relationships among variables of a program. *Acta Inf.*, 1976.
7. A. A. Lamb, W. Thies, and S.P.Amarasinghe. Linear analysis and optimisation of stream programs. In *Proc. PLDI'03*. ACM Press, 2003.
8. X. Leroy, D. Doligez, J. Garrigue, D. Rémy, and J. Vouillon. The Objective Caml system, documentation and user's manual. Technical report, INRIA, 2002.
9. A. Miné. The octagon abstract domain. In *Proc. WCRE'01(AST'01)*, IEEE, 2001.
10. A. Miné. Relational abstract domains for the detection of floating-point run-time errors. In *Proc. ESOP'04*, LNCS. Springer, 2004. © Springer.

Sound and Decidable Type Inference for Functional Dependencies

Gregory J. Duck[1], Simon Peyton-Jones[2], Peter J. Stuckey[1], and Martin Sulzmann[3]

[1] Department of Computer Science and Software Engineering
The University of Melbourne, Vic. 3010, Australia
{gjd,pjs}@cs.mu.oz.au
[2] Microsoft Research Ltd
7 JJ Thomson Avenue, Cambridge CB3 0FB, England
simonpj@microsoft.com
[3] School of Computing, National University of Singapore
S16 Level 5, 3 Science Drive 2, Singapore 117543
sulzmann@comp.nus.edu.sg

Abstract. Functional dependencies are a popular and useful extension to Haskell style type classes. In this paper, we give a reformulation of functional dependencies in terms of Constraint Handling Rules (CHRs). In previous work, CHRs have been employed for describing user-programmable type extensions in the context of Haskell style type classes. Here, we make use of CHRs to provide for the first time a concise result that under some sufficient conditions, functional dependencies allow for sound and decidable type inference. The sufficient conditions imposed on functional dependencies can be very limiting. We show how to safely relax these conditions.

1 Introduction

Functional dependencies, introduced by Mark Jones [Jon00], have proved to be a very attractive extension to multi-parameter type classes in Haskell. For example, consider a class intended to describe a collection of type `c` containing values of type `e`:

```
class Coll c e | c -> e where
  empty :: c
  insert :: c -> e -> c
  member :: c -> e -> Bool
```

The part "`| c->e`" is a functional dependency, and indicates that fixing the collection type `c` should fix the element type `e`. These functional dependencies have proved very useful, because they allow the programmer to control the type inference process more precisely. We elaborate in Section 2.

The purpose of this paper is to explore and consolidate the design space of functional dependencies (FDs). The main tool we use in this exploration is the reformulation of FDs in terms of *Constraint Handling Rules* (CHRs) [Frü95, SS02], an idea that we review in Section 3. This reformulation allows us to make several new contributions:

D.A. Schmidt (Ed.): ESOP 2004, LNCS 2986, pp. 49–63, 2004.

– Despite their popularity, functional dependencies have never been formalised, so far as we know. CHRs give us a language in which to explain more precisely what functional dependencies *are*. In particular, we are able to make the so-called "improvement rules" implied by FDs explicit in terms of CHRs.
– Based on this understanding, we provide the first concise proof that the restrictions imposed by Jones on functional dependencies [Jon00] ensure sound and decidable type inference (Section 3).
– Jones's restrictions can be very limiting. We propose several useful extensions (Section 4) such as *more liberal FDs* (Section 4.1). We establish some concise conditions under which liberal FDs are sound.

Throughout, we provide various examples to support the usefulness of our improvement strategies. Related work is discussed in Section 5. We conclude in Section 6.

We refer the interested reader to [DPJSS03] for proofs and additional material.

2 Background: Functional Dependencies in Haskell

We begin by reviewing functional dependencies, as introduced by Jones [Jon00], assuming some basic familiarity with Haskell-style type classes.

Example 1. Recall the collection class

```
class Coll c e | c -> e where
  empty :: c
  insert :: c -> e -> c
  member :: c -> e -> Bool
```

plus the following

```
instance Eq a => Coll [a] a where ...
ins2 xs a b = insert (insert xs a) b
```

Consider the function ins2. In the absence of functional dependencies, type inference would give

```
ins2 :: (Coll c e1, Coll c e2) => c -> e1 -> e2 -> c
```

which is of course not what we want: we expect a and b to have the same type. The functional dependency c->e expresses the idea that the collection type c fixes the element type e, and hence that e1 and e2 must be the same type. In such a situation, we commonly say that types are "*improved*" [Jon95].

Functional dependencies are useful in many different contexts. Here are some representative examples.

Example 2. Consider the following class for representing state monads and two instances

```
class SM m r | m->r, r->m where
  new   :: a -> m (r a)
  read  :: r a -> m a
  write :: r a -> a -> m ()

instance SM IO IORef where
  new   = newIORef
  read  = readIORef
  write = writeIORef

instance SM (ST s) (STRef s) where
  new   = newSTRef
  read  = readSTRef
  write = writeSTRef
```

The part "`| m->r, r->m`" gives two functional dependencies, and indicates that fixing the monad type `m` should fix the reference type `r` as well, and vice versa. Now consider the code

```
f x = do { r <- new x; print "Hello"; return r }
```

The call to `print`, whose type is `String -> IO ()`, makes it clear that `f` is in the `IO` monad, and hence, by the functional dependency, that `r` must be an `IORef`. So we infer the type

```
f :: a -> IO (IORef a)
```

From this example we can see the main purpose of functional dependencies: they allow the programmer to place stronger conditions on the set of constraints generated during type inference, and thus allow more accurate types to be inferred. In their absence, we would infer the type

```
f :: (SM IO r) => IO (r a)
```

which is needlessly general. In other situations, ambiguity would be reported. For example:

```
g :: a -> IO a
g x = do { r <- new x ; read r }
```

Without functional dependencies, the type system cannot work out which reference type to use, and so reports an ambiguous use of `new` and `read`.

Example 3. Consider the following application allowing for (overloaded) multiplication among base types such as `Int` and `Float` and user-definable types such as vectors. For simplicity, we omit the obvious function bodies.

```
class Mul a b c | a b -> c where
    (*)::a->b->c
instance Mul Int Int Int where ...
instance Mul Int Float Float where ...
type Vec b = [b]
instance Mul a b c => Mul a (Vec b) (Vec c) where ...
```

The point here is that the argument types of `(*)` determine its result type. In the absence of this knowledge an expression such as `(a*b)*c` cannot be typed, because the type of the intermediate result, `(a*b)`, is not determined. The type checker would report type ambiguity, just as it does when faced with the classic example of ambiguity, `(read (show x))`.

Example 4. Here is an another useful application of FDs to encode a family of zip functions.

```
zip2 :: [a]->[b]->[(a,b)]
zip2 (a:as) (b:bs) = (a,b) : (zip2 as bs)
zip2 _      _      = []

class Zip a b c | a c -> b, b c -> a where
    zip :: [a] -> [b] -> c
instance Zip a b [(a,b)] where
    zip = zip2
instance Zip (a,b) c e => Zip a b ([c]->e) where
    zip as bs cs = zip (zip2 as bs) cs
```

These definitions make `zip` into an n-ary function. For example, we may write

```
e1 :: (Bool,Char)
e1 = head (zip [True,False] ['a','b','c'])
e2 :: ((Bool,Char),Int)
e2 = head (zip [True,False] ['a','b','c'] [1::Int,2])
```

2.1 Functional Dependencies Are Tricky

As we have seen, functional dependencies allow the programmer to exert control over the type inference process. However, used uncritically, this additional control can have unexpected consequences. Specifically: they may lead to *inconsistency*, whereby the type inference engine deduces nonsense such as `Int` = `Bool`; and they may lead to *non-termination*, whereby the type inference engine goes into an infinite loop. We illustrate each of these difficulties with an example.

Example 5. Suppose we add `instance Mul Int Float Int` to Example 3. That is, we have the following declarations:

```
class Mul a b c | a b -> c
instance Mul Int Float Float   -- (I1)
instance Mul Int Float Int     -- (I2)
```

Note that the first two parameters are meant to uniquely determine the third parameter. In case type inference encounters `Mul Int Float a` we can either argue that `a=Int` because of instance declaration `(I2)`. However, declaration `(I1)` would imply `a=Float`. These two answers are inconsistent, so allowing both `(I1)` and `(I2)` makes the whole program inconsistent, which endangers soundness of type inference.

Example 6. Assume we add the following function to the classes and instances in Example 3.

```
f b x y = if b then (*) x [y] else y
```

The program text gives rise to the constraint `Mul a (Vec b) b`. The improvement rules connected to `instance Mul a b c => Mul a (Vec b) (Vec c)` imply that `b=Vec c` for some `c`; applying this substitution gives the constraint `Mul a (Vec (Vec c)) (Vec c)`. But this constraint can be simplified using the instance declaration, giving rise to the simpler constraint `Mul a (Vec c) c`. Unfortunately, now the entire chain of reasoning simply repeats! We find that type inference becomes suddenly non-terminating. Note that the instances (without the functional dependency) are terminating.

The bottom line is this. We want type inference to be *sound* and *decidable.* Functional dependencies threaten this happy situation. The obvious solution is to place restrictions on how functional dependencies are used, so that type inference remains well-behaved, and that is what we discuss next.

2.2 Jones's Functional Dependency Restrictions

We assume that $fv(t)$ takes a syntactic term t and returns the set of *free variables* in t. A *substitution* $\theta = [t_1/a_1, \ldots, t_n/a_n]$ simultaneously replaces each a_i by its corresponding t_i.

In Jones's original paper [Jon00], the following restrictions are imposed on functional dependencies.

Definition 1 (Haskell-FD Restrictions). *Consider a class declaration*

$$\texttt{class } C \texttt{ => TC } a_1 \ldots a_n \mid fd_1, \ldots, fd_m$$

where the a_i are type variables and C is the class context consisting of a (possibly empty) set of type class constraints. Each fd_i is a functional dependency *of the form*[1] $a_{i_1}, \ldots, a_{i_k}$ `->` a_{i_0} *where* $\{i_0, i_1, \ldots, i_k\} \subseteq \{1 \ldots n\}$. *We commonly refer to* $a_{i_1}, \ldots, a_{i_k}$ *as the* domain *and* a_{i_0} *as the* range.

The following conditions must hold for functional dependency fd_i:

Consistency. *Consider every pair of instance declarations*

$$\texttt{instance} \ldots \texttt{ => TC } t_1 \ldots t_n$$
$$\texttt{instance} \ldots \texttt{ => TC } s_1 \ldots s_n$$

for a particular type class TC. Then, for any substitution ϕ such that

$$\phi(t_{i_1}, \ldots, t_{i_k}) = \phi(s_{i_1}, \ldots, s_{i_k})$$

we must have that $\phi(t_{i_0}) = \phi(s_{i_0})$.

[1] Haskell systems that allow functional dependencies usually allow dependencies of the form `a -> b c`, with multiple type variables to the right of the arrow. But this is equivalent to the form `a -> b, a -> c`, so in the rest of the paper we only deal with the case where there is a single type variable to the right of the arrow.

Termination. *For each* `instance ... => TC` $t_1 \dots t_n$ *we must have that*

$$fv(t_{i_0}) \subseteq fv(t_{i_1}, \dots, t_{i_k})$$

The first of these conditions rules out inconsistent instance declarations (see Example 5); and it turns out that the second ensures termination, although the informal argument in Jones's original paper does not mention termination as an issue. In particular, the second restriction makes illegal the recursive `Vec` instance in Example 3 (since $fv(c) \not\subseteq fv(a,b)$), and hence prevents the divergence of Example 6.

To the best of our knowledge, no one has proved that the restrictions given above ensure sound and decidable type inference. We do so, for the first time, in Section 3.

While these two restrictions make the system well-behaved, it is natural to ask whether either condition could be weakened. The consistency condition seems entirely reasonable, but we have seen many examples in which the termination restriction excludes entirely reasonable and useful programs. Besides Examples 3 (which appears in Jones's original paper) and 4, there are a number of other examples in the literature which break the termination condition [Kar03,WW03, CK03]. In Section 4.1, we propose a more liberal form of FDs which allows for breaking the termination condition under some additional conditions.

3 Functional Dependencies Expressed Using CHRs

In this section we explain how to translate functional dependencies into a lower-level notation, called *Constraint Handling Rules* (CHRs) [Frü98]. This translation has two benefits: it allows us to give a more precise account of exactly what functional dependencies mean; and it allows us to formally verify that Jones's conditions are sufficient to ensure sound and decidable type inference.

Example 7. Let us return to the collection example:

```
class Coll c e | c -> e where
  empty :: c
  insert :: c -> e -> c
  member :: c -> e -> Bool

class Eq a => Ord a where
  (>=) :: a -> a -> Bool

instance Ord a  => Coll [a] a where ...
```

From the functional dependency `c->e` we generate the two improvement rules which we shall express using the following CHRs:

```
rule  Coll c e1, Coll c e2 ==> e1=e2
rule  Coll [a] b           ==> a=b
```

Informally, the first rule says that if the two constraints `(Coll c e1)` and `(Coll c e2)` both hold, then it must be that `e1` and `e2` are the same type. This rule is generated from the `class` declaration alone, and expresses the idea that `c` uniquely determines `e`. The second rule is generated from the `instance` declaration, together with the functional dependency, and states that if `(Coll [a] b)` holds, then it follows that `a = b`. During type inference, the inference engine is required to solve sets of constraints, and it can apply these improvement rules to narrow its choices.

These CHRs have one or more type-class constraints on the left hand side, and one or more equality constraints on the right. The *logical* interpretation of `==>` is implication. Its *operational* interpretation — that is, its effect on the type inference process — is this: when the type inference engine sees constraints matching the left hand side, it adds the constraints found on the right-hand side.

Superclass relations also generate CHR rules. The superclass relationship `class Eq a => Ord a where...` generates the CHR

```
rule Ord a ==> Eq a
```

Informally, the rule states that if the constraint `Ord a` holds then also the constraint `Eq a` holds. During typing this rule is used to check that all superclass constraints are also satisfied.

The instance declaration above also generates the following CHR rule, which allows us to simplify sets of constraints to remove class constraints which are known to hold.

```
rule Coll [a] a <==> Ord a
```

Informally, the rule states that the constraint `Coll [a] a` holds if and only if `Ord a` holds. The logical interpretation of the `<==>` is bi-implication, while the operational interpretation is to replace the constraints on the left hand side by those on the right hand side.

Although not relevant to the content of this paper, the rule generated from the instance is also intimately connected to the evidence translation for the program above, we refer readers to [SS02] for more details.

3.1 Translation to CHRs

Formalising the translation given above, `class` and `instance` declarations are translated into CHRs as follows:

Definition 2 (CHR Translation). *Consider a class declaration*

$$\texttt{class } C \texttt{ => TC } a_1 \ \dots \ a_n \ \texttt{|} \ fd_1, \dots, fd_m$$

where the a_i are type variables and each functional dependency fd_i is of the form $a_{i_1}, \dots, a_{i_k}$ `->` a_{i_0}, where $\{i_0, i_1, \dots, i_k\} \subseteq \{1 \dots n\}$. From the class declaration we generate the following CHRs:

Class CHR: `rule TC` $a_1 \dots a_n$ `==>` C

Functional dependency CHR: *for each functional dependency fd_i in the class declaration, we generate*

`rule TC` $a_1 \dots a_n$`,` `TC` $\theta(b_1) \dots \theta(b_n)$ `==>` $a_{i_0} = b_{i_0}$

where $\theta(b_{i_j}) = a_{i_j}$, $j > 0$ and $\theta(b_l) = b_l$ if $\neg\exists j. l = i_j$.

In addition, for each instance declaration of the form

`instance` C `=>` `TC` $t_1 \ldots t_n$

we generate the following CHRs:

Instance CHR: `rule TC` $t_1 \ldots t_n$ `<==>` C. *In case the context C is empty, we introduce the always-satisfiable constraint True on the right-hand side of generated CHRs.*

Instance improvement CHR: *for each functional dependency fd_i in the class declaration,*
`rule TC` $\theta(b_1) \ldots \theta(b_n)$ `==>` $t_{i_0} = b_{i_0}$
where $\theta(b_{i_j}) = t_{i_j}$, $j > 0$ *and* $\theta(b_l) = b_l$ *if* $\neg\exists j.l = i_j$.

If p is a set of `class` *and* `instance` *declarations, we define* Simp(p) *to be the set of all instance CHRs generated from p; and* Prop(p) *to be the set of all class, functional-dependency and instance-improvement CHRs generated from p*[2]. *We define* $\text{Prop}_{class}(\text{p})$ *to be the set of all class CHRs in* Prop(p), *and similarly* $\text{Prop}_{inst}(\text{p})$ *to be the set of all instance improvement CHRs in* Prop(p),

The class and instance CHRs, $Prop_{class}(p) \cup Simp(p)$, are standard Haskell, while the functional-dependency and instance-improvement CHRs arise from the functional-dependency extension to Haskell.

For convenience, in the case where the functional dependency $a_{i_1}, ..., a_{i_k}$ `->` a_{i_0} imposed on `TC` is *full*, that is, when $k = n - 1$, we are able to combine the instance improvement and instance rule into one rule. In such a situation, for each `instance` C `=>` `TC` $t_1 \ldots t_n$ and full functional dependency $a_{i_1}, ..., a_{i_k}$ `->` a_{i_0} we generate the following CHR: `rule TC` $\theta(b_1) \ldots \theta(b_n)$ `<==>` $t_{i_0} = b_{i_0}$, `C` where $\theta(b_{i_j}) = t_{i_j}$, $j > 0$ and $\theta(b_l) = b_l$ if $\neg\exists j.l = i_j$.

By having a uniform description of (super) class and instance relations and FDs in terms of CHRs, we can establish some important criteria (in terms of CHRs) under which type inference is sound and decidable.

3.2 Main Result

The translation to CHRs allows us to phrase the entire type inference process as CHR solving. We know from earlier work that if a set of CHRs is (a) *confluent*, (b) *terminating*, and (c) *range-restricted* (all terms that we explain shortly) we achieve type inference that is *sound* (all answers are correct), *complete* (if there is an answer then type inference will provide us with an answer), and *decidable* (the type inference engine always terminates) [SS02].

Then our main result is as follows:

Theorem 1 (Soundness and Decidability). *Let p be a set of Haskell class and instance declarations which satisfies the Haskell-FD restrictions (see Definition 1). Let Simp(p) and Prop(p) be the sets of CHRs defined by Definition 2. If the set* $Prop_{class}(p) \cup Simp(p)$ *of CHRs is confluent, terminating and range-restricted then* $Simp(p) \cup Prop(p)$ *is confluent, terminating and range-restricted.*

[2] "Simp" is short for "simplification rule" and "Prop" for "propagation rule", terminology that comes from the CHR literature.

The design of Haskell 98 ensures that the CHRs $Prop_{class}(p) \cup Simp(p)$, which represent the Haskell type system with no FD extension, are indeed confluent, terminating and range-restricted. Hence, our theorem says that provide the FDs satisfy the Jones restrictions, then type inference is sound and decidable.

To explain this result we need to say what we mean for a set of CHRs to be confluent, terminating, and range restricted.

Confluence. Recall Example 5 whose translation to CHRs is as follows (note that the functional dependency is fully imposed).

```
rule Mul a b c, Mul a b d ==> c=d  -- (M1)
rule Mul Int Float c <==> c=Float  -- (M2)
rule Mul Int Float c <==> c=Int    -- (M3)
```

We find two contradicting CHR derivations. We write $C \rightarrowtail_R D$ to denote the CHR derivation which applies rule (R) to constraint store C yielding store D. E.g. consider $Mul\ Int\ Float\ c \rightarrowtail_{M2} c = Float$ and $Mul\ Int\ Float\ c \rightarrowtail_{M3} c = Int$. The problem with the code of Example 5 manifests itself in the CHR rules as *non-confluence*. That is there are two possible sequences of applying rules, that lead to different results. Just considering the rules as logical statements, the entire system is unsatisfiable; that is, there are no models which satisfy the above set of rules.

Non-confluence also arises in case of "overlapping" instances. Assume we add the following declaration to the code of Example 7.

```
instance Eq a ==> Coll [a] a where
```

In case type inference encounters `Coll [t] t` we can either reduce this constraint to `Ord t` (by making use of the original instance) or `Eq t` (by making use of the above instance). However, both derivations are non-joinable. In fact, a common assumption is that instances must be non-overlapping, in which case non-confluence only occurs due to "invalid" FDs.

We note that the consistency condition *alone* is not sufficient to guarantee confluence (assuming that instances and super classes are already confluent of course).

Example 8. The following code fragment forms part of a type-directed evaluator.

```
data Nil        = Nil
data Cons a b   = Cons a b
data ExpAbs x a = ExpAbs x a
-- env represents environment, exp expression
-- and t is the type of the resulting value
class Eval env exp t | env exp -> t where
    eval :: env->exp->t
instance Eval (Cons (x,v1) env) exp v2
      => Eval env (ExpAbs x exp) (v1->v2) where
    eval env (ExpAbs x exp) = \v -> eval (Cons (x,v) env) exp
```

The translation to CHRs yields

```
rule Eval env exp t1, Eval env exp t2 ==> t1=t2  -- (E1)
rule Eval env (ExpAbs x exp) v <==>
     v=(v1->v2), Eval (Cons (x,v1) env) exp v2   -- (E2)
```

Note that the termination condition is violated but the consistency condition is trivially fulfilled (there is only one instance). However, we find that CHRs are terminating but non-confluent. E.g. we find that (applying (E2) twice)

$$
\begin{aligned}
& \mathit{Eval}\ \mathit{env}\ (\mathit{ExpAbs}\ x\ \mathit{exp})\ t_1, \mathit{Eval}\ \mathit{env}\ (\mathit{ExpAbs}\ x\ \mathit{exp})\ t_2 \\
\rightarrowtail^* \ & t_1 = v_1 \to v_2, \mathit{Eval}\ (\mathit{Cons}\ (x, v_1)\ \mathit{env})\ \mathit{exp}\ v_2, \\
& t_2 = v_3 \to v_4, \mathit{Eval}\ (\mathit{Cons}\ (x, v_3)\ \mathit{env})\ \mathit{exp}\ v_4
\end{aligned}
$$

Note that rule (E1) cannot be applied on constraints in the final store. But there is also another non-joinable derivation (applying rule (E1) then (E2))

$$
\begin{aligned}
& \mathit{Eval}\ \mathit{env}\ (\mathit{ExpAbs}\ x\ \mathit{exp})\ t_1, \mathit{Eval}\ \mathit{env}\ (\mathit{ExpAbs}\ x\ \mathit{exp})\ t_2 \\
\rightarrowtail^* \ & t_1 = t_2, t_1 = v_5 \to v_6, \mathit{Eval}\ (\mathit{Cons}\ (x, v_5)\ \mathit{env})\ \mathit{exp}\ v_6
\end{aligned}
$$

So the "termination condition" is perhaps mis-named; in this example, its violation leads to non-confluence rather than non-termination.

Termination. Recall Example 3. The translation to CHRs yields (among others) the following.

```
rule Mul a (Vec b) d <==> d=Vec c, Mul a b c -- (M4)
```

The program text in Example 6 gives rise to `Mul a (Vec b) b`. We find that

$$
\begin{aligned}
& \mathit{Mul}\ a\ (\mathit{Vec}\ b)\ b \\
\rightarrowtail_{M4}\ & \mathit{Mul}\ a\ (\mathit{Vec}\ c)\ c, c = \mathit{Vec}\ b \\
\rightarrowtail_{M4}\ & \mathit{Mul}\ a\ (\mathit{Vec}\ d)\ d, d = \mathit{Vec}\ c, c = \mathit{Vec}\ b \\
& \ldots
\end{aligned}
$$

That is, the CHR derivation, and hence type inference, is non-terminating. The important point here is that non-termination was introduced through the FD.

For the purpose of this paper, we generally assume that instance CHRs are terminating. There exists some sufficient criteria to ensure that instance CHRs are terminating, e.g. consider [Pey99]. Clearly, we can possibly identify further classes of terminating instance CHRs which we plan to pursue in future work. Note that, when a set of CHRs are terminating, we can easily test for confluence by checking that all "critical pairs" are joinable [Abd97].

Range restriction. Range-restrictedness is the third condition we impose on CHRs. We say a CHR is *range-restricted* iff grounding all variables on the left-hand side of a CHR, grounds all variables on the right-hand side.

Example 9. Consider

```
class C a b c
class D a b
instance C a b c => D [a] [b]
```

Our translation to CHRs yields

```
rule D [a] [b] <==> C a b c  -- (D1)
```

Note that rule (D1) is not range-restricted. After grounding the left-hand side, we still find non-ground variable `c` on the right-hand side. Range-restrictedness ensures that no unconstrained variables are introduced during a derivation and is a necessary condition for complete type inference. We refer readers to [SS02] for more details.

4 Extensions

In turn we discuss several extensions and variations of functional dependencies.

4.1 More Liberal Functional Dependencies

Earlier in the paper we argued that, while Jones's consistency condition is reasonable, the termination condition is more onerous than necessary, because it excludes reasonable and useful programs (Section 2.2). In this section we suggest replacing the termination restriction with the following weaker one, with the goal of making these useful programs legal.

Definition 3 (Liberal-FD). *Consider a class declaration*

$$\texttt{class } C \texttt{ => TC } a_1 \ldots a_n \texttt{ | } fd_1, \ldots, fd_m$$

where the a_i are type variables and C is the class context consisting of a (possibly empty) set of type class constraints. Each fd_i is a functional dependency *of the form $a_{i_1}, \ldots, a_{i_k}$ `->` a_{i_0} where $\{i_0, i_1, \ldots, i_k\} \subseteq \{1 \ldots n\}$.*

In addition to the consistency condition (see Definition 1), the following condition must hold for more liberal functional dependency fd_i:

Context Consistency. *For each* `instance` C `=>` `TC` $t_1 \ldots t_n$ *we must have that* $fv(t_{i0}) \subseteq closure(C, fv(t_{i1}, \ldots, t_{ik}))$ *where*

$$closure(C, vs) = \bigcup_{\substack{\texttt{TC } t_1 \ldots t_n \in C \\ \texttt{TC } a_1 \ldots a_n \,|\, a_{i_1}, \ldots, a_{i_k} \texttt{ -> } a_{i_0}}} \{fv(t_{i_0}) \mid fv(t_{i_1}, \ldots, t_{i_k}) \subseteq vs\}$$

The basic idea of the context consistency condition is that the variables in the range are captured by some FDs imposed on type classes present in the context. Note that although the context consistency condition resembles a more "liberal" version of the termination condition, context consistency does not prevent non-termination. Example 3 satisfies both of the above conditions, however, resulting CHRs are non-terminating. More precisely, adding the improvement rules *Prop(p)* to a terminating set *Simp(p)* of instance CHRs yields a non-terminating set *Simp(p)* ∪ *Prop(p)*. Hence, for the following result to hold we need to assume that CHRs are terminating.

Theorem 2 (More Liberal FDs Soundness). *Let p be a set of Haskell class and instance declarations which satisfies the Liberal-FD restrictions. Let Simp(p) and Prop(p) be defined by Definition 2. If the set $Simp(p) \cup Prop(p)_{class}$ is confluent and range-restricted and $Simp(p) \cup Prop(p)$ is terminating, then $Simp(p) \cup Prop(p)$ is confluent and range-restricted.*

Note that Example 4 also satisfies the more liberal FD conditions. According to Definition 2 we generate the following improvement rules. Note that the functional dependency imposed is full. For simplicity, we only focus on improvement rules.

```
rule Zip a b c, Zip a d c ==> b=d          -- (Z1)
rule Zip a b c, Zip d b c ==> a=d          -- (Z2)
rule Zip a d [(a,b)]      ==> d=b          -- (Z3)
rule Zip d b [(a,b)]      ==> d=a          -- (Z4)
rule Zip a d ([c]->e)     ==> d=b          -- (Z5)
rule Zip d b ([c]->e)     ==> d=a          -- (Z6)
```

Rules (Z5) and (Z6) are generated from the second instance. Note that both rules introduce some new variables since we violate the termination condition. However, both rules are harmless. Effectively, we can replace them by

```
rule Zip a d ([c]->e)     ==> True         -- (Z5')
rule Zip d b ([c]->e)     ==> True         -- (Z6')
```

which makes them trivial. Hence, we can omit them altogether. We observe that we can "safely" violate the termination condition (without breaking termination) in case the improvement rules generated are trivial, i.e. the right-hand side of CHRs can be replaced by the always true constraint. This is always the case if the range component of an instance is a variable.

4.2 Stronger Improvement

There are situations where FDs do not enforce sufficient improvement. Note that the inferred types of `e1` and `e2` in Example 4 are

```
e1 :: Zip Bool Char [a] => a
e2 :: Zip (Bool,Char) Int [a] => a
```

rather than

```
e1 :: (Bool,Char)
e2 :: ((Bool,Char),Int)
```

For example rule (Z3) states that only if we see `Zip a d [(a,b)]` we can improve `d` by `b`. However, in case of `e1` we see `Zip Bool Char [a]`, and we would like to improve `a` to `(Bool,Char)`. Indeed, in this context it is "safe" to replace rules (Z3) and (Z4) by

```
rule Zip a b [c] ==> c=(a,b)    -- (Z34)
```

which imposes stronger improvement to achieve the desired typing of `e1` and `e2`. Note that rule (Z34) respects the consistency and termination conditions (assuming we enforce these conditions for user-provided improvement rules). Hence, we retain confluence and termination of CHRs.

Of course, if a user-provided improvement violates any of the sufficient conditions, it is the user's responsibility to ensure that resulting CHRs are confluent and terminating.

4.3 Instance Improvement Only

Instead of *stronger* improvement it might sometimes be desirable to *omit* certain improvement rules. For example, in case the context consistency condition is violated, we can recover confluence by dropping the functional dependency rule.

Theorem 3 (Instance Improvement Soundness). *Let p be a set of Haskell class and instance declarations which satisfies the Haskell-FD consistency restriction. If the set* $Simp(p) \cup Prop_{class}(p)$ *is confluent and range-restricted and* $Simp \cup Prop_{class}(p) \cup Prop_{inst}(p)$ *is terminating, then* $Simp(p) \cup Prop_{class}(p) \cup Prop_{inst}(p)$ *is confluent and range-restricted.*

Here is a (confluent) variation of Example 8 where we only impose the instance improvement rule.

```
data Nil         = Nil
data Cons a b    = Cons a b
data ExpAbs x a = ExpAbs x a
-- env represents environment, exp expression
-- and t is the type of the resulting value
class Eval env exp t where  eval :: env->exp->t
-- we only impose the instance improvement rule but NOT
-- the class FD
rule Eval env (ExpAbs x exp) v ==> v=v1->v2
instance Eval (Cons (x,v1) env) exp v2
      => Eval env (ExpAbs x exp) (v1->v2) where
    eval env (ExpAbs x exp) = \v -> eval (Cons (x,v) env) exp
```

5 Related Work

The idea of improving types in the context of Haskell type classes is not new. For example, Chen, Hudak and Odersky [CHO92] introduce type classes which can be parameterized by a specific parameter. For example, the declaration `class SM m r | m->r` from Example 2 can be expressed as the parametric declaration `class m::SM r`. Interestingly, they impose conditions similar to Jones's consistency and termination condition to achieve sound and decidable type inference. However, their approach is more limited than ours. Functional dependencies must be always of the form `a->b` where `b` is not allow to appear in the domain of any other functional dependency. Furthermore, they do not consider any extensions such as more liberal FDs.

In [Jon95], Jones introduces a general theory of simplifying and improving types as a refinement of his theory of qualified types [Jon92]. However, he does not provide any formal results which improvement strategies lead to sound and decidable type inference.

Subsequently, Jones extends multi-parameter type classes with functional dependencies [Jon00]. He states some conditions (consistency and termination) which in this paper we finally verify as sufficient to ensure sound and decidable type inference. Surprisingly, he introduces Example 3 (which breaks the termination condition) as a motivation for functional dependencies.

Duggan and Ophel [DO02] describe an improvement strategy, domain-driven unifying overload resolution, which is very similar to functional dependencies. Indeed, they were the first to point out the potential problem of non-termination of type inference. However, they do not discuss any extensions such as more liberal FDs nor do they consider how to cope with the termination problem.

Stuckey and Sulzmann [SS02] introduce a general CHR-based formulation for type classes. They establish some general conditions, e.g. termination and confluence, in terms of CHRs under which type inference is sound and decidable. Here, we rephrase functional dependencies as a particular instance of their framework.

6 Conclusion

We have given a new perspective on functional dependencies by expressing the improvement rules implied by FDs in terms of CHRs. We have verified, for the first time, that the conditions (termination and consistency, see Definition 1) stated by Jones are sufficient to guarantee sound and decidable type inference (see Theorem 1).

There are many examples which demand dropping the termination condition. For this purpose, we have introduced more liberal FDs in Section 4.1. We have identified an additional condition (context consistency) which guarantees confluence (see Theorem 2). We have also discussed further useful extensions such as stronger improvement rules (Section 4.2) and instance improvement rules only (Section 4.3).

For such extensions it becomes much harder to guarantee decidability (unless the generated improvement rules are trivial). For example, the more liberal FD conditions only ensure soundness but not decidability. We are already working on identifying further decidable classes of CHRs. We expect to report results on this topic in the near future.

In another line of future work we plan to investigate how to safely drop the consistency condition. Consider

```
class Insert ce e | ce -> e where insert :: e->ce->ce
instance Ord a => Insert [a] a
instance Insert [Float] Int
```

Our intention is to insert elements into a collection. The class declaration states that the collection type uniquely determines the element type. The first instance states that we can insert elements into a list if the list elements enjoy an ordering relation. The second instance states that we have a special treatment in case we insert `Int`s into a list of `Float`s (for example, we assume that `Int`s are internally represented by `Float`s). This sounds reasonable, however, the above program is rejected because the consistency condition is violated. To establish confluence we seem to require a more complicated set of improvement rules. We plan to pursue this topic in future work.

Acknowledgements. We thank Jeremy Wazny and the reviewers for their comments.

References

[Abd97] S. Abdennadher. Operational semantics and confluence of constraint propagation rules. In *Proc. of CP'97*, volume 1330 of *LNCS*, pages 252–266. Springer-Verlag, 1997.

[CHO92] K. Chen, P. Hudak, and M. Odersky. Parametric type classes. In *Proc. of ACM Conference on Lisp and Functional Programming*, pages 170–191. ACM Press, June 1992.

[CK03] M. Chakravarty and S. Keller. Classy type analysis, 2003.

[DO02] D. Duggan and J. Ophel. Type-checking multi-parameter type classes. *Journal of Functional Programming*, 12(2):133–158, 2002.

[DPJSS03] G. J. Duck, S. Peyton-Jones, P. J. Stuckey, and M. Sulzmann. Sound and decidable type inference for functional dependencies. Technical report, National University of Singapore, 2003. `http://www.comp.nus.edu.sg/~sulzmann/chr/download/fd-chr.ps.gz`.

[Frü95] T. Frühwirth. Constraint handling rules. In *Constraint Programming: Basics and Trends*, volume 910 of *LNCS*. Springer-Verlag, 1995.

[Frü98] T. Frühwirth. Theory and practice of constraint handling rules. *Journal of Logic Programming*, 37(1–3):95–138, 1998.

[Jon92] M. P. Jones. *Qualified Types: Theory and Practice.* PhD thesis, Oxford University, September 1992.

[Jon95] M. P. Jones. Simplifying and improving qualified types. In *FPCA '95: Conference on Functional Programming Languages and Computer Architecture.* ACM Press, 1995.

[Jon00] M. P. Jones. Type classes with functional dependencies. In *Proc. of the 9th European Symposium on Programming Languages and Systems, ESOP 2000*, volume 1782 of *LNCS*. Springer-Verlag, March 2000.

[Kar03] J. Karczmarczuk. Structure and interpretation of quantum mechanics – a functional framework. In *Proc. of Haskell Workshop'03*, pages 50–61. ACM Press, 2003.

[Pey99] S. Peyton Jones et al. Report on the programming language Haskell 98, February 1999. http://haskell.org.

[SS02] P. J. Stuckey and M. Sulzmann. A theory of overloading. In *Proc. of ICFP'02*, pages 167–178. ACM Press, 2002.

[WW03] G. Washburn and S. Weirich. Boxes go bananas: encoding higher-order abstract syntax with parametric polymorphism. In *Proc. of ICFP'03*, pages 249 – 262. ACM Press, 2003.

Call-by-Value Mixin Modules*

Reduction Semantics, Side Effects, Types

Tom Hirschowitz[1], Xavier Leroy[2], and J.B. Wells[3]

[1] École Normale Supérieure de Lyon
[2] INRIA Rocquencourt
[3] Heriot-Watt University

Abstract. Mixin modules are a framework for modular programming that supports code parameterization, incremental programming via late binding and redefinitions, and cross-module recursion. In this paper, we develop a language of mixin modules that supports call-by-value evaluation, and formalize a reduction semantics and a sound type system for this language.

1 Introduction

For programming "in the large", it is desirable that the programming language offers linguistic support for the decomposition and structuring of programs into modules. A good example of such linguistic support is the ML module system and its powerful support for parameterized modules. Nevertheless, this system is weak on two important points.

- Mutual recursion: Mutually recursive definitions cannot be split across separate modules. There are several cases where this hinders modularization [7].
- Modifiability: The language does not propose any mechanism for incremental modification of an already-defined module, similar to inheritance and overriding in object-oriented languages.

Class-based object-oriented languages provide excellent support for these two features. Classes are naturally mutually recursive, and inheritance and method overriding answer the need for modifiability. However, viewed as a module system, classes have two weaknesses: they do not offer a general parameterization mechanism (no higher-order functions on classes), and the mechanisms they offer to describe pre-computations (initialization of static and instance variables) lack generality, since a module system should allow to naturally alternate function definitions with computational definitions using these functions.

Mixin modules [4] (hereafter simply called mixins) provide an alternative approach to modularity that combines some of the best aspects of classes and ML-style modules. Mixins are modules with "holes" (not-yet-defined components), where the holes can be plugged later by composition with other mixins, following a late-binding semantics. However, the handling of pre-computations and

* Partially supported by EPSRC grant GR/R 41545/01

D.A. Schmidt (Ed.): ESOP 2004, LNCS 2986, pp. 64–78, 2004.

initializations in mixins is still problematic. Most of the previous work on mixins, notably by Ancona and Zucca [2] and Wells and Vestergaard [26], is better suited to a call-by-name evaluation strategy. This strategy makes it impossible to trigger computations at initialization time.

Our goal in this paper is to define a call-by-value semantics for mixins that supports cleanly the evaluation of mixin components into values in a programmer-controlled evaluation order. In an earlier paper, Hirschowitz and Leroy [17] define a a typed language of mixins in a call-by-value setting, whose semantics is given by type-directed translation into an enriched λ-calculus. The present paper improves over this first attempt in the following ways:

- Reduction semantics: We give a source-to-source, small-step reduction semantics for the mixin language. This semantics is simpler than the translation-based semantics, and is untyped. It also simplifies the proof of type soundness to a standard argument by subject reduction and progress.
- Side effects: The semantics makes it easy for the programmer to (1) know when side-effects occur, and (2) control the order in which they occur.
- Anonymous definitions: Our system features anonymous definitions, that is, definitions that are evaluated, but not exported as components of the final module.[1] The translation-based semantics cannot handle anonymous definitions, because it is type-directed and anonymous definitions do not appear in mixin types.
- Practicality of mixin types: The type of a mixin must carry some dependency information about its contents. Requiring the dependency information to match exactly between the declared type of a mixin and its actual type, like Hirschowitz and Leroy did, is not practical. To address this issue, we introduce a new notion of subtyping w.r.t. dependencies, allowing a mixin to be viewed with more dependencies than it actually has. Furthermore, appropriate syntactic sugar allows to specify the dependencies of a large class of mixins with low syntactic overhead.

Section 2 informally presents *MM*. Section 3 defines the language and its dynamic semantics. Section 4 presents the type system and the soundness result. Section 5 emphasizes the importance of subtyping of dependency graphs. Section 6 examines related work. Section 7 concludes with some future work.

2 Overview

2.1 An Operational Semantics of Mixins

Our central idea for bringing mutual recursion and modifiability to modules is to adapt the distinction between classes and objects to the context of mixins. Following this idea, this paper designs a kernel language of mixins called

[1] *Anonymous* is not exactly the same as *private*, since private definitions are generally mentioned in the types as private, whereas anonymous ones are not mentioned at all.

MM, which distinguishes mixins from actual modules. *Mixins* are dedicated to modularity operations, and feature parameterization, modifiability and mutual recursion. The contents of mixins are never reduced, so no computation takes place at the mixin level. *Modules* are dedicated to computation, contain fully evaluated values, and can be obtained by mixin instantiation, written close.

For the sake of simplicity, *MM* does not explicitly include a module construct. Instead, modules are encoded by a combination of records and value binding. Roughly, a module struct $x_1 = e_1 \ldots x_n = e_n$ end is implemented by let rec $x_1 = e_1 \ldots x_n = e_n$ in $\{x_1 = e_1 \ldots x_n = e_n\}$. Based on previous work on value binding in a call-by-value setting [18], *MM* features a single value binding construct that expresses both recursive and non-recursive definitions. Basically, this construct evaluates the definitions from left to right, considering variables as values.

A mixin is a pair of a set of input variables $x_1 \ldots x_n$, and a list of output definitions $y_1 = e_1 \ldots y_m = e_m$, written $\langle x_1 \ldots x_n; y_1 = e_1 \ldots y_m = e_m \rangle$.

Operators on mixins are adapted from previous works [4,2,26]. The main one is composition: given two mixins e_1 and e_2, their composition $e_1 + e_2$ returns a new mixin whose outputs are the concatenation of those of e_1 and e_2, and whose inputs are the inputs of e_1 or e_2 that have not been filled by any output.

When closing a mixin $\langle \emptyset; y_1 = e_1 \ldots y_m = e_m \rangle$ without inputs (called *concrete*), the order in which to evaluate the definitions is not obvious. Indeed, the syntactic order arises from previous compositions, and does not necessarily reflect the intention of the programmer. For instance, the expression $\langle f; x = f\ 0 \rangle + \langle \emptyset; f = \lambda x.x + 1 \rangle$ evaluates to $\langle \emptyset; x = f\ 0, f = \lambda x.x + 1 \rangle$, which should be instantiated into struct $f = \lambda x.x + 1, x = f\ 0$ end (since definitions are evaluated from left to right). Thus, the close operator reorders definitions before evaluating them, thus turning a mixin into a module. It approximates an order in which the evaluation of each definition only needs previous definitions.

Unfortunately, this makes instantiation quite unintuitive in the presence of side effects. For example, if we are programming a ticket-vending machine for buying train tickets, it is reasonable to expect that the machine asks for the destination before asking whether the customer is a smoker or not. Indeed, the second question is useless if the trains to the requested destination are full. However, asking the second question does not require any information on the answer to the first one. So, if the program is built as an assembly of mixins, dependencies do not impose any order on the two questions, which can be a source of error. To handle this issue, our language of mixins provides programmer control over the order of evaluation: a definition can be annotated with the name of another one, to indicate that it should be evaluated after that one. For example, we can define $s = \langle destination; smoker[destination] = \ldots \rangle$. Intuitively, the annotation tells the system to do as if *smoker* depended on *destination*. This is why we call these annotations *fake dependencies*. Additionally, the system provides an operation for adding such dependencies *a posteriori*. For instance, assume our mixin was initially provided without the dependency annotation above: $s_0 = \langle destination; smoker = \ldots \rangle$. It is then important to be able to add it without modifying the source code. This is written $s_1 = s_{0\, smoker[destination]}$, which evaluates to the previous mixin s. Fake dependencies make *MM* ready for imperative features, although the formalization given in this paper does not include imperative features to keep it simpler.

2.2 Typing *MM*

The natural way to type-check mixins is via sets of type declarations for input and output components. For instance, let $m_1 = \langle x; y = e_1 \rangle$ and $m_2 = \langle y; x = e_2 \rangle$, where e_1 and e_2 denote two arbitrary expressions. It appears natural to give them the types $m_1 : \langle x : M_2; y : M_1 \rangle$ and $m_2 : \langle y : M_1; x : M_2 \rangle$, where M_1 and M_2 denote the types of e_1 and e_2, respectively, and the semi-colon separates the inputs from the outputs. The type of their composition is then $m : \langle \emptyset; x : M_2, y : M_1 \rangle$. While adequate for call-by-name mixins, this type system is not sound for call-by-value evaluation, because it does not guarantee that bindings generated at close time contain only well-founded recursive definitions that can be safely evaluated using call-by-value. In the example above, we could have x bound to $y+1$ and y bound to $x+1$, which is not well-founded. Yet, nothing in the type of m signals this problem.

In Sect. 4, we enrich these naive mixin types with dependency graphs describing the dependencies between definitions, and we formalize a simple (monomorphic) type system for *MM*. These graphs distinguish *strong dependencies*, which are forbidden in dependency cycles, from *weak dependencies*, which are allowed. For instance, $x+1$ strongly depends on x, while $\lambda y.x$ only weakly depends on it. The graphs are updated at each mixin operation, and allow to detect ill-founded recursions, while retaining most of the expressive power of *MM*.

Moreover, as mixin types carry dependency graphs, the types assigned to inputs may also contain graphs, and thus constrain the future mixins filling these inputs to have exactly the same graph. This policy is rather inflexible. To recover some flexibility, we introduce a notion of subtyping over dependency graphs: a mixin with a dependency graph G can be viewed as having a more constraining graph. The type system of *MM* is the first to handle both subtyping over dependency graphs and anonymous definitions in mixins.

3 Syntax and Dynamic Semantics of *MM*

3.1 Syntax

We now formally define our kernel language of call-by-value mixin modules, called *MM*. Following Harper and Lillibridge [14], we distinguish *names* X from *variables* x. Variables are α-convertible, but names are not. *MM* expressions are defined in Fig. 1. Expressions include variables x, records (labeled by names) $\{X_1 = e_1 \dots X_n = e_n\}$, and record selection $e.X$, which are standard.

The basic mixins are called *mixin structures*, which we abbreviate as simply *structures*. A structure $\langle \iota; o \rangle$ is a pair of an *input* ι of the shape $X_1 \triangleright x_1 \dots X_n \triangleright x_n$, and of an *output* o of the shape $d_1 \dots d_m$. The input ι maps external names

Expression:	$e ::= x$	Variable
	$\mid \{X_1 = e_1 \ldots X_n = e_n\}$	Record
	$\mid e.X$	Record selection
	$\mid \langle X_1 \triangleright x_1 \ldots X_n \triangleright x_n; d_1 \ldots d_m \rangle$	Structure
	$\mid e_1 + e_2$	Composition
	$\mid \mathsf{close}\, e$	Closure
	$\mid e_{\mid -X_1 \ldots X_n}$	Deletion
	$\mid e_{X[Y]}$	Fake dependency
	$\mid \mathsf{let\ rec}\ x_1 = e_1 \ldots x_n = e_n\ \mathsf{in}\ e$	let rec
Definition:	$d ::= X[x_1 \ldots x_n] \triangleright x = e$	Named definition
	$\mid \_[x_1 \ldots x_n] \triangleright x = e$	Anonymous definition

Fig. 1. Syntax of *MM*

imported by the structure to internal variables (used in o). The output o is an ordered list of *definitions* d. A definition is of the shape $L[\boldsymbol{x}\,] \triangleright x = e$, where e is the *body* of the definition, and the *label* L is either a name X or the anonymous label $\_$. The symbol $\boldsymbol{x}$ stands for a possibly empty finite list of variables $x_1 \ldots x_n$, the list of *fake dependencies* of this definition on other definitions of the structure.

We provide four representative operators over mixins: compose $e_1 + e_2$, close $\mathsf{close}\, e$, delete $e_{\mid -X_1 \ldots X_n}$, and fake dependency $e_{X[Y]}$. Additional operators are formalized in Hirschowitz's PhD thesis [16].

Finally, *MM* features a single value binding construct let rec b in e, where b is a list of recursive definitions $x_1 = e_1 \ldots x_n = e_n$, called a *binding.* As in previous work [18], this construct encompasses ML recursive and non-recursive binding constructs. Moreover, we restrict recursion syntactically as follows.

Backward dependencies. In a binding $b = (x_1 = e_1 \ldots x_n = e_n)$, we say that there is a *backward dependency* of x_i on x_j if $1 \leq i \leq j \leq n$ and $x_j \in FV(e_i)$, where $FV(e_i)$ denotes the set of free variables of e_i. A backward dependency of x_i on x_j is syntactically incorrect, except when e_j is of *predictable shape.*

Predictable shape. Expressions of predictable shape are defined by $e_\downarrow \in$ *Predictable* $::= \{s_v\} \mid \langle \iota; o \rangle \mid \mathsf{let\ rec}\ b\ \mathsf{in}\ e_\downarrow$, where s_v ranges over evaluated record sequences (see below the definition of values).

In the sequel, we only consider syntactically correct bindings. Moreover, we consider expressions equivalent up to α-conversion of variables bound in structures and let rec expressions. We also consider inputs equivalent up to reordering, and fake dependency lists equivalent up to reordering and repetition. Further, we assume that bindings, inputs, outputs, and structures (resp. records, inputs, outputs, and structures) do not define the same variable (resp. name) twice.

3.2 Dynamic Semantics

Values and answers. *MM* values are defined by

$$v ::= x \mid \{s_v\} \mid \langle X_1 \triangleright x_1 \ldots X_n \triangleright x_n; d_1 \ldots d_n \rangle$$

where $s_v ::= X_1 = v_1 \ldots X_1 = v_1$.

Evaluation answers are values, possibly surrounded by an evaluated binding: $a ::= v \mid \mathsf{let\ rec}\ b_v\ \mathsf{in}\ v$, where $b_v ::= x_1 = v_1 \ldots x_n = v_n$.

Contraction relation. In preparation for the reduction relation, we first define a local *contraction relation* $\leadsto$ by the rules in Fig. 2. Reduction will contain the closure of contraction under evaluation contexts.

Rule Compose defines composition. Outputs o are viewed as finite maps from pairs (L, x) to pairs $(\boldsymbol{y}, e)$. For any ι and o, we let $Bind(\iota, o) = \iota \cup dom(o)$. Moreover, the restriction of $dom(o)$ to pairs with a name as first component is a finite map from names to variables, which we denote by $Input(o)$. The composition of two structures $\langle \iota_1; o_1 \rangle$ and $\langle \iota_2; o_2 \rangle$ is a structure $\langle \iota; o \rangle$, defined as follows: ι is the union of ι_1 and ι_2, where names defined in o_1 or o_2 are removed. The result output o is defined as the concatenation of o_1 and o_2. There is a side condition checking that the obtained mixin is well-formed, and that no variable capture occurs. (Given a binary relation R, $rng(R)$ denotes its range, i.e. the set of all of the right-hand-sides of the pairs in R.) For example, let $e_1 = \langle X \triangleright x; Y \triangleright y = z + x \rangle$ and $e_2 = \langle X \triangleright x; Z \triangleright z = x \rangle$. After suitable α-conversion, the composition $e_1 + e_2$ reduces to $\langle X \triangleright x; Y \triangleright y = z + x, Z \triangleright z' = x \rangle$.

Rule Close defines the instantiation of a structure $\langle \iota; o \rangle$. The input ι must be empty. The instantiation is in three steps.

- First, o is reordered according to its dependencies, its fake dependencies, and its syntactic ordering, thus yielding a new output $Reorder(o)$. This is done by considering the syntactic definition order in o, written $\triangleright_o$, and the *unlabeled dependency graph* of o, written $\rightharpoonup_o$, and defined by the following rules:

$$\frac{x' \in FV(e) \quad (L[\boldsymbol{y}] \triangleright x = e), (L'[\boldsymbol{z}] \triangleright x' = e') \in o}{x' \rightharpoonup_o x} \qquad \frac{(L[x_1 \ldots x_n] \triangleright x = e) \in o \quad (L'[\boldsymbol{z}] \triangleright x_i = e') \in o}{x_i \rightharpoonup_o x}$$

(Here, $x' \rightharpoonup x$ means that x depends on x'.) Given an unlabeled graph $\rightharpoonup$ on variables, we define the binary relation $\rightarrowtail_{\rightharpoonup}$ by $\{x \rightarrowtail_{\rightharpoonup} y \mid x \rightharpoonup^+ y \text{ and } y \not\rightharpoonup^* x\}$, where $\rightharpoonup^+$ and $\rightharpoonup^*$ respectively are the transitive and reflexive-transitive closure of $\rightharpoonup$, and $\not\rightharpoonup^*$ is the complementary relation to $\rightharpoonup^*$. It defines a partial order on the variables defined by o, which respects dependencies, in the sense that if $x \rightarrowtail_{\rightharpoonup} y$, then x does not depend on y. The output $Reorder(o)$ is then o, reordered w.r.t. the left-to-right lexicographical order $(\rightarrowtail_{\rightharpoonup_o}, \triangleright_o)$. Thus, when dependencies do not impose an order, we choose the syntactic definition order as a default. By construction, in $Reorder(o)$,

Contraction rules

$$\frac{e = \langle(\iota_1 \cup \iota_2) \setminus \mathit{Input}(o_1, o_2); o_1, o_2\rangle \qquad e \text{ is well-formed} \quad \mathit{rng}(\mathit{Bind}(\iota_1, o_1)) \perp \mathit{FV}(\langle\iota_2; o_2\rangle) \qquad \mathit{rng}(\mathit{Bind}(\iota_2, o_2)) \perp \mathit{FV}(\langle\iota_1; o_1\rangle)}{\langle\iota_1; o_1\rangle + \langle\iota_2; o_2\rangle \rightsquigarrow e} \ (\text{COMPOSE})$$

$$\mathsf{close}\langle\emptyset; o\rangle \rightsquigarrow \mathsf{let\ rec}\ \mathit{BofO}(\mathit{Reorder}(o))\ \mathsf{in}\ \mathit{RofO}(\mathit{Reorder}(o)) \quad (\text{CLOSE})$$

$$\langle\iota; o\rangle_{|-X_1\ldots X_n} \rightsquigarrow \langle\iota \cup \mathit{Input}(o)_{|\{X_1\ldots X_n\}}; o_{|\,\mathsf{dom}(o)\setminus(\{X_1\ldots X_n\}\times \mathsf{Vars})}\rangle \quad (\text{DELETE})$$

$$\frac{(Y, y) \in \mathit{Input}(\iota, (o_1, X[z^*] \triangleright x = e, o_2))}{\langle\iota; o_1, X[z^*] \triangleright x = e, o_2\rangle_{X[Y]} \rightsquigarrow \langle\iota; o_1, X[yz^*] \triangleright x = e, o_2\rangle} \ (\text{FAKE})$$

$$\{s_v\}.X \rightsquigarrow s_v(X) \quad (\text{SELECT}) \qquad \frac{\mathit{dom}(b) \perp \mathit{FV}(\mathbb{L})}{\mathbb{L}\,[\mathsf{let\ rec}\ b\ \mathsf{in}\ e] \rightsquigarrow \mathsf{let\ rec}\ b\ \mathsf{in}\ \mathbb{L}\,[e]} \ (\text{LIFT})$$

Reduction rules

$$\frac{e \rightsquigarrow e'}{\mathbb{E}\,[e] \to \mathbb{E}\,[e']} \ (\text{CONTEXT}) \qquad \frac{\mathbb{E}\,[\mathbb{D}\,](x) = v}{\mathbb{E}\,[\mathbb{D}\,[x]] \to \mathbb{E}\,[\mathbb{D}\,[v]]} \ (\text{SUBST})$$

$$\frac{\mathit{dom}(b_1) \perp (\{x\} \cup \mathit{dom}(b_v, b_2) \cup \mathit{FV}(b_v, b_2) \cup \mathit{FV}(e'))}{\mathsf{let\ rec}\ b_v, x = (\mathsf{let\ rec}\ b_1\ \mathsf{in}\ e), b_2\ \mathsf{in}\ e' \to \mathsf{let\ rec}\ b_v, b_1, x = e, b_2\ \mathsf{in}\ e'} \ (\text{IM})$$

$$\frac{\mathit{dom}(b) \perp (\mathit{dom}(b_v) \cup \mathit{FV}(b_v))}{\mathsf{let\ rec}\ b_v\ \mathsf{in\ let\ rec}\ b\ \mathsf{in}\ e \to \mathsf{let\ rec}\ b_v, b\ \mathsf{in}\ e} \ (\text{EM})$$

Evaluation contexts

Evaluation context:

$\mathbb{E} ::= \mathbb{F} \mid \mathsf{let\ rec}\ b_v\ \mathsf{in}\ \mathbb{F} \mid \mathsf{let\ rec}\ b_v, x = \mathbb{F}, b\ \mathsf{in}\ e$

Nested lift context:

$\mathbb{F} ::= \square \mid \mathbb{L}\,[\mathbb{F}]$

Lift context:

$\mathbb{L} ::= \{s_v, X = \square, s\} \mid \square.X \mid \mathsf{close}\,\square \mid \square_{X[Y]} \mid \square_{|-X_1\ldots X_n} \mid \square + e \mid v + \square$

Dereferencing context:

$\mathbb{D} ::= \square.X \mid \mathsf{close}\,\square \mid \square_{|-X_1\ldots X_n} \mid \square_{X[Y]} \mid \square + v_1 \mid v_2 + \square$ (v_2 is not a variable).

Access in evaluation contexts

$$(\mathsf{let\ rec}\ b_v\ \mathsf{in}\ \mathbb{F}\,)(x) = b_v(x) \quad (\text{EA}) \qquad (\mathsf{let\ rec}\ b_v, y = \mathbb{F}, b\ \mathsf{in}\ e)(x) = b_v(x) \quad (\text{IA})$$

Fig. 2. Dynamic semantics of *MM*

all backward dependencies are part of cycles. For example, consider the mixin $e = \langle\emptyset; X \triangleright x = e_1(z), Y \triangleright y = e_2(x, z), Z \triangleright z = e_3(x)\rangle$. Its instantiation will evaluate X, then Z, then Y.

– Second, a binding $\mathit{BofO}(\mathit{Reorder}(o))$ is generated, defining, for each definition $d = (L[\boldsymbol{y}\,] \triangleright x = e)$ in $\mathit{Reorder}(o)$, the definition $x = e$, in the same order as in *Reorder*(o). As we only write syntactically correct expressions, the rule has an implicit side condition that *BofO*(*Reorder*(o)) be syntactically correct. For instance, the reduction of the expression $\mathsf{close}\langle\emptyset; X \triangleright x = x + x\rangle$ is stuck, since $x + x$ is not of predictable shape.

- Third, the values of the named definitions of *Reorder*(o) are grouped in a record *RofO*(*Reorder*(o)), with, for each named definition $X[\boldsymbol{y}] \triangleright x = e$, a field $X = x$. This record is the result of the instantiation.

Rule DELETE describes how *MM* deletes a finite set of names $\{X_1 \dots X_n\}$ from a structure $\langle\iota; o\rangle$. Let *Vars* denote the set of all variables. First, o is restricted to the other definitions. Second, the removed definitions remain bound as inputs, by adding the corresponding inputs to ι.

Rule FAKE describes the fake dependency operation, which allows adding a fake dependency to a mixin *a posteriori*. Let *Input*(ι, o) denote $\iota \cup$ *Input*(o), and assume given an input ι and an output $o = (o_1, X[\boldsymbol{z}] \triangleright x = e, o_2)$. Further assume that $(Y, y) \in$ *Input*(ι, o). Then, the expression $\langle\iota; o\rangle_{X[Y]}$ adds a fake dependency on y to the definition of X, thus yielding $\langle\iota; o_1, X[y\boldsymbol{z}] \triangleright x = e, o_2\rangle$.

The record selection rule SELECT is standard.

Finally, in *MM*, there is no rule for eliminating $\mathsf{let\ rec}$. Instead, evaluated bindings remain at top-level in the expression as a kind of run-time environment. Bindings that are not at top-level in the expression must be lifted before their evaluation can begin, as defined by rule LIFT and *lift contexts* $\mathbb{L}$.

Reduction relation. We now define the dynamic semantics of *MM* by the global *reduction relation* $\longrightarrow$, defined by the rules in Fig. 2.

First, by rule CONTEXT, it extends contraction to evaluation contexts. Moreover, as mentioned above, only the top-level binding can be evaluated. As soon as one of its definitions gets evaluated, evaluation can proceed with the next one, or with the enclosed expression if there is no definition left. This is enforced by the definition of *evaluation contexts* $\mathbb{E}$: evaluation happens under (if evaluated) or inside an optional top-level binding, and a *nested lift context* $\mathbb{F}$ (which is simply a series of lift contexts). If evaluation meets a binding inside the considered expression, then this binding is lifted to the top level of the expression, or just before the top-level binding if there is one. In this case, it is merged with the latter, either internally or externally, as described by rules IM and EM, respectively. External and internal substitutions (rules SUBST, EA and IA) allow to copy one of the already evaluated definitions of the top-level binding, when they are needed by the evaluation, i.e. when they appear in a *dereferencing context*. The condition that v_2 is not a variable in the grammar ensures determinism of the reduction in cases such as $x + y$. The left argument is always copied first.

4 Static Semantics of *MM*

Types are defined by $M \in \mathit{Types} ::= \{O\} \mid \langle I; O; G\rangle$, where I and O are *signatures*, that is, finite maps from names to types, and where G is a graph over names, labeled by *degrees*. A degree χ is one of $\bullet$ and $\circ$, respectively representing strong and weak dependencies. There are only two kinds of types: record types $\{O\}$ and mixin types $\langle I; O; G\rangle$. *Environments* Γ are finite maps from variables to types. Type, signature, and environment well-formedness only require that for any mixin type $\langle I; O; G\rangle$, G is *safe*, in the sense that its cycles only contain weak dependencies (labeled by $\circ$), and $O \leq I_{|\,dom(O)}$, in the sense of signature subtyping, defined below.

The type system is defined in Fig. 3. After the standard typing rule T-VARIABLE for variables, rule T-STRUCT defines the typing of structures $\langle \iota; o\rangle$. The rule introduces a well-formed input signature I corresponding to ι, and a well-formed type environment Γ_o corresponding to o. Given I and Γ_o, the rule checks that the definitions in o indeed have the types mentioned in Γ_o. The types of named definitions of o, obtained by composing Γ_o with *Input*(o), are retained both as inputs and outputs. Finally, the condition $\vdash \rightarrow_{\langle \iota; o\rangle}$ checks that the dependencies of the structure are safe. It relies on the labeled dependency graph of $\langle \iota; o\rangle$, which is defined by the following rules:

$$\frac{(L', x') \in \mathit{Bind}(\iota, o) \qquad (L[\boldsymbol{y}] \rhd x = e) \in o}{\mathit{Node}(L', x') \xrightarrow{\mathit{Degree}(x', e)}_{\langle \iota; o\rangle} \mathit{Node}(L, x)} \qquad \frac{(L_i, x_i) \in \mathit{Bind}(\iota, o) \qquad (L[x_1 \ldots x_n] \rhd x = e) \in o}{\mathit{Node}(L_i, x_i) \xrightarrow{\bullet}_{\langle \iota; o\rangle} \mathit{Node}(L, x)}$$

where $\mathit{Node}(L, x)$ denotes L if L is a name, and x otherwise. The edges of this graph are labeled by degrees, which are computed by the *Degree* function, defined if $x \in \mathit{FV}(e)$ by $\mathit{Degree}(x, e) = \circ$ if $e \in \mathit{Predictable}$ and $\mathit{Degree}(x, e) = \bullet$ otherwise. Finally, variables should not appear in types, so we *lift* the graph to a labeled graph over names written $\lfloor \rightarrow_{\langle \iota; o\rangle} \rfloor$. Namely, we extend edges through anonymous components: for each path $N_1 \xrightarrow{\chi_1} x \xrightarrow{\chi_2} N_2$, we add the edge $N_1 \xrightarrow{\chi} N_2$, where χ is the minimum of χ_1 and χ_2, given that $\bullet < \circ$. Then, $\lfloor \rightarrow_{\langle \iota; o\rangle} \rfloor$ denotes the restriction of the obtained graph to names.

The subsumption rule T-SUB materializes the presence of subtyping in *MM*. Subtyping is defined by the following rules:

$$\frac{I_2 \leq I_1 \qquad O_1 \leq O_2 \qquad G_1 \subset G_2}{\langle I_1; O_1; G_1\rangle \leq \langle I_2; O_2; G_2\rangle} \qquad \frac{O_1 \leq O_2}{\{O_1\} \leq \{O_2\}}$$

where subtyping between signatures is defined component-wise. Subtyping allows a dependency graph to be replaced by a more constraining graph. Section 5 illustrates the practical importance of subtyping between dependency graphs.

Rule T-COMPOSE types the composition of two expressions. It guesses a lower bound I of the input signatures I_1 and I_2 of its arguments, such that $\mathit{dom}(I) = \mathit{dom}(I_1) \cup \mathit{dom}(I_2)$. This lower bound is used as the input signature of the result. Checking that it is a lower bound implies that common names between I_1 and I_2 have compatible types. The rule also checks that the union of the two dependency graphs is safe, and that no name is defined twice (i.e. appears in both outputs). The result type shares the inputs and takes the disjoint union, written $+$, of the outputs and the union of the dependency graphs.

Expressions

$$\frac{x \in dom(\Gamma)}{\Gamma \vdash x : \Gamma(x)} \quad (\text{T-VARIABLE})$$

$$\frac{\begin{array}{c} dom(\iota) = dom(I) \qquad \vdash I \qquad \vdash \Gamma_o \qquad \vdash \longrightarrow_{\langle \iota; o \rangle} \\ \Gamma\langle I \circ \iota^{-1} \cup \Gamma_o \rangle \vdash o : \Gamma_o \qquad O = \Gamma_o \circ Input(o) \end{array}}{\Gamma \vdash \langle \iota; o \rangle : \langle I \cup O; O; \lfloor \longrightarrow_{\langle \iota; o \rangle} \rfloor \rangle} \quad (\text{T-STRUCT})$$

$$\frac{\Gamma \vdash e : M' \qquad M' \leq M \qquad \vdash M}{\Gamma \vdash e : M} \quad (\text{T-SUB})$$

$$\frac{\begin{array}{c} \Gamma \vdash e_1 : \langle I_1; O_1; G_1 \rangle \qquad \Gamma \vdash e_2 : \langle I_2; O_2; G_2 \rangle \\ \vdash G_1 \cup G_2 \qquad dom(I) = dom(I_1) \cup dom(I_2) \qquad \vdash I \\ I_{\mid dom(I_1)} \leq I_1 \qquad I_{\mid dom(I_2)} \leq I_2 \qquad (O_1 + O_2) \leq I_{\mid dom(O_1 + O_2)} \end{array}}{\Gamma \vdash e_1 + e_2 : \langle I; O_1 + O_2; G_1 \cup G_2 \rangle} \quad (\text{T-COMPOSE})$$

$$\frac{\Gamma \vdash e : \langle I; O; G \rangle \qquad dom(I) = dom(O)}{\Gamma \vdash \mathsf{close}\, e : \{O\}} \quad (\text{T-CLOSE})$$

$$\frac{\Gamma \vdash e : \langle I; O; G \rangle}{\Gamma \vdash e_{\mid - X_1 \ldots X_n} : \langle I; O_{\setminus \{X_1 \ldots X_n\}}; G_{\mid - \{X_1 \ldots X_n\}} \rangle} \quad (\text{T-DELETE})$$

$$\frac{\Gamma \vdash e : \langle I; O; G \rangle \qquad X \in dom(O) \qquad Y \in dom(I) \qquad \vdash G_{X[Y]}}{\Gamma \vdash e_{X[Y]} : \langle I; O; G_{X[Y]} \rangle} \quad (\text{T-FAKE})$$

$$\frac{\vdash b \qquad \vdash \Gamma_b \qquad \Gamma\langle \Gamma_b \rangle \vdash b : \Gamma_b \qquad \Gamma\langle \Gamma_b \rangle \vdash e : M}{\Gamma \vdash \mathsf{let\ rec}\ b\ \mathsf{in}\ e : M} \quad (\text{T-LETREC})$$

$$\frac{\forall X \in dom(s), \Gamma \vdash s(X) : O(X)}{\Gamma \vdash \{s\} : \{O\}} \quad (\text{T-RECORD}) \qquad \frac{\Gamma \vdash e : \{O\}}{\Gamma \vdash e.X : O(X)} \quad (\text{T-SELECT})$$

Sequences

$$\Gamma \vdash \epsilon : \emptyset \qquad \frac{\Gamma \vdash e : M \qquad \Gamma \vdash o : \Gamma_o}{\Gamma \vdash (L[x^*] \rhd x = e, o) : \{x : M\} \cup \Gamma_o}$$

$$\frac{\Gamma \vdash e : M \qquad \Gamma \vdash b : \Gamma_b}{\Gamma \vdash (x = e, b) : \{x : M\} \cup \Gamma_b}$$

Fig. 3. Static semantics of *MM*

Rule T-CLOSE transforms a mixin type whose inputs are all matched by its outputs into a record type.

Rule T-DELETE, exactly as the corresponding contraction rule, removes the selected names from the output types, reporting the other ones in the input signature. The abstract graph is modified accordingly by the operation $G_{|-\{X_1 \ldots X_n\}}$, which removes the edges leading to the deleted components.

Rule T-FAKE types an expression of the shape $e_{X[Y]}$. If e has a type $\langle I; O; G \rangle$, with $X \in \mathit{dom}(O)$, and $Y \in \mathit{dom}(I)$, then adding a fake dependency of X on Y only modifies the graph G: $G_{X[Y]}$ denotes G, augmented with a strong edge from Y to X. The rule checks that this does not make the graph unsafe.

Rule T-LETREC for typing bindings let rec b in e is standard, except for its side condition: $\vdash b$ means that b does not contain backward dependencies on definitions of unpredictable shape, and is well ordered with respect to its dependencies, in the following sense. The labeled dependency graph $\rightarrow_b$ of $b = (x_1 = e_1 \ldots x_n = e_n)$ is defined as the labeled dependency graph of the equivalent output $(\_[\,] \triangleright x_1 = e_1 \ldots \_[\,] \triangleright x_n = e_n)$. Then, we require that all paths of $\rightarrow_b$ whose last edge is labeled by $\bullet$ are forward. This is sufficient to ensure that b contains no dependency problem.

The T-SELECT and T-RECORD rules for typing record construction and selection are standard. Rule T-SELECT implicitly requires that $X \in \mathit{dom}(O)$.

Finally, Fig. 3 also presents the typing of outputs and bindings, which is straightforward, since it consists in successively typing their definitions.

Theorem 1 (Soundness). *A closed, well-typed expression must either not terminate or reach an answer.*

The proof of this theorem (via the standard subject reduction and progress properties) can be found in Hirschowitz's PhD thesis [16].

5 Practical Syntactic Signatures and Subtyping w.r.t. Dependencies

As mentioned in the introduction, enriching mixin types with dependency graphs without graph subtyping would make the type system too rigid. Assuming such a system, consider a mixin e which imports a mixin X. The type of e has an input declaration named X that associates a graph to X. If we later want to use e twice in the program, composing it with two different mixins e' and e'', it is unlikely that X has exactly the same dependency graph in e' and e'', so we cannot attribute a graph to X in e that allows both compositions. Furthermore, from the standpoint of separate development, the dependency graph is part of the specification of a mixin. It informs clients of dependencies, but also of non-dependencies. Thus, definitions must depend exactly on the components that the graph claims they depend on. So, if the implementation of a mixin changes for any reason such as optimization, bug fix, etc, then probably its specification will also have to change. This is undesirable for separate development, which encourages the independent development of mixins, based on stable specifications.

Our previous type systems for mixins [17,19] suffer from this drawback: they require the dependency graph of an output to exactly match the one of the input it fills. We improve over these type systems here, by incorporating a simple notion of subtyping in our type system for *MM*, which allows to see a mixin with dependency graph G as a mixin with a more constraining dependency graph, that is, a super graph of G. The idea is that when giving the type of an input, the programmer (or possibly a type inference algorithm, although we have no such algorithm to propose yet) chooses a reasonably constraining dependency graph that remains compatible with the uses made of the input. Subtyping, then, allows the input to be filled by less constrained definitions.

Another related problem is that dependency graphs, and *a fortiori* the constraining graphs mentioned above, are very cumbersome to write by hand for the programmer. To alleviate this issue, we propose the introduction of appropriate syntactic sugar: we define the new form of mixin type $\mathsf{mixsig}\ Q_1 \ldots Q_n\ \mathsf{end}$, with

$$Q ::= U \mid [U_1 \ldots U_n]$$
$$U ::= ?X : M \mid !X : M$$

This new form is a list of enriched specifications Q. An enriched specification Q is either a single declaration U, or a block of single declarations $[U_1 \ldots U_n]$. A single declaration assigns a type to a name, with a flag ? or !, to indicate that it is an input or an output, respectively. Blocks are considered equivalent modulo the order, and they represent groups of potentially recursive definitions of predictable shape. Single declarations represent arbitrary definitions.

This construct can be elaborated to core *MM* types: basically, ? declarations are inputs, and ! declarations are both inputs and outputs. A single ! declaration strongly depends on all the preceding declarations. A ! declaration in a block strongly depends on the preceding declarations, and weakly depends on all the declarations of its block. This form makes mixin types more concise and intuitive.

6 Related Work

Mixin-based inheritance. The notion of mixin originates in the object-oriented language Flavors [22], and was further investigated both as a linguistic device addressing many of the shortcomings of inheritance [13,11,3] and as a semantic foundation for inheritance [6]. Here, we call this kind of mixins *mixin classes.* An issue with mixin classes that is generally not addressed is the treatment of instance fields and their initialization. Mixin classes where instance fields can be initialized by arbitrary expressions raise exactly the same problems of finding a correct evaluation order and detecting cyclic dependencies that we have addressed in this paper in the context of call-by-value mixins. Initialization can also be performed by an initialization method with a standard name (say, `init`), but this breaks data encapsulation. Instead, *MM* naturally allows interleaving function definitions and arbitrary computations.

Recursive modules. Harper et al. [7,9] and Russo [25] extend the ML module system with recursive definitions of modules. This addresses the mutual recursion issue we mentioned in introduction, but not the modifiability (open recursion) issue. Russo relies on lazy evaluation for the recursive definitions and makes no attempt to statically detect ill-founded recursions. Harper et al. use a standard call-by-value fixed-point operator, and statically constrain components of recursively-defined modules to be *valuable*. This is less flexible than our proposal, since module components can only weakly depend on the recursive variable. Recent work by Dreyer [8] lifts this restriction by using an effect system to track strong dependencies on recursively-defined variables.

Language designs with mixins. Bracha [4] formulated the concept of mixin-based inheritance (composition) independently of an object-oriented setting. His mixins do not address the initialization issue. Duggan and Sourelis [10] extended his proposal and adapted it to ML. In their system, a mixin comprises a body, containing only function and data-type definitions, surrounded by a prelude and an initialization section, containing arbitrary computations. During composition, only the bodies of the two mixins are connected, but neither the preludes nor the initialization sections. This ensures that mixin composition never creates ill-founded recursive definitions, but forbids to alternate standard definitions and composable definitions.

Flatt and Felleisen [12] introduce the closely related concept of *units*. A first difference with our proposal is that units do not feature late binding. Moreover, the initialization problem is handled differently. The formalization of units in [12, Sect. 4] restricts definitions to syntactic values, but includes in each unit an initialization expression that can perform arbitrary computations. Like Duggan and Sourelis's approach, this approach prevents the creation of ill-founded recursive definitions, but is less flexible than our approach. The implementation of units for Scheme allows arbitrary computations within the definitions of unit components. The defined variables are implicitly initialized to `nil` before evaluating the right-hand sides of the definitions and updating the defined variables with the results of the computation. Ill-founded recursions are thus not prevented statically, and result either in a run-time type error or in a value that is not a fixed-point of the recursive definition.

Linking calculi and mixin calculi. Cardelli [5] initiated the study of linking calculi. His system is a first-order linking model, that is, modules are compilation units and cannot be nested. His type system does not restrict recursion at all, but the operational semantics is sequential in nature and does not appear to handle cross-unit recursion. As a result, the system seems to lack the progress property.

Machkasova and Turbak [21] explore a very expressive linking calculus, which is not confluent. Instead, it is argued that it is computationally sound, in the sense that all strategies lead to the same outcome. The system is untyped, and does not feature nested modules.

Ancona and Zucca [2] propose a call-by-name module system called *CMS*. As *MM*, *CMS* extends Jigsaw by allowing any kind of expressions as mixin definitions, not just values. Unlike in *MM*, in *CMS*, there is no distinction between modules and mixin modules, which makes sense in call-by-name languages, since the contents of modules are not evaluated until selection. In call-by-value, the contents of a module are eagerly evaluated, so *CMS* is not a suitable model. From the standpoint of typing, *CMS*, unlike *MM*, and consistently with most call-by-name languages, does not control recursive definitions.

In a more recent calculus [1], Ancona et al. do distinguish mixins from modules. They propose to handle side effects using monadic operators. However, they do not attempt to statically reject faulty recursive definitions. Moreover, in their system, given a composition $e_1 + e_2$, the monadic definitions of e_1 are necessarily evaluated before those of e_2, which is less flexible than our proposal.

As *CMS*, Wells and Vestergaard's **m**-calculus [26] is targeted to call-by-name evaluation. Nevertheless, it has a rich equational theory that allows to see *MM* as a strongly-typed version of the **m**-calculus specialized to call-by-value plus built-in late binding behavior (encoded in the **m**-calculus), explicit distinction between mixins and modules, programmer control over the order of evaluation, and a sound and flexible type system.

7 Conclusion

We have presented a language of call-by-value mixin modules, equipped with a reduction semantics and a sound type system. Some open issues remain to be dealt with, which are related to different practical uses of mixin modules. If mixin modules are used as first-class, core language constructs, then the simple type system presented here is not expressive enough. Some form of polymorphism over mixin module types seems necessary, along the lines of type systems for record concatenation proposed by Harper and Pierce [15] and by Pottier [24]. If one wants to build a module system based on mixin modules, then type abstraction and user-defined type components have to be considered. We are working on extending the type systems for ML modules [20,14] to mixin modules with type components. For this, we plan to build on previous work on recursive, non-mixin modules [7,9]. Nevertheless, an issue appears for finding the inputs of a composition, which involves a kind of greatest lower bound operation on types. In a similar context, Odersky et al. [23] resort to explicit annotations, which is not entirely satisfactory.

References

[1] D. Ancona, S. Fagorzi, E. Moggi, E. Zucca. Mixin modules and computational effects. In *Int'l Col. on Automata, Lang. and Progr.*, 2003.

[2] D. Ancona, E. Zucca. A calculus of module systems. *J. Func. Progr.*, 12(2), 2002.

[3] V. Bono, A. Patel, V. Shmatikov. A core calculus of classes and mixins. In R. Guerraoui, ed., *Europ. Conf. on Object-Oriented Progr.*, vol. 1628 of *LNCS*. Springer-Verlag, 1999.

[4] G. Bracha. *The Programming Language Jigsaw: Mixins, Modularity and Multiple Inheritance.* PhD thesis, University of Utah, 1992.
[5] L. Cardelli. Program fragments, linking, and modularization. In *24th symp. Principles of Progr. Lang.* ACM Press, 1997.
[6] W. R. Cook. *A Denotational Semantics of Inheritance.* PhD thesis, Department of Computer Science, Brown University, 1989.
[7] K. Crary, R. Harper, S. Puri. What is a recursive module? In *Prog. Lang. Design and Impl.* ACM Press, 1999.
[8] D. Dreyer. A type system for well-founded recursion. In *31st symp. Principles of Progr. Lang.* ACM Press, 2004. To appear.
[9] D. R. Dreyer, R. Harper, K. Crary. Toward a practical type theory for recursive modules. Technical Report CMU-CS-01-112, Carnegie Mellon University, Pittsburgh, PA, 2001.
[10] D. Duggan, C. Sourelis. Mixin modules. In *Int. Conf. on Functional Progr.* ACM Press, 1996.
[11] R. B. Findler, M. Flatt. Modular object-oriented programming with units and mixins. In *Int. Conf. on Functional Progr.* ACM Press, 1998.
[12] M. Flatt, M. Felleisen. Units: cool modules for HOT languages. In *Prog. Lang. Design and Impl.* ACM Press, 1998.
[13] M. Flatt, S. Krishnamurthi, M. Felleisen. Classes and mixins. In *25th symp. Principles of Progr. Lang.* ACM Press, 1998.
[14] R. Harper, M. Lillibridge. A type-theoretic approach to higher-order modules with sharing. In *21st symp. Principles of Progr. Lang.* ACM Press, 1994.
[15] R. Harper, B. Pierce. A record calculus based on symmetric concatenation. In *18th symp. Principles of Progr. Lang.*, Orlando, Florida, 1991.
[16] T. Hirschowitz. *Modules mixins, modules et récursion étendue en appel par valeur.* PhD thesis, University of Paris VII, 2003.
[17] T. Hirschowitz, X. Leroy. Mixin modules in a call-by-value setting. In D. Le Métayer, ed., *Europ. Symp. on Progr.*, vol. 2305 of *LNCS*, 2002.
[18] T. Hirschowitz, X. Leroy, J. B. Wells. Compilation of extended recursion in call-by-value functional languages. In *Princ. and Practice of Decl. Prog.* ACM Press, 2003.
[19] T. Hirschowitz, X. Leroy, J. B. Wells. A reduction semantics for call-by-value mixin modules. Research report RR-4682, INRIA, 2003.
[20] X. Leroy. Manifest types, modules, and separate compilation. In *21st symp. Principles of Progr. Lang.* ACM Press, 1994.
[21] E. Machkasova, F. A. Turbak. A calculus for link-time compilation. In *Europ. Symp. on Progr.*, vol. 1782 of *LNCS*. Springer-Verlag, 2000.
[22] D. A. Moon. Object-oriented programming with Flavors. In *OOPSLA*, 1986.
[23] M. Odersky, V. Cremet, C. Röckl, M. Zenger. A nominal theory of objects with dependent types. FOOL'03.
[24] F. Pottier. A versatile constraint-based type inference system. *Nordic Journal of Computing*, 7(4), 2000.
[25] C. V. Russo. Recursive structures for Standard ML. In *Int. Conf. on Functional Progr.* ACM Press, 2001.
[26] J. B. Wells, R. Vestergaard. Equational reasoning for linking with first-class primitive modules. In *Europ. Symp. on Progr.*, vol. 1782 of *LNCS*. Springer-Verlag, 2000.

ML-Like Inference for Classifiers

Cristiano Calcagno[1], Eugenio Moggi[2*], and Walid Taha[3**]

[1] Imperial College, London, UK ccris@doc.ic.ac.uk
[2] DISI, Univ. of Genova, Italy moggi@disi.unige.it
[3] Rice University, TX, USA taha@cs.rice.edu

Abstract. Environment classifiers were proposed as a new approach to typing multi-stage languages. Safety was established in the simply-typed and let-polymorphic settings. While the motivation for classifiers was the feasibility of inference, this was in fact not established. This paper starts with the observation that inference for the full classifier-based system fails. We then identify a subset of the original system for which inference is possible. This subset, which uses *implicit classifiers*, retains significant expressivity (e.g. it can embed the calculi of Davies and Pfenning) and eliminates the need for classifier names in terms. Implicit classifiers were implemented in MetaOCaml, and no changes were needed to make an existing test suite acceptable by the new type checker.

1 Introduction

Introducing explicit staging constructs into programming languages is the goal of research projects including 'C [9], Popcorn [25], MetaML [30,20], MetaOCaml [4, 19], and Template Haskell [23]. Staging is an essential ingredient of macros [10], partial evaluation [15], program generation [16], and run-time code generation [12]. In the untyped setting, the behavior of staging constructs resembles the quasi-quotation mechanisms of LISP and Scheme [2]. But in the statically-typed setting, such quotation mechanisms may prohibit static type-checking of the quoted expression. Some language designs, such as that of 'C, consider this acceptable. In Template Haskell, this is considered a feature; namely, a form of staged type inference [24]. But in the design of MetaML and MetaOCaml, it is seen as a departure from the commitment of ML and OCaml to static prevention of runtime errors.[1]

Multi-stage Basics. The use of staging constructs can be illustrated in a multi-stage language such as MetaOCaml [19] with a classic example[2]:

* Supported by MIUR project NAPOLI, EU project DART IST-2001-33477 and thematic network APPSEM II IST-2001-38957

** Supported by NSF ITR-0113569 and NSF CCR-0205542.

[1] Dynamic typing can be introduced as orthogonal and non-pervasive feature [1].

[2] Dots are used around brackets and escapes to disambiguate the syntax in the implementation, but they are dropped when we consider the underlying calculus.

D.A. Schmidt (Ed.): ESOP 2004, LNCS 2986, pp. 79–93, 2004.

```
let rec power n  x = (* : int -> int code -> int code *)
  if n=0 then .<1>. else .<.~x * .~(power (n-1) x)>.
let power72 : int -> int = .! .<fun x -> .~(power 72 .<x>.)>.
```

Ignoring the type constructor *t* code and the three staging annotations *brackets* .<*e*>., *escapes* .~*e*, and *run* .!, the above code is a standard definition of a function that computes x^n, which is then used to define the specialized function x^{72}. Without staging, however, the last step just produces a closure that invokes the power function every time it gets a value for x. To understand the effect of the staging annotations, it is best to start from the end of the example. Whereas a term fun x -> *e* x is a value, an annotated term .<fun x -> .~(*e* .<x>.)>. is not. Brackets indicate that we are constructing a future stage computation, and an escape indicates that we must perform an immediate computation *while* building the enclosing bracketed computation. The application *e* .<x>. has to be performed first, even though x is still an uninstantiated *symbol*. In the power example, power 72 .<x>. is performed immediately, once and for all, and not repeated every time we have a new value for x. In the body of the definition of the power function, the recursive application of power is escaped to make sure that it is performed immediately. The run construct (.!) on the last line invokes the compiler on the generated code fragment, and incorporates the result of compilation into the runtime system.

Background. Starting with the earliest statically typed languages supporting staging (including those of Gomard and Jones [11] and Nielson and Nielson [22]), most proposals to date fall under two distinct approaches: one treating code as always open, the other treating code as always closed. The two approaches are best exemplified by two type systems corresponding to well-known logics:

- $\lambda^{\bigcirc}$ Motivated by the next modality $\bigcirc$ of linear time temporal logic, this system provides a sound framework for typing constructs that have the same operational semantics as bracket and escape [6]. As illustrated above, brackets and escapes can be used to annotate λ-abstractions so as to force evaluation under lambda. This type system supports code generation but does not provide a construct for code execution.
- $\lambda^{\Box}$ Motivated by the necessity modality $\Box$ of S4 modal logic, this system provides constructs for generating and executing closed code [7]. The exact correspondence between the constructs of $\lambda^{\Box}$ and LISP-style quotation mechanism is less immediate than for $\lambda^{\bigcirc}$.

Combining the two approaches to realize a language that allows evaluation under lambda *and* a run construct is challenging [26]. In particular, evaluation under lambda gives rise to code fragments that contain free variables that are not yet "linked" to any fixed value. Running such open code fragments can produce a runtime error. Several type systems [3,29,21] have been proposed for safely combining the key features of $\lambda^{\bigcirc}$ (the ability to manipulate open code) and $\lambda^{\Box}$ (the ability to execute closed code). But a practical solution to the problem requires meeting a number of demanding criteria simultaneously:

- **Safety:** the extension should retain static safety;
- **Conservativity:** the extension should not affect programs that do not use multi-stage facilities;
- **Inference:** the extension should support type inference;
- **Light annotations:** the extension should minimize the amount of programmer annotations required to make type inference possible.

All the above proposals were primarily concerned with the safety criterion, and were rarely able to address the others. Because previous proposals seemed notationally heavy, implementations of multi-stage languages (such MetaML and MetaOCaml) often chose to sacrifice safety. For example, in MetaOCaml `.! e` raises an exception, when the evaluation of `e` produces open code.

The type system for environment classifiers λ^{α} of [29] appears to be the most promising starting point towards fulfilling all criteria. The key feature of λ^{α} is providing a code type $\langle\tau\rangle^{\alpha}$ decorated with a classifier α that constrains the unresolved variables that may occur free in code. Intuitively, in the type system of λ^{α}, variables are declared at levels annotated by classifiers, and code of type $\langle\tau\rangle^{\alpha}$ may contain only unresolved variables declared at a level annotated with α. Classifiers are also used explicitly in terms. Type safety for λ^{α} was established [29], but type inference was only conjectured.

Contributions and Organization of this Paper. The starting point for this work is the observation that inference for full λ^{α} fails. To address this problem, a subset of the original system is identified for which inference is not only possible but is in fact *easy*. This subset uses *implicit classifiers*, thus eliminates the need for classifier names in terms, and retains significant expressivity (e.g. it embeds the paradigmatic calculi $\lambda^{\bigcirc}$ and $\lambda^{\Box}$). Implicit classifiers have been implemented in MetaOCaml, and no changes were needed to make an existing test suite acceptable by the type checker. The paper proceeds as follows:

- Section 2 extends a core subset of ML with environment classifiers. The new calculus, called λ^{i}_{let}, corresponds to a proper subset of λ^{α} but eliminates classifier names in terms. This is an improvement on λ^{α} in making annotations lighter, and the proof of type safety for λ^{α} adapts easily to λ^{i}_{let}.
- Section 3 gives two inference algorithms:
  1. a principal typing algorithm for λ^{i}, the simply-typed subset of λ^{i}_{let} (i.e. no type schema and let-binding), which extends Hindley's principal typing algorithm for the λ-calculus.
  2. a principal type algorithm for λ^{i}_{let}, which extends Damas and Milner's algorithm W.

  Therefore classifiers are a natural extension to well-established type systems.
- Section 4 relates λ^{i} to λ^{α} and exhibits some terms typable in λ^{α} that fail to have a principal type (thus, λ^{α} fails to meet the inference criterion). It also shows that λ^{i} retains significant expressivity, namely there are *typability-preserving* embeddings of $\lambda^{\bigcirc}$ and a variant of $\lambda^{\Box}$ into λ^{i} (similar to the embeddings into λ^{α} given in [29]). However, if one restricts λ^{i}_{let} further, by considering a runClosed construct similar to Haskell's runST [17], then the embedding of $\lambda^{\Box}$ is lost (but term annotations disappear completely).

Variables	$x \in \mathsf{X}$
Classifiers	$\alpha \in \mathsf{A}$
Named Levels	$A \in \mathsf{A}^*$
Terms	$e, v \in \mathsf{E} ::= x \mid \lambda x.e \mid e\ e \mid \langle e \rangle \mid \tilde{\ } e \mid$ $\mathsf{run}\ e \mid \%e \mid \mathsf{open}\ e \mid \mathsf{close}\ e \mid \mathsf{let}\ x = e_1\ \mathsf{in}\ e_2$
Type Variables	$\beta \in \mathsf{B}$
Types	$\tau \in \mathsf{T} ::= \beta \mid \tau_1 \to \tau_2 \mid \langle \tau \rangle^\alpha \mid \langle \tau \rangle$
Type Schema	$\sigma \in \mathsf{S} ::= \tau \mid \forall \alpha.\sigma \mid \forall \beta.\sigma$ or equivalently $\forall \overline{\kappa}.\tau$ with $\overline{\kappa}$ sequence of distinct α and β
Assignments	$\Gamma \in \mathsf{X} \overset{fin}{\to} (\mathsf{T} \times \mathsf{A}^*)$ of types and named levels
Assignments	$\Delta \in \mathsf{X} \overset{fin}{\to} (\mathsf{S} \times \mathsf{A}^*)$ of type schema and named levels

Fig. 1. Syntax of λ^i_{let}

Notation. Throughout the paper we use the following notation and conventions:

- We write m to range over the set N of natural numbers. Furthermore, $m \in \mathsf{N}$ is identified with the set of its predecessors $\{i \in \mathsf{N} | i < m\}$.
- We write $\overline{a}$ to range over the set A^* of finite sequences $(a_i | i \in m)$ with $a_i \in \mathsf{A}$, and $|\overline{a}|$ denotes its length m. We write $\emptyset$ for the empty sequence and $\overline{a}_1, \overline{a}_2$ for the concatenation of $\overline{a}_1$ and $\overline{a}_2$.
- We write $f : A \overset{fin}{\to} B$ to say that f is a partial function from A to B with a finite domain, written $\mathrm{dom}(f)$. We write $A \to B$ to denote the set of total functions from A to B. We use the following operations on partial functions:
  - $\{a_i : b_i | i \in m\}$ is the partial function mapping a_i to b_i (where the a_i are distinct, i.e. $a_i = a_j$ implies $i = j$); in particular, $\emptyset$ is the everywhere undefined partial function;
  - $f \backslash a$ denotes the partial function g s.t. $g(a') = b$ iff $f(a') = b$ when $a' \neq a$, and undefined otherwise;
  - $f\{a : b\}$ denotes the (possibly) partial function g s.t. $g(a) = b$ and $g(a') = f(a')$ when $a' \neq a$;
  - f, g denotes the union of two partial functions with disjoint domains.
  - $f = g \bmod X$ means that $\forall x \in X. f(x) = g(x)$.
- We write $X \# X'$ to mean that X and X' are disjoint sets, and $X \uplus X'$ for their disjoint union.

2 λ^i_{let}: A Calculus with Implicit Classifiers

This section defines λ^i_{let}, an extension of the functional subset of ML with environment classifiers. In comparison to λ^α [29], classifier names do not appear in terms. In particular, the constructs of λ^α for explicit abstraction $(\alpha)e$ and instantiation $e[\alpha]$ of classifiers are replaced by the constructs $\mathsf{close}\ e$ and $\mathsf{open}\ e$, but with more restrictive typing rules. As we show in this paper, this makes it possible to support ML-style inference of types and classifiers in a straightforward manner.

Figure 1 gives the syntax of λ^i_{let}. Intuitively, *classifiers* allow us to name parts of the environment in which a term is typed. Classifiers are described as *implicit* in λ^i_{let} because they do not appear in terms. *Named levels* are sequences of environment classifiers. They are used to keep track of the environments used as we build nested code. Named levels are thus an enrichment of the traditional notion of levels in multi-stage languages [6,30,28], the latter being a natural number which keeps track only of the depth of nesting of brackets. Terms include:

- the standard λ-terms, i.e. variables, λ-abstraction and application;
- the staging constructs of MetaML [30], i.e. Brackets $\langle e \rangle$, escape $\tilde{}e$, and run $\mathsf{run}\ e$, and a construct $\%e$ for cross-stage persistence (CSP) [3,29];
- the constructs $\mathsf{close}\ e$ and $\mathsf{open}\ e$ are the implicit versions of the λ^α constructs for classifiers abstraction $(\alpha)e$ and instantiation $e[\alpha]$ respectively;
- the standard let-binding for supporting Hindley-Milner polymorphism.

Types include type variables, functional types, and code types $\langle \tau \rangle^\alpha$ annotated with a classifier (exactly as in λ^α of [29], thus refining open code types). The last type $\langle \tau \rangle$ is for executable code (it is used for typing $\mathsf{run}\ e$) and basically corresponds to the type $(\alpha)\langle \tau \rangle^\alpha$ of λ^α (as explained in more detail in Section 4.1).

As in other Hindley-Milner type systems, type schema restrict quantification at the outermost level of types. Since the types of λ^i_{let} may contain not only type variables but also classifiers, type schema allow quantification of both.

Notation. The remainder of the paper makes use of the following definitions:

- We write $\{x_i : \tau_i^{A_i} | i \in m\}$ and $\{x_i : \sigma_i^{A_i} | i \in m\}$ to describe type and schema assignments, and in this context τ^A denotes the pair (τ, A).
- FV(_) denotes the set of variables free in _. In λ^i_{let}, there are three kinds of variables: term variables x, classifiers α, and type variables β. The definition of FV(_) for terms, types, and type schema is standard, and it extends in the obvious way to A, Γ, and Δ, e.g. $\mathrm{FV}(\Delta) = \cup\{\mathrm{FV}(\sigma) \cup \mathrm{FV}(A) \mid \Delta(x) = \sigma^A\}$.
- We write $\equiv$ for equivalence up to α-conversion on terms, types, and type schema. $\_[x : e]$ denotes substitution of x with e in _ modulo $\equiv$, i.e. the bound variables in _ are automatically renamed to avoid clashes with FV(e). Similarly we write $\_[\alpha : \alpha']$ and $\_[\beta : \tau]$ for classifiers and type variables.
- We write $\rho \in \mathsf{Sub}$ for the set of *substitutions*, i.e. functions (with domain $\mathsf{A} \cup \mathsf{B}$) mapping classifiers α to classifiers and type variables β to types τ, and having a finite *support* defined as $\{\alpha | \rho(\alpha) \neq \alpha\} \cup \{\beta | \rho(\beta) \neq \beta\}$. Then $\_[\rho]$ denotes *parallel substitution*, where each free occurrence in _ of a classifier α and type variable β is replaced by its ρ-image. With some abuse of notation, we write $e[\rho]$ also when ρ is a partial function with finite domain, by extending it as the identity outside dom(ρ).
- $\sigma \succ \tau$ means that type τ is an *instance* of σ, i.e. $\forall\overline{\kappa}.\tau \succ \tau' \stackrel{\text{def}}{\Longleftrightarrow} \tau[\rho] = \tau'$ for some $\rho \in \mathsf{Sub}$ with support $\overline{\kappa}$ (the order in $\overline{\kappa}$ is irrelevant).
  $\succ$ extends to a relation on type schemas and type schema assignments:

$$\text{var}\ \frac{\sigma \succ \tau}{\Delta \overset{A}{\vdash} x : \tau}\ \Delta(x) = \sigma^A \qquad \text{lam}\ \frac{\Delta\{x : \tau_1^A\} \overset{A}{\vdash} e : \tau_2}{\Delta \overset{A}{\vdash} \lambda x.e : \tau_1 \to \tau_2} \qquad \text{app}\ \frac{\Delta \overset{A}{\vdash} e_1 : \tau_1 \to \tau_2 \quad \Delta \overset{A}{\vdash} e_2 : \tau_1}{\Delta \overset{A}{\vdash} e_1 e_2 : \tau_2}$$

$$\text{brck}\ \frac{\Delta \overset{A,\alpha}{\vdash} e : \tau}{\Delta \overset{A}{\vdash} \langle e \rangle : \langle \tau \rangle^\alpha} \qquad \text{esc}\ \frac{\Delta \overset{A}{\vdash} e : \langle \tau \rangle^\alpha}{\Delta \overset{A,\alpha}{\vdash} {}^\sim e : \tau} \qquad \text{run}\ \frac{\Delta \overset{A}{\vdash} e : \langle \tau \rangle}{\Delta \overset{A}{\vdash} \mathsf{run}\ e : \tau} \qquad \text{csp}\ \frac{\Delta \overset{A}{\vdash} e : \tau}{\Delta \overset{A,\alpha}{\vdash} \% e : \tau}$$

$$\text{open}\ \frac{\Delta \overset{A}{\vdash} e : \langle \tau \rangle}{\Delta \overset{A}{\vdash} \mathsf{open}\ e : \langle \tau \rangle^\alpha} \qquad \text{close}\ \frac{\Delta \overset{A}{\vdash} e : \langle \tau \rangle^\alpha}{\Delta \overset{A}{\vdash} \mathsf{close}\ e : \langle \tau \rangle}\ \alpha \notin \mathrm{FV}(\Delta, A, \tau)$$

$$\text{let}\ \frac{\Delta \overset{A}{\vdash} e_1 : \tau_1 \quad \Delta\{x : (\forall \overline{\kappa}.\tau_1)^A\} \overset{A}{\vdash} e_2 : \tau_2}{\Delta \overset{A}{\vdash} \mathsf{let}\ x = e_1\ \mathsf{in}\ e_2 : \tau_2}\ \mathrm{FV}(\Delta, A) \# \overline{\kappa}$$

Fig. 2. Type System for λ^i_{let}

- $\forall \overline{\kappa}.\tau \succ \forall \overline{\kappa}'.\tau' \overset{\text{def}}{\iff} \forall \overline{\kappa}.\tau \succ \tau'$, where we assume $\overline{\kappa}' \# \mathrm{FV}(\forall \overline{\kappa}.\tau)$ by α-conversion
- $\Delta_1 \succ \Delta_2 \overset{\text{def}}{\iff} \mathrm{dom}(\Delta_1) = \mathrm{dom}(\Delta_2)$ and, for all x, whenever $\Delta_1(x) = \sigma_1^{A_1}$ and $\Delta_2(x) = \sigma_2^{A_2}$ then it is also the case that $\sigma_1 \succ \sigma_2$ and $A_1 = A_2$.

2.1 Type System

Figure 2 gives the type system for λ^i_{let}. The first three rules are mostly standard. As in ML, a polymorphic variable x whose type schema is σ can be assigned any type which is an instance of σ. In these constructs the named level A is propagated without alteration to the sub-terms. In the variable rule, the named level associated with the variable being typed-checked is required to be the *same* as the current level. In the lambda abstraction rule, the named level of the abstraction is recorded in the environment.

The rule for brackets is almost the same as in previous type systems. First, for every code type a classifier must be assigned. Second, while typing the body of the code fragment inside brackets, the named level of the typing judgment is extended by the name of the "current" classifier. This information is used in both the variable and the escape rules to make sure that only variables and code fragments with the same classification are ever incorporated into this code fragment. The escape rule at named level A, α only allows the incorporation of code fragments of type $\langle \tau \rangle^\alpha$. The rule for CSP itself is standard: It allows us to incorporate a term e at a "higher" level. The rule for run allows to execute a code fragment that has type $\langle \tau \rangle$.

The *close* and *open* rules are introduction and elimination for the runnable code type $\langle \tau \rangle$ respectively. One rule says that close e is runnable code when e can be classified with *any* α, conversely the other rule says that code open e can be classified by any α provided e is runnable code. The rule for let is standard and allows the introduction of variables of polymorphic type.

The following proposition summarizes the key properties of the type system relevant for type safety as well as type inference.

Proposition 1 (Basic Properties). *The following rules are admissible:*

– $\alpha\tau$-subst $\dfrac{\Delta \overset{A}{\vdash} e : \tau}{(\Delta \overset{A}{\vdash} e : \tau)[\rho]} \rho \in \mathsf{Sub}$ $\qquad$ Δ-sub $\dfrac{\Delta_2 \overset{A}{\vdash} e : \tau}{\Delta_1 \overset{A}{\vdash} e : \tau} \Delta_1 \succ \Delta_2$

– strength $\dfrac{\Delta \overset{A}{\vdash} e : \tau}{\Delta \backslash x \overset{A}{\vdash} e : \tau} x \notin \mathrm{FV}(e)$ $\qquad$ weaken $\dfrac{\Delta \overset{A}{\vdash} e : \tau}{\Delta, x : \sigma_1^{A_1} \overset{A}{\vdash} e : \tau} x \notin dom(\Delta)$

– e-subst $\dfrac{\Delta \overset{A_1}{\vdash} e_1 : \tau_1 \qquad \Delta, x : (\forall \overline{\kappa}.\tau_1)^{A_1} \overset{A_2}{\vdash} e_2 : \tau_2}{\Delta \overset{A_2}{\vdash} e_2[x : e_1] : \tau_2} \overline{\kappa}\#\mathrm{FV}(\Delta, A_1)$

3 Inference Algorithms

This section describes two inference algorithms. The first algorithm extends Hindley's principal typing algorithm [13] for the simply typed λ-calculus with type variables to λ^i (the simply-typed subset of λ^i_{let}, i.e. without type schema and let-binding). Existence of principal typings is very desirable but hard to get (see [14,31]). Thus it is reassuring that it is retained after the addition of classifiers. The second algorithm extends Damas and Milner's algorithm W [5] to λ^i_{let} and proves that it is sound and complete for deriving principal types. Damas and Milner's algorithm is at the core of type inference for languages such as ML, OCaml, and Haskell. That this extension is possible (and easy) is of paramount importance to the practical use of the proposed type system.

Both algorithms make essential use of a function $mgu(T)$ computing a most general unifier $\rho \in \mathsf{Sub}$ for a finite set T of equations between types or between classifiers. For convenience, we also introduce the following derived notation for sets of equations (used in side-conditions to the rules describing the algorithms):

- (A_1, A_2) denotes $\{(\alpha_{1,j}, \alpha_{2,j}) \mid j \in n\}$ when $n = |A_1| = |A_2|$ and $\alpha_{i,j}$ is the j-th element of A_i, and is undefined when $|A_1| \neq |A_2|$
- (Γ_1, Γ_2) denotes $\cup\{(\tau_{1,x}, \tau_{2,x}), (A_{1,x}, A_{2,x}) | x \in \mathrm{dom}(\Gamma_1) \cap \mathrm{dom}(\Gamma_2)\}$ where $\Gamma_i(x) = \tau_{i,x}^{A_{i,x}}$.

3.1 Principal Typing

We extend Hindley's principal typing algorithm for the simply typed λ-calculus with type variables to λ^i. Wells [31] gives a general definition of principal typing and related notions, but we need to adapt his definition of Hindley's principal typing to our setting, mainly to take into account levels.

Definition 1 (Typing). *A triple (Γ, τ, A) is a typing of (e, n) $\overset{def}{\iff}$ $\Gamma \overset{A}{\vdash} e : \tau$ is derivable and $n = |A|$. A Hindley principal typing of (e, n) is a typing (Γ, τ, A) of (e, n) s.t. for every other typing (Γ', τ', A') of (e, n)*

– *$\Gamma[\rho] \subseteq \Gamma'$ and $\tau' = \tau[\rho]$ and $A' = A[\rho]$ for some $\rho \in \mathsf{Sub}$.*

Remark 1. Usually one assigns typings to terms. We have chosen to assign typings to a pair (e, n), because the operational semantics of a term is level-dependent. However, one can easily assign typings to terms (and retain the existence of principal typings). First, we introduce an infinite set of variables $\phi \in \Phi$ ranging over annotated levels. Then, we modify the BNF for annotated levels to become $A ::= \phi \mid A, \alpha$. Unification will also have to deal with equations for annotated levels, e.g. $\phi_1 = \phi_2, \alpha$. A posteriori, one can show that a principal typing will contain exactly one variable ϕ.

Figure 3 defines the algorithm by giving a set of rules (directed by the structure of e) for deriving judgments of the form $\mathcal{K}, (e, n) \Rightarrow \mathcal{K}', (\Gamma, \tau, A)$. $\mathcal{K} \subseteq_{fin} \mathsf{A} \uplus \mathsf{B}$ is an auxiliary parameter (instrumental to the algorithm), which is threaded in recursive calls for recording the classifiers and type variables used so far. The algorithm computes a typing (and updates $\mathcal{K}$) or fails, and it enjoys the following properties (which imply that every (e, n) with a typing has a principal typing).

Theorem 1 (Soundness). *If $\mathcal{K}, (e, n) \Rightarrow \mathcal{K}', (\Gamma', \tau', A')$, then $\Gamma' \overset{A'}{\vdash} e : \tau'$ and $n = |A'|$, moreover $dom(\Gamma') = \mathrm{FV}(e)$, $\mathcal{K} \subseteq \mathcal{K}'$ and $\mathrm{FV}(\Gamma', \tau', A') \subseteq \mathcal{K}' \setminus \mathcal{K}$.*

Theorem 2 (Completeness). *If $\Gamma' \overset{A'}{\vdash} e : \tau'$, then $\mathcal{K}, (e, n) \Rightarrow \mathcal{K}', (\Gamma, \tau, A)$ is derivable (for any choice of $\mathcal{K}$) and exists $\rho' \in \mathsf{Sub}$ s.t. $\Gamma[\rho'] \subseteq \Gamma'$, $\tau' = \tau[\rho']$ and $A' = A[\rho']$.*

Moreover, from general properties of the most general unifier and the similarity of our principal typing algorithm with that for the λ-calculus, one can also show

Theorem 3 (Conservative Extension). *If $e ::= x \mid \lambda x.e \mid e\ e$ is a λ-term, then (Γ, τ) is a principal typing of e in $\lambda \iff (\Gamma, \tau, \emptyset)$ is a principal typing of $(e, 0)$ in λ^i, where we identify $x : \tau$ with $x : \tau^{\emptyset}$.*

3.2 Principal Type Inference

In this section, we extend Damas and Milner's [5] principal type algorithm to λ^i_{let} and prove that it is sound and complete. Also in this case we have to adapt to our setting the definition of Damas-Milner principal type in [31].

Definition 2 (Principal Type). *A Damas-Milner principal type of (Δ, A, e) is a type τ s.t. $\Delta \overset{A}{\vdash} e : \tau$ and for every $\Delta \overset{A}{\vdash} e : \tau'$*

- *$\tau' = \tau[\rho]$ for some $\rho \in \mathsf{Sub}$ with support $\mathrm{FV}(\tau) - \mathrm{FV}(\Delta, A)$*

We define a principal type algorithm $W(\Delta, A, e, \mathcal{K})$, where $\mathcal{K} \subseteq_{fin} \mathsf{A} \uplus \mathsf{B}$ is an auxiliary parameter that is threaded in recursive calls for recording the classifiers and type variables used so far. The algorithm either computes a type and a substitution for Δ and A (and updates $\mathcal{K}$) or fails. Figure 4 derives judgments of the form $\mathcal{K}, (\Delta, e, A) \Rightarrow \mathcal{K}', (\rho, \tau)$. When the judgment is derivable, it means that $W(\Delta, A, e, \mathcal{K}) = (\rho, \tau, \mathcal{K}')$. The rules use the following notation:

- $\text{close}(\tau, \Delta, A) \stackrel{\text{def}}{\equiv} \forall\overline{\kappa}.\tau$, where $\overline{\kappa} = \text{FV}(\tau) - \text{FV}(\Delta, A)$
- $\rho'\rho$ denotes composition of substitutions, i.e. $e[\rho'\rho] = (e[\rho])[\rho']$

The algorithm enjoys the following soundness and completeness properties.

Theorem 4 (Soundness). *If* $W(\Delta, A, e, \mathcal{K}) = (\rho, \tau, \mathcal{K}')$ *and* $\text{FV}(\Delta, A) \subseteq \mathcal{K}$ *then* $\Delta[\rho] \stackrel{A[\rho]}{\vdash} e : \tau$, *moreover* $\mathcal{K} \subseteq \mathcal{K}'$ *and* $\text{FV}(\tau, \Delta[\rho], A[\rho]) \subseteq \mathcal{K}'$.

Theorem 5 (Completeness). *If* $\Delta[\rho'] \stackrel{A[\rho']}{\vdash} e : \tau'$ *and* $\text{FV}(\Delta, A) \subseteq \mathcal{K}$ *and* $\mathcal{K} \subseteq_{fin} \mathsf{A} \cup \mathsf{B}$ *then* $W(\Delta, A, e, \mathcal{K}) = (\rho, \tau, \mathcal{K}')$ *is defined and exists* $\rho'' \in \mathsf{Sub}$ *s.t.* $\tau' = \tau[\rho'']$ *and* $\Delta[\rho'] \equiv \Delta[\rho''\rho]$ *and* $A[\rho'] = A[\rho''\rho]$.

Remark 2. In practice, one is interested in typing a complete program e, i.e. in computing $W(\emptyset, \emptyset, e, \emptyset)$. If the algorithm returns $(\rho, \tau, \mathcal{K}')$, then τ is the principal type and ρ and $\mathcal{K}'$ can be ignored. Even when the program uses a library, one can ignore the substitution ρ, since $\text{FV}(\Delta) = \emptyset$.

$$\frac{\beta \text{ and } A = (\alpha_i | i \in n) \text{ distinct and } \notin \mathcal{K}}{\mathcal{K}, (x, n) \Rightarrow \mathcal{K} \uplus \{\beta, A\}, (x : \beta^A, \beta, A)}$$

$$\frac{\begin{array}{c}\mathcal{K}, (e_1, n) \Rightarrow \mathcal{K}', (\Gamma_1, \tau_1, A_1) \\ \mathcal{K}', (e_2, n) \Rightarrow \mathcal{K}'', (\Gamma_2, \tau_2, A_2) \\ \rho = mgu((\tau_1, \tau_2 \to \beta), (\Gamma_1, \Gamma_2), (A_1, A_2))\end{array}}{\mathcal{K}, (e_1\ e_2, n) \Rightarrow \mathcal{K}'' \uplus \{\beta\}, (\Gamma_1 \cup \Gamma_2, \beta, A_1)[\rho]}$$

$$\frac{\begin{array}{c}\mathcal{K}, (e, n) \Rightarrow \mathcal{K}', (\Gamma, \tau, A) \\ x \notin \text{FV}(e) \text{ and } \beta \notin \mathcal{K}'\end{array}}{\mathcal{K}, (\lambda x.e, n) \Rightarrow \mathcal{K}' \uplus \{\beta\}, (\Gamma, \beta \to \tau, A)}$$

$$\frac{\begin{array}{c}\mathcal{K}, (e, n) \Rightarrow \mathcal{K}', (\Gamma, \tau_2, A_2) \\ x \in \text{FV}(e)\ ,\ \Gamma(x) = \tau_1^{A_1} \text{ and } \rho = mgu(A_1, A_2)\end{array}}{\mathcal{K}, (\lambda x.e, n) \Rightarrow \mathcal{K}', (\Gamma \setminus x, \tau_1 \to \tau_2, A_2)[\rho]}$$

$$\frac{\mathcal{K}, (e, n+) \Rightarrow \mathcal{K}', (\Gamma, \tau, (A, \alpha))}{\mathcal{K}, (\langle e \rangle, n) \Rightarrow \mathcal{K}', (\Gamma, \langle \tau \rangle^\alpha, A)}$$

$$\frac{\begin{array}{c}\mathcal{K}, (e, n) \Rightarrow \mathcal{K}', (\Gamma, \tau, A) \\ \rho = mgu(\tau, \langle \beta \rangle^\alpha) \text{ and } \beta, \alpha \notin \mathcal{K}'\end{array}}{\mathcal{K}, ({\tilde{}}e, n+) \Rightarrow \mathcal{K}' \uplus \{\beta, \alpha\}, (\Gamma, \beta, (A, \alpha))[\rho]}$$

$$\frac{\begin{array}{c}\mathcal{K}, (e, n) \Rightarrow \mathcal{K}', (\Gamma, \tau, A) \\ \alpha \notin \mathcal{K}'\end{array}}{\mathcal{K}, (\%e, n+) \Rightarrow \mathcal{K}' \uplus \{\alpha\}, (\Gamma, \tau, (A, \alpha))}$$

$$\frac{\begin{array}{c}\mathcal{K}, (e, n) \Rightarrow \mathcal{K}', (\Gamma, \tau, A) \\ \rho = mgu(\tau, \langle \beta \rangle) \text{ and } \beta \notin \mathcal{K}'\end{array}}{\mathcal{K}, (\mathsf{run}\ e, n) \Rightarrow \mathcal{K}' \uplus \{\beta\}, (\Gamma, \beta, A)[\rho]}$$

$$\frac{\begin{array}{c}\mathcal{K}, (e, n) \Rightarrow \mathcal{K}', (\Gamma, \tau, A) \\ \rho = mgu(\tau, \langle \beta \rangle^\alpha) \text{ and } \beta, \alpha \notin \mathcal{K}'\end{array}}{\mathcal{K}, (\mathsf{open}\ e, n) \Rightarrow \mathcal{K}' \uplus \{\beta, \alpha\}, (\Gamma, \langle \beta \rangle^\alpha, A)[\rho]}$$

$$\frac{\begin{array}{l}\mathcal{K}, (e, n) \Rightarrow \mathcal{K}', (\Gamma, \tau, A) \\ \rho = mgu(\tau, \langle \beta \rangle^\alpha)\ ,\ \beta, \alpha \notin \mathcal{K}' \text{ and } \alpha[\rho] \notin \text{FV}((\Gamma, \beta, A)[\rho])\end{array}}{\mathcal{K}, (\mathsf{close}\ e, n) \Rightarrow \mathcal{K}'' \uplus \{\beta, \alpha\}, (\Gamma, \langle \beta \rangle, A)[\rho]}$$

Fig. 3. Principal Typing Algorithm

4 Relation to Other Calculi

This section studies the expressivity of the type system for λ^i, the simply-typed subset of λ^i_{let} (i.e. no let-binding and no quantification in type schema). The typing judgment for λ^i takes the form $\Gamma \stackrel{A}{\vdash} e : \tau$, since type schema collapse into types, and the typing rules are restricted accordingly. In summary, we have the following results:

- λ^i is a proper subset of λ^α, but the additional expressivity of λ^α comes at a price: the type system has *no principal types.*
- λ^i retains significant expressivity, namely, the embeddings given in [29] for two paradigmatic calculi $\lambda^{\bigcirc}$ and λ^{S4} (a variant of $\lambda^{\Box}$) factor through λ^i.
- λ^i can be simplified further, by replacing run e with a construct runClosed e similar to Haskell's runST, and then removing $\langle\tau\rangle$, close e and open e, but doing so implies that the embedding of λ^{S4} no longer holds.

$$\frac{\Delta(x) \equiv (\forall\overline{\kappa}.\tau)^{A_1} \quad \rho = mgu(A, A_1) \quad \overline{\kappa}\#\mathcal{K}}{\mathcal{K}, (\Delta, x, A) \Rightarrow \mathcal{K} \uplus \{\overline{\kappa}\}, (\rho, \tau[\rho])} \qquad \frac{\mathcal{K} \uplus \{\beta\}, (\Delta\{x : \beta^A\}, e, A) \Rightarrow \mathcal{K}', (\rho, \tau) \quad \beta \notin \mathcal{K}}{\mathcal{K}, (\Delta, \lambda x.e, A) \Rightarrow \mathcal{K}', (\rho, \beta[\rho] \to \tau)}$$

$$\frac{\mathcal{K}, (\Delta, e_1, A) \Rightarrow \mathcal{K}', (\rho_1, \tau_1) \quad \mathcal{K}', (\Delta[\rho_1], e_2, A[\rho_1]) \Rightarrow \mathcal{K}'', (\rho_2, \tau_2) \quad \rho = mgu(\tau_1[\rho_2], \tau_2 \to \beta) \quad \beta \notin \mathcal{K}''}{\mathcal{K}, (\Delta, e_1 e_2, A) \Rightarrow \mathcal{K}'' \uplus \{\beta\}, (\rho\rho_2\rho_1, \beta[\rho])}$$

$$\frac{\mathcal{K} \uplus \{\alpha\}, (\Delta, e, (A, \alpha)) \Rightarrow \mathcal{K}', (\rho, \tau) \quad \alpha \notin \mathcal{K}}{\mathcal{K}, (\Delta, \langle e\rangle, A) \Rightarrow \mathcal{K}', (\rho, \langle\tau\rangle^{\alpha[\rho]})} \qquad \frac{\mathcal{K}, (\Delta, e, A) \Rightarrow \mathcal{K}', (\rho, \tau) \quad \rho' = mgu(\tau, \langle\beta\rangle^\alpha) \quad \beta \notin \mathcal{K}'}{\mathcal{K}, (\Delta, \tilde{\ } e, (A, \alpha)) \Rightarrow \mathcal{K}' \uplus \{\beta\}, (\rho'\rho, \beta[\rho'])}$$

$$\frac{\mathcal{K}, (\Delta, e, A) \Rightarrow \mathcal{K}', (\rho, \tau)}{\mathcal{K}, (\Delta, \%e, (A, \alpha)) \Rightarrow \mathcal{K}', (\rho, \tau)} \qquad \frac{\mathcal{K}, (\Delta, e, A) \Rightarrow \mathcal{K}', (\rho, \tau) \quad \rho' = mgu(\tau, \langle\beta\rangle) \quad \beta \notin \mathcal{K}'}{\mathcal{K}, (\Delta, \mathsf{run}\ e, A) \Rightarrow \mathcal{K}' \uplus \{\beta\}, (\rho'\rho, \beta[\rho'])}$$

$$\frac{\mathcal{K}, (\Delta, e, A) \Rightarrow \mathcal{K}', (\rho, \tau) \quad \rho' = mgu(\tau, \langle\beta\rangle) \quad \alpha, \beta \notin \mathcal{K}'}{\mathcal{K}, (\Delta, \mathsf{open}\ e, A) \Rightarrow \mathcal{K}' \uplus \{\alpha, \beta\}, (\rho'\rho, \langle\beta[\rho']\rangle^\alpha)}$$

$$\frac{\mathcal{K}, (\Delta, e, A) \Rightarrow \mathcal{K}', (\rho, \tau) \quad \rho' = mgu(\tau, \langle\beta\rangle^\alpha) \quad \alpha, \beta \notin \mathcal{K}' \quad \alpha[\rho'] \notin \mathrm{FV}(\Delta[\rho'\rho], A[\rho'\rho], \beta[\rho'])}{\mathcal{K}, (\Delta, \mathsf{close}\ e, A) \Rightarrow \mathcal{K}' \uplus \{\alpha, \beta\}, (\rho'\rho, \langle\beta[\rho']\rangle)}$$

$$\frac{\mathcal{K}, (\Delta, e_1, A) \Rightarrow \mathcal{K}', (\rho_1, \tau_1) \quad \mathcal{K}', (\Delta[\rho_1]\{x : \mathsf{close}(\tau_1, \Delta[\rho_1], A[\rho_1])^{A[\rho_1]}\}, e_2, A[\rho_1]) \Rightarrow \mathcal{K}'', (\rho_2, \tau_2)}{\mathcal{K}, (\Delta, \mathsf{let}\ x = e_1\ \mathsf{in}\ e_2, A) \Rightarrow \mathcal{K}'', (\rho_2\rho_1, \tau_2)}$$

Fig. 4. Principal Type Algorithm

4.1 Relation to λ^α

The key feature of λ^α is the inclusion of a special quantifier $(\alpha)\tau$ in the language of types, representing universal quantification over classifiers. Figure 5 recalls the BNF for terms and types, and the most relevant typing rules [29]. In λ^i the main difference is that the quantifier $(\alpha)\tau$ of λ^α is replaced by the runnable code type $\langle\tau\rangle$. In fact, $\langle\tau\rangle$ corresponds to a restricted form of quantification, namely $(\alpha)\langle\tau\rangle^\alpha$ with $\alpha \notin \mathrm{FV}(\tau)$. It is non-trivial to define formally a typability-preserving embedding of λ^i into λ^α, since we need to recover classifier names in terms. Therefore, we justify the correspondence at the level of terms only informally:

- The terms close e and open e of λ^i correspond to $(\alpha)e$ and $e[\alpha]$ of λ^α. Since λ^i has no classifier names in terms, these constructs record that a classi-

Terms $e \in \mathsf{E} ::= x \mid \lambda x.e \mid e\ e \mid \langle e \rangle^{\alpha} \mid \tilde{\ } e \mid \%e \mid \mathsf{run}\ e \mid (\alpha)e \mid e[\alpha]$
Types $\tau \in \mathsf{T} ::= \beta \mid \tau_1 \to \tau_2 \mid \langle \tau \rangle^{\alpha} \mid (\alpha)\tau$

$$\text{brck}\ \frac{\Gamma \overset{A,\alpha}{\vdash} e : \tau}{\Gamma \overset{A}{\vdash} \langle e \rangle^{\alpha} : \langle \tau \rangle^{\alpha}} \quad \text{esc}\ \frac{\Gamma \overset{A}{\vdash} e : \langle \tau \rangle^{\alpha}}{\Gamma \overset{A,\alpha}{\vdash} \tilde{\ } e : \tau} \quad \text{csp}\ \frac{\Gamma \overset{A}{\vdash} e : \tau}{\Gamma \overset{A,\alpha}{\vdash} \%e : \tau} \quad \text{all-run}\ \frac{\Gamma \overset{A}{\vdash} e : (\alpha)\langle \tau \rangle^{\alpha}}{\Gamma \overset{A}{\vdash} \mathsf{run}\ e : (\alpha)\tau}$$

$$\text{all-close}\ \frac{\Gamma \overset{A}{\vdash} e : \tau}{\Gamma \overset{A}{\vdash} (\alpha)e : (\alpha)\tau}\ \alpha \notin \mathrm{FV}(\Gamma, A) \quad \text{all-open}\ \frac{\Gamma \overset{A}{\vdash} e : (\alpha)\tau}{\Gamma \overset{A}{\vdash} e[\alpha'] : \tau[\alpha : \alpha']}$$

Fig. 5. Type System for λ^{α} (adapted from [29])

fier abstraction and instantiation has occurred *without* naming the classifier involved. (Similarly, the term $\langle e \rangle$ in λ^i corresponds to $\langle e \rangle^{\alpha}$ in λ^{α}.)
- The term $\%e$ has exactly the same syntax and meaning in the two calculi.
- The term $\mathsf{run}\ e$ of λ^i corresponds to $(\mathsf{run}\ e)[\alpha']$ of λ^{α}, where α' can be chosen arbitrarily without changing the result type. In fact, the type of run in λ^{α} is $((\alpha)\langle \tau \rangle^{\alpha}) \to (\alpha)\tau$, while in λ^i it is $\langle \tau \rangle \to \tau$, which corresponds to $((\alpha)\langle \tau \rangle^{\alpha}) \to \tau$ with $\alpha \notin \mathrm{FV}(\tau)$.

We conclude the comparison between λ^i and λ^{α} by showing that type inference in λ^{α} is problematic.

Lack of principal types in λ^{α}. Consider the closed term $e \equiv (\lambda x.\mathsf{run}\ x)$. We can assign to e exactly the types of the form $((\alpha)\langle \tau \rangle^{\alpha}) \to (\alpha)\tau$ with an arbitrary type τ, including ones with $\alpha \in \mathrm{FV}(\tau)$. However, e does not have a *principal type*, i.e. one from which one can recover all other types (modulo α-conversion of bound classifiers) by applying a substitution $\rho \in \mathsf{Sub}$ for classifiers and type variables. In fact, the obvious candidate for the principal type, i.e. $((\alpha)\langle \beta \rangle^{\alpha}) \to (\alpha)\beta$, allows us to recover only the types of the form $((\alpha)\langle \tau \rangle^{\alpha}) \to (\alpha)\tau$ with $\alpha \notin \mathrm{FV}(\tau)$, since substitution should be capture avoiding.

Lack of principal types in previous polymorphic extensions of λ^{α}. A more expressive type system for λ^{α} was previously proposed [29], where type variables β are replaced by variables β^n ranging over types parameterized w.r.t. n classifiers. Thus, the BNF for types becomes:

$$\tau \in \mathsf{T} ::= \beta^n[A] \mid \tau_1 \to \tau_2 \mid \langle \tau \rangle^{\alpha} \mid (\alpha)\tau \quad \text{with } |A| = n$$

In this way, there is a better candidate for the principal type of e, namely $((\alpha)\langle \beta^1[\alpha] \rangle^{\alpha}) \to (\alpha)\beta^1[\alpha]$.

In this extension, standard unification techniques are no longer applicable, and some form of higher-order unification is needed. However, even in this system, there are typable terms that do not have a principal type. For instance, the term $e = (x(x_1[\alpha]), f(x_2[\alpha]))$ (for simplicity, we assume that we have pairing and product types) has no principal typing, in fact

Terms	$e \in \mathsf{E} ::= x \mid \lambda x.e \mid e\ e \mid \mathsf{box}\ e \mid \mathsf{unbox}_n\ e$
Types	$\tau \in \mathsf{T} ::= \beta \mid \tau_1 \to \tau_2 \mid \Box\tau$
Assignments	$\Gamma \in \mathsf{X} \xrightarrow{fin} \mathsf{T}$ of types
Stacks	$\Psi \in (\mathsf{X} \xrightarrow{fin} \mathsf{T})^*$ of type assignments

$$\frac{}{\Psi;\Gamma \vdash x : \tau}\ \Gamma(x) = \tau \qquad \frac{\Psi;\Gamma, x : \tau_1 \vdash e : \tau_2}{\Psi;\Gamma \vdash \lambda x.e : \tau_1 \to \tau_2} \qquad \frac{\Psi;\Gamma \vdash e_1 : \tau_1 \to \tau_2 \quad \Psi;\Gamma \vdash e_2 : \tau_1}{\Psi;\Gamma \vdash e_1 e_2 : \tau_2}$$

$$\frac{\Psi;\Gamma;() \vdash e : \tau}{\Psi;\Gamma \vdash \mathsf{box}\ e : \Box\tau} \qquad \frac{\Psi;\Gamma \vdash e : \Box\tau}{\Psi;\Gamma;\Gamma_1;\ldots;\Gamma_n \vdash \mathsf{unbox}_n\ e : \tau}$$

Fig. 6. Type system for λ^{S4} [8, Section 4.3]

- x must be a function, say of type $\tau \to \tau'$
- x_i must be of type $(\alpha_i)\tau_i$, among them the most general is $(\alpha_i)\beta_i^1[\alpha_i]$
- τ and $\tau_i[\alpha_i : \alpha]$ must be the same, but there is no most general unifier for $\beta_1^1[\alpha] = \beta_2^1[\alpha]$.

4.2 Embedding of $\lambda^{\bigcirc}$

The embedding of $\lambda^{\bigcirc}$ [6] into λ^i is direct. We pick one arbitrary classifier α and define the embedding as follows:

$$[\![\beta]\!] \equiv \beta, \quad [\![\bigcirc\tau]\!] \equiv \langle[\![\tau]\!]\rangle^{\alpha}, \quad [\![\tau_1 \to \tau_2]\!] \equiv [\![\tau_1]\!] \to [\![\tau_2]\!]$$
$$[\![n]\!] \equiv \alpha^n, \quad [\![x_i : \tau_i^{n_i}]\!] \equiv x_i : [\![\tau_i]\!]^{[\![n_i]\!]}$$
$$[\![x]\!] \equiv x, \quad [\![\lambda x.e]\!] \equiv \lambda x.[\![e]\!], \quad [\![e_1\ e_2]\!] \equiv [\![e_1]\!]\ [\![e_2]\!]$$
$$[\![\mathsf{next}\ e]\!] \equiv \langle[\![e]\!]\rangle \quad [\![\mathsf{prev}\ e]\!] \equiv \tilde{}\,[\![e]\!]$$

The translation preserves the typing, i.e.

Theorem 6. *If* $\Gamma \overset{n}{\vdash} e : \tau$ *is derivable in* $\lambda^{\bigcirc}$*, then* $[\![\Gamma]\!] \overset{[\![n]\!]}{\vdash} [\![e]\!] : [\![\tau]\!]$ *is derivable in* λ^i.

The translation preserves also the big-step operational semantics.

4.3 Embedding of λ^{S4}

Figure 6 recalls the type system of λ^{S4} [8, Section 4.3]. This calculus is *equivalent* to $\lambda^{\Box}$ [7], but makes explicit use of levels in typing judgments. The operational semantics of λ^{S4} is given indirectly [8, Section 4.3] via the translation into $\lambda^{\Box}$. The embedding of this calculus into λ^i is as follows: the embedding maps types to types:

$$[\![\Box\tau]\!] \equiv \langle[\![\tau]\!]\rangle \quad [\![\tau_1 \to \tau_2]\!] \equiv [\![\tau_1]\!] \to [\![\tau_2]\!] \quad [\![\beta]\!] \equiv \beta$$

The embedding on terms is parameterized by a level m:

$$[\![x]\!]_m \equiv x \quad [\![\lambda x.e]\!]_m \equiv \lambda x.[\![e]\!]_m \quad [\![e_1 e_2]\!]_m \equiv [\![e_1]\!]_m [\![e_2]\!]_m$$
$$[\![\mathsf{box}\ e]\!]_m \equiv \mathsf{close}\ \langle[\![e]\!]_{m+1}\rangle$$
$$[\![\mathsf{unbox}_0\ e]\!]_m \equiv \mathsf{run}\ [\![e]\!]_m \quad [\![\mathsf{unbox}_{n+1}\ e]\!]_{m+n+1} \equiv \%^n(\tilde{}(\mathsf{open}\ [\![e]\!]_m))$$
$$\%^0(e) \equiv e \quad \%^{n+1}(e) \equiv \%^n(\%e)$$

The translation of unbox_m depends on the subscript m. unbox_0 corresponds to running code. When $m > 0$ the term unbox_m corresponds to ˜−, but if $m > 1$ it also digs into the environment stack to get code from previous stages, and thus the need for the sequence of %s. To define the translation of typing judgments, we must fix a sequence of distinct classifiers $\alpha_1, \alpha_2, \ldots$, and we write A_i for the prefix of the first i classifiers, i.e. $A_i = \alpha_1, \ldots, \alpha_i$:

$$[\![\Gamma_0; \ldots; \Gamma_n \vdash e : \tau]\!] \equiv [\![\Gamma_0]\!]^{A_0}, \ldots, [\![\Gamma_n]\!]^{A_n} \overset{A_n}{\vdash} [\![e]\!]_n : [\![\tau]\!]$$

where $[\![x_1 : \tau_1, \ldots, x_n : \tau_n]\!]^A \equiv x_1 : [\![\tau_1]\!]^A, \ldots, x_n : [\![\tau_n]\!]^A$. The translation preserves the typing, i.e.

Theorem 7. *If $\Gamma_0; \ldots; \Gamma_n \vdash e : \tau$ is derivable in λ^{S4}, then $[\![\Gamma_0; \ldots; \Gamma_n \vdash e : \tau]\!]$ is derivable in λ^i.*

4.4 Relation to Haskell's runST

The typing rules for close and run can be combined into one rule analogous to that for the Haskell's runST [17,18], namely,

$$\text{runClosed}\ \frac{\Delta \overset{A}{\vdash} e : \langle\tau\rangle^{\alpha}}{\Delta \overset{A}{\vdash} \mathsf{runClosed}\ e : \tau}\ \alpha \notin \mathrm{FV}(\Delta, A, \tau)$$

With this rule in place, there is no need to retain the type $\langle\tau\rangle$ and the terms close e and open e, thus resulting in a proper fragment of λ^i. There is a loss in expressivity, because the embedding of λ^{S4} does not factor through this fragment. In fact, the term $\lambda x.\mathsf{runClosed}\ x$ is not typable, while $\lambda x.\mathsf{run}\ x$ is typable in λ^i_{let} (but $\lambda x.\mathsf{close}\ x$ is still not typable). This variant was implemented in the MetaOCaml system (giving .! the typing of runClosed), and it was found that it required no change to the existing code base of multi-stage programs.

References

1. M. Abadi, L. Cardelli, B. Pierce, and G. Plotkin. Dynamic typing in a statically typed language. *ACM Transactions on Programming Languages and Systems*, 13(2):237–268, April 1991.
2. Alan Bawden. Quasiquotation in LISP. In O. Danvy, editor, *Proceedings of the Workshop on Partial Evaluation and Semantics-Based Program Manipulation*, pages 88–99, San Antonio, 1999. University of Aarhus, Dept. of Computer Science. Invited talk.
3. Cristiano Calcagno, Eugenio Moggi, and Tim Sheard. Closed types for a safe imperative MetaML. *Journal of Functional Programming*, 2003. To appear.
4. Cristiano Calcagno, Walid Taha, Liwen Huang, and Xavier Leroy. Implementing multi-stage languages using asts, gensym, and reflection. In Krzysztof Czarnecki, Frank Pfenning, and Yannis Smaragdakis, editors, *Generative Programming and Component Engineering (GPCE)*, Lecture Notes in Computer Science. Springer-Verlag, 2003.

5. Luís Damas and Robin Milner. Principal type schemes for functional languages. In *9th ACM Symposium on Principles of Programming Languages*. ACM, August 1982.
6. Rowan Davies. A temporal-logic approach to binding-time analysis. In *the Symposium on Logic in Computer Science (LICS '96)*, pages 184–195, New Brunswick, 1996. IEEE Computer Society Press.
7. Rowan Davies and Frank Pfenning. A modal analysis of staged computation. In *the Symposium on Principles of Programming Languages (POPL '96)*, pages 258–270, St. Petersburg Beach, 1996.
8. Rowan Davies and Frank Pfenning. A modal analysis of staged computation. *Journal of the ACM*, 48(3):555–604, 2001.
9. Dawson R. Engler, Wilson C. Hsieh, and M. Frans Kaashoek. 'C: A language for high-level, efficient, and machine-independent dynaic code generation. In *In proceedings of the ACM Symposium on Principles of Programming Languages (POPL)*, pages 131–144, St. Petersburg Beach, 1996.
10. Steven Ganz, Amr Sabry, and Walid Taha. Macros as multi-stage computations: Type-safe, generative, binding macros in MacroML. In *the International Conference on Functional Programming (ICFP '01)*, Florence, Italy, September 2001. ACM.
11. Carsten K. Gomard and Neil D. Jones. A partial evaluator for untyped lambda calculus. *Journal of Functional Programming*, 1(1):21–69, 1991.
12. Brian Grant, Matthai Philipose, Markus Mock, Craig Chambers, and Susan J. Eggers. An evaluation of staged run-time optimizations in DyC. In *Proceedings of the Conference on Programming Language Design and Implementation*, pages 293–304, 1999.
13. J. Roger Hindley. *Basic Simple Type Theory*, volume 42 of *Cambridge Tracts in Theoretical Computer Science*. Cambridge University Press, Cambridge, 1997.
14. Trevor Jim. What are principal typings and what are they good for? In *Conf. Rec. POPL '96: 23rd ACM Symp. Princ. of Prog. Langs.*, 1996.
15. Neil D. Jones, Carsten K. Gomard, and Peter Sestoft. *Partial Evaluation and Automatic Program Generation*. Prentice-Hall, 1993.
16. Sam Kamin, Miranda Callahan, and Lars Clausen. Lightweight and generative components II: Binary-level components. In *[27]*, pages 28–50, 2000.
17. John Launchbury and Simon L. Peyton Jones. State in haskell. *LISP and Symbolic Computation*, 8(4):293–342, 1995.
18. John Launchbury and Amr Sabry. Monadic state: Axiomatization and type safety. In *Proceedings of the International Conference on Functional Programming*, Amsterdam, 1997.
19. MetaOCaml: A compiled, type-safe multi-stage programming language. Available online from http://www.cs.rice.edu/ taha/MetaOCaml/, 2001.
20. The MetaML Home Page, 2000. Provides source code and documentation online at http://www.cse.ogi.edu/PacSoft/projects/metaml/index.html.
21. A. Nanevski and F. Pfenning. Meta-programming with names and necessity. submitted, 2003.
22. Flemming Nielson and Hanne Riis Nielson. Two-level semantics and code generation. *Theoretical Computer Science*, 56(1):59–133, 1988.
23. Tim Sheard and Simon Peyton-Jones. Template meta-programming for haskell. In *Proc. of the workshop on Haskell*, pages 1–16. ACM, 2002.
24. Mark Shields, Tim Sheard, and Simon L. Peyton Jones. Dynamic typing through staged type inference. In *In proceedings of the ACM Symposium on Principles of Programming Languages (POPL)*, pages 289–302, 1998.

25. Frederick Smith, Dan Grossman, Greg Morrisett, Luke Hornof, and Trevor Jim. Compiling for run-time code generation. *Journal of Functional Programming*, 2003.
26. Walid Taha. *Multi-Stage Programming: Its Theory and Applications*. PhD thesis, Oregon Graduate Institute of Science and Technology, 1999.
27. Walid Taha, editor. *Semantics, Applications, and Implementation of Program Generation*, volume 1924 of *Lecture Notes in Computer Science*, Montréal, 2000. Springer-Verlag.
28. Walid Taha. A sound reduction semantics for untyped CBN multi-stage computation. Or, the theory of MetaML is non-trivial. In *Proceedings of the Workshop on Partial Evaluation and Semantics-Based Program Maniplation (PEPM)*, Boston, 2000. ACM Press.
29. Walid Taha and Michael Florentin Nielsen. Environment classifiers. In *The Symposium on Principles of Programming Languages (POPL '03)*, New Orleans, 2003.
30. Walid Taha and Tim Sheard. Multi-stage programming with explicit annotations. In *Proceedings of the Symposium on Partial Evaluation and Semantic-Based Program Manipulation (PEPM)*, pages 203–217, Amsterdam, 1997. ACM Press.
31. Joe Wells. The essence of principal typings. In *Proc. 29th Int'l Coll. Automata, Languages, and Programming*, volume 2380 of *Lecture Notes in Computer Science*, pages 913–925. Springer-Verlag, 2002.

From Constraints to Finite Automata to Filtering Algorithms

Mats Carlsson[1] and Nicolas Beldiceanu[2*]

[1] SICS, P.O. Box 1263, SE-752 37 KISTA, Sweden
matsc@sics.se

[2] LINA FRE CNRS 2729
École des Mines de Nantes
La Chantrerie
4, rue Alfred Kastler, B.P. 20722
FR-44307 NANTES Cedex 3, France
Nicolas.Beldiceanu@emn.fr

Abstract. We introduce an approach to designing filtering algorithms by derivation from finite automata operating on constraint signatures. We illustrate this approach in two case studies of constraints on vectors of variables. This has enabled us to derive an incremental filtering algorithm that runs in $O(n)$ plus amortized $O(1)$ time per propagation event for the lexicographic ordering constraint over two vectors of size n, and an $O(nmd)$ time filtering algorithm for a chain of $m-1$ such constraints, where d is the cost of certain domain operations. Both algorithms maintain hyperarc consistency. Our approach can be seen as a first step towards a methodology for semi-automatic development of filtering algorithms.

1 Introduction

The design of filtering algorithms for global constraints is one of the most creative endeavors in the construction of a finite domain constraint programming system. It is very much a craft and requires a good command of e.g. matching theory [1], flow theory [2] scheduling theory [3], or combinatorics [4], in order to successfully bring to bear results from these areas on specific constraints. As a first step towards a methodology for semi-automatic development of filtering algorithms, we introduce an approach to designing filtering algorithms by derivation from finite automata operating on constraint signatures, an approach that to our knowledge has not been used before. We illustrate this approach in two case studies of constraints on vectors of variables, for which we have developed one filtering algorithm for $\vec{x} \leq_{\text{lex}} \vec{y}$, the lexicographic ordering constraint over two vectors $\vec{x}$ and $\vec{y}$, and one filtering algorithm for lex_chain, a chain of $\leq_{\text{lex}}$ constraints.

The rest of the article is organized as follows: We first define some necessary notions and notation. We proceed with the two case studies: Sect. 3 treats $\leq_{\text{lex}}$, and Sect. 4 applies the approach to lex_chain, or more specifically to the constraint $\vec{a} \leq_{\text{lex}} \vec{x} \leq_{\text{lex}} \vec{b}$, where $\vec{a}$ and $\vec{b}$ are vectors of integers. This latter constraint is the central building-block of

* This research was carried out while N. Beldiceanu was at SICS.

D.A. Schmidt (Ed.): ESOP 2004, LNCS 2986, pp. 94–108, 2004.

lex_chain. Filtering algorithms for these constraints are derived. After quoting related work, we conclude with a discussion.

For reasons of space, lemmas and propositions are given with proofs omitted. Full proofs and pseudocode algorithms can be found in [5] and [6]. The algorithms have been implemented and are part of the CLP(FD) library of SICStus Prolog [7].

2 Preliminaries

We shall use the following notation: $[i,j]$ stands for the interval $\{v \mid i \leq v \leq j\}$; $[i,j)$ is a shorthand for $[i,j-1]$; (i,j) is a shorthand for $[i+1,j-1]$; the *subvector* of $\vec{x}$ with start index i and last index j is denoted by $\vec{x}_{[i,j]}$.

A *constraint store* (X, D) is a set of variables, and for each variable $x \in X$ a domain $D(x)$, which is a finite set of integers. In the context of a current constraint store: $\underline{x}$ denotes $\min(D(x))$; $\overline{x}$ denotes $\max(D(x))$; next_value(x,a) denotes $\min\{i \in D(x) \mid i > a\}$, if it exists, and $+\infty$ otherwise; and prev_value(x,a) denotes $\max\{i \in D(x) \mid i < a\}$, if it exists, and $-\infty$ otherwise. The former two operations run in constant time whereas the latter two have cost d[1]. If for $\Gamma = (X,D)$ and $\Gamma' = (X,D')$, $\forall x \in X : D'(x) \subseteq D(x)$, we say that $\Gamma' \sqsubseteq \Gamma$, Γ' is *tighter* than Γ.

The constraint store is *pruned* by applying the following operations to a variable x: fix_interval(x,a,b) removes from $D(x)$ any value that is not in $[a,b]$, and prune_interval(x,a,b) removes from $D(x)$ any value that is in $[a,b]$. Each operation has cost d and succeeds iff $D(x)$ remains non-empty afterwards.

For a constraint C, a variable x mentioned by C, and a value v, the assignment $x = v$ *has support* iff $v \in D(x)$ and C has a solution such that $x = v$. A constraint C is *hyperarc consistent* iff, for each such variable x and value $v \in D(x)$, $x = v$ has support. A filtering algorithm maintains hyperarc consistency of C iff it removes any value $v \in D(x)$ such that $x = v$ does not have support. By convention, a filtering algorithm returns one of: *fail*, if it discovers that there are no solutions; *succeed*, if it discovers that C will hold no matter what values are taken by any variables that are still nonground; and *delay* otherwise.

A constraint satisfaction problem (CSP) consists of a set of variables and a set of constraints connecting these variables. The solution to a CSP is an assignment of values to the variables that satisfies all constraints. In solving a CSP, the constraint solver repeatedly calls the filtering algorithms associated with the constraints. The removal by a filtering algorithm of a value from a domain is called a *propagation event*, and usually leads to the resumption of some other filtering algorithms. The constraint kernel ensures that all propagation events are eventually served by the relevant filtering algorithms.

A *string* S over some alphabet A is a finite sequence $\langle S_0, S_1, \ldots \rangle$ of letters chosen from A. A *regular expression* E denotes a *regular language* $L(E)$, i.e. a subset of all the possible strings over A, recursively defined as usual: a single letter a denotes the language with the single string $\langle a \rangle$; EE' denotes $L(E)L(E')$ (concatenation); $E \mid E'$ denotes $L(E) \cup L(E')$ (union); and $E^\star$ denotes $L(E)^\star$ (closure). Parentheses are used for grouping.

[1] E.g. if a domain is represented by a bit array, d is linear in the size of the domain.

Let $\mathcal{A}$ be an alphabet, C a constraint over vectors of length n, and Γ a constraint store. We will associate to C a string $\sigma(C, \Gamma, \mathcal{A})$ over $\mathcal{A}$ of length $n+1$ called the *signature of* C.

3 Case Study: $\leq_{\text{lex}}$

Given two vectors, $\vec{x}$ and $\vec{y}$ of n variables, $\langle x_0, \ldots, x_{n-1}\rangle$ and $\langle y_0, \ldots, y_{n-1}\rangle$, let $\vec{x} \leq_{\text{lex}} \vec{y}$ denote the lexicographic ordering constraint on $\vec{x}$ and $\vec{y}$. The constraint holds iff $n = 0$ or $x_0 < y_0$ or $x_0 = y_0$ and $\langle x_1, \ldots, x_{n-1}\rangle \leq_{\text{lex}} \langle y_1, \ldots, y_{n-1}\rangle$. Similarly, the constraint $\vec{x} <_{\text{lex}} \vec{y}$ holds iff $x_0 < y_0$ or $x_0 = y_0$ and $\langle x_1, \ldots, x_{n-1}\rangle <_{\text{lex}} \langle y_1, \ldots, y_{n-1}\rangle$. We now present an alphabet and a finite automaton for this constraint, and an incremental filtering algorithm.

3.1 Signatures

Let $\mathcal{A}$ be the alphabet $\{\boxed{<}, \boxed{=}, \boxed{>}, \boxed{\leq}, \boxed{\geq}, \boxed{?}, \boxed{\$}\}$. It is worth noting that each symbol except $\boxed{\$}$ corresponds to a subset of the fundamental arithmetic relations. The signature $S = \sigma(C, \Gamma, \mathcal{A})$ of a constraint $C \equiv \vec{x} \leq_{\text{lex}} \vec{y}$ wrt. a constraint store Γ is defined by $S_n = \boxed{\$}$, to mark the end of the string, and for $0 \leq i < n$:

$$S_i = \begin{cases} \boxed{<}, \text{ if } \Gamma \models x_i < y_i \\ \boxed{=}, \text{ if } \Gamma \models x_i = y_i \\ \boxed{>}, \text{ if } \Gamma \models x_i > y_i \\ \boxed{\leq}, \text{ if } \Gamma \models x_i \leq y_i \wedge \Gamma \not\models x_i < y_i \wedge \Gamma \not\models x_i = y_i \\ \boxed{\geq}, \text{ if } \Gamma \models x_i \geq y_i \wedge \Gamma \not\models x_i > y_i \wedge \Gamma \not\models x_i = y_i \\ \boxed{?}, \text{ if } \Gamma \text{ does not entail any relation on } x_i, y_i \end{cases}$$

From a complexity point of view, it is important to note that the tests $\Gamma \models x_i \circ y_i$ where $\circ \in \{<, \leq, =, \geq, >\}$ can be implemented by domain bound inspection, and are all $O(1)$ in any reasonable domain representation; see left part of Fig. 1.

S_i	**Condition**
$\boxed{<}$	$\overline{x_i} < \underline{y_i}$
$\boxed{=}$	$\underline{x_i} = \overline{x_i} = \underline{y_i} = \overline{y_i}$
$\boxed{>}$	$\underline{x_i} > \overline{y_i}$
$\boxed{\leq}$	$\overline{x_i} = \underline{y_i} \wedge \underline{x_i} < \overline{y_i}$
$\boxed{\geq}$	$\overline{y_i} = \underline{x_i} \wedge \underline{y_i} < \overline{x_i}$
$\boxed{?}$	otherwise

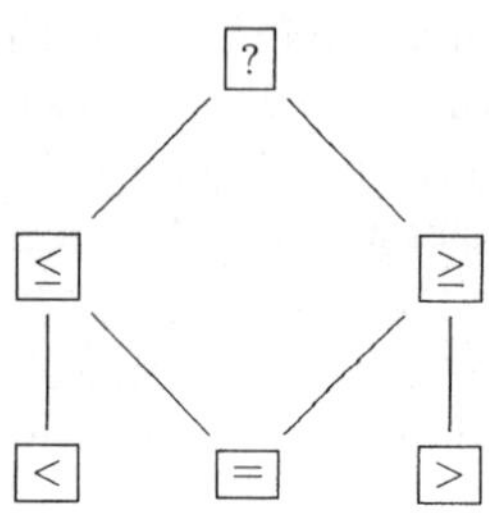

$D(x)$	$D(y)$	**Signature letter**
$\{0,1\}$	$\{0,1\}$	$\boxed{?}$
$\{0\}$	$\{0,1\}$	$\boxed{\leq}$
$\{0\}$	$\{1\}$	$\boxed{<}$

Fig. 1. Computing the signature letter at position i

The letters of $\mathcal{A}$ (except $\boxed{\$}$) form the partially ordered set $(\mathcal{A}, \preceq)$ of Fig. 1. For all $\leq_{\text{lex}}$ constraints C and all i $(0 \leq i < n)$, we have that:

$$\Gamma' \sqsubseteq \Gamma \Rightarrow \sigma(C, \Gamma', \mathcal{A})_i \preceq \sigma(C, \Gamma, \mathcal{A})_i$$

The right part of Fig. 1 also illustrates how a signature letter becomes more ground (smaller wrt. $\preceq$) as the constraint store gets tighter.

3.2 Finite Automaton

Fig. 2 shows a deterministic finite automaton LFA for signature strings, from which we shall derive the filtering algorithm, and the automaton at work on a small example. State 1 is the initial state. There are seven terminal states, F, T1–T3 and D1–D3, each corresponding to a separate case. Case F is the failure case; cases T1–T3 are cases where the algorithm detects that either C must hold or C can be replaced by a $<$ or a $\leq$ constraint; cases D1–D3 are cases where ground instances of C can be either true or false, and so the algorithm must suspend.

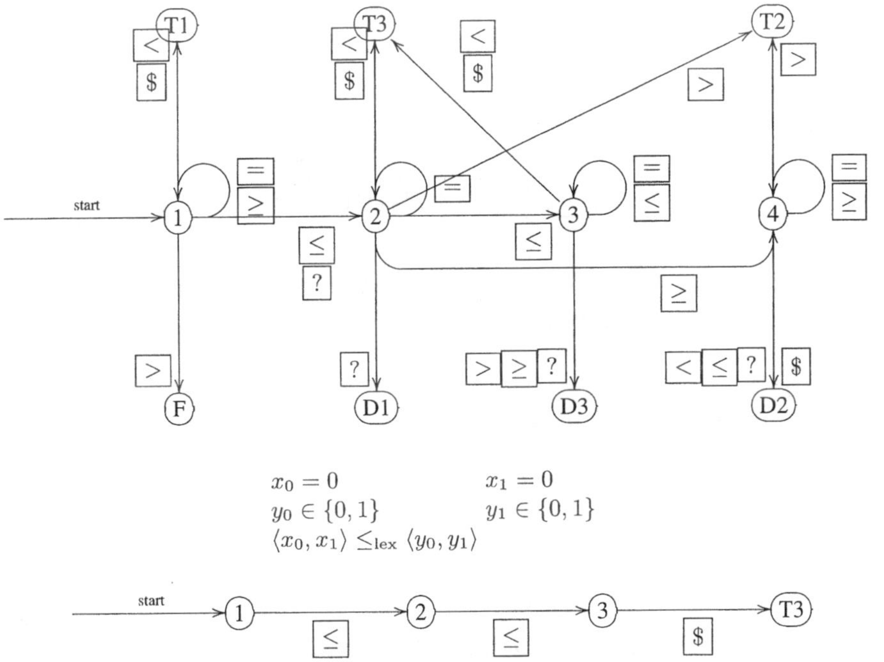

Fig. 2. Case analysis of $\leq_{\text{lex}}$ as finite automaton LFA and an example, where the automaton stops in state T3, detecting entailment.

3.3 Case Analysis

We now discuss seven regular expressions covering all possible cases of signatures of C. Where relevant, we also derive pruning rules for maintaining hyperarc consistency. Each regular expression corresponds to one of the terminal states of LFA. Note that, without loss of generality, each regular expression has a common prefix $P = (\boxed{=}\mid\boxed{\geq})^{\star}$. For C to hold, clearly for each position $i \in P$ where $S_i = \boxed{\geq}$, we must enforce $x_i = y_i$. We assume that the filtering algorithm does so in each case. In the regular expressions, q denotes the position of the transition out of state 1, r denotes the position of the transition out of state 2, and s denotes the position of the transition out of state 3 or 4. We now discuss the cases one by one.

Case F.

$$(\boxed{=}\mid\boxed{\geq})^{\star}\,\boxed{>}\,\mathcal{A}^{\star} \tag{F}$$

Clearly, if the signature of C is accepted by F, the signature of any ground instance will contain a $\boxed{>}$ before the first $\boxed{<}$, if any, so C has no solution.

Case T1.

$$\underbrace{(\boxed{=}\mid\boxed{\geq})^{\star}}_{P}\,\underbrace{(\boxed{<}\mid\boxed{\$})}_{q}\,\mathcal{A}^{\star} \tag{T1}$$

C will hold; we are done.

Case T2.

$$\underbrace{(\boxed{=}\mid\boxed{\geq})^{\star}}_{P}\,\underbrace{(\boxed{\leq}\mid\boxed{?})}_{q}\,(\boxed{=}\mid\boxed{\geq})^{\star}\,\boxed{>}\,\mathcal{A}^{\star} \tag{T2}$$

For C to hold, we must enforce $x_q < y_q$, in order for there to be at least one $\boxed{<}$ preceding the first $\boxed{>}$ in any ground instance.

Case T3.

$$\underbrace{(\boxed{=}\mid\boxed{\geq})^{\star}}_{P}\,\underbrace{(\boxed{\leq}\mid\boxed{?})}_{q}\,(\boxed{=}\mid\boxed{\leq})^{\star}\,(\boxed{<}\mid\boxed{\$})\,\mathcal{A}^{\star} \tag{T3}$$

For C to hold, all we have to do is to enforce $x_q \leq y_q$.

Case D1.

$$\underbrace{(\boxed{=}\mid\boxed{\geq})^{\star}}_{P}\,\underbrace{(\boxed{\leq}\mid\boxed{?})}_{q}\,\boxed{=}^{\star}\,\underbrace{\boxed{?}}_{r}\,\mathcal{A}^{\star} \tag{D1}$$

Consider the possible ground instances. Suppose that $x_q > y_q$. Then C is false. Suppose instead that $x_q < y_q$. Then C holds no matter what values are taken at r. Suppose instead that $x_q = y_q$. Then C is false iff $x_r > y_r$. Thus, the only relation at q and r that doesn't have support is $x_q > y_q$, so we enforce $x_q \leq y_q$.

Case D2.

$$\underbrace{\left(\boxed{=}\mid\boxed{\geq}\right)^\star}_{P}\ \underbrace{\left(\boxed{\leq}\mid\boxed{?}\right)}_{q}\ \boxed{=}^\star\ \underbrace{\boxed{\geq}}_{r}\ \left(\boxed{=}\mid\boxed{\geq}\right)^\star\ \underbrace{\left(\boxed{<}\mid\boxed{\leq}\mid\boxed{?}\mid\boxed{\$}\right)}_{s}\ \mathcal{A}^\star \tag{D2}$$

Consider the possible ground instances. Suppose that $x_q > y_q$. Then C is false. Suppose instead that $x_q < y_q$. Then C holds no matter what values are taken in $[r, s]$. Suppose instead that $x_q = y_q$. Then C is false iff $x_r > y_r \vee \cdots \vee x_{s-1} > y_{s-1} \vee (s < n \wedge x_s > y_s)$. Thus, the only relation in $[q, s]$ that doesn't have support is $x_q > y_q$, so we enforce $x_q \leq y_q$.

Case D3.

$$\underbrace{\left(\boxed{=}\mid\boxed{\geq}\right)^\star}_{P}\ \underbrace{\left(\boxed{\leq}\mid\boxed{?}\right)}_{q}\ \boxed{=}^\star\ \underbrace{\boxed{\leq}}_{r}\ \left(\boxed{=}\mid\boxed{\leq}\right)^\star\ \underbrace{\left(\boxed{>}\mid\boxed{\geq}\mid\boxed{?}\right)}_{s}\ \mathcal{A}^\star \tag{D3}$$

Consider the possible ground instances. Suppose that $x_q > y_q$. Then C is false. Suppose instead that $x_q < y_q$. Then C holds no matter what values are taken in $[r, s]$. Suppose instead that $x_q = y_q$. Then C is false iff $x_r = y_r \wedge \cdots \wedge x_{s-1} = y_{s-1} \wedge x_s > y_s$. Thus, the only relation in $[q, s]$ that doesn't have support is $x_q > y_q$, so we enforce $x_q \leq y_q$.

3.4 Non-incremental Filtering Algorithm

By augmenting LFA with the pruning actions mentioned in Sect. 3.3, we arrive at a filtering algorithm for $\leq_{\text{lex}}$, `FiltLex`. When a constraint is posted, the algorithm will succeed, fail or delay, depending on where LFA stops. In the delay case, the algorithm will restart from scratch whenever a propagation event (a bounds adjustment) arrives, until it eventually succeeds or fails. We summarize the properties of `FiltLex` in the following proposition.

Proposition 1.

1. `FiltLex` *covers all cases of* $\leq_{\text{lex}}$.
2. `FiltLex` *doesn't remove any solutions.*
3. `FiltLex` *doesn't admit any non-solutions.*
4. `FiltLex` *never suspends when it could in fact decide, from inspecting domain bounds, that the constraint is necessarily true or false.*
5. `FiltLex` *maintains hyperarc consistency.*
6. `FiltLex` *runs in* $O(n)$ *time.*

3.5 Incremental Filtering Algorithm

In a tree search setting, it is reasonable to assume that each variable is fixed one by one after posting the constraint. In this scenario, the total running time of `FiltLex` for reaching a leaf of the search tree would be $O(n^2)$. We can do better than that. In this section, we shall develop incremental handling of propagation events so that the total running time is $O(n+m)$ for handling m propagation events after posting the constraint.

Assume that a $C \equiv \vec{x} \leq_{\text{lex}} \vec{y}$ constraint has been posted, `FiltLex` has run initially, has reached one of its suspension cases, possibly after some pruning, and has suspended, recording: the state $u \in \{2, 3, 4\}$ that preceded the suspension, and the positions q, r, s. Later on, a propagation event arrives on a variable x_i or y_i, i.e. one or more of $\underline{x_i}, \overline{x_i}, \underline{y_i}$ and $\overline{y_i}$ have changed.

We assume that updates of the constraint store and of the variables u, q, r, s are trailed [8], so that their old values can be restored on backtracking. Thus whenever the algorithm resumes, the constraint store will be tighter than last time (modulo backtracking). We shall now discuss the various cases for handling the event.

Naive Event Handling. Our first idea is to simply restart the automaton at position i, in state u. The reasoning is that either everything up to position i is unchanged, or there is a pending propagation event at position $j < i$, which will be dealt with later:

- $i \in P$ is impossible, for after enforcing $x_i = y_i$ for all $i \in P$, all those variables are ground. This follows from the fact that:

$$\begin{array}{l} \underline{x_i} = \overline{x_i} = \underline{y_i} = \overline{y_i}, \text{ if } \Gamma \models x_i = y_i \\ \underline{x_i} = \overline{y_i}, \text{ if } \Gamma \models x_i \geq y_i \end{array} \quad (1)$$

  for any constraint store Γ.
- If $i = q$, we resume in state 1 at position i.
- If $i = r$, we resume in state 2 at position i.
- If $u > 2 \wedge i = s$, we resume in state u at position i.
- If $u > 2 \wedge r < i < s$:
  - If the signature letter at position i is unchanged or is changed to $\boxed{=}$, we do nothing.
  - Otherwise, we resume in state u at position i, immediately reaching a terminal state.
- Otherwise, we just suspend, as LFA would perform the same transitions as last time.

Better Event Handling. The problem with the above event handling scheme is that if $i = q$, we may have to re-examine any number of signature letters in states 2, 3 and 4 before reaching a terminal state. Similarly, if $i = r$, we may have to re-examine any number of positions in states 3 and 4. Thus, the worst-case total running time remains $O(n^2)$. We can remedy this problem with a simple device: when the finite automaton resumes, it simply ignores the following positions:

- In state 2, any letter before position r is ignored. This is safe, for the ignored letters will all be $\boxed{=}$.
- In states 3 and 4, any letter before position s is ignored. Suppose that there is a pending propagation event with position j, $r < j < s$ and that S_j has changed to $\boxed{<}$ (in state 3) or $\boxed{>}$ (in state 4), which should take the automaton to a terminal state. The pending event will lead to just that, when it is processed.

Incremental Filtering Algorithm. Let `FiltLexI` be the `FiltLex` algorithm augmented with the event handling described above. As before, we assume that each time the algorithm resumes, the constraint store will be tighter than last time. We summarize the properties of `FiltLexI` in Proposition 2.

Proposition 2.

1. `FiltLex` *and* `FiltLexI` *are equivalent.*
2. *The total running time of* `FiltLexI` *for posting a* $\leq_{\text{lex}}$ *constraint followed by* m *propagation events is* $O(n+m)$.

4 Case Study: lex_chain

In this section, we consider a chain of $\leq_{\text{lex}}$ constraints, $\text{lex\_chain}(\vec{x}_0, \ldots, \vec{x}_{m-1}) \equiv \vec{x}_0 \leq_{\text{lex}} \cdots \leq_{\text{lex}} \vec{x}_{m-1}$. As mentioned in [9], chains of lexicographic ordering constraints are commonly used for breaking symmetries arising in problems modelled with matrices of decision variables. The authors conclude that finding an hyperarc consistency algorithm for lex_chain "may be quite challenging". This section addresses this open question. Our contribution is a filtering algorithm for lex_chain, which maintains hyperarc consistency and runs in $O(nmd)$ time per invocation, where d is the cost of certain domain operations (see Sect. 1).

The key idea of the filtering algorithm is to compute feasible lower and upper bounds for each vector $\vec{x}_i$, and to prune the domains of the individual variables wrt. these bounds. Thus at the heart of the algorithm is the ancillary constraint $\text{between}(\vec{a}, \vec{x}, \vec{b})$, which is a special case of a conjunction of two $\leq_{\text{lex}}$ constraints. The point is that we have to consider globally both the lower and upper bound, lest we miss some pruning, as illustrated by Fig. 3.

We devote most of this section to the between constraint, applying the finite automaton approach to it. We then give some additional building blocks required for a filtering algorithm for lex_chain, and show how to combine it all.

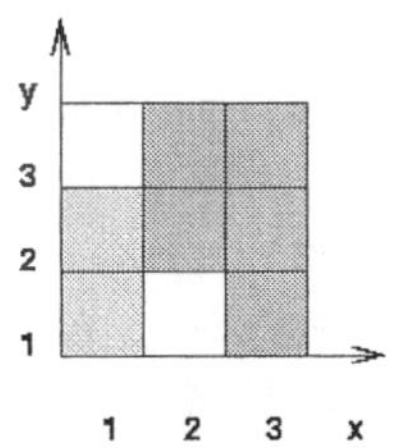

$x \in 1..3$
$y \in 1..3$
$\text{between}(\langle 1, 3\rangle, \langle x, y\rangle, \langle 2, 1\rangle)$

Fig. 3. The between constraint. $\langle 1, 3\rangle \leq_{\text{lex}} \langle x, y\rangle \leq_{\text{lex}} \langle 2, 1\rangle$ has no solution for $y = 2$, but the conjunction of the two $\leq_{\text{lex}}$ constraints doesn't discover that.

4.1 Definition and Declarative Semantics of between

Given two vectors, $\vec{a}$ and $\vec{b}$ of n integers, and a vector $\vec{x}$ of n variables, let $C \equiv \text{between}(\vec{a}, \vec{x}, \vec{b})$ denote the constraint $\vec{a} \leq_{\text{lex}} \vec{x} \leq_{\text{lex}} \vec{b}$.

For technical reasons, we will need to work with tight, i.e. lexicographically largest and smallest, as well as feasible wrt. $\vec{x}$[2], versions $\vec{a'}$ and $\vec{b'}$ of $\vec{a}$ and $\vec{b}$, i.e.:

$$\forall i \in [0, n) : a'_i \in D(x_i) \wedge b'_i \in D(x_i) \tag{2}$$

This is not a problem, for under these conditions, the $\text{between}(\vec{a}, \vec{x}, \vec{b})$ and $\text{between}(\vec{a'}, \vec{x}, \vec{b'})$ constraints have the same set of solutions. Algorithms for computing $\vec{a'}$ and $\vec{b'}$ from $\vec{a}$, $\vec{b}$ and $\vec{x}$ are developed in Sect. 4.6.

It is straightforward to see that the declarative semantics is:

$$C \equiv \bigvee \begin{cases} n = 0 & (3.1) \\ a'_0 = x_0 = b'_0 \wedge \vec{a'}_{[1,n)} \leq_{\text{lex}} \vec{x}_{[1,n)} \leq_{\text{lex}} \vec{b'}_{[1,n)} & (3.2) \\ a'_0 = x_0 < b'_0 \wedge \vec{a'}_{[1,n)} \leq_{\text{lex}} \vec{x}_{[1,n)} & (3.3) \\ a'_0 < x_0 = b'_0 \wedge \vec{x}_{[1,n)} \leq_{\text{lex}} \vec{b'}_{[1,n)} & (3.4) \\ a'_0 < x_0 < b'_0 & (3.5) \end{cases} \tag{3}$$

and hence, for all $i \in [0, n)$:

$$C \wedge (a'_0 = b'_0) \wedge \cdots \wedge (a'_{i-1} = b'_{i-1}) \Rightarrow a'_i \leq x_i \leq b'_i \tag{4}$$

4.2 Signatures of between

Let $\mathcal{B}$ be the alphabet $\{\boxed{<}, \boxed{\hat{<}}, \boxed{=}, \boxed{\hat{=}}, \boxed{>}, \boxed{\hat{>}}, \boxed{\$}\}$. The signature $S = \sigma(C, \Gamma, \mathcal{B})$ of C wrt. a constraint store Γ is defined by $S_n = \boxed{\$}$, to mark the end of the string, and for $0 \leq i < n$:

$$S_i = \begin{cases} \boxed{<}, \text{ if } a'_i < b'_i \wedge \Gamma \models (x_i \leq a'_i \vee x_i \geq b'_i) \\ \boxed{\hat{<}}, \text{ if } a'_i < b'_i \wedge \Gamma \not\models (x_i \leq a'_i \vee x_i \geq b'_i) \\ \boxed{=}, \text{ if } a'_i = b'_i \wedge \Gamma \models a'_i = x_i = b'_i \\ \boxed{\hat{=}}, \text{ if } a'_i = b'_i \wedge \Gamma \not\models a'_i = x_i = b'_i \\ \boxed{>}, \text{ if } a'_i > b'_i \wedge \Gamma \models b'_i \leq x_i \leq a'_i \\ \boxed{\hat{>}}, \text{ if } a'_i > b'_i \wedge \Gamma \not\models b'_i \leq x_i \leq a'_i \end{cases}$$

From a complexity point of view, we note that the tests $\Gamma \models a'_i = x_i = b'_i$ and $\Gamma \models b'_i \leq x_i \leq a'_i$ can be implemented with domain bound inspection and run in constant time, whereas the test $\Gamma \models (x_i \leq a'_i \vee x_i \geq b'_i)$ requires the use of next_value or prev_value, and has cost d; see Table 1.

[2] The adjective *feasible* refers to the requirement that $\vec{a'}$ and $\vec{b'}$ be instances of $\vec{x}$.

Table 1. Computing the signature letter at position i. Note that if $a < b$ then $\text{next\_value}(x, a) \geq b$ holds iff $D(x)$ has no value in (a, b).

S_i	**Condition**
$<$	$a'_i < b'_i \wedge \text{next\_value}(x_i, a'_i) \geq b'_i$
$\hat{<}$	$a'_i < b'_i \wedge \text{next\_value}(x_i, a'_i) < b'_i$
$=$	$\underline{x_i} = \overline{x_i} = a'_i = b'_i$
$\hat{=}$	$\underline{x_i} \neq a'_i = b'_i \vee \overline{x_i} \neq a'_i = b'_i$
$>$	$a'_i > b'_i \wedge b'_i \leq \underline{x_i} \leq \overline{x_i} \leq a'_i$
$\hat{>}$	$a'_i > b'_i \wedge (\underline{x_i} < b'_i \vee a'_i < \overline{x_i})$

4.3 Finite Automaton for between

Fig. 4 shows a deterministic finite automaton BFA for signature strings, from which we shall derive the filtering algorithm. State 1 is the initial state. There are three terminal states, F, T1 and T2, each corresponding to a separate case. State F is the failure case, whereas states T1–T2 are success cases.

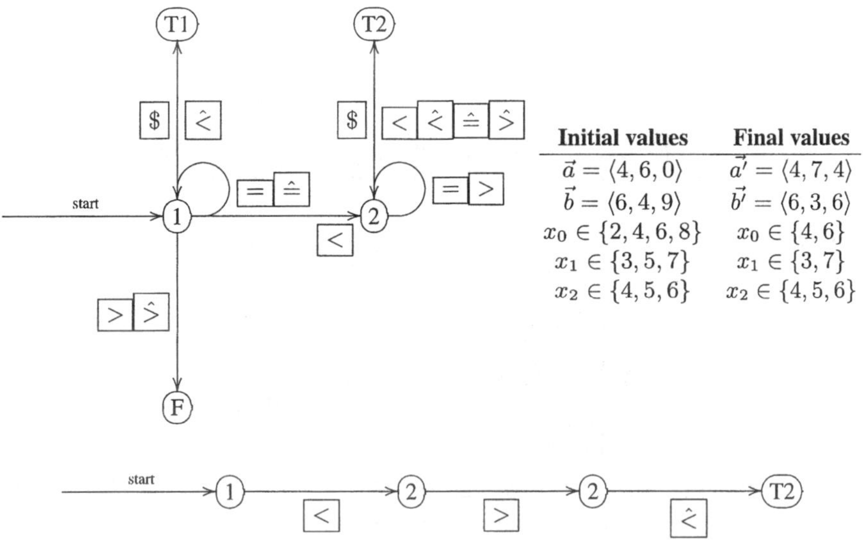

Fig. 4. Case analysis of $\text{between}(\vec{a}, \vec{x}, \vec{b})$ as finite automaton BFA, and an example, where BFA stops in state T2.

4.4 Case Analysis of between

We now discuss three regular expressions covering all possible cases of signatures of C. Where relevant, we also derive pruning rules for maintaining hyperarc consistency. Each regular expression corresponds to one of the terminal states of BFA. Note that, without loss of generality, each regular expression has a common prefix $P = (\boxed{=} \mid \boxed{\hat{=}})^\star$. For C to hold, clearly for each position i in the corresponding prefix of $\vec{x}$, by (3.2) the filtering algorithm must enforce $a'_i = x_i = b'_i$. In the regular expressions, q and r denote the position of the transition out of state 1 and 2 respectively. We now discuss the cases one by one.

Case F.

$$\underbrace{(\boxed{=} \mid \boxed{\hat{=}})^\star}_{P} \underbrace{(\boxed{>} \mid \boxed{\hat{>}})}_{q} \mathcal{B}^\star \tag{F}$$

We have that $a'_0 = b'_0 \wedge \cdots \wedge a'_{q-1} = b'_{q-1} \wedge a'_q > b'_q$, and so by (4), C must be false.

Case T1.

$$\underbrace{(\boxed{=} \mid \boxed{\hat{=}})^\star}_{P} \underbrace{(\boxed{\hat{<}} \mid \boxed{\$})}_{q} \mathcal{B}^\star \tag{T1}$$

We have that $a'_0 = b'_0 \wedge \cdots \wedge a'_{q-1} = b'_{q-1} \wedge (q = n \vee a'_q < b'_q)$. If $q = n$, we are done by (3.1) and (3.2). If $q < n$, we also have that $(a'_q, b'_q) \cap D(x_q) \neq \emptyset$. Thus by (3.5), all we have to do after P for C to hold is to enforce $a'_q \le x_q \le b'_q$.

Case T2.

$$\underbrace{(\boxed{=} \mid \boxed{\hat{=}})^\star}_{P} \underbrace{\boxed{<}}_{q} (\boxed{>} \mid \boxed{=})^\star \underbrace{(\boxed{<} \mid \boxed{\hat{<}} \mid \boxed{\hat{=}} \mid \boxed{\hat{>}} \mid \boxed{\$})}_{r} \mathcal{B}^\star \tag{T2}$$

We have that:

$$\bigwedge \begin{cases} a'_0 = b'_0 \wedge \cdots \wedge a'_{q-1} = b'_{q-1} \\ a'_q < b'_q \\ (a'_q, b'_q) \cap D(x_q) = \emptyset \\ a'_{q+1} \ge b'_{q+1} \wedge \cdots \wedge a'_{r-1} \ge b'_{r-1} \\ \forall i \in (q, r) : b'_i \le \underline{x_i} \le \overline{x_i} \le a'_i \end{cases}$$

Consider position q, where $a'_q < b'_q$ and $(a'_q, b'_q) \cap D(x_q) = \emptyset$ hold. Since by (4) $a'_q \le x_q \le b'_q$ should also hold, x_q must be either a'_q or b'_q, and we know from (2) that both $x_q = a'_q$ and $x_q = b'_q$ have support.

It can be shown by induction that there are exactly two possible values for the subvector $\vec{x}_{[0,r)}$: $\vec{a'}_{[0,r)}$ and $\vec{b'}_{[0,r)}$.

Thus for C to hold, after P we have to enforce $x_i \in \{a'_i, b'_i\}$ for $q \le i < r$. From (3.3) and (3.4), we now have that C holds iff

$$\bigvee \begin{cases} \vec{x}_{[0,r)} = \vec{a'}_{[0,r)} \wedge \vec{a'}_{[r,n)} \preceq_{\text{lex}} \vec{x}_{[r,n)} \\ \vec{x}_{[0,r)} = \vec{b'}_{[0,r)} \wedge \vec{x}_{[r,n)} \preceq_{\text{lex}} \vec{b'}_{[r,n)} \end{cases}$$

i.e.

$$\bigvee \begin{cases} r = n \wedge \vec{x}_{[0,r)} = \vec{a'}_{[0,r)} & (5.1) \\ r = n \wedge \vec{x}_{[0,r)} = \vec{b'}_{[0,r)} & (5.2) \\ r < n \wedge \vec{x}_{[0,r)} = \vec{a'}_{[0,r)} \wedge x_r > a'_r & (5.3) \\ r < n \wedge \vec{x}_{[0,r)} = \vec{a'}_{[0,r)} \wedge x_r = a'_r \wedge \vec{a'}_{(r,n)} \leq_{\text{lex}} \vec{x}_{(r,n)} & (5.4) \\ r < n \wedge \vec{x}_{[0,r)} = \vec{b'}_{[0,r)} \wedge x_r < b'_r & (5.5) \\ r < n \wedge \vec{x}_{[0,r)} = \vec{b'}_{[0,r)} \wedge x_r = b'_r \wedge \vec{x}_{(r,n)} \leq_{\text{lex}} \vec{b'}_{(r,n)} & (5.6) \end{cases} \quad (5)$$

Finally, consider the possible cases for position r, which are:

- $r = n$, signature letter $\boxed{\$}$. We are done by (5.1) and (5.2).
- $a'_r < b'_r$, signature letters $\boxed{<}$ and $\boxed{\hat{<}}$. Then from (2) we know that we have solutions corresponding to both (5.3) and (5.5). Thus, all values for $\vec{x}_{[r,n)}$ have support, and we are done.
- $a'_r \geq b'_r$, signature letters $\boxed{\hat{>}}$ and $\boxed{\hat{=}}$. Then from (2) and from the signature letter, we know that we have solutions corresponding to both (5.4), (5.6), and one or both of (5.3) and (5.5). Thus, all values v for x_r such that $v \leq b'_r \vee v \geq a'_r$, and all values for $\vec{x}_{(r,n)}$, have support. Hence, we must enforce $x_r \notin (b'_r, a'_r)$.

4.5 Filtering Algorithm for between

By augmenting BFA with the pruning actions mentioned in Sect. 4.4, we arrive at a filtering algorithm `FiltBetween` ([5, Alg. 1]) for $\text{between}(\vec{a}, \vec{x}, \vec{b})$. When a constraint is posted, the algorithm will delay or fail, depending on where BFA stops. The filtering algorithm needs to recompute feasible upper and lower bounds each time it is resumed. We summarize the properties of `FiltBetween` in the following proposition.

Proposition 3.

1. `FiltBetween` *doesn't remove any solutions.*
2. `FiltBetween` *removes all domain values that cannot be part of any solution.*
3. `FiltBetween` *runs in* $O(nd)$ *time.*

4.6 Feasible Upper and Lower Bounds

We now show how to compute the tight, i.e. lexicographically largest and smallest, and feasible vectors $\vec{a'}$ and $\vec{b'}$ that were introduced in Sect. 4.1, given a constraint $\text{between}(\vec{a}, \vec{x}, \vec{b})$.

Upper Bounds. The algorithm, $\texttt{ComputeUB}(\vec{x}, \vec{b}, \vec{b'})$, has two steps. The key idea is to find the smallest i, if it exists, such that b'_i must be less than b_i.

1. Compute α as the smallest $i \geq -1$ such that one of the following holds:
   a) $i \geq 0 \wedge b_i \notin D(x_i) \wedge b_i > \underline{x_i}$
   b) $\vec{b}_{(i,n)} <_{\text{lex}} \underline{\vec{x}}_{(i,n)}$

In both cases, a value $b'_i < b_i$ must be chosen from $D(x_i)$. If no such i exists, let $\alpha = n$. If $\alpha = -1$, the algorithm fails, meaning that $\vec{x} \leq_{\mathrm{lex}} \vec{b}$ can't hold. For example, $\alpha = 1$ in the example shown in Fig. 4. See [5, Alg. 2].

2. b'_i is computed as follows for $0 \leq i < n$:

$$b'_i = \begin{cases} b_i, \text{ if } i < \alpha \\ \text{prev\_value}(x_i, b_i), \text{ if } i = \alpha \\ \overline{x_i}, \text{ if } i > \alpha \end{cases}$$

We summarize the properties of `ComputeUB` in the following lemma.

Lemma 1. `ComputeUB` *is correct and runs in* $O(n + d)$ *time.*

Lower Bounds. The feasible lower bound algorithm, `ComputeLB`, is totally analogous to `ComputeUB`, and not discussed further.

4.7 Filtering Algorithm

We now have the necessary building blocks for constructing a filtering algorithm for lex_chain; see [5, Alg. 3]. The idea is as follows. For each vector in the chain, we first compute a tight and feasible upper bound by starting from $\vec{x}_{m-1}$. We then compute a tight and feasible lower bound for each vector by starting from $\vec{x}_0$. Finally for each vector, we restrict the domains of its variables according to the bounds that were computed in the previous steps. Any value removal is a relevant propagation event. We summarize the properties of `FiltLexChain` in the following proposition.

Proposition 4.

1. `FiltLexChain` *maintains hyperarc consistency.*
2. *If there is no variable aliasing,* `FiltLexChain` *reaches a fixpoint after one run.*
3. *If there is no variable aliasing,* `FiltLexChain` *runs in* $O(nmd)$ *time.*

5 Related Work

Within the area of logic, automata have been used by associating with each formula defining a constraint an automaton recognizing the solutions of the constraint [10].

An $O(n)$ filtering algorithm maintaining hyperarc consistency of the $\leq_{\mathrm{lex}}$ constraint was described in [9]. That algorithm is based on the idea of using two pointers α and β. The α pointer gives the position of the most significant pair of variables that are not ground and equal, and corresponds to our q position. The β pointer, if defined, gives the most significant pair of variables from which $\leq_{\mathrm{lex}}$ cannot hold. It has no counterpart in our algorithm. As the constraint store gets tighter, α and β get closer and closer, and the algorithm detects entailment when $\alpha + 1 = \beta \vee \overline{x_\alpha} < \underline{y_\alpha}$. The algorithm is only triggered on propagation events on variables in $[\alpha, \beta)$. It does not detect entailment as eagerly as ours, as demonstrated by the example in Fig. 2. `FiltLex` detects entailment on this example, whereas Frisch's algorithm does not. Frisch's algorithm is shown to run in $O(n)$ on posting a constraint as well as for handling a propagation event.

6 Discussion

The main result of this work is an approach to designing filtering algorithms by derivation from finite automata operating on constraint signatures. We illustrated this approach in two case studies, arriving at:

- A filtering algorithm for $\leq_{\text{lex}}$, which maintains hyperarc consistency, detects entailment or rewrites itself to a simpler constraint whenever possible, and runs in $O(n)$ time for posting the constraint plus amortized $O(1)$ time for handling each propagation event.
- A filtering algorithm for lex_chain, which maintains hyperarc consistency and runs in $O(nmd)$ time per invocation, where d is the cost of certain domain operations.

In both case studies, the development of the algorithms was mainly manual and required several inspired steps. In retrospect, the main benefit of the approach was to provide a rigorous case analysis for the logic of the algorithms being designed. Some work remains to turn the finite atomaton approach into a methodology for semi-automatic development of filtering algorithms. Relevant, unsolved research issues include:

1. **What class of constraints is amenable to the approach?** It is worth noting that $\leq_{\text{lex}}$ and between can both be defined inductively, so it is tempting to conclude that any inductively defined constraint is amenable. Constraints over sequences [11,12] would be an interesting candidate for future work.
2. **Where does the alphabet come from?** In retrospect, this was the most difficult choice in the two case studies. In the $\leq_{\text{lex}}$ case, the basic relations used in the definition of the constraint are $\{<, =, >\}$, each symbols of $\mathcal{A}$ denoting a set of such relations. In the between case, the choice of alphabet was far from obvious and was influenced by an emerging understanding of the necessary pruning rules. As a general rule, the cost of computing each signature letter has a strong impact on the overall complexity, and should be kept as low as possible.
3. **Where does the finite automaton come from?** Coming up with a regular language and corresponding finite automaton for *ground* instances is straightforward, but there is a giant leap from there to the nonground case. In our case studies, it was mainly done as a rational reconstruction of an emerging understanding of the necessary case analysis.
4. **Where do the pruning rules come from?** This was the most straightforward part in our case studies. At each non-failure terminal state, we analyzed the corresponding regular language, and added pruning rules that prevented there from being failed ground instances, i.e. rules that removed domain values with no support.
5. **How do we make the algorithms incremental?** The key to incrementality for $\leq_{\text{lex}}$ was the observation that the finite automaton could be safely restarted at an internal state. This is likely to be a general rule for achieving some, if not all, incrementality. We could have done this for between$(\vec{a}, \vec{x}, \vec{b})$, except in the context of lex_chain, between is not guaranteed to be resumed with $\vec{a}$ and $\vec{b}$ unchanged, and the cost of checking this would probably outweigh the savings of an incremental algorithm.

Acknowledgements. We thank Justin Pearson and Zeynep Kızıltan for helpful discussions on this work, and the anonymous referees for their helpful comments.

References

1. J.-C. Régin. A filtering algorithm for constraints of difference in CSPs. In *Proc. of the National Conference on Artificial Intelligence (AAAI-94)*, pages 362–367, 1994.
2. J.-C. Régin. Generalized arc consistency for global cardinality constraint. In *Proc. of the National Conference on Artificial Intelligence (AAAI-94)*, pages 209–215, 1996.
3. P. Baptiste, C. LePape, and W. Nuijten. *Constraint-Based Scheduling*. Kluwer Academic Publishers, 2001.
4. Alan Tucker. *Applied Combinatorics*. John Wiley & Sons, 4th edition, 2002.
5. Mats Carlsson and Nicolas Beldiceanu. Arc-consistency for a Chain of Lexicographic Ordering Constraints. Technical Report T2002-18, Swedish Institute of Computer Science, 2002.
6. Mats Carlsson and Nicolas Beldiceanu. Revisiting the Lexicographic Ordering Constraint. Technical Report T2002-17, Swedish Institute of Computer Science, 2002.
7. Mats Carlsson et al. *SICStus Prolog User's Manual*. Swedish Institute of Computer Science, 3.10 edition, January 2003. `http://www.sics.se/sicstus/`.
8. N. Beldiceanu and A. Aggoun. Time stamps techniques for the trailed data in CLP systems. In *Actes du Séminaire 1990 - Programmation en Logique*, Tregastel, France, 1990. CNET.
9. A. Frisch, B. Hnich, Z. Kızıltan, I. Miguel, and T. Walsh. Global Constraints for Lexicographic Orderings. In Pascal Van Hentenryck, editor, *Principles and Practice of Constraint Programming – CP'2002*, volume 2470 of *LNCS*, pages 93–108. Springer-Verlag, 2002.
10. H. Comon, M. Dauchet, R. Gilleron, F. Jacquemard, D. Lugiez, S. Tison, and M. Tommasi. Tree automata techniques and applications. `http://www.grappa.univ-lille3.fr/tata/`.
11. COSYTEC S.A. *CHIP Reference Manual*, version 5 edition, 1996. The *sequence* constraint.
12. J.-C. Régin and J. F. Puget. A filtering algorithm for global sequencing constraints. In G. Smolka, editor, *Principles and Practice of Constraint Programming – CP'97*, volume 1330 of *LNCS*, pages 32–46. Springer-Verlag, 1997.

A Memoizing Semantics for Functional Logic Languages

Salvador España and Vicent Estruch

Departamento de Sistemas Informáticos y Computación-DSIC
Technical University of Valencia, C. de Vera s/n, 46022 Valencia, Spain.
{sespana,vestruch}@dsic.upv.es

Abstract. Declarative multi-paradigm languages combine the main features of functional and logic programming, like laziness, logic variables and non-determinism. The operational semantics of these languages is based on a combination of narrowing and residuation. In this article, we introduce a non-standard *memoizing* semantics for multi-paradigm declarative programs and prove its equivalence with the standard operational semantics. Both pure functional and pure logic programming have for long time taken advantage of tabling or memoizing schemes [15,19,7], which motivates the interest in the adapation of this technique to the integrated paradigm.

Keywords: Programming languages, formal semantics, memoization.

1 Introduction

Declarative multi-paradigm languages [11] (like Curry [10]) combine the main features of functional and logic programming. In comparison with functional languages, such integrated languages are more expressive thanks to the ability to perform function inversion and to implement partial data structures by means of logical variables. With respect to logic languages, multi-paradigm languages have a more efficient operational behaviour since functions allow more deterministic evaluations than predicates.

The operational semantics of these languages is usually based on a combination of two different operational principles: narrowing and residuation [12]. The *residuation* principle is based on the idea of delaying function calls until they are ready for a deterministic evaluation (by rewriting). On the other hand, the *narrowing* mechanism allows the instantiation of variables in input expressions and, then, applies reduction steps to the function calls of the instantiated expression. Each function specifies a concrete *evaluation annotation* (see [12,10]) in order to indicate whether it should be evaluated by residuation (for functions annotated as *rigid*) or by narrowing (for *flexible* functions). Due to its optimality properties w.r.t. the length of derivations and the number of computed solutions, *needed narrowing* [5] is currently the best narrowing strategy for multi-paradigm functional logic programs. The formulation of needed narrowing is based on the use of *definitional trees* [3], which define a strategy to evaluate functions by applying narrowing steps. Recently, [13] introduced a *flat* representation for functional

D.A. Schmidt (Ed.): ESOP 2004, LNCS 2986, pp. 109–123, 2004.

logic programs in which definitional trees are embedded in the rewrite rules by means of case expressions. The interest in using the flat representation arises because it provides more explicit control (hence the associated calculus is simpler than needed narrowing), while source programs can be still automatically translated to the new representation.

Several techniques from pure functional and pure logic languages have been extended to implement multi-paradigm languages. In particular, both pure paradigms have exploited memoization[1] to memoize sub-computations and reuse their results later. In some situations [15] a reduction of the asymptotic cost can be obtained[2]. The advantages of memoization have long been known to the functional programming community [15,8]. Tamaki and Sato [19] proposed an interpretation for logic programming based on memoization; this seminal paper has stimulated a large body of work [7,18,16,6]. In addition to reuse previous computed sub-goals, infinite paths in the search space can be detected, enabling better termination properties [7].

These properties motivate the adaptation of the memoization technique to the integrated functional logic paradigm. This adaptation is not straightforward due to some differences between functional evaluation and narrowing. Firstly, in addition to the computed normal form, functional logic programs also produce a computed answer. Secondly, non-determinism of narrowing computations leads to a large, possibly infinite, set of results arising from different sequences of narrowing steps. Previous work attempting to introduce memoization in narrowing [4] focused in finding a finite representation of a (possibly infinite) narrowing space by means of a graph representing the narrowing steps of a goal.

In this article, we define a new *memoizing* semantics for flat programs, the MLNT calculus, and prove its equivalence with the standard operational semantics.

The rest of the paper is organized as follows. In the next section we briefly introduce a *flat* representation for multi-paradigm functional logic programs and its operational semantics based on the LNT (Lazy Narrowing with definitional Trees) calculus [13]. Section 3 presents the proposed memoizing semantics and proves the completeness w.r.t. LNT calculus. Finally, Section 4 offers some conclusions.

2 The Flat Language

This section briefly introduces a *flat* representation for multi-paradigm functional logic programs and its standard operational semantics. Similar representations are considered in [13,14,17]. Unlike them, here we distinguish two kinds of case expressions in order to make also explicit the *flexible/rigid* evaluation annotations of source programs. The syntax for programs in the flat representation is as follows:

[1] Other terms (tabling, caching, etc.) are used to refer to the same concept too.

[2] Memoization can be viewed as an automatic technique for applying dynamic programming optimization [9].

$$
\begin{array}{lll}
\mathcal{R} & ::= D_1 \ldots D_m & \text{(program)} \\
\mathcal{D} & ::= f(\overline{x_n}) = e & \text{(rule)} \\
e & ::= x & \text{(variable)} \\
 & \mid c(\overline{e_n}) & \text{(constructor)} \\
 & \mid f(\overline{e_n}) & \text{(function call)} \\
 & \mid case\ e\ of\ \{\overline{p_n \to e_n}\} & \text{(rigid case)} \\
 & \mid fcase\ e\ of\ \{\overline{p_n \to e_n}\} & \text{(flexible case)} \\
 & \mid e_1\ or\ e_2 & \text{(disjunction)} \\
p & ::= c(\overline{x_n}) & \text{(flat pattern)}
\end{array}
$$

Here, we write $\overline{o_n}$ for the sequence of objects $o_1, \ldots, o_n$. Thus, a program $\mathcal{R}$ consists of a sequence of function definitions D such that the left-hand side is linear and has only variable arguments, i.e., pattern matching is compiled into case expressions. The right-hand side of each function definition is an expression e composed of variables ($\mathcal{X}$), constructors ($\mathcal{C}$), function calls ($\mathcal{F}$), and case expressions for pattern-matching. Variables are denoted by $x, y, z \ldots$, constructors by $a, b, c \ldots$, and defined functions by $f, g, h \ldots$ The general form of a case expression is:

$$(f)case\ e\ of\ \{c_1(\overline{x_{n_1}}) \to e_1; \ldots; c_k(\overline{x_{n_k}}) \to e_k\}$$

where e is an expression, $c_1, \ldots, c_k$ are different constructors of the type of e, and $e_1, \ldots, e_k$ are expressions (possibly containing case structures). The variables $\overline{x_{n_i}}$ are local variables which occur only in the corresponding expression e_i. The difference between *case* and *fcase* only shows up when the argument e is a free variable: *case* suspends (which corresponds to residuation) whereas *fcase* nondeterministically binds this variable to the pattern in a branch of the case expression (which corresponds to narrowing). Functions defined only by *fcase* (resp. *case*) expressions are called *flexible* (resp. *rigid*).

Without loss of generality, we will assume some restrictions in flat programs in the following: on the one hand, all $(f)case$ arguments are variables; on the other hand, *or* and $(f)case$ expressions appear at the outermost positions i.e., they do not appear inside function and constructor calls. Every flat program can be automatically transformed to one which satisfies these restrictions.

Example 1. The following flat program will be used to illustrate some examples throughout the paper. It defines some functions on natural numbers which are represented by terms built from `Zero` and `Succ`. `double` is defined by means of the addition, `coin` nondeterministically computes `Zero` or `Succ(Zero)`. `add` is the arithmetic addition and `leq` defines the relation "less than or equal to".

```
double(x) = add(x, x)
coin      = Zero or Succ(Zero)
add(x, y) = fcase x of {Zero → y; Succ(m) → Succ(add(m, y))}
leq(x, y) = fcase x of {Zero → True;
                        Succ(m) → fcase y of {Zero → False;
                                              Succ(n) → leq(m, n)}}
```

Case Select		
$[\![(f)case\ c(\overline{e_n})\ of\ \{\overline{p_k \to e'_k}\}]\!]$	$\Rightarrow_{id}$	$[\![\sigma(e'_i)]\!]$ if $p_i = c(\overline{x_n})$ and $\sigma = \{\overline{x_n \mapsto e_n}\}$
Case Guess		
$[\![fcase\ x\ of\ \{\overline{p_k \to e_k}\}]\!]$	$\Rightarrow_\sigma$	$[\![\sigma(e_i)]\!]$ if $\sigma = \{x \mapsto p_i\}$, $i = 1, \ldots, k$
Case Eval		
$[\![(f)case\ e\ of\ \{\overline{p_k \to e_k}\}]\!]$	$\Rightarrow_\sigma$	$[\![\sigma((f)case\ e'\ of\ \{\overline{p_k \to e_k}\})]\!]$ if $[\![e]\!] \Rightarrow_\sigma [\![e']\!]$, $e \notin \mathcal{X}$, and $root(e) \notin \mathcal{C}$
Function Eval		
$[\![f(\overline{e_n})]\!]$	$\Rightarrow_{id}$	$[\![\sigma(e')]\!]$ if $f(\overline{x_n}) = e' \in \mathcal{R}$ and $\sigma = \{\overline{x_n \mapsto e_n}\}$
Or		
$[\![e_1\ or\ e_2]\!]$	$\Rightarrow_{id}$	$[\![e_i]\!], i = 1, 2$

Fig. 1. LNT calculus

The operational semantics of flat programs is based on the LNT (Lazy Narrowing with definitional Trees) calculus [13]. In Figure 1, we present a slight extension of this calculus in order to cope with case expressions including evaluation annotations and disjunction; nevertheless, we still use the name "LNT calculus" for simplicity. First, let us note that the symbols "$[\![$" and "$]\!]$" in an expression like $[\![e]\!]$ are purely syntactical (i.e., they do not denote "the value of e"). Indeed, they are only used to *guide* the inference rules. LNT steps are labelled with the substitution computed in the step. The empty substitution is denoted by *id*. Let us briefly describe the LNT rules:

Case Select. It is used to select the appropriate branch of the current case expression.

Case Guess. It non-deterministically selects a branch of a flexible case expression and instantiates the variable at the case argument to the appropriate constructor pattern. The step is labelled with the computed substitution σ. Rigid case expressions with a variable argument *suspend*, giving rise to an abnormal termination.

Case Eval. It is used to evaluate case expressions with a function call or another case expression in the argument position. Here, $root(e)$ denotes the outermost symbol of e. This rule initiates the evaluation of the case argument by creating a (recursive) call for this subexpression.

Function Eval. This rule performs the unfolding of a function call. As in logic programming, we assume that rules are renamed so that they only contain fresh variables.

Or. It non-deterministically selects a choice of a disjunction expression.

Arbitrary LNT *derivations* are denoted by $e \Rightarrow^*_\sigma e'$ which is a shorthand for the sequence of steps $e \Rightarrow_{\sigma_1} \ldots \Rightarrow_{\sigma_n} e'$ with $\sigma = \sigma_n \circ \cdots \circ \sigma_1$ (if $n = 0$ then $\sigma = id$). We say that a LNT derivation $e \Rightarrow^*_\sigma e'$ is *successful* when e' is in *head normal form* (i.e., it is rooted by a constructor symbol) or it is a variable; in this case, we say that e evaluates to e' with *answer* σ. This calculus can be easily extended to evaluate expressions to normal form, but we keep the above presentation in both calculi for simplicity. In the rest of the paper, a *value* will denote a term in head normal form or a variable.

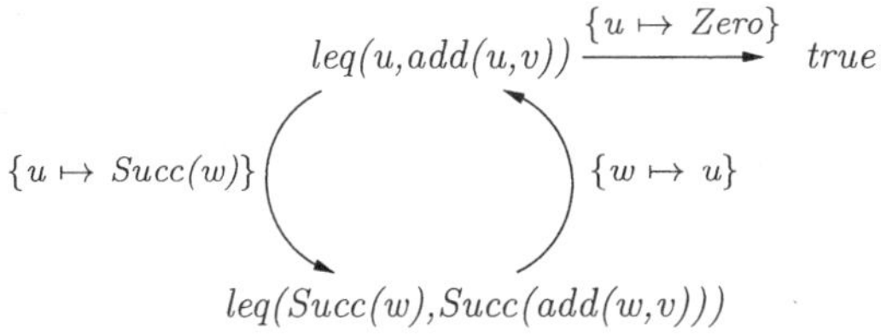

Fig. 2. Graph representation of the narrowing space of the goal $leq(u, add(u, v))$

3 MLNT Calculus

Previous work aiming at introducing memoization in narrowing [4] focused in finding a finite representation of a (possibly infinite) narrowing space by means of a graph representing the narrowing steps of a goal. Let us consider the example of Figure 2 extracted from [4]. This figure shows the graph representation[3] of the narrowing space of the goal $leq(u, add(u, v))$.

The vertices of this graph are goals i.e., terms being narrowed, and the edges are narrowing steps between these goals. Terms are considered the same vertex if they differ only by a renaming of variables. Solutions can be obtained by composing the set of substitutions which appear in any path in the graph whose origin is the goal vertex and whose destination vertex is a value.

Our proposal is based in a graph representation too, but in contrast to [4], every subgoal is explicitly introduced in the graph in order to take advantage of memoization. Therefore, the graph represents no longer the search space of the original goal, but also contains the search space of *all derived subgoals*. The sets of results are pairs composed by a value and a computed answer.

Furthermore, search spaces from different goals may share common parts in order to further improve memoization. For instance, consider the narrowing space of the goal *double*(*coin*) shown in Figure 3. The term *add*(*coin*, *coin*) denoted by `v2` requires subgoal *coin* at position 1 to be reduced, thus a new vertex `v3` associated to *coin* is introduced in the graph. Later, `v2` is reduced to `v3`. Therefore, `v3` has played a double role.

The proposed calculus consists of a state transition system MLNT where a MLNT-State is a 4-tuple from

$$Eval \times Ready \times Suspended \times Graph$$

Eval may be a special symbol *void* or an *EvaluationState*. An *EvaluationState* is a 3-tuple composed by a goal to be solved, a flat expression and a substitution.

Non-determinism (for instance, variable instantiation in a $(f)case$) is addressed by considering every possible choice and creating a different *EvaluationState* associated to it. Note that despite non-determinism, *only one* graph is

[3] For simplicity, we omitted some intermediate steps which basically correspond to $(f)case$ reductions.

considered which memoizes the information of all these branches as soon as they are computed.

Since the computation process must pursue only a single branch at a given moment, we maintain a set of ready *EvaluationStates* which are stored to be selected later. This set is the second component of a MLNT-State.

Every goal evaluation that needs a subgoal to be solved is suspended and stored in a "suspended table". This table maps every suspended *EvaluationState* to the set of subgoal's solutions already used to continue this *EvaluationState*. These sets of solutions are needed to avoid resuming the suspended *EvaluationState* several times with the same subgoal's solution.

Given an initial goal e, the initial MLNT-state associated to it is the tuple: $\langle void, \{\langle e, e, id\rangle\}, \emptyset, \emptyset\rangle$. A sequence of steps is applied and the calculus proceeds until *Eval* is *void*, the set *Ready* is empty and no rules can be applied.

The aim of this calculus is to obtain a graph which contains the original goal e as a vertex and also value vertices connected to it by a path. The edges of the graph are labelled with substitutions. The composition of substitutions in a path, in reverse order, gives the computed answer. This scheme can be easily adapted to evaluate expressions to normal form.

Let us briefly describe the MLNT rules shown in Figure 4. (sel) and (sol) are the only ones which overlap and the only non-deterministic too. They may be applied to a MLNT-state with *void* in the *Eval* field:

- (sel) This rule takes an *EvaluationState* element of the set *Ready* and puts it in the field *Eval* to be used later by other rules.
- (sol) A solution may be generated whenever a path appears in the graph from a goal to a value vertex. A new solution is searched in the graph for some vertex v corresponding to a goal appeared in the $(f)case$ argument of some suspended *EvaluationState*. A new *EvaluationState* is created from the suspended one by replacing its goal argument by the solution previously found, and is stored in the set *Ready* to be selected later. The mapping *Suspended* is updated to reflect the fact that this solution has already been used.

The rest of the rules are applied when *Eval* is not *void*, they are non-overlapping and deterministic:

- (or) The outermost position of the second component of *Eval* is an *or* expression. This rule breaks this expression into two who are introduced in the set *Ready* to be selected later.
- (val) The second component of *Eval* must be a value (head normal form or a variable) in order to apply this rule. A new edge in the graph is inserted connecting the goal being solved to the value.
- (goal) The outermost position of the second component of *Eval* is a function call $f(\overline{t_n})$. This expression is always a term because of the restrictions imposed to flat programs. An edge is added from the goal being solved to this

function call when they are different. If the goal was not in the graph, a new *EvaluationState* $Unfold(f(\overline{t_n}))$ is introduced in the set *Ready* to be selected later.

The three following rules (casec), (casef) and (casev) correspond to the case where an expression of the form $(f)case\ e\ of\ \{c_1(\overline{x_{n_1}}) \rightarrow e_1; \ldots; c_k(\overline{x_{n_k}}) \rightarrow e_k\}$ is at the outermost position of the second component of *Eval*.

(casec) This rule is used when e in the above expression is constructor rooted (with root c_i). The corresponding pattern $c_i(\overline{x_{n_i}})$ is selected and matched against e. The associated expression e_i replaces the current expression of the field *Eval*. Other fields remain unchanged.

(casef) In this case, e is a function call $f(\overline{t_n})$ which must be computed. The current *EvaluationState* of field *Eval* is stored in the mapping *Suspended*. The evaluation $\langle f(\overline{t_n}), f(\overline{t_n}), id\rangle$ is also introduced in the set *Ready*.

(casev) This rule is applied to a *fcase* expresion whenever e is an unbound variable. This variable may be bound to every $c_i(\overline{x_{n_i}})$ pattern. Thus, a new *EvaluationState* is inserted in the set *Ready* for every possible variable instantiation. This set of *EvaluationState*s is finite and equal to the arity of the *fcase* expression. Note that this rule does not consider a rigid *case*, the evaluation is suspended whenever this situation is produced.

To illustrate this calculus, a trace of *double*(*coin*) is shown in Figure 3. The following domains and auxiliary functions are used to simplify the MLNT rules shown in Figure 4:

Eval: is $(EvaluationState \cup \{void\})$
EvaluationState: $Term \times Expr \times Substitution$.
Ready: $2^{EvaluationState}$.
Suspended: set of partial mappings from *EvaluationState* to $2^{Substitution \times Term}$.
Graph: set of partial mappings from *Term* to $2^{Substitution \times Term}$ a set of pairs ⟨edge label, destination vertex⟩. $Vertices(G)$ will denote $Dom(G)$

The partial mappings Suspended and Graph described above consider terms modulo variable renaming.

ObtainSolution: Searches a path in the graph from a given vertex to a value vertex. Returns a pair ⟨computed answer,value ⟩, where the computed answer is obtained by composing the path's sequence of substitutions (taken in reverse orden). This function is non-deterministic, but it must guarantee that every solution will be found eventually.

UnionMap: This function performs the union of two partial mappings and is used to update *Suspended* and *Graph* mappings. $Dom(UnionMap(G,H)) = Dom(G) \cup Dom(H)$. $UnionMap(G,H)(x) = G(x)$ if $x \notin Dom(H)$ and $UnionMap(G,H)(x) = H(x)$ if $x \notin Dom(G)$. $UnionMap(G,H)(x) = G(x) \cup H(x)$ whenever both exists. For instance, $UnionMap(G,\{t \rightarrow \emptyset\})$ adds vertex t to G.

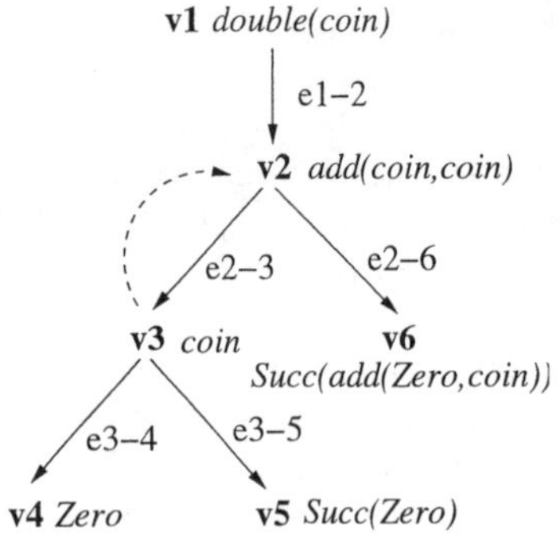

ev1	= ⟨double(coin), double(coin), {}⟩
ev2	= ⟨double(coin), add(coin, coin), {}⟩
ev3	= ⟨add(coin, coin), *fcase* coin *of* {Zero → coin; Succ(m) → Succ(add(m, coin)), {}⟩
ev4	= ⟨coin, coin, {}⟩
ev5	= ⟨coin, Zero *or* Succ(Zero), {}⟩
ev6	= ⟨coin, Zero, {}⟩
ev7	= ⟨coin, Succ(Zero), {}⟩
ev8	= ⟨add(coin, coin), *fcase* Zero *of* {Zero → coin; Succ(m) → Succ(add(m, coin)), {}⟩
ev9	= ⟨add(coin, coin), coin, {}⟩
ev10	= ⟨add(coin, coin), *fcase* Succ(Zero) *of* {Zero → coin; Succ(m) → Succ(add(m, coin)), {}⟩
ev11	= ⟨add(coin, coin), Succ(add(Zero, coin)), {}⟩

Step	Rule	Eval	Ready	Suspended	Graph
		void	{ev1}	∅	∅
1	sel	ev1	∅	∅	∅
2	goal	*void*	{ev2}	∅	⟨{v1}, {}⟩
3	sel	ev2	∅	∅	⟨{v1}, {}⟩
4	goal	*void*	{ev3}	∅	⟨{v1,v2}, {e1-2}⟩
5	sel	ev3	∅	∅	⟨{v1,v2}, {e1-2}⟩
6	casef	*void*	{ev4}	{ev3 → {}}	⟨{v1,v2}, {e1-2}⟩
7	sel	ev4	∅	{ev3 → {}}	⟨{v1,v2}, {e1-2}⟩
8	goal	*void*	{ev5}	{ev3 → {}}	⟨{v1,v2,v3}, {e1-2}⟩
9	sel	ev5	∅	{ev3 → {}}	⟨{v1,v2,v3}, {e1-2}⟩
10	or	*void*	{ev6, ev7}	{ev3 → {}}	⟨{v1,v2,v3}, {e1-2}⟩
11	sel	ev6	{ev7}	{ev3 → {}}	⟨{v1,v2,v3}, {e1-2}⟩
12	val	*void*	{ev7}	{ev3 → {}}	⟨{v1,v2,v3,v4}, {e1-2,e3-4}⟩
13	sel	ev7	∅	{ev3 → {}}	⟨{v1,v2,v3,v4}, {e1-2,e3-4}⟩
14	val	*void*	∅	{ev3 → {}}	⟨{v1,v2,v3,v4,v5}, {e1-2,e3-4,e3-5}⟩
15	sol	*void*	{ev8}	{ev3 → {Zero}}	⟨{v1,v2,v3,v4,v5}, {e1-2,e3-4,e3-5}⟩
16	sel	ev8	∅	{ev3 → {Zero}}	⟨{v1,v2,v3,v4,v5}, {e1-2,e3-4,e3-5}⟩
17	casec	ev9	∅	{ev3 → {Zero}}	⟨{v1,v2,v3,v4,v5}, {e1-2,e3-4,e3-5}⟩
18	goal	*void*	∅	{ev3 → {Zero}}	⟨{v1,v2,v3,v4,v5}, {e1-2,e3-4,e3-5,e2-3}⟩
19	sol	*void*	{ev10}	{ev3 → {Zero, Succ(Zero)}}	⟨{v1,v2,v3,v4,v5}, {e1-2,e3-4,e3-5,e2-3}⟩
20	sel	ev10	∅	{ev3 → {Zero, Succ(Zero)}}	⟨{v1,v2,v3,v4,v5}, {e1-2,e3-4,e3-5,e2-3}⟩
21	casec	ev11	∅	{ev3 → {Zero, Succ(Zero)}}	⟨{v1,v2,v3,v4,v5}, {e1-2,e3-4,e3-5,e2-3}⟩
22	val	*void*	∅	{ev3 → {Zero, Succ(Zero)}}	⟨{v1,v2,v3,v4,v5,v6}, {e1-2,e3-4,e3-5,e2-3,e2-6}⟩

Fig. 3. Trace of the goal *double*(*coin*). Bottom table corresponds to the sequence of MLNT-states. The graphs in this sequence are represented as pairs of sets: The first component is the set of vertices. The second component is the set of edges. Both sets use the notation of the graph in the top-left part of the figure. Top-left is the search space graph; dashed edges represent dependence relations between goals and suspended evaluations in these vertices; edges are no labeled since this example has no variables. Top-right table corresponds to *EvaluationStates* used in the trace.

Rule	*Eval*	*Ready*	*Suspended*	*Graph*
(sel)	$void$	R	S	G
	$\Rightarrow e$	$R - \{e\}$	S	G
	where $e \in R$			
(sol)	$void$	R	S	G
	$\Rightarrow void$	$R \cup \{e\}$	S'	G
	where $s = \langle t, (f)case\ f(\overline{t_n})\ of\ \{\overline{p_n \to e_n}\}, \sigma\rangle \in Dom(S)$ $f(\overline{t_n}) \in Vertices(G)$ $\langle \varphi, r\rangle = ObtainSolution(G, f(\overline{t_n})) \notin S(s)$ $e = \langle t, (f)case\ r\ of\ \{\overline{p_n \to \varphi(e_n)}\}, \varphi \circ \sigma\rangle$ $S' = UnionMap(S, \{s \to \{\langle \varphi, r\rangle\}\})$			
(or)	$\langle t, e_1\ or\ e_2, \sigma\rangle$	R	S	G
	$\Rightarrow void$	R'	S	G
	where $R' = R \cup \{\langle t, e_1, \sigma\rangle, \langle t, e_2, \sigma\rangle\}$			
(val)	$\langle t, val, \sigma\rangle$	R	S	G
	$\Rightarrow void$	R	S	G'
	where val in head normal form, $G' = UnionMap(G, \{t \to \{\langle \sigma, val\rangle\}\})$			
(goal)	$\langle t, f(\overline{t_n}), \sigma\rangle$	R	S	G
	$\Rightarrow void$	R'	S	G'
	where $G' = \begin{cases} UnionMap(G, \{t \to \{\langle \sigma, f(\overline{t_n})\rangle\}\}) & \text{if } t \neq f(\overline{t_n}) \vee \sigma \neq id \\ UnionMap(G, \{t \to \emptyset\}) & \text{otherwise} \end{cases}$ $R' = \begin{cases} R \cup \{Unfold(f(\overline{t_n}))\} & \text{if } f(\overline{t_n}) \notin vertices(G) \\ R & \text{otherwise} \end{cases}$			
(casec)	e	R	S	G
	$\Rightarrow e'$	R	S	G
	where $e = \langle t, (f)case\ c(\overline{b_k})\ of\ \{\overline{p_n \to e_n}\}, \sigma\rangle$ $p_i = c(\overline{x_k})$ is the pattern that matches $c(\overline{b_k})$ $e' = \langle t, \varphi(e_i), \varphi \circ \sigma\rangle$, $\varphi = \{\overline{x_k \mapsto b_k}\}$			
(casef)	e	R	S	G
	$\Rightarrow void$	R'	S'	G
	where $e = \langle t, (f)case\ f(\overline{t_n})\ of\ \{\overline{p_n \to e_n}\}, \sigma\rangle$ $S' = UnionMap(S, \{e \to \emptyset\})$, $R' = R \cup \{\langle f(\overline{t_n}), f(\overline{t_n}), id\rangle\}$			
(casev)	e	R	S	G
	$\Rightarrow void$	R'	S	G
	where $e = \langle t, fcase\ x\ of\ \{\overline{p_n \to e_n}\}, \sigma\rangle$ $\varphi_i = \{x \mapsto p_i\}$, $\forall i = 1, \ldots, n$ $R' = R \cup \{\langle t, \varphi_i(e_i), \varphi_i \circ \sigma\rangle : i \in \{1, \ldots, n\}\}$			

Fig. 4. MLNT Calculus

Unfold: Given a function call $f(\overline{t_n})$, creates a new *EvaluationState* $\langle f(\overline{t_n}), e, \sigma \rangle$ where e is obtained by unfolding $f(\overline{t_n})$ and σ is the associated substitution. Example: *Unfold*(add(coin, coin)) is:

$$\langle \texttt{add(coin, coin)},\ \textit{fcase}\ \texttt{coin}\ \textit{of}\ \{\ \texttt{Zero} \to \texttt{coin}; \quad \texttt{Succ(m)} \to \texttt{Succ(add(m, coin))}\}, \texttt{id}\rangle$$

Theorem 1 (Completeness). *Let e be an expression, e′ a value, and $\mathcal{R}$ a flat program. For each LNT derivation $e \Rightarrow^*_\sigma e'$ in $\mathcal{R}$, there exists a sequence of MLNT transition steps $\langle void, \{\langle e, e, id\rangle\}, \emptyset, \emptyset, \emptyset\rangle = st_1 \Rightarrow st_2 \Rightarrow \ldots \Rightarrow st_k = \langle void, R, S, G\rangle$ such that G contains e and e′ as vertices connected by a path $e = e_1, \ldots, e_r = e'$, and the composition of edge labels of this path (taken in reverse order) $label(e_{r-1}, e_r) \circ \cdots \circ label(e_1, e_2)$ is the computed answer σ. Where label(edge) denotes the substitution that labels an edge.*

Informally speaking, we would like to reason by induction over the length of the LNT derivation relating the application of a rule in LNT calculus to the application of one or more steps in MLNT calculus. This is not easy because the graph in the MLNT derivation is not updated every step. Only the MLNT rules (val) and (goal) update the graph (a composition of substitutions is stored in every *EvaluationState* and is used later to label the edges created by these rules). This is the reason why the proof is decomposed in three stages. First, we demonstrate for arbitrary sequences of LNT rules Case Select, Case Guess and Or. In a second stage, the LNT rule Function Eval is also considered. Finally, the LNT rule Case Eval is included.

Note also that memoization should be taken into account in this proof. For instance, whenever the MLNT rule (goal) is applied, the unfolding of the corresponding function call expression is inserted into the set *Ready* only the first time this function is to be evaluated (the graph allows the MLNT state transition system to check it). For simplicity, the proof of Lemma 2 considers only the case when every function call appears in the graph for the first time. The general case should take into account *EvaluationStates* that remain in the set *Ready* but which are not taken into account in the induction steps of the proof.

Lemma 1. *Let e and e′ be two expressions and $\mathcal{R}$ a flat program. For each (not necessarily successful) LNT derivation $e \Rightarrow^*_\sigma e'$ in $\mathcal{R}$ which only uses the rules* Case Select, Case Guess *and* Or, *there exists a sequence of MLNT transition steps $\langle\langle h, e, \varphi\rangle, R, S, G\rangle = st_1 \Rightarrow \ldots \Rightarrow st_k = \langle\langle h, e', \sigma \circ \varphi\rangle, R', S, G\rangle$.*

Proof. The proof proceeds by induction on the length n of this LNT derivation.

Base case $(n = 0)$. Trivial.

Inductive case $(n > 0)$. Assume that the LNT derivation has the form

$$e \Rightarrow_\theta e^a \Rightarrow^*_\gamma e'$$

where $\sigma = \gamma \circ \theta$. Now, we distinguish several cases depending on the applied rule in the first step:

Case Select. Then, e has the form $[\![(f)case\ c(\overline{e_n})\ of\ \{\overline{p_k \to e'_k}\}]\!]$ and $e^a = [\![\theta(e'_i)]\!]$ if $p_i = c(\overline{x_n})$ and $\theta = \{\overline{x_n \mapsto e_n}\}$. A single MLNT step suffices: $\langle\langle h, (f)case\ c(\overline{e_n})\ of\ \{\overline{p_k \to e'_k}\}, \varphi\rangle, R, S, G\rangle \Rightarrow_{casec} \langle\langle h, \theta(e'_i), \theta\circ\varphi\rangle, R, S, G\rangle$.

Case Guess. Then, e has the form $[\![fcase\ x\ of\ \{\overline{p_k \to e_k}\}]\!]$ and $e^a = [\![\theta(e_j)]\!]$, where $\theta = \{x \mapsto p_j\}$ for some $j \in \{1, \ldots, k\}$. In this case the corresponding MLNT steps are: $\langle\langle h, e, \varphi\rangle, R, S, G\rangle \Rightarrow_{casev} \langle void, R^I, S, G\rangle \Rightarrow_{sel} \langle\langle h, e^a, \theta \circ \varphi\rangle, R^{II}, S, G\rangle$.

Case Or. In this case, e has the form $[\![e_1\ or\ e_2]\!]$ and, in one LNT-step, non-deterministically we get $e^a = e_i$, $i \in \{1, 2\}$ with $\theta = id$. In this case the corresponding MLNT steps are: $\langle\langle h, e_1\ or\ e_2, \varphi\rangle, R, S, G\rangle \Rightarrow_{or} \langle void, R^I, S, G\rangle \Rightarrow_{sel} \langle\langle h, e^a, \varphi\rangle, R^{II}, S, G\rangle$, where $R^I = R \cup \{\langle e, e_1, \varphi\rangle, \langle e, e_2, \varphi\rangle\}$ and the *EvaluationState* with the adequate e_i is selected by rule (sel). □

Lemma 2. *Let e and e' be two expressions and $\mathcal{R}$ a flat program. For each (not necessarily successful) LNT derivation $e \Rightarrow^*_\sigma e'$ in $\mathcal{R}$ which does not use the rule* Case Eval, *there exists a sequence of MLNT transition steps $\langle\langle h, e, \varphi\rangle, R, S, G\rangle = st_1 \Rightarrow \ldots, \Rightarrow st_k = \langle\langle h', e', \varphi'\rangle, R', S, G'\rangle$ such that there exist a path in G' from h to h' and $\varphi' \circ \sigma' \circ \varphi = \sigma \circ \varphi$, where σ' is the composition of edge labels of this path (taken in reverse order).*

Proof. If the rule Function Eval has not been used in the LNT derivation, it suffices to apply Lemma 1. Now, let us suppose that Function Eval has been used at least once in the derivation. In this case, the derivation $e = e_1 \Rightarrow_{\sigma_1} e_2 \Rightarrow_{\sigma_2} \ldots \Rightarrow_{\sigma_{n-1}} e_n = e'$ may be expressed:

$$e_1 \Rightarrow^*_{\varphi_1} e_{i_1} \Rightarrow_{\theta_1} e_{i_1+1} \Rightarrow^*_{\varphi_2} e_{i_2} \Rightarrow_{\theta_2} e_{i_2+1} \ldots e_{i_k+1} \Rightarrow^*_{\varphi_{k+1}} e_{i_{k+1}} = e_n$$

where $e_{i_j} \Rightarrow_{\theta_j} e_{i_j+1}$, $j = 1, \ldots, k$ are the only steps where the rule Function Eval has been applied. Therefore, by Lemma 1, the derivations $e_{i_j+1} \Rightarrow^*_{\varphi_{j+1}} e_{i_{j+1}}$ are equivalent to MLNT-sequences:

$$\langle\langle h_j, e_{i_j+1}, \rho_j\rangle, R_j, S, G_j\rangle \Rightarrow^* \langle\langle h_j, e_{i_{j+1}}, \varphi_{j+1} \circ \rho_j\rangle, R'_j, S, G_j\rangle$$

Now, it suffices to join these sequences of MLNT transitions by applying the MLNT-rules (goal) and (sel) whenever LNT rule Function Eval has been applied, so that $e_{i_j} \Rightarrow_{\theta_j} e_{i_j+1}$ is associated to $\langle\langle h_j, e_{i_{j+1}}, \varphi_{j+1} \circ \rho_j\rangle, R^I_j, S, G_j\rangle \Rightarrow_{goal} \langle void, R^{II}_j, S, G_{j+1}\rangle \Rightarrow_{sel} \langle\langle h_{j+1}, e_{i_{j+1}+1}, \rho_{j+1}\rangle, R_{j+1}, S, G_{j+1}\rangle$. □

Lemma 3. *Let e be an expression, $\mathcal{R}$ a flat program and e' a value. For each LNT derivation $e \Rightarrow^*_\sigma e'$ in $\mathcal{R}$, there exists a sequence of MLNT transition steps $\langle\langle h, e, \varphi\rangle, R, S, G\rangle = st_1 \Rightarrow \ldots \Rightarrow st_k = \langle\langle h', e', \varphi'\rangle, R', S, G'\rangle$ such that there exist a path in G' from h to h' and $\varphi' \circ \sigma' \circ \varphi = \sigma \circ \varphi$, where σ' is the composition of edge labels of this path (taken in reverse order).*

Proof. The proof proceeds by induction on the number of times the rule Case Eval has been used.

Base case. Lemma 2.

Inductive case. Assume that the LNT derivation has the form

$$e = e_1 \Rightarrow_{\sigma_1} e_2 \Rightarrow_{\sigma_2} \dots \Rightarrow_{\sigma_{n-1}} e_n = e'$$

and the rule Case Eval is used in the derivation. There is a maximal subsequence of k contiguous Case Eval derivations:

$$e_{i+1} \Rightarrow_{\sigma_i+1} \dots e_{i+k-1} \Rightarrow_{\sigma_{i+k-1}} e_{i+k}$$

where $e_{i+j} = [\![(f)case\ e^j\ of\ \{\overline{p_m \to e_m}\}]\!]$, $j = 0, \dots, k$
Note that $k < n$ since e_n is a value and, by the condition of maximality, e^k is also a value. Therefore, the sequence

$$e^1 \Rightarrow_{\sigma_{i+1}} e^2 \Rightarrow_{\sigma_{i+2}} \dots \Rightarrow_{\sigma_{i+k}} e^k$$

is also a *successful derivation* of length less than n, therefore the induction hypothesis can be applied: $\langle\langle h, e_1, \varphi\rangle, R, S, G\rangle \Rightarrow^* \langle\langle h', e_{i+1}, \varphi'\rangle, R^I, S^I, G^I\rangle$ $\Rightarrow_{casef} \langle void, R^{II}, S^{II}, G^I\rangle \Rightarrow_{sel} \langle\langle e^1, e^1, id\rangle, R^{III}, S^{II}, G^I\rangle \Rightarrow_{Ind.\ Hypothesis}$ $\langle\langle h'', e^k, \varphi''\rangle, R^{IV}, S^{III}, G^{II}\rangle \Rightarrow_{val} \langle void, R^{IV}, S^{III}, G^{III}\rangle \Rightarrow_{sol} \langle\langle h''', e_{i+k}\varphi'''\rangle,$ $R^V, S^{IV}, G^{III}\rangle \Rightarrow^* \langle void, R^{VI}, S^V, G^{IV}\rangle$
such that G^{IV} contains the path $e_1, \dots, e_n$. □

Proof (of Theorem 1). $\langle void, \{\langle e, e, id\rangle\}, \emptyset, \emptyset\rangle \Rightarrow_{sel} \langle\langle e, e, id\rangle, \emptyset, \emptyset, \emptyset\rangle$ $\Rightarrow_{Lemma3} \langle\langle h, e', \varphi\rangle, R, S, G'\rangle \Rightarrow_{val} \langle void, R, S, G\rangle$ □

Note that a successful LNT derivation obtains a single solution whereas MLNT can obtain a set of solutions and is complete. Despite these differences, soundness may be formulated as follows:

Theorem 2 (Soundness). *Let e be a goal, $\mathcal{R}$ be a flat program and let $st_1 = \langle void, \{\langle e, e, id\rangle\}, \emptyset, \emptyset, \emptyset\rangle \Rightarrow \dots \Rightarrow \langle void, R, S, G\rangle = st_k$ be a sequence of MLNT transition steps. For every path $e = e_1, \dots, e_r = e'$ in G such that e' is a value and $label(e_{r-1}, e_r) \circ \cdots \circ label(e_1, e_2) = \sigma$, there exists a successful LNT derivation $e \Rightarrow^*_\sigma e'$*

Proof. The proof is decomposed in two parts. First, we introduce the notion of *restricted* subsequence of MLNT transition steps associated to an edge and show how this sequence can be obtained. This sequence allow us to relate MLNT and LNT steps in a more direct manner than the original MLNT sequence[4].

In a second part, we obtain a sequence of LNT steps from the restricted sequence of MLNT transition steps. This part proceeds by induction when MLNT

[4] The sequence of MLNT and LNT steps cannot be related in a direct way for several reasons. On the one hand, some MLNT steps are used to construct parts of the graph which are not needed to obtain the solution e' (they may be used to construct other solutions). On the other hand, MLNT steps may appear in many different arrangements. For instance, steps associated to different solutions or even to different subgoals might be interleaved.

rules (casef) and (sol) does not appear in the sequence. This special case is a base case for a recursive, constructive, procedure that covers the general case.

Given an edge of G, a *restricted* subsequence[5] of MLNT transition steps $m_1, \ldots, m_p$ associated to this edge is composed by those steps from the original sequence $st_1, \ldots, st_k$ satisfying the following conditions:

- The step is needed to construct the edge assuming that the origin vertex already exists and the *EvaluationState* associated to the unfolding of this edge is in the set *Ready* in the first MLNT state of the restricted sequence.
- The steps needed to construct subgoals are not included.

In order to obtain a restricted sequence of an edge, note that only MLNT rules (val) and (goal) update the graph and both create an edge (and the destination vertex, if necessary). This step can be traced back obtaining previous *EvaluationStates* until a (val) or (goal) rule has been applied. Whenever a (sel) rule is used to obtain an *EvaluationState* e, we need to search for the previous step that put e in the set *Ready*. If the rule that put e was (sol), we consider the (casef) step that inserted the *EvaluationState* in *Suspended* that later was used to create e by (sol).

In the second part of the proof, we will relate a *restricted* sequence of MLNT steps to the corresponding LNT steps. In a first stage, we prove by induction for sequences where (casef) and (sol) rules have not been applied. We distinguish several cases depending on the applied rule in the first step. We show here only two rules, since they are similar Lemma 1:

(or) Since the sequence is *restricted*, this step is always followed by a (sel) step: $\langle\langle t, e_1 \; or \; e_2, \sigma\rangle, R, S, G\rangle \Rightarrow_{or} \langle void, R \cup \{\langle t, e_1, \sigma\rangle, \langle t, e_2, \sigma\rangle\}, S, G\rangle \Rightarrow_{sel} \langle\langle t, e_i, \sigma\rangle, R \cup \{\langle t, e_j, \sigma\rangle\}, S, G\rangle$ where $i, j \in \{1, 2\}$, $i \neq j$. The corresponding sequence of LNT steps is a single Case or step: $[\![e_1 \; or \; e_2]\!] \Rightarrow_{id} [\![e_i]\!]$.

(casev) This step is also followed by a (sel) step: $\langle\langle t, fcase \; x \; of \; \{\overline{p_k \rightarrow e_k}\}, \sigma\rangle, \sigma\rangle, R, S, G\rangle \Rightarrow_{casev} \langle void, R', S, G\rangle \Rightarrow_{sel} \langle\langle t, \varphi_i(e_i), \varphi_i \circ \sigma\rangle, R'', S, G\rangle$ where $i \in \{1, \ldots, k\}$. The corresponding sequence of LNT steps is a single Case Guess step: $[\![fcase \; x \; of \; \{\overline{p_k \rightarrow e_k}\}]\!] \Rightarrow_{\varphi_i} [\![\varphi_i(e_i)]\!]$.

By simple concatenation of the associated LNT steps, we can prove the result for any path in the graph which does not need pairs of (casef) and (sol) rules.

In a second stage, the rules (casef) and (sol) are considered. This part is proved in a constructive manner using recursion. The base case (there are no pairs of (casef) and (sol) rules) is guaranteed because there is a partial dependence relation between goals and subgoals. This case corresponds to the second stage.

Let us consider the transition steps $\langle\langle h, (f)case \; r_1 \; of \; \{\overline{p_k \rightarrow e_k}\}, \theta\rangle, R, S, G\rangle \Rightarrow_{casef} \langle void, R', S', G\rangle \Rightarrow_{sol} \langle void, R'', S'', G'\rangle \Rightarrow_{sel} \langle\langle h, (f)case \; r_j \; of \; \{\overline{p_k \rightarrow e_k}\}, \varphi \circ \theta\rangle, R''', S'', G'\rangle$ where $r_1 = f(\overline{t_n})$ is a goal. The rule (sol) uses a tuple $\langle \varphi, r\rangle$ given by *ObtainSolution* which has traversed a path $r_1, \ldots, r_j$ in G. By recursion, we obtain a sequence of LNT steps $s_1 \Rightarrow^* s_p$ associated to

[5] By subsequence we do not mean contiguous.

$r_1, \ldots, r_j$. Now, it suffices to create the following LNT steps to obtain the LNT sequence associated to the MLNT transition steps:

$$\begin{array}{l} (f)case\ s_1\ of\ \{\overline{p_k \to e_k}\} \\ \Rightarrow (f)case\ s_2\ of\ \{\overline{p_k \to e_k}\} \\ \quad\vdots \\ \Rightarrow (f)case\ s_p\ of\ \{\overline{p_k \to e_k}\} \end{array}$$

and the claim follows. □

4 Conclusions

This work presents a non-standard memoizing semantics for functional logic programs (for a class of flat programs, with no loss of generality) and demonstrates the equivalence w.r.t. a standard operational semantics for such programs. This coud provide the theoretical basis for a complete sequential implementation of a functional logic language with memoization.

This work considers a pure memoization approach where every goal is memoized. In some situations, memoizing all subgoals is not feasible from a practical point of view. Therefore, an obvious extension is a mixed approach which allows memoizing only some subgoals, as is done in most logic programming systems [18].

Other extensions to this work could consider the computed graph which may be used for other purposes such as partial evaluation [1] and debugging [2].

Acknowledgements. We gratefully acknowledge Germán Vidal for many useful questions, suggestions and helpful discussions.

References

1. E. Albert and G. Vidal. The Narrowing-Driven Approach to Functional Logic Program Specialization. *New Generation Computing*, 20(1):3–26, 2002.
2. M. Alpuente, F. J. Correa, and M. Falaschi. Debugging Scheme of Functional Logic Programs. In M. Hanus, editor, *Proc. of International Workshop on Functional and (Constraint) Logic Programming, WFLP'01*, volume 64 of *Electronic Notes in Theoretical Computer Science*. Elsevier Science Publishers, 2002.
3. S. Antoy. Definitional Trees. In H. Kirchner and G. Levi, editors, *Proc. of the 3rd International Conference on Algebraic and Logic Programming*, volume Springer LNCS 632, pages 143–157, 1992.
4. S. Antoy and Z. M. Ariola. Narrowing the narrowing space. In *9th Int'l Symp. on Prog. Lang., Implementations, Logics, and Programs (PLILP'97)*, volume Springer LNCS 1292, pages 1–15, 1997.
5. S. Antoy, R. Echahed, and M. Hanus. A Needed Narrowing Strategy. In *Journal of the ACM (JACM)*, volume 47, pages 776–822. ACM Press New York, NY, USA, 2000.

6. J. Barklund. Tabulation of Functions in Definite Clause Programs. In Manuel Hermenegildo and Jaan Penjam, editors, *Proc. of the Sixth International Symposium on Programming Language Implementation and Logic Programming*, pages 465–466. Springer Verlag, 1994.
7. W. Chen and D. S. Warren. Tabled Evaluation with Delaying for General Logic Programs. *Journal of the ACM*, 43(1):20–74, 1996.
8. B. Cook and J. Launchbury. Disposable Memo Functions. *ACM SIGPLAN Notices*, 32(8):310–318, 1997.
9. T. H. Cormen, C. E. Leiserson, and R. L. Rivest. *Introduction to Algorithms*. MIT Press, 1992.
10. M. Hanus. Curry: An Integrated Functional Logic Language. Available at: `http://www.informatik.uni-kiel.de/~mh/curry` (2000).
11. M. Hanus. The Integration of Functions into Logic Programming: From Theory to Practice. *Journal of Logic Programming*, 19&20:583–628, 1994.
12. M. Hanus. A Unified Computation Model for Functional and Logic Programming. In *Proc. 24st ACM Symposium on Principles of Programming Languages (POPL'97)*, pages 80–93, 1997.
13. M. Hanus and C. Prehofer. Higher-Order Narrowing with Definitional Trees. *Journal of Functional Programming*, 9(1):33–75, 1999.
14. T. Hortalá-González and E. Ullán. An abstract machine based system for a lazy narrowing calculus. In *Proc. of the 5th Int'l Symp. on Functional and Logic Programming (FLOPS'2001)*, volume Springer LNCS 2024, pages 216–232, 2001.
15. J. Hughes. Lazy memo-functions. Proc. of the 2nd Conference on Functional Programming Languages and Computer Architecture (FPCA). *Lecture Notes in Computer Science*, 201:129–146, 1985.
16. M. Leuschel, B. Mertens, and K. Sagonas. Preserving termination of tabled logic programs while unfolding. in proc. of lopstr'97: Logic program synthesis and transformation, n. fuchs,ed. lncs 1463:189–205, 1997.
17. W. Lux and H. Kuchen. An Efficient Abstract Machine for Curry. In *Proc. of the 8th Int'l Workshop on Functional and Logic Programming (WFLP'99)*, pages 171–181, 1999.
18. I. V. Ramakrishnan, P. Rao, K. F. Sagonas, T. Swift, and D. S. Warren. Efficient access mechanisms for tabled logic programs. *Journal of Logic Programming*, 38(1):31–54, 1999.
19. H. Tamaki and T. Sato. Old Resolution with Tabulation. In *3rd International Conference on Logic Programming*, volume Springer LNCS 225, pages 84–98, 1986.

Adaptive Pattern Matching on Binary Data*

Per Gustafsson and Konstantinos Sagonas

Department of Information Technology, Uppsala University, Sweden
{pergu,kostis}@it.uu.se

Abstract. Pattern matching is an important operation in functional programs. So far, pattern matching has been investigated in the context of structured terms. This paper presents an approach to extend pattern matching to terms without (much of a) structure such as binaries which is the kind of data format that network applications typically manipulate. After introducing a notation for matching binary data against patterns, we present an algorithm that constructs a tree automaton from a set of binary patterns. We then show how the pattern matching can be made adaptive, how redundant tests can be avoided, and how we can further reduce the size of the resulting automaton by taking interferences between patterns into account. The effectiveness of our techniques is evaluated using implementations of network protocols taken from actual telecom applications.

1 Introduction

Binary data are omnipresent in telecom and computer network applications. Many formats for data exchange between nodes in distributed computer systems (MPEG, ELF, PGP keys, yEnc, JPEG, MP3, GIF, ...) as well as most network protocols use binary representations. The main reason for using binaries is size; a binary is a much more compact format than the symbolic or textual representation of the same information. Consequently, less resources are required to transmit binaries over the network.

When binaries are received, they typically need to be processed. Their processing can either be performed in a low-level language such as C (which can directly manipulate these objects), or binaries need to be converted to some non-binary term representation and manipulated by a high-level language such as a functional programming language. The main problem with the second approach is that most high-level languages do not provide adequate support for binary data. As a result, programming tends to become pretty low level anyway (e.g., use of bit-shifts) and the necessary conversion takes time and results in a format which requires more space to be stored. So, both for convenience and out of performance considerations, it is frequent that the first approach is followed; despite the fact that this practice is possibly error-prone and a security risk.

Our aim is to make programming of telecom and packet filter applications using high-level languages both easier and more efficient than its counterpart in low-level languages such as C. More specifically, given a functional programming language which has been enriched with a binary data type and a convenient notation to perform pattern matching on binaries, we propose methods to extend a key feature of functional programs, pattern matching, to binary terms.

* Research supported in part by grants from ASTEC, Vetenskapsrådet, Ericsson, and T-Mobile.

D.A. Schmidt (Ed.): ESOP 2004, LNCS 2986, pp. 124–139, 2004.

Doing so is not straightforward for the following two reasons. First, unlike pattern matching on structured terms where arities and argument positions of constructors are statically known, binary pattern matching needs to deal with the fact that binaries have a totally amorphous structure. Second, typical uses of binaries (e.g. in network protocols) are such that certain parts of the binary (typically its headers) encode information about how many parts the remaining binary contains and how these parts are to be interpreted. An effective binary pattern matching scheme has to effectively cater for these uses.

On the other hand, the potential performance advantages of our approach should be clear: indeed, hand-coded pattern matchers, even in C, can hardly compete with those derived automatically using a systematic algorithm, once the sizes of the patterns becomes significant.

This paper presents an adaptive binary pattern matching scheme, based on *decision trees*, that is tailored to the characteristics of binaries in typical applications. The reason we use decision trees is that they result in fast execution (since each constraint on the matching is tested at most once).[1] Our implementation is based on the Erlang/OTP system; a system which is used to develop large telecom applications where binary pattern matching allows implementation of network protocols using high-level specifications.

The structure of the rest of the paper is as follows: the next section overviews a notation for matching binary data against patterns. Although the notation is that of ERLANG, the ideas behind it are generic. After introducing a definition of what binary pattern matching is (Sect. 3), we present an algorithm that constructs a tree automaton from a set of binary patterns (Sect. 4). We then show how to perform effective pruning (Sect. 4.2), how pattern matching can be made adaptive (Sect. 4.3), how redundant tests can be avoided, and how the size of the resulting automaton can be further reduced by taking interferences between patterns into account (Sect. 5). After reviewing related work (Sect. 6), we evaluate the effectiveness of our techniques (Sect. 7), and conclude.

2 Binaries in Erlang

ERLANG's bit syntax allows the user to conveniently construct binaries and match these against binary patterns. A simplified introduction to ERLANG's bit syntax appears below; for more information, see [12,17].

In ERLANG, a binary is written with the syntax `<<Seg`$_1$`,Seg`$_2$`,...,Seg`$_n$`>>` and represents a sequence of machine bits that are byte-aligned. Each of the `Seg`$_i$'s specifies a *segment* of the binary, which represents an arbitrary number of contiguous bits in the binary. Segments are placed next to each other in the same order as they appear in the bit syntax expression.

Each segment expression has the general syntax `Value:Size/Specifiers` where both the `Size` and the `Specifiers` fields can be omitted since there are default values for them; see [12]. The `Value` field must however always be specified. In a binary matching expression, the `Value` can either be an Erlang term (of any type) or an unbound variable. The `Size` field, which denotes the number of bits of the segment, can either be statically

[1] However, since the size of the tree automaton is exponential in the worst case, the full version of this paper [8] also presents an alternative approach to compiling binary pattern matching which is conservative, and more specifically linear, in space.

an integer or a variable that will be bound to an integer. The Specifiers can be used to specify how the segment should be interpreted (e.g., what is its type). For simplicity of presentation, only integer and binary specifiers will be used in this paper; see [12] for the complete set of specifiers. Moreover, a binary type specifier will mean that this segment is viewed as the *tail* (i.e., the complete remaining part) of the binary. Binary tail segments will have no explicit size specified for them.

Binary Matching. The syntax for matching with a binary if Binary is a variable bound to a binary is <<Seg$_1$,Seg$_2$,...,Seg$_n$>> = Binary. The Value$_i$ fields of the Seg$_i$ expressions, which describe each segment, will be matched to corresponding segments in Binary. For example, if the Value$_1$ field in Seg$_1$ contains an unbound variable and the size of this segment is 16, this variable will be bound to the first 16 bits of Binary.

Example 1. As shown below, binaries are often constructed as a sequence of comma-separated unsigned 8 bit integers inside <<>>'s, but pattern matching can select parts of binaries whose size is less than a byte long (and actually there are no byte-alignment restrictions). The ERLANG code:

```
<<A1:3/integer, A2:5/integer, B/binary>> = <<42,43,44>>
```

results in the binding A1=1, A2=10, B=<<43,44>>. Here A1 matches the first three bits. These bits are interpreted as an unsigned, big-endian integer. Similarly, A2 matches the next five bits. B is matched to the rest of the bits of the binary <<42,43,44>>. These bits are interpreted as a binary since the segment has this type specifier.

Example 2. Size fields of segments are not always statically known. This occurs quite often and complicates the pattern matching operation in our context. The code:

```
<<Sz:8/integer, Vsn:Sz/integer, Msg/binary>> = <<16,2,154,11,12>>
```

results in the binding Sz=16, Vsn=666, and Msg=<<11,12>>.

Example 3. Naturally, pattern matching against a binary can occur in a function head or in a case statement just like any other matching operation as in the code below:

```
case Binary of
  <<42:8/integer, X1/binary>> -> X = X1, handle1(X);
  <<Sz:8, V:Sz/integer, X2/binary>> when Sz > 16 -> X = X2, handle2(V,X);
  <<_:8, X3:16/integer, Y:8/integer>> -> X = X3, handle3(X,Y)
end.
```

Here Binary will match the pattern in the first branch of the case statement if its first 8 bits represented as an unsigned integer have the value 42. In this case, X1 (and later X) will be bound to a binary consisting of the rest of the bits of Binary. If this is not the case, then Binary will match the second pattern if the first 8 bits of Binary interpreted as an unsigned integer are greater than 16. Notice that this is a non-linear and guarded binary pattern. Finally, if Binary is exactly 32 bits long, X (through X3) will be bound to an integer consisting of the second and third byte of the Binary (taken in big-endian order). If neither of the patterns match, the whole match expression will fail. On the right, we show three examples of matchings and a failure to match using this code.

Binary	matching of X
<<42,14,15>>	<<14,15>>
<<24,1,2,3,10,20>>	<<10,20>>
<<12,1,2,20>>	258
<<0,255>>	*failure*

3 Binary Pattern Matching Definitions

We assume the usual definition of when two non-binary terms (integers, compound terms, ...) match. A binary pattern matching is defined by a binary term and a set of binary patterns, which is ordered with respect to the priority of the patterns.

In a binary pattern matching compiler, each binary pattern b_i consists of a list of segments $[seg_1, \ldots, seg_n]$ and is associated with a success label which is denoted by $SL(b_i)$.[2] Each segment is represented by a tuple $seg_i = \langle v_i, t_i, p_i, s_i \rangle, i \in \{1, \ldots, n\}$ consisting of a value, a type, a position, and a size field. The value and type fields contain the term in the `Value` field and the type `Specifier` of the corresponding segment, respectively. The size field s_i represents the `Size` of the segment in bits. When the size is statically known, s_i is an integer constant. Otherwise, s_i is either a variable which will be bound to an integer at runtime, or the special don't care variable (denoted as $\_$) which is used when the last segment, seg_n, is of `binary` type without any constraint on its size (cf. the first two binary patterns of Ex. 3). The p_i field denotes the position where segment seg_i starts in the binary. If the size values of all preceding segments are statically known, then p_i is just an integer constant and is defined as $p_i = \sum_{j=1}^{i-1} s_j$. However, the presence of variable-sized segments complicates the calculation of a segment's position. In such cases, we will denote p_i's as $c + V$ where c is the sum of all sizes of preceding segments which are statically known and V is a symbolic representation of the sum of all s_j terms of preceding segments whose values are variables. For example, the binary pattern of Ex. 2 is represented as $[\langle \mathtt{Sz}, \mathtt{integer}, 0, 8 \rangle, \langle \mathtt{Vsn}, \mathtt{integer}, 8, \mathtt{Sz} \rangle, \langle \mathtt{Msg}, \mathtt{binary}, 8{+}\mathtt{Sz}, \_ \rangle]$.

Each binary pattern corresponds to a sequence of *actions* obtained by concatenating the actions of its segments. The actions of each segment generally consist of a size and a match test. Each match test includes an associated read action which is to be performed before the actual match test. These are defined below.

Definition 1 (Size test). *For each segment $seg_i = \langle v_i, t_i, p_i, s_i \rangle$ of a binary pattern $[seg_1, \ldots, seg_n]$, if $s_i \neq \_$, we associate a size test st defined as*

$$st = \begin{cases} \mathtt{size}(=, p_i + s_i) & \textit{if } i = n \\ \mathtt{size}(\geq, p_i + s_i) & \textit{otherwise} \end{cases}$$

Given a binary b, st succeeds if the size of b in bits is equal to (resp. at least) $p_i + s_i$.

Note that no size test is associated with a tail binary segment (a segment where $s_i = \_$). Also, although positions and sizes might not be integer constants statically, in type-correct programs, they will be so at runtime. Thus the second argument of a size test will always be (evaluable to) an integer constant at runtime.

Definition 2 (Read action). *For a segment $\langle v, t, p, s \rangle$, the corresponding read action (denoted* $\mathtt{read}(p, s, t)$*) is as follows: given a binary b, the action reads s bits starting at position p of b, constructs a term of type t out of them, and returns the constructed term. When $s = \_$ the action reads the remaining part of the binary.*

[2] The fail labels are implicitly defined by the order of the patterns; the fail labels of every $b_k, 1 \leq k \leq n-1$ point to b_{k+1} except for the fail label of b_n which points to a *failure* action.

Definition 3 (Match test). *For a segment $\langle v, t, p, s\rangle$, a match test (which is denoted* $\mathtt{match}(v, ra)$ *where* ra *is the corresponding read action) succeeds if the term* r *returned by* ra *matches* v*. If the match test is successful, the variables of* v *get bound to the corresponding subterms of* r*.*

Example 4. Action sequences for the three binary patterns in the case statement of Ex. 3 are shown below:

```
b1 = {size(≥,8), match(42,read(0,8,integer)), match(X1,read(8,_,binary))}
b2 = {size(≥,8), match(Sz,read(0,8,integer)),
      size(≥,8+Sz), match(V,read(8,Sz,integer)), match(X2,read(8+Sz,_,binary))}
b3 = {size(=,32), match(X3,read(8,24,integer)), match(Y,read(24,32,integer))}
```

Note that the above action sequences are optimized. Size tests which are implied by other ones have been removed and match tests which do not influence the binary matching have also been eliminated. For example, without any optimizations, b_3 is:

```
b3 = {size(≥, 8), match(_,read(0,8,integer)),
      size(≥,24), match(X3,read(8,24,integer)),
      size(=,32), match(Y,read(24,32,integer))}
```

Since there is a tight correspondence between segments and action sequences, representing a binary pattern using segments is equivalent to representing it using actions. Since actions are what is guiding the binary pattern matching compilation, we henceforth represent binary patterns using action sequences and use the terms binary patterns and action sequences to mean the same thing.

Definition 4 (Static size equality). *Two sizes* s_1 *and* s_2 *are statically equal (denoted* $s_1 = s_2$*) if they are either the same integer or the same variable.*

Definition 5 (Static position equality). *Two positions* p_1 *and* p_2 *are statically equal (denoted* $p_1 = p_2$*) if their representations are identical (i.e., if they are either the same constant, or they are of the form* $c_1 + V_1$ *and* $c_2 + V_2$ *where* $c_1 = c_2$ *and* V_1 *is the same multiset of variables as* V_2*).*

Definition 6 (Statically equal read actions). *Two read actions* $ra_1 = \mathtt{read}(p_1, s_1, t_1)$ *and* $ra_2 = \mathtt{read}(p_2, s_2, t_1)$ *are statically equal (denoted* $ra_1 = ra_2$*) if* $s_1 = s_2$*,* $p_1 = p_2$*, and* $t_1 = t_2$*.*

Definition 7 (Size test compatibility). *Let* $|b|$ *denote the size of a binary* b*. A size test* $st = \mathtt{size}(op, p+s)$ *where* $op \in \{=, \geq\}$ *is compatible with a binary* b *(denoted* $st \sqsubseteq b$*) if* $(p + s)\ op\ |b|$*. If the condition does not hold, we say that the size test is incompatible with the binary (*$st \not\sqsubseteq b$*).*

Definition 8 (Match test compatibility). *Let* $ra = \mathtt{read}(p, s, t)$ *be a read action. A match test* $mt = \mathtt{match}(v, ra)$ *is compatible with a binary* b *(denoted* $mt \sqsubseteq b$*) if* ra *(or more generally a read action which is statically equal to* ra*) has been performed and the sub-binary of size* s *starting at position* p *of* b *when read as a term of type* t *matches with the term* v*. If the term* v *does not match, we say that the match test is incompatible with the binary (*$mt \not\sqsubseteq b$*).*

We can now formally define what binary pattern matching is. In the following definitions, let B denote a set of binary patterns ordered by their textual priority.

Definition 9 (Instance of binary pattern). *A binary b is an instance of a binary pattern $b_i \in B$ if b is compatible with all the tests of b_i.*

Definition 10 (Binary pattern matching). *A binary pattern $b_i \in B$ matches a binary b if b is an instance of b_i and b is not an instance of any $b_j \in B, j < i$.*

4 From a Set of Binary Patterns to a Tree Automaton

The construction of the tree automaton begins with an ordered set of k binary patterns which have been transformed to the corresponding action sequences $B = \{b_1, \dots, b_k\}$. The construction algorithm, shown below, builds the tree automaton for B and returns its start node. Each node of the automaton consists of an action and two branches (a success and a failure branch) to its children nodes. In interior nodes, the action is a test. In leaf nodes, the action is a goto a success label, or a *failure* action.

Given an action a and a set of action sequences B, the action implicitly creates two sets, B_s and B_f. Action sequences in B_s are sequences from B that either do not contain a, or sequences which are created by removing a from them. B_f are action sequences from B that do not contain a. These two sets are driving the construction of the tree automaton. More specifically, the success and failure branches of an interior node point to subtrees that are created by calling the construction algorithm with B_s and B_f, respectively.

```
Procedure Build(B)
 1. u := new_node()
 2. if B = ∅ then
 3.   u.action := failure
 4. else
 5.   b0 := the action sequence of the
              highest priority pattern in B
 6.   if current_actions(b0) = ∅ then
 7.     u.action := goto(SL(b0))
 8.   else
 9.     a := select_action(B)
10.     u.action := a
11.     Bs := prune_compatible(a, B)
12.     u.success := Build(Bs)
13.     Bf := prune_incompatible(a, B)
14.     u.fail := Build(Bf)
15. return u
```

The tree automaton operates on an incoming binary b. The algorithm that constructs the tree is quite straightforward. A given node u corresponds to a set of patterns that could still match b when u has been reached. If this set is empty, then no match is possible and a fail leaf is created (lines 2–3). When there are still patterns which can match, the action sequence of the highest priority pattern (b_0) is examined. If it is now empty, then a match has been found (lines 5–7). Otherwise, the `select_action` procedure chooses one of the remaining actions a (a size or match test) from an action sequence in B. This is the action associated with the current node. Based on a, procedures `prune_compatible` and `prune_incompatible` construct the B_s and B_f sets described above. The success and failure branches of the node are then obtained by recursively calling the construction algorithm with B_s and B_f, respectively (lines 9–14).

The `select_action` procedure controls the traversal order of patterns, making the pattern matching adaptive. It is discussed in Sect. 4.3. The `prune_*` procedures can be more effective in the amount of pruning that they perform. This is discussed in Sect. 4.2.

Notice that the match tests naturally handle non-linearity in the binary patterns. Also, although not shown here, it is quite easy to extend this algorithm to allow it to handle guarded binary patterns. The only change that needs to be made is to add guard actions to the action sequences.

4.1 Complexity

The worst case for this algorithm is when no conclusions can be drawn to prune actions and patterns from B. In this case, the size of the constructed tree automaton is exponential in the number of actions (segments) in a pattern. The time complexity for the worst case path through this tree is linear in the total number of segments.

4.2 Pruning

Let a be an action of a node. Based on a, procedure `prune_compatible` creates a pruned set of action sequences by removing a (or more generally actions which are implied by a) and action sequences which contain a test a' that will fail if a succeeds. Similarly, procedure `prune_incompatible` creates a pruned set of action sequences by removing action sequences which contain a test a' that will fail if a fails, and actions that succeed if a fails. The functionality of these procedures can be described as follows:

`prune_compatible(`a, B`)` Removes all actions from action sequences in B which can be proven to be compatible with any binary b such that $a \sqsubseteq b$ and all action sequences that contain an action which can be proven to be incompatible with any binary b such that $a \sqsubseteq b$.

`prune_incompatible(`a, B`)` Removes all actions from action sequences in B which can be proven to be compatible with any binary b such that $a \not\sqsubseteq b$ and all action sequences that contain an action which can be proven to be incompatible with any binary b such that $a \not\sqsubseteq b$.

Size test pruning. Using size tests to prune the tree automaton for binary pattern matching is similar to switching on the arity of constructors when performing pattern matching on structured terms. If $=$ were the only comparison operator in size tests, the similarity would be exact. Since in binary pattern matching the size test operator can also be $\geq$ and sizes of segments might not be statically known, the situation in our context is more complicated.

To effectively perform size test pruning we need to setup rules that allow us to infer the compatibility or incompatibility of some size test st_1 with any binary b given that another size test st_2 is either compatible or incompatible with b.

In order to construct these rules we need to describe how size tests can be compared at compile time. Consider a size test, $st = \texttt{size}(op, se)$ where op is a comparison operator and se a size expression. In the general case, the size expression will have the form $c+V$

Table 1. Size pruning rules.

(a) Rules for `prune_compatible`(st, B)

op	op_i	relation	conclusion
$\geq$	$\geq$	$se \geq se_i$	$st_i \sqsubseteq b$
$\geq$	$=$	$se > se_i$	$st_i \not\sqsubseteq b$
$=$	$\geq$	$se \geq se_i$	$st_i \sqsubseteq b$
$=$	$\geq$	$se < se_i$	$st_i \not\sqsubseteq b$
$=$	$=$	$se = se_i$	$st_i \sqsubseteq b$
$=$	$=$	$se \neq se_i$	$st_i \not\sqsubseteq b$

(b) Rules for `prune_incompatible`(st, B)

op	op_i	relation	conclusion
$\geq$	$\geq$	$se_i \geq se$	$st_i \not\sqsubseteq b$
$\geq$	$=$	$se_i \geq se$	$st_i \not\sqsubseteq b$
$=$	$=$	$se = se_i$	$st_i \not\sqsubseteq b$

where c is a constant and V is a multiset of variables. The following definition of how to statically compare size expressions is based on what can be inferred about two different size expressions $c_1 + V_1$ and $c_2 + V_2$, assuming that during run-time, all variables in V_1 and V_2 will be bound to non-negative integers (or else a runtime type exception will occur).

Definition 11 (Comparing size expressions statically). *Let $se_1 = c_1 + V_1$ and $se_2 = c_2 + V_2$ be two size expressions.*

- *se_1 is statically equal to se_2 (denoted $se_1 = se_2$) if $c_1 = c_2$ and V_1 is the same multiset as V_2;*
- *se_1 is statically bigger than se_2 (denoted $se_1 > se_2$) if $c_1 > c_2$ and V_1 is a superset of V_2;*
- *se_1 is statically bigger or equal to se_2 (denoted $se_1 \geq se_2$) if $se_1 > se_2$ or $se_1 = se_2$ or $c_1 = c_2$ and V_1 is a superset of V_2;*
- *se_1 is statically different than se_2 (denoted $se_1 \neq se_2$) if either $se_1 > se_2$ or $se_1 < se_2$.*

Let b be any binary such that a size test $st \sqsubseteq b$ (is compatible with b). In the `prune_compatible`(st, B) procedure we want to prune all size tests st_i such that st_i is contained in some action sequence in B and $st_i \sqsubseteq b$. We also want to prune all action sequences in B that contain a size test st_j such that $st_j \not\sqsubseteq b$. If $st = \texttt{size}(op, se)$ and $st_i = \texttt{size}(op_i, se_i)$ then Table 1(a) presents the conclusion which can be drawn about the compatibility of st_i with b given values for op and op_i and a static comparison of size expressions se and se_i.

Now let b be any binary such that a size test $st \not\sqsubseteq b$ (is incompatible with b). The `prune_incompatible`(st, B) procedure will prune all action sequences in B that contain a size test st_i such that $st_i \not\sqsubseteq b$. Table 1(b) presents when it is possible to infer this size test incompatibility given values for op, op_i, and a static comparison of se and se_i.

The following example illustrates size test pruning.

Example 5. Let $st = \texttt{size}(=, 24 + \texttt{Sz})$ and $B = \{b_1, b_2, b_3, b_4\}$ where:

$$
\begin{aligned}
b_1 &= \{\texttt{size}(=, 24 + \texttt{Sz}), a_{1,2}, \ldots, a_{1,n_1}\} \\
b_2 &= \{\texttt{size}(\geq, 24), a_{2,2}, \ldots, a_{2,n_2}\} \\
b_3 &= \{\texttt{size}(=, 16), \ldots\} \\
b_4 &= \{\texttt{size}(\geq, 32 + \texttt{Sz}), \ldots\}
\end{aligned}
$$

and let $a_{i,j}$ be actions whose size expressions cannot be compared with the size expression of st statically. Then $\texttt{prune\_compatible}(st, B) = \{b'_1, b'_2\}$ where $b'_1 = \{a_{1,2}, \ldots, a_{1,n_1}\}$, and $b'_2 = \{a_{1,2}, \ldots, a_{2,n_2}\}$. Why the size test st is removed from b_1 should be obvious. In b_2, the size test $\texttt{size}(\geq, 24)$ is implied by st (see third row of Table 1(a)) and is removed. Sequences b_3 and b_4 each contain a size test which is false if st succeeds (this is found by looking at rows six and four of Table 1(b)) and are pruned. We also have that $\texttt{prune\_incompatible}(st, B) = \{b_2, b_3, b_4\}$.

Match test pruning. A simple form of match test pruning can be based on the concept of similarity. Let b be a binary and $mt_1 = \texttt{match}(v_1, ra_1)$ and $mt_2 = \texttt{match}(v_2, ra_2)$ be two match tests whose read actions ra_1 and ra_2 are statically equal. If $v_1 = v_2$, then we have the following rules:

$$mt_1 \sqsubseteq b \Rightarrow mt_2 \sqsubseteq b$$
$$mt_1 \not\sqsubseteq b \Rightarrow mt_2 \not\sqsubseteq b$$

If both v_1 and v_2 are constants and $v_1 \neq v_2$, we get the additional rule:

$$mt_1 \sqsubseteq b \Rightarrow mt_2 \not\sqsubseteq b$$

In Sect. 5.3 we describe how to extract more information from the success or failure of a match test by taking interference of actions into account. Doing so, increases the effectiveness of match test pruning.

4.3 Selecting an Action

The `select_action` procedure controls the traversal order of actions and makes the binary pattern matching adaptive. It also allows discussion of the binary matching algorithm without an *a priori* fixed traversal order.

For the binary pattern matching problem, there are constraints on which actions can be selected from the action sequences. A size test can not be chosen unless its size expression can be evaluated to a constant. Similarly, match tests whose read actions have a yet unknown size cannot be selected. More importantly, a match test cannot be selected unless all size tests which precede it have either been selected or pruned. This ensures the safety of performing the read action which a match test contains: otherwise a read action could access memory which lies outside the memory allocated to the binary.

What we are looking for is to select actions which perform effective pruning and thus make the size of the resulting tree automaton small. Since both constructing an optimal decision tree and a minimal order-containing pruned trie are NP-complete problems [9, 5], we employ heuristics. One such heuristic is to select an action which makes the size of the success subtree of a node small. Such actions are defined below.

Definition 12 (Eliminators). *Let $B = \{b_1, \ldots, b_k\}$ be a set of action sequences. A test α (of some $b_j \in B$) is an eliminator of m sequences if exactly m members of B contain a test which will not succeed if α succeeds. A test α is a perfect eliminator if it is an eliminator of $k-1$ sequences. A test α is a good eliminator if it is an eliminator of m sequences and for all $l > m$ there do not exist eliminators of l sequences.*

So, what we are looking for is good eliminators; ideally, for perfect ones. If a perfect eliminator exists each time the `select_action` procedure is called, then the size of the tree automaton will be linear in the total number of actions. Also, the height of the tree (which controls the worst time it takes to find a matching) will be no greater than the number of patterns plus the maximum number of actions in one sequence.

In the absence of perfect eliminators, the heuristics below can be used. Some of them reduce the size of the tree and some the time needed to find a matching.

Eliminator A good eliminator is chosen. As a tie-breaker, a top-down, left-to-right order of selecting good eliminators is followed.

Pruning The action which minimizes the size of the sets of action sequences returned by the `prune_*` procedures is chosen. A top-down, left-to-right order is used as a tie-breaker.

Left-to-Right This is the commonly used heuristic of selecting actions in a top-down, left-to-right fashion. This heuristic does not result in adaptive binary pattern matching, but on the other hand it is typically effective as the traversal order is the one that most programmers would expect (and often program for!); see also [13].

5 Optimizations

The algorithm presented in Sect. 4 is quite inefficient when it comes to the size of the resulting tree automaton. We now present some optimizations that can decrease its size; often very effectively.

5.1 Generating Shorter Action Sequences

Simple ways to avoid unnecessary work are to eliminate size tests which are implied by other ones and to not generate match tests (and their corresponding read actions) for variables that are unused. We have already shown these optimizations in Ex. 4. Another easy way to make the tree more compact is to preprocess the original binary patterns so that they contain fewer segments. Two adjacent segments with constant terms as values can be coalesced into one so that only one match test is generated for them. For example, the pattern `<<0:8, 1:8, B/binary>>` can be source-transformed to the equivalent binary pattern `<<1:16, B/binary>>`.

5.2 Turning the Tree Automaton into a DAG

Creating a directed acyclic graph (DAG) instead of a tree is a standard way to decrease the size of a matching automaton. One possible choice is to construct the tree automaton first, and then use standard FSA minimization techniques to create the optimal DAG. This is however impractical, since it requires that a tree automaton of possibly exponential size is first constructed. Instead, we can use a concept similar to memoization to construct the DAG directly. We simply remember the results we got from calling the `Build` procedure, and if the procedure is called again with the same input argument we return the subtree that was constructed at that time.

Turning a tree into a DAG does not affect the time it takes to perform binary pattern matching. This is evident since the length of paths from the root to each leaf is not changed. It is difficult to formalize the size reduction obtained by this optimization, as it depends on the characteristics of the action sequences and its interaction with action pruning. In general, the more the pruning that the selected actions perform, the harder it is to share subtrees. However, in our experience, turning the tree into a DAG is an effective size-reducing optimization in practice.

5.3 Pruning Based on Interference of Match Tests

Pruning based on match tests (Sect. 4.2) takes place when two match tests contain read actions which are statically equal. We can increase the amount of pruning performed based on match tests by taking interferences between match tests into account. Consider the following example:

Example 6. In binary patterns $b_1 =$ `<<Sz:4,0:12,X:Sz>>` and $b_2 =$ `<<255:8,...>>` there are not any statically equal read actions in match tests. However, it is clear that if the match test associated with the second segment of b_1 succeeds, then b_2 cannot possibly match the incoming binary. This is because these match tests *interfere*. The notion is formalized below.

Definition 13 (Interference). *Let p_1 and p_2 be statically known positions and $p_1 \leq p_2$. Also, let s_1 and s_2 be statically known sizes. Match tests* $\mathtt{match}(v_1, \mathtt{read}(p_1, s_1, t_1))$ *and* $\mathtt{match}(v_2, \mathtt{read}(p_2, s_2, t_2))$ *interfere if $p_1 + s_1 > p_2$. Their common bits are bits in the range $[p_2, \ldots, min(p_2 + s_2, p_1 + s_1)]$.*

For pruning purposes, the concept of interfering match tests is only interesting when both terms v_1, v_2 of the match tests are known. Let us denote the common bits of v_1 and v_2 by v_1' and v_2', respectively.

Definition 14 (Enclosing match test). *Let $mt_1 =$* $\mathtt{match}(v_1, \mathtt{read}(p_1, s_1, t_1))$ *and $mt_2 =$* $\mathtt{match}(v_2, \mathtt{read}(p_2, s_2, t_2))$ *be two match tests which interfere and let $p_1 \leq p_2$. We say that mt_1 encloses mt_2 (denoted $mt_1 \supseteq mt_2$) if $p_1 + s_1 \geq p_2 + s_2$.*

Let mt_1 and mt_2 be match tests which interfere and v_1' and v_2' be their common bits. Then mt_2 will be:

1. compatible with all binaries that mt_1 is compatible with if $v_1' = v_2'$ and $mt_1 \supseteq mt_2$;
2. incompatible with all binaries that mt_1 is compatible with if $v_1' \neq v_2'$;
3. incompatible with all binaries that mt_1 is incompatible with if $mt_2 \supseteq mt_1$ and $v_1' = v_2'$.

The first two rules can be used in the $\mathtt{prune\_compatible}(mt_1, B)$ procedure to prune interfering match tests. Similarly, the last rule can be used to guide the pruning in the $\mathtt{prune\_incompatible}(mt_1, B)$ procedure.

5.4 Factoring Read Actions

To ease exposition of the main ideas, we have thus far presented read actions as tightly coupled with match actions although they need not really be. Indeed, read actions can appear in the action field of tree nodes. Such tree nodes need a success branch only (their failure branch is null). With this as the only change, read actions can also be selected by the `select_action` procedure, statically equal read actions can be factored, and read actions can be moved around in the tree (provided of course that they are still protected by the size test that makes them safe).

Since, especially in native code compilers, accessing memory is quite expensive, one important optimization is to avoid unnecessary read actions. This can be done if there is a read action that is statically equal to a read action which has already been performed. Then the result of the first read action can be saved in some temporary register, and the second read action can be replaced by a use of that register. Our experience is that in practice this optimization significantly reduces the time to perform binary pattern matching.

Also, to reduce code size, standard compiler techniques like *code hoisting* can be used to move a read action to a node in the tree where a statically equal read action will be performed on all successful paths from that node to a leaf. These read actions can then be removed, reducing the code size.

6 Related Work

In functional languages, compilation schemes for efficient pattern matching over structured terms have been developed and deployed for more than twenty years. Their main goal has been to make the right trade-off between time and space costs. The *backtracking automaton* approach [1,15] is *a priori* economical in space usage (because patterns never get compiled more than once) but is inefficient in time (since the same symbols can be inspected several times). This is the approach used in implementations of typed functional languages such as Caml and Haskell. In the context of the Objective-Caml compiler, [10] suggested using exhaustiveness and incompatibility characteristics of patterns to improve the time behavior of backtracking automata. Exhaustiveness is only applicable when constructor-based type definitions are available, and thus cannot be used in binary pattern matching. In our context, a kind of incompatibility-based pruning is obtained by taking advantage of match test interference (Sect. 5.3).

Deterministic tree automata approaches have been proposed before; e.g. [3,14]. Such tree-based approaches guarantee that no constructor symbol is inspected twice, but doing so leads to exponential upper bounds on the automaton size. One way of dealing with this problem is to try to construct an optimal traversal order to minimize the size of the tree. However, since the optimization problem is NP-complete, [3] argues that heuristics should be employed to find near-optimal trees. In the same spirit, [14] also suggests several different heuristics to synthesize an adaptive traversal order that results in a tree automaton of small size. To further decrease the size of the automaton they generate a directed acyclic graph (DAG) automaton by sharing all isomorphic subtrees. Finally, [13] also examines several different match-compilation heuristics (including those of [3,14]) and measures their effects on different benchmarks. However, all these works heavily rely on being able to do a constructor-based decomposition of patterns, and to inspect terms in positions which are known statically.

By exploiting the foreign language interface, an API for a bit stream data structure for Haskell is introduced in [16]. Pattern matching on these bit streams is however not explored. Some of the techniques presented here could likely be used to implement pattern matching on bit streams for Haskell which would allow for a less imperative style of programming. There are however some fundamental differences between our work and [16] as the lazy setting of [16] might restrict the traversal order of tests.

Several packet filtering frameworks have been developed by the networking community. Some of them, e.g., PATHFINDER [2], DPF [6] and BPF+ [4], use the backtracking automaton approach to pattern matching to filter packets. To achieve better performance common prefixes are collapsed in [2,6]. In contrast, [4] employs low level optimizations such as redundant predicate elimination to produce efficient pattern matching code. As far as we know, the tree automaton approach to pattern matching compilation has not been used in packet filters. We intend to investigate the effectiveness of our scheme in a packet filter setting. Finally, [11] proposes an external type system for packet data which allows for type checking of packets and suggests a scheme to use pattern matching based on type refinement to construct efficient packet filters.

7 Some Experiments

In [7], we presented a scheme for efficient just-in-time compilation of BEAM instructions that manipulate binaries to native code.[3] On a set of benchmarks, when executing native code but without pattern matching compilation, speedups ranging from 20% to four times faster compared with BEAM were obtained. With [7] providing an efficient basis for compiling binary instructions to native code, and with adaptive pattern matching complementing nicely that work, we felt there is no need to do extensive benchmarking in this paper. We just report on two issues.

7.1 Impact of Pruning Heuristics and Optimizations

As benchmark programs we selected three different (parts of) actual protocol applications that perform binary pattern matching. The `BER-decode` matching code is quite complicated; it contains 14 different patterns and 10 distinct read actions. `BS-extract` contains just 4 patterns and 11 distinct read actions (each pattern contains a perfect eliminator; adaptive selection is required to benefit from it). The `PPP-config` matching code contains 8 different patterns and 7 distinct read actions. Using these benchmarks, we measured the impact of different heuristics used in the `select_action` function. The Eliminator, Pruning, and Left-to-Right heuristics are as described in Sect. 4.3. Both size (the number of nodes in the resulting DAG) and two time-related aspects of the heuristics are reported: the average (resp. maximum) height of the DAG measured as the average length of paths (resp. longest path) from a start node to a leaf node.

[3] BEAM is the virtual machine of the Erlang/OTP (Open Telecom Platform) system. Native code compilation of binaries is available in Erlang/OTP since Oct. 2002; see www.erlang.org.

Table 2. Impact of heuristics and optimizations.

	`BER-decode`			`BS-extract`			`PPP-config`		
Heuristic	Size	Avg. H	Max H	Size	Avg. H	Max H	Size	Avg. H	Max H
Eliminator	101	15.30	17	28	17.5	19	40	8.73	10
Pruning	74	14.31	17	28	17.5	19	41	8.73	10
Left-to-Right	78	14.36	17	43	17.5	19	46	10.93	16
Read Hoisting	66	15.50	17	22	17.5	19	28	10.90	15

Table 3. Comparison between programs manipulating binary data written in C and in ERLANG.

Program written in	Time
C returning its result as a binary	2220
ERLANG using binary pattern matching	2580
C returning its result as an Erlang term	4110
ERLANG processing the data in the binary represented using a list of integers	41060

In Table 2, the Read Hoisting row refers to an optimization which aggressively uses code hoisting to move read actions up to a node if statically equal read actions exist on at least two paths from that node. Therefore this optimization yields tree automata that are small in size. However, the time properties of these automata are rarely better and actually sometimes worse than those for automata created using the Left-to-Right heuristic. The Eliminator and Pruning heuristics give similar time characteristics for these benchmarks, but it seems that the Pruning heuristic yields automata which are both small in size and with better matching times. As optimizing for time is our current priority, we find the Pruning heuristic to be the most suitable choice. We are currently using it as default.

7.2 Speed of Binary Pattern Matching in Erlang

Speed is critical in programs implementing telecom and network protocols. It is quite common for developers to resort to low-level languages such as C in order to speed up the time-critical parts of their applications, and indeed manipulating bit sequences is considered C's bread and butter. So, we were curious to know how well binary pattern matching in ERLANG compares with manipulating binaries in C.

We found four different versions of the same program whose input is a binary. The benchmark is taken from the ASN.1 library available in the Erlang/OTP distribution. Two versions written in C exist: one which is a stand alone program (first row of Table 3) and one which is used as a linked in C-driver in an application which is otherwise written in ERLANG. The latter thus needs to return its output in the form of an ERLANG term, and a translation step takes place as the last step of the C program. The other two versions are written completely in ERLANG: one manipulates its input as a binary, performs binary pattern matching and returns a result as an ERLANG term for further processing, while the last version receives its input as a list of integers (a representation which could be a reasonable choice if binaries were not part of the language).

As seen in Table 3, showing times in msecs, the stand-alone C program (compiled using `gcc -O3`) is the fastest program but is only about 15% faster than the ERLANG code using adaptive binary pattern matching. When the rest of the application is written in ERLANG, and a translation step in needed for the C program to be used as a linked-in driver, the ERLANG code with binary pattern matching is about 60% faster. Using a list of integers representation rather than a binary data type results in a program with a rather poor performance. It should be mentioned that the ERLANG programs have been run with a rather large heap to avoid garbage collections (which C does not perform).

8 Concluding Remarks

From the performance data in Table 3, it should be clear that enriching a functional programming language with a binary data type and implementing a binary pattern matching compilation scheme such as the ones described in this paper are additions to the language which are worth their while. Indeed, since 2000 when a notation for binary pattern matching was introduced to ERLANG [12], binaries have been heavily used in commercial applications and programmers have often found innovative uses for them.

Our adaptive binary pattern matching compilation scheme will soon find its way into Erlang/OTP R10 (release 10) from Ericsson, and ERLANG programmers will no doubt benefit from it. However, the ideas we presented are generic and as we have shown there is nothing that prevents binaries from being first-class citizens in declarative languages. For this reason, we hope that other high-level programming languages, which employ pattern matching, will also benefit from them.

References

1. L. Augustsson. Compiling pattern matching. In *Functional Programming Languages and Computer Architecture*, number 201 in LNCS, pages 368–381. Springer-Verlag, Sept. 1985.
2. M. Bailey, B. Gopal, M. Pagels, L. Peterson, and P. Sarkar. PATHFINDER: A pattern-based packet classifier. In *Proceedings of USENIX OSDI Symposium*, pages 115–123, Nov. 1994.
3. M. Baudinet and D. MacQueen. Tree pattern matching for ML. Unpublished paper, 1985.
4. A. Begel, S. McCanne, and S. L. Graham. BPF+: Exploiting global data-flow optimization in a generalized packet filter architecture. In *ACM SIGCOMM*, pages 123–134, Aug. 1999.
5. D. Comer and R. Sethi. The complexity of trie index construction. *Journal of the ACM*, 24(3):428–440, July 1977.
6. D. R. Engler and M. F. Kaashoek. DPF: Fast, flexible message demultiplexing using dynamic code generation. In *Proceedings of ACM SIGCOMM*, pages 53–59. Aug. 1996.
7. P. Gustafsson and K. Sagonas. Native code compilation of Erlang's bit syntax. In *Proceedings of ACM SIGPLAN Erlang Workshop*, pages 6–15. ACM Press, Nov. 2002.
8. P. Gustafsson and K. Sagonas. Adaptive pattern matching on binary data. Technical Report, Department of Information Technology, Uppsala University, Sweden, Dec. 2003.
9. L. Hyafil and R. L. Rivest. Constructing optimal binary decision tress is NP-complete. *Information Processing Letters*, 5(1):15–17, May 1976.
10. F. Le Fessant and L. Maranget. Optimizing pattern matching. In *Proceedings of the ACM SIGPLAN International Conference on Functional programming*, pages 26–37. Sept. 2001.
11. P. J. McCann and S. Chandra. Packet types: Abstract specification of network protocol messages. In *Proceedings of ACM SIGCOMM*, pages 321–333. Aug./Sept. 2000.

12. P. Nyblom. The bit syntax - the released version. In *Proceedings of the Sixth International Erlang/OTP User Conference*, Oct. 2000. Available at http://www.erlang.se/euc/00/.
13. K. Scott and N. Ramsey. When do match-compilation heuristics matter? Technical Report CS-2000-13, Department of Computer Science, University of Virginia, May 2000.
14. R. C. Sekar, R. Ramesh, and I. V. Ramakrishnan. Adaptive pattern matching. *SIAM Journal of Computing*, 24(6):1207–1234, Dec. 1995.
15. P. Wadler. Efficient compilation of pattern matching. In S. L. Peyton Jones, editor, *The Implementation of Functional Programming Languages*, chapter 7. Prentice-Hall, 1987.
16. M. Wallace and C. Runciman. The bits between the lambdas: Binary data in a lazy functional language. In *Proceedings of ACM SIGPLAN ISMM*, pages 107–117. ACM Press, Oct. 1998.
17. C. Wikström and T. Rogvall. Protocol programming in Erlang using binaries. In *the Erlang/OTP User Conference*, Oct. 1999. Available at http://www.erlang.se/euc/99/.

Compositional Analysis of Authentication Protocols*

Michele Bugliesi, Riccardo Focardi, and Matteo Maffei

Dipartimento di Informatica, Università Ca' Foscari di Venezia,
Via Torino 155, I-30172 Mestre (Ve), Italy
{michele,focardi,maffei}@dsi.unive.it

Abstract. We propose a new method for the static analysis of entity authentication protocols. We develop our approach based on a dialect of the spi-calculus as the underlying formalism for expressing protocol narrations. Our analysis validates the honest protocol participants against static (hence decidable) conditions that provide formal guarantees of entity authentication. The main result is that the validation of each component is provably sound and fully compositional: if all the protocol participants are successfully validated, then the protocol as a whole guarantees entity authentication in the presence of Dolev-Yao intruders.

1 Introduction

Security protocols are designed to provide diverse security guarantees in possibly hostile environments: typical guarantees include the secrecy of a message exchange between two trusted entities, the freshness and authenticity of a message, the authenticity of a claimed identity, ... and more. The presence of hostile entities makes protocol design complex and often error prone, as shown by many attacks to long standing protocols reported in the literature (see, e.g., [10,13,20,25,26]). In most cases, such attacks dwell on flaws in the protocols' logic, rather than on breaches in the underlying cryptosystem. Indeed, even when cryptography is assumed as a fully reliable building-block, an intruder can engage a number of potentially dangerous actions, notably, intercepting/replaying/forging messages, to break the intended protocol invariants. Formal methods have proved very successful as tools for protocol design and validations. On the one hand, failures to model-check protocols against formal specifications have lead to the discovery of several attacks (see, e.g., [24,26]). On the other hand, static techniques, based on type systems and control-flow analyses have proved effective in providing static guarantees of correctness [1,2,5,16,17].

Overview and main results. Static analysis is also at the basis of our present technique: we target the analysis of (shared-key) *entity authentication* protocols, i.e. protocols that enable one entity to prove its presence and claimed identity to a remote party [14,22]. Our approach is based on a new tagging mechanism for messages that we introduce to support an analysis of the role that certain message components play in the authentication protocol. Based on that, and drawing on our earlier work in [8], we formulate a set of decidable conditions on the protocols' executions that imply formal

* Work partially supported by MIUR project 'Modelli formali per la sicurezza' and EU Contract IST-2001-32617 'Models and Types for Security in Mobile Distributed Systems' (MyThS).

D.A. Schmidt (Ed.): ESOP 2004, LNCS 2986, pp. 140–154, 2004.

guarantees of entity authentication for a large class of protocols. Interestingly, such conditions may be checked by means of a static, and fully compositional, analysis that inspects the protocol participants and the structure of the tagged messages they exchange. The analysis is carried out in isolation on each participant: each validated principal is decreed *locally correct*. Our main result, then, is a *safety theorem* stating that protocols composed of *locally correct* principals are safe, i.e., immune to attacks mounted by any protocol intruder[1]. The safety theorem relies critically on the assumption that the messages exchanged in the protocol are tagged: hence our tags play a static as well a dynamic role, and the safety theorem assumes that the semantics of protocols is itself tagged. While this may be seen as a limitation, our tagging mechanism turns out to be less demanding than those employed to resolve message ambiguities in many existing protocol implementations (cf. §6).

We formalize our technique in a new process calculus, named ρ-spi, that we use to specify the authentication protocols of interest: ρ-spi is a dialect of the spi-calculus [2] and includes a set of authentication-specific constructs inspired by the process calculus *Lysa* [5]. Our approach appears interesting in several respects:

(i) The compositional nature of the analysis makes it applicable for validating unboundedly many protocol sessions: a safety proof for one protocol session is also a safety proof for an unbounded number of sessions;

(ii) The only human effort needed for the analysis is the encoding of the protocol narration in ρ-spi, which in turn requires one to identify the correct tags for the ciphertext components. On the one hand, this is a relatively straightforward task; on the other hand, we argue that stating the purpose of message components explicitly in the tags represents a good practice for the design of robust protocols.

(iii) Even though we focus on shared-key authentication protocols, our approach is fairly general and can easily be extended to deal with a wider class of authentication protocols (e.g. based on public-key cryptography).

Structure of the paper. §2 motivates and illustrates our mechanism for the tagging of messages. §3 introduces ρ-spi and its operational semantics. §4 gives a formal description of our static analysis, and its main properties. §5 illustrates the analysis with a simple example. §6 concludes the presentation with final remarks.

2 Tagged Messages

A typical source of flaws in security protocols, and specifically in authentication protocols, is a poor interpretation of messages, by which certain messages are believed to convey more guarantees than they actually do. Prudent protocol engineering principles [3] suggest instead that "every message should say what it means, i.e., its interpretation should depend only on its content". A simple instance of a message exchange that fails to comply with this principle is the one-step protocol $A \to B : \{M\}_{K_{AB}}$. Here *Alice* is sending to *Bob* the message M encrypted with a long-term key shared between them.

[1] We implicitly appeal to a Dolev-Yao intruder model [11]: intruders may intercept, reply and forge new messages, but never decrypt messages without knowing the corresponding keys.

When Bob receives the message, he could be misled into believing that the message has been generated by Alice since it is encrypted with a key that only Alice (besides Bob himself) knows. However, this is not true if Bob previously ran the same protocol with Alice (with exchanged roles). In that case, the following, well-known, *reflection attack* could be exploited by an intruder E:

$$a)\; B \to E(A) : \{M\}_{K_{AB}} \qquad\qquad b)\; E(A) \to B : \{M\}_{K_{AB}}$$

In the first run a, E pretends to be A (denoted with $E(A)$) and intercepts the message sent by Bob; in the second run b, $E(A)$ replays the same message back to Bob. As a consequence, B erroneously interprets his own message as sent by Alice. The problem is that Bob is assuming that the message has been generated by Alice without that being explicitly indicated in the message. A simple solution is to provide this additional information within the message, as in $A \to B : \{A, M\}_{K_{AB}}$, where the first component now signals that A is the 'claimant' of the protocol. Our approach is best understood as a generalization of this idea: we envision a tagging mechanism for messages that makes the interpretation of certain, critical message components unambiguous. The untagged part of a message forms the message's payload, while the tagged components include entity identifiers, tagged with Id, session keys, tagged with Key, and nonces (quantities generated for the purpose of being recent, or *fresh*). Nonce tags are more elaborate, as they convey information on the role that nonces play in the authentication protocol: Claim, in messages authenticating a claimant, Verif, in messages specifying an intended verifier, or Owner in messages authenticating a session key.

To motivate, consider a message $\{A, N, M\}_{K_{BS}}$ encrypted under a long-term key K_{BS} shared by a principal B and a server S. A naive tagging of this message, such as one signaling that A is an identifier, N a nonce, and M the payload would still leave several, reasonable, interpretations of the function of this message: (i) B is asking S to authenticate with A; (ii) S is telling B that A wants to authenticate with him; and (iii) S is telling B that M is or contains a fresh session key shared with A. Our nonce tags eliminate such ambiguity: the tagging $\{A : \mathsf{Id}, N : \mathsf{Claim}, M\}_{K_{BS}}$ enforces interpretation (i), while the taggings $\{A : \mathsf{Id}, N : \mathsf{Verif}, M\}_{K_{BS}}$ and $\{A : \mathsf{Id}, N : \mathsf{Owner}, M : \mathsf{Key}\}_{K_{BS}}$ enforce interpretations (ii) and (iii), respectively.

3 The ρ-Spi Calculus

The ρ-spi calculus derives from the spi calculus [2], and inherits many of the features of *Lysa*, a version of the spi calculus proposed in [5] for the analysis of authentication protocols. ρ-spi differs from both calculi in several respects: it incorporates the notion of tagged message exchange from [8], it provides new authentication-specific constructs, and primitives for declaring process identities and (shared) long-term keys.

Syntax. The syntax of the calculus is presented in Table 1. We presuppose two countable sets: $\mathcal{N}$, of names and $\mathcal{V}$ of variables. We reserve a, b, k, m, n for names and x, y, z for variables. Both names and variables can be tagged, noted $n : C$ and $x : C$, respectively. Tags, denoted by C, are a special category of names and include roles (the three special names Claim, Owner, Verif), the identity tag Id and the session key tag Key. *Identities*

Table 1. The syntax of ρ-spi calculus.

Notation: d ranges over untagged names and variables, I over identity labels, D over, possibly tagged, names and variables

P, Q ::= *Processes*		S ::= *Sequential processes*	
$I \rhd S$	(principal)	$\mathbf{0}$	(nil)
$I \rhd !S$	(replication)	$\mathsf{in}(D_1, \dots, D_m).S$	(input)
$P \mid Q$	(composition)	$\mathsf{out}(D_1, \dots, D_m).S$	(output)
let k = $\mathsf{key}(I_1, I_2).P$	(key assignment)	$\mathsf{new}(n).S$	(restriction)
		decrypt x as $\{D_1, \dots, D_m\}_d.S$	(decryption)
		encrypt $\{D_1, \dots, D_m\}_d$ as $x.S$	(encryption)
		$\mathsf{run}(I_1, I_2).S$	(run)
		$\mathsf{commit}(I_1, I_2).S$	(commit)

$\mathcal{ID}$ are a subset of names, further partitioned into *principals* $\mathcal{I}_\mathcal{P}$, ranged over A and B, and *trusted third parties* (TTPs) $\mathcal{I}_\mathcal{T}$, ranged over by T.

Processes (or *protocols*), ranged over by P, Q are formed as parallel composition of principals. To allow the sharing of long-term keys among principals, we provide ρ-spi with let-bindings as in let $k = \mathsf{key}(I_1, I_2).P$ to declare (and bind) the long-term key k shared between I_1 and I_2 in the scope P. Each principal is a sequential process with an associated identity, noted $I \rhd S$. The replicated form $I \rhd !S$ indicates an arbitrary number of copies of S associated with identity I.

Sequential processes may never fork into parallel components: this assumption helps assign unique identities to (sequential) processes, and involves no significant loss of expressive power as protocol principals are typically specified as sequential processes, possibly sharing some long-term keys. The sequential process $\mathbf{0}$ is the null process that does nothing, as usual. Process $\mathsf{new}(n).S$ generates a fresh name n local to S. The constructs for input, output and decryption are essentially the same as in the calculus *Lysa*. In particular, we presuppose a unique (anonymous) public channel, the network, from/to which all principals, including intruders, read/send messages. Similarly to *Lysa*, our input and decryption constructs may test part of the message read (decrypted), by pattern-matching. The pattern matching mechanism is so defined as to ensure that untagged patterns only match untagged messages, while tagged patterns only match tagged messages (provided that the tags also match). Accordingly, the pattern x matches the message n (and binds x to n) but it does not match n : Claim (as x is untagged, while n : Claim is tagged). Similarly, x : Claim matches n : Claim but does not match n : Verif.

Distinctive of ρ-spi is the presence of an explicit construct for encryption: process encrypt $\{D_1, \dots, D_m\}_d$ as $x.S$ binds variable x to the encrypted message $\{D_1, \dots, D_m\}_d$ in the continuation S. The syntactic structure of ρ-spi requires all the encrypted messages to be explicitly formed in an encryption prefix, and forbids ciphertexts to be sent directly on the output channel. These restrictions are useful for our analysis, as they ease the reasoning based on the structural inspection of the encrypted messages of a protocol. Finally, the process forms $\mathsf{run}(I_1, I_2).S$ and $\mathsf{commit}(I_1, I_2).S$ declare that the sequential process I_1 is starting, respectively committing, a protocol session with I_2. These constructs are used to check the *correspondence assertions* as done in [16].

Table 2. A sample protocol narration ρ-spi

Protocol	$\triangleq$ let k_{AB} = key$(A, B)(A \triangleright$ *Initiator*$(A, B) \mid B \triangleright$ *Responder*$(B, A))$
Initiator(A,B)	$\triangleq$ new(m).in(x).run(A, B).encrypt$\{x, m\}_{k_{AB}}$ as y.out(y)
Responder(B, A)	$\triangleq$ new(n_B).out(n_B).in(y).decrypt y as $\{n_B, z\}_{k_{AB}}$.commit(B, A)

We use a number of notation conventions. The restriction operator is a binder for names, while the input and decryption prefixes are binders for the variables that occur in components D_i; in all cases the scope of the binders is the continuation process. The notions of free/bound names and variables arise as expected.

Example 1. We illustrate ρ-spi with a simple (flawed) authentication protocol:

$$1)\ B \to A : n_B \qquad 2)\ A \to B : \{n_B, m\}_{k_{AB}}$$

We assume k_{AB} to be known only by A and B and n_B to be a fresh nonce generated by B. The intention of the protocol is to give guarantee to B that the last message has been (recently) generated by A as only A should be able to encrypt the freshly generated nonce n_B. This protocol can be formalized in our calculus as shown in Table 2. Process $Initiator$, generates a fresh message $m \in \mathcal{N}$. After receiving x, it signals the start of a new authentication run with B, encrypts x and m with the long term key k_{AB}, and then sends out the encrypted message. Similarly, *Responder* generates a fresh nonce n_B and sends it out. Then, it reads y from the net and decrypts it with the long term key k_{AB}, checking the nonce n_B (through the pattern-matching mechanism of decryption). If the match is successful, the variable z gets bound to a message (from A) and the principal commits through commit(B, A). Notice that we are only modeling one protocol session. However, as we will see, multiple sessions can be easily achieved by just replicating the $Initiator$ and *Responder* processes.

Operational Semantics. We define the operational semantics of ρ-spi in terms of *traces*, after [6], and formalize it by means of a transition relation between *configurations*, i.e., pairs $\langle s, P\rangle$, where $s \in Act^*$ is a trace, P is a (closed) process. Each transition $\langle s, P\rangle \longrightarrow \langle s :: \alpha, P'\rangle$ simulates one computation step in P and records the corresponding action in the trace. The transitions involving a sequential process preserve the identity identifiers associated with the process, as in $\langle s, I \triangleright \pi.S\rangle \longrightarrow \langle s :: \alpha, I \triangleright S\rangle$, where α is the action corresponding to the prefix π. The transitions, in Table 3, are mostly standard. As in companion transition systems, see, e.g. [7], we identify processes up to renaming of bound variables and names, i.e., up to α-equivalence. Moreover we assume two infinite sets of bound names and free names so that bound names are distinct from free names and not touched by substitutions. The INPUT rule requires that any messages read by a process must be computable using the output generated so far using the available keys. The rules for message manipulation formalize the power of a Dolev-Yao intruder. Rule ENV provides the environment with the power of generating a new bound name not occurring in the trace.

Table 3. Transition System for ρ-spi

Transition rules: $P[M/x]$ is the result of substituting M for all the free occurrences of x in P, and define $P[M : C/x : C] \triangleq P[M/x]$; the category M of *Messages* is defined by the following productions: $M ::= x \mid n \mid \{M_1, \ldots, M_m\}_M \mid M : C$; bn($s$) is the set of bound names in s; the symmetric rule of PAR is omitted.

REPLICATION
$$\langle s, I \triangleright !S\rangle \rightarrow \langle s, I \triangleright S | I \triangleright !S\rangle$$

PAR
$$\frac{\langle s, P\rangle \rightarrow \langle s', P'\rangle}{\langle s, P|Q\rangle \rightarrow \langle s', P'|Q\rangle}$$

RES
$$\frac{n \notin \text{bn}(s)}{\langle s, I \triangleright \mathsf{new}(n).S\rangle \rightarrow \langle s :: I \triangleright \mathit{new}(n)\,, I \triangleright S\rangle}$$

RUN
$$\langle s, A \triangleright \mathsf{run}(A, B).S\rangle \rightarrow \langle s :: \mathit{run}(A, B), A \triangleright S\rangle$$

COMMIT
$$\langle s, A \triangleright \mathsf{commit}(A, B).S\rangle \rightarrow \langle s :: \mathit{commit}(A, B), A \triangleright S\rangle$$

INPUT
$$\frac{\forall i = 1, \ldots, m \quad s \vdash M_i \quad D_i \text{ matches } M_i}{\langle s, I \triangleright \mathsf{in}(D_1, \ldots, D_m).S\rangle \rightarrow \langle s :: I \triangleright \mathit{in}(M_1, \ldots, M_m), I \triangleright S\,[M_1/D_1, \ldots M_m/D_m]\rangle}$$

OUTPUT
$$\langle s, I \triangleright \mathsf{out}(M_1, \ldots, M_m).S\rangle \rightarrow \langle s :: I \triangleright \mathit{out}(M_1, \ldots, M_m), I \triangleright S\rangle$$

KEY
$$\frac{k \notin \text{bn}(s)}{\langle s, \mathsf{let}\ k = \mathsf{key}(I_1, I_2).P\rangle \rightarrow \langle s :: \mathit{key}(k, I_1, I_2), P\rangle}$$

DECRYPTION
$$\frac{\forall i = 1, \ldots, m \quad D_i \text{ matches } M_i \quad \mathsf{key}(M, I_1, I_2) \in s \Rightarrow I \in \{I_1, I_2\}}{\langle s, I \triangleright \mathsf{decrypt}\{M_1, \ldots, M_m\}_M \ \mathsf{as}\ \{D_1, \ldots, D_m\}_M.S\rangle \rightarrow \langle s :: I \triangleright \mathit{dec}\{M_1, \ldots, M_m\}_M, I \triangleright S\,[M_i/D_i]\rangle}$$

ENCRYPTION
$$\frac{\mathsf{key}(M, I_1, I_2) \in s \Rightarrow I \in \{I_1, I_2\}}{\langle s, I \triangleright \mathsf{encrypt}\{M_1, \ldots, M_m\}_M \ \mathsf{as}\ x.S\rangle \rightarrow \langle s :: I \triangleright \mathit{enc}\{M_1, \ldots, M_m\}_M, I \triangleright S\,[\{M_1, \ldots, M_m\}_M/x]\rangle}$$

Message manipulation rules: required by rule INPUT.

AX
$$\frac{I \triangleright \mathit{out}(M_1, \ldots, M_m) \in s}{s \vdash M_l \quad l = 1 \ldots m}$$

TAG
$$\frac{s \vdash M}{s \vdash M : C}$$

UNTAG
$$\frac{s \vdash M : C}{s \vdash M}$$

ENV
$$\frac{n \notin \text{bn}(s)}{s \vdash n}$$

DEC
$$\frac{s \vdash \{M_1, \ldots, M_m\}_M \qquad s \vdash M}{s \vdash M_l \quad l = 1 \ldots m}$$

ENC
$$\frac{s \vdash M_l \quad l = 1, \ldots, m \qquad s \vdash M}{s \vdash \{M_1, \ldots, M_m\}_M}$$

Definition 1 (Traces). *The set $T(P)$ of traces of process P is the set of all the traces that may be generated by a finite sequence of transitions from the configuration $\langle \epsilon, P\rangle$. Formally, $T(P) = \{s \mid \exists P' \text{ s.t. } \langle \epsilon, P\rangle \longrightarrow^* \langle s, P'\rangle\}$*

The notion of safety is standard (cf. [16]) and based on correspondence assertions. We say that a trace is *safe* if every $commit(B, A)$ is preceded by a distinct $run(A, B)$.

Definition 2 (Safety). A trace s is safe if and only if whenever $s = s_1 :: commit(B, A) :: s_2$, then $s_1 = s_1' :: run(A, B) :: s_1''$, and $s_1' :: s_1'' :: s_2$ is safe. A process P is safe if, $\forall s \in T(P)$, s is safe.

Example 2. We look again at the protocol of Example 1, and now consider a multiple-session version of the protocol, with A and B running both as Initiator and as Responder: the new version of the protocol is subject to the following, well-known, *reflection* attack.

1.a) $B \rightarrow E(A) : n_B$	2.a) $B \rightarrow E(A) : \{m, n_B\}_{k_{AB}}$
1.b) $E(A) \rightarrow B : n_B$	2.b) $E(A) \rightarrow B : \{m, n_B\}_{k_{AB}}$

We show that the attack is captured by our notion of safety. As we mentioned earlier, we can model multiple sessions, directly by replication. For the protocol in question, this amounts to analyzing the following process:

$$\begin{aligned} Protocol_2 \triangleq \ & \mathsf{let}\ k_{AB} = \mathsf{key}(A, B).\ (A \triangleright !Initiator(A, B)\ |A \triangleright !Responder(A, B))| \\ & B \triangleright !Responder(B, A)\ |B \triangleright !Initiator(B, A)) \end{aligned}$$

where A and B run both as Initiator and as Responder (the two processes $Initiator(B, A)$ and $Responder(A, B)$ model B running as Initiator and A running as Responder, respectively). Consider now the following trace for $Protocol_2$:

$$\begin{gathered} \text{key}(k_{AB}, A, B) :: \mathbf{B} \triangleright \text{new}(m) :: B \triangleright \text{new}(n_B) :: B \triangleright \text{out}(n_B) :: \mathbf{B} \triangleright \text{in}(n_B) :: \text{run}(\mathbf{B}, \mathbf{A}) :: \\ \mathbf{B} \triangleright \text{enc}\{n_B, m\}_{k_{AB}} :: \mathbf{B} \triangleright \text{out}(\{n_B, m\}_{k_{AB}}) :: B \triangleright \text{in}(\{n_B, m\}_{k_{AB}}) :: \\ B \text{ dec } \{n_B, m\}_{k_{AB}} :: \text{commit}(B, A) \end{gathered}$$

where B is running as initiator instead of A (as pointed out in bold font). The trace is easily seen to be unsafe, as commit(B, A) is not matched by any run(A, B). Indeed, B is running the protocol with himself while A is doing nothing. Interestingly, the unsafe trace corresponds to the attack displayed above.

4 A Compositional Proof Technique

The proof technique we propose applies to protocol narrations that may be coded as ρ-spi terms of the form $\mathbf{keys}(k_1, \ldots, k_n).(I_1 \triangleright ! S_1 \ | \ \ldots \ | \ I_m \triangleright ! S_m)$, where $\mathbf{keys}(k_1, \ldots, k_n)$ represents a sequence of let binding for the long-term keys $k_1, \ldots, k_n$. As we noted earlier, the protocols of interest may directly be represented as processes in the above form: hence there is no significant loss of expressive power in our choice of a specific process format. The analysis proceeds by examining each process $\mathbf{keys}(k_1, \ldots, k_n).I_i \triangleright S_i$, and attempts to validate S_i under the key assignment determined by $\mathbf{keys}(k_1, \ldots, k_n)$.

4.1 Proof Rules

The proof rules (tables 4 and 5) derive judgments of the form $I; \Gamma; \Pi \vdash S$ validating the sequential process S relative to the identity I and the two environments Γ and Π. The history environment Π traces the ordered list of encryptions, decryptions, run and key assignment events performed by the party in question. The nonce environment Γ holds the nonces that the party generates. A nonce is first included in Γ as *unchecked*, when it is introduced by a new prefix. Subsequently, the nonce may be *checked* by pattern matching, and marked as such: the proof rules are so defined as to ensure that each nonce may be checked at most once, as desired. We make a few, important, assumptions

Table 4. Local correctness: Principal and TTP rules

$\Pi(x) = enc\{\dots\}_d$ indicates that $x \mapsto enc\{\dots\}_d \in \Pi$, and similarly for the other entries. We write $\Pi(\bullet) = enc\{\dots\}_d$ to mean that there exists x such that $\Pi(x) = enc\{\dots\}_d$.

Claimant and Verifier Rules.

AUTHENTICATE CLAIM
$$\frac{A;\Gamma,n:\text{checked};\Pi\vdash S \qquad \Pi(\bullet)=dec\{B:\mathsf{Id},n:\mathsf{Claim},\dots\}_k \qquad \Pi(k)\in\{key(A,T),key(A,B)\}}{A;\Gamma,n:\text{unchecked};\Pi\vdash \mathsf{commit}(A,B).S}$$

AUTHENTICATE OWNER
$$\frac{\begin{array}{c}A;\Gamma,n:\text{checked};\Pi\vdash S \qquad \Pi(\bullet)=dec\{B:\mathsf{Id},n:\mathsf{Owner},y:\mathsf{Key},\dots\}_k \qquad \Pi(k)=key(A,T)\\ \Pi(\bullet)=dec\{D_1,\dots,D_m\}_y \qquad (\Pi(\bullet)=enc\{D'_1,\dots,D'_m\}_{y'} \text{ implies } \exists i \text{ s.t. } D'_i \text{ does not match } D_i)\end{array}}{A;\Gamma,n:\text{unchecked};\Pi\vdash \mathsf{commit}(A,B).S}$$

CLAIMANT
$$\frac{A;\Gamma;\Pi,B\mapsto run,y\mapsto enc\{A:\mathsf{Id},x:\mathsf{Claim}\}_k\vdash S \qquad \Pi(k)=key(A,B)}{A;\Gamma;\Pi,B\mapsto run\vdash \mathsf{encrypt}\{A:\mathsf{Id},x:\mathsf{Claim},\dots\}_k \text{ as } y.S}$$

VERIFIER
$$\frac{A;\Gamma;\Pi,B\mapsto run,y\mapsto enc\{B:\mathsf{Id},x:\mathsf{Verif}\}_k\vdash S \qquad \Pi(k)=\mathrm{key}(A,T)}{A;\Gamma;\Pi,B\mapsto run\vdash \mathsf{encrypt}\{B:\mathsf{Id},x:\mathsf{Verif},\dots\}_k \text{ as } y.S}$$

OWNER
$$\frac{\begin{array}{c}A;\Gamma;\Pi,B\mapsto run,y\mapsto enc\{D_1,\dots,D_m\}_x\vdash S\\ \Pi(\bullet)=dec\{B:\mathsf{Id},n:\mathsf{Owner},x:\mathsf{Key},\dots\}_k \qquad \Pi(k)=key(A,T)\end{array}}{A;\Gamma;\Pi,B\mapsto run\vdash \mathsf{encrypt}\{D_1,\dots,D_m\}_x \text{ as } y.S}$$

RUN
$$\frac{A;\Gamma;\Pi,B\mapsto run\vdash S}{A;\Gamma;\Pi\vdash \mathsf{run}(A,B).S}$$

TTP Rules.

TTP FORWARD & CHECK
$$\frac{\begin{array}{c}T;\Gamma,n:\text{checked};\Pi,y\mapsto enc\{A:\mathsf{Id},x:\mathsf{Claim}\}_{k_{BT}}\vdash S\\ \Pi(\bullet)=dec\{B:\mathsf{Id},n:\mathsf{Verif},\dots\}_{k_{AT}} \qquad \Pi(k_{BT})=key(B,T) \qquad \Pi(k_{AT})=key(A,T)\end{array}}{T;\Gamma,n:\text{unchecked};\Pi\vdash \mathsf{encrypt}\ \{A:\mathsf{Id},x:\mathsf{Claim},\dots\}_{k_{BT}} \text{ as } y.S}$$

TTP FORWARD
$$\frac{\begin{array}{c}T;\Gamma;\Pi,y\mapsto enc\{A:\mathsf{Id},x:\mathsf{Claim}\}_{k_{BT}}\vdash S\\ \Pi(\bullet)=dec\{B:\mathsf{Id},x:\mathsf{Verif},\dots\}_{k_{AT}} \qquad \Pi(k_{BT})=key(B,T) \qquad \Pi(k_{AT})=key(A,T)\end{array}}{T;\Gamma;\Pi\vdash \mathsf{encrypt}\ \{A:\mathsf{Id},x:\mathsf{Claim},\dots\}_{k_{BT}} \text{ as } y.S}$$

TTP DISTRIBUTE
$$\frac{T;\Gamma;\Pi,y\mapsto enc\{A:\mathsf{Id},x:\mathsf{Owner},k_s:\mathsf{Key}\}_k\vdash S}{T;\Gamma;\Pi\vdash \mathsf{encrypt}\ \{A:\mathsf{Id},x:\mathsf{Owner},k_s:\mathsf{Key},\dots\}_k \text{ as } y.S}$$

which we leave implicit in the rules to avoid cluttering the notation. The environments Γ and Π may contain at most one binding for each name (key, nonce) or variable in their domain: this may require alpha renaming on the processes being analyzed. In addition, all the output or encrypted tuples as well as all the tuples of input or decryption patterns occurring in the rules are assumed to contain at most one component with tag Id, at most one component with tag $R \in \{\mathsf{Claim},\mathsf{Verif},\mathsf{Owner}\}$ and at most one component with tag Key. The relative order among the encrypted elements is immaterial.

Table 5. Local Correctness: Generic Rules

NIL
$$\frac{}{I;\Gamma;\Pi \vdash \mathbf{0}}$$

NEW
$$\frac{I;\Gamma,n:\text{unchecked};\Pi \vdash S \qquad n \text{ fresh in } \Gamma}{I;\Gamma;\Pi \vdash \mathsf{new}(n).S}$$

INPUT
$$\frac{I;\Gamma;\Pi \vdash S}{I;\Gamma;\Pi \vdash \mathsf{in}(\ldots).S}$$

OUTPUT
$$\frac{I;\Gamma;\Pi \vdash S}{I;\Gamma;\Pi \vdash \mathsf{out}(\ldots).S}$$

ENCRYPTION
$$\frac{\begin{array}{c}I;\Gamma;\Pi.y \mapsto enc\{d_1,\ldots,d_m\}_d \vdash S \\ \Pi(\bullet) = dec\{\ldots,d:\mathsf{Key},\ldots\}_k \text{ implies } \Pi = \Pi'.B \mapsto run.x \mapsto enc\{\ldots\}_d, \Pi''\end{array}}{I;\Gamma;\Pi \vdash \mathsf{encrypt}\{d_1,\ldots,d_m\}_d \text{ as } y.S}$$

DECRYPTION
$$\frac{I;\Gamma;\Pi, y \mapsto dec\{D_1,\ldots,D_m\}_d \vdash S}{I;\Gamma;\Pi \vdash \mathsf{decrypt}\ y \text{ as } \{D_1,\ldots,D_m\}_d.S}$$

The first two rules in Tables 4 formalize the two possible ways for a principal A to authenticate another principal B. Specifically, rule (AUTHENTICATE CLAIM) states that A may legally commit (hence authenticate) B only if A has previously generated a nonce n and decrypted a message $\{B : \mathsf{Id}, n : \mathsf{Claim}\ldots\}_k$ (with the same nonce) with k shared either with T or with B. Rule (AUTHENTICATE OWNER), in turn, states that A may commit B if she has decrypted (i) a message $\{B : \mathsf{Id}, n : \mathsf{Owner}, y : \mathsf{Key}, \ldots\}_k$, encrypted by a TTP and including a fresh session key y owned by B and nonce n that A previously generated; and (ii) at least one message $\{D_1, \ldots, D_m\}_y$ that she did not generate. The first decryption guarantees that the session key y is fresh and shared by A and B; then, with the second decryption she is guaranteed that the message comes from B. Since the encryption key is fresh, so must be the message, and A may safely authenticate B.

The authentication guarantees we just discussed require a very careful use of the role tags attached to the encrypted message components. In particular, the message $\{B : \mathsf{Id}, n : \mathsf{Claim}, \ldots\}_k$ should be generated only if B is indeed willing to authenticate with A; similarly, $\{B : \mathsf{Id}, n : \mathsf{Owner}, k_s : \mathsf{Key}, \ldots\}_k$ should only be generated if k_s is a fresh session key shared between A and B. This intended use of role tags is enforced by the remaining rules in Table 4, which we comment below.

Rules (CLAIMANT), (VERIFIER) and (OWNER) formalize the ways in which A may declare her willingness to authenticate with B. In particular, in rule (CLAIMANT), A may request B to authenticate herself as claimant by sending a message $\{A : \mathsf{Id}, x : \mathsf{Claim}, \ldots\}_k$ directly to B using a long-term key k she shares with B. In an ideal protocol run, x is intended to be a nonce sent as a challenge by B, that B will check with (AUTHENTICATE CLAIM). On the other hand, rule (CLAIMANT) in itself does not impose any condition on x as it is B, rather than A, which is in charge of checking the nonce for the purpose of authentication.

In rule (VERIFIER), A may request a TTP T to authenticate herself with B as verifier, by sending a message $\{B : \mathsf{Id}, x : \mathsf{Verif}, \ldots\}_k$ to T using a long-term key k shared with

T. The role Verif informs T about A's intention of authenticating with someone else (B), while x is again meant to represent the challenge, originated by T.

In rule (OWNER), A may send a message $\{D_1, \dots, D_m\}_y$ to confirm to have received the fresh session key y, provided that (i) she has previously decrypted a message $\{B : \mathsf{Id}, n : \mathsf{Owner}, y : \mathsf{Key}, \dots\}_k$ originated by a TTP T and declaring that y is a fresh key shared with B, and (ii) she has previously performed a run with B.

The three rules all validate the start of new runs. Correspondingly, they all require A to have previously marked the start of a run by issuing run(A, B), with rule (RUN). The *run* event must be the last action performed, to guarantee that these rules are applied only once for each protocol run.

Rules (TTP FORWARD & CHECK), (TTP FORWARD) and (TTP DISTRIBUTE) govern the behavior of TTPs. In rule (TTP FORWARD & CHECK), T generates a message $\{A : \mathsf{Id}, x : \mathsf{Claim}, \dots\}_{k_{BT}}$ if it has previously decrypted (and checked the nonce n of) a message of the form $\{B : \mathsf{Id}, n : \mathsf{Verif}, \dots\}_{k_{AT}}$, with k_{AT} and k_{BT} shared with A and B respectively.

In rule (TTP FORWARD), T may generate a message $\{A : \mathsf{Id}, x : \mathsf{Claim}, \dots\}_{k_{BT}}$ if it has previously decrypted (without checking the nonce) a message of the form $\{B : \mathsf{Id}, x : \mathsf{Verif}, \dots\}_{k_{AT}}$ (again k_{AT} and k_{BT} are shared with A and B); notice that x is forwarded to B so that B can check the freshness of the first message.

Finally, in rule (TTP DISTRIBUTE), T declares new session keys through messages of the form $\{A : \mathsf{Id}, x : \mathsf{Owner}, k_s : \mathsf{Key}, \dots\}_k$.

The rules in Table 5 complete the axiomatization. Rules (NEW), (OUTPUT), (KEY) and (INPUT) are standard. Rules (DECRYPTION) and (ENCRYPTION) handle the cases of the corresponding constructs in which none of the rules in Table 4 apply. In fact, the rule (ENCRYPTION) does overlap with (OWNER) in case of encryptions with session keys: this is safe only if the start of the authentication session has previously been asserted (with a *run* event), in which case (OWNER) must have previously been applied for another encryption with the same session key. The safety check is implemented by requiring that the two consecutive bindings $A \mapsto \mathrm{run}(B).x \mapsto enc\{\dots\}_d$ be part of the history environment Π.

4.2 Safety Theorem

The safety proof for a protocol requires further hypotheses on the way that long-term and session keys are circulated among principals and trusted third parties. Specifically, given a process $\mathbf{keys}(k_1, \dots, k_n).I \rhd S$, we make the following assumptions: (a) long-term keys are never circulated in clear or within encrypted messages; (b) only principals (not TTP's) may receive session keys, without leaking them; and (c) fresh session keys are only distributed by TTP's at most to two parties, only once. When these assumptions are satisfied, we say that $I \rhd S$ is $\{k_1, \dots, k_n\}$-safe.

Definition 3 (Local Correctness). Let P be the process $\mathbf{keys}(k_1, \dots, k_n).I \rhd S$, with k_i shared between I_i and J_i. We say that P is *locally correct* iff $I \rhd S$ is $\{k_1, \dots, k_n\}$-safe and the judgment $I; \varnothing; \Pi_{k_1,\dots,k_n} \vdash S$ is derivable, for $\Pi_{k_1,\dots,k_n} = k_1 \mapsto key(I_1, J_1), \dots, k_n \mapsto key(I_n, J_n)$.

Table 6. A variant of the ISO Two-steps Unilateral Authentication Protocol

$Protocol_{ISO} \triangleq \mathsf{let}\ k_{AB} = \mathsf{key}(A, B).(A \rhd Initiator_{ISO}(k_{AB}, A, B) \,|\, B \rhd Responder_{ISO}(k_{AB}, B, A))$

$Initiator_{ISO}(k_{AB}, A, B) \triangleq$		$Responder_{ISO}(k_{AB}, B, A) \triangleq$	
$\mathsf{new}(m).$	NEW	$\mathsf{new}(n_B).$	NEW
$\mathsf{in}(x).$	IN	$\mathsf{out}(n_B).$	OUT
$\mathsf{run}(A, B).$	RUN	$\mathsf{in}(y).$	IN
$\mathsf{enc}.\{A : \mathsf{Id}, x : \mathsf{Claim}, m\}_{k_{AB}}\ \mathsf{as}\ y.$	CLAIM	$\mathsf{dec}.\ y\ \mathsf{as}\ \{A : \mathsf{Id}, n_B : \mathsf{Claim}, z\}_{k_{AB}}.$	DEC
$\mathsf{out}(y)$	OUT	$\mathsf{commit}(B, A)$	AUTH CLAIM

A protocol is correct if all of its sequential components are locally correct. Formally, the process $\mathbf{keys}(k_1, \ldots, k_n).(I_1 \rhd !S_1 \mid \cdots \mid I_m \rhd !S_m)$. is *correct* if for all $i \in \{1, \ldots, m\}$ the process $\mathbf{keys}(k_1, \ldots, k_n).I_i \rhd S_i$ is locally correct. Our safety theorem states that correct processes are safe: hence, the local correctness of the protocol participants is a sufficient condition for the safety of the protocol as a whole (the proof, worked out in the full version of the paper, is omitted here for the lack of space).

Theorem 1 (Safety). *Let* $P = \mathbf{keys}(k_1, \ldots, k_n).(I_1 \rhd !S_1 \mid \cdots \mid I_m \rhd !S_m)$. *If* P *is correct, then it is safe.*

5 An Example

We illustrate the analysis on the ρ-spi specification of the protocol in Table 2. As discussed in Example 2, the protocol is subject to attacks when running in multiple sessions: with our analysis the flaw is unveiled by a failure to validate the responder, as we illustrate showing that the principal $\mathsf{let}\ k_{AB}{=}\mathsf{key}(k_{AB}, A, B).B \rhd Responder(B, A)$ is not locally correct. To see that, note that for $B; \Gamma; \Pi \vdash \mathsf{commit}(B, A)$ to be derivable, by rules (AUTHENTICATE CLAIM) and (AUTHENTICATE OWNER), there must exists y such that $\Pi(y) = dec\{A : \mathsf{Id}, n_b : R, \ldots\}_{k_{AB}}$, with $R \in \{\mathsf{Claim}, \mathsf{Owner}\}$. On the other hand, the only decryption in S is $\mathsf{decrypt}\ y\ \mathsf{as}\ \{n_B, z\}_{k_{AB}}$, which implies $B; \Gamma; \Pi \nvdash \mathsf{commit}(B, A)$. The failure of local correctness persists when we add a role $R \in \{\mathsf{Claim}, \mathsf{Owner}\}$ to the ciphertext. In fact, even in that case, the hypotheses of the two authentication rules do not hold because the ciphertext is still missing the identity label A. Interestingly, the attack presented in Section 3 exploits precisely this flaw. The reflection attack is prevented in the ISO Two-Pass Unilateral Authentication Protocol [21] which fixes the problem by including the identity label A in the ciphertext sent by A (in fact the original version from [21] includes B instead of A in the ciphertext).

$$1)\ B \to A : n_B \qquad 2)\ A \to B : \{A, n_B, m\}_{k_{AB}}$$

The specification of the new protocol in ρ-spi is given in Table 6. The only non-obvious aspect of the specification is in the choice of the claimant role for the label A in the encrypted message. Given this choice the protocol is easily proved correct, as we outline next. The second and fourth columns in Table 6 refer to the rules applied for verifying local correctness of the two principals. In particular, for $A; \emptyset; \Pi_{k_{AB}} \vdash Initiator_{ISO}(k_{AB}$

$, A, B)$, the hypotheses of the rules (NEW), (INPUT), (RUN) and (OUTPUT) are trivially verified. The only interesting case is rule (CLAIMANT), which is applied in the proof of

$$A; \{m : \text{unchecked}\}; \Pi_A \vdash \text{encrypt}\{A : \text{Id}, x : \text{Claim}, m\}_{k_{AB}} \text{ as } y.\text{out}(y)$$

Rule (CLAIMANT) requires $\Pi_A = \Pi'_A.B \mapsto run$ and $\Pi_A(k_{AB}) = key(A, B)$, which are both true. As for $Responder_{ISO}(k_{AB}, B, A)$, proving $B; \Gamma_B; \Pi_B \vdash \text{commit}(B, A)$ is straightforward. The hypotheses for rule (AUTHENTICATE CLAIM) hold since $\Pi_B(\bullet) = dec\{A : \text{Id}, n_B : \text{Claim}, z\}_{k_{AB}}$, $\Gamma_B(n_b) = unchecked$, and $\Pi_B(k_{AB}) = key(A, B)$. Now one derives $B; \emptyset; \Pi_{k_{AB}} \vdash Responder_{ISO}\,(k_{AB}, B, A)$, routinely, by rules (NEW), (OUTPUT), (INPUT) and (DECRYPTION).

Finally, both principals handle keys safely, as they use no session keys and never send long term keys on the net or encrypted. By Theorem 1, we know that every trace of $Protocol_{ISO}$ is safe, hence the protocol is immune to authentication attacks.

The specification can easily be generalized to an arbitrary number m of entities, acting both as initiator and as responder and arbitrarily replicated.

$$Protocol_{ISO} - m \triangleq \text{let}^{m}_{i,j=1,i<j} k_{ij} = \text{key}(I_i, I_j).$$
$$(|^{m}_{i,j=1,i\neq j} I_i \triangleright !Initiator_{ISO}(k_{ij}, I_i, I_j) | I_i \triangleright !Responder_{ISO}(k_{ij}, I_i, I_j)))$$

Here k_{ij} represents a long term key shared between entities I_i and I_j. We assume that $k_{ij} = k_{ji}$ (and correspondingly define the key assignment only for keys k_{ij} with $i < j$). The correctness proof for this version of the protocol derives directly, by compositionality, from the correctness proof we just outlined.

6 Conclusion

We have proposed a new, compositional, analysis of entity authentication protocols, based on a new tagging mechanism for encrypted messages. The impact of the tagging mechanism is twofold. On one hand, it is a specification tool: stating the purpose of message components explicitly leads to more robust protocol design. On the other hand, it is directly useful as an implementation technique which allows a non-ambiguous interpretation of messages, as other tagging techniques employed in protocol implementations, while at the same time supporting formal correctness proofs.

The analysis is appealing for its relative simplicity: verifying the conditions of local correctness is intuitive and easily implemented by an automatic tool. We have conducted various (hand written) tests on authentication protocols from the literature, some of which are given in Table 7: for all the correct versions of the protocols the analysis admits safety proofs, while it consistently fails to validate the flawed versions.

The authentication patterns we have investigated are certainly not exhaustive, but fairly general. Also, the framework is scalable, as new patterns may be added, as needed. Desirable extensions include new patterns needed to validate, e.g, protocols based on public-key encryption and other kinds of nonce-challenges [18,19]. Our current work shows that the approach fits very well these extensions.

Related Work. Tagging is not a new idea and it is proposed and used for verification purposes in [3,4,16,17,20]. Typically, tagging amounts to add a different label to each

Table 7. Case Studies

Protocols	Correct	Flawed
Iso Symmetric Key Two-Pass Unilateral Authentication Protocol	X	
Iso Symmetric Key Three-Pass Mutual Authentication Protocol	X	
Andrew Secure RPC Protocol		X
Needham Schroeder Protocol		X
Needham Schroeder Amended Version	X	
Otway and Rees Protocol		X
Carlsen's Secret Key Initiator Protocol	X	
Wide Mouthed Frog Protocol,Nonce Based Version	X	
Woo and Lam Protocol		X
Woo and Lam Amended Version	X	

encrypted protocol message, so that ciphertexts cannot be confused. Our tagging is less demanding, as we do not require that every message is unambiguously tagged since we tag only certain components. In particular, for protocols implemented with stronger tagging techniques, our tags can be safely removed without compromising the protocols' safety. Our tagging seems also well suited for multi-protocol systems. In [23], Syverson and Meadows observe that "problems can arise when a protocol is interacting with another protocol that does not use a tagging scheme, or tags data in a different way". Our tagging does not require that different protocols use different tags, since it is related to the security informations conveyed by a ciphertext. If it was uniformly applied in every protocol the safety result would scale up to the parallel composition of different authentication protocols.

In [16,17] Gordon and Jeffrey define a type system for the analysis of authentication protocols (with symmetric and asymmetric encryption) expressed in a dialect of the spi calculus. Their approach is related to our work in several aspects. As ours, their authentication analysis is a safety analysis based on correspondence assertions. Also, as in our approach, the reasoning is guided by a tagging mechanism for messages that provides enough redundancy for the analysis to identify and distinguish different messages. There are, however, important differences. Their tags are applied uniformly, so as to distinguish any pair of encrypted messages, and are used by a dependent type system to form traces of dependent effects which are then inspected to verify protocols by checking a correspondence assertion property similar to ours. Their type analysis is inherently compositional, as ours, but the safety result requires a further inspection of the effects associated with a complete protocol trace. Moreover the human effort required for the type definitions is relevant, while our tags range on a finite set and their definition is simple and relatively mechanical.

The recent work by Bodei *et al.* on a control-flow analysis for message authentication in *Lysa* [5] is also strongly related to our present approach. The motivations and goals, however, are different, since message authentication concerns the origin of a message, while entity authentication also provides guarantees about the presence of a given entity during an authentication session. Indeed, our analysis provides a strong form of entity authentication guarantee [22,28]: not only the presence of the claimant is analyzed, but also its intention to authenticate itself with the verifier.

Further related work is based on employing belief logics , like, e.g., BAN [9], GNY [15], as formal tools for reasoning about authentication guarantees provided by messages. The main difference with these papers is that we do not have any kind of protocol idealization. Indeed, we reason about 'concrete' execution traces, directly connected to the structure of ciphertexts. An interesting paper that goes in the direction of eliminating the idealization step in analyses based on (belief) logics is [12] by Durgin, Mitchell and Pavlovic. They propose a logic for security protocols which is designed around a process calculus derived from Strand Spaces [19,27], and built on top of an asymmetric encryption system. As in our framework, the semantics of the calculus is formalized in terms of a trace semantics. The formalization of authentication is, however, largely different, and not easily comparable to ours.

References

1. M. Abadi and B. Blanchet. Secrecy types for asymmetric communication. *Theor. Comput. Sci.*, 298(3):387–415, 2003.
2. M. Abadi and A. D. Gordon. A calculus for cryptographic protocols: The spi calculus. *Information and Computation*, 148(1):1–70, 1999.
3. M. Abadi and R. Needham. Prudent engineering practice for cryptographic protocols. *IEEE Transactions on Software Engineering*, 22(1):6–15, 1996.
4. B. Blanchet and A. Podelski. Verification of cryptographic protocols: Tagging enforces termination. *Proceedings of Foundations of Software Science and Computation Structures*, pages 136–152, 2003.
5. C. Bodei, M. Buchholtz, P. Degano, F. Nielson, and H. Riis Nielson. Automatic validation of protocol narration. In *In proceedings of 16th IEEE Computer Security Foundations Workshop (CSFW 16)*, pages 126–140, June 2003.
6. M. Boreale. Symbolic trace analysis of cryptographic protocols. In *Proceedings of ICALP 01*, volume 2076, pages 667–681. LNCS 2076, Springer Verlag, 2001.
7. M. Boreale, R. De Nicola, and R. Pugliese. Proof techniques for cryptographic processes. In *Logic in Computer Science*, pages 157–166, 1999.
8. M. Bugliesi, R. Focardi, and M. Maffei. Principles for entity authentication. In *Proceedings of 5th International Conference Perspectives of System Informatics (PSI 2003)*, volume 2890, pages 294–307, July 2003.
9. M. Burrows, M. Abadi, and R. Needham. "A Logic of Authentication". *Proceedings of the Royal Society of London*, 426(1871):233–271, 1989.
10. J. Clark and J. Jacob. A survey of authentication protocol literature: Version 1.0. http://www.cs.york.ac.uk/~jac/papers/drareview.ps.gz, November 1997.
11. D. Dolev and A. Yao. On the security of public key protocols. *IEEE Transactions on Information Theory*, 29(2):198–208, 1983.
12. N. Durgin, J. Mitchell, and D. Pavlovic. A compositional logic for proving security properties of protocols. *Journal of Computer Security*, 11, 2003.
13. R. Focardi, R. Gorrieri, and F. Martinelli. Non interference for the analysis of cryptographic protocols. In *Proceedings of ICALP'00*, pages 354–372. Springer LNCS 1853, July 2000.
14. D. Gollmann. "What do we mean by Entity Authentication". In *Proceedings of the 1996 Symposium on Security and Privacy*, pages 46–54. IEEE Computer Society Press, 1996.
15. L. Gong, R. Needham, and R. Yahalom. Reasoning About Belief in Cryptographic Protocols. In Deborah Cooper and Teresa Lunt, editors, *Proceedings 1990 IEEE Symposium on Research in Security and Privacy*, pages 234–248. IEEE Computer Society, 1990.
16. A. Gordon and A. Jeffrey. Authenticity by typing for security protocols. In 14th IEEE Computer Security Foundations Workshop (CSFW-14),pages 145-159, June 2001.
17. A. Gordon and A. Jeffrey. Types and effects for asymmetric cryptographic protocols. In *15th IEEE Computer Security Foundations Workshop — CSFW'01*, pages 77–91. IEEE Computer Society Press, 24–26 June 2002.

18. J. Guttman. Security protocol design via authentication tests. In *15th IEEE Computer Security Foundations Workshop — CSFW'01*, pages 92–103, Cape Breton, Canada, 24–26 June 2002. IEEE Computer Society Press.
19. Joshua D. Guttman and F. Javier Thayer. Authentication tests and the structure of bundles. *Theoretical Computer Science*, 283(2):333–380, 2002.
20. J. Heather, G. Lowe, and S. Schneider. How to prevent type flaw attacks on security protocols. In *13th IEEE Computer Security Foundations Workshop — CSFW'00*, pages 255–268, Cambridge, UK, 3–5 July 2000. IEEE Computer Society Press.
21. ISO/IEC. "Entity Authentication Using Symmetric Techniques". Report ISO/IEC JTC1.27.02.2 (20.03.1.2), June 1990.
22. G. Lowe. "A Hierarchy of Authentication Specification". In *Proceedings of the 10th Computer Security Foundation Workshop*, pages 31–44. IEEE press, 1997.
23. C. Meadows and P. Syverson. Formal specification and analysis of the group domain of intrepretation protocol using npatrl and the nrl protocol analyzer, 2003. to appear in Journal of Computer Security.
24. J. C. Mitchell, M. Mitchell, and U. Stern. Automated analysis of cryptographic protocols using murϕ. In *Proceedings of the 1997 IEEE Symposium on Research in Security and Privacy*, pages 141–153. IEEE Computer Society Press, 1997.
25. R M Needham and M D Schroeder. Authentication revisited. *ACM SIGOPS Operating Systems Review*, 21(1):7–7, 1987.
26. L. C. Paulson. Relations between secrets: Two formal analyses of the yahalom protocol. *Journal of Computer Security*, 9(3):197–216, 2001.
27. J. Thayer, J. Herzog, and J. Guttman. Strand spaces: Proving security protocols correct. Journal of Computer Security, 1999. 15.
28. T.Y.C. Woo and S.S. Lam. Authentication for distributed systems. *IEEE Computer*, 25(3):39–51, 1992.

A Distributed Abstract Machine for Boxed Ambient Calculi

Andrew Phillips, Nobuko Yoshida, and Susan Eisenbach

Department of Computing, 180 Queen's Gate,
Imperial College London, SW7 2AZ, UK
{anp,yoshida,sue}@doc.ic.ac.uk

Abstract. Boxed ambient calculi have been used to model and reason about a wide variety of problems in mobile computing. Recently, several new variants of Boxed Ambients have been proposed, which seek to improve on the original calculus. In spite of these theoretical advances, there has been little research on how such calculi can be correctly implemented in a distributed environment. This paper bridges a gap between theory and implementation by defining a distributed abstract machine for a variant of Boxed Ambients with channels. The abstract machine uses a *list semantics*, which is close to an implementation language, and a *blocking semantics*, which leads to an efficient implementation. The machine is proved sound and complete with respect to the underlying calculus. A prototype implementation is also described, together with an application for tracking the location of migrating ambients. The correctness of the machine ensures that the work done in specifying and analysing mobile applications is not lost during their implementation.

1 Introduction

Boxed ambient calculi have been used to model and reason about a wide variety of problems in mobile computing. The original paper on Boxed Ambients [2] shows how the Ambient calculus can be complemented with finer-grained and more effective mechanisms for ambient interaction. In [3], Boxed Ambients are used to reason about resource access control, and in [9] a sound type system for Boxed Ambients is defined, which provides static guarantees on information flow. Recently, several new variants of Boxed Ambients have been proposed, which seek to improve on the foundations of the original calculus. In particular, [14] introduces Safe Boxed Ambients, which uses co-capabilities to express explicit permissions to access ambients, and [4] introduces the NBA calculus, which seeks to limit communication and migration interferences in Boxed Ambients.

In spite of these theoretical advances, there has been little research on how boxed ambient calculi can be correctly implemented in a distributed environment. In general, such an implementation can be achieved by defining an Application Programming Interface (API), which maps the constructs of the calculus to a chosen programming language. Examples of this approach include [5], which describes a Java API for the Ambient calculus, and [17], which describes a Java

D.A. Schmidt (Ed.): ESOP 2004, LNCS 2986, pp. 155–170, 2004.

API for a variant of Boxed Ambients. The main advantage of the approach is that the API can be smoothly integrated into an existing programming language. The main disadvantage, however, is that the constructs of the chosen language often extend beyond the scope of the calculus model. Therefore, when method calls to the API are combined with arbitrary program code, e.g. code which generates exceptions, the resulting program is unpredictable. As a result, most of the benefits of using a calculus model are lost, since any security or correctness properties that hold for the model may not hold for its implementation.

An alternative approach for implementing boxed ambient calculi uses an interpreter to execute calculus expressions. Although this approach constrains the programmer to use a custom language (which may not be compatible with existing code or libraries), support for language interoperability can be provided in the implementation, allowing the non-distributed aspects of a mobile application to be written in any chosen language, and the mobile and distributed aspects to be written in the calculus. The interaction between these two aspects can be achieved using the communication primitives of the calculus, allowing a clean separation of concerns in the spirit of modern coordination languages such as [1]. More importantly, this approach ensures that any security or correctness properties of the calculus model are preserved during execution, provided the interpreter is implemented correctly. This can be achieved by defining an *abstract machine* to specify how the interpreter should behave. The correctness of the machine can then be verified with respect to the underlying calculus.

This paper presents a distributed abstract machine for a variant of Boxed Ambients with channels, known as the Channel Ambient calculus (CA). [1]To our knowledge, a correct abstract machine for a variant of Boxed Ambients has not yet been implemented in a distributed environment. The remainder of the paper is structured as follows: Section 2 introduces the Channel Ambient calculus, and Section 3 defines the syntax and semantics of the Channel Ambient Machine (CAM), an abstract machine for CA. Section 4 outlines the proof of correctness of CAM with respect to the calculus CA. Due to space limitations the full proofs have been omitted, but can be found in [15]. Section 5 describes a distributed runtime system that has been implemented based on CAM, and Section 6 describes an example application. Finally, Section 7 compares CA and CAM with related calculi and abstract machines.

2 The Channel Ambient Calculus

The Channel Ambient calculus is a variant of the Boxed Ambient calculus in which ambients can interact using named channels. The main constructs of CA are illustrated in the following example:

$$Network \mid client\boxed{C \mid \nu login\,(server \cdot request\langle client, login\rangle \mid \overline{\texttt{in}}\, login.P)}$$

$$\mid server\boxed{S \mid !\overline{\texttt{out}}\, logout \mid !request^{\uparrow}(c,x).service\boxed{\texttt{out}\, logout.\texttt{in}\, c \cdot x.Q}}$$

[1] The work presented here forms part of the first author's forthcoming PhD thesis [16]

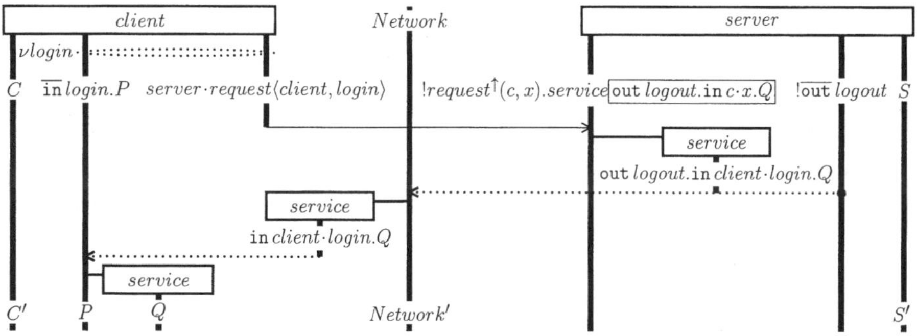

Fig. 1. Execution Scenario

The example uses a polyadic variant of CA to model a *client* machine, which downloads a *service* ambient from a *server* machine over a *Network*. An execution scenario for this system is illustrated in Fig. 1, in which the vertical lines represent parallel processes, the boxes represent ambients, the horizontal arrows represent interaction, and the flow of time proceeds from top to bottom. Initially, the client creates a new *login* channel and sends its name and login channel to the server on the *request* channel. In parallel, it allows an ambient to enter via the login channel. The server receives the request and creates a new *service* ambient, which leaves via the *logout* channel and enters the client via the login channel. Once inside the client, the service ambient executes process Q, and the client executes process P. In parallel, the *Network* evolves to *Network′*, and the processes C and S inside the client and server evolve to C' and S' respectively. The system has a high degree of parallelism. In particular, the network can contain multiple clients and the server can handle multiple requests simultaneously.

The full syntax of CA is defined in terms of processes P, Q, R and actions α:

$P, Q, R ::=$	$\mathbf{0}$	Null	$\alpha ::=$	$a{\cdot}x\langle n\rangle$	Sibling Output
$\mid$	$P \mid Q$	Parallel	$\mid$	$x^{\uparrow}\langle n\rangle$	Parent Output
$\mid$	$\nu n\, P$	Restriction	$\mid$	$x(m)$	Internal Input , $x \neq m$
$\mid$	$a\boxed{P}$	Ambient	$\mid$	$x^{\uparrow}(m)$	External Input , $x \neq m$
$\mid$	$\alpha.P$	Action	$\mid$	$\mathtt{in}\, a{\cdot}x$	Enter
$\mid$	$!\alpha.P$	Replication	$\mid$	$\mathtt{out}\, x$	Leave
			$\mid$	$\overline{\mathtt{in}}\, x$	Accept
			$\mid$	$\overline{\mathtt{out}}\, x$	Release

Processes in CA have the same structure as processes in the Ambient calculus [7], except that replicated actions $!\alpha.P$ are used instead of general replication $!P$. The definition of the set of free names $fn(P)$ of a process P is standard, where restriction $\nu m\, P$ and inputs $x(m).P$ and $x^{\uparrow}(m).P$ act as binders for the name m. Standard notational conventions are used, including assigning the lowest precedence to the parallel composition operator, and writing α as syntactic sugar for $\alpha.\mathbf{0}$. In addition, local output $x\langle n\rangle$ and child output $a/x\langle n\rangle$ are written as syntactic sugar for $\nu b\, b\boxed{x^{\uparrow}\langle n\rangle}$ and $\nu b\, b\boxed{a{\cdot}x\langle n\rangle}$ respectively, where $b \notin \{a, x, n\}$.

The semantics of CA is defined in terms of structural congruence ($\equiv$) and reduction ($\longrightarrow$). The definition of structural congruence is mostly standard:

$$P \mid \mathbf{0} \equiv P \tag{1}$$
$$P \mid Q \equiv Q \mid P \tag{2}$$
$$P \mid (Q \mid R) \equiv (P \mid Q) \mid R \tag{3}$$
$$!\alpha.P \equiv \alpha.(P \mid !\alpha.P) \tag{4}$$
$$\nu n\, \mathbf{0} \equiv \mathbf{0} \tag{5}$$
$$\nu n\, n\boxed{\mathbf{0}} \equiv \mathbf{0} \tag{6}$$
$$\nu n\, \nu m\, P \equiv \nu m\, \nu n\, P \tag{7}$$
$$n \notin fn(P) \Rightarrow P \mid \nu n\, Q \equiv \nu n\, (P \mid Q) \tag{8}$$
$$a \neq n \Rightarrow a\boxed{\nu n\, P} \equiv \nu n\, a\boxed{P} \tag{9}$$
$$n \notin fn(P) \Rightarrow \nu m\, P \equiv \nu n\, P_{\{n/m\}} \tag{10}$$
$$n \notin fn(P) \Rightarrow x(m).P \equiv x(n).P_{\{n/m\}} \tag{11}$$
$$n \notin fn(P) \Rightarrow x^{\uparrow}(m).P \equiv x^{\uparrow}(n).P_{\{n/m\}} \tag{12}$$
$$P \equiv Q \Rightarrow a\boxed{P} \equiv a\boxed{Q} \tag{13}$$
$$P \equiv Q \Rightarrow P \mid R \equiv Q \mid R \tag{14}$$

Rule (6) allows empty ambients to be garbage-collected, and (11) and (12) allow bound names to be substituted, where $P_{\{n/m\}}$ substitutes the name n for m in process P. The only non-standard rule is (4), which allows a replicated action $!\alpha.P$ to be expanded to $\alpha.(P \mid !\alpha.P)$. This ensures that only a single copy of $\alpha.P$ can be created at a time, since $!\alpha.P$ is unable to spawn a new copy while inside the prefix α. This is useful from an implementation perspective, and differs from the standard rule for replication, $!\alpha.P \equiv \alpha.P \mid !\alpha.P$, which allows an infinite number of copies of $\alpha.P$ to be created. The definition of reduction is also standard:

$$(Q \equiv P \wedge P \longrightarrow P' \wedge P' \equiv Q') \Rightarrow Q \longrightarrow Q' \tag{15}$$
$$(P \longrightarrow P') \Rightarrow P \mid Q \longrightarrow P' \mid Q \tag{16}$$
$$(P \longrightarrow P') \Rightarrow \nu n\, P \longrightarrow \nu n\, P' \tag{17}$$
$$(P \longrightarrow P') \Rightarrow a\boxed{P} \longrightarrow a\boxed{P'} \tag{18}$$
$$a\boxed{b{\cdot}x\langle n\rangle.P \mid P'} \mid b\boxed{x^{\uparrow}(m).Q \mid Q'} \longrightarrow a\boxed{P \mid P'} \mid b\boxed{Q_{\{n/m\}} \mid Q'} \tag{19}$$
$$a\boxed{x^{\uparrow}\langle n\rangle.P \mid P'} \mid x(m).Q \longrightarrow a\boxed{P \mid P'} \mid Q_{\{n/m\}} \tag{20}$$
$$a\boxed{\mathbf{in}\, b{\cdot}x.P \mid P'} \mid b\boxed{\overline{\mathbf{in}}\, x.Q \mid Q'} \longrightarrow b\boxed{Q \mid Q' \mid a\boxed{P \mid P'}} \tag{21}$$
$$b\boxed{a\boxed{\mathbf{out}\, x.P \mid P'} \mid \overline{\mathbf{out}}\, x.Q \mid Q'} \longrightarrow b\boxed{Q \mid Q'} \mid a\boxed{P \mid P'} \tag{22}$$

Rule (15) allows structurally congruent processes to perform the same reductions. Rules (16) - (18) allow a reduction to take place inside a parallel composition, inside a restriction or inside an ambient. Rules (19) and (20) allow an ambient to send a message to a sibling or to its parent on a given channel. Rules (21) and (22) allow an ambient to enter a sibling or to leave its parent on a given channel.

A brief comparison of CA with related calculi is given in Section 7. One distinguishing feature of CA is that it allows sibling ambients to communicate synchronously. This is often desirable within a single machine, or between machines in a local area network. Even over a wide area network, certain protocols such as TCP/IP provide a useful abstraction for synchronous communication. In cases where asynchronous communication is required, such as the UDP protocol, sibling ambients can communicate via an intermediate *router* ambient.

3 The Channel Ambient Machine

The Channel Ambient Machine is inspired by the Pict abstract machine [19], which is used as a basis for implementing the asynchronous π-calculus. Like the Pict machine, CAM uses a list syntax to represent the parallel composition of processes. It also uses a notion of *blocked processes*, which are a generalisation of the *channel queues* in Pict.

The machine executes a given process P by extending the scope of each unguarded restriction in P to the top level and converting each unguarded parallel composition in P to a list form. The resulting term is of the form $\nu n \ldots \nu n'\, A$, where A is a tree of the form $\alpha_1.P_1 :: \ldots \alpha_N.P_N :: a_1\boxed{A_1} :: \ldots :: a_M\boxed{A_M}$. The leaves of the tree are actions $\alpha_i.P_i$ and the nodes are ambients $a_i\boxed{A_i}$. Once a process has been converted to this form, the machine attempts to execute an action somewhere in the tree. If the chosen action $\alpha.P$ is able to interact with a corresponding *blocked* co-action then a reduction is performed. If not, the action $\alpha.P$ is *blocked* to $\underline{\alpha.P}$. The machine then non-deterministically schedules a different action to be executed. If all the actions in a given ambient $a\boxed{A}$ are blocked then the ambient itself is blocked to $\underline{a}\boxed{A}$. Execution terminates when all the actions and ambients in the tree are blocked.

Blocking significantly improves the efficiency of the machine by labelling those ambients and actions that are not able to initiate a reduction. This partitions the search space, allowing the machine to ignore the entire contents of a blocked ambient when looking for an unblocked action to schedule. Blocking also simplifies the condition for termination, since the machine only needs to check for the presence of an unblocked action to know whether a reduction is possible.

The machine can be used to execute the example from Section 2. First, it converts the calculus process to the following term, where $login \notin fn(S, C, Network)$:

$$\nu login\ (server\boxed{!\overline{\texttt{out}}\, logout :: !request^{\uparrow}(c,x).service\boxed{\texttt{out}\, logout.\texttt{in}\, c\cdot x.Q} :: S}$$

$$:: client\boxed{server\cdot request\langle client, login\rangle :: \overline{\texttt{in}}\, login.P :: C} :: Network)$$

Then, the machine tries to execute one of the actions in the tree. For example, it can try to execute the replicated release $!\overline{\texttt{out}}\, logout$. If this action is unable to interact with a corresponding blocked co-action it will block to $\underline{!\overline{\texttt{out}}\, logout}$. Similarly, the replicated input on the *request* channel will block if there is no corresponding blocked output. The machine can then execute the sibling output $server{\cdot}request\langle client, login\rangle$, which will interact with the blocked input on the server. The model scales smoothly to the case where the server and client processes are executing on two different machines. In this case, the interaction between machines is implemented by socket libraries, which provide an interface to the physical network layer. When a given machine can no longer perform any reductions it goes into a blocked state, waiting for an interrupt from the network announcing the arrival of new messages or ambients.

The full syntax of CAM is defined below, in terms of machine terms V, U, lists A, B, C and blocked lists $\underline{A}, \underline{B}, \underline{C}$:

$$\begin{array}{rcll} V, U & ::= & A & \text{List} \\ & \mid & \nu n\, V & \text{Restriction} \end{array}$$

$$\begin{array}{rcll} \underline{A}, \underline{B}, \underline{C} & ::= & [] & \text{Empty List} \\ & \mid & \underline{a}\boxed{\underline{A}} :: \underline{C} & \text{Blocked Ambients} \\ & \mid & \underline{\alpha.P} :: \underline{C} & \text{Blocked Actions} \end{array}$$

$$\begin{array}{rcll} A, B, C & ::= & [] & \text{Empty List} \\ & \mid & a\boxed{A} :: C & \text{Ambient} \\ & \mid & \underline{a}\boxed{\underline{A}} :: C & \text{Blocked Ambient} \\ & \mid & P :: C & \text{Process} \\ & \mid & \underline{\alpha.P} :: C & \text{Blocked Action} \end{array}$$

A machine term V is a list with a number of restricted names. Each list A can contain processes, blocked actions, ambients or blocked ambients. By definition, blocked ambients can only contain blocked actions or blocked sub-ambients. In addition, $\underline{!\alpha.P}$ is written as syntactic sugar for $\underline{\alpha.(P \mid !\alpha.P)}$ and $\underset{..}{a}$ is used to denote either a blocked ambient $\underline{a}$ or an unblocked ambient a.

The semantics of CAM is defined in Fig. 2 in terms of structural congruence ($\equiv$) and reduction ($\longrightarrow$). The structural congruence rules are used to find an element in a list that matches a specific pattern. Rule (23) allows an element X at the head of a list to be placed at the back of the list, where (@) denotes the list append function, and (24) allows the list A inside an ambient to be replaced with a list B that is structurally congruent to A.

The reduction rules of the machine are derived from the reduction rules of the calculus, and use standard definitions for free names $fn(A)$ and substitution $A_{\{n/m\}}$. Each rule is defined over the entire length of a list and there is no rule to allow reduction across the (::) operator. Rule (28) ensures that all restricted names are moved to the top-level, by substituting each restricted name with a globally unique name generated by the machine. In practice, such a name can be created using a secret key, together with a time stamp or a suitable counter. Rule (29) is used to label an ambient as blocked, indicating that it does not contain any unblocked actions. Rules (31) - (34) allow CA processes to be converted to list form, and rules (35) - (42) allow an action to interact with a blocked co-action. The latter rules are derived from rules (19) - (22) in CA, where each rule in CA is mapped to two corresponding rules in CAM. Rules (39) - (42) make use of an *unblocking function* $\lfloor A \rfloor$, which unblocks all of the top-level actions in a given list A. The main rule for unblocking is given by $\lfloor \underline{\alpha.P} :: C \rfloor \triangleq \alpha.P :: \lfloor C \rfloor$, and the full definition is given in Section 4. The unblocking function is used to unblock the contents of an ambient when it moves to a new location, allowing the ambient to *re-bind* to its new environment by giving any blocked actions it contains the chance to interact with their new context. Additionally, for each

$$X :: A \;\equiv\; A@X \tag{23}$$
$$A \equiv B \Rightarrow \underset{\cdot\cdot}{a}\boxed{A} :: C \;\equiv\; \underset{\cdot\cdot}{a}\boxed{B} :: C \tag{24}$$

$$(U \equiv V \wedge V \longrightarrow V') \Rightarrow U \longrightarrow V' \tag{25}$$
$$(V \longrightarrow V') \Rightarrow \nu n\, V \longrightarrow \nu n\, V' \tag{26}$$
$$(A \longrightarrow A') \Rightarrow a\boxed{A} :: C \longrightarrow a\boxed{A'} :: C \tag{27}$$
$$n \notin fn(a\boxed{A'} :: C) \wedge A \longrightarrow \nu m\, A' \Rightarrow a\boxed{A} :: C \longrightarrow \nu n\, (a\boxed{A'_{\{n/m\}}} :: C) \tag{28}$$
$$a\boxed{\underline{A}} :: C \longrightarrow \underline{a}\boxed{\underline{A}} :: C \tag{29}$$
$$!\alpha.P :: C \longrightarrow \alpha.(P \mid !\alpha.P) :: C \tag{30}$$
$$\mathbf{0} :: C \longrightarrow C \tag{31}$$
$$(P \mid Q) :: C \longrightarrow P :: Q :: C \tag{32}$$
$$n \notin fn(P :: C) \Rightarrow (\nu m\, P) :: C \longrightarrow \nu n\, (P_{\{n/m\}} :: C) \tag{33}$$
$$a\boxed{P} :: C \longrightarrow a\boxed{P :: []} :: C \tag{34}$$
$$C \equiv \underset{\cdot\cdot}{b}\boxed{\underline{x^{\uparrow}(m).Q} :: B} :: C' \Rightarrow a\boxed{b\cdot x\langle n\rangle.P :: A} :: C \longrightarrow a\boxed{P :: A} :: b\boxed{Q_{\{n/m\}} :: B} :: C' \tag{35}$$
$$C \equiv \underset{\cdot\cdot}{a}\boxed{\underline{b\cdot x\langle n\rangle.P} :: A} :: C' \Rightarrow b\boxed{x^{\uparrow}(m).Q :: B} :: C \longrightarrow b\boxed{Q_{\{n/m\}} :: B} :: a\boxed{P :: A} :: C' \tag{36}$$
$$C \equiv \underline{x(m).Q} :: C' \Rightarrow a\boxed{x^{\uparrow}\langle n\rangle.P :: A} :: C \longrightarrow a\boxed{P :: A} :: Q_{\{n/m\}} :: C' \tag{37}$$
$$C \equiv \underset{\cdot\cdot}{a}\boxed{\underline{x^{\uparrow}\langle n\rangle.P} :: A} :: C' \Rightarrow x(m).Q :: C \longrightarrow Q_{\{n/m\}} :: a\boxed{P :: A} :: C' \tag{38}$$
$$C \equiv \underset{\cdot\cdot}{b}\boxed{\underline{\overline{\mathbf{in}}\, x.Q} :: B} :: C' \Rightarrow a\boxed{\mathbf{in}\, b\cdot x.P :: A} :: C \longrightarrow b\boxed{Q :: a\boxed{P :: \lfloor A \rfloor} :: B} :: C' \tag{39}$$
$$C \equiv \underset{\cdot\cdot}{a}\boxed{\underline{\mathbf{in}\, b\cdot x.P} :: A} :: C' \Rightarrow b\boxed{\overline{\mathbf{in}}\, x.Q :: B} :: C \longrightarrow b\boxed{Q :: a\boxed{P :: \lfloor A \rfloor} :: B} :: C' \tag{40}$$
$$B \equiv \underline{\overline{\mathbf{out}}\, x.Q} :: B' \Rightarrow b\boxed{a\boxed{\mathbf{out}\, x.P :: A} :: B} :: C \longrightarrow b\boxed{Q :: B'} :: a\boxed{P :: \lfloor A \rfloor} :: C \tag{41}$$
$$B \equiv \underset{\cdot\cdot}{a}\boxed{\underline{\mathbf{out}\, x.P} :: A} :: B' \Rightarrow b\boxed{\overline{\mathbf{out}}\, x.Q :: B} :: C \longrightarrow b\boxed{Q :: B'} :: a\boxed{P :: \lfloor A \rfloor} :: C \tag{42}$$

Fig. 2. Machine Semantics

of the rules (35) - (42) there is a corresponding rule to block an action that is unable to interact with a corresponding co-action. The blocking rule for (35) is as follows:

$$C \not\equiv \underset{\cdot\cdot}{b}\boxed{\underline{x^{\uparrow}(m).Q} :: B} :: C' \Rightarrow a\boxed{b\cdot x\langle n\rangle.P :: A} :: C \longrightarrow a\boxed{\underline{b\cdot x\langle n\rangle.P} :: A} :: C \tag{43}$$

The blocking rules for the remaining actions are defined in a similar fashion.

The abstract machine can be used in both local and distributed settings. Local execution of a term A on a device a is modeled as $a\boxed{A}$. Distributed execution of terms $A_1, ..., A_N$ on devices $a_1, ..., a_N$, respectively, is modeled as $network\boxed{a_1\boxed{A_1} :: ... :: a_N\boxed{A_N}}$, where each identifier a_i corresponds to the address of a device in the network. Nested ambients inside a given term A_i can be executed independently, since only top-level processes in A_i can interact with other devices in the network. These interactions between devices are implemented using socket libraries, according to the reduction rules of CAM. For example, in a local area network a device a performs a sibling output to a device b by checking if b contains a corresponding blocked input, according to (35). Similarly, a performs an external input by checking if any of the devices in the network contain a corresponding blocked output, according to (36). In a wide area network, devices send all sibling outputs to an intermediate router device, and therefore only need to check the router for blocked outputs in order to perform an external input. Note also that CA, and ambient calculi in general, allow migrating ambients to interact while in transit between devices. Such interactions can either be prevented using type systems for single-threaded migration [18], or they can be implemented by defining a default *network* device where migrating ambients can execute while waiting to be admitted to a new host.

4 Correctness of the Channel Ambient Machine

The correctness of the Channel Ambient Machine is expressed in terms of three main properties: soundness, completeness and termination. Due to space limitations the full proofs have been omitted, but can be found in [15].

The soundness of the machine relies on a decoding function $[V]$, which maps a given machine term V to a calculus process, and the unblocking function $\lfloor V \rfloor$ described in Section 3. Decoding and unblocking are defined as follows:

$$\begin{aligned}
[\nu n\, V] &\triangleq \nu n\, [V] & \lfloor \nu n\, V \rfloor &\triangleq \nu n\, \lfloor V \rfloor \\
[[]] &\triangleq \mathbf{0} & \lfloor [] \rfloor &\triangleq [] \\
[\underset{..}{a}\boxed{A} :: C] &\triangleq a\boxed{[A]} \mid [C] & \lfloor \underset{..}{a}\boxed{A} :: C \rfloor &\triangleq \underset{..}{a}\boxed{A} :: \lfloor C \rfloor \\
[P :: C] &\triangleq P \mid [C] & \lfloor P :: C \rfloor &\triangleq P :: \lfloor C \rfloor \\
[\underline{\alpha.P} :: C] &\triangleq \alpha.P \mid [C] & \lfloor \underline{\alpha.P} :: C \rfloor &\triangleq \alpha.P :: \lfloor C \rfloor
\end{aligned}$$

Proposition 1 states that reduction in CAM is sound with respect to reduction in CA. The proof relies on Lemma 1, which states that machine terms are reduction-closed.

Proposition 1. $\forall V. V \in \text{CAM} \wedge V \longrightarrow^* V' \Rightarrow [V] \longrightarrow^* [V']$

Proof. By Lemma 1 and by induction on reduction in CAM. The decoding function is applied to the left and right hand side of each reduction rule and the result is shown to be a valid reduction in CA. □

Lemma 1. $\forall V.V \in \text{CAM} \wedge V \longrightarrow V' \Rightarrow V' \in \text{CAM}$

Proof. By definition of structural congruence, by definition of unblocking, and by induction on reduction in CAM. □

The completeness of the Channel Ambient Machine relies on a notion of well-formedness to describe invariants on machine terms. The set of well-formed terms $\text{CAM}^{\checkmark}$ is defined with respect to the set of ill-formed terms $\text{CAM}^{\times}$, such that $V \in \text{CAM}^{\checkmark} \Rightarrow V \in \text{CAM} \wedge V \notin \text{CAM}^{\times}$. Ill-formed terms $V^{\times}$ are defined as follows:

$$
\begin{array}{lll}
V^{\times} ::= & A^{\times} & \text{Bad List} \\
\mid & \nu n\, V^{\times} & \text{Bad Restriction}
\end{array}
$$

$$
\begin{array}{lll}
A^{\times} ::= & \underset{..}{a}\boxed{A^{\times}} :: C & \text{Bad Ambient} \\
\mid & C & \text{Bad Enter}, C \equiv \underset{..}{a}\boxed{\underline{\mathbf{in}\, b{\cdot}x.P} :: A} :: C' \wedge C' \equiv \underset{..}{b}\boxed{\underline{\overline{\mathbf{in}}\, x.Q} :: B} :: C'' \\
\mid & C & \text{Bad Leave}, C \equiv \underset{..}{b}\boxed{\underset{..}{a}\boxed{\underline{\mathbf{out}\, x.P} :: A} :: B} :: C' \wedge B \equiv \underline{\overline{\mathbf{out}}\, x.Q} :: B' \\
\mid & C & \text{Bad Sibling}, C \equiv \underset{..}{a}\boxed{\underline{b{\cdot}x\langle n\rangle.P} :: A} :: C' \wedge C' \equiv \underset{..}{b}\boxed{\underline{x^{\uparrow}(m).Q} :: B} :: C'' \\
\mid & C & \text{Bad Parent}, C \equiv \underset{..}{a}\boxed{\underline{x^{\uparrow}\langle n\rangle.P} :: A} :: C' \wedge C' \equiv \underline{x(m).Q} :: C''
\end{array}
$$

A term is ill-formed if it contains both a blocked action $\underline{\alpha.P}$ and a corresponding blocked co-action. Therefore, a well-formed term cannot contain a blocked action $\underline{\alpha.P}$ that could participate in a reduction if it were unblocked to $\alpha.P$.

Proposition 2 states that reduction in $\text{CAM}^{\checkmark}$ is complete with respect to reduction in CA. The proof relies on Lemma 2, which states that well-formed machine terms are reduction-closed. The proof of reduction closure relies on Lemma 3, which states that a term V' inside an arbitrary context K cannot become ill-formed as a result of a reduction.

Proposition 2. $\forall V.(V \in \text{CAM}^{\checkmark} \wedge [V] \longrightarrow^{*} P') \Rightarrow \exists V'.V \longrightarrow^{*} V' \wedge [V'] \equiv P'$

Proof. By Lemma 2 and by induction on reduction in CA. For each reduction rule in CA, any machine term that corresponds to the left hand side of the rule can reduce to a term that corresponds to the right hand side. □

Lemma 2. $\forall V.V \in \text{CAM}^{\checkmark} \wedge V \longrightarrow V' \Rightarrow V' \in \text{CAM}^{\checkmark}$

Proof. By Lemma 3 and by definition of $\text{CAM}^{\checkmark}$. □

Lemma 3. $\forall V.\forall K.V \longrightarrow V' \wedge K(V') \in \text{CAM}^{\times} \Rightarrow K(V) \in \text{CAM}^{\times}$

Proof. By definition of unblocking and by induction on reduction in CAM. □

Proposition 3 states that reduction in CAM$^{\checkmark}$ terminates if reduction in CA terminates. For a given well-formed machine term V, if the corresponding calculus process $[V]$ is unable to reduce then V will be unable to reduce after a finite number of steps.

Proposition 3. $\forall V. V \in \text{CAM}^{\checkmark} \wedge [V] \not\longrightarrow \Rightarrow V \not\longrightarrow^*$

Proof. Reductions in CAM can be classified into housekeeping, interaction and blocking reductions. By definition of well-formedness, an action is blocked if it cannot interact with a suitable co-action. Therefore, if no interactions are possible then all the actions in a given machine term will eventually block and execution will terminate after a finite number of housekeeping reductions. □

5 Implementation

The Channel Ambient Machine has been used to implement a runtime system, which executes programs written in the Channel Ambient language. The runtime is implemented in OCaml, and the language is based on polyadic CA with built-in base types from OCaml. The language also uses a type system for channel communication based on the polymorphic type system of Pict [19]. The runtime is invoked by the command `cam.exe sourcefile portnumber`. This starts a new runtime, which executes the contents of `sourcefile.ca` and accepts connections on `portnumber` of the host machine. Before a given source file is executed, it is statically checked by the CA type-checker, which reports any type errors to the user. The current state of the runtime is regularly streamed to `sourcefile.html`, which can be viewed in a web browser and periodically refreshed to display the latest state information. A beta version of the runtime can be downloaded from [15], together with a user guide.

The main functionality of the runtime is illustrated by the following example, which lists the contents of two source files, *server.ca* and *client.ca*, respectively:

```
    let request = request:<site,<void>>
in
    let service = service:ambient in
    let logout = logout:<void> in
    (  !request(c:site,x:<void>);
         applet[out logout; in c.x; Q<>]
    || !-out logout )
```

```
    let server = 192.168.0.2(3145) in
    let client = 192.168.0.3(3145) in
    let request = request:<site,<void>>
in
    new login:<void>
    (  server.request<client,login>
    || -in login; P<> )
```

These files contain source code corresponding to the *server* and *client* ambients of the example described in Section 2. The syntax of the code is similar to the syntax of CA, with minor variations such as using a semi-colon instead of a dot for action prefixes. The code also contains type annotations of the form $n : T$, where n is a variable name and T is a type expression, and value declarations of the form $let\ n\ = V\ in\ P$, where V is a value expression. Site values are of the form $IP(i)$, where IP is an IP address and i is a port number. Channel values are of the form $n : \langle T \rangle$, where n is a name and T is the type of values carried by the channel, and ambient values are of the form $n : ambient$ where n is a name. The additional type information helps to preserve type safety when remote machines interact over global channels, since two channels are only equal if both their names and types coincide. The code also contains process macros $P\langle\rangle$ and $Q\langle\rangle$, whose definitions are omitted. The example is executed by invoking the commands `cam.exe server 3145` and `cam.exe client 3145` on two different machines with IP addresses 192.168.0.2 and 192.168.0.3 respectively. The behaviour of the program is as described in Section 2: after a certain number of executions steps, the client receives a service ambient from the server.

The runtime also provides support for system calls, which are modeled using a sibling output of the form $system \cdot call\langle parameters\rangle$. For example, the call $system{\cdot}print\langle n\rangle$ prints the value n on the runtime console. For security reasons, system calls can only be executed by the top-level ambient. This ambient can then provide an interface to a given system call by means of forwarder channels. A separate forwarder channel can be defined for each user or group of users, enabling fine-grained security policies to be implemented for each system call. The runtime also allows files to be stored in an ambient in binary form and sent over channels like ordinary values. This feature is used in the call $system \cdot java\langle file\rangle$, which invokes the Java runtime with the specified file. This can be used to program a wide range of applications. For example, it can be used to program an ambient that moves to a remote site, retrieves a Java class file and then moves to a new site to execute the retrieved file. A similar approach can be used to coordinate the execution of multiple Prolog queries on different sites, or coordinate the distribution and retrieval of multiple HTML forms. Section 6 describes an ambient tracker application, which illustrates the kind of application that can be executed by the runtime system.

6 Ambient Tracker Application

The Channel Ambient calculus can be used to model an *ambient tracker* application, which keeps track of the location of registered client ambients as they move between trusted sites $s_0, ..., s_N$ in a network. The application is inspired by previous work on location-independence, studied in the context of the Nomadic π-calculus [21] and the Nomadic Pict programming language [22]. This section describes a decentralised version of the algorithm given in [20]. The algorithm uses multiple *home servers* to track the location of mobile clients, and relies on a locking mechanism to prevent race conditions. The locking mechanism ensures that messages are not forwarded to a client while it is migrating between sites, and that the client does not migrate while messages are in transit.

The application is modeled using the *Site*, *Tracker* and *Client* processes defined in Fig. 3. The *Site* process describes the services provided by each trusted site in the network. An ambient at a trusted site can receive a message m on channel x from a remote ambient via the *child* channel. Likewise, it can forward a message m on channel x to a remote ambient a at a site s via the fwd channel. Visiting ambients can enter and leave a trusted site via the *login* and *logout* channels respectively. An ambient at a trusted site can check whether a given site s is trusted by sending an output on channel s. A *client* ambient can register

$$
\begin{array}{l}
Site(s_i) \triangleq \\
(!child^{\uparrow}(a,x,m).a/x\langle m\rangle \\
\mid !fwd(s,a,x,m).s{\cdot}child\langle a,x,m\rangle \\
\mid !\overline{\texttt{in}}\,login \mid !\overline{\texttt{out}}\,logout \\
\mid !s_0() \mid \ldots \mid !s_N() \\
\mid !register(client,ack).\nu tracker\,\nu send\,\nu move\,\nu deliver\,\nu lock \\
\quad (tracker\boxed{Tracker\langle client,send,move,deliver,lock\rangle} \\
\quad \mid client/ack\langle tracker,send,move,deliver,lock\rangle \\
\quad \mid tracker/lock\langle s_i\rangle))
\end{array}
$$

$$
\begin{array}{l}
Tracker(client,send,move,deliver,lock) \triangleq \\
(!send^{\uparrow}(x,m).lock^{\uparrow}(s).fwd^{\uparrow}\langle s,client,deliver,(s,x,m)\rangle \\
\mid !move^{\uparrow}(s').s'^{\uparrow}\langle\rangle.lock^{\uparrow}(s).fwd^{\uparrow}\langle s,client,lock,s'\rangle)
\end{array}
$$

$$
\begin{array}{l}
Client(home,tracker,deliver,lock) \triangleq \\
(!lock^{\uparrow}(s).\texttt{out}\,logout.\texttt{in}\,s{\cdot}login.fwd^{\uparrow}\langle home,tracker,lock,s\rangle.moved\langle s\rangle \\
\mid !deliver^{\uparrow}(s,x,m).fwd^{\uparrow}\langle home,tracker,lock,s\rangle.x\langle m\rangle)
\end{array}
$$

Fig. 3. Tracker Definitions

with a trusted site via the *register* channel, which creates a new *tracker* ambient to keep track of the location of the client. The *Tracker* and *Client* processes describe the services provided by the tracker and client ambients respectively.

Figure 4 describes a scenario in which a client registers with its home site. The client c sends a message to its home site s_0 on the *register* channel, consisting of its name and an acknowledgement channel *ack*. The site creates a new ambient name t_c and new send, move, deliver and lock channels s_c, m_c, d_c, l_c respectively. It then sends these names to the client on channel *ack*, and in parallel creates a new tracker ambient t_c for keeping track of the location of the client. The tracker is initialised with the *Tracker* process and the current location of the client is stored as an output to the tracker on the lock channel l_c. When the client receives the acknowledgement it spawns a new *Client* process in parallel with process P.

A message can be sent to the client by sending a request to its corresponding tracker ambient on the home site s_0. The request is sent to the tracker ambient t_c on the send channel s_c, asking the tracker to send a message n to its client on channel x. The tracker then inputs the current location s_i of its client via the lock channel l_c, thereby acquiring the lock and preventing the client from moving. The tracker then forwards the request to the deliver channel d_c of the

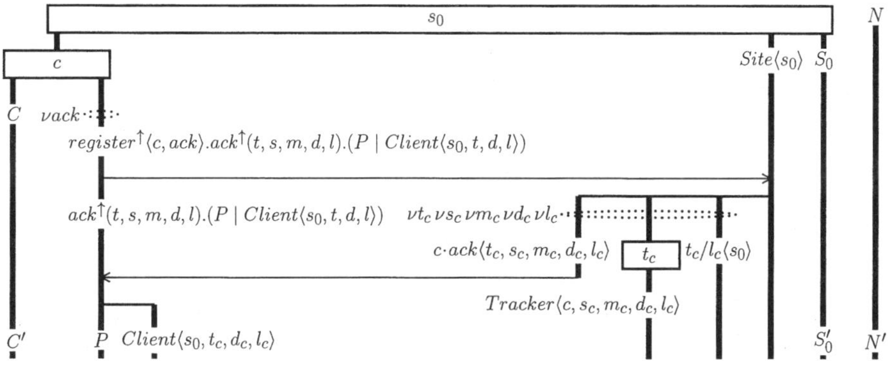

Fig. 4. Tracker Registration

client. When the client receives the request, it forwards its current location to the tracker on the lock channel, thereby releasing the lock, and then locally sends the message n on channel x.

When the client wishes to move to a site s_j, it forwards the name s_j to the tracker ambient on the move channel m_c. The tracker ambient first checks whether this site is trusted by trying to send an output on channel s_j. If the output succeeds, the tracker then inputs the current location of its client on the lock channel, thereby acquiring the lock and preventing subsequent messages from being forwarded to the client. It then forwards the name s_j to the client on the lock channel, giving it permission to move to site s_j. When the client receives permission to move, it leaves on the *logout* channel and enters site s_j on the *login* channel. It then forwards its new location to the tracker ambient on the lock channel, thereby releasing the lock.

The above application has been implemented in the channel ambient programming language, and preliminary trials have been performed. Multiple clients were initialised on a number of different machines and registered with a tracker service. These clients were programmed to migrate between the various sites and perform local tasks, including retrieving files and launching Java applications, whilst communicating with each other on the move.

7 Comparison with Related Work

The Channel Ambient calculus is a variant of Boxed Ambients inspired by recent developments in the design of process calculi for mobility. The calculus uses guarded replication, which is present in modern variants of Boxed Ambients such as [4]. Actions in CA are similar to actions in Boxed Ambients [9], except that ambients in CA can interact using named channels and sibling ambients can communicate directly. This form of sibling communication is inspired by the

Nomadic π-calculus, although agents in Nomadic π are not nested. A similar form of channel communication is also used in the Seal calculus [8], although sibling seals cannot communicate directly. The use of channels for mobility is inspired by the mechanism of passwords, first introduced in [13] and subsequently adopted in [4]. The main advantage of CA over existing variants of Boxed Ambients is its ability to express high-level constructs such as channel-based interaction and sibling communication directly. These constructs seem to be at the right level of abstraction for writing mobile applications such as the tracker application outlined in Section 6. The main advantage of CA over the Nomadic π-calculus is its ability to regulate access to an ambient by means of named channels, and its ability to model computation within nested locations, both of which are lacking in Nomadic π.

The Channel Ambient Machine extends the list semantics of the Pict machine, to provide support for nested ambients and ambient migration. Pict uses channel queues in order to store blocked inputs and outputs that are waiting to synchronise. In CAM these channel queues are generalised to a notion of blocked processes, in order to allow both communication and migration primitives to synchronise. A notion of unblocking is also defined, to allow mobile ambients in CAM to re-bind to new environments. The Pict machine does not require a notion of restriction, since all names in Pict are local to a single machine. In contrast, CAM requires an explicit notion of restriction in order to manage the scope of names across ambient boundaries, as given by rules (26), (28) and (33). By definition, the Pict abstract machine is deterministic and, although it is sound with respect to the π-calculus, it is not complete. In contrast, CAM is non-deterministic and is both sound and complete with respect to CA.

A number of abstract machines have also been defined for variants of the Ambient calculus. In [5] an abstract machine for Ambients is presented, which has not been proved sound or complete. In [11] a distributed implementation of Ambients is described, which uses JoCaml as an implementation language. The implementation relies on a formal translation of Ambients into the Distributed Join calculus. However, it is not clear how such a translation can be adapted to boxed ambient calculi, which use more sophisticated communication primitives. Furthermore, the implementation is tied to a particular programming language (JoCaml), which limits the scope in which it can be used. In [18] a distributed abstract machine for Safe Ambients is presented, which uses logical forwarders to represent mobility. Physical mobility can only occur when an ambient is *opened*. However, such an approach is not applicable to boxed ambient calculi, where the *open* primitive is non-existent.

The ambient tracker application described in Section 6 is inspired by work on mobile applications presented in [21]. This work identifies a key role for process calculi in modelling communication infrastructures for mobile agent systems. Such infrastructures can be used as a foundation for building robust applications in the areas of data mining and resource monitoring, among others. In [21] the Nomadic π-calculus is used to model an infrastructure for reliably forwarding messages to mobile agents, and a centralised version of this algorithm is proved correct in [20]. In Section 6, a decentralised version of this algorithm is modeled in CA. The main advantage of Channel Ambients over Nomadic Pict lies in the correctness of the Channel Ambient Machine, which ensures that any properties satisfied by the calculus model will also hold in its implementation.

8 Conclusions and Future Work

In this paper we presented a distributed abstract machine for a variant of the Boxed Ambient calculus with channels, and proved the soundness and completeness of the machine with respect to the calculus. We then described a prototype implementation, together with an application for tracking the location of mobile ambients. The prototype is a useful tool for experimenting with the development of mobile applications based on a formal model, which we hope will provide insight into the design of future programming languages for mobile computing. To our knowledge, this is the first time that a correct abstract machine for a variant of Boxed Ambients has been implemented in a distributed environment. The correctness of the machine ensures that the work done in specifying and analysing mobile applications is not lost during their implementation.

We are currently using the techniques outlined in this paper to define abstract machines for other variants of boxed ambients, such as those described in [9] and [4]. We also believe that similar techniques can be used to define an abstract machine for Safe Ambients [12]. It would be interesting to see how the resulting machine compares with those defined in [11] and [18].

Another area for future research is the choice between a deterministic and a non-deterministic implementation. Non-determinism guarantees completeness, but requires a random scheduling algorithm to be implemented. Determinism is more efficient, but leads to weaker correctness properties. The machine defined in this paper allows both alternatives to be implemented. It would be interesting to investigate whether the more efficient deterministic machine provides sufficient guarantees for correctness.

The main motivation for defining an abstract machine for CA, as opposed to another variant of boxed ambients, was the desire to express high-level constructs such as channel-based interaction and sibling communication directly. In future, we plan to investigate whether these constructs can be encoded in other variants of Boxed Ambients. We also intend to ascertain whether existing type theories for boxed ambient calculi can be smoothly to applied to CA.

More generally, we plan to investigate whether existing program analysis techniques can be used to prove properties of applications written in CA. Examples of such techniques include equivalence-based analysis of mobile applications [20], model-checking techniques based on ambient logic [6] and security types for mobile ambients [10].

Acknowledgements. The authors would like to thank the ESOP referees and the members of the Imperial College Concurrency group for their comments and suggestions. Nobuko Yoshida is partially supported by EPSRC grants GR/R33465 and GR/S55538.

References

1. L. Bettini, R. D. Nicola, and R. Pugliese. Xklaim and klava: Programming mobile code. In M. Lenisa and M. Miculan, editors, *ENTCS*, volume 62. Elsevier, 2002.
2. M. Bugliesi, G. Castagna, and S. Crafa. Boxed ambients. In *TACS'01*, number 2215 in LNCS, pages 38–63. Springer, 2001.
3. M. Bugliesi, G. Castagna, and S. Crafa. Reasoning about security in mobile ambients. In *CONCUR'01*, number 2154 in LNCS, pages 102–120. Springer, 2001.
4. M. Bugliesi, S. Crafa, M. Merro, and V. Sassone. Communication interference in mobile boxed ambients. In *FSTTCS'02*, volume 2556 of *LNCS*, pages 71–84. Springer, 2002.
5. L. Cardelli. Mobile ambient synchronization. Technical Report SRC-TN-1997-013, Hewlett Packard Laboratories, July 25 1997.
6. L. Cardelli and A. D. Gordon. Anytime, anywhere: Modal logics for mobile ambients. In *Proceedings of POPL '00*, pages 365–377. ACM, Jan. 2000.
7. L. Cardelli and A. D. Gordon. Mobile ambients. *Theoretical Comput. Sci.*, 240(1):177–213, 2000. An extended abstract appeared in *FoSSaCS '98*: 140–155.
8. G. Castagna, J. Vitek, and F. Zappa. The seal calculus. 2003. Available from ftp://ftp.di.ens.fr/pub/users/castagna/seal.ps.gz.
9. S. Crafa, M. Bugliesi, and G. Castagna. Information flow security for boxed ambients. In *F-WAN'02*, number 66(3) in ENTCS, 2002.
10. M. Dezani-Ciancaglini and I. Salvo. Security types for mobile safe ambients. In *ASIAN'00*, volume 1961 of *LNCS*, pages 215–236. Springer, 2000.
11. C. Fournet, J.-J. Lévy, and A. Schmitt. An asynchronous distributed implementation of mobile ambients. In J. van Leeuwen, O. Watanabe, M. Hagiya, P. Mosses, and T. Ito, editors, *Proceedings of TCS 2000*, volume 1872 of *LNCS*, pages 348–364. IFIP, Springer, Aug. 2000.
12. F. Levi and D. Sangiorgi. Controlling interference in ambients. In *POPL'00*. ACM Press, 2000.
13. M. Merro and M. Hennessy. Bisimulation congruences in safe ambients. In *POPL'02*, pages 71–80. ACM Press, 2002.
14. M. Merro and V. Sassone. Typing and subtyping mobility in boxed ambients. In *CONCUR'02*, volume 2421 of *LNCS*, pages 304–320. Springer, 2002.
15. A. Phillips. *The Channel Ambient System*, 2003. Runtime system and related documentation available from http://www.doc.ic.ac.uk/~anp/ca.html.
16. A. Phillips. *The Channel Ambient Calculus: From Process Algebra to Mobile Code.* PhD thesis, Imperial College London, 2004. Forthcoming.
17. A. Phillips, S. Eisenbach, and D. Lister. From process algebra to java code. In *ECOOP Workshop on Formal Techniques for Java-like Programs*, 2002.
18. D. Sangiorgi and A. Valente. A distributed abstract machine for Safe Ambients. In *ICALP'01*, volume 2076 of *LNCS*. Springer, 2001.
19. D. N. Turner. *The Polymorphic Pi-Calculus: Theory and Implementation.* PhD thesis, LFCS, University of Edinburgh, June 1996. CST-126-96 (also published as ECS-LFCS-96-345).
20. A. Unyapoth and P. Sewell. Nomadic Pict: Correct communication infrastructures for mobile computation. In *POPL'01*, pages 116–127, 2001.
21. P. T. Wojciechowski. *Nomadic Pict: Language and Infrastructure Design for Mobile Computation.* PhD thesis, University of Cambridge, June 2000. Also appeared as Technical Report 492, Computer Laboratory, University of Cambridge, June 2000.
22. P. T. Wojciechowski. *The Nomadic Pict System*, 2000. Available electronically as part of the Nomadic Pict distribution.

A Dependently Typed Ambient Calculus*

Cédric Lhoussaine and Vladimiro Sassone

University of Sussex, UK

Abstract. *The Ambient calculus is a successful model of distributed, mobile computation, and has been the vehicle of new ideas for resource access control. Mobility types have been used to enforce elementary access control policies, expressed indirectly via classification of ambients in groups by means of 'group types.' The paper presents a theory of dependent types for the Ambient calculus which allows greater flexibility, while keeping the complexity away from the programmer into the type system.*

1 Introduction

The work on types for *Mobile Ambients* [6] (MA), initiated in [7], has introduced some interesting innovations. In particular, it led to natural concepts of mobility types (cf., e.g. [4,3,12,8]). The common framework proposed so far in the literature for mobility control relies on *groups* and *group types*. Groups represent collections of ambients with uniform access rights, and policies like 'n *CanMoveTo* m' are expressed by saying, for instance, 'n *belongs to group* G and all ambients of *group* G *can move to* m.' These and similar simple constraints, such as 'm *accepts ambients of group* G,' are then enforced statically by embodying groups in types. This approach's merit is to simplify considerably the type system. It allows to avoid the difficulties of dependent types, since it replaces (variable) ambient names with (constant) group names. The loss in expressiveness and flexibility, however, is self-evident.

This paper generalises the approaches to access control based on groups by using types explicitly dependent on ambient names, so that policies like 'n *CanMoveTo* m' can be expressed directly. The task involves issues of technical complexity, and we believe that our approach contributes significantly to advance the theory of type-based resource access control in the Ambient calculus. The guiding principle behind our work is to allow for flexibility in control policies, while pushing the complexity to the type system. We elaborate further on this below.

Dependent types vs groups. At the formal level, dependent types are indeed trickier to work with than groups, as already suggested in [4]. However, they are very expressive and ultimately, at the programming level, not necessarily more difficult to use than groups. It may indeed be challenging, if not impossible, to

* Research supported by 'MyThS: Models and Types for Security in Mobile Distributed Systems', EU FET-GC IST-2001-32617.

D.A. Schmidt (Ed.): ESOP 2004, LNCS 2986, pp. 171–187, 2004.

partition ambient names into groups in order to implement the desired security policy in complex applications. By referring directly to names, instead, a programmer avoids a level of indirection, and is less prone to policy specification errors. The type systems we propose here aim at harnessing the complexity of dependent types and relegating it to inner working of the type system, so as to keep the burden off the programmer, and consequently make programs more robust.

To illustrate the point, let us consider a naive and specialised taxi server whose intention is to provide a taxi service usable only by ambient n:

$$\mathit{TaxiServ}(n) = !(\nu\, \mathit{taxi}\colon A)\,(\mathit{taxi}[] \mid n[\mathsf{in}\ \mathit{taxi}]).$$

The process creates a new ambient called *taxi*, with some type A, together with an ambient n which can move to it. Due to the scoping rules, an external ambient $m[P]$ can move into the taxi by first moving to n and then escaping it after being transported to *taxi*. To avoid this, A must restrict the children allowed of *taxi* to, say, only ambient n. Using groups – for instance in the setting of [12], where an ambient type $a : \mathsf{amb}[G, \mathsf{mob}[\mathcal{G}]]$ assigns group G to a and specifies that $\mathcal{G}$ is the set of groups of those ambients which a is allowed to move to – to prevent any ambient other than n to occupy the taxi, n must be the *only* ambient with a type of the form $\mathsf{amb}[H, \mathsf{mob}[\{G\} \cup \mathcal{H}]]$, where G is the group of *taxi*. This condition is clearly beyond the control of the $\mathit{TaxiServ}(n)$ application, as the environment may create new names with types that violate it. Making G private is not a solution, as it forces n to be confined too, so defeating its very purpose. Indeed, in a term such as $(\nu\, G)\,(\nu\, n\colon A)\, P \mid Q$, with G in A, n can not be passed to Q (not even via subtyping [12]), as the type of any suitable receiving variable would contain G.

With dependent types we would simply and directly mention n as a possible (or perhaps the only) child for *taxi*. This leads to ambient types of the form $\mathsf{amb}[\mathsf{mob}[\mathcal{P}, \mathcal{C}]]$, where $\mathcal{P}$ is the set of names of those ambients allowed to contain *taxi* and, dually, $\mathcal{C}$ is the set of names of those ambients allowed to reside within *taxi*. Type A above can be simply $\mathsf{amb}[\mathsf{mob}[\{\mathit{top}\}, \{n\}]]$, where name *top* represents the top-level ambient. Yet, the *taxi* ambient would be guaranteed to have n and only n as a possible child, with no need for n to be private. Of course, such simplicity in expressing types comes at the cost of additional complexity at the type system level. Primarily, we need to enforce consistency between the type of a parent ambient and those of its children. To exemplify, when a taxi is created, n receives a new capability to have *taxi* as its parent; the type of n – which actually predates the creation of the fresh instance of *taxi* – must then be updated accordingly. Observe that in a conventional type system, the effect of the new name would be confined inside the scope of its definition, and would certainly not affect the type of n. In our case, however, leaving n's type unchanged leads to an unsound system (cf. Example 1).

In order for n to be aware of any additional capability it may acquire over time, we introduce the pivotal notion of *abstract names*. Such names are used only in the derivation of typing judgements, to record potential name creations, either by a process or by its environment. As it will be clear later, abstract names intuitively play the role of group names in their ability to cross the scope of name restrictions.

Flexibility. The main contribution of this paper is the use of dynamic types to increase expressiveness, which can be fleshed out as the ability to deploy security policies at run time. More precisely, we want servers flexible enough to provide services specialised to each particular client, so leading towards secure, highly modular programming. In other words, a service specifically provided for client c_1 must be unusable by client c_2. Such objectives may be achieved in several different ways, as for instance by adding special operators to the calculus. In this paper we stick to the basic primitives of the Ambient calculus and investigate the issue of personalised services at the level of types.

The taxi server discussed above is not particularly interesting, because it is hardly a server at all: it does not interact with generic clients, but provides again and again the same 'secure' service to the same client. A brief reflection proves that if we were to design a 'true' server using groups, we would need to exchange group names, yielding soon a form of (group) dependent types. The type system we propose for dynamic types is a natural extension of the one we illustrated above, for mobility only. Namely, we simply require that communications of ambient names and variables be reflected in the types. For instance, the dynamic taxi server will have the form:

$$!(x)\,\mathit{TaxiServ}(x) = !(x)(\nu\, \mathit{taxi}\colon \mathsf{amb}[\mathsf{mob}[\{\mathit{top}\},\{x\}]])\,(\mathit{taxi}[] \mid x[\mathsf{in}\ \mathit{taxi}]).$$

Communication increases the complexity of the type system, because the rules need to track information about receivers, too. It makes little sense to type communication via the usual exchange types, because receiving different names may lead to orthogonal behavioural and mobility properties. Subtyping does not help towards a unifying treatment (cf. Example 2). We approach the problem by tracking the names that may be received at a given variable. This enriches ambient types which, in addition to a mobility component, acquire a communication one. A typing assignment $n\colon \mathsf{amb}[\,\mathsf{mob}[\mathcal{P},\mathcal{C}],\mathsf{com}[\mathcal{E},\mathcal{L}]\,]$, where $\mathcal{E}$ and $\mathcal{L}$ are sets of ambient names, means that n may be communicated inside any ambient in $\mathcal{E}$, and dually, that any ambient in $\mathcal{L}$ may be communicated within n. It is important to remark that even if such components only carry finite sets, the volume of information exchanged is in general not bounded: the joint effect of name creation and the use of abstract names, allows to distribute new communication capabilities at run time, and communicate infinitely many names.

Plan. The paper proceeds as follows. Section 2 presents a simple type system with dependent types. We focus on mobility, that is the Ambient calculus with no communication at all. Then, in Section 3, we investigate dynamic types allowing communication of ambient names. For the sake of simplicity, we do not address the issue of communication of capabilities, even though this can easily be integrated in our approach.

2 A Simple Dependent Type System

In the paper we use the standard Ambient calculus with *asynchronous, monadic* communication. (We remark that our results do not depend on such choice.) Syntax and reduction semantics can be found in [6]. In this section we consider the pure Ambient calculus, that is the calculus restricted to the mobility features. Communication will be studied in Section 3.

2.1 Types and Definitions

The syntax of types is given in Figure 1 where N denotes an infinite set of *abstract ambient names* and the symbol $\star$ stands for the *self*-ambient, whose meaning is explained below. The type $\mathsf{cap}[\mathcal{P}]$ denotes the type of a capability which can be exercised within any ambient whose name occurs in $\mathcal{P}$. An ambient type has, for the moment, just one component: a mobility type. Ambient n with mobility type $\mathsf{mob}[\mathcal{P},\mathcal{C}]$ is allowed to be a sub-ambient of all ambients whose name occurs in $\mathcal{P}$; i.e. $\mathcal{P}$ is the set of *possible parents* of n. Moreover, an ambient is allowed to occur as sub-ambient of n if its name occurs in $\mathcal{C}$, the set of *possible children* of n. We define some useful notations on types:

$$\mathsf{amb}[M]^{\mathsf{mob}} = M \qquad \mathsf{mob}[\mathcal{P},\mathcal{C}]^{\uparrow} = \mathcal{P} \qquad \mathsf{mob}[\mathcal{P},\mathcal{C}]^{\downarrow} = \mathcal{C}$$

We use two kinds of typing contexts: *abstract contexts* (ranged over by $\Xi, \Theta, \dots$) and *concrete contexts* (ranged over by $\Gamma, \Delta, \dots$), which map respectively abstract and concrete names to ambient types. We use Π to denote either an abstract or a concrete context. We note by (Π, Π') the union of disjoint contexts of the same kind. According to the informal meaning of types, type assignments in concrete typing contexts are related to each other. Consider for instance

$$\Gamma = n\colon \mathsf{amb}[\,\mathsf{mob}[\mathcal{P},\mathcal{C}]\,],\ m\colon \mathsf{amb}[\,\mathsf{mob}[\emptyset,\{n\}]\,],$$

where the type of m allows it to have n as a child. Coherently, the type of n should allow n to have m as a parent, i.e. $m \in \mathcal{P}$. This can be expressed by the central notion of *context update* $\Gamma^{(n:A)}$, which updates Γ with respect to a fresh type assignment $n : A$:

$$\begin{aligned}(\Gamma, \Delta)^{(n:A)} &= \Gamma^{(n:A)}, \Delta^{(n:A)}\\ (m\colon \mathsf{amb}[M_0])^{(n:\mathsf{amb}[N])} &= m\colon \mathsf{amb}[M_1],\end{aligned} \tag{1}$$

where

$$M_1^{\uparrow} = \begin{cases} M_0^{\uparrow} \cup \{n\} & \text{if } m \in N^{\downarrow},\\ M_0^{\uparrow} & \text{otherwise;}\end{cases} \qquad \text{and} \qquad M_1^{\downarrow} = \begin{cases} M_0^{\downarrow} \cup \{n\} & \text{if } m \in N^{\uparrow},\\ M_0^{\downarrow}. \end{cases}$$

Context update is pivotal in our type systems to express the typing of name creation. We define union (resp. inclusion and equality) of types as component-wise set union (resp. inclusion and equality); the notation $nm(A)$ (resp. $an(A)$) stands for the set of (abstract) names occurring in A. It is extended to all types and typing contexts.

Ambient (concrete) names $n, m, \ldots \in \mathcal{N}$		*Abstract names* $\mathsf{n}, \mathsf{m}, \ldots \in \mathsf{N}$	
Capability types	$K ::= \mathsf{cap}[\mathcal{P}]$	*Mobility types*	$M, N ::= \mathsf{mob}[\mathcal{P}, \mathcal{C}]$
Ambient types	$A ::= \mathsf{amb}[M]$	where $\mathcal{P}, \mathcal{C} \subseteq \mathcal{N} \cup \mathsf{N} \cup \{\star\}$	

Fig. 1. Types

$$\frac{A \in \mathit{Types}(\Gamma, \Theta, a)}{\Gamma \vdash^{\Theta} a : A}\ (\text{VAMB}) \qquad \frac{\Gamma \vdash^{\Theta} U : K, V : K}{\Gamma \vdash^{\Theta} U.V : K}\ (\text{VPFX})$$

$$\frac{\Gamma \vdash^{\Theta} a : A, a_i : A_i \quad A^{\mathsf{mob}\uparrow} \subseteq A_i^{\mathsf{mob}\uparrow} \quad 1 \leq i \leq n}{\Gamma \vdash^{\Theta} \mathsf{out}\, a : \mathsf{cap}[\{a_1, \ldots, a_n\}]}\ (\text{VOUT}) \qquad \frac{\Gamma \vdash^{\Theta} a : A \qquad \mathcal{P} \subseteq A^{\mathsf{mob}\downarrow}}{\Gamma \vdash^{\Theta} \mathsf{in}\, a : \mathsf{cap}[\mathcal{P}]}\ (\text{VIN})$$

$$\frac{\Gamma \vdash^{\Theta} a : A, a_i : A_i \qquad A^{\mathsf{mob}} \subseteq A_i^{\mathsf{mob}} \qquad 1 \leq i \leq n}{\Gamma \vdash^{\Theta} \mathsf{open}\, a : \mathsf{cap}[\{a_1, \ldots, a_n\}]}\ (\text{VOPEN})$$

$$\frac{\Gamma \vdash_a^{\Xi;\Theta} P \quad \Gamma \vdash^{\Xi,\Theta} a : A \quad b \in A^{\mathsf{mob}\uparrow}}{\Gamma \vdash_b^{\Xi;\Theta} a[P]}\ (\text{AMB}) \qquad \frac{}{\Gamma \vdash_a^{\emptyset;\Theta} \mathbf{0}}\ (\text{NIL}) \qquad \frac{\Gamma \vdash_a^{\Xi;\Theta,\Xi\sigma} P}{\Gamma \vdash_a^{\Xi;\Theta} !P}\ (\text{REP})$$

$$\frac{\Gamma \vdash_a^{\Xi;\Theta} P \quad \Gamma \vdash^{\Theta,\Xi} V : \mathsf{cap}[a]}{\Gamma \vdash_a^{\Xi;\Theta} V.P}\ (\text{PFX}) \qquad \frac{\Gamma \vdash_a^{\Xi_1;\Xi_2,\Theta} P \qquad \Gamma \vdash_a^{\Xi_2;\Xi_1,\Theta} Q}{\Gamma \vdash_a^{\Xi_1,\Xi_2;\Theta} P \mid Q}\ (\text{PAR})$$

$$\frac{\Gamma^{(n:A)}, n : A\{{}^{n}/_{\star}\} \vdash_a^{\Xi\{n/\mathsf{n}\};\Theta} P}{\Gamma \vdash_a^{\mathsf{n}:A,\Xi;\Theta} (\nu\, n : A)\, P}\ (\text{RES})$$

Fig. 2. Simple Type System

2.2 The Type System

Our type system deals with typing judgements for values and processes, that is

$$\Gamma \vdash^{\Theta} V : T \qquad \text{and} \qquad \Gamma \vdash_a^{\Xi;\Theta} P,$$

where T is either an ambient or a capability type. The first judgement reads as "V has type T with respect to the concrete context Γ and the abstract context Θ." In the second one, ambient name a stands for the ambient where P is running, which we call the *current location* of P. In other words, P is guaranteed to be well-typed if run in a. Abstract contexts Ξ and Θ are used to account for potential name creations: those arising from P are registered in the *local* abstract context Ξ, those performed by the environment appear in the *external* abstract context Θ. The role of such contexts is to "internalise" (a dynamic notion of) group names, which move from being part of the language to being a inner mechanism of the type system.

Example 1. Let

$$\mathit{TaxiServ}(n) = !(\nu\, \mathit{taxi}\colon A)\,(\mathit{taxi}[] \mid n[\mathsf{in}\ \mathit{taxi}]), \quad \text{for} \quad A = \mathsf{amb}[\,\mathsf{mob}[\{\mathit{top}\}, \{n\}]\,].$$

Let $Q = n[\,\mathsf{in}\, n \mid m[\mathsf{out}\, n.\mathsf{out}\, n]\,]$. We study the system $P = \mathit{TaxiServ}(n) \mid Q$, which we assume running in some ambient named *top*. The server $\mathit{TaxiServ}(n)$ creates an ambient *taxi* whose type allows it to accept only n as a child. The scope (or "visibility") of *taxi* is $(\mathit{taxi}[] \mid n[\mathsf{in}\, \mathit{taxi}])$. We assume that Q is an ambient n which may move in an ambient of the same name n and contains a child ambient m, willing to escape twice out n. Thus, m must be allowed to run at the same level of n, and a type system should ensure that any possible parent for n is also a possible one for m. This leads to an assignment like Γ below.

$$\Gamma = \begin{cases} \mathit{top}\colon \mathsf{amb}[\,\mathsf{mob}[\emptyset, \{n, m\}]\,] \\ \quad n\colon \mathsf{amb}[\,\mathsf{mob}[\{\mathit{top}, n\}, \{n, m\}]\,] \\ \quad m\colon \mathsf{amb}[\,\mathsf{mob}[\{\mathit{top}, n\}, \emptyset]\,] \end{cases} \quad \Delta = \begin{cases} \mathit{top}\colon \mathsf{amb}[\,\mathsf{mob}[\emptyset, \{n, m, \mathit{taxi}\}]\,] \\ \quad n\colon \mathsf{amb}[\,\mathsf{mob}[\{\mathit{top}, n, \mathit{taxi}\}, \{n, m\}]\,] \\ \quad m\colon \mathsf{amb}[\,\mathsf{mob}[\{\mathit{top}, n\}, \emptyset]\,], \\ \mathit{taxi}\colon \mathsf{amb}[\,\mathsf{mob}[\{\mathit{top}\}, \{n\}]\,] \end{cases}$$

In $(\mathit{taxi}[] \mid n[\mathsf{in}\, \mathit{taxi}])$, ambient n gains access to *taxi* by means of name creation, viz. *taxi*, and the type assignment must evolve to Δ above (which actually is of the form $\Gamma^{(\mathit{taxi}:A)}, \mathit{taxi}\colon A$). However, running P may obviously lead to m becoming a child of *taxi*, thus violating the specification expressed by the type of *taxi*. So, P must be considered ill-typed. A naive approach would however try to typecheck $(\mathit{taxi}[] \mid n[\mathsf{in}\, \mathit{taxi}])$ (against Δ) and Q (against Γ) independently, and therefore accept P. Indeed, from Q's point of view, *taxi* does not exist (it is bound in $\mathit{TaxiServ}(n)$), and Q behaves well. From the viewpoint of $\mathit{TaxiServ}(n)$, although *taxi* exists, the specification given by its type is respected: ambient n is allowed to move into *taxi*. Considering $\mathit{TaxiServ}(n)$ and Q as stand-alone processes prevents from realising that their interaction may lead to a breach of the intended access policy. □

Example 1 motivates the use of abstract contexts. They are a means to record the new capabilities which may potentially arise from name creations performed in external processes. Since such names are bound, they cannot be referred to by name in typing contexts: we use *abstract names* to represent them. The typechecking of process Q in Example 1 must then be carried out with an *external* abstract context $\Theta = \mathsf{taxi}\colon A$, representing the potential creation of a name of type A, and an empty *local* abstract context, as Q does not create names. In other words, we are led to prove $\Gamma \vdash^{\emptyset;\Theta}_{\mathit{top}} Q$. From Γ and Θ, we can deduce a more informative type for n, viz. its *global type* $\mathsf{amb}[\,\mathsf{mob}[\{\mathit{top}, n, \mathsf{taxi}\}, \{n, m\}]\,]$, which states that n is allowed to run within *top*, n and some ambient taxi, to be created by its environment and whose actual name we do not known yet. (We stress that the name taxi is just a placeholder; the information that leads to the global type is carried by A.) Since m does not appear in Θ, its global type remains $\mathsf{amb}[\mathsf{mob}[\{\mathit{top}, n\}, \emptyset]]$, and we can conclude that Q is ill-typed. Indeed, there exists a possible parent of n which is not a possible one for m, namely taxi.

We define the *symmetric type* $\Pi[\alpha]$ of a name α with respect to a typing context Π, as $\mathsf{amb}[\mathsf{mob}[\mathcal{P},\mathcal{C}]]$, where $\mathcal{P}=\{\beta \mid \alpha\in\Pi(\beta)^{\mathsf{mob}\downarrow}\}$ and $\mathcal{C}=\{\beta \mid \alpha\in\Pi(\beta)^{\mathsf{mob}\uparrow}\}$.

Definition 1. The *global type* of a name α with respect to typing contexts Γ and Θ is defined as

$$gt(\Gamma;\Theta)(\alpha)=\begin{cases}\Gamma(\alpha)\cup\Theta[\alpha] & \textit{if } \alpha\in\mathcal{N}\\ \Theta(\alpha)\{\alpha/\star\}\cup\Theta[\alpha] & \textit{if } \alpha\in\mathsf{N}\end{cases}$$

We define $\mathit{Types}(\Gamma,\Theta,a)=\{gt(\Gamma;\Theta)(a)\}$. (We use a singleton set here for uniformity with next section.) Turning back to the previous discussion, one can verify that indeed

$$gt(\Gamma;\Theta)(n)=\mathsf{amb}[\mathsf{mob}[\{\mathit{top},n,\mathsf{taxi}\},\{n,m\}]].$$

The notion of symmetric type leads to the definition of *symmetric typing context.*

Definition 2. A concrete typing context Γ is said *symmetric* if $\Gamma(n)=\Gamma[n]$, for all $n\in nm(\Gamma)$.

Symmetric typing context formalises the notion of "consistency" of a typing context. It ensures that a name n has a type allowing m as a child of n if and only if m itself has a type allowing n as a parent. It also guarantees that a typing context is "complete," i.e. that any name occurring in it has a type assignment. In the following we will assume all concrete typing contexts to be symmetric, and all abstract contexts to be "complete" for abstract names, that is $dom(\Theta)=an(\Theta)$.

Symmetric typing replicates parenthood information both in children and in parents types. Nevertheless, both components of mobility types are necessary to give sufficient access control in the presence of name creation. We remark that comparable mechanisms play in groups based approaches via the assignment of names to groups. Using the types of [12] to exemplify, recall that $\mathcal{G}$ in $n\colon\mathsf{amb}[G,\mathsf{mob}[\mathcal{G}]]$ is the set of groups of ambients allowed as parents of n. Therefore, assigning n to G to has the effect of determining the children allowed of n: namely, those ambients whose mobility component contains G.

Let us now comment on the rules of the Figure 2, starting with the judgements for values. We look at the rules from conclusions to premises. A judgement $\Gamma\vdash^{\Theta} U\colon T, V\colon T'$ stands for $\Gamma\vdash^{\Theta} U\colon T$ and $\Gamma\vdash^{\Theta} V\colon T'$. Axiom (VAMB) simply gives the global type of a name, while (VPFX) asserts that the prefix $U.V$ has the capability type K if both U and V have such type. In order to type a $\mathsf{out}\,a$ performed in some ambient a_i, (VOUT) checks that the possible parents of a are allowed for a_i (for $i\in\{1,\dots,n\}$). Rule (VIN) typechecks the capability of ambient b (a member of $\mathcal{P}$) to move to ambient a. This is allowed if b is a possible child of a. Finally, (VOPEN) states that some ambient a_i can open a if both the allowed parents and children of a are allowed for a_i, $i\in\{1,\dots,n\}$. This ensures that whatever happens to a_i because of the capabilities inherited from a via the open is compatible with its specification.

A process is always typed with respect to a current location. Process $a[P]$ is well-typed in ambient b (rule AMB) if b is allowed as a's parent and P is well-typed in a. Process $\mathbf{0}$ is always well-typed with local abstract context empty. Process $V.P$ is well-typed in a if P is well-typed in a and V is a capability that can be exercised in a. In order to type a parallel composition of processes (rule (PAR)), the local abstract context must be split in two parts: in the typing of each component one of these remains local, the other becomes external.

Rule (RES) deserves a close analysis. The typing of $(\nu n\colon A)\,P$ requires the local abstract context to assign type A to some abstract name (here n). The rule consumes such assignment, and P is then typed with its concrete typing context updated with n's typing. We apply the substitution $\{n/\star\}$ to A, where $\star$ is an "alias" for the self ambient (n here). This is necessary, since in the conclusion n cannot occur in A. Indeed, we make the usual assumption that a bound name does not occur in the typing contexts and in the current location (which here means $n \neq a$). Finally, the substitution $\{n/\mathsf{n}\}$ is applied to the local abstract context, as types in Ξ may refer to n. This would be the case of, e.g., the term

$$(\nu n\colon \mathsf{amb}[\,\mathsf{mob}[\{\mathit{top}\},\emptyset]\,])\,(\nu m\colon \mathsf{amb}[\,\mathsf{mob}[\{n\},\emptyset]\,])\,P$$

typed with the local abstract context $\mathsf{n}\colon \mathsf{amb}[\,\mathsf{mob}[\{\mathit{top}\},\emptyset]\,],\ \mathsf{m}\colon \mathsf{amb}[\,\mathsf{mob}[\{\mathsf{n}\},\emptyset]\,]$.

In Rule (REP) we assume that σ is an *abstract renaming*. By this we mean an injective substitution whose domain is the set of abstract names occurring in Ξ and whose codomain is a set of fresh abstract names. In other words, if σ is an abstract renaming, then $\Xi\sigma$ is a fresh copy of Ξ. Process $!P$ can be seen as an infinite parallel composition of copies of P. Therefore, typing $!P$ is equivalent to typing P in an environment which can provide new capabilities as P can. These are represented by the local abstract context of $!P$, which explains why we add a copy of the local abstract context to the external one. It is easy to prove that one copy is sufficient.

It is worth remarking that there are behavioural properties which are expressible with groups but not with this system of dependent types. This is because in the present system, name creation assigns types which may only refer to names already in the scope of the created name. For instance, in

$$(\nu n\colon A)\,P \mid (\nu m\colon A')\,Q$$

m (resp. n) can not occur in A (resp. A'). This means that n and m will not be able to interact. With group types one may use group names shared by m and n, i.e. whose scope contains both names. The extension of the type system to dynamic types introduced in the next section circumvents the problem by the usual mechanisms of scope extrusion in name passing calculi. Indeed, in order for m to give (and acquire) new capabilities to n, we send n to m, which then may refer in A' to the received name.

3 Dynamic Types

As illustrated in the previous section, name creation is itself a means to dynamically change ambient capabilities. In the type system, abstract names are used

Abstract variables $\mathsf{x}, \mathsf{y}, \ldots \in \mathsf{X}$		*Capability types*	$K ::= \mathsf{cap}[\mathcal{P}]$
Mobility types	$M, N ::= \mathsf{mob}[\mathcal{P}, \mathcal{C}]$	*Communication types*	$C ::= \mathsf{com}[\mathcal{E}, \mathcal{L}]$
Ambient types	$A ::= \mathsf{amb}[M, C]$	*Variable types*	$B ::= \mathsf{var}[\mathcal{B}]$

$$\text{where } \mathcal{P}, \mathcal{C} \subseteq \mathcal{N} \cup \mathsf{N} \cup \mathcal{X} \cup \mathsf{X} \cup \{\star\} \quad \text{and} \quad \mathcal{B}, \mathcal{E}, \mathcal{L} \subseteq \mathcal{N} \cup \mathsf{N} \cup \{\star\}$$

Fig. 3. New types for communication

to track the relevant changes outside the actual scope of the name. New names may refer directly in their types to known ambient names. For instance, the taxi server

$$(\nu\, taxi\colon \mathsf{amb}[\mathsf{mob}[\{top\}, \{n\}]])\,(taxi[] \mid n[\mathsf{in}\ taxi])$$

creates a name *taxi* which may have n as a child. At the same time, the type of n is enriched with the capability to have *taxi* as a parent. This process, however, is restricted in that it provides a private taxi for one and only one ambient, namely n. By enabling communication of ambient names, types in name creation constructs may also refer to a received name, so boosting the dynamic aspects of the calculus. This allows, for instance, to write a *generic* taxi server which dynamically provides private taxis for any ambient whose name is received by a communication:

$$DTaxiServ = !(x)(\nu\, taxi\colon \mathsf{amb}[\,\mathsf{mob}[\{top\}, \{x\}]\,])\,(taxi[] \mid x[\mathsf{in}\ taxi]),$$

Such an increase in dynamic adaptation, and therefore in expressiveness, comes with a corresponding increase in the complexity of the typing system. There are two reasons:

- ▷ firstly, types may now refer to ambients indirectly, via variables;
- ▷ secondly, upon communication a variable may become instantiated by a name or by another, thus leading to different capabilities, that is different access control policies. Moreover, such policies are not necessarily comparable, which, for instance, makes subtyping useless.

Example 2. Let *DTaxiServ* be as above, and consider $P = \langle n \rangle \mid \langle m \rangle \mid DTaxiServ$. Process P may evolve to either

$$P_1 = \langle n \rangle \mid taxi[] \mid m[\mathsf{in}\ taxi] \mid DTaxiServ \quad \text{or} \quad P_2 = \langle m \rangle \mid taxi[] \mid n[\mathsf{in}\ taxi] \mid DTaxiServ$$

according to whether *DTaxiServ* receives m or n. As regards to the type assigned to *taxi*, in P_1 only m – that is the received name – is allowed to go inside *taxi*, whereas in P_2 only n is. Such situations are orthogonal and thus incomparable: in the first one, m acquires a new capability (‘*CanMoveTo*’ *taxi*) and n remains unchanged, whereas in the second it is the other way around. This means that the type system will have to deal with all possible communications. □

Example 2 suggests that an ambient name may have different possible types depending on the communications that may happen.

3.1 New Types and Definitions

The needed additional types are given in Figure 3, where X is an infinite set of *abstract variables.* Ambient types have now two components: one for mobility, which remains unchanged, and one for communication. Following our "symmetric style" for types, a communication type consists of two sets of names: an *external* one, $\mathcal{E}$, which describes the ambients where the name in object may be communicated, and a *local* one, $\mathcal{L}$, which describes the names which may be communicated within the object ambient. For instance, if n has type $\mathsf{amb}[M, \mathsf{com}[\{m\}, \{o\}]]$, then n can be exchanged inside m, and o can be communicated inside n; two terms which satisfy such specification are: $m[\langle n\rangle]$ and $n[\langle o\rangle]$.

A variable type is the set of ambients where a variable may be bound. For instance, in $n[(x)P]$ the variable x may have type $\mathsf{var}[\{n\}]$. Because we deal with an ambient calculus with the open capability, a variable may of course be bound in several places. Variable x in

$$n[\langle o_1\rangle \mid \mathsf{open}\, m \mid m[\langle o_2\rangle \mid (x)P]$$

may be bound in n or in m, depending on whether m is opened before x is bound or not. The type of x in the term above must therefore be $\mathsf{var}[\{m, n\}]$.

We remark that, contrary to usual type systems, but as in [1], we do not use the so-called *exchange* types, which build on the notion of "topic of conversation" permitted within a given ambient. This is a particular type (modulo subtyping) which all processes within that ambient agree to exchange. Indeed, suppose that n is an ambient whose exchange type is A, and m_1 and m_2 have type A. Then, the term

$$n[\langle m_1\rangle \mid \langle m_2\rangle \mid (x\colon A)P]$$

would be well-typed. However, if an external process gives a new capabilities to m_1 via name creation, then $\langle m_1\rangle$ may become ill-typed. An instance of this is the following term.

$$(\nu\, o\colon \mathsf{amb}[\mathsf{mob}[\{m_1\}, \emptyset], C])\, Q \mid n[\langle m_1\rangle \mid \langle m_2\rangle \mid (x\colon A)P]$$

Here, $\langle m_2\rangle$ is still well-typed, but $\langle m_1\rangle$ is manifestly not. In fact, after scope extrusion, m_1 has not anymore type A, but A enriched with the capability to admit o as a child, which leads to a type error when trying to bind x to m_1. Our type system does not feature uniform exchange types, but it allows in principle to bind a variable to names which may have completely different types. This also leads to an increase in expressiveness.

Assuming the set of communicable ambient names to appear in types may at first appear to give a very restricted form of communication, where only finitely many names can be communicated in a given ambient. Due to the dynamic nature of types, this is actually not the case: name creation can give new communication capabilities to existing ambients. For instance, if ambient n has a communication type $\mathsf{com}[\emptyset, \{o\}]$ – that is, only o may be sent in n – the creation of name m with communication type $\mathsf{com}[\{n\}, \emptyset]$ gives n the new capability to have m has communicable ambient. Combining name creation with replication leads to potentially infinite communicable names in a given ambient.

Finally, we remark that variable and communication types, contain only ambient names and no variables. This means that communication is forbidden inside ambients created using a received name, as in $(x)x[P]$. We embraced such restriction for the sake of simplicity: allowing variables in such types is possible, at the price of a more complex definition of the set of types (Definition 7) and of additional side conditions in the type system's rules.

We introduce notations for communication types corresponding to those given for mobility types in (1). We define $\mathsf{amb}[M,C]^{\mathsf{com}} = C$, and then $C^{\uparrow}$, $C^{\downarrow}$ and $(\Gamma,\Delta)^{(n:A)}$, where $(x:B)^{(n:A)} = x:B$, as obvious. The notion of *symmetric type* is extended to communication types straightforwardly.

No variable occurs in symmetric types, therefore the notion of symmetric typing context must be defined accordingly.

Definition 3. A concrete typing context Γ is *symmetric* if, for all $n \in nm(\Gamma)$, we have $\Gamma(n) - (\mathsf{X} \cup \mathcal{X}) = \Gamma[n]$.

Here $\Gamma(n) - (\mathsf{X} \cup \mathcal{X})$ denotes the type of n in Γ with all variables removed. Definition 1 of global types for ambient names remains unchanged; we complete it below for variables.

Definition 4. The *global type* of a variable α with respect to typing contexts Γ and Θ is defined by

$$gt(\Gamma;\Theta)(\alpha) = \begin{cases} \Gamma[\alpha] \cup \Theta[\alpha] & \textit{if } \alpha \in \mathcal{X} \\ \Theta[\alpha] & \textit{if } \alpha \in \mathsf{X} \end{cases}$$

The global type of a variable is the ambient type constructed from the capabilities the variable is given by typing contexts. In case of an abstract variable, only the abstract context provides the information, as no abstract variable occurs in the concrete context.

We finally define the *local type* of a name, as the usual notion of type provided by a typing context.

Definition 5. The *local type* of a name α with respect to typing contexts Γ and Θ is defined by

$$lt(\Gamma;\Theta)(\alpha) = \begin{cases} \Gamma(\alpha) & \textit{if } \alpha \in dom(\Gamma) \\ \Theta(\alpha) & \textit{if } \alpha \in dom(\Theta) \\ \text{undefined otherwise.} \end{cases}$$

For $B = \mathsf{var}[\mathcal{B}]$, we usually identify B and $\mathcal{B}$ writing, for instance, $\alpha \in B$ instead of $\alpha \in \mathcal{B}$.

$$\frac{\Gamma \vdash^{\Theta} a : A, a_i : A_i \qquad \begin{array}{c}\text{for any } \alpha,\ \text{if } lt(\Gamma;\Theta)(\alpha) = B \text{ then } a \in B \text{ iff } a_i \in B \\ A^{\mathsf{mob}} \subseteq A_i^{\mathsf{mob}} \qquad A^{\mathsf{com}} = A_i^{\mathsf{com}} \qquad \forall i \in \{1, \dots n\}\end{array}}{\Gamma \vdash^{\Theta} \mathsf{open}\, a : \mathsf{cap}[\{a_1, \dots, a_n\}]} \ (\text{VOPEN'})$$

$$\frac{\Gamma, x : B \vdash_a^{\Xi\{x/x\};\Theta} P \qquad a \in B}{\Gamma \vdash_a^{x:B,\Xi;\Theta} (x)P} \ (\text{INPUT}) \qquad \frac{\Gamma \vdash^{\Theta} V : A \qquad a \in A^{\mathsf{com}\uparrow}}{\Gamma \vdash_a^{\emptyset;\Theta} \langle V \rangle} \ (\text{OUPUT})$$

Fig. 4. Revised typing system and additional ones for communication

3.2 Revised Typing System

The type system for the calculus with communication of ambient names is obtained from Figure 2 adding rules (INPUT) and (OUPUT) for communication in Figure 4, and replacing (VOPEN) with (VOPEN').

Rule (VOPEN') has two new conditions. The first verifies that the communication type is the same in the opened ambient and in the enclosing one. The condition on the top line checks that variables may be bound in the opened ambient if and only if they may in the opening one. Rule (INPUT) is similar to (RES): we pick up an abstract variable from the local abstract context whose type contains the current location. We do not perform any context update, since such updates only concern ambient names. Finally, rule (OUTPUT) says that we can send the value V inside a if that is allowed by the type of V.

The most significant revision is in the definition of $\mathit{Types}(\Gamma, \Theta, a)$, which is not anymore just a singleton, since names may now have several types. This means that any typing derivation with an axiom (VAMB) as a premise has to be read as: "for all types A such that $\Gamma \vdash^{\Theta} a : A$." Before we give the formal definition of $\mathit{Types}(\Gamma, \Theta, a)$, let us focus on an example to gather some intuition.

Example 3. Let us consider a non-replicated version of the taxi server of Example 2, but with the new communication types:

$$\mathit{DTaxiServ}_1 = (x)(\nu\, \mathit{taxi} : \mathsf{amb}[M, C])\, (\mathit{taxi}[] \mid x[\mathsf{in}\ \mathit{taxi}]),$$

with $M = \mathsf{mob}[\{\mathit{top}\}, \{x\}]$ and $C = \mathsf{com}[\emptyset, \emptyset]$. Let $P = \langle n \rangle \mid \langle m \rangle \mid \mathit{DTaxiServ}_1$, and suppose to work with the following typing context which assigns types to the free ambient names:

$$\Gamma = \begin{cases} n : A_n, \\ m : A_m, \\ \mathit{top} : \mathsf{amb}[\,\mathsf{mob}[\emptyset, \{m, n\}], \mathsf{com}[\emptyset, \{m, n\}]\,], \end{cases}$$

where

$$A_n = \mathsf{amb}[\,\mathsf{mob}[\{\mathit{top}\}, \{m\}], \mathsf{com}[\{\mathit{top}\}, \emptyset]\,]$$
$$A_m = \mathsf{amb}[\,\mathsf{mob}[\{\mathit{top}, n\}, \emptyset], \mathsf{com}[\{\mathit{top}\}, \emptyset]\,].$$

Here, n and m can be communicated in top, and have top as a parent. Moreover, n may have m as child and, consequently, m may have n as parent. One can verify that Γ is symmetric. In order to type $DTaxiServ_1$ we need an abstract context which assigns variable type $\mathsf{var}[\{top\}]$ to an abstract variable, say x, because x may be bound in top. Also, it has to assign an ambient type A to an abstract ambient name, say taxi. Type A has to match $\mathsf{amb}[M, C]$, but we cannot directly use the latter, since M contains x which is initially bound. However, we can refer to the abstract name x, meant to correspond to x. Therefore the abstract context is

$$\Xi = \mathsf{x} : \mathsf{var}[\{top\}], \mathsf{taxi} : \mathsf{amb}[N, C],$$

for $N = \mathsf{mob}[\{top\}, \{\mathsf{x}\}]$. It is easy to check that the proof of $\Gamma \vdash^{\Xi;\emptyset}_{top} DTaxiServ_1$ leads to the judgement $\Delta \vdash^{\emptyset;\emptyset}_{top} (taxi[] \mid x[\mathsf{in}\, taxi])$, by application of the rules (INPUT) and (RES), where

$$\Delta = \begin{cases} n : A_n, \\ m : A_m, \\ top : \mathsf{amb}[\,\mathsf{mob}[\emptyset, \{m, n, taxi\}], \mathsf{com}[\emptyset, \{m, n\}]\,], \\ x : \mathsf{var}[\{top\}], \\ taxi : \mathsf{amb}[\,\mathsf{mob}[\{top\}, \{x\}], \mathsf{com}[\emptyset, \emptyset]\,]. \end{cases}$$

In $(taxi[] \mid x[taxi])$, x is an ambient whose global *ambient* type is

$$A_x = \Delta[x] = \mathsf{amb}[\,\mathsf{mob}[\{taxi\}, \emptyset], \mathsf{com}[\emptyset, \emptyset]\,].$$

This is actually the least type assignable to x, since x is intended to be instantiated by an ambient name. Indeed, x may be bound to n or m, which means that the global types it may possibly assume include

$$A_x \cup A_n = \mathsf{amb}[\,\mathsf{mob}[\{top, taxi\}, \{m\}], \mathsf{com}[\{top\}, \emptyset]\,],$$

if n is received for x, and

$$A_x \cup A_m = \mathsf{amb}[\,\mathsf{mob}[\{top, taxi, n\}, \emptyset], \mathsf{com}[\{top\}, \emptyset]\,],$$

if m is received for x. Type $A_x \cup A_n$ is possible for n in the scope of the restriction. Indeed, if n is received, then the newly created ambient $taxi$ gives to n – the received name – the capability to be its child. Outside the scope of the restriction, a possible type for n is rather

$$\Xi[\mathsf{x}] \cup A_n = \mathsf{amb}[\,\mathsf{mob}[\{top, \mathsf{taxi}\}, \{m\}], \mathsf{com}[\{top\}, \emptyset]\,].$$

Since $taxi$ is not visible, we have to refer to its abstract representative taxi. Inspecting the various possibilities, we are therefore led to consider the following sets of possible ambient types.
(1) Outside the scope of $taxi$:

$$Types(\Gamma, \Xi, n) = \{\, A_n, A_n \cup \Xi[\mathsf{x}] \,\} \quad \text{and} \quad Types(\Gamma, \Xi, m) = \{A_m, A_m \cup \Xi[\mathsf{x}] \,\};$$

(2) Inside the scope of $taxi$:

$$Types(\Delta, \emptyset, n) = \{\, A_n, A_n \cup \Delta[x] \,\}, \qquad Types(\Delta, \emptyset, m) = \{\, A_m, A_m \cup \Delta[x] \,\}$$

$$\text{and} \quad Types(\Delta, \emptyset, x) = \{\, A_x \cup A_n, A_x \cup A_m \,\}. \square$$

3.3 Estimating the Set of Possible Types

In this section we give the formal estimate of the set of possible types for name a with respect to chosen typing contexts. As illustrated by Example 3, the possible types of an ambient name n are given by its global type merged with those of the variables n might instantiate. Consider the term

$$R = !\langle n\rangle \mid \langle m\rangle \mid (x)P \mid (y)Q,$$

and suppose that n and m have respectively global types A_n and A_m. Then, n may instantiate variables x and y with global types, say, A_x and A_y respectively. The possible types of n are, therefore, A_n, $A_n \cup A_x$, $A_n \cup A_y$ and $A_n \cup A_x \cup A_y$. The latter corresponds to the case in which n instantiates both x and y. The possible types of m are A_m, $A_m \cup A_x$, $A_m \cup A_y$, and $A_m \cup A_x \cup A_y$. (Observe that the latter is actually impossible, since m may instantiate at most one variable; it is an approximation error introduced by our estimation of possible types.) Symmetrically, the possible types for x are $A_x \cup A_n$, $A_x \cup A_m$, $A_x \cup A_y \cup A_n$ and $A_x \cup A_y \cup A_m$.

We first define the set of names which a given name may possibly instantiate or be instantiated by. To this aim we use binary relations over names. Intuitively, if a name α can instantiate a variable β, then the pair (α, β) is in one such a relation. We focus exclusively on so-called binding relations, which only depend on types and typing contexts. Basically, this amounts to saying that α is related to β if β is a variable which might be bound in some ambient where α may be communicated, as formalised by the definition below.

Definition 6. The *binding relation* with respect to typing contexts Γ and Θ is

$$\mathit{Bind}(\Gamma;\Theta) = \{\, (\alpha,\beta) \mid gt(\Gamma;\Theta)(\alpha) = A \text{ and } gt(\Gamma;\Theta)(\beta) = B \text{ with } A^{\mathsf{com}\uparrow}\{\alpha/\star\} \cap B \neq \emptyset \,\}.$$

Observe that $\mathit{Bind}(\Gamma,\Theta)$ is actually a subset of $(\mathsf{N} \cup \mathcal{N}) \times (\mathsf{X} \cup \mathcal{X})$. Indeed, due to our restrictions, the global (ambient) type of a variable is always empty – more precisely, it is always $\mathsf{com}[\emptyset,\emptyset]$. It follows that a variable cannot be related to another variable.

Relying on binding relations, we can estimate which variables may be instantiated by a given ambient name, and which ambient names may instantiate a given variable.

$$\mathit{Vars}(\Gamma;\Theta;\alpha) = \{\, \beta \mid (\alpha,\beta) \in \mathit{Bind}(\Gamma;\Theta) \,\};$$
$$\mathit{Ambs}(\Gamma;\Theta;\alpha) = \{\, \beta \mid (\beta,\alpha) \in \mathit{Bind}(\Gamma;\Theta) \,\}.$$

We use the notation $A \rhd \mathcal{T}$, for $\mathcal{T}$ a set of ambient types, to denote the set $\{A \cup B \mid B \in \mathcal{T}\}$, and $A \rhd^{\star} \mathcal{T}$ for $\{A\} \cup A \rhd \mathcal{T}$.

Definition 7. The set $\mathit{Types}(\Gamma;\Theta;\alpha)$ of possible types for α with respect to typing contexts Γ and Θ is defined by

$$\mathit{Types}(\Gamma;\Theta;\alpha) = gt(\Gamma;\Theta)(\alpha) \rhd^{\star} \Big\{\, gt(\Gamma;\Theta)(\beta) \;\Big|\; \beta \in \mathit{Vars}(\Gamma;\Theta;\alpha) \,\Big\}, \qquad \text{if } \alpha \in \mathsf{N} \cup \mathcal{N}, \text{ and}$$

$$\mathit{Types}(\Gamma;\Theta;\alpha) = \bigcup_{\beta \in \mathit{Ambs}(\Gamma;\Theta;\alpha)} gt(\Gamma;\Theta)(\alpha) \rhd \mathit{Types}(\Gamma;\Theta;\beta), \qquad \text{if } \alpha \in \mathsf{X} \cup \mathcal{X}.$$

Observe that the constraints on our typing rules are expressed essentially as type inclusion constraints. Therefore, we do not really need to consider all the possible types of an ambient name. In practice, as well as in proofs, it is more convenient the use notions of maximum and minimum types which are respectively the union and the intersection of all possible types. Due to space limitation, we leave to the reader to reformulate our rules in such terms. For instance, rule (VAMB) can be removed, whilst (VIN) is rewritten by replacing A (standing for all possible types for a) by the minimum type for a.

The main result of this paper is a 'Subject Reduction' theorem for the type systems we introduced. Write $\Gamma \vdash_a P$ if there exist some abstract contexts Ξ and Θ such that $\Gamma \vdash_a^{\Xi;\Theta} P$, it can be expressed as follows.

Theorem 1 (Subject Reduction). If $\Gamma \vdash_n P$ and $P \to Q$, then $\Gamma \vdash_n Q$.

4 Conclusion, Related and Future Work

The paper proposed a type system to describe access control policies and related behavioural properties of processes in the Ambient calculus. Whilst all type systems in the literature make use of groups to describe such properties [4,12,8], ours is based on dependent types. Despite an additional complexity in building typing derivations, our system has simple, natural types which may make policy specifications easier, and, therefore, simplify the programming task.

The major technical device of our approach is the novel notion of *abstract names*, which mimic the role of groups internally to typing derivations. More precisely, they keep track of – and dynamically embody in an ambient's type – any new capability that the ambient may gain during its lifespan. Abstract names are, in a sense, a dynamic notion of group, made internal to the type system rather than part of the language.

We showed how to extend a basic system to deal with communication of ambient names. The resulting type system is, we believe, the main contribution of this paper. It allows modular, per-client programming and is, to the best of our knowledge, the first one dealing at such a level with dynamic specifications of security policies in the ambient calculus. Communication types come together with a noticeable increase of complexity of typing derivations in the system. Indeed, when typing a communication, one has to consider all ambient names that can possibly instantiate a given variable. However, only a finite number of names are necessary for the proofs, and the notions of maximum and minimum types simplify the matter considerably.

We plan to study in future work the question of decidability of type checking, as a positive answer would make our type system usable in practice. We conjecture that it should be possible to devise a type checking algorithm, for the following reasons.

▷ The use of abstract contexts is not a concern: for a typeable term P, it is easy to provide (algorithmically or "by hand"), an abstract context Θ, such that $\Gamma \vdash_n^{\Theta;\emptyset} P$ for some Γ and n. Indeed, Θ is essentially the collection of bound names in P.

▷ Communication is quite hard to manage "manually" because it requires the synthesis of several global types. However, given variable types and communication types, it does not seem difficult to design an algorithm that does the job.

Because processes are typed against an environment – represented by the external abstract contexts – our type system is not compositional, in that $\Gamma \vdash_a P$ and $\Gamma \vdash_a Q$ does not imply $\Gamma \vdash_a P \mid Q$. This may be problematic in the framework of open (or partially typed) systems which have to deal with the arrival of unknown agents. Thus, the following questions arises: if $\Gamma \vdash_n^{\Xi;\emptyset} P$ is provable, does a class exist of external abstract contexts Θ such that $\Gamma \vdash_n^{\Xi;\Theta} P$? Such a class would determine the environments which make P typeable. Another question concerns the design of a type inference algorithm, which is a crucial component in open systems, where information coming from external sources cannot always be trusted. As studied in [11] for $D\pi$, dependent types call for a very accurate treatment, which would certainly be required for our type system as well. Such challenging questions are topics of our current and future research.

Related work. Beside the already mentioned work on groups [4,12,8], which provided direct inspiration for our research, related work includes [14,10]. These papers introduce dynamic and dependent types for a distributed π calculus, and study their impact on behavioural semantics. A difficulty arises in [14] with referring to bound names created in external processes, at all analogous to the one we tackled here with the introduction of *abstract names*. As a matter of fact, it is pointed out in *loc. cit.* as the main limitation of their work. The problem has been addressed in [13], completely independently of our work, using existential types. There appear to be analogies between Yoshida's existential types and our approach, although at this stage it is difficult to assess them in the details.

Since our type system works linearly on internal abstract contexts, and classically on external ones, the closest match appears to be with Yoshida's linear type discipline. However, while we conjecture we can reformulate local abstract names with (some form of) existential types, it looks as though they cannot provide a notion corresponding to our external abstract contexts. But such contexts are the keystones of our work. They allow, in particular, a correct treatment of parallel composition and replication (cf. Figure 2), where it is not always the case that if P is correct, so is $P \mid P$ or, a fortiori, $!P$. We plan to investigate this matter further.

Concerning typing systems for the ambient calculus, [1] uses dependent types for communication in order to achieve advanced type polymorphism of the sort usually encountered in lambda calculi. Types in *loc. cit.* track – like ours – all messages exchanged, and not rely on topics of conversation. They are also used to bound the nesting of ambients.

We conclude by observing that, as pointed out in [5] there are intriguing connections between groups and channels and binders of the flow analysis, as in [2,9]. Indeed, our approach has a lot to share with control flow analysis, and we believe our work can shed further light on such connections.

References

1. T. Amtoft and J. Wells. Mobile processes with dependent communication types and singleton types for names and capabilities. Technical Report 2002-3, Kansas State University, 2002.
2. C. Bodei, P. Degano, F. Nielson, and H. R. Nielson. Static analysis for the π calculus with applications to security. *Information and Computation*, 168:68–92, 2001.
3. M. Bugliesi, G. Castagna, and S. Crafa. Boxed ambients. In *TACS'01*, volume 2215 of *Lecture Notes in Computer Science*, pages 38–63. Springer, 2001.
4. L. Cardelli, G. Ghelli, and A. Gordon. Ambient groups and mobility types. In *International Conference IFIP TCS*, volume 1872 of *Lecture Notes in Computer Science*, pages 333–347. Springer, 2000.
5. L. Cardelli, G. Ghelli, and A. Gordon. Secrecy and group creation. In *CONCUR'00*, volume 1877 of *Lecture Notes in Computer Science*, pages 365–379. Springer, 2000.
6. L. Cardelli and A. Gordon. Mobile ambients. In *FOSSACS'98*, volume 1378 of *Lecture Notes in Computer Science*, pages 140–155. Springer, 1998.
7. L. Cardelli and A. Gordon. Types for mobile ambients. In *POPL'99*, pages 79–92. ACM Press, 1999.
8. M. Coppo, M. Dezani-Ciancaglini, E. Giovannetti, and I. Salvo. M3: Mobility types for mobile processes in mobile ambients. In *CAT'03*, volume 78 of *Electronic Notes in Theoretical Computer Science*. Elsevier, 2003.
9. P. Degano, F. Levi, and C. Bodei. Safe ambients: Control flow analysis and security. In *Proceedins of ASIAN'00*, volume 1961 of *LNCS*, pages 199–214. Springer-Verlag, 2000.
10. M. Hennessy, M. Merro, and J. Rathke. Towards a behavioural theory of access and mobility control in distributed systems. In *FOSSACS'03*, Lecture Notes in Computer Science. Springer, 2003.
11. C. Lhoussaine. Type inference for a distributed π-calculus. In *ESOP'03*, volume 2618 of *Lecture Notes in Computer Science*, pages 253–268. Springer, 2003.
12. M. Merro and V. Sassone. Typing and subtyping mobility in boxed ambients. In *CONCUR'02*, volume 2421 of *Lecture Notes in Computer Science*, pages 304–320. Springer, 2002.
13. N. Yoshida. Channel dependent types for higher-order mobile processes. In *POPL'04*, 2004. To appear.
14. N. Yoshida and M. Hennessy. Assigning types to processes. In *LICS'00*, pages 334–345, 2000.

A Control Flow Analysis for Safe and Boxed Ambients*

Francesca Levi[1] and Chiara Bodei[2]

[1] DISI, Università di Genova
[2] Dpt. di Informatica, Università di Pisa

Abstract. We present two main contributions: (i) an encoding of Boxed Ambients into a variant of Safe Ambients; (ii) a new Control Flow Analysis for Safe Ambients. Then, we show that the analysis, when applied to the encoded processes, permits to accurately verify Mandatory Access Control policies of the source processes.

1 Introduction

Mobile Ambients (MA) [9] is one of the most relevant linguistic answers, in literature, to the problem of modelling mobility. *Ambients* are bounded places, where multi-threaded computations happen, and represent its central notion. They are characterized by a name, and by a collection of local processes and of sub-ambients, therefore generalizing both the idea of agent and the idea of location. The ambients hierarchy can be dynamically modified, according to the three following *capabilities*: $\mathtt{in}\, n$ allows an ambient to enter into an ambient (named) n: $(m[\,\mathtt{in}\, n.\, P_1 \mid P_2\,] \mid n[\,Q\,] \longrightarrow n[\,m[\,P_1 \mid P_2\,] \mid Q\,])$; $\mathtt{out}\, n$ allows an ambient to exit from an ambient (named) n: $(n[\,m[\,\mathtt{out}\, n.\, P_1 \mid P_2\,] \mid Q\,] \longrightarrow m[\,P_1 \mid P_2\,] \mid n[\,Q\,])$; $\mathtt{open}\, n$ allows to destroy the boundary of an ambient (named) n: $(\mathtt{open}\, n.\, P \mid n[\,Q\,] \longrightarrow P \mid Q)$. The previous rules show that the affected ambient n undergoes the action and has no control on whether or not the action takes place. This is a serious drawback which is overcome in *Safe Ambients* (SA) [20, 21], a variant of MA, where a movement or an ambient dissolution can take place only when the affected ambient, named n, allows it, offering the corresponding *coaction*. This modification does not change the expressiveness of the calculus, yet makes it easier both to write programs and to formally prove their correctness, by using behavioural equivalences [20,22]. Furthermore, the existing static techniques of MA, based on Type Systems [7,8] and Control Flow Analysis (CFA) [24], can straightforwardly transplanted to SA, and typically give more precise results due to the coactions [20,12,11,3,15,1,17].

Recently, another modification of MA has been proposed, called *Boxed Ambients* (BA). In BA there is no ambient dissolution and new primitives are introduced for exchanging values across ambient boundaries (in MA/SA only processes local to the same ambient can communicate). Specifically, the *downward* actions, $\langle M \rangle^n$ and $(x)^n\, P$, indicate an output for and an input from a

* Work partially supported by EU-project DEGAS (IST-2001-32072)

D.A. Schmidt (Ed.): ESOP 2004, LNCS 2986, pp. 188–203, 2004.

sub-ambient (named) n; and the *upward* actions, $\langle M\rangle^{\uparrow}$ and $(x)^{\uparrow}\, P$, indicate an output for and an input from the parent ambient.

To understand the relevant difference between the BA and the MA/SA model it is convenient to consider a simple situation. Assume that an ambient (named) a is willing to communicate a message to an ambient (named) b. The following MA and BA (using the semantics of [10]) processes show two typical protocols,

$$a[\,\mathtt{in}\, b.\, m[\,\mathtt{out}\, a.\, \langle M\rangle\,] \mid P\,] \mid b[\,\mathtt{open}\, m \mid (x)\, S \mid Q\,] \tag{1}$$

$$a[\,\mathtt{in}\, b.\, \langle M\rangle^{\uparrow} \mid P\,] \mid b[\,(x)^{a}\, S \mid Q\,] \tag{2}$$

In (1) ambient a moves inside ambient b; then an auxiliary ambient (named) m exits from ambient a, thus ending up within ambient b, where it is opened; consequently, the input $(x)\, S$ and the output $\langle M\rangle$ can locally interact. The role of the open capability here is crucial, but at the same time may not give security guarantees. In fact, any process contained within ambient m is unleashed inside ambient b; ambient m could for instance contain a malicious process, which may cause ambient b to move inside possibly hostile locations and to be there damaged. Further problems arise when we try to understand the opening, according to the principles of mandatory access control (MAC) policies in multi-level security. As the ambient interested by the action is dissolved, it is rather difficult to classify standard read and write operations. In (2) instead there is no need of the auxiliary ambient m, because ambient a enters inside ambient b, and can directly communicate. Moreover, the MAC properties have a natural interpretation: there is clearly a write access from ambient a to ambient b, and symmetrically a read access from ambient b to ambient a.

As this example shows, the new forms of inter-level communication offer a valid alternative to the delicate primitive of opening of MA/SA. Nevertheless, the introduction of a different model for a given language – as BA w.r.t. MA/SA - suggests the following questions: (i) is it possible to rebuild for the former model (BA) the techniques previously developed for the latter (MA/SA)? (ii) does it exist an encoding from the former into the latter model? and, consequently, (iii) which of the techniques for the latter model keep giving the expected results when applied to the encoded processes?

The first issue has been investigated: [4,23] introduce type systems for BA, inspired from those of MA, controlling the consistency of communications and the mobility of ambients; [5] extends [4] for checking precisely the MAC properties. In this paper instead we address the other approach and we investigate whether it is possible to apply the same static techniques for both languages. We present the following contributions: – an encoding of BA (w.r.t. the semantics of [10]) into a variant of SA, in Sect. 3; – a new Control Flow Analysis for SA, in Sect. 4, which is an adaptation of the CFA of [24] for MA, obtained by profitably exploiting the presence of coactions. It computes a sound approximation of the run-time behaviour of processes, by giving information about the evolution of the ambients hierarchy, and about which capabilities may be exercised and which messages may be exchanged inside any ambient.

We finally show that our analysis can safely be applied to the encoded BA processes to verify the MAC policies, and that it is particularly adequate for this application. First, it can be more precise than the types for BA of [5] [1]. Moreover, when compared to the other static techniques for MA/SA, our analysis is a good compromise between complexity and accuracy.

Some formal statements, here omitted for lack of space, can be found in [18].

2 Syntax and Semantics of SA and BA

With the aim of compacting as much as possible the presentation, we give the common productions and rules, needed both for (the variant) of SA and for BA, and then the additional productions and semantic rules specific of any calculus.

We note that the variant of SA is a combination of recent proposals [14,15,22, 23,6] where: the coaction for opening does not refer to the name of the affected ambient; the coactions for movements reside in the target ambient, and either refer to the name of the ambient authorized to move or allow any ambient to move. These modifications are necessary only for the encoding, meaning that the CFA can be easily adapted to standard SA.

Syntax. As common in CFA, we discipline the α-renaming of bound names and variables by partitioning names and variables as follows. For SA, we consider names $\widehat{\mathcal{N}} = \uplus_{n \in \mathcal{N}} \mathcal{N}_n$, where $\mathcal{N}_n = \{n_0, n_1, \ldots\}$ for the infinite set of names $\mathcal{N} = \{n, h, k, \ldots\}$; similarly for variables, given the set $\mathcal{V} = \{x, y, z \ldots\}$ and $\widehat{\mathcal{V}} = \uplus_{x \in \mathcal{V}} \mathcal{V}_x$. Analogously, for BA we consider names $\widehat{\mathcal{N}_{BA}}$ and variables $\widehat{\mathcal{V}_{BA}}$ partitioned as in SA. Hereafter, we may use the name n and the variable x for a generic element of $\mathcal{N}_n$ and demand that a name $n_i \in \mathcal{N}_n$ can only be α-converted with a name $n_j \in \mathcal{N}_n$. Moreover, to define the CFA it is convenient to label the SA ambients, using a set of labels $\mathcal{L}$ (ranged over by elements λ, μ ...), where $\top \in \mathcal{L}$ represents the outermost ambient.

The following productions define the syntax of SA and BA, processes and expressions (for simplicity we omit capability paths),

Common Part

$P ::=$	*Processes*	$M ::=$	*Expressions*
$\mathbf{0}$	nil	$\mathsf{in}\, M$	enter M
$\mid M.P$	prefix	$\mid \mathsf{out}\, M$	exit M
$\mid P \mid P$	parallel	$\mid n$	name
$\mid (\nu n)P$	restriction	$\mid x$	variable
$\mid\ !P$	replication	$\mid (M_1, \ldots, M_n)$	tuple
$\mid \langle M \rangle$	message		
$\mid (x_1, \ldots, x_n)\, P$	abstraction		

Additional Productions for SA

$P ::=$	*Processes*	$M ::=$	*Expressions*
$M_\lambda[P]$	ambient	$\overline{\mathsf{in}}\, M$	let M enter
		$\mid \overline{\mathsf{out}}\, M$	let M exit
		$\mid \mathsf{open}\, M$	open M
		$\mid \overline{\mathsf{open}}$	let open
		$\mid \overline{\mathsf{in}}$	let enter
		$\mid \overline{\mathsf{out}}$	let exit

[1] The type system is defined for a slightly different semantics of BA [4]. In this paper we refer to its easy adaptation to the semantics considered here (see [10]).

Additional Productions for BA

$P ::=$	*Processes*	$\eta ::= M \mid \uparrow$
$M[\,P\,]$	ambient	
$\mid \langle M \rangle^{\eta}$	message up-down	
$\mid (x_1, \ldots, x_n)^{\eta} P$	abstraction up-down	

For both calculi, we adopt standard syntactical conventions. We often omit the trailing **0** in processes, and we assume that parallel composition has the least syntactic precedence. As usual, the operators $(\nu n)P$, $(x_1, \ldots, x_n)P$ and $(x_1, \ldots, x_n)^{\eta} P$ act as static binders for name n and for variables $x_1, \ldots, x_n$; the free and bound names of processes and expressions are defined, accordingly. Moreover, we use the standard notation $P\{M/x\}$ for substitution. We use $\tilde{M}$ to denote tuples of expressions $(M_1, \ldots, M_k)$, and we assume that $(\nu \tilde{n})$ stands for $(\nu n_1) \ldots (\nu n_k)$ and $P\{\tilde{M}/\tilde{x}\}$ for $P\{M_1/x_1\} \ldots \{M_k/x_k\}$. We recall also that in the untyped calculi bad-formed processes may occur, such as $\mathtt{in}\, n[\,P\,]$ and $n.\,P$.

Table 1. Reduction Axioms of BA and SA

Common part (`Com`) $\langle \tilde{M} \rangle \mid (\tilde{x})\, P \longrightarrow P\{\tilde{M}/\tilde{x}\}$

Additional axioms of SA

(`In`) for $\mathsf{cap} \in \{\overline{\mathtt{in}}, \overline{\mathtt{in}}\, n\}$

$$n_\lambda[\,\mathtt{in}\, m.\, P_1 \mid P_2\,] \mid m_\mu[\,\mathsf{cap}.\, Q_1 \mid Q_2\,] \longrightarrow m_\mu[\,n_\lambda[\,P_1 \mid P_2\,] \mid Q_1 \mid Q_2\,]$$

(`Out`) for $\mathsf{cap} \in \{\overline{\mathtt{out}}, \overline{\mathtt{out}}\, n\}$

$$m_\mu[\,n_\lambda[\,\mathtt{out}\, m.\, P_1 \mid P_2\,] \mid Q_2\,] \mid \mathsf{cap}.\, Q_1 \longrightarrow n_\lambda[\,P_1 \mid P_2\,] \mid m_\mu[\,Q_2\,] \mid Q_1$$

(`Open`) $\mathtt{open}\, n.\, Q \mid n_\lambda[\,\overline{\mathtt{open}}.\, P_1 \mid P_2\,] \longrightarrow Q \mid P_1 \mid P_2$

Additional axioms of BA

(`Input` $\uparrow$) $\langle \tilde{M} \rangle^n \mid n[\,(\tilde{x})^{\uparrow}\, P \mid R\,] \longrightarrow n[\,P\{\tilde{M}/\tilde{x}\} \mid R\,]$

(`Output` $\uparrow$) $(\tilde{x})^n\, P \mid n[\,\langle \tilde{M} \rangle^{\uparrow} \mid R\,] \longrightarrow P\{\tilde{M}/\tilde{x}\} \mid n[\,R\,]$

Semantics. For lack of space, we comment only the top-level reductions (the main ones are reported in Tab. 1); the auxiliary relation of structural congruence $\equiv$ and the inference rules, which propagate the reductions, are fairly standard (for more details [9,4]). The rules (`In`), (`Out`) and (`Open`) of SA model the movements, in and out, and the opening of ambients. The rules of movement for BA are analogous to those for MA, outlined in the Introduction. Rule (`Com`), common to both languages, models local communication, and the additional rules for BA (`Output` $\uparrow$) and (`Input` $\uparrow$) model the inter-level communications.

In the following, $\Longrightarrow$ stands for the transitive and reflexive closure of $\longrightarrow$. Moreover, to simplify the encoding and the CFA, we consider SA and BA processes where all the bound names and variables are distinct one from each other and from the free names and variables, respectively.

3 Encoding Boxed Ambients into Safe Ambients

We define the encoding of BA into SA in two steps: we give the translation into unlabeled processes; then we introduce *a posteriori* a suitable annotation [2].

The encoding, defined in Tab. 2, depends on the enclosing ambient (in general an expression N) and works compositionally on the structure of the process. The inter-level communications are simulated by processes which use auxiliary sets of names $\mathcal{N}_{aux}$ and variables $\mathcal{V}_{aux}$. We define $\mathcal{N}_{aux} = \mathcal{N}_{\mathcal{G}^{\uparrow,\downarrow}} \cup \mathcal{N}_e$, where $\mathcal{G}^{\uparrow,\downarrow} = \{\mathtt{r}_1^{\downarrow}, \mathtt{r}_2^{\downarrow}, \mathtt{w}^{\uparrow}, \mathtt{w}_1^{\downarrow}, \mathtt{w}_2^{\downarrow}, \mathtt{r}^{\uparrow}\}$, $\mathcal{N}_{\mathcal{G}^{\uparrow,\downarrow}} = \{n^g \mid n \in \mathcal{N}_{BA}, g \in \mathcal{G}^{\uparrow,\downarrow}\}$ and $\mathcal{N}_e = \{\mathtt{t}^{\mathtt{rd}}, \mathtt{t}^{\mathtt{wd}}, \mathtt{c}^{\mathtt{ru}}, \mathtt{c}^{\mathtt{rd}}\}$; analogously, we define $\mathcal{V}_{aux} = \mathcal{V}_{\mathcal{G}^{\uparrow,\downarrow}}$.

Table 2. The encoding.

Expressions

$\llbracket M \rrbracket = (M, M^{\mathtt{r}_1^{\downarrow}}, M^{\mathtt{r}_2^{\downarrow}}, M^{\mathtt{w}^{\uparrow}}, M^{\mathtt{w}_1^{\downarrow}}, M^{\mathtt{w}_2^{\downarrow}}, M^{\mathtt{r}^{\uparrow}})$

$(M_i)^g = (M^g)_i$ if $M \in \mathcal{V}_{BA} \cup \mathcal{N}_{BA}$ $\quad (\mathsf{cap}\ M)^g = \mathsf{cap}\ M^g$ if $\mathsf{cap} \in \{\mathtt{in}, \mathtt{out}\}$

Processes

$\llbracket \mathbf{0} \rrbracket^N = \mathbf{0} \quad \llbracket M.\,P \rrbracket^N = M.\,\llbracket P \rrbracket^N \quad \llbracket P \mid Q \rrbracket^N = \llbracket P \rrbracket^N \mid \llbracket Q \rrbracket^N \quad \llbracket !P \rrbracket^N = !\llbracket P \rrbracket^N$

$\llbracket (\nu n)\, P \rrbracket^N = (\nu \llbracket n \rrbracket)\, \llbracket P \rrbracket^N \quad \llbracket M[\, P\,] \rrbracket^N = M[\, \llbracket P \rrbracket^M \mid !\overline{\mathtt{out}} \mid !\overline{\mathtt{in}}\,] \mid !\overline{\mathtt{out}}$

$\llbracket \langle M \rangle^{\uparrow} \rrbracket^N = \mathtt{wu}(\llbracket M \rrbracket, N, N^{\mathtt{r}_1^{\downarrow}}, N^{\mathtt{r}_2^{\downarrow}}, N^{\mathtt{w}^{\uparrow}}) \quad \llbracket (\tilde{x})^{N'}\, P \rrbracket^N = \mathtt{rd}((\llbracket \tilde{x} \rrbracket)\, \llbracket P \rrbracket^N, N'^{\mathtt{r}_1^{\downarrow}}, N'^{\mathtt{r}_2^{\downarrow}}, N'^{\mathtt{w}^{\uparrow}})$

$\llbracket (\tilde{x})^{\uparrow}\, P \rrbracket^N = \mathtt{ru}((\llbracket \tilde{x} \rrbracket)\, \llbracket P \rrbracket^N, N, N^{\mathtt{w}_1^{\downarrow}}, N^{\mathtt{w}_2^{\downarrow}}, N^{\mathtt{r}^{\uparrow}}) \quad \llbracket (\tilde{x})\, P \rrbracket^N = (\llbracket \tilde{x} \rrbracket)\, \llbracket P \rrbracket^N$

$\llbracket \langle M \rangle^{N'} \rrbracket^N = \mathtt{wd}(\langle \llbracket M \rrbracket \rangle, N'^{\mathtt{w}_1^{\downarrow}}, N'^{\mathtt{w}_2^{\downarrow}}, N'^{\mathtt{r}^{\uparrow}}) \qquad \llbracket \langle M \rangle \rrbracket^N = \langle \llbracket M \rrbracket \rangle$

Names and variables are translated into the corresponding tuple in $\mathcal{N}_{\mathcal{G}^{\uparrow,\downarrow}}$ and $\mathcal{V}_{\mathcal{G}^{\uparrow,\downarrow}}$; the other expressions are translated accordingly. The encoding of prefix, parallel composition, bang, restriction and local communications are fairly standard. An ambient is translated into a corresponding one, with the same name; generic coactions $\overline{\mathtt{in}}$ and $\overline{\mathtt{out}}$ are introduced to properly preserve the feature that a BA ambient can be traversed by any other ambient. More interesting and difficult is the encoding of inter-level communications, rendered by the four basic protocols, defined in Tab. 3, using the auxiliary ambients. More in details, *upward* and *downward* messages and abstractions, located inside an ambient N, are modelled as follows: – $\mathtt{wu}(\langle \llbracket M \rrbracket \rangle, N, N^{\mathtt{r}_1^{\downarrow}}, N^{\mathtt{r}_2^{\downarrow}}, N^{\mathtt{w}^{\uparrow}})$ and $\mathtt{ru}((\llbracket x \rrbracket)\, \llbracket P \rrbracket^N, N, N^{\mathtt{w}_1^{\downarrow}}, N^{\mathtt{w}_2^{\downarrow}}, N^{\mathtt{r}^{\uparrow}})$ realise $\langle M \rangle^{\uparrow}$ and $(x)^{\uparrow}\, P$, respectively; – and, $\mathtt{wd}(\langle \llbracket M \rrbracket \rangle, N'^{\mathtt{w}_1^{\downarrow}}, N'^{\mathtt{w}_2^{\downarrow}}, N'^{\mathtt{r}^{\uparrow}})$ and $\mathtt{rd}((\llbracket x \rrbracket)\, \llbracket P \rrbracket^N, N'^{\mathtt{r}_1^{\downarrow}}, N'^{\mathtt{r}_2^{\downarrow}}, N'^{\mathtt{w}^{\uparrow}})$ realise $\langle M \rangle^{N'}$ and $(x)^{N'}\, P$ for sub-ambients (named) N', respectively.

We now explain how the protocols of Tab. 3 suitably model the inter-level communications corresponding to (Output $\uparrow$) and (Input $\uparrow$). We mean that their

[2] Notice that the labels are used only by the CFA and do not affect at all the semantics.

Table 3. Protocols for inter-level communication

$$\mathtt{wu}(\langle M\rangle, N, N^{\mathtt{r}^{\downarrow}_{1}}, N^{\mathtt{r}^{\downarrow}_{2}}, N^{\mathtt{w}^{\uparrow}}) = \mathtt{in}\, N^{\mathtt{r}^{\downarrow}_{1}} . \mathtt{in}\, N^{\mathtt{r}^{\downarrow}_{2}} . (N^{\mathtt{w}^{\uparrow}}[\, \mathtt{out}\, N . \overline{\mathtt{open}} . \langle M\rangle \,] \mid \mathtt{out}\, N^{\mathtt{r}^{\downarrow}_{2}})$$

$$\mathtt{rd}((\tilde{x})\, P, N^{\mathtt{r}^{\downarrow}_{1}}, N^{\mathtt{r}^{\downarrow}_{2}}, N^{\mathtt{w}^{\uparrow}}) = (\nu \mathtt{t}^{\mathtt{rd}})\, (\nu \mathtt{c}^{\mathtt{rd}}) \Big(\mathtt{t}^{\mathtt{rd}}[\, \overline{\mathtt{in}}\, N^{\mathtt{r}^{\downarrow}_{1}} . \mathtt{open}\, N^{\mathtt{r}^{\downarrow}_{1}} . \overline{\mathtt{open}} \,] \mid$$
$$\mathtt{open}\, \mathtt{t}^{\mathtt{rd}} . \mathtt{open}\, \mathtt{c}^{\mathtt{rd}} \mid N^{\mathtt{r}^{\downarrow}_{1}}[\, \overline{\mathtt{in}} . (N^{\mathtt{r}^{\downarrow}_{2}}[\, \overline{\mathtt{in}} . \overline{\mathtt{out}}\, N^{\mathtt{w}^{\uparrow}} . \mathtt{open}\, N^{\mathtt{w}^{\uparrow}} . (\tilde{x})\, \mathtt{c}^{\mathtt{rd}}[\, \mathtt{out}\, N^{\mathtt{r}^{\downarrow}_{2}} . \overline{\mathtt{open}} . P \,]\,] \mid$$
$$\overline{\mathtt{out}}\, \mathtt{c}^{\mathtt{rd}} . \overline{\mathtt{out}} . \mathtt{in}\, \mathtt{t}^{\mathtt{rd}} . \overline{\mathtt{open}} \,)\,] \Big)$$

$$\mathtt{ru}((\tilde{x})\, P, N, N^{\mathtt{w}^{\downarrow}_{1}}, N^{\mathtt{w}^{\downarrow}_{2}}, N^{\mathtt{r}^{\uparrow}}) = (\nu \mathtt{c}^{\mathtt{ru}})$$
$$\Big(\mathtt{in}\, N^{\mathtt{w}^{\downarrow}_{1}} . \mathtt{in}\, N^{\mathtt{w}^{\downarrow}_{2}} . (N^{\mathtt{r}^{\uparrow}}[\mathtt{out}\, N . \overline{\mathtt{open}} . (\tilde{x})\, \mathtt{c}^{\mathtt{ru}}[\, \mathtt{in}\, N . \overline{\mathtt{open}} . P \,]\,] \mid \mathtt{open}\, \mathtt{c}^{\mathtt{ru}} . \mathtt{out}\, N^{\mathtt{w}^{\downarrow}_{2}}) \Big)$$

$$\mathtt{wd}(\langle M\rangle, N^{\mathtt{w}^{\downarrow}_{1}}, N^{\mathtt{w}^{\downarrow}_{2}}, N^{\mathtt{r}^{\uparrow}}) = (\nu \mathtt{t}^{\mathtt{wd}}) \Big(\mathtt{t}^{\mathtt{wd}}[\, \overline{\mathtt{in}}\, N^{\mathtt{w}^{\downarrow}_{1}} . \mathtt{open}\, N^{\mathtt{w}^{\downarrow}_{1}} . \overline{\mathtt{open}} \,] \mid \mathtt{open}\, \mathtt{t}^{\mathtt{wd}} \mid$$
$$N^{\mathtt{w}^{\downarrow}_{1}}[\, \overline{\mathtt{in}} . (N^{\mathtt{w}^{\downarrow}_{2}}[\, \overline{\mathtt{in}} . \overline{\mathtt{out}}\, N^{\mathtt{r}^{\uparrow}} . \mathtt{open}\, N^{\mathtt{r}^{\uparrow}} . \langle M\rangle \,] \mid \mathtt{in}\, \mathtt{t}^{\mathtt{wd}} . \overline{\mathtt{out}} . \overline{\mathtt{open}} \,)\,] \Big)$$

execution lead to the expected communication and also that their steps cannot be interfered by the interactions with the external context.

To illustrate (`Output` $\uparrow$) we consider a process $m[\, n[\, \langle M\rangle^{\uparrow} \,] \mid (x)^{n}\, P \,]$. The communication is realised by the processes $\mathtt{rd}((\llbracket x\rrbracket)\, \llbracket P\rrbracket^{m}, n^{\mathtt{r}^{\downarrow}_{1}}, n^{\mathtt{r}^{\downarrow}_{2}}, n^{\mathtt{w}^{\uparrow}})$, running inside m, and $\mathtt{wu}(\langle \llbracket M\rrbracket\rangle, n, n^{\mathtt{r}^{\downarrow}_{1}}, n^{\mathtt{r}^{\downarrow}_{2}}, n^{\mathtt{w}^{\uparrow}})$, running inside the sub-ambient n. Ambient $n^{\mathtt{r}^{\downarrow}_{1}}$, located within m, is a sort of isolating box, which protects the interaction between the ambients $n^{\mathtt{w}^{\uparrow}}$, containing the output $\langle \llbracket M\rrbracket\rangle$, and $n^{\mathtt{r}^{\downarrow}_{2}}$, containing the input $(\llbracket x\rrbracket)\, \llbracket P\rrbracket^{m}$. The protocol is started by the sub-ambient n that moves inside $n^{\mathtt{r}^{\downarrow}_{1}}$, and then inside $n^{\mathtt{r}^{\downarrow}_{2}}$. At this point, ambient $n^{\mathtt{w}^{\uparrow}}$ goes out of n, and therefore ends up inside $n^{\mathtt{r}^{\downarrow}_{2}}$, where it is opened; consequently, the message $\langle \llbracket M\rrbracket\rangle$ is unleashed and can be consumed. After the communication has been realised, both the continuation of the abstraction (contained inside $\mathtt{c}^{\mathtt{rd}}$) and ambient n go out from ambient $n^{\mathtt{r}^{\downarrow}_{2}}$. Finally, the boundary of $n^{\mathtt{r}^{\downarrow}_{1}}$ is dissolved, thus liberating the ambients n and $\mathtt{c}^{\mathtt{rd}}$ within ambient m. To avoid the observation of the opening of $n^{\mathtt{r}^{\downarrow}_{1}}$ from the external context, its name is changed into a fresh name $\mathtt{t}^{\mathtt{rd}}$ by using a well-known renaming protocol [9].

The interaction (`Input` $\uparrow$) is realised by a similar protocol using the symmetric processes and auxiliary ambients. Only slight modifications are necessary, since here the continuation of the abstraction (that is $\mathtt{c}^{\mathtt{ru}}$) has to end up inside the sub-ambient rather than inside the enclosing ambient.

To annotate the BA and auxiliary ambients, resp., we adopt sets of labels $\mathcal{L}_{BA}$ and $\mathcal{L}_{aux}$, where $\mathcal{L}_{aux} = \{(g_{\lambda}, i) \mid g \in \mathcal{G}^{\uparrow,\downarrow} \cup \mathcal{N}_{e},\ \lambda \in \mathcal{L}_{BA}, i \in N\}$. Formally, we require that, for any ambient $M_{\chi}[\, Q \,]$, occurring in the labelled process: (i) if M is a BA expression, then $\chi \in \mathcal{L}_{BA}$; (ii) if M is either a name $g \in \mathcal{N}_{e}$ or an expression N^{g} for $g \in \mathcal{G}^{\uparrow,\downarrow}$, then χ is (g_{λ}, i), where λ is the label of the surrounding BA ambient (possibly $\top$).

Notice that, by condition (ii), the labels of the auxiliary ambients (used in Tab. 3) depend on the label of the BA ambient, which is ready to engage into the inter-level communication action (see e. g. Sect. 5). Moreover, different equivalent labellings can be given, we therefore use $[\![P]\!]^N$ for the canonical representative. As common in CFA, in order to obtain a more precise analysis it is convenient to assign distinct labels to the ambients.

The encoding is operationally correct, meaning that any reduction of a BA process is properly simulated by its SA encoding, and that the steps of the encoding simulating any BA reduction cannot be interfered. We omit here the formalization of this property, as it requires to introduce additional notions (including behavioural equivalence), and we refer the reader to [18]. We only mention that coactions are necessary to control the interferences, which may damage the protocols, similarly as in the coalescing encoding of π-calculus [20].

4 Control Flow Analysis for *SA*

The analysis approximates the run-time behaviour of a process, by predicting for each ambient, its possible sub-ambients, and which capabilities may be exercised and which messages may be exchanged locally. Our CFA does not distinguish among different elements of the same equivalence class $\mathcal{N}_n$ and $\mathcal{V}_x$: it only considers their canonical representatives n and x, respectively.

Solutions. A *local solution* I is either on the form $\langle L, U, C\rangle$ or on the form $\langle L, U \cup \{\overline{\texttt{open}}\}, C\rangle; \langle L', U', C'\rangle$, for $L, L' \subseteq \mathcal{L}$, $C, C' \subseteq \mathcal{CE}$ and $U, U' \subseteq \mathcal{L} \cup \mathcal{CE}$, where $\mathcal{CE}$ is the set of closed SA expressions. A *solution* of the analysis is a triple (ρ, ϕ, σ), where : $\rho : \mathcal{L} \to \mathcal{CE}$, describes the relation between an ambient label and its possible names; $\phi : \mathcal{L} \to \mathcal{I}$ assigns a local solution to any ambient label (here $\mathcal{I}$ is the set of local solutions); and $\sigma : \mathcal{V} \to \mathcal{CE}$, predicts which expressions may be bound to any variable.

The local solution $\phi(\lambda)$ reports the information about the ambients with label $\lambda \in L$; more in details, it describes the possible behaviour both of the processes running inside, and of the processes which may be unleashed, when they are opened. It may be either (a) $\langle L, U, C\rangle$ or (b) $\langle L, U, C\rangle; \langle L', U', C'\rangle$, provided that $\lambda \in L$. In both cases, the sets U and C approximate the behaviour of the internal processes: U reporting the labels of the possible sub-ambients and the expressions (in particular the capabilities), which may be exercised; C reporting the expressions which may be communicated. Local solutions (a) and (b) differ in the information they give about the opening: (a) says that the ambients may be opened (if $\overline{\texttt{open}} \in U$) inside the ambients with label $\mu \in L$, and that the process unleashed is described by U and C; while (b) says that the ambients may be opened (indeed $\overline{\texttt{open}} \in U$) within the ambients with label $\mu \in L'$, and that the process unleashed is described by U' and C'.

Technically, to distinguish, inside a local solution I, between what happens before and after the possible opening, we use the following functions $\texttt{pre}(I)$ and $\texttt{post}(I)$. We let $\texttt{pre}(\langle L, U, C\rangle) = \texttt{pre}(\langle L, U, C\rangle; \langle L', U', C'\rangle) = \langle L, U, C\rangle$,

$\mathtt{post}(\langle L,U,C\rangle;\langle L',U',C'\rangle) = \langle L',U',C'\rangle$ and $\mathtt{post}(\langle L,U,C\rangle) = \langle L,U,C\rangle$, if $\overline{\mathtt{open}} \in U$, $\mathtt{post}(\langle L,U,C\rangle) = \emptyset$, otherwise.

The following example is intended to illustrate both the different meaning of the two forms of local solutions and the role of the coaction $\overline{\mathtt{open}}$, which is exploited, in our CFA, to have a more precise treatment of the critical opening action. This is the main relevant difference with the analysis of [24] for MA, and follows the lines of the type systems for SA [20,12,15,1,17], in particular the proposal of [15] adding more flexibility to the single-threaded types of [20].

Example 1. The following process is similar to the process (1) of the Introduction: $a_\lambda[\,\mathtt{in}\,b.\,m_\mu[\,(\mathtt{out}\,a.\,\overline{\mathtt{open}}\,.\,\langle\mathtt{in}\,h\rangle)\mid \mathtt{out}\,k\,]\,]\mid b_\chi[\,\overline{\mathtt{in}}\,a.\,\overline{\mathtt{out}}\,m.\,\mathtt{open}\,m.\,(x)\,x\,]$. The only difference is that, when ambient m is opened inside ambient b, both the message $\langle\mathtt{in}\,h\rangle$ and the capability $\mathtt{out}\,k$ are unleashed. A valid solution for this process is (ρ,ϕ,σ), where $\rho(\lambda)=a,\ \rho(\mu)=m,\ \rho(\chi)=b$, $\sigma(x)=\{\mathtt{in}\,h\}$,

$$\phi(\top)=\langle\{\top\},\{\lambda,\mu,\chi\},\emptyset\rangle\quad \phi(\chi)=\langle\{\chi\},\{\overline{\mathtt{in}}\,a,\overline{\mathtt{out}}\,m,\mathtt{open}\,m,\mathtt{in}\,h,\mathtt{out}\,k,\mu,\lambda\},\{\mathtt{in}\,h\}\rangle$$
$$\phi(\mu)=\langle\{\mu\},\{\mathtt{out}\,a,\overline{\mathtt{open}}\,,\mathtt{out}\,k\},\emptyset\rangle;\langle\{\chi\},\{\mathtt{out}\,k\},\{\mathtt{in}\,h\}\rangle\quad \phi(\lambda)=\langle\{\lambda\},\{\mu,\mathtt{in}\,b\},\emptyset\rangle$$

Here, $\rho(\lambda) = a$ says that a may be the name of the ambient with label λ (similarly $\rho(\mu) = m,\ldots$); $\sigma(x)$ contains the expression $\mathtt{in}\,h$, meaning that variable x may be bound to $\mathtt{in}\,h$; the function ϕ describes the possible contents of any ambient. For instance,

- $\phi(\mu)$ says that the capabilities $\mathtt{out}\,a$, $\overline{\mathtt{open}}$ and $\mathtt{out}\,k$ may run inside m; moreover, ambient m may be opened inside ambient b, and, when opened, it may unleash the capability $\mathtt{out}\,k$ and the message $\langle\mathtt{in}\,h\rangle$.
- $\phi(\chi)$ says that inside ambient b: the ambients m and a may appear; the capabilities $\overline{\mathtt{in}}\,a, \overline{\mathtt{out}}\,m, \mathtt{open}\,m, \mathtt{in}\,h$ and $\mathtt{out}\,k$ may be exercised; and the expression $\mathtt{in}\,h$ may be communicated.

Note that in the local solution for ambient m (that is $\phi(\mu)$) there is a clear distinction between what may end up *before* and *after* the capability $\overline{\mathtt{open}}$. This information is exploited by the CFA to predict that ambient b, when opening ambient m, acquires *only* the capability $\mathtt{out}\,k$ and the message $\langle\mathtt{in}\,h\rangle$ (see $\phi(\chi)$). We could also adopt a local solution (as in the CFA of [24]) $\phi(\mu) = \langle\{\mu,\chi\},\{\mathtt{out}\,a,\overline{\mathtt{open}}\,,\mathtt{out}\,k\},\{\mathtt{in}\,h\}\rangle$. In this case, there is no distinction between what may run inside the ambient and what may be unleashed, when the ambient is opened (inside m or b). This would therefore lead to a less precise result. In particular, $\phi(\chi)$ should be modified taking into account that also the capabilities $\mathtt{out}\,a$ and $\overline{\mathtt{open}}$ may end up within ambient b, as a consequence to the opening of ambient m.

Validation. The validation of a given solution, as we will see in a while, is established by a set of clauses, that bring the validation of a compound process back to the validations of its sub-processes. To capture the distinction between what happens before and after the opening, it is necessary to keep the local solutions of the sub-processes and to combine them in a proper way. This is not a trivial task and can be intuitively introduced by considering Ex. 1 and the validation of the internal process of ambient m, w.r.t. (ρ,ϕ,σ) and $\phi(\mu)$.

The local solution $I_1 = \langle\{\mu\}, \{\texttt{out}\, a, \overline{\texttt{open}}\}, \emptyset\rangle; \langle\{\chi\}, \emptyset, \{\texttt{in}\, h\}\rangle$ approximates the behaviour of $\texttt{out}\, a.\, \overline{\texttt{open}}\,.\, \langle \texttt{in}\, h\rangle$, and is obtained by combining the following local solutions: $\langle\{\mu\}, \{\texttt{out}\, a\}, \emptyset\rangle$ describing the presence of $\texttt{out}\, a$ inside m; $\langle\{\mu\}, \{\overline{\texttt{open}}\}, \emptyset\rangle; \langle\{\chi\}, \emptyset, \emptyset\rangle$ saying that ambient m may be opened inside b; $\langle\{\chi\}, \emptyset, \{\texttt{in}\, h\}\rangle$ describing the presence of message $\langle \texttt{in}\, h\rangle$ inside b. The position of the processes establishes the ordering of composition and therefore what may end up before $\overline{\texttt{open}}$ (that is inside m) and after $\overline{\texttt{open}}$ (that is inside the ambient opening m, named b).

Furthermore, $\phi(\mu) = \langle\{\mu\}, \{\texttt{out}\, a, \overline{\texttt{open}}, \texttt{out}\, k\}, \emptyset\rangle; \langle\{\chi\}, \{\texttt{out}\, k\}, \{\texttt{in}\, h\}\rangle$ approximates the behaviour of process $\texttt{out}\, a.\, \overline{\texttt{open}}\,.\, \langle \texttt{in}\, h\rangle \mid \texttt{out}\, k$, and is obtained by combining I_1 with the local solution $I_2 = \langle\{\chi, \mu\}, \{\texttt{out}\, k\}, \emptyset\rangle$ describing the process $\texttt{out}\, k$. Note that, since the capability $\texttt{out}\, k$ may be executed (at runtime) either before (inside m) or after opening (inside b), then I_2 correctly predicts that it may be enclosed in both ambients and $\phi(\mu)$ says that it may end up both before and after opening. We also note that the solution (ρ, ϕ, σ) is valid for this process w.r.t. $\phi(\mu)$, provided that the possible effects of the capabilities of movement on their enclosing ambients are properly recorded in the ambients hierarchy. For instance, $\texttt{out}\, a$ could cause the ambient m to move out of ambient a (see the discussion below about rule (**move**)).

To realise the technique explained above, following the type systems for SA [15,1,17], we introduce two main technical concepts. First, we define two operators of *parallel and sequential* composition ($|$) and (.) to properly combine local solutions. We order components by letting $\langle L_1, U_1, C_1\rangle \sqsubseteq \langle L_2, U_2, C_2\rangle$ iff $L_2 \subseteq L_1$, $U_1 \subseteq U_2$ and $C_1 \subseteq C_2$, and we define

$$
\begin{array}{l}
\langle L_1, U_1, C_1\rangle \sqcup \langle L_2, U_2, C_2\rangle = \langle L_1, U_1, C_1\rangle \mid \langle L_2, U_2, C_2\rangle = \langle L_1, U_1, C_1\rangle.\, \langle L_2, U_2, C_2\rangle \\
\langle L_1, U_1, C_1\rangle; \langle L_2, U_2, C_2\rangle \mid I = \\
\qquad \begin{cases} (\texttt{pre}(I) \mid \langle L_1, U_1, C_1\rangle); (\texttt{pre}(I) \mid \langle L_2, U_2, C_2\rangle) & \text{if } \texttt{post}(I) = \emptyset \\ (\texttt{pre}(I) \mid \langle L_1, U_1, C_1\rangle); (\texttt{pre}(I) \mid \langle L_1, U_1, C_1\rangle \mid \langle L_2, U_2, C_2\rangle \mid \texttt{post}(I)) & \end{cases} \\
\langle L, U, C\rangle.\, \langle L_1, U_1, C_1\rangle; \langle L_2, U_2, C_2\rangle = \\
\qquad \begin{cases} ((\langle L, U, C\rangle.\, \langle L_1, U_1, C_1\rangle)); \langle L_2, U_2, C_2\rangle & \text{if } \overline{\texttt{open}} \notin U \\ ((\langle L, U, C\rangle.\, \langle L_1, U_1, C_1\rangle)); (\langle L_1, U_1, C_1\rangle \sqcup \langle L_2, U_2, C_2\rangle) & \end{cases} \\
\langle L_1, U_1, C_1\rangle; \langle L_2, U_2, C_2\rangle.\, I = \\
\qquad \begin{cases} \langle L_1, U_1, C_1\rangle; (\langle L_2, U_2, C_2\rangle \sqcup \texttt{pre}(I) \sqcup \texttt{post}(I)) & \text{if } \texttt{post}(I) \neq \emptyset \\ \langle L_1, U_1, C_1\rangle; (\langle L_2, U_2, C_2\rangle \sqcup \texttt{pre}(I)) & \end{cases}
\end{array}
$$

Two local solutions of the shape $\langle L, U, C\rangle$ are composed by taking the least upper bound with respect to $\sqsubseteq$ (denoted by $\sqcup$), because we have to collect enough information to validate both processes. The parallel and sequential composition with a local solution of the shape $\langle L_1, U_1, C_1\rangle; \langle L_2, U_2, C_2\rangle$ are based on the ideas explained above. Thus, any parallel process may end up both before and after the $\overline{\texttt{open}}$, also when two $\overline{\texttt{open}}$ may appear we don't know which of them will be executed first; in sequential composition the ordering establishes whether the process may end up either before or after the $\overline{\texttt{open}}$.

Moreover, we introduce *contexts*, which are expressions, built from local solutions and from the special expression $\diamond$ (denoting the hole) using parallel ($|$) and sequential composition (.) operators. Formally, a context is either $\diamond$, or $I.\, Z$

Table 4. Control Flow Analysis for SA

move: $\models \mathsf{cap} : \langle L, U, C\rangle . \diamond$ iff $\mathsf{cap} \in U \wedge \mathsf{cap} \in \{\overline{\mathtt{in}}\, n, \overline{\mathtt{out}}\, n, \overline{\mathtt{out}}\,, \overline{\mathtt{in}}\,, n, \mathtt{out}\, n, \mathtt{in}\, n\}$
$\wedge\ (\mathsf{cap} = \mathtt{in}\, n \Rightarrow\ \forall \lambda \in L, \forall \mu$
$(n \in \rho(\mu) \wedge \mathcal{E}_{in}(\lambda, \mu) \Rightarrow \lambda \mathsf{E}\, \phi(\mu)))$
$\wedge\ (\mathsf{cap} = \mathtt{out}\, n \Rightarrow \forall \lambda \in L, \forall \mu, \chi$
$(n \in \rho(\mu) \wedge \mathcal{E}_{out}(\lambda, \mu, \chi) \Rightarrow \lambda \mathsf{E}\, \phi(\chi)))$

open: $\models \mathsf{open}\, n : \langle L, U, C\rangle . (\diamond \mid \langle L_1, U_1, C_1\rangle)$ iff $\mathsf{open}\, n \in U \wedge \forall \lambda \in L, \forall \mu$
$(n \in \rho(\mu) \wedge\ \mathcal{E}_{open}(\lambda, \mu) \Rightarrow$
$\mathtt{post}(\phi(\mu)) \sqsubseteq \langle L_1, U_1, C_1\rangle)$

co-open: $\models \overline{\mathsf{open}} : \langle L, U, C\rangle ; \langle L', U', C'\rangle . \diamond$ iff $\overline{\mathsf{open}} \in U$

nil: $\models \mathbf{0} : \langle L, U, C\rangle$ iff true **res:** $\models (\nu n)P : I$ iff $\models P : I$

amb: $\models M_\lambda[P] : \langle L, U, C\rangle$ iff $\lambda \in U\ \wedge M\sigma \subseteq \rho(\lambda) \wedge \models P : \phi(\lambda) \wedge$
$\mathtt{pre}(\phi(\lambda)) = \langle L' \cup \{\lambda\}, U', C'\rangle$

msg : $\models \langle M\rangle : \langle L, U, C\rangle$ iff $M\sigma \subseteq C$ **bang :** $\models !P : I$ iff $I \mid I_1 = I \wedge \models P : I_1$

abs: $\models (\tilde{x})\, P : I$ iff $\mathtt{pre}(I) = \langle L, U, C\rangle \wedge \models P : I \wedge \forall \lambda \in L$
$(\mathtt{pre}(\phi(\lambda)) = \langle L', U', C' \cup \{\tilde{M}\}\rangle\ \Rightarrow \forall i \in \{1, k\} M_i \in \sigma(x_i))$

par : $\models P_1 \mid P_2 : I_1 \mid I_2$ iff $\models P_1 : I_1 \wedge \models P_2 : I_2$

pref: $\models M.P : Z[I]$ iff $\forall N \in M\sigma \models N : Z' \wedge Z' \preceq Z \wedge \models P : I$

or $I \mid Z$, where I is a local solution and Z is a context. Contexts are needed to analyse the capabilities, appearing in a prefix; the hole actually shows where the local solution of the continuation has to be inserted (see rule **(pref)** of Tab. 4). A context Z filled with a local solution I, denoted by $Z[I]$, is evaluated to a local solution by applying the composition operators defined above.

The clauses for validation are shown in Tab. 4[3]. The judgments for: *expressions* are on the form $(\rho, \phi, \sigma) \models M : I.Z$, where M is a closed expression (without free variables) and $I.Z$ is a context; *processes* are on the form $(\rho, \phi, \sigma) \models P : I$, where P is a process and I a local solution. The rules for processes check whether (ρ, ϕ, σ) is a valid solution for P w.r.t local solution I, meaning that I contains enough information to approximate the behaviour of P, when enclosed inside any ambient with label λ, such that $\lambda \in L$ and $\mathtt{pre}(I) = \langle L, U, C\rangle$. Analogously for expressions.

The rules for *expressions* use also the following auxiliary notions: the function $\mathtt{f}$ collects, for any label λ, the labels of the possible fathers; the next three conditions check whether the capabilities of movement and opening are enabled. Let $\mathtt{f}(\lambda) = \{\mu \mid \mathtt{pre}(\phi(\mu)) = \langle L, U \cup \{\lambda\}, C\rangle\}$.

[3] In the rules we write $\models M : Z$ for $(\rho, \phi, \sigma) \models M : Z$; similarly for processes.

- $\mathcal{E}_{in}(\lambda,\mu) \equiv (\overline{\mathtt{in}} \in U_1 \vee (\overline{\mathtt{in}}\, m \in U_1 \wedge m \in \rho(\lambda)) \wedge (\mathtt{f}(\lambda) \cap \mathtt{f}(\mu) \neq \emptyset)$ where $\mathtt{pre}(\phi(\mu)) = \langle L_1, U_1, C_1\rangle$;
- $\mathcal{E}_{out}(\lambda,\mu,\chi) \equiv (\mu \in \mathtt{f}(\lambda)) \wedge (\chi \in \mathtt{f}(\mu)) \wedge (\overline{\mathtt{out}} \in U_1 \vee (\overline{\mathtt{out}}\, m \in U_1 \wedge m \in \rho(\lambda)))$ where $\mathtt{pre}(\phi(\chi)) = \langle L_1, U_1, C_1\rangle$;
- $\mathcal{E}_{open}(\lambda,\mu) \equiv (\lambda \in \mathtt{f}(\mu)) \wedge \overline{\mathtt{open}} \in U_1$, where $\mathtt{pre}(\phi(\mu)) = \langle L_1, U_1, C_1\rangle$.

In all the clauses the expression, appearing at top-level, is properly recorded in the local solution. Rule (**move**) handles the actions and coactions of movement; the context is simply $\langle L, U, C\rangle.\diamond$. The additional conditions verify the possible movements produced by the capabilities, $\mathtt{in}\, n$ and $\mathtt{out}\, n$, on their possible enclosing ambients (those with label $\lambda \in L$). For instance, for $\mathtt{in}\, n$ we control whether there exists an ambient (named) n and with label μ, which may be a sibling of that with label λ and which offers the right coaction. When the ambient (with label λ) may move, it has to be recorded as possible sub-ambient of the target ambient (with label μ). To this aim, we use $\lambda \mathrel{\mathsf{E}} I$, where $\lambda \mathrel{\mathsf{E}} I$ iff, either $I = \langle L, U, C\rangle$ and $\lambda \in U$, or $I = \langle L_1, U_1, C_1\rangle; \langle L_2, U_2, C_2\rangle$ and $\lambda \in U_1 \cap U_2$.

In rule (**co-open**) the context is $\langle L, U, C\rangle; \langle L', U', C'\rangle.\diamond$, where $\overline{\mathtt{open}} \in U$, because the continuation ends up after $\overline{\mathtt{open}}$. In rule (**open**) the context $\langle L, U, C\rangle.(\diamond \mid \langle L_1, U_1, C_1\rangle)$ shows that the process unleashed by the opening of an ambient n (approximated by $\langle L_1, U_1, C_1\rangle$) may end up in parallel with the continuation.

In the clauses for *processes* the following notion is also used. Given an expression M, we define $M\sigma = \{N \in \mathcal{CE} \mid N = M\eta$ for a substitution η such that $\eta(x) \in \sigma(x)\}$. The set $M\sigma$ reports the closed expressions, that may appear in place of M at run-time. The rules (**amb**) and (**msg**) are rather standard; the ambient and the message appear at top-level, and therefore have to be properly recorded in the local solution. Rule (**abs**) says that any message, which may be communicated inside the possible enclosing ambients, has to be recorded by the function σ. The rules for parallel, sequential composition and bang, (**par**), (**pref**) and (**bang**), exploit the auxiliary composition operations to properly combine the local solutions of the sub-processes. Rule (**pref**) says that the local solution of a process $M.P$ is obtained by filling the context, modelling the capability, with the local solution of the continuation. In order to find out a common context that correctly approximates the behaviour of all the capabilities that may belong to $M\sigma$ we use a relation $\preceq$ over contexts. The relation $\preceq$ is the least transitive and reflexive relation such that: (i) $\langle L, U, C\rangle.\diamond \preceq \langle L, U, C\rangle.(\diamond \mid \langle L', U', C'\rangle)$; and (ii) $\langle L, U, C\rangle; \langle L, U, C\rangle.\diamond \preceq \langle L, U, C\rangle.\diamond$.

Properties. A solution (ρ, ϕ, σ) is *valid* for a process P iff $(\rho, \phi, \sigma) \models P : \phi(\top)$, s.t. $\mathtt{pre}(\phi(\top)) = \langle L, U, C\rangle$ and $\top \in L$. The CFA satisfies standard properties (see [24,18]); i.e. Subject Reduction (validity of solutions is preserved under reduction) and soundness (the static behaviour is a sound approximation of the dynamic one). Furthermore, there always exists a least (in terms of precision) solution which is valid [4]. To formalise soundness we use contexts, that are standard process expressions with a hole. A context is said *enabling* whenever the hole does not appear underneath a prefix, an abstraction or a bang.

[4] We omit for lack of space the formal definition of the ordering.

Theorem 1 (Subject Reduction and Soundness). *Let (ρ, ϕ, σ) be a valid solution for process P. For any process P', s.t. $P \Longrightarrow P'$, we have that*

1. *(ρ, ϕ, σ) is a valid solution also for P';*
2. *if $P' \equiv C[n_\lambda[\,R\,]]$, for some enabling context C, then $n \in \rho(\lambda)$. Moreover, if $\mathtt{pre}(\phi(\lambda)) = \langle L, U, C\rangle$, we have also that: (a) if $R = M.\,P_1 \mid P_2$ and $M \in \mathcal{CE}$, then $M \in U$; (b) if $R = m_\mu[\,P_1\,] \mid P_2$, then $\mu \in U$; (c) if $R = \langle M\rangle \mid (x)P_1 \mid P_2$ and $M \in \mathcal{CE}$, then $M \in C$ and $M \in \sigma(x)$.*

5 Applying the CFA to the Encoding

We show how the MAC properties of BA [5] can be verified by analysing the encoding. A MAC policy is specified by a boolean predicate $\mathcal{P} \subseteq \mathcal{N}_{BA} \times \mathcal{N}_{BA} \times \mathcal{AM}$, where $\mathcal{AM} = \{r, w, rw\}$ defines the access modes (read, write, read-write).

Definition 1 (MAC Properties). *A BA process P* satisfies *the property $\mathcal{P}$ iff for any $P \Longrightarrow P'$, s.t. $P' \equiv C[m[\,R_1 \mid n[\,R_2 \mid Q_2\,] \mid Q_3\,]]$ for an enabling context C, we have that: (i) if $R_1 = (x)^n\,Q_1$ and $R_2 = \langle M\rangle^\uparrow$, then $\mathcal{P}(n, m, \alpha)$ and $\mathcal{P}(m, n, \beta)$, for $\alpha \in \{w, rw\}$ and $\beta \in \{r, rw\}$; (ii) if $R_1 = \langle M\rangle^n$ and $R_2 = (x)^\uparrow\,Q_1$, then $\mathcal{P}(n, m, \alpha)$ and $\mathcal{P}(m, n, \beta)$, for $\alpha \in \{r, rw\}$ and $\beta \in \{w, rw\}$.*

We introduce a *static property* on the solutions of the analysis that is *safe*, i.e. : if a solution for the encoding passes the test, then the source BA process satisfies the security property of Def. 1. The basic idea is to translate the conditions of Def. 1 into equivalent conditions on the behaviour of the auxiliary ambients that realise the inter-level communication actions. We examine, as an example, case (ii) corresponding to (`Input` $\uparrow$); (`Output` $\uparrow$) is analogous.

To this aim, we focus on the following process $Q = c[\,\langle M_2\rangle^a\,] \mid a[\,\mathtt{in}\,c \mid \mathtt{in}\,b \mid (x)^\uparrow\,P \mid b[\,\langle M_1\rangle^a\,]\,]$, and we consider its encoding (w.r.t k)

$$\begin{aligned}\llbracket Q\rrbracket^k \equiv\ & !\overline{\mathtt{out}} \mid c_c[\,!\overline{\mathtt{out}} \mid !\overline{\mathtt{in}} \mid \mathtt{wd}_c(\langle\llbracket M_2\rrbracket\rangle, a^{\mathtt{w}_1^\downarrow}, a^{\mathtt{w}_2^\downarrow}, a^{\mathtt{r}^\uparrow})\,] \mid a_a[\,!\overline{\mathtt{out}} \mid !\overline{\mathtt{in}} \mid \mathtt{in}\,c \mid \mathtt{in}\,b \mid \\ & \mathtt{ru}_a((\llbracket x\rrbracket)\,\llbracket P\rrbracket^a, a, a^{\mathtt{w}_1^\downarrow}, a^{\mathtt{w}_2^\downarrow}, a^{\mathtt{r}^\uparrow}) \mid b_b[\,!\overline{\mathtt{out}} \mid !\overline{\mathtt{in}} \mid \mathtt{wd}_b(\langle\llbracket M_1\rrbracket\rangle, a^{\mathtt{w}_1^\downarrow}, a^{\mathtt{w}_2^\downarrow}, a^{\mathtt{r}^\uparrow})\,]\,]\end{aligned}$$

For simplicity, we adopt in the encoding the following labels: for the BA ambients their names; for the auxiliary ambients the derived labels (see Sect. 3), where indexes are omitted (they usually are necessary to have distinct labels, but here are not relevant.). For instance, the ambients $a^{\mathtt{w}_1^\downarrow}$ and $a^{\mathtt{w}_2^\downarrow}$ appearing in $\mathtt{wd}_c(\langle\llbracket M_2\rrbracket\rangle, a^{\mathtt{w}_1^\downarrow}, a^{\mathtt{w}_2^\downarrow}, a^{\mathtt{r}^\uparrow})$ have labels $\mathtt{w}_{1c}^\downarrow$ and $\mathtt{w}_{2c}^\downarrow$, resp.; while those occurring in $\mathtt{wd}_b(\langle\llbracket M_1\rrbracket\rangle, a^{\mathtt{w}_1^\downarrow}, a^{\mathtt{w}_2^\downarrow}, a^{\mathtt{r}^\uparrow})$ have labels $\mathtt{w}_{1b}^\downarrow$ and $\mathtt{w}_{2b}^\downarrow$, resp.. Similarly, in $\mathtt{ru}_a((\llbracket x\rrbracket)\,\llbracket P\rrbracket^a, a, a^{\mathtt{w}_1^\downarrow}, a^{\mathtt{w}_2^\downarrow}, a^{\mathtt{r}^\uparrow})$ the ambient $a^{\mathtt{r}^\uparrow}$ has label $\mathtt{r}_a^\uparrow$.

Process Q obviously satisfies the MAC policy, specified only by $\mathcal{P}(a, c, r)$ and $\mathcal{P}(c, a, w)$ (meaning that a can read from c and c can write to a). In fact, ambient a may move inside ambient c, and there communicate; while it does not enter inside and communicate with ambient b (b is a sub-ambient of a).

The condition on the encoded process has to capture whether ambient a may communicate with ambient c (or analogously with ambient b). The most relevant auxiliary ambients used in the simulation of (Input $\uparrow$) are: the ambient $a^{\mathtt{r}^{\uparrow}}$, containing the upward abstraction $(\llbracket x \rrbracket)\, \llbracket P \rrbracket^{a}$; the ambients $a^{\mathtt{w}_2^{\downarrow}}$, one for b and one for c, containing the downward outputs $\langle \llbracket M_1 \rrbracket \rangle$ and $\langle \llbracket M_2 \rrbracket \rangle$ resp.. The communication between a and c takes place whenever $a^{\mathtt{r}^{\uparrow}}$ ends up (by exiting from a) inside the ambient $a^{\mathtt{w}_2^{\downarrow}}$, local to c (as shown by the label $\mathtt{w}^{\downarrow}_{2c}$), and there is opened; similarly, for the communication between a and b. Therefore, one way to capture these interactions is to detect inside which ambients $a^{\mathtt{w}_2^{\downarrow}}$ the ambient $a^{\mathtt{r}^{\uparrow}}$ may end up. This is formalised by the following definition, according to the labelling of the auxiliary ambients, explained in Sect. 3.

Definition 2 (Static Property). *Let (ρ, ϕ, σ) be a solution. We say that (ρ, ϕ, σ)* satisfies *the property $\mathcal{P}$ when the following conditions hold:*
(i) if $\mathtt{pre}(\phi((\mathtt{r}^{\downarrow}_{2\mu}, j))) = \langle L, U, C \rangle$, $(\mathtt{w}^{\uparrow}{}_{\lambda}, i) \in U$, $n^{\mathtt{r}_2^{\downarrow}} \in \rho((\mathtt{r}^{\downarrow}_{2\mu}, j))$, $n^{\mathtt{w}^{\uparrow}} \in \rho((\mathtt{w}^{\uparrow}{}_{\lambda}, i))$ and $n \in \rho(\lambda)$, then for any $m \in \rho(\mu)$, we have $\mathcal{P}(n, m, \alpha)$ and $\mathcal{P}(m, n, \beta)$, where $\alpha \in \{w, rw\}$ and $\beta \in \{r, rw\}$;
(ii) if $\mathtt{pre}(\phi((\mathtt{w}^{\downarrow}_{2\mu}, j))) = \langle L, U, C \rangle$, $(\mathtt{r}^{\uparrow}{}_{\lambda}, i) \in U$, $n^{\mathtt{w}_2^{\downarrow}} \in \rho((\mathtt{w}^{\downarrow}_{2\mu}, j))$, $n^{\mathtt{r}^{\uparrow}} \in \rho((\mathtt{r}^{\uparrow}{}_{\lambda}, i))$ and $n \in \rho(\lambda)$, then for any $m \in \rho(\mu)$, we have $\mathcal{P}(n, m, \alpha)$ and $\mathcal{P}(m, n, \beta)$, where $\alpha \in \{r, rw\}$ and $\beta \in \{w, rw\}$.

Theorem 2 (Safeness). *Let (ρ, ϕ, σ) be a valid solution for $\llbracket P \rrbracket^{N}$. If (ρ, ϕ, σ) satisfies the property $\mathcal{P}$, then the BA process P satisfies the property $\mathcal{P}$.*

We apply this approach to the example above, by analysing the encoding of Q. The following is a valid solution [5], where (ρ, ϕ, σ), and $\sigma(x) = \{M_2\}$, $\rho(\mathtt{r}^{\uparrow}_{a}) = a^{\mathtt{r}^{\uparrow}}$, $\rho(\mathtt{c}^{\mathtt{ru}}_{a}) = \mathtt{c}^{\mathtt{ru}}$, $\rho(g_b) = \rho(g_c) = a^{g}$ for $g \in \{\mathtt{w}^{\downarrow}_{1}, \mathtt{w}^{\downarrow}_{2}\}$, $\rho(\mathtt{t}^{\mathtt{wd}}{}_{b}) = \rho(\mathtt{t}^{\mathtt{wd}}{}_{c}) = \mathtt{t}^{\mathtt{wd}}$,

$$
\begin{array}{l}
\phi(\top) = \langle \{\top\}, \{\overline{\mathtt{out}}, a, c, \mathtt{r}^{\uparrow}_{a}\}, \emptyset \rangle \quad \phi(b) = \langle \{b\}, \{\overline{\mathtt{out}}, \overline{\mathtt{in}}, \mathtt{w}^{\downarrow}_{1b}, \mathtt{w}^{\downarrow}_{2b}, \mathtt{t}^{\mathtt{wd}}_{b}, \mathtt{open}\, \mathtt{t}^{\mathtt{wd}}\}, \emptyset \rangle \\
\phi(a) = \langle \{a\}, \{\overline{\mathtt{out}}, \overline{\mathtt{in}}, \mathtt{in}\, b, \mathtt{in}\, c, b, \mathtt{in}\, a^{\mathtt{w}_1^{\downarrow}}, \mathtt{in}\, a^{\mathtt{w}_2^{\downarrow}}, \mathtt{r}^{\uparrow}_{a}, \mathtt{open}\, \mathtt{c}^{\mathtt{ru}}, \mathtt{out}\, a^{\mathtt{w}_2^{\downarrow}}, \mathtt{c}^{\mathtt{ru}}_{a}\}, \emptyset \rangle \\
\phi(c) = \langle \{c\}, \{\overline{\mathtt{out}}, \overline{\mathtt{in}}, a, \mathtt{r}^{\uparrow}_{a}, \mathtt{w}^{\downarrow}_{1c}, \mathtt{w}^{\downarrow}_{2c}, \mathtt{t}^{\mathtt{wd}}_{c}, \mathtt{open}\, \mathtt{t}^{\mathtt{wd}}\}, \emptyset \rangle \\
\phi(\mathtt{r}^{\uparrow}_{a}) = \langle \{\mathtt{r}^{\uparrow}_{a}\}, \{\mathtt{out}\, a, \overline{\mathtt{open}}\}, \emptyset \rangle ; \langle \{\mathtt{w}^{\downarrow}_{2c}\}, \{\mathtt{c}^{\mathtt{ru}}_{a}\}, \emptyset \rangle \\
\phi(\mathtt{c}^{\mathtt{ru}}_{a}) = \langle \{\mathtt{c}^{\mathtt{ru}}_{a}\}, \{\mathtt{in}\, a, \overline{\mathtt{open}}\}, \emptyset \rangle ; \langle \{a\}, \emptyset, \emptyset \rangle \\
\phi(\mathtt{w}^{\downarrow}_{1b}) = \langle \{\mathtt{w}^{\downarrow}_{1b}\}, \{\overline{\mathtt{in}}, \overline{\mathtt{out}}, \mathtt{in}\, \mathtt{t}^{\mathtt{wd}}, \overline{\mathtt{open}}, \mathtt{w}^{\downarrow}_{2b}\}, \emptyset \rangle ; \langle \{\mathtt{t}^{\mathtt{wd}}{}_{b}\}, \{\mathtt{w}^{\downarrow}_{2b}\}, \emptyset \rangle \\
\phi(\mathtt{w}^{\downarrow}_{2b}) = \langle \{\mathtt{w}^{\downarrow}_{2b},\}, \{\overline{\mathtt{in}}, \overline{\mathtt{out}}\, a^{\mathtt{r}^{\uparrow}}, \mathtt{open}\, a^{\mathtt{r}^{\uparrow}}\} \rangle \{M_1\} \\
\phi(\mathtt{t}^{\mathtt{wd}}{}_{b}) = \langle \{\mathtt{t}^{\mathtt{wd}}{}_{b}\}, \{\overline{\mathtt{in}}\, a^{\mathtt{w}_1^{\downarrow}}, \mathtt{open}\, a^{\mathtt{w}_1^{\downarrow}}, \overline{\mathtt{open}}, \mathtt{w}^{\downarrow}_{1b}, \mathtt{w}^{\downarrow}_{2b}\}, \emptyset \rangle ; \langle \{b\}, \{\mathtt{w}^{\downarrow}_{1b}, \mathtt{w}^{\downarrow}_{2b}\}, \emptyset \rangle \\
\phi(\mathtt{w}^{\downarrow}_{1c}) = \langle \{\mathtt{w}^{\downarrow}_{1c}\}, \{\overline{\mathtt{in}}, \overline{\mathtt{out}}, \mathtt{in}\, \mathtt{t}^{\mathtt{wd}}, \overline{\mathtt{open}}, \mathtt{w}^{\downarrow}_{2c}, \mathtt{r}^{\uparrow}_{a}, a\}, \emptyset \rangle ; \langle \{\mathtt{t}^{\mathtt{wd}}{}_{c}\}, \{\mathtt{w}^{\downarrow}_{2c}, \mathtt{r}^{\uparrow}_{a}, a\}, \emptyset \rangle \\
\phi(\mathtt{w}^{\downarrow}_{2c}) = \langle \{\mathtt{w}^{\downarrow}_{2c}\}, \{\overline{\mathtt{in}}, \overline{\mathtt{out}}\, a^{\mathtt{r}^{\uparrow}}, \mathtt{open}\, a^{\mathtt{r}^{\uparrow}}, \mathtt{r}^{\uparrow}_{a}, a, \mathtt{c}^{\mathtt{ru}}_{a}\}, \{M_2\} \rangle \\
\phi(\mathtt{t}^{\mathtt{wd}}{}_{c}) = \langle \{\mathtt{t}^{\mathtt{wd}}{}_{c}\}, \{\overline{\mathtt{in}}\, a^{\mathtt{w}_1^{\downarrow}}, \mathtt{open}\, a^{\mathtt{w}_1^{\downarrow}}, \overline{\mathtt{open}}, \mathtt{w}^{\downarrow}_{1c}, \mathtt{w}^{\downarrow}_{2c}, \mathtt{r}^{\uparrow}_{a}, a\}, \emptyset \rangle ; \langle \{c\}, \{\mathtt{w}^{\downarrow}_{1c}, \mathtt{w}^{\downarrow}_{2c}, \mathtt{r}^{\uparrow}_{a}, a\}, \emptyset \rangle
\end{array}
$$

The solution says that the ambient $a^{\mathtt{r}^{\uparrow}}$ (with label $\mathtt{r}^{\uparrow}_{a}$) can enter only inside the ambient $a^{\mathtt{w}_2^{\downarrow}}$ with label $\mathtt{w}^{\downarrow}_{2c}$, as shown by $\phi(\mathtt{w}^{\downarrow}_{2c})$ and $\phi(\mathtt{w}^{\downarrow}_{2b})$. Since this kind of access among a and c is authorised, the policy is satisfied according to Def. 2.

Note that the crucial information to achieve this result is that the capability $\mathtt{in}\, b$ cannot be exercised (since ambients a and b cannot be siblings); and

[5] We assume for simplicity that $P = \mathbf{0}$ and that M_1 and M_2 are two closed expressions. Also, we omit ρ for the BA ambients (it is the identity).

therefore ambient a cannot enter inside ambient b (see $\phi(b)$). Moreover, the local solutions are essential $\langle L_1, U_1, C_1 \rangle ; \langle L_2, U_2, C_2 \rangle$ for the auxiliary ambients to accurately distinguish what happens before and after their dissolution. A weaker analysis as [24] (see Ex. 1) cannot argue that $\mathtt{in}\, a$ has been consumed before $\mathtt{c}^{\mathtt{ru}}$ (carrying the continuation of the abstraction) is opened inside ambient a (see $\phi(\mathtt{c}^{\mathtt{ru}}_a)$ and $\phi(a)$). As a consequence, it would report that ambient a may enter inside itself, by exercising $\mathtt{in}\, a$, and that the MAC property may be violated (as $\mathtt{in}\, b$ may run ambient a inside its possible sibling b). Also the types of [5] for BA cannot prove this property, precisely because they do not capture that $\mathtt{in}\, b$ cannot be exercised inside a.

6 Conclusions

We have presented: – an encoding of BA into a variant of SA; – a CFA for SA that refines the proposal of [24] with a finer treatment of the critical opening action, along the lines of the type systems for SA [20,12,15,1,17] (see Ex. 1). The CFA is sufficiently informative to capture the typical security properties of SA [7,12,3,11,2] controlling which boundaries an ambient may cross and which ambients it may open.

These results are interesting by themselves, but also when combined together, given that, by means of the translation, the CFA can be applied to verify security properties also of BA, in particular the MAC properties. Other properties can probably be verified this way, e.g. the mobility property of [23]. The relevance of our CFA for this application is demonstrated by the example, discussed in Sect. 5, which cannot be proved using either the types of [5] for BA or the adaptation of CFA of [24] to SA. Several refinements [16,25,11,19,13] of [24] have been proposed. The analyses of [11,13,19] for MA/SA further restrict the space of possible interactions, by exploiting more contextual information, and better handle replication. It is not clear whether their treatment of the opening is sufficiently accurate for analysing the encoding. The CFA for MA of [16, 25] are more complex than [24] (and also of our CFA), as they exploit more detailed information about the possible run-time shape of processes, and could be profitably applied to the encoding to derive more accurate predictions. The CFA in [2] verifies an information flow property, which does not seem adequate to capture the MAC properties. The type systems of MA/SA [7,8,20,3,1,12,15,17] are typically simpler and more elegant than the analyses. They cannot however distinguish the auxiliary ambients with the same name and therefore cannot give better results than the types for BA [5], when applied to the encoded processes (see e.g. the use of labels in the example of Sect. 5).

Finally, we mention that in [4,5,23] a different semantics for the BA inter-level communications is used, where downward-upward communication actions interact with local prefixes rather than with each other. In [18] we have adapted the approach of this paper to the BA version of [4], which seems more expressive, and we have obtained similar results w.r.t [5]. Although the encoding of [4] is much more complex, it can be derived along the lines of Sect. 3. It is enough to modify the translation of local and inter-level communication actions, by using different auxiliary ambients in the protocols of Tab. 3 and by introducing sum between non-prefixed terms in SA, reflecting the intrinsic non-determinism on local prefixes of this model. We intend to study the encoding also of another version of BA [6], which extends [10] with special coactions using passwords.

References

1. T. Amtoft and A. J. Kfoury and S. M. Pericas-Geertsen. *What are Polymorphically-Typed Ambients?* Proc. of ESOP'01, LNCS 2028, 2001.
2. C. Braghin, A. Cortesi and R. Focardi. *Control Flow Analysis for information flow security in mobile ambients.* Proc. of FMOODS'02, pp. 197-212, 2002.
3. M. Bugliesi and G. Castagna. *Secure safe ambients.* Proc. of POPL '01, pp. 222-235, 2001.
4. M. Bugliesi, G. Castagna, S. Crafa. *Boxed Ambients.* Proc. of TACS'01, LNCS 2225, pp. 36-61, 2001.
5. — *Reasoning about Security in Mobile Ambients.* Proc. of CONCUR'01, LNCS 2154, pp. 102-120, 2001.
6. M. Bugliesi, S. Crafa, M. Merro and V. Sassone. *Communication Interference in Boxed Ambients.* Proc. of FSTTCS'02, LNCS 2556, pp. 71–84, 2002.
7. L. Cardelli, G. Ghelli, and A.D. Gordon. *Mobility types for mobile ambients.* Proc. of ICALP'99, LNCS 1644, pp. 230-239, 1999.
8. — *Types for the ambient calculus.* Information and Computation, 177(2), 2002.
9. L. Cardelli and A.D. Gordon. *Mobile ambients.* Proc. of FoSSaCS '98, LNCS 1378, pp. 140-155, 1998.
10. S. Crafa, M. Bugliesi and G. Castagna. *Information Flow Security in Boxed Ambients.* Proc. of FWAN '02, ENTCS, 66(3), 2002.
11. P. Degano, F. Levi and C. Bodei. *Safe Ambients: Control Flow Analysis and Security.* Proc. of ASIAN '00, LNCS 1961, pp. 199-214, 2000.
12. M. Dezani-Ciancaglini and I. Salvo. *Security Types for Mobile Safe Ambients.* Proc. of ASIAN '00, LNCS 1961, pp. 215-236, 2000.
13. J. Feret. *Abstract Interpretation-Based Static Analysis of Mobile Ambients.* Proc. of SAS'01, LNCS 2126, pp. 412-430, 2001.
14. X. Guan, Y. Yang, and J. You. *Making Ambients More Robust.* Proc. of the International Conference on Software: Theory and Practise, 377–384, 2000.
15. — *Typing Evolving Ambients.* Inf. Processing Letters, 80(5), pp. 265–270, 2001.
16. R. R. Hansen and J. G. Jensen and F. Nielson and H. R.Nielson. *Abstract Interpretation of Mobile Ambients.* Proc. of SAS'99, LNCS 1694, pp. 135-148, 1999.
17. F. Levi. *Types for Evolving Communication in Safe Ambients.* Proc. of VMCAI '03, LNCS 2575, pp. 102-115, 2003.
18. F. Levi and C. Bodei *A Control Flow Analysis for Safe and Boxed Ambients (Extended Version).* Available at `http://www.di.unipi.it/~ levifran/papers.html`
19. F. Levi and S. Maffeis. *An Abstract Interpretation Framework for Analysing Mobile Ambients.* Proc. of SAS '01, LNCS 2126, pp. 395-411, 2001.
20. F. Levi and D. Sangiorgi. *Controlling Interference in Ambients.* Proc. of POPL '00, pp. 352-364, 2000.
21. — *Mobile Safe Ambients.* TOPLAS, 25(1), 1–69, 2003.
22. M. Merro and M. Hennessy. *Bisimulation congruences in Safe Ambients.* Proc. of POPL '02, 2002.

23. M. Merro and V. Sassone. *Typing and Subtyping Mobility in Boxed Ambients.* Proc. of CONCUR'02, LNCS 2421, pp. 304-320, 2002.
24. F. Nielson, H.R. Nielson, R.R. Hansen. *Validating firewalls using flow logics.* Theoretical Computer Science, 283(2), 381-418, 2002. Also (joint work also with J.G. Jensen) appeared in the Proc. of CONCUR'99, LNCS 1664, 1999.
25. H. R. Nielson and F. Nielson. *Shape Analysis for Mobile Ambients.* Proc. of POPL' 00, pp. 135-148, 2000.

Linear Types for Packet Processing

Robert Ennals[1], Richard Sharp[2], and Alan Mycroft[1]

[1] Computer Laboratory, Cambridge University
15 JJ Thomson Avenue, Cambridge, CB3 0FD, UK.
{robert.ennals,am}@cl.cam.ac.uk
[2] Intel Research Cambridge,
15 JJ Thomson Avenue, Cambridge, CB3 0FD, UK.
richard.sharp@intel.com

Abstract. We present PacLang: an imperative, concurrent, linearly-typed language designed for expressing packet processing applications. PacLang's linear type system ensures that no packet is referenced by more than one thread, but allows multiple references to a packet *within a thread*. We argue (*i*) that this property greatly simplifies compilation of high-level programs to the distributed memory architectures of modern Network Processors; and (*ii*) that PacLang's type system captures that style in which imperative packet processing programs are already written. Claim (*ii*) is justified by means of a case-study: we describe a PacLang implementation of the IPv4 unicast packet forwarding algorithm.
PacLang is formalised by means of an operational semantics and a Unique Ownership theorem formalises its correctness with respect to the type system.

1 Introduction

Network Processors (NPs) [1,10,17] are programmable, application-specific hardware architectures designed to facilitate high-speed packet processing. NPs typically contain multiple processor cores (allowing multiple network packets to be processed concurrently) and multiple memory banks. The majority of NPs are based on what is known as a *distributed memory architecture*: not all memory banks are accessible from all processor cores.

State-of-the-art programming techniques for NPs are invariably low-level, requiring programmers to specify explicitly how data will be mapped to, and dynamically moved between, complex arrays of available memory banks. This results in design flows which are difficult to master, error prone and inextricably tied to one particular architecture. Our research attempts to address this problem by developing higher-level languages and tools for programming NPs.

This paper formally defines an imperative language which provides an architecturally neutral concurrent programming model—multiple parallel threads accessing a shared heap—and considers the problem of compiling this language to NP-based architectures. We argue that although, *in general*, the efficient compilation of a high-level concurrent language to a diverse range of NP architectures is very difficult, *in the domain of packet processing* the problem is more

D.A. Schmidt (Ed.): ESOP 2004, LNCS 2986, pp. 204–218, 2004.

tractable. Our argument is based on the observation that a great deal of network processing code is written in a restricted data-flow style, in which network packets can be seen to "flow" through a packet processing system. We formalise this restricted style of programming by means of a linear type system and state a *unique ownership property*: if a program is typeable then at any given point in its execution, each packet in the heap is referenced by exactly one thread. It is this property that we argue simplifies the process of compiling for network processors.

Contributions of this paper: (*i*) the formalisation of a concurrent, first-order, imperative language which we argue is well suited for compiling to a diverse range of NP architectures; (*ii*) a simple, intuitive linear type system in which no packet is referenced by more than one thread but multiple references to packets *within a thread* are allowed; and (*iii*) a case-study that demonstrates both that the type system is applicable to the domain of packet processing (i.e. not overly restrictive) and that the resulting code is comprehensible to C/C++ programmers.

Previous research [16] has shown that (*i*) locking is unnecessary for linearly typed objects; and (*ii*) memory leaks can be detected statically as type errors. Although these are not direct contributions of this paper, they are nevertheless benefits enjoyed by PacLang programmers.

Structure of this paper: We outline the design of an NP-based platform and explain how our unique ownership property helps us target such architectures (Section 1.1). Section 2 gives formal syntax and types for PacLang and Section 3 defines its linear typing judgements along with more intuitive explanation. An operational semantics for the language is presented and the *unique ownership property* formalised (Section 4). To justify that our linear type system is not overly restrictive in the domain of packet processing applications, we present a case study which shows how PacLang can be used to implement an IPv4 packet forwarder (Section 5). Finally we consider related work (Section 6) and conclude, giving directions for future research/development (Section 7).

1.1 Compiling for Network Processors

Figure 1 gives a concrete example of an NP-based system: the Intel IXDP2400 [9]. The platform consists of two Intel IXP2400 NPs [10] connected in a pipeline configuration. Each NP contains 16 small RISC processors called *micro-engines* (labelled μE-1,. . .,μE-16), a single Intel X-Scale processor and some on-chip shared RAM. Each micro-engine[1] has its own local memory. The external SRAM and DRAMs can be accessed by all the cores on the NP to which they are connected. Micro-engines are equipped with *next neighbour registers*. The next neighbour

[1] Note that each micro-engine actually supports 8 hardware-level threads. This level of detail is beyond the scope of the paper.

registers of μE-i are accessible to μE-$(i+1)$, forming a uni-directional datapath between consecutive micro-engines.

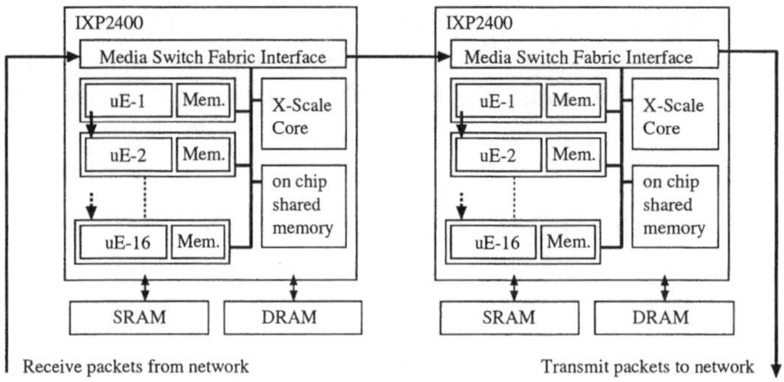

Fig. 1. Simplified diagram of IXDP2400 NP evaluation board

When programming for architectures such as this a great deal of low-level knowledge is required to decide how packets should be represented in memory and how packets should be transferred between different memory banks[2]. For example, if a small amount of data needs to be transferred between two threads running on μE-1 and μE-2, then the most efficient mechanism may well be to move the data across the serial datapath connecting μE-1 and μE-2. Conversely, if we have data already in DRAM that needs to be transferred between threads running on μE-1 and the X-Scale core then leaving the data where it is and passing a reference to it is the obvious choice. When passing data between the two separate IXP2400s we *must* pass-by-value since the two processors have no memories in common.

Clearly, if we are to succeed in our goal of designing a high-level language that can be compiled to a variety of different NP architectures then a compiler must be *free to choose* how data will be passed between threads (e.g. pass a reference pointing to shared memory, or pass the data itself over a shared bus). Unfortunately, conventional imperative languages (e.g. C/C++) are unsatisfactory in this respect since they force the programmer to *explicitly specify* whether data will be passed by value or passed by reference. Note that a compiler cannot simply transform pass-by-value into pass-by-reference (or vice versa); sophisticated *alias analysis* is required to determine whether this transformation is semantics-preserving—an analysis that is undecidable in general.

In contrast, in the PacLang framework, the unique ownership property (provided by our linear type system) gives us two key benefits: (i) a thread

[2] Moving a packet between different memories as it "flows" through a packet processing application is crucial to achieving efficient implementation on the IXP (and other NPs). Data should be located "as close as possible" to the thread operating on it in order to reduce memory latency.

$v \leftarrow i$	*integer constant*
$\quad \mid b$	*boolean constant*
$\quad \mid x$	*variable*
$e \leftarrow \texttt{if}\ v\ \texttt{then}\ e_1\ \texttt{else}\ e_2$	*conditional*
$\quad \mid \texttt{let}\ (x_1,\ldots,x_j) = f(v_1,\ldots,v_k)\ \texttt{in}\ \mathrm{e}\quad (j,k \geq 0)$	*call*
$\quad \mid \texttt{return}\ (v_1,\ldots,v_k)\quad (k \geq 0)$	*return*
$d \leftarrow (\sigma_1,\ldots,\sigma_j)\ f(\rho_1\ x_1,\ldots,\rho_k\ x_k)\{e\}\quad (j,k \geq 0)$	*function definition*
$\quad \mid \mathit{packetQueue}\ q;$	*queue definition*
$p \leftarrow d_1 \ldots d_n$	*top-level program*
$\rho,\ \sigma,\ \tau \leftarrow \mathit{int} \mid \mathit{bool} \mid \mathit{packet} \mid \mathit{!packet}$	*types*

Fig. 2. Syntax of PACLANG, our simple first-order CBV language.

can dynamically move an object it owns to a new location without worrying about dangling references; and *(ii)* pass-by-value and pass-by-reference are semantically indistinguishable when transferring data between threads. This gives a PACLANG compiler the freedom to make decisions regarding both the flow of packets between available memory banks and the low-level mechanisms employed to implement these transfers, on a per-architecture basis.

2 A Packet Processing Language

PACLANG is a concurrent, first-order, imperative language with a linear type system; its syntax is presented in Figure 2. Concurrency is supported by the simple expedient of treating functions whose name is spelt $\texttt{main}_1,\ldots,\texttt{main}_n$, as representing the entry points of n static threads $(n \geq 1)$[3]. Such functions take no arguments and return no results. Statically allocated, synchronous (blocking) packet queues are provided to facilitate inter-thread communication.

Expressions, e, comprise conditionals, function calls and `return`s. Note that PACLANG syntax forces all function return values to be explicitly bound to variables (cf. A-Normal Form [7]); this simplifies subsequent typing and semantic rules. In addition to function names defined by *function definitions* we assume some functions to be built-in, e.g. arithmetic and queue manipulation primitives (see later); both forms may be called using the `let` construct. We use v to range over simple expressions (constants and variables). A program, p, consists of a sequence of function and queue definitions, d. Note that functions take multiple arguments and return multiple results.

In contrast to most languages in the linear types literature, PACLANG has imperative features. Given a packet reference p, an integer offset i and a value

[3] In practice a compiler may wish to transform a single programmer-specified thread into several finer-grained threads for efficient implementation on certain NP architectures. Such *automated partitioning* is beyond the scope of this paper.

v, the built-in function `update(`p`,`i`,`v`)` updates p to contain v at offset i. The packet read function `read(`p`,`i`)` returns the value stored at offset i in packet p.

Global queues also provide side-effecting enqueue and dequeue operations. To simplify the presentation we assume built-in `enq` and `deq` functions replicated over queue names. We write `q.enq(`p`)` to enqueue a packet p in the queue declared with name `q`. Similarly, `q.deq()` returns a packet dequeued from `q`. The semantics of queues are formalised in Section 4.

We also provide built-in functions `new(`i`)` which given an integer size i, creates a new packet buffer of size i, returning its associated *packet reference*; and `kill(`p`)`, which takes a packet reference p, consumes it, deallocates the associated packet and returns nothing. In PACLANG packets are simply dynamically created arrays. As well as representing network packets, they can also be used as containers for arbitrary (non-pointer) data within a PACLANG program.

Syntactic sugaring is employed to increase readability for those familiar with C. We write "$f(v_1, \ldots, v_k); e$" to abbreviate "`let` $() = f(v_1, \ldots, v_k)$ `in` e". We allow nested function calls to be written directly, assuming a left-to-right evaluation order. For example, the expression "`let x =` $f(g(x), h(y))$ `in` e", becomes "`let` z_1 `=` $g(x)$ `in let` z_2 `=` $h(y)$ `in let x =` $f(z_1, z_2)$ `in` e" where $z_1, z_2 \notin fv(e)$. We add types to the variables following `let` (corresponding to the return type of the called function) as usual in C, and also drop the `let` keyword and parentheses entirely. We write `void` in place of `()` in the signature of functions that return an empty tuple of values and adopt the convention that an expression without an explicit `return` implicitly returns a value of type `void`. We also introduce a `switch/case` construct which is translated into nested `if`s in the usual way. We write `update(`p`,`a`,`v`)` using C-like syntax, p`[`a`] =` v, and use array subscript notation, p`[`a`]`, for `read(`p`,`a`)`. To avoid the extra syntax required for explicit while-loops, we use recursion to model iteration in this presentation. (Of course, a PACLANG compiler would implement tail-call optimisation to ensure the generated code is as efficient as if it had been written with while-loops.)

3 Linear Type System

An industrial NP programming textbook [11] observes: *"In most designs processing of a packet by multiple threads simultaneously is rare, but using multiple threads to process packets at different points in the packet's lifetime is common."* This quote summarises the philosophy behind PACLANG's linear type system: we (i) *guarantee* that, in a well typed program, a packet, p, cannot be accessed by multiple threads simultaneously; whilst (ii) allowing p to be transferred between threads as it flows through an application. Unlike many linear type systems, we allow p to be referenced multiple times (aliasing). However, we require that all references to p reside in the same thread. Allowing intra-thread aliasing is crucial to the readability of PACLANG code. It is this property that allows PACLANG programmers to write in the familiar imperative (pass-by-reference) style—see

Section 5. In many ways, PACLANG's type system is inspired by Kobayashi's work on *Quasi-Linear Types* [12].

We start by defining some terminology. A variable, x, that holds a reference to a packet p, will either be of type *packet* or *!packet*:

- If x has type *packet* then, at any point where x is in scope, there are no other references to p. We say that x is an *owning variable* and holds an *owning reference* for p. If one has an owning reference to p then one can safely move p to another thread without creating dangling references.
- If x has type *!packet* then other references to p may exist, but they must be on the same thread as x. We say that x is an *alias* for p. An alias cannot escape from its enclosing scope.

Value types, *int* and *bool*, are non-linear and behave as is normal.

Our type rules use arrow-notation for vectors. We write $\vec{\tau}$ to represent a vector of types and similarly $\vec{x}$ and $\vec{v}$ for vectors of variables and values respectively. We let ρ, σ, τ range over types. Function types are written $\rho_1 \times \ldots \times \rho_k \rightarrow \sigma_1 \times \ldots \times \sigma_j$ or more briefly as $\vec{\rho} \rightarrow \vec{\sigma}$. Given a function name f, $\mathcal{F}(f)$ gives its type signature. For user-defined functions this comes from the textual definition; the types of built-in functions are given in Figure 4.

Typing judgements for expressions ($\overset{e}{\vdash}$) take the form $\Gamma \overset{e}{\vdash} e : \vec{\tau}$ where Γ is a typing environment, e is an expression (generally returning a tuple) and $\vec{\tau}$ is the return type (generally a tuple type). Γ can be regarded as the set of *capabilities* that e requires during its execution. Each capability in Γ takes the form $x : \rho$ specifying that x is used as ρ in e. We adopt the usual notation of writing $\Gamma, x:\tau$ to represent Γ extended to include the capability $x:\tau$ (note that scope shadowing is problematic in linear type systems so we will simply presume that all variable names are distinct).

The typing rules for PACLANG, rely on two partial binary operators, "+" and ";" which operate on type environments. An expression which requires capabilities in Γ_1 and then subsequently the capabilities in Γ_2, can equivalently be said to require the capabilities in environment $\Gamma_1; \Gamma_2$. Similarly, if an expression requires capabilities in both Γ_1 and Γ_2 in an unordered fashion, it requires $\Gamma_1 + \Gamma_2$. We first define, "+" and ";" over *types*:

$$
\begin{array}{ccc}
\mathit{int} + \mathit{int} = \mathit{int} & \qquad & \mathit{int} \ ; \ \mathit{int} = \mathit{int} \\
\mathit{bool} + \mathit{bool} = \mathit{bool} & & \mathit{bool} \ ; \ \mathit{bool} = \mathit{bool} \\
\mathit{!packet} + \mathit{!packet} = \mathit{!packet} & & \mathit{!packet} \ ; \ \mathit{!packet} = \mathit{!packet} \\
 & & \mathit{!packet} \ ; \ \mathit{packet} = \mathit{packet}
\end{array}
$$

If no rule is given then that signifies a type error. Note that ";" is a strict superset of "+". We extend these operators to type environments by the following definitions (here $\otimes$ ranges over "+" and ";"):

$$
\begin{aligned}
\Gamma_1 \otimes \Gamma_2 \overset{def}{=} & \{x : \tau \mid x : \tau \in \Gamma_1 \wedge x \notin \mathrm{dom}\ \Gamma_2\} \ \cup \\
& \{x : \tau \mid x : \tau \in \Gamma_2 \wedge x \notin \mathrm{dom}\ \Gamma_1\} \ \cup \\
& \{x : \tau_1 \otimes \tau_2 \mid x : \tau_1 \in \Gamma_1 \wedge x : \tau_2 \in \Gamma_2\}
\end{aligned}
$$

$$\frac{}{\{x:\tau\} \overset{v}{\vdash} x:\tau}\,(var) \qquad \frac{}{\emptyset \overset{v}{\vdash} i : int}\,(int)\ (i \in \mathbb{Z}) \qquad \frac{}{\emptyset \overset{v}{\vdash} b : bool}\,(bool)\ (i \in \mathbb{B})$$

$$\frac{\Gamma_1 \overset{v}{\vdash} v_1 : \rho_1 \quad \ldots \quad \Gamma_k \overset{v}{\vdash} v_k : \rho_k \qquad \Gamma_0, x_1 {:} \sigma_1, \ldots, x_j {:} \sigma_j \overset{e}{\vdash} e : \vec{\tau}}{(\Gamma_1 + \ldots + \Gamma_k); \Gamma_0 \overset{e}{\vdash} \texttt{let}\ (x_1, \ldots, x_j) = f(v_1, \ldots, v_k)\ \texttt{in}\ e : \vec{\tau}}\,(apseq)$$

$$\text{provided } \mathcal{F}(f) = (\rho_1 \times \ldots \times \rho_k) \rightarrow (\sigma_1 \times \ldots \times \sigma_j)$$

$$\frac{\Gamma_1 \overset{v}{\vdash} v_1 : \tau_1 \quad \ldots \quad \Gamma_j \overset{v}{\vdash} v_j : \tau_j}{\Gamma_1 + \ldots + \Gamma_j \overset{e}{\vdash} \texttt{return}\ (v_1, \ldots, v_j) : \tau_1 \times \ldots \times \tau_j}\,(ret)$$

$$\text{provided no } \tau_j \text{ is } !packet$$

$$\frac{\Gamma_1 \overset{v}{\vdash} v : bool \quad \Gamma_2 \overset{e}{\vdash} e_1 : \vec{\tau} \quad \Gamma_2 \overset{e}{\vdash} e_2 : \vec{\tau}}{\Gamma_1; \Gamma_2 \overset{e}{\vdash} \texttt{if}\ v\ \texttt{then}\ e_1\ \texttt{else}\ e_2 : \vec{\tau}}\,(if) \qquad \frac{\Gamma \overset{e}{\vdash} e : \vec{\tau}}{\Gamma, x : \rho \overset{e}{\vdash} e : \vec{\tau}}\,(weak)$$

$$\text{provided } \rho \text{ is not } packet$$

$$\frac{\{x_1 {:} \rho_1, \ldots, x_k {:} \rho_k\} \overset{e}{\vdash} e : \sigma_1 \times \ldots \times \sigma_j}{\overset{d}{\vdash} (\sigma_1, \ldots, \sigma_j)\ f(\rho_1\ x_1, \ldots, \rho_k\ x_k)\{e\}}\,(fundef) \qquad \frac{}{\overset{d}{\vdash} packetQueue\ q;}\,(qdef)$$

$$\frac{\overset{d}{\vdash} d_1 \quad \ldots \quad \overset{d}{\vdash} d_n}{\overset{p}{\vdash} d_1 \ldots d_n}\,(prog)$$

Fig. 3. Linear typing rules

Figure 3 presents the linear type rules. Typing rules for definitions ($\overset{d}{\vdash}$), programs ($\overset{p}{\vdash}$) and simple expressions ($\overset{v}{\vdash}$) are self-explanatory, although note that, in contrast to non-linear type systems, the (*var*) rule only holds if the environment contains the *single* assumption, $x{:}\tau$.

The typing rules for expressions ($\overset{e}{\vdash}$) deserve more detailed explanation. Essentially they ensure (*i*) that an owning variable x for a packet p goes out of scope for the lifetime of any aliases to p; and (*ii*) that an owning variable x may no longer be used if its owning reference is passed to another owning variable.

For a variable x to be of type *!packet*, x must be bound as a formal parameter of its enclosing function definition. When calling a function, f, the (*apseq*) rule allows aliases to be created from an owning variable provided that the owning variable goes out of scope[4] during the call, and that the alias dies before the function returns. It is the use of the environment sequencing operator ";" in the consequent of the (*apseq*) rule that facilitates the creation of aliases from an owning variable. (Recall that $!packet\ ;\ packet = packet$).

The (*ret*) rule types its subexpressions in environments $\Gamma_1, \ldots, \Gamma_j$ respectively, and uses the "+" operator to combine these environments in the antecedent. The "+" operator is used in this context to prevent owning references

[4] In PACLANG this is ensured by the absence of nested function definitions and the absence of global packet variables.

being duplicated. We prevent values of type *!packet* being returned because the enclosing scope may contain the corresponding owning variable.

```
int ⟨arith-op⟩ (int x, int y);        bool ⟨bool-op⟩ (bool x, bool y);
bool ⟨rel-op⟩ (int x, int y);
packet new(int size);                 void kill(packet p);
packet q.deq();                       void q.enq(packet p);
int read(!packet p, int offset);
void update(!packet p, int offset, int value);
```

Fig. 4. Type signatures of the built-in functions expressed in C-like syntax

The type signatures of built-in functions are given in Figure 4. Note that inter-thread communication primitives, *q.enq* and *q.deq*, enqueue and dequeue values of type *packet* (i.e. owning references). Thus when transferring a packet between threads, the packet can be physically relocated.

We assume the existence of special queues, `receive` and `transmit` which represent the external network interface. `receive.deq()` reads a packet from the network; `transmit.enq(p)` schedules packet `p` for transmission. In reality a network appliance would typically contain multiple network interfaces and one would expect a variety of more sophisticated range of read/write calls. However, since this does not affect the fundamental concepts expressed in PacLang, we stick to the simple interface above for the purposes of this paper.

The following two examples (in de-sugared form) help to illustrate PacLang's linear type system. First consider the following valid PacLang expression:

```
let packet x = new(10) in
let () = update(x,0,5) in
let () = update(x,1,10) in
let () = transmit.enq(x) in return ()
```

This code will type check successfully as, although `x` is accessed multiple times, `update` only requires a local alias to `x` (*!packet*) and so does not prevent `x` being passed as type *packet* to `transmit.enq`.

Conversely, consider the following *invalid* PacLang expression:

```
let packet x = new(10) in
let () = kill(x) in
let () = transmit.enq(x) in return ()
```

The type system rejects this program since `x` is passed twice as type *packet*: once to the `kill` function and then again to the `transmit.enq` function. Once `x` has been passed as type *packet*, it effectively disappears and cannot be used again.

4 Operational Semantics

In this section we define the language formally by means of a small-step operational semantics modelled on the Chemical Abstract Machine [2]. States of the machine are a chemical solution of reacting molecules. We let W range over machine states. The "|" operator separates molecules in the multiset solution (cf. parallel composition). Molecules take the following forms:

$$\begin{array}{lll} M \leftarrow & [\![\{\vec{x}\}e]\!]_f & \text{(function definition)} \\ \mid & \langle\!\langle Q \rangle\!\rangle_q & \text{(queue)} \\ \mid & \langle H \rangle & \text{(shared heap)} \\ \mid & (\!| e, \Sigma |\!) & \text{(thread: expression and its stack frames)} \end{array}$$

We let α range over an infinite set of heap-bound packet reference values[5]. We extend the syntactic category, v, allowing values also to be packet references, α, in addition to integer and boolean constants.

A *function molecule*, $[\![\{\vec{x}\}e]\!]_f$, corresponds to a source-level function definition for f, with formal parameters, $\vec{x}$, and body e. Function molecules themselves do not perform computation, they exist merely to provide their bodies to callers.

A *queue molecule*, $\langle\!\langle Q \rangle\!\rangle_q$ has name q and contents Q, where Q takes the form of a list of elements separated by the associative operator $\bullet$. An empty queue is written ϵ. In the semantics presented here, queues are unbounded with synchronous (blocking) behaviour.

A *heap molecule*, $\langle H \rangle$, maps *packet references*, α, onto packets, p. A packet, p, is a finite mapping from integer offsets, i, to integer values, $p(i)$[6]. We define $empty_k$ as the empty packet of size k: $empty_k = \{0 \mapsto 0, \ldots, (k-1) \mapsto 0\}$. We write $\langle H \backslash \alpha \rangle$ for the heap which is as $\langle H \rangle$ but no longer contains an entry for α. The heap, which is as $\langle H \rangle$ but maps α to p, is written $\langle H[\alpha \mapsto p]\rangle$. Thus, updating the ith element of the packet referenced by α to value 42 is written $\langle H[\alpha \mapsto H(\alpha)[i \mapsto 42]]\rangle$. The reader should note that the heap molecule need not be implemented as a single shared memory. The central result of this paper is that, due to PacLang's unique ownership property, a compiler is free to map the packets in $\langle H \rangle$ to the multiple memory banks of a distributed memory architecture.

A *thread molecule*, $(\!| e, \Sigma |\!)$, corresponds to one of the `main`-functions (see Section 2) where e is an *evaluation state* and Σ is a stack of (function-return) continuations as in Landin's SECD machine. As with queue molecules, we use the associative operator, $\bullet$, to separate elements on the stack and write ϵ for the empty stack. The syntax of evaluation states, e, is essentially the same as the syntax of expressions given in Figure 2, save that as noted above unbound variables do not occur but values may also be packet references, α. We write "$\{\vec{x}\}e$" for the continuation that binds variables $\vec{x}$ and continues as evaluation state e.

---

[5] There is no syntactic (compile-time) form of such values.

[6] If the offset is outside the domain of the packet the result is undefined.

Core language primitives:

$$[\![\{\vec{x}\}e_1]\!]_f \mid (\!|\texttt{let } \vec{y} = f(\vec{v}) \texttt{ in } e_2, \Sigma|\!) \rightsquigarrow [\![\{\vec{x}\}e_1]\!]_f \mid (\!|e_1\{\vec{v}/\vec{x}\}, (\{\vec{y}\}e_2) \bullet \Sigma|\!) \quad (\textit{user-call})$$
$$(\!|\texttt{let } x = v_1 \; op \; v_2 \texttt{ in } e, \Sigma|\!) \rightsquigarrow (\!|e\{v/x\}, \Sigma|\!) \text{ where } v = v_1 \; op \; v_2 \quad (\textit{basic-op})$$
$$(\!|\texttt{return } \vec{v}, (\{\vec{x}\}e) \bullet \Sigma|\!) \rightsquigarrow (\!|e\{\vec{v}/\vec{x}\}, \Sigma|\!) \quad (\textit{ret})$$
$$(\!|\texttt{if } \textit{true} \texttt{ then } e_1 \texttt{ else } e_2, \Sigma|\!) \rightsquigarrow (\!|e_1, \Sigma|\!) \quad (\textit{if}_1)$$
$$(\!|\texttt{if } \textit{false} \texttt{ then } e_1 \texttt{ else } e_2, \Sigma|\!) \rightsquigarrow (\!|e_2, \Sigma|\!) \quad (\textit{if}_2)$$

Packet manipulation:

$$\langle H\rangle \mid (\!|\texttt{let } x = \textit{new}(i) \texttt{ in } e, \Sigma|\!) \rightsquigarrow \langle H[\alpha \mapsto \textit{empty}_i]\rangle \mid (\!|e\{\alpha/x\}, \Sigma|\!) \quad (\textit{new})$$
where α is a fresh name

$$\langle H\rangle \mid (\!|\texttt{let } () = \textit{kill}(\alpha) \texttt{ in } e, \Sigma|\!) \rightsquigarrow \langle H\backslash\alpha\rangle \mid (\!|e, \Sigma|\!) \quad (\textit{kill})$$
$$\langle H\rangle \mid (\!|\texttt{let } x = \textit{read}(\alpha, i) \texttt{ in } e, \Sigma|\!) \rightsquigarrow \langle H\rangle \mid (\!|e\{H(\alpha)(i)/x\}, \Sigma|\!) \quad (\textit{read})$$
$$\langle H\rangle \mid (\!|\texttt{let } () = \textit{update}(\alpha, i, v) \texttt{ in } e, \Sigma|\!) \rightsquigarrow \langle H[\alpha \mapsto H(\alpha)[i \mapsto v]]\rangle \mid (\!|e, \Sigma|\!) \quad (\textit{update})$$

Queues:

$$\langle\!\langle \alpha \bullet Q\rangle\!\rangle_q \mid (\!|\texttt{let } x = q.\textit{deq}() \texttt{ in } e, \Sigma|\!) \rightsquigarrow \langle\!\langle Q\rangle\!\rangle_q \mid (\!|e\{\alpha/x\}, \Sigma|\!) \quad (\textit{deq})$$
$$\langle\!\langle Q\rangle\!\rangle_q \mid (\!|\texttt{let } () = q.\textit{enq}(\alpha) \texttt{ in } e, \Sigma|\!) \rightsquigarrow \langle\!\langle Q \bullet \alpha\rangle\!\rangle_q \mid (\!|e, \Sigma|\!) \quad (\textit{enq})$$

Fig. 5. Operational Semantics for PacLang

We write *init*(P) to denote the initial state for program P. It consists of a function molecule, $[\![\{\vec{x}\}e]\!]_f$, for each function definition, $f(\vec{x})\{e\}$, in P; a thread molecule, $(\!|e_j, \epsilon|\!)$, for each definition $\texttt{main}_j()\{e_j\}$ in P; an empty queue molecule $\langle\!\langle\epsilon\rangle\!\rangle_q$ for each queue definition in P; and an empty heap $\langle\;\rangle$.

The semantics is given as a transition relation, $\rightarrow$, on states (multisets of molecules). For convenience, we define $\rightarrow$ in terms of an operator, $\rightsquigarrow$, which operates on only a subset of the molecules in a complete state:

$$\frac{M_1 \mid \ldots \mid M_n \rightsquigarrow M_1' \mid \ldots \mid M_n'}{\Delta_1 \mid \ldots \mid \Delta_k \mid M_1 \mid \ldots \mid M_n \rightarrow \Delta_1 \mid \ldots \mid \Delta_k \mid M_1' \mid \ldots \mid M_n'} \; (\rightsquigarrow)$$

where $\Delta_1, \ldots, \Delta_k$ are molecules that form part of the state, but are not of interest to the $\rightsquigarrow$-transition. Figure 5 gives transition rules for PacLang. Capture-free substitution of values $\vec{v}$ for variables $\vec{x}$ in expression e is written $e\{\vec{v}/\vec{x}\}$.

The outside world interacts with the program by placing network packets on the `receive` queue and removing network packets from the `transmit` queue. In reality these queues would be filled and emptied by hardware. However, to avoid extra semantic rules to express this, we can model a generic network interface as if it were two system-provided threads, one of which dequeues packets from `transmit` and frees them; the other of which constructs and allocates appropriate packets and enqueues them on `receive`.

4.1 Unique Ownership

Recall from Section 1 that the primary motivation for our type-system is to ensure that every packet in the heap is referenced by exactly one thread. We have argued that this *unique ownership* property makes practical the mapping of a high-level program to a variety of diverse hardware architectures (see Section 1.1). In this section we define unique ownership formally.

Let, $pr(M)$, be the set of packet references, α, that occur in molecule M. (This is empty for function molecules, but generally non-empty for thread and queue molecules; $pr(\cdot)$ is not applied to the heap molecule.) We write $S_1 \uplus S_2$ to be the union of sets S_1 and S_2 under the condition that the elements of S_1 and S_2 are disjoint ($S_1 \cap S_2 = \emptyset$).

Definition 1 (Unique Ownership).

$$UniqueOwn(M_1 \mid \ldots \mid M_n \mid \langle H \rangle) \iff pr(M_1) \uplus \ldots \uplus pr(M_n) = \text{dom } H$$

Theorem 1 (Preservation of Unique Ownership). *If a program, P, types then any state, W, resulting from execution of P satisfies unique ownership:*

$$\vdash^{p} P \quad \wedge \quad init(P) \overset{*}{\rightarrow} W \quad \Rightarrow \quad UniqueOwn(W)$$

A proof of this theorem is presented in an accompanying technical report [6].

5 Case Study: An IPv4 Packet Forwarder

In this section we outline the PacLang implementation of the IP (version 4) uni-cast packet forwarding algorithm. The precise details of IP packet forwarding are not the focus of this section and, indeed, due to space constraints are not described here (the interested reader is referred to the IETF standards [13,14]). Instead, the purpose of the example is to outline the implementation of a realistic application, demonstrating that (*i*) packets are indeed treated as linear objects in real-life applications; and (*ii*) that the PacLang type-system is intuitive and easy to use.

Figure 6 shows the top-level structure of our PacLang IPv4 packet forwarder; we omit many of the function bodies, giving only their signatures. Function `eth_readAndClassify()` reads ethernet packets from the network interface and classifies them according to their type. Function `ip_lookup` performs a route lookup (on an externally defined routing table) returning both the next hop IP address and the network interface on which to forward the packet. (Note that since the external routing table component only contains `int`s, we do not have to worry about it breaking unique ownership.)

The program is divided into two separate threads (`main1` and `main2`). The `main1` thread sits in a tight loop, repeatedly calling the read/classify function. Packets which require ICMP processing are written to the `icmpQ` queue. The `main2` thread reads packets from `icmpQ` and performs the ICMP processing. The details of this thread are omitted. An example of a side-effecting function that manipulates packets is given by the `ip_dec_ttl` function which decrements the IP Time-To-Live field.

The PacLang code given here demonstrates that our linear type system naturally models the way packets flow through the system as a whole. Note

```
int eth_type(!packet p); // read type-field of ethernet frame
void eth_gen_arp_response(packet p); // generate response to ARP query
void eth_proc_arp_response(packet p); // process ARP response packet
void ip_local_packet(packet p); // send packet to local network stack
void ip_process_options(!packet p); // process IP options
void ip_transmit(packet p, int tx_interface, int ip_nexthop);
  // do MAC-level processing, get MAC address of next hop and transmit
int eth_rx_iface(!packet p); // which interface was packet from?

packetQueue icmpQ; // queue for packets which require ICMP processing

(int, int) ip_lookup(int dest_ip_addr);
     // lookup IP address and network interface for next-hop in route

void eth_readAndClassify() {
   packet p = receive.deq();
   switch (eth_type(p)) of {
      case ARP_QUERY: eth_gen_arp_response(p);
      case ARP_RES: eth_proc_arp_response(p);
      case IP: ip_forward(p);
      default: kill(p); }}

void ip_forward(packet p) {
   if (ip_packet_for_localhost(p)) ip_local_packet(p);
   else {
     (int nexthop, int iface) = ip_lookup(eth_ip_dest_addr(p));
     if (nexthop == 0) icmpQ.enq(p);
     else { if (iface==eth_rx_iface(p)) icmpQ.enq(p);
            else ip_forward_packet(p,iface,nexthop); }}}

void ip_forward_packet(Packet p, int iface, int nexthop) {
   if (ip_dec_ttl(p)) icmpQ.enq(p);
   else { ip_process_options(p);
          ip_transmit(p,tx_iface,ip_nexthop); }}}

bool ip_dec_ttl(!packet p) {
   if (p[ip_ttl]==0) return true;
   else { p[ip_ttl] = p[ip_ttl]-1; return false; }}

// thread 1 -- read, process, transmit loop:
void main1() { eth_readAndClassify(); main1(); }

// thread 2 -- process icmp packets:
void main2() { packet p = icmpQ.deq(); ... ICMP processing ...; main2(); }
```

Fig. 6. Top-level structure of an IPv4-over-ethernet packet forwarding engine

particularly that aliases (*!packet* types) allow us to express imperative operations on packets without requiring a packet's owning reference to be tediously threaded through all imperative operations (cf. the Clean language [8]).

Let us now consider compiling the PacLang IPv4 packet forwarder to the architecture shown in Figure 1.1. Due to PacLang's unique ownership property a compiler is free to choose between either (say) implementing both threads on a single IXP2400, implementing the queue using a shared memory; or placing `main1` on the first IXP2400, and `main2` on the second, passing packets by value between the two. In the latter case the queue itself could be located on either the first or second network processor and, further, as soon as a packet is transmitted from the first to the second IXP it can be immediately deallocated from the memory of the first. Although PacLang makes these tradeoffs very easy to reason about, recall that this is not the case in the framework of traditional imperative languages (e.g. C/C++)—see Section 1.1.

6 Related Work

There has been a great deal of work in the area of linear types. Of this, our research is most closely related to Kobayashi's quasi-linear type system [12]. Aliases in our work (*!packet*) correspond to δ-uses in the quasi-linear framework. Similarly, owning references (of type *packet*) correspond to 1-use types. There are three major differences between our work and Kobayashi's. Firstly, we do not deal with higher-order functions: these add much of the perceived complication of linear types; hence this makes our type system much simpler and, we argue, more accessible to industrial software engineers. Secondly, we work with a concurrent language. Thirdly, whereas Kobayashi is primarily concerned with eliminating garbage collection, we use linear types to assist in the mapping of high-level specifications to distributed memory architectures.

Clarke et al. have proposed *ownership types* [5,4] for object-oriented languages. Each ownership type is annotated with a *context declaration*. The type system ensures that types with different declared contexts cannot alias. Ownership types have been applied to the detection of data races and deadlocks [3].

The `auto_ptr` template in the C++ standard library [15] exploits the notion of "unique ownership" *dynamically*. Suppose `p1` and `p2` are of type `auto_ptr`, then the assignment `p2 = p1` copies `p1` to `p2` as usual but also nulls `p1` so it cannot be used again. Similarly, if an `auto_ptr` is passed to a function it is also nulled. In this framework violation of the unique ownership constraint is only detected at run-time by a null pointer check. However, the widespread use of `auto_ptrs` in practical C++ programming suggests that working software engineers find the notion of object ownership intuitive and useful.

Further discussion of related work, including a comparison with *region*-based memory management approaches, is included in an associated technical report [6].

7 Conclusions and Future Work

We have formally defined the PacLang language and claimed, with reference to a case-study, that it is capable of specifying realistic packet processing applications. Our linear type system enforces a unique ownership property whilst allowing software engineers to program in a familiar style. We have argued that unique ownership greatly simplifies the compilation of a high-level program to a diverse range of NP architectures.

There are a number of ways in which PacLang must be extended if it is to be used on an industrial-scale. For example, the type system needs to be able to differentiate between different types of *packet* (e.g. IP packets, UDP packets etc.); support for structured types (such as records and tuples) and a module system are also required. However, much of this work amounts to engineering rather than research effort. We believe that PacLang, as presented in this paper, captures the essence of packet-processing, providing a solid foundation for the development of an industrial-scale packet processing framework.

Our current work focuses on the implementation of a PacLang compiler which targets a variety of platforms, including Network Processors. This implementation effort will provide insights that can be fed back into the PacLang language design.

We hope that the ideas presented in this paper can be applied to the automatic partitioning of high-level code across multi-core architectures more generally (i.e. not just Network Processors). Since industrial trends suggest that such architectures will become more prevalent (as silicon densities continue to increase) we believe that this is an important topic for future research.

Acknowledgements. The authors wish to thank Tim Griffin and Lukas Kencl for their valuable comments and suggestions. We are grateful for the generous suppport of Microsoft Research, who funded the studentship of the first author.

References

1. Allen, J *et al.* PowerNP network processor: Hardware, software and applications. *IBM Journal of research and development 47*, 2–3 (3003), 177–194.
2. Berry, G., and Boudol, G. The chemical abstract machine. *Theoretical Computer Science 96* (1992), 217–248.
3. Boyapati, C., Lee, R., and Rinard, M. Ownership types for safe programming: Preventing data races and deadlocks. In *Proceedings of the 17th Conference on Object-Oriented Programming, Systems, Languages, and Applications (OOPSLA-02)* (November 2002), ACM Press.
4. Clarke, D., and Wrigstad, T. External uniqueness is unique enough. In *Proceedings of the 17th European Conference for Object-Oriented Programming (ECOOP)* (July 2003), vol. 2743 of *LNCS*, Springer-Verlag.
5. Clarke, D. G., Potter, J. M., and Noble, J. Ownership types for flexible alias protection. In *Proceedings of the 13th Conference on Object-Oriented Programming, Systems, Languages, and Applications (OOPSLA-98)* (New York, 1998), vol. 33:10 of *ACM SIGPLAN Notices*, ACM Press, pp. 48–64.
6. Ennals, R., Sharp, R., and Mycroft, A. Linear types for packet processing (extended version). Tech. Rep. UCAM-CL-TR-578, University of Cambridge Computer Laboratory, 2004.
7. Flanagan, C., Sabry, A., Duba, B. F., and Felleisen, M. The essence of compiling with continuations. In *Proceedings ACM SIGPLAN 1993 Conf. on Programming Language Design and Implementation, PLDI'93, Albuquerque, NM, USA, 23–25 June 1993*, vol. 28(6). ACM Press, New York, 1993, pp. 237–247.
8. Hilt High Level Software Tools B.V. Concurrent clean language report. Available from: `ftp://ftp.cs.kun.nl/pub/Clean/Clean20/doc/CleanRep2.0.pdf`.
9. Intel Corporation. Intel IXDP2400 & IXDP2800 advanced development platforms product brief. Available from: `http://www.intel.com/design/network/prodbrf/ixdp2x00.htm`.

10. Intel Corporation. Intel IXP2400 Network Processor: Flexible, high-performance solution for access and edge applications.
Available from: `http://www.intel.com/design/network/papers/ixp2400.htm`.
11. Johnson, E. J., and Kunze, A. *IXP-1200 Programming: The Microengine Coding Guide for the Intel IXP1200 Network Processor Family.* Intel Press, 2002.
12. Kobayashi, N. Quasi-linear types. In *Conference Record of POPL 99: The 26th ACM SIGPLAN-SIGACT Symposium on Principles of Programming Languages, San Antonio, Texas* (New York, NY, 1999), pp. 29–42.
13. Postel, J. Internet Protocol RFC 791. Internet Engineering Task Force, September 1981. Available from: `http://www.ietf.org/rfc.html`.
14. Postel, J. Internet Control Message Protocol, RFC 792. Internet Engineering Task Force, September 1981. Available from: `http://www.ietf.org/rfc.html`.
15. Stroustrup, B. *The C++ programming language (third edition).* Addison-Wesley.
16. Turner, D. N., Wadler, P., and Mossin, C. Once upon a type. In *Functional Programming Languages and Computer Architecture* (1995), ACM Press.
17. Yavatkar, R., and H. Vin (eds.). *IEEE Network Magasine. Special issue on Network Processors: Architecture, Tools, and Applications 17*, 4 (July 2003).

Modal Proofs as Distributed Programs*
(Extended Abstract)

Limin Jia and David Walker

Princeton University
35 Olden St., Princeton, NJ 08544, USA
{ljia,dpw}@cs.princeton.edu

Abstract. We develop a new foundation for distributed programming languages by defining an intuitionistic, modal logic and then interpreting the modal proofs as distributed programs. More specifically, the proof terms for the various modalities have computational interpretations as *remote procedure calls*, commands to *broadcast* computations to all nodes in the network, commands to use *portable* code, and finally, commands to invoke computational *agents* that can find their own way to safe places in the network where they can execute. We prove some simple meta-theoretic results about our logic as well as a safety theorem that demonstrates that the deductive rules act as a sound type system for a distributed programming language.

1 Introduction

One of the characteristics of distributed systems that makes developing robust software for them far more difficult than developing software for single standalone machines is *heterogeneity*. Different places in the system may have vastly different properties and resources. For instance, different machines may be attached to different hardware devices, have different software installed and run different services. Moreover, differing security concerns may cause different hosts to provide different interfaces to distributed programs, even when the underlying computational resources are similar.

In order to model such heterogeneous environments, programming language researchers usually turn to formalisms based on one sort of process algebra or another. Prime examples include the distributed join calculus [1] and the ambient calculus [2]. These calculi often have rich theories of process equivalence and are useful tools for reasoning about distributed systems. However, a significant disadvantage of starting with process algebras as a foundation for distributed computing is that they immediately discard the wealth of logical principles that underlie conventional sequential programming paradigms and that form the sequential core of any distributed computation.

In this paper, we develop a foundation for safe distributed programming, which rather than rejecting the logical foundations of sequential (functional)

* This research was supported in part by NSF Career Award CCR-0238328, NSF Trusted Computing Grant CCR-0208601 and DARPA award F30602-99-1-0519.

D.A. Schmidt (Ed.): ESOP 2004, LNCS 2986, pp. 219–233, 2004.

programming, extends them with new principles tuned to programming in heterogeneous distributed environments. More specifically, we develop an intuitionistic, modal logic and provide an operational interpretation of the logical proofs as distributed programs. Our logic has the property that at any given place all of the intuitionistic propositional tautologies are provable. Consequently, our correspondence between proofs and programs implies we can safely execute any (closed) functional program at any place in our distributed programming environment.

We extend these simple intuitionistic proofs with modal connectives and provide computational interpretations of the connectives as operations for remote code execution:

- Objects with type $\tau\,@\,p$ are return values with type τ. They are the results of *remote procedure calls* from the place p.
- Objects with type $\Box\,\tau$ are computations that can safely run everywhere, and may be *broadcast* to all places in the network.
- Objects with type $\boxplus\tau$ are logically equivalent to those objects with type $\Box\,\tau$, but are treated operationally simply as *portable* code that can run everywhere, but is not actually broadcast.
- Objects with type $\Diamond\tau$ are computational *agents* that have internalized the place p where they may execute safely to produce a value with type τ.

The central technical contributions of our work may be summarized as follows.

- We develop an intuitionistic, modal logic from first principles following the logical design techniques espoused by Martin Löf [3] and Frank Pfenning [4, 5]. Our logic is a relative of the hybrid logics, which are discussed in more detail at the end of the paper (see Section 4).
- Each connective in the logic is defined orthogonally to all others, is shown to be locally sound and complete, and supports the relevant substitution principles.
- This paper concentrates on the natural deduction formulation of the logic due to its correspondence with functional programs. However, we have also developed a sequent calculus that has cut elimination and shown that the sequent calculus is sound and complete with respect to the natural deduction system.
- We give an operational interpretation of the proofs in our logic as distributed functional programs. We prove that the logical deduction rules are sound when viewed as a type system for the programming language.

Due to space considerations, we have omitted many details from this extended abstract. Proofs of our theorems, language extensions (including references and recursive functions), and further programming examples may be found in our extended technical report [6].

2 A Logic of Places

2.1 Preliminaries

The central purpose of our logic is to facilitate reasoning about heterogeneous distributed systems where different nodes may have different properties and may contain different resources. Hence, the primary judgment in the logic not only considers *whether* a formula is true, but also *where* it is true. More precisely, each primitive judgment has the form

$$\vdash^P F \textsf{ at } p$$

where F is a formula from the logic and p is a particular place in the system. These places are drawn from the set P. When P is unimportant or easy to guess from the context (i.e., most of the time) we omit them from the judgment and simply write $\vdash F \textsf{ at } p$. For any syntactic object X, $\textsf{FP}(X)$ denotes the set of free places that appear in X. We consider judgments $\vdash^P F \textsf{ at } p$ to have no meaning if $\textsf{FP}(F) \cup \{p\} \not\subseteq P$.

To gain some intuition about this preliminary set up, consider a network of five computers (A, B, C, D, E). Each of these computers may have different physical devices attached to it. For instance, E may have a printer attached to it and B may have a scanner. If $\textsf{sc}$ ("there is a scanner here") and $\textsf{pt}$ ("there is a printer here") are propositions in the logic, we might assert judgments such as $\vdash \textsf{pt at } E$ and $\vdash \textsf{sc at } B$ to describe this situation.

Hypothetical Judgments. In order to engage in more interesting reasoning about distributed resources, we must define hypothetical judgments and facilities for reasoning from hypotheses. To begin with, hypothetical judgments have the form $\Delta \vdash^P F \textsf{ at } p$ where Δ is a list of (variable-labeled) assumptions:

$$\textit{contexts } \Delta ::= \cdot \mid \Delta, x : F \textsf{ at } p$$

We do not distinguish between contexts that differ only in the order of assumptions. We use hypotheses according to the following inference rule (where L stands for use of a Local hypothesis).

$$\frac{}{\Delta, x : F \textsf{ at } p \vdash F \textsf{ at } p}\ L$$

Intuitionistic Connectives. With the definition of hypothetical judgments in hand, we may proceed to give the meaning of the usual intuitionistic connectives for truth ($\top$), implication ($F_1 \to F_2$) and conjunction ($F_1 \wedge F_2$) in terms of their introduction and elimination rules.

$$\frac{}{\Delta \vdash \top \textsf{ at } p}\ \top I$$

$$\frac{\Delta, x : F_1 \textsf{ at } p \vdash F_2 \textsf{ at } p}{\Delta \vdash F_1 \to F_2 \textsf{ at } p} \to I \qquad \frac{\Delta \vdash F_1 \to F_2 \textsf{ at } p \quad \Delta \vdash F_1 \textsf{ at } p}{\Delta \vdash F_2 \textsf{ at } p} \to E$$

$$\frac{\Delta \vdash F_1 \textsf{ at } p \quad \Delta \vdash F_2 \textsf{ at } p}{\Delta \vdash F_1 \wedge F_2 \textsf{ at } p}\ \wedge I$$

$$\frac{\Delta \vdash F_1 \wedge F_2 \textsf{ at } p}{\Delta \vdash F_1 \textsf{ at } p}\ \wedge E1 \qquad \frac{\Delta \vdash F_1 \wedge F_2 \textsf{ at } p}{\Delta \vdash F_2 \textsf{ at } p}\ \wedge E2$$

None of the rules above are at all surprising: each rule helps explain how one of the usual intuitionistic connectives operates at a particular place. Hence, if we limit the set of places to a single place "_" the logic will reduce to ordinary intuitionistic logic. So far, there is no interesting way to use assumptions at multiple different places, but we will see how to do that in a moment.

As a simple example, consider reasoning about the action of the printer at place E in the network we introduced earlier. Let pdf be a proposition indicating the presence of a PDF file waiting to be printed and po be a proposition indicating the presence of a printout. The following derivation demonstrates how we might deduce the presence of a printout at E. The context Δ referenced below is

$$\mathsf{f}_E : \mathsf{pdf\ at}\ E,\ \mathsf{ptr}_E : \mathsf{pt\ at}\ E,\ \mathsf{print} : \mathsf{pdf} \wedge \mathsf{pt} \to \mathsf{po\ at}\ E$$

This context represents the presence of a PDF file and printer at E as well as some software (a function) installed at E that can initiate the printing process.

$$\dfrac{\dfrac{}{\Delta \vdash \mathsf{pdf} \wedge \mathsf{pt} \to \mathsf{po\ at}\ E}\,L \qquad \dfrac{\dfrac{}{\Delta \vdash \mathsf{pdf\ at}\ E}\,L \quad \dfrac{}{\Delta \vdash \mathsf{pt\ at}\ E}\,L}{\Delta \vdash \mathsf{pdf} \wedge \mathsf{pt\ at}\ E}\,\wedge I}{\Delta \vdash \mathsf{po\ at}\ E}\,\to E$$

2.2 Inter-place Reasoning

To reason about relationships between objects located at different places we introduce a modal connective, which describes objects in terms of their location in the system.

We derive our modal connective by internalizing the judgmental notion that a formula is true at a particular place, but not necessarily elsewhere. We write this new modal formula as $F\,@\,p$. The introduction and elimination rules follow.

$$\dfrac{\Delta \vdash F\ \mathsf{at}\ p}{\Delta \vdash F\,@\,p\ \mathsf{at}\ p'}\,@\,I \qquad \dfrac{\Delta \vdash F\,@\,p\ \mathsf{at}\ p'}{\Delta \vdash F\ \mathsf{at}\ p}\,@\,E$$

This connective allows us to reason about objects, software or devices "from a distance." For instance, in our printer example, it is possible to refer to the printer located at E while reasoning at D; to do so we might assert $\Delta \vdash \mathsf{pt}\,@\,E$ at D. Moreover, we can relate objects at one place to objects at another. For instance, in order to share E's printer, D needs to have software that can convert local PDF files at D to files that may be used and print properly at E (perhaps this software internalizes some local fonts, inaccessible to E). An assumption of the form $\mathsf{DtoE} : \mathsf{pdf} \to \mathsf{pdf}\,@\,E\ \mathsf{at}\ D$ would allow us to reason about such software.[1] If Δ' is the assumption DtoE above together with an assumption $\mathsf{f}_\mathsf{D} : \mathsf{pdf\ at}\ D$, the following derivation allows us to conclude that we can get the PDF file to E. We can easily compose this proof with the earlier one to demonstrate that PDF files at D can not only be sent to E, but actually printed there.

[1] We assume that "@" binds tighter than implication or conjunction. When fully parenthesized, the assumption above has the following form: $(\mathsf{pdf} \to (\mathsf{pdf}\,@\,E))\ \mathsf{at}\ D$.

$$\dfrac{\dfrac{}{\Delta' \vdash \mathsf{pdf} \to \mathsf{pdf}\,@\,E \text{ at } D}\,L \quad \dfrac{}{\Delta' \vdash \mathsf{pdf} \text{ at } D}\,L}{\dfrac{\Delta' \vdash \mathsf{pdf}\,@\,E \text{ at } D}{\Delta' \vdash \mathsf{pdf} \text{ at } E}\,@E}\,\to E$$

2.3 Global Reasoning

While our focus is on reasoning about networks with heterogeneous resources, we cannot avoid the fact that certain propositions are true *everywhere*. For instance, the basic laws of arithmetic do not change from one machine to the next, and consequently, we should not restrict the application of these laws to any particular place. Just as importantly, we might want to reason about distributed applications deployed over a network of machines, all of which support a common operating system interface. The functionality provided by the operating system is available everywhere, just like the basic laws of arithmetic, and use of the functionality need not be constrained to one particular place or another.

Global Judgments. To support global reasoning, we generalize the judgment considered so far to include a second context that contains assumptions that are valid everywhere. Our extended judgments have the form $\Gamma; \Delta \vdash^P F \text{ at } p$ where Γ is a global context and Δ is the local context we considered previously.

$$\begin{array}{ll} \textit{Global Contexts}\ \Gamma ::= \cdot \mid \Gamma, x : F \\ \textit{Local Contexts}\ \ \Delta ::= \cdot \mid \Delta, x : F \text{ at } p \end{array}$$

Our extended logic contains two sorts of hypothesis rules, one for using each sort of assumption. Rule L is identical to the hypothesis rule used in previous sections (modulo the unused global context Γ). Rule G specifies how to use global hypotheses; they may be placed in any location and used there.

$$\dfrac{}{\Gamma; \Delta, x : F \text{ at } p \vdash F \text{ at } p}\,L \qquad \dfrac{}{\Gamma, x : F; \Delta \vdash F \text{ at } p}\,G$$

All rules from the previous sections are included in the new system unchanged aside from the fact that Γ is passed unused from conclusion to premises.

Internalizing Global Truth. The modal connective $\Box F$ internalizes the notion that the formula F is true everywhere. If a formula may be proven true at a new place p, which by definition can contain no local assumptions, then that formula must be true everywhere:[2]

$$\dfrac{\Gamma; \Delta \vdash^{P+p} F \text{ at } p}{\Gamma; \Delta \vdash^P \Box F \text{ at } p'}\,\Box I$$

[2] By convention, judgments are meaningless when they contain places not contained in the sets P that annotate the judgment. Consequently, this rule requires that $p \notin \mathsf{FP}(\Gamma) \cup \mathsf{FP}(\Delta) \cup \mathsf{FP}(F)$.

Here, we use $P+p$ to denote the disjoint union $P \cup \{p\}$. If $p \in P$, we consider $P+p$, and any judgment containing such notation, to be undefined. If we can prove $\Box F$, we can assume that F is globally true in the proof of any other judgment F' at p':

$$\frac{\Gamma; \Delta \vdash^{P} \Box F \ \mathsf{at}\ p \quad \Gamma, x : F; \Delta \vdash^{P} F' \ \mathsf{at}\ p'}{\Gamma; \Delta \vdash^{P} F' \ \mathsf{at}\ p'} \ \Box E$$

Returning to our printing example, suppose node E decides to allow *all* machines to send PDF files to it. In order to avoid hiccups in the printing process, E intends to distribute software to all machines that allows them to convert local PDF files to files that will print properly on E's printer. We might represent this situation with a hypothesis $\mathsf{ToE} : \Box(\mathsf{pdf} \rightarrow \mathsf{pdf} @ E)$ at E. Now, given a PDF file at any other node q in the network (coded as the assumption $\mathsf{f}_q : \mathsf{pdf}$ at q), we can demonstrate that it is possible to send the PDF file to E using the following proof, where Δ'' contains assumptions ToE and f_q. The global context Γ contains the single assumption $\mathsf{ToE}' : \mathsf{pdf} \rightarrow \mathsf{pdf} @ E$.

$$\frac{\mathcal{D} \qquad \dfrac{\dfrac{\dfrac{}{\Gamma; \Delta'' \vdash \mathsf{pdf} \rightarrow \mathsf{pdf} @ E \ \mathsf{at}\ q}\ G \quad \dfrac{}{\Gamma; \Delta'' \vdash \mathsf{pdf}\ \mathsf{at}\ q}\ L}{\Gamma; \Delta'' \vdash \mathsf{pdf} @ E \ \mathsf{at}\ q}\ \rightarrow E}{\Gamma; \Delta'' \vdash \mathsf{pdf}\ \mathsf{at}\ E}\ @E}{\cdot; \Delta'' \vdash \mathsf{pdf}\ \mathsf{at}\ E} \ \Box E$$

where the derivation $\mathcal{D} = \dfrac{}{\cdot; \Delta'' \vdash \Box(\mathsf{pdf} \rightarrow \mathsf{pdf} @ E) \ \mathsf{at}\ E}\ L$

The Truth Is Out There. The dual notion of a globally true proposition F is a proposition that is true *somewhere*, although we may not necessarily know where. We already have all the judgmental apparatus to handle this new idea; we need only internalize it in a connective ($\Diamond F$). The introduction rule states that if the formula holds at any particular place p in the network, then it holds somewhere. The elimination rule explains how we use a formula F that holds somewhere: we introduce a new place p and assume F holds there.

$$\frac{\Gamma; \Delta \vdash^{P} F \ \mathsf{at}\ p}{\Gamma; \Delta \vdash^{P} \Diamond F \ \mathsf{at}\ p'} \ \Diamond I \qquad \frac{\Gamma; \Delta \vdash^{P} \Diamond F \ \mathsf{at}\ p' \quad \Gamma; \Delta, x : F \ \mathsf{at}\ p \vdash^{P+p} F' \ \mathsf{at}\ p''}{\Gamma; \Delta \vdash^{P} F' \ \mathsf{at}\ p''} \ \Diamond E$$

Modal Axioms. We can begin to understand the relationship between our modal logic and other intuitionistic modal logics presented in the literature by considering the axioms provable in our logic. The following axioms, taken from Simpson's thesis [7], can all be proven in our logic, indicating that it is a relative of intuitionistic S5.[3]

[3] The modal logics in Simpson's thesis [7] include disjunction, negation and falsehood, which we do not treat in this paper. In the presence of these additional connectives, S5 and other modal logics should satisfy two further axioms (IK3, IK4).

IK1	$\Box(F_1 \to F_2) \to (\Box F_1 \to \Box F_2)$ at p
IK2	$\Box(F_1 \to F_2) \to (\Diamond F_1 \to \Diamond F_2)$ at p
IK5	$(\Diamond F_1 \to \Box F_2) \to \Box(F_1 \to F_2)$ at p
T	$(\Box F \to F) \land (F \to \Diamond F)$ at p
5	$(\Diamond\Box F \to \Box F) \land (\Diamond F \to \Box\Diamond F)$ at p

2.4 Properties

We have proved local soundness and completeness properties (i.e., subject reduction for beta-reduction and eta-expansion of proofs) for each of the connectives in our logic, as well as standard substitution properties. In addition, we have developed a sequent calculus and proved the following two theorems:

Theorem 1. *The natural deduction system is sound and complete with regard to the sequent calculus (SEQ).*

Theorem 2. *The cut rule is admissible in SEQ.*

3 λ_{rpc}: A Distributed Programming Language

The previous section developed an intuitionistic, modal logic capable of concisely expressing facts about the placement of various objects in a network. Here, we present the proof terms of the logic and show how they may be given an operational interpretation as a distributed programming language, which we call λ_{rpc}. The logical formulas serve as types that prevent distributed programs from "going wrong" by attempting to access resources that are unavailable at the place where the program is currently operating.

3.1 Syntax and Typing

Figure 1 presents the syntax of programs and their types, and Figure 2 presents the typing rules for the language, which are the natural deduction-style proof rules for the logic.

Types and Typing Judgments. The types correspond to the formulas of the logic; we use the meta variable τ rather than F to indicate a shift in interpretation. We also included a set of base types (**b**).

Since we have discovered two different operational interpretations of $\Box F$, and we would like to explain both of them in this paper, we have extended the language of formulas (types) to include an extra modality $\boxtimes\tau$ to handle the second interpretation. To support the two universal modalities, we also separate the logical context Γ into two parts, $\Gamma_\Box$ and $\Gamma_\boxtimes$, during type checking. Hence the overall type checking judgment has the following form: $\Gamma_\Box ; \Gamma_\boxtimes ; \Delta \vdash^P e : \tau$ at p. By deleting either $\Box\tau$ or $\boxtimes\tau$ (and the associated context), we recover *exactly the same logic* as discussed in the previous section.[4]

[4] We could have defined two languages, one language for each interpretation of $\Box F$, where the typing rules of each language correspond exactly to the logical inference

Types τ ::=
$\mathbf{b} \mid \top \mid \tau_1 \to \tau_2 \mid \tau_1 \wedge \tau_2 \mid \tau @ p \mid \Box\tau \mid ⌑\tau \mid \Diamond\tau$

Proof Terms/Programs e ::=

$c \mid x \mid \mathbf{sync}\,(x) \mid \mathbf{run}\,(\,x\,[p]\,) \mid ()$	*const/var/*$\top$
$\mid \lambda x{:}\tau.e \mid e_1\ e_2$	*functions*$(\to)$
$\mid \langle\, e_1\,,\, e_2 \,\rangle \mid \pi_i e$	*pairs* $(\wedge)$
$\mid \mathbf{ret}(e,p) \mid \mathbf{rpc}(e,p)$	*rpc* $(\,@\,)$
$\mid \mathbf{close}(\lambda p.\,e) \mid \mathbf{bc}\, e_1 \ \mathsf{at}\ p\ \mathbf{as}\ x\ \mathbf{in}\ e_2$	*broadcast* $(\Box)$
$\mid \mathbf{port}(\lambda p.\,e) \mid \mathbf{pull}\, e_1\ \mathsf{at}\ p\ \mathbf{as}\ x\ \mathbf{in}\ e_2$	*portable* (⌑)
$\mid \mathbf{agent}[e,p] \mid \mathbf{go}\, e_1\ \mathsf{at}\ p\ \mathbf{return}\ x, q\ \mathbf{in}\ e_2$	*agent* $(\Diamond)$

Fig. 1. The syntax of λ_{rpc}

Programs. The programs include an unspecified set of constants (c), and the standard introduction and elimination forms for unit, functions and pairs.

Variables from each different context are used in different ways. We have added some syntactic sugar to the standard proof terms as a mnemonic for the different sorts of uses. Uses of local variables from Δ are just like ordinary uses of variables in your favorite (call-by-value) functional language so they are left undecorated. Variables in $\Gamma_\Box$ refer to computations that have been broadcast at some earlier point. In order to use such a variable, the program must *synchronize* with the concurrently executing computation. Hence, we write $\mathbf{sync}\,(x)$ for such uses. Variables in $\Gamma_{⌑}$ refer to portable closures. The use of a variable in this context corresponds to *running* the closure with the current place p as an argument. Hence, we write $\mathbf{run}\,(\,x\,[p]\,)$ for such uses.

Our first modality $\tau @ p$ has an operational interpretation as a remote procedure call. The introduction form $\mathbf{ret}(e,p)$ constructs a "return value" for a remote procedure call. This "return value" can actually be an arbitrary expression e, which will be returned to and run at the place p. The elimination form $\mathbf{rpc}(e,p')$ is the remote procedure call itself. It sends the expression e to the remote site p' where e will be evaluated. If the expression is well typed, it will eventually evaluate to $\mathbf{ret}(e',p)$: a return value that can be run safely at the caller's place, which, in this case is place p.

The introduction form for $\Box\, F$ is $\mathbf{close}(\lambda p.\,e)$. It creates a closure that may be *broadcast* by the elimination form $\mathbf{bc}\, e_1\ \mathsf{at}\ p_1\ \mathbf{as}\ x\ \mathbf{in}\ e_2$ to every node in the network. More specifically, the elimination form executes e_1 at p_1, expecting e_1 to evaluate to $\mathbf{close}(\lambda p.\,e)$. When it does, the broadcast expression chooses a new universal reference for the closure, which is bound to x, and sends $\lambda p.e$ to every place in the network where it is applied to the current place and the resulting expression is associated with its universal reference. Finally, expression e_2 is executed with the universal reference bound to x. Remote procedure calls or

rules. However, we obtain a more powerful result by showing that these two interpretations inter-operate.

$$\frac{}{\Gamma_\square;\Gamma_\boxtimes;\Delta, x:\tau \text{ at } p \vdash^P x:\tau \text{ at } p}\ L$$

$$\frac{}{\Gamma_\square, x:\tau;\Gamma_\boxtimes;\Delta \vdash^P \mathbf{sync}\,(x):\tau \text{ at } p}\ G\square$$

$$\frac{}{\Gamma_\square;\Gamma_\boxtimes, x:\tau;\Delta \vdash^P \mathbf{run}\,(\,x\,[p]\,):\tau \text{ at } p}\ G\boxtimes$$

$$\frac{}{\Gamma_\square;\Gamma_\boxtimes;\Delta \vdash^P ():\top \text{ at } p}\ \mathit{Unit} \qquad \frac{}{\Gamma_\square;\Gamma_\boxtimes;\Delta \vdash^P c:\mathbf{b} \text{ at } p}\ \mathit{Const}$$

$$\frac{\Gamma_\square;\Gamma_\boxtimes;\Delta, x:\tau_1 \text{ at } p \vdash^P e:\tau_2 \text{ at } p}{\Gamma_\square;\Gamma_\boxtimes;\Delta \vdash^P \lambda x{:}\tau_1.e:\tau_1 \to \tau_2 \text{ at } p}\ \to I$$

$$\frac{\Gamma_\square;\Gamma_\boxtimes;\Delta \vdash^P e_1:\tau_1 \to \tau_2 \text{ at } p \quad \Gamma_\square;\Gamma_\boxtimes;\Delta \vdash^P e_2:\tau_1 \text{ at } p}{\Gamma_\square;\Gamma_\boxtimes;\Delta \vdash^P e_1\,e_2:\tau_2 \text{ at } p}\ \to E$$

$$\frac{\Gamma_\square;\Gamma_\boxtimes;\Delta \vdash^P e_1:\tau_1 \text{ at } p \quad \Gamma_\square;\Gamma_\boxtimes;\Delta \vdash^P e_2:\tau_2 \text{ at } p}{\Gamma_\square;\Gamma_\boxtimes;\Delta \vdash^P \langle\, e_1\,,\, e_2\,\rangle:\tau_1 \times \tau_2 \text{ at } p}\ \wedge I$$

$$\frac{\Gamma_\square;\Gamma_\boxtimes;\Delta \vdash^P e:\tau_1 \times \tau_2 \text{ at } p}{\Gamma_\square;\Gamma_\boxtimes;\Delta \vdash^P \pi_i e:\tau_i \text{ at } p}\ \wedge E$$

$$\frac{\Gamma_\square;\Gamma_\boxtimes;\Delta \vdash^P e:\tau \text{ at } p}{\Gamma_\square;\Gamma_\boxtimes;\Delta \vdash^P \mathbf{ret}(e,p):\tau\,@\,p \text{ at } p'}\ @\,I \qquad \frac{\Gamma_\square;\Gamma_\boxtimes;\Delta \vdash^P e:\tau\,@\,p \text{ at } p'}{\Gamma_\square;\Gamma_\boxtimes;\Delta \vdash^P \mathbf{rpc}(e,p'):\tau \text{ at } p}\ @\,E$$

$$\frac{\Gamma_\square;\Gamma_\boxtimes;\Delta \vdash^{P+p} e:\tau \text{ at } p}{\Gamma_\square;\Gamma_\boxtimes;\Delta \vdash^P \mathbf{close}(\lambda p.\, e):\square\,\tau \text{ at } p'}\ \square I$$

$$\frac{\Gamma_\square;\Gamma_\boxtimes;\Delta \vdash^P e_1:\square\,\tau \text{ at } p \quad \Gamma_\square, x:\tau;\Gamma_\boxtimes;\Delta \vdash^P e_2:\tau' \text{ at } p'}{\Gamma_\square;\Gamma_\boxtimes;\Delta \vdash^P \mathbf{bc}\,e_1 \text{ at } p \text{ } \mathbf{as}\, x \,\mathbf{in}\, e_2:\tau' \text{ at } p'}\ \square E$$

$$\frac{\Gamma_\square;\Gamma_\boxtimes;\Delta \vdash^{P+p} e:\tau \text{ at } p}{\Gamma_\square;\Gamma_\boxtimes;\Delta \vdash^P \mathbf{port}(\lambda p.\, e):\boxtimes\tau \text{ at } p'}\ \boxtimes I$$

$$\frac{\Gamma_\square;\Gamma_\boxtimes;\Delta \vdash^P e_1:\boxtimes\tau \text{ at } p \quad \Gamma_\square;\Gamma_\boxtimes, x:\tau;\Delta \vdash^P e_2:\tau' \text{ at } p'}{\Gamma_\square;\Gamma_\boxtimes;\Delta \vdash^P \mathbf{pull}\,e_1 \text{ at } p \text{ } \mathbf{as}\, x \,\mathbf{in}\, e_2:\tau' \text{ at } p'}\ \boxtimes E$$

$$\frac{\Gamma_\square;\Gamma_\boxtimes;\Delta \vdash^P e:\tau \text{ at } p}{\Gamma_\square;\Gamma_\boxtimes;\Delta \vdash^P \mathbf{agent}[e,p]:\Diamond\tau \text{ at } p'}\ \Diamond I$$

$$\frac{\Gamma_\square;\Gamma_\boxtimes;\Delta \vdash^P e_1:\Diamond\tau \text{ at } p' \quad \Gamma_\square;\Gamma_\boxtimes;\Delta, x:\tau \text{ at } p \vdash^{P+p} e_2:\tau' \text{ at } p''}{\Gamma_\square;\Gamma_\boxtimes;\Delta \vdash^P \mathbf{go}\,e_1 \text{ at } p' \text{ } \mathbf{return}\, x, p \,\mathbf{in}\, e_2:\tau' \text{ at } p''}\ \Diamond E$$

Fig. 2. The typing rules for λ_{rpc}

broadcasts generated during evaluation of e_2 may refer to the universal reference bound to x, which is safe, since x has been broadcast everywhere.

Objects of type $\boxtimes\tau$ are portable closures; they may be run anywhere. The elimination form $\mathbf{pull}\, e_1$ at p_1 $\mathbf{as}\, x\, \mathbf{in}\, e_2$ takes advantage of this portability by first computing e_1 at p_1, which should result in a value with the form $\mathbf{port}(\lambda p.\, e)$. Next, it pulls the closure $\lambda p.e$ from p_1 and substitutes it for x in e_2. The typing rules will allow x to appear anywhere, including in closures in e_2 that will eventually be broadcast or remotely executed. Once again, this is safe since e is portable and runs equally well everywhere.

Our last connective $\Diamond\tau$ is considered the type of a computational agent that is smart enough to know where it can go to produce a value with type τ. We introduce such an agent by packaging an expression with a place where the expression may successfully be run to completion. The elimination form $\mathbf{go}\, e_1$ at p_1 $\mathbf{return}\, x, p\, \mathbf{in}\, e_2$ first evaluates e_1 at p_1, producing an agent $\mathbf{agent}[e, p_2]$. Next, it commands the agent to go to the hidden place p_2 and execute its encapsulated computation there. When the agent has completed its task, it synchronizes with the current computation and e_2 continues with p bound to p_2 and x bound to the value that is safe to use at p_2.

Simple Examples. To gain a little more intuition about how to write programs in this language, consider computational interpretations of some of the proofs from the previous section. The context Δ referenced below contains the following assumptions.

$$\begin{array}{ll} \mathsf{f}_D : \mathsf{pdf}\ \mathsf{at}\ D & \mathsf{print} : \mathsf{pdf} \wedge \mathsf{pt} \to \mathsf{po}\ \mathsf{at}\ E \\ \mathsf{f}_E : \mathsf{pdf}\ \mathsf{at}\ E & \mathsf{DtoE} : \mathsf{pdf} \to \mathsf{pdf} \mathbin{@} E\ \mathsf{at}\ D \\ \mathsf{ptr}_E : \mathsf{pt}\ \mathsf{at}\ E & \mathsf{ToE} : \Box\,(\mathsf{pdf} \to \mathsf{pdf} \mathbin{@} E)\ \mathsf{at}\ E \end{array}$$

Printing a PDF file (involving local computation only):

$$\cdot; \Delta \vdash \mathsf{print}(\mathsf{f}_E, \mathsf{ptr}_E) : \mathsf{po}\ \mathsf{at}\ E$$

Fetching a PDF file (involving a remote procedure call in which the computation DtoE f_D is executed at D):

$$\cdot; \Delta \vdash \mathbf{rpc}(\mathsf{DtoE}\ \mathsf{f}_D, D) : \mathsf{pdf}\ \mathsf{at}\ E$$

Fetching then printing:

$$\cdot; \Delta \vdash (\lambda x{:}\mathsf{pdf}.\mathsf{print}\ (x, \mathsf{ptr}_E))(\mathbf{rpc}(\mathsf{DtoE}\ \mathsf{f}_D, D)) : \mathsf{po}\ \mathsf{at}\ E$$

Broadcasting E's PDF conversion function to all nodes then fetching a PDF file from node q (recall that in general, uses of these global variables involve synchronizing with the broadcast expression; below the broadcast expression is a value, but we synchronize anyway):

$$\cdot; \Delta, \mathsf{f}_q : \mathsf{pdf}\ \mathsf{at}\ q \vdash \mathbf{bc}\, \mathsf{ToE}\ \mathsf{at}\ E\ \mathbf{as}\, \mathsf{ToE}'\, \mathbf{in}\, \mathbf{rpc}(\mathbf{sync}\,(\mathsf{ToE}')\ \mathsf{f}_q, q) : \mathsf{pdf}\ \mathsf{at}\ E$$

Another way to manage PDF files is to make them portable. For instance, if C and D contain portable PDF files, then E can pull these files from their resident locations and print them on its local printer. Remember that portable values are polymorphic closures that are "run" when used. In this case, the closure simply returns the appropriate PDF file.

$$
\begin{array}{l}
\cdot; \Delta, \mathsf{f}_C : \maltese\mathsf{pdf}\ \mathsf{at}\ C, \mathsf{f}_D : \maltese\mathsf{pdf}\ \mathsf{at}\ D \vdash \\
\quad \mathbf{pull}\, \mathsf{f}_C\ \mathsf{at}\ C\ \mathbf{as}\, \mathsf{f}'_C\ \mathbf{in} \\
\quad \mathbf{pull}\, \mathsf{f}_D\ \mathsf{at}\ D\ \mathbf{as}\, \mathsf{f}'_D\ \mathbf{in} \\
\quad \mathbf{let}\ \_\ = \mathsf{print}(\mathbf{run}\,(\mathsf{f}'_C\,[E]), \mathsf{ptr}_E)\ \mathbf{in} \\
\quad \mathbf{let}\ \_\ = \mathsf{print}(\mathbf{run}\,(\mathsf{f}'_D\,[E]), \mathsf{ptr}_E)\ \mathbf{in} \\
\quad \ldots \qquad\qquad\qquad\qquad\qquad\qquad : \tau\ \mathsf{at}\ E
\end{array}
$$

3.2 Operational Semantics and Safety

When one defines an operational semantics for a language, it is essential to choose the correct level of abstraction. When the level of abstraction is too low, details get in the way of understanding the larger issues; when the level of abstraction is too high, there may be confusion as to how the semantics relates to reality. In our case, we could give an operational semantics based directly on proof reduction, but this semantics would be at too high a level of abstraction to observe important details concerning the distribution of values over a network. In particular, we would not be able to distinguish between the two very different interpretations of $\Box$. Consequently, we give an operational semantics at a lower level of abstraction than proof reduction by including an explicit, concrete network in the semantics as shown in Figure 3.[5] Nevertheless, the basis for the semantics is the interaction of introduction and elimination rules as the proof theory suggests. The various new syntactic objects we use to specify our operational model are listed below.

$$
\begin{array}{lll}
\textit{Networks} & \mathcal{N} & ::= (P, \mathcal{L}) \\
\textit{Process Envs.} & \mathcal{L} & ::= \cdot \mid \mathcal{L}, \ell \to e\ \mathsf{at}\ p \\
\textit{Values} & v & ::= c \mid \lambda x{:}\tau.e \mid \langle v_1\,,\, v_2 \rangle \mid \mathbf{ret}(e,p) \\
 & & \quad \mid \mathbf{close}(\lambda p.\, e) \mid \mathbf{port}(\lambda p.\, e) \mid \mathbf{agent}[e,p] \\
\textit{RT Terms} & e & ::= \cdots \mid \mathbf{sync}\,(\ell) \mid \mathbf{run}\,(\,\lambda p.e\,[p_1\,]) \mid \mathbf{sync}\,(\mathbf{rpc}(\ell,p)) \\
 & & \quad \mid \mathbf{sync}\,(\mathbf{bc}\,\ell\ \mathsf{at}\ p\ \mathbf{as}\, x\, \mathbf{in}\, e_2) \mid \mathbf{sync}\,(\mathbf{pull}\,\ell\ \mathsf{at}\ p\ \mathbf{as}\, x\ \mathbf{in}\, e_2) \\
 & & \quad \mid \mathbf{sync}_{\,1}(\mathbf{go}\,\ell\ \mathsf{at}\ p\ \mathbf{return}\, x, q\ \mathbf{in}\, e) \\
 & & \quad \mid \mathbf{sync}_{\,2}(\mathbf{go}\,\ell\ \mathsf{at}\ p\ \mathbf{return}\, x, q\ \mathbf{in}\, e) \\
\textit{Contexts} & C & ::= [\,] \mid C\, e_2 \mid v_1\, C \mid \langle C\,,\, e_2 \rangle \mid \langle v_1\,,\, C \rangle \mid \pi_i\, C
\end{array}
$$

[5] Our choice here is also informed by the history of operational interpretations of linear logic. Several researchers [8,9] gave interpretations of linear logic using a store-less semantics derived directly from logical proof reduction. These semantics led to *significant* confusion about the memory management properties of the languages: How many pointers to a linear object could there be, and can linear objects be deallocated after they are used? It was impossible to say because the operational models did not contain pointers! Only when Chirimar et al. [10] and Turner and Wadler [11] later gave interpretations that deviated from the proof-theoretic interpretation by including an explicit store was the story made clear. Our interpretation of modal logic deviates from the proof theory in a similar way to these latter works as we include an explicit network.

	$\mathcal{L} \longmapsto \mathcal{L}'$
sync *OS*	$\mathcal{L},\, \ell' \to C\,[\,\mathbf{sync}\,(\ell)\,]$ at $p,\ \ell \to v$ at p $\longmapsto \mathcal{L},\, \ell' \to C\,[\,v\,]$ at $p,\ \ell \to v$ at p
run *OS*	$\mathcal{L},\, \ell \to C\,[\,\mathbf{run}\,(\,\lambda p.e\,[\,p_1\,]\,)\,]$ at p_2 $\longmapsto \mathcal{L},\, \ell \to C\,[\,e\,[\,p_1\,/\,p\,]\,]$ at p_2
$\to$ *OS*	$\mathcal{L},\, \ell \to C\,[\,(\lambda x{:}\tau.e)\,v\,]$ at p $\longmapsto \mathcal{L},\, \ell \to C\,[\,e\,[\,v\,/\,x\,]\,]$ at p
$\wedge$ *OS*	$\mathcal{L},\, \ell \to C\,[\,\pi_i\langle\, v_1\,,\, v_2\,\rangle\,]$ at p $\longmapsto \mathcal{L},\, \ell \to C\,[\,v_i\,]$ at p
@ *OS1*	$\mathcal{L},\, \ell \to C\,[\,\mathbf{rpc}(e, p_1)\,]$ at p_0 $\longmapsto \mathcal{L},\, \ell \to C\,[\,\mathbf{sync}\,(\mathbf{rpc}(\ell_1, p_1))\,]$ at $p_0,\ \ell_1 \to e$ at p_1
@ *OS2*	$\mathcal{L},\, \ell \to C\,[\,\mathbf{sync}\,(\mathbf{rpc}(\ell_1, p_1))\,]$ at $p_0,\ \ell_1 \to \mathbf{ret}(e, p_0)$ at p_1 $\longmapsto \mathcal{L},\, \ell \to C\,[\,e\,]$ at $p_0,\ \ell_1 \to \mathbf{ret}(e, p_0)$ at p_1
$\Box$ *OS1*	$\mathcal{L},\, \ell \to C\,[\,\mathbf{bc}\, e_1$ at p_1 $\mathbf{as}\, x\, \mathbf{in}\, e_2\,]$ at p_0 $\longmapsto \mathcal{L},\, \ell \to C\,[\,\mathbf{sync}\,(\mathbf{bc}\, \ell_1$ at p_1 $\mathbf{as}\, x\, \mathbf{in}\, e_2)\,]$ at $p_0,\ \ell_1 \to e_1$ at p_1
$\Box$ *OS2*	$\mathcal{L},\, \ell \to C\,[\,\mathbf{sync}\,(\mathbf{bc}\, \ell_1$ at p_1 $\mathbf{as}\, x\, \mathbf{in}\, e_2)\,]$ at $p_0,\ \ell_1 \to \mathbf{close}(\lambda p.\, e)$ at p_1 $\longmapsto \mathcal{L},\, \ell \to C\,[\,e_2\,[\,\ell_2\,/\,x\,]\,]$ at $p_0,\ \ell_1 \to \mathbf{close}(\lambda p.\, e)$ at p_1, $\{\,\ell_2 \to e\,[\,q\,/\,p\,]$ at $q\,\}\ (\forall q\, \in\, P)$
⌑ *OS1*	$\mathcal{L},\, \ell \to C\,[\,\mathbf{pull}\, e_1$ at p_1 $\mathbf{as}\, x\, \mathbf{in}\, e_2\,]$ at p_0 $\longmapsto \mathcal{L},\, \ell \to C\,[\,\mathbf{sync}\,(\mathbf{pull}\, \ell_1$ at p_1 $\mathbf{as}\, x\, \mathbf{in}\, e_2)\,]$ at $p_0,\ \ell_1 \to e_1$ at p_1
⌑ *OS2*	$\mathcal{L},\, \ell \to C\,[\,\mathbf{sync}\,(\mathbf{pull}\, \ell_1$ at p_1 $\mathbf{as}\, x\, \mathbf{in}\, e_2)\,]$ at $p_0,\ \ell_1 \to \mathbf{port}(\lambda p.\, e)$ at p_1 $\longmapsto \mathcal{L},\, \ell \to C\,[\,e_2\,[\,\lambda p.e\,/\,x\,]\,]$ at $p_0,\ \ell_1 \to \mathbf{port}(\lambda p.\, e)$ at p_1
$\Diamond$ *OS1*	$\mathcal{L},\, \ell \to C\,[\,\mathbf{go}\, e_1$ at p_1 $\mathbf{return}\, x, q\, \mathbf{in}\, e_2\,]$ at p_0 $\longmapsto \mathcal{L},\, \ell \to C\,[\,\mathbf{sync}_1(\mathbf{go}\, \ell_1$ at p_1 $\mathbf{return}\, x, q\, \mathbf{in}\, e_2)\,]$ at $p_0,\ \ell_1 \to e_1$ at p_1
$\Diamond$ *OS2*	$\mathcal{L},\, \ell \to C\,[\,\mathbf{sync}_1(\mathbf{go}\, \ell_1$ at p_1 $\mathbf{return}\, x, q\, \mathbf{in}\, e_2)\,]$ at p_0, $\ell_1 \to \mathbf{agent}[e, p_2]$ at p_1 $\longmapsto \mathcal{L},\, \ell \to C\,[\,\mathbf{sync}_2(\mathbf{go}\, \ell_2$ at p_2 $\mathbf{return}\, x, q\, \mathbf{in}\, e_2)\,]$ at p_0, $\ell_1 \to \mathbf{agent}[e, p_2]$ at $p_1,\ \ell_2 \to e$ at p_2
$\Diamond$ *OS3*	$\mathcal{L},\, \ell \to C\,[\,\mathbf{sync}_2(\mathbf{go}\, \ell_1$ at p_1 $\mathbf{return}\, x, q\, \mathbf{in}\, e_2)\,]$ at $p_0,\ \ell_1 \to v$ at p_1 $\longmapsto \ell \to C\,[\,e_2\,[\,p_1\,/\,q\,]\,[\,v\,/\,x\,]\,]$ at $p_0,\ \ell_1 \to v$ at p_1

Fig. 3. The operational semantics of λ_{rpc}

Networks $\mathcal{N}$ are pairs consisting of a set of places P, and a distributed process environment $\mathcal{L}$. We have seen places before. The process environment $\mathcal{L}$ is a finite partial map from places p in P to process IDs to expressions. We write these partial maps as lists of elements with the form $\ell \to e$ at p. We assume that no pair of place and location (p and ℓ) appears in two different components of the map. We do not distinguish between maps that differ only in the ordering of their elements. $\mathcal{L}(p)(\ell)$ denotes e when $\mathcal{L} = \mathcal{L}', \ell \to e$ at p. We use the notation $\mathcal{L} \setminus \ell$ to denote the mapping $\mathcal{L}$ with all elements of the form $\ell \to e$ at p removed.

We also introduce new expressions (the RT terms above) that only occur at run time to give an operation semantics to our program. Run-time terms are used to represent expressions, which are suspended part-way through evaluation and are waiting to synchronize with remotely executing expressions. Lastly, we define evaluation contexts C to specify the order of evaluation.

In order to show that the network is well-typed at every step in evaluation, we add typing rules to give types to the RT terms and we also give well-formedness conditions for the network as a whole. The typing judgment for a network has the form $\vdash \mathcal{L} : \Gamma_{\Box}; \cdot; \Delta$. See the technical report [6] for further details.

Operational Rules and Type Safety. The state of a network $\mathcal{N} = (P, \mathcal{L})$ evolves according to the operational rules listed in Figure 3. These rules specify a relation with the form $\mathcal{L} \longmapsto \mathcal{L}'$.

The type system is sound with respect to our operational semantics for distributed program evaluation. The proofs of Preservation and Progress theorems, stated below, follow the usual strategy.

Theorem 3 (Preservation). *If $\vdash \mathcal{L} : \Gamma_{\Box}; \cdot; \Delta$ and $\mathcal{L} \longmapsto \mathcal{L}'$ then there exists $\Gamma'_{\Box}$ and Δ' such that $\vdash \mathcal{L}' : \Gamma'_{\Box}; \cdot; \Delta'$.*

Theorem 4 (Progress). *If $\vdash \mathcal{L} : \Gamma_{\Box}; \cdot; \Delta$ then either*

- $\mathcal{L} \longmapsto \mathcal{L}'$*, or*
- *for all places p in P, and for all ℓ in* $\mathsf{Dom}(\mathcal{L}(p))$, $\mathcal{L}(p)(\ell)$ *is a value.*

4 Discussion

Extensions and Variations. This paper presents a solid foundation on which to build a distributed functional programming language. However, in terms of language design, it is only the beginning. For instance, the current work assumes that the set of network places and the network topology is fixed. While this is a reasonable assumption for some distributed programming environments, others allow the topology to evolve. An interesting challenge for future work is to extend our logic and language with features that allow allocation of new places and handling of failures.

Related Work. Hybrid logics are an old breed of logic that date back to Arthur Prior's work in the 1960s [12]. As does our logic, they mix modal necessity and possibility with formulas such as $F @ p$ that are built from pure names. More recently, researchers have developed a rich semantic theory for these logics and studied both tableau proofs and sequents; many resources on these topics and others are available off the hybrid logics web page.[6] However, work on hybrid logics is usually carried out in a classical setting and we have not found an intuitionistic, natural deduction style proof theory like ours that can serve as a foundation for distributed functional programming languages.

Cardelli and Gordon's ambient logic [13] highlights the idea that modalities for possibility and necessity need not only be interpreted *temporally*, but can also be interpreted *spatially*, and this abstract idea was a central influence in our work. However, at a more technical level, the ambient logic is entirely different from the logic we develop here: The ambient logic has a widely different set of

[6] See `http://www.hylo.net`.

connectives, is classical as opposed to intuitionistic, and is defined exclusively by a sequent calculus rather than by natural deduction. Moreover, it does not serve as a type system for ambient programs; rather, it is a tool for reasoning about them.

Much effort has been invested in interpreting proof search in sequent calculus of linear logic as concurrent computation. Recently along this line of research, Kobayshi et al. have explained how modal linear logic can be viewed as a distributed concurrent programming language [14]. In this work, they introduce a formula similar to our $F @ p$ but they define it axiomatically rather than through introduction and elimination rules (or left and right rules), as we have done. Consequently, their formulation cannot serve as the basis for a functional programming language. They did not consider modal necessity and possibility.

Another major influence on our work is Pfenning and Davies' judgmental reconstruction of modal logic [5], which is developed in accordance with Martin Löf's design patterns for type theory [3]. Alex Simpson's thesis [7] is also an indispensable reference on intuitionistic modal logic; we used it to help us understand the pure fragment of our logic. Pfenning and Davies interpret modal necessity temporally (as opposed to spatially) in their work on staged computation [15]. The most significant technical difference between our logic and theirs is that our logic hybrid and is founded on local judgments that include the specific place where a proposition is true whereas their logic is not.

Concurrently with this research, Jonathan Moody [16] has been investigating the relationship between modal logics and type systems for distributed computing, particularly Grid computing. Moody interprets objects with type $\Box \tau$ as jobs that may be injected into the Grid and run anywhere. This interpretation resembles our portable code, but there are some technical differences: his type system is based on S4 rather than S5 and, whereas we assume all nodes are connected to all other nodes, Moody's networks may have a more refined accessibility relation. Moody has not considered an interpretation of $\Box \tau$ as broadcast.

Another important difference between systems is that Moody only considers the pure modal logic. He does not have the hybrid logic connective $\tau @ p$ and the associated commands for remote procedure calls. The advantage of programming exclusively in Moody's pure fragment is that the types are simpler (they do not involve explicit places) and the run-time system takes care of the entire distribution strategy for the programmer. The disadvantage of working exclusively in the pure fragment is that the programmer does not have as much control over how computations are evaluated and where resources are placed.

Acknowledgments. We would like to thank Frank Pfenning for helping us understand the status of the pure fragment of our modal logic.

References

1. Fournet, C., Gonthier, G., Lévy, J.J., Maranget, L., Rémy, D.: A calculus of mobile agents. In: 7th International Conference on Concurrency Theory (CONCUR'96). Volume 1119 of Lecture Notes in Computer Science., Springer (1996) 406–421

2. Cardelli, L., Gordon, A.D.: Mobile ambients. Theoretical Computer Science **240** (2000) 177–213
3. Löf, M.: On the meanings of the logical constants and the justifications of the logical laws. Technical Report 2, University of Siena (1985)
4. Pfenning, F.: Logical frameworks. In Robinson, A., Voronkov, A., eds.: Handbook of Automated Reasoning. Elsevier Science and MIT Press (2001) 977–1061
5. Pfenning, F., Davies, R.: A judgmental reconstruction of modal logic. Mathematical Structures in Computer Science **11** (2001) 511–540
6. Jia, L., Walker, D.: Modal proofs as distributed programs. Technical Report TR-671-03, Princeton University (2003)
7. Simpson, A.K.: The Proof Theory and Semantics of Intuitionistic Modal Logic. PhD thesis, University of Edinburgh, Edinburgh (1994)
8. Abramsky, S.: Computational interpretations of linear logic. Theoretical Computer Science **111** (1993) 3–57
9. Lincoln, P., Mitchell, J.: Operational aspects of linear lambda calculus. In: IEEE Symposium on Logic in Computer Science. (1992) 235–246
10. Chirimar, J., Gunter, C.A., Riecke, J.G.: Proving memory management invariants for a language based on linear logic. In: ACM Conference on Lisp and Functional Programming. (1992) 139–150
11. Turner, D.N., Wadler, P.: Operational interpretations of linear logic. Theoretical Computer Science **227** (1999) 231–248 Special issue on linear logic.
12. Prior, A.: Past, present and future. Oxford University press (1967)
13. Cardelli, L., Gordon, A.: Anytime, anywhere: Modal logics for mobile ambients. In: Twenty-Seventh ACM Symposium on Principles of Programming Languages, ACM Press (2000) 365–377
14. Kobayashi, N., Shimizu, T., Yonezawa, A.: Distributed concurrent linear logic programming. Theoretical Computer Science **227** (1999) 185–220
15. Davies, R., Pfenning, F.: A modal analysis of staged computation. Journal of the ACM **48** (2001) 555–604
16. Moody, J.: Modal logic as a basis for distributed computation. Technical Report CMU-CS-03-194, Carnegie Mellon University (2003)

ULM:* A Core Programming Model for Global Computing
(Extended Abstract)

Gérard Boudol

INRIA Sophia Antipolis

Abstract. We propose a programming model to address the unreliable character of accessing resources in a global computing context, focusing on giving a precise semantics for a small, yet expressive core language. To design the language, we use ideas and programming constructs from the synchronous programming style, that allow us to deal with the suspensive character of some operations, and to program reactive behaviour. We also introduce constructs for programming mobile agents, that move together with their state, which consists of a control stack and a store. This makes the access to references also potentially suspensive.

1 Introduction

According to the *global computing* vision, "*In the future most objects that we work with will be equipped with processors and embedded software* [...] *Many of these objects will be able to communicate with each other and to interact with the environment*" [15]. In a word: processors everywhere. This is gradually becoming a reality: besides computers and laptops, or personal assistants, nowadays telephones and smart cards also are equipped with processors, as well as cars, planes, audio and video devices, household appliances, etc. Then a question is: will we be able to exploit such a highly distributed computing power? How will we compute in such a context? There are clearly many new features to deal with, and many problems to address in order to be able to "compute globally". As pointed out by Cardelli [8,9], the global computing context introduces new observables, "*so radically different from the current computational norm that they amount to a new model of computation*".

In this paper we address one specific aspect of this global computing vision, namely the fact that "*The availability and responsiveness of resources* [...] *are unpredictable and difficult to control*" [15]. This is indeed something that everybody can already experiment while browsing the web: quite often we observe that an URL appears inaccessible, for various reasons which are not always clearly identified – failure of a node, insufficient bandwidth, congestion, transient

* ULM is the acronym for the french words "*Un Langage pour la Mobilité*". Work partially supported by the MIKADO project of the IST-FET Global Computing Initiative, and the CRISS project of the ACI Sécurité Informatique.

D.A. Schmidt (Ed.): ESOP 2004, LNCS 2986, pp. 234–248, 2004.

disconnection, impossibility to cross a firewall, etc. We would like to have some ability to react and take actions to bypass these obstacles. This is what Cardelli provided for us, with service combinators for scripting the activity of web browsing [10]. Cardelli's combinators are quite specific, however: only the time and rate of transmission can be used as parameters for a reaction. We would like to have programming constructs to deal with more general situations where the availability and responsiveness of resources is not guaranteed. This is not provided by traditional computing models. For instance, in a LAN, the fact that some file is unreachable is considered as an error – unless this is prescribed by some security policy –, and a latency period that exceeds normal response times and communication delays is the sign of a failure. In global computing, by contrast, trying to access something which is, maybe temporarily, absent or unavailable appears to be the rule, rather than the exception. Such a failure should not be regarded as a fatal error. We should rather have means to detect and react to the lack of something.

A typical scenario where these partial failures occur is the one of *mobile code*, which is thought of as a general technique to cope with the new observable features of the global computing context [9,13]. For instance, a mobile code (which may be code embedded in a mobile device) may fail to link with some specific libraries it might need at a visited site, if the site does not provide them. In this case, a default behaviour should be triggered. Conversely, the mobile code may be unreachable from a site which is supposed to maintain connections with it. In such a case, the user who has delegated the mobile agent, or who tries to contact a remote mobile device, for instance, has to wait and, after a while, take some decisions.

The model we shall use to deal with absence, waiting, and reactions is basically that of *synchronous programming* [2,14]. This does not mean that, in our approach, something like the web is to be regarded as a synchronous system. We rather take the view that the global computing world is a (wide) GALS, that is, a "Globally Asynchronous, Locally Synchronous" network. Only at a local level does a notion of time make sense, which serves as the basis for taking decisions to react. As regards the way to program reactions, we follow the ESTEREL imperative (or control-oriented) style [3], which seems more appropriate for our purpose than the LUSTRE data flow style [14]. However, in ESTEREL a program is not always "causally correct", and a static analysis is needed to check correctness. This checking is not compositional, and more specifically, the parallel composition of causally correct programs is not always correct. From the point of view of global computing, this is unfortunate, because this makes it impossible to dynamically add new components, like mobile agents, to a system. Therefore, we shall use the *reactive* variant of ESTEREL designed by Boussinot [5,6], which is slightly less expressive, but is well suited for dynamically evolving concurrent systems. The main ingredients of the synchronous/reactive model, in its control-oriented incarnation – as we see it – are the following:

- *broadcast signals.* Program components react according to the absence or presence of signals, by computing, and emitting signals. These signals are broadcast to all the components of a synchronous area, which is a limited area where a local control over all the components exists.
- *suspension.* Program components may be in a suspended state, either because of the presence of a signal, or because they are waiting for a signal which is absent at the moment.
- *preemption.* There are means to abort the execution of a program component, depending on the presence or absence of a signal.
- *instants.* These are successive periods of the execution of the program, where the signals are consistently seen as present or absent by all the components.

Suspension is what we need to signify the lack of something, and preemption allows us to program reactive behaviours, aborting suspended parts of a program in order to trigger alternative tasks[1]. Notice that a notion of time – the instants – is needed to give meaning to actions depending on the absence of a signal: otherwise, when could we decide that we have waited for too long, and that the signal is to be considered as really absent? This last notion of an instant is certainly the main innovation of the synchronous programming model, and also the less easy to grasp. In our formalization, an "instant", or, better, a *time slot* – or simply a slot –, is an interval in the execution of a program, possibly involving many (micro-)steps, the end of which is determined by the fact that all the components are either terminated or suspended, and therefore unable to activate any other component. Moreover, only at the very beginning of an "instant" interactions with the environment may take place. By contrast with ESTEREL, in the reactive programming style of Boussinot, the absence of a signal can only be determined at the end of the "instant", and therefore one cannot suspend a component on the presence of a signal (that is, run it only if the signal is absent), and one can only abort its execution at the end of a time slot. The following example illustrates the use of reactive programming in a global computing perspective:

$$\begin{array}{l}\mathsf{agent}\ \lambda a.\mathsf{let}\ s = \mathsf{sig}\ \mathsf{in}\ \mathsf{thread}\ \lambda t.\mathsf{if}\ \mathsf{present}\ s\ \mathsf{then}\ ()\ \mathsf{else}\ (\mathsf{migrate\_to}\,\ell)a;\\ \qquad\qquad\qquad\qquad P\,;\mathsf{emit}\ s\end{array}$$

This is the code of an agent, named a, that, in some site, tries to executes a program P for one time slot. It spawns a thread (named t) that terminates if executing P succeeds, and otherwise moves the agent elsewhere. To trigger the migration, we use a local signal s which is only present when the task P terminates. One can also easily program a similar migration behaviour triggered by the presence of a failure signal emitted in a site:

$$\mathsf{agent}\ \lambda a.(\mathsf{thread}\ \lambda t.(\mathsf{when}\ \mathit{failure})(\mathsf{migrate\_to}\,\ell)a)\ ;P$$

Here the migration instruction is suspended, by means of the when construct, until the *failure* signal is emitted.

[1] This is surely not new from a system or network programming point of view, where one needs to deal with suspended or stuck tasks. However, the relevant mechanisms are usually not integrated in high-level programming languages.

The main novelty in this paper is in the way we deal with the *state*, and more generally the context of a program. Apart from the reactive constructs, we adopt a fairly conventional style of programming, say the ML or SCHEME imperative and functional style, where a memory (or heap) is associated with a program, to store mutable values. Then, in the presence of mobile code, a problem arises: when a code migrates, what happens with the portion of the store it may share with other, mobile or immobile components? There are three conceivable solutions:

- *network references.* The owner of a reference (a pointer) keeps it with him, and remote accesses are managed by means of proxies, forwarding the requests through the network.
- *distributed references.* A shared reference is duplicated and each copy is directly accessible, by local operations. Its value is supposed to be the same in all the copies.
- *mobile references.* The owner of a reference keeps it with him, and all non local accesses to the reference fail.

All the three solutions have their own flaws, the last one being the simplest to implement, but also the worse, according to the current computing model: it amounts to systematically introducing dangling pointers upon migration, thus causing run-time errors. Indeed, as far as I can see, this solution has never been used. Regarding the first, the construction and use of chains of forwarders may be costly, but, more importantly, network references rely on the implicit assumption that the network is reliable, in the sense that a distant site is always accessible (otherwise this solution is as bad as the last one). As we have seen, this assumption does not hold in a global computing context, where it is, for instance, perfectly normal for a mobile device to be sometimes disconnected from a given network. Similarly, maintaining the coherence of replicated references in a large network may be very difficult and costly, especially if connections may be temporarily broken. Moreover, with mobile code, the conflicts among several values for a given reference are not easy to solve: if a user possesses such a reference, and launches several agents updating it, which is the right value?

We adopt mobile references in our programming model for global computing, but with an important new twist: trying to access an absent reference is not an error, it is a suspended operation, like waiting for an absent signal in synchronous/reactive programming. Then the reactive part of the model allows us to deal with programs suspended on absent references, exactly as with signals. Although we do not investigate them in this paper, we think that for many other aspects of distributed and global computing, a programming model taking into account suspension as an observable, and offering preemption constructs, is indeed relevant. For instance, we will not consider communications between nodes of a network (apart from the asynchronous migration of code), but it should be clear that, from a local point of view, remote communication operations should have a suspensive character. In particular, this should be the case in an implementation of network references. Similarly, we do not consider the dynamic linking phase that an agent should perform upon migration (we assume that the sites provide the implementation of the constructs of our core model), but clearly an agent using some (supposedly ubiquitous) libraries for instance should involve some backup behaviour in case linking fails. In fact, in a global computing perspective, every operation engaging some code in an interaction with its environment should, from the point of view of this code, be considered as potentially suspensive. Therefore we think that, although they have been developed for radically different purposes – namely, hard real-time computations, and circuit design – the ideas of synchronous programming that we integrate in our ULM core programming model should prove also useful in the highly interactive and "odd-time" world of global computing.

2 The Computing Model

2.1 Asynchronous Networks of Synchronous Machines

Since the focus in this paper is on local reactive programming, and mobility, we have only minimal requirements on the network model. We assume that computing takes place in a network which is a collection of named nodes (or sites, or localities). Besides the nodes, the network also contains "packets", which merely consist here of frozen programs asynchronously migrating to some destination node. Then, assuming given a set $\mathcal{L}$ of node names, we describe a network using the following syntax:

$$R \ ::= \ \ell[\mathcal{M}] \ \mid \ \ell\langle p \rangle \ \mid \ (R_0 \parallel R_1)$$

where ℓ is any node name. We denote by $\ell[\mathcal{M}]$ a site, named ℓ, containing the configuration $\mathcal{M}$ of a reactive machine, while $\ell\langle p \rangle$ is a packet, en route to the site called ℓ. The syntax of the content of packets, as well as machine configurations, will be given below, and we shall see in a next section how packets are introduced in the network. We denote by $(R_0 \parallel R_1)$ the juxtaposition of the nodes of the two networks R_0 and R_1. We make the assumption that the sets of node names – that is, ℓ in $\ell[\mathcal{M}]$ – are disjoint when joining two networks. This is supposed to be guaranteed by some name service.

As we said in the introduction, our model is the one of a GALS network, a concept that we formalize as follows. The behaviour exhibited by a network is represented by transitions $R \rightarrow R'$, and is determined by the behaviour of its nodes. To account for the asynchronous character of network computations, we assume that juxtaposition is associative and commutative. (This also means that all the nodes, and packets, are considered here as neighbours, with no security barrier filtering communication, for instance.) Then, denoting by $\equiv$ the least congruence on networks for which $\parallel$ is associative and commutative, we have:

$$\frac{R_0 \rightarrow R_0'}{(R_0 \parallel R_1) \rightarrow (R_0' \parallel R_1)} \ (\textsc{Ntwk1}) \qquad \frac{R_0 \rightarrow R_0' \quad R_1 \equiv R_0 \quad R_1' \equiv R_0'}{R_1 \rightarrow R_1'} \ (\textsc{Ntwk2})$$

Now let us say a few words about the "locally synchronous" aspect of a GALS network. In Section 2.3 we shall define transitions between machine configurations, and we shall see that the behaviour of a synchronous machine, starting from an initial configuration $\mathcal{M}_0$, can be described as a sequence of *time slots*:

$$\ell[\mathcal{M}_0] \to \cdots \to \ell[\mathcal{M}'_0] \to \ell[\mathcal{M}_1] \qquad \textit{first slot}$$
$$\ell[\mathcal{M}_1] \to \cdots \to \ell[\mathcal{M}'_1] \to \ell[\mathcal{M}_2] \qquad \textit{second slot}$$
$$\vdots \qquad \textit{and so on.}$$

where the transitions $\ell[\mathcal{M}_i] \xrightarrow{*} \ell[\mathcal{M}'_i]$ represent purely local (micro)-steps to a "stable" configuration, and the last step $\ell[\mathcal{M}'_i] \to \ell[\mathcal{M}_{i+1}]$ is a special "*tick*" transition. During the local steps of computation, the machine behaves in isolation from its environment. This normally ends up with a state $\mathcal{M}'_i$ where all the concurrent threads running in the machine are either terminated or suspended, waiting for some information, so that no further local computation may occur. Then all the interactions with the environment take place, during the "tick" transition, where the machine by itself does not perform any computation. Therefore one can say that during a time slot, the threads running in the machine have a coherent vision of the outside world. In this paper the interactions between a machine and its environment only consist in the management of migration – incorporating immigrant agents, and sending emigrating agents as packets in the network. However, one could easily imagine other forms of interactions, like receiving input signals or sending calls to remote procedures.

2.2 The Language: Syntax

As we suggested above, a reactive machine $\mathcal{M}$ runs a collection of concurrent threads – among which mobile threads, that we call agents –, organized in a queue which we denote by T. These threads share a common store S and a context (a set) of signals E. Moreover, the configuration of the machine records a set P of emigrating agents. That is, a machine configuration has the form

$$\mathcal{M} = (S, E, T, P)$$

In this section we introduce the core language used to program agents and threads. As in ML or SCHEME, this core language is a call-by-value λ-calculus, enriched with imperative and reactive programming constructs, and with constructs to create and manage threads, including mobile ones. The syntax is given in Figure 1. Let us comment briefly on the primitive constructs of the language.

• Regarding the λ-calculus part of the language, we shall use the standard abbreviations and notations. We denote $\lambda x M$ by $\lambda.M$ when x is not free in M. The capture avoiding substitution of N for x in M is denoted $\{x \mapsto N\}M$.
• The imperative constructs, that is ref, ? and set are quite standard, except that we denote by ? the dereferencing operation (which is denoted ! in ML), to emphasize the fact that this is a potentially suspensive operation. As usual, we also write $M := N$ for $(\mathsf{set}\, M)N$.
• The intuitive semantics of the reactive constructs sig, emit, when and watch is as follows. The constant sig creates, much like the ref construct, a new signal, that is a name. The created signal is initially absent, and one uses the emit function to make a signal present for the current time slot. The function when

$$
\begin{array}{rcl}
M, N \ldots & ::= & V \mid (MN) \mid \mathsf{sig} \\
V, W \ldots & ::= & \ell \mid x \mid \lambda x M \mid () \\
& \mid & \mathsf{ref} \mid \,?\, \mid \mathsf{set} \mid (\mathsf{set}\, V) \\
& \mid & \mathsf{emit} \mid \mathsf{when} \mid (\mathsf{when}\, V) \mid \mathsf{watch} \mid (\mathsf{watch}\, V) \\
& \mid & \mathsf{thread} \mid \mathsf{agent} \mid \mathsf{migrate\_to} \mid (\mathsf{migrate\_to}\, V)
\end{array}
$$

Fig. 1. Syntax

is intended to be applied to two arguments, the first one being a signal. It *suspends* the evaluation of its second argument when the first one is absent. The preemption function watch is also a function of a signal and an expression. At the end of the current slot, it *aborts* the execution of its second argument if the watched signal is present.

• The thread function spawns a new thread, as well as the agent function which, in addition, creates an agent name. Agent names are used by the migrate_to function to cause the migration of the designated thread.

As we have suggested in these informal explanations, the evaluation of several constructs of the language, namely ref, sig and agent (and also thread) will create various kinds of names at run-time. These names are values in an extended, run-time language. They are defined as follows. First, we assume given a denumerable set $\mathcal{N}$ of names, disjoint from $\mathcal{L}$. Then, besides node names in $\mathcal{L}$, used in the source language, we shall use three kinds of names:

(i) Simple names, belonging to $\mathcal{N}$ and ranged over by $u, v, w \ldots$. These are used to name immobile threads, that is, the threads created using the thread construct.

(ii) Compound names of the form $\ell.u$, thus belonging to $\mathcal{L}.\mathcal{N}$. They are used to name signals, immobile references (that is, references created by an immobile thread), and agents. All these names may be imported in a node by a mobile agent, and this is why we use the name ℓ of the creation node as a prefix, to avoid conflicts whith names created elsewhere.

(iii) Compound names of the form $\ell.u.v$, belonging to $\mathcal{L}.\mathcal{N}.\mathcal{N}$. These are the names of references created by agents. As we will see, an agent will carry with it its own portion of the memory upon migration, and it is therefore convenient to distinguish the references created by an agent, by prefixing their name v with the name $\ell.u$ of their creator.

2.3 Operational Semantics

We have already described the semantics of networks, which relies on machine transitions. To introduce the latter, let us first define more precisely the components of a configuration:

• As usual, the *store* S is a mapping from a finite set $\mathsf{dom}(S) \subseteq \mathcal{L}.\mathcal{N} \cup \mathcal{L}.\mathcal{N}.\mathcal{N}$ of memory addresses to values.

• The signal environment $E \subseteq \mathcal{L}.\mathcal{N}$ is the set of names of signals that are *present* during the current time slot.
• The threads queue T is a sequence of named programs M^t, where M is an expression of the run-time language and t is the name of a thread executing M (so that $t \in \mathcal{N} \cup \mathcal{L}.\mathcal{N}$). We denote by $T \cdot T'$ the concatenation of two threads sequences, and by ε the empty sequence.
• The set P of emigrating agents consists in named programs together with a destination, denoted $(\mathsf{to}\,\ell)M^t$.

To run an expression M of the language in a locality ℓ, we start from an initial configuration where M is the only thread in the queue, with an arbitrary (simple) name, and everything else is empty, that is:

$$\ell[\emptyset, \emptyset, M^u, \emptyset]$$

For the sake of exposition, we distinguish four kinds of machine transitions. These transitions generally concern the head of the thread queue (on the left), that is the code M if $T = M^t \cdot T'$. First, we have purely functional transitions that occur in the active code part M of a configuration, and are essentially independent from the rest, like β-reduction. Then we have the imperative and reactive behaviour, where the code M interacts with the store S or the signal environment E. Next there are transitions having an effect on the thread queue, like thread creation, migration, and scheduling. Last but not least, there are transitions from one time slot to the next. As we said, all interactions with the "outside world" take place at this moment, and in particular the P part of the configuration is only considered at this point. The functional transitions, denoted $M \rightarrow_f M'$, are given by the following axioms:

$$(\lambda x M V) \rightarrow_f \{x \mapsto V\}M \qquad (\beta_{\mathrm{v}})$$

$$((\mathsf{when}\, W)V) \rightarrow_f V \qquad (\textsc{When})$$

$$((\mathsf{watch}\, W)V) \rightarrow_f () \qquad (\textsc{Watch})$$

The two transitions regarding when and watch mean that, when the code they control terminates, then the whole expression terminates.

To define the imperative and reactive transitions, acting on tuples (S, E, M^t), we need some auxiliary notions. First, we shall use the standard notion of an *evaluation context*, analogous to a "control stack". Evaluation contexts in our language are defined by the following grammar:

$$\mathbf{E} ::= [] \mid (\mathbf{E}N) \mid (V\mathbf{E})$$

Besides the evaluation contexts, we need the predicate $(S, E, M)\dagger$ of *suspension*. In our language, there are two ways in which a code M may be suspended in the context of a store S and a signal environment E: either M tries to access, for reading or writing it, a reference which is not in the domain of the store, or M waits for a signal which is absent. This is easily formalized, see [4].

To abbreviate the notations, in the rules below we will use the predicate $(E, \mathbf{E})\not\dagger$, meaning that, given the signal environment E, the evaluation context $\mathbf{E}$ is not suspensive, that is, if $\mathbf{E} = \mathbf{E}_0[((\mathsf{when}\, s)\mathbf{E}_1)]$ then $s \in E$. In the rules we also need, in some cases, the knowledge of the name of the locality where they occur. Therefore the imperative and reactive transitions are of the form

$$\vdash_\ell (S, E, M^t) \rightarrow_{ir} (S', E', M'^t)$$

For lack of space, we omit here some of the rules of the operational semantics. The complete design has to be found in [4]. For instance, there is a rule by which functional transitions are allowed in any non suspensive context. Then we have rules to create a reference and enlarge the store, and to get or update the value of a reference. These are more or less standard, except that dereferencing and updating are suspensive operations when the reference is not in the domain of the store (again, see [4] for the details). The creation of a signal is similar to the creation of a reference, that is, a fresh signal name is returned as a value:

$$\frac{(E, \mathbf{E}) \not\downarrow \qquad \ell.u \text{ fresh}}{\vdash_\ell (S, E, \mathbf{E}[\mathsf{sig}]^t) \rightarrow_{ir} (S, E, \mathbf{E}[\ell.u]^t)} \quad (\textsc{Sig})$$

Notice that the signal is still absent, that is $\ell.u \notin E$. The signal is present, for the rest of the current slot, when it has been emitted:

$$\frac{(E, \mathbf{E}) \not\downarrow}{\vdash_\ell (S, E, \mathbf{E}[(\mathsf{emit}\, s)]^t) \rightarrow_{ir} (S, E \cup \{s\}, \mathbf{E}[()]^t)} \quad (\textsc{Emit})$$

One can see that, following these transitions, it may happen that the evaluation of M gets suspended at some point. In this case, we have to look for other threads to execute, or to notice that the current slot has ended. This is decribed by the next rules, for transitions of the form

$$\ell[\mathcal{M}] \rightarrow \ell[\mathcal{M}']$$

that we mentioned in Section 2.1. A first rule says that an imperative or reactive transition is also a machine transition, if this transition is performed by the first thread in the queue (see [4]). Then, when the first thread is suspended, it is put at the end of the queue, provided that there is still some computation to perform, that is, there is another thread in the queue which is not terminated, and not suspended. By abuse of notation, we shall denote by $(S, E, T) \not\downarrow$ the fact that there is a thread in the queue T which is active in the context of S and E. The rule for scheduling the queue of threads is as follows:

$$\frac{\neg(S, E, M^t) \not\downarrow \qquad (S, E, T) \not\downarrow}{\ell[S, E, M^t \cdot T, P] \rightarrow \ell[S, E, T \cdot M^t, P]} \quad (\textsc{Sched})$$

We have adopted a round-robin scheduling, placing the current thread at the end of the queue when it is terminated or suspended. We could obviously use any other (fair) strategy, but we think it is important, in a language with effects, to have a deterministic strategy, in order to have some understanding of the semantics. One may notice that if a thread is suspended, waiting for a signal on a (when s) statement, and if this signal is emitted during the current time slot, then the thread will always be activated during this slot.

It remains to see how threads are created, and how migration is managed. The thread function takes a thunk – that is, a frozen expression $\lambda.M$ – as argument, creates a new thread, the body of which is the unfrozen thunk, and terminates. The body of the created thread is subject to the control (by signals, that is by means of when and watch functions) exercized by the context that created it. To formulate this, let us define the control context $\mathbf{E}^w$ extracted from an evaluation context $\mathbf{E}$ as follows:

$$\begin{aligned}
[]^w &= [] \\
(\mathbf{E}N)^w &= \mathbf{E}^w \\
(V\mathbf{E})^w &= \begin{cases} (V\mathbf{E}^w) & \text{if } V = (\mathsf{when}\,W) \text{ or } V = (\mathsf{watch}\,W) \\ \mathbf{E}^w & \text{otherwise} \end{cases}
\end{aligned}$$

One can see that $\mathbf{E}^w$ is a sequence of $(\mathsf{when}\,W)$ and $(\mathsf{watch}\,W)$ statements. The rule for thread creation is as follows:

$$\frac{(E,\mathbf{E})\not\downarrow}{\ell[S,E,\mathbf{E}[(\mathsf{thread}\,V)]^t\cdot T,P] \to \ell[S,E,\mathbf{E}[()]^t\cdot T\cdot \mathbf{E}^w[(V())]^u,P]} \quad (\textsc{Thread})$$

Notice that the newly created thread is put at the end of the queue, and therefore it cannot prevent the existing threads to execute, since the thread queue is scanned from left to right by the scheduler.

The agent function also creates threads, but with a different semantics. It is intended to have as argument a function of an agent name, say λxN. Then $(\mathsf{agent}\,\lambda xN)$ creates a new agent name, returned as a value, and a new thread, the body of which is N where x is instantiated by the created agent name. Unlike with threads created by thread, the control exercized by the creating context is not transferred on the created agent. The idea is that a thread, created by thread, is intended to cooperate with its creation context in the achievement of some task, while an agent is thought of as detached from a main task, and is intended to move (maybe just to escape from abortion of the main task). The rule is:

$$\frac{(E,\mathbf{E})\not\downarrow \qquad \ell.u \text{ fresh}}{\ell[S,E,\mathbf{E}[(\mathsf{agent}\,V)]^t\cdot T,P] \to \ell[S,E,\mathbf{E}[\ell.u]^t\cdot T\cdot (V\ell.u)^{\ell.u},P]} \quad (\textsc{Agent})$$

As one can see, the created name $\ell.u$ is known from both the creating context, and the agent itself. This name could be used to control the behaviour of the agent in various ways. We could for instance have primitive constructs to kill, or resume/suspend the execution of an agent. In this paper, the only construction of this kind we consider is the statement causing the migration of an agent. When we have to execute a $(\mathsf{migrate\_to}\,\ell')t$ instruction, where ℓ' is a node name and t is a thread name (it should be guaranteed by typing that migrate_to only applies to such values), we look in the thread queue for a component named t, and put it, with destination ℓ', in the set of emigrating agents:

$$\frac{(E,\mathbf{E})\not\downarrow \qquad \mathbf{E}[()]^r\cdot T = T'\cdot N^t\cdot T''}{\ell[S,E,\mathbf{E}[((\mathsf{migrate\_to}\,\ell')t)]^r\cdot T,P] \to \ell[S,E,T'\cdot T'',P\cup\{(\mathsf{to}\,\ell')N^t\}]} \quad (\textsc{Migr})$$

(There is also a rule in the case where the agent is not there, which is omitted.) If $t = r$, we have $N = \mathbf{E}[()]$, and we say that the migration is subjective, since it is performed by the agent itself. Otherwise, that is if the migration instruction is exercized by another thread, we say that the migration is objective. We also observe that (subjective) migration in our model may be qualified as "strong mobility" [13], since the "control stack", that is the evaluation context $\mathbf{E}$ of the migration instruction, is moving (together with the memory of the agent, as we shall see).

The last rule describes what happens at the end of a time slot, which is also the beginning of the next one – we call this the *tick* transition. One can see that no rule applies if the thread queue only consists of terminated or suspended threads. In this case, that is when $\neg(S, E, T) \not\downarrow$, the current slot is terminated, and the computation restarts for a new one, after the following actions have been done:

• The signal environment is reset to the empty set

Note 1. One could also imagine that signals could be emitted from the external environment. In this case, they would be incorporated as input signals for the next slot, but only during the "tick" transition..

• The preemption actions take place. That is, a sub-expression $((\mathsf{watch}\, s)M)$ (in a non suspensive context) terminates if the signal s was present in the signal environment at the end of the slot. Otherwise – that is, if s is absent –, this expression is resumed for the next slot, as well as the when guards.

• The immigrant agents, that is the contents of network packets $\ell\langle p\rangle$, are incorporated. In a more realistic language, one should have a buffering mechanism, involving a security check, to receive the asynchronously incoming agents. The contents p of a packet is a pair (S, M^t) of a store and a named program. The intuition is that M is the code of a migrating agent, and S is its own, local store. Then the code M is put at the end of the threads queue, and the S store is added to the one of the host machine (thus possibly activating threads suspended on trying to access an absent reference).

• The emigrant agents, in P, are sent in the outside world. More precisely, an element $(\mathsf{to}\, \ell')N^t$ of P is transformed into a packet $\ell'\langle S', N^t\rangle$ where S' is the portion of the store that is owned by the agent N^t. This portion is removed from the store of the locality where the tick transition is performed. Notice that a machine waits until it reaches a stable configuration to send the emigrating agents in the network. This is to maintain a coherent view of the store, as far as the presence or absence of references is concerned, during each time slot (notice also that the other threads may modify the store carried by the agent, even after it has been put in the P part of the configuration).

The precise formulation of the "tick" transition is given in [4].

3 Some Examples

In this section, we examine some examples, to illustrate the expressive power of the constructs of the language. We begin with examples related to the reactive programming primitives. There has been many variations, sometimes just notational, in the choice of primitives in synchronous, imperative programming. To obtain a "minimal" language, suited for formal reasoning, we have chosen to have only two primitives for reactive programming in ULM, one for introducing suspension, and the other for programming preemption. However, the other constructs, functional and imperative, of the language allow us to encode most of the standard constructs of synchronous/reactive programming. Let us see this now.

First we notice that our preemption construct $(\mathsf{watch}\, s)M$ exists in some versions of ESTEREL [2], where it is written ($\mathsf{abort}\ M\ \mathsf{when}\ s$), and also in SL [6], where it is written ($\mathsf{do}\ M\ \mathsf{kill}\ s$). In synchronous programming, there is a statement, called stop in [6] and pause in [2] (it is not a primitive, but is easily derived in the language of [3]), which lasts just one instant, that is, in our setting, which is suspended until the end of the current time slot, and terminates at the tick transition. To express this in ULM, it is convenient to first introduce a now construction which, when applied to a thunk, executes it for the current time slot only, so that ($\mathsf{now}\, M$) always terminates at the end of the slot, at the latest. This is easy to code: we just have to preempt the argument of now on a signal that is immediately emitted:

$$\mathsf{now} =_{\mathsf{def}} \lambda x(\mathsf{let}\ s = \mathsf{sig}\ \mathsf{in}\ (\mathsf{watch}\, s)(\mathsf{emit}\, s\, ;\, x()))$$

Another useful notation, that exists in ESTEREL (see [2]) is

$$\mathsf{await} =_{\mathsf{def}} \lambda s.(\mathsf{when}\, s)()$$

Then the pause construct is easily defined, as waiting for an absent signal, for the current slot only:

$$\mathsf{pause} =_{\mathsf{def}} (\mathsf{let}\ s = \mathsf{sig}\ \mathsf{in}\ (\mathsf{now}\, \lambda.\mathsf{await}\, s))$$

Using a pause statement, a thread suspends itself until the next time slot. We can also define a statement by which a thread just gives its turn, as if it were put at the end of the queue. This is easily done by spawning a new thread (thus put at the end of the queue) that emits a signal on which the "self-suspending" thread waits:

$$\mathsf{yield} =_{\mathsf{def}} (\mathsf{let}\ x = \mathsf{sig}\ \mathsf{in}\ (\mathsf{thread}\ \lambda.\mathsf{emit}\ x)\ ;\ \mathsf{await}\ x)$$

We can also use the now construct to define a present predicate whose value, when applied to a signal, is true (assuming that the language is extended with truth values *tt* and *ff*) if the signal is present, and false otherwise. Notice that since we can only determine that a signal is absent at the end of the current time slot, the value false can only be returned at the beginning of the next slot. The code is, using a reference to record the presence or absence of the signal:

$$\begin{aligned}\mathsf{present} =_{\mathsf{def}} \lambda s\, \mathsf{let}\ r = \mathsf{ref}\, ff \\ \mathsf{in}\ (\mathsf{now}\, \lambda.(\mathsf{when}\, s)\, r := tt)\ ;\ ?r\end{aligned}$$

In a conditional construct if present s then M else N, the code M is started in the current slot if s is present, and otherwise N is executed at the next one.

To finish with the examples, let us briefly discuss the mobile code aspect of the language. Imagine that we want to send, from a main program at site ℓ, an agent to a site ℓ', with the task of collecting some information there and coming back to communicate this to the sender (like we would do with a proxy for a network reference, for instance). We cannot write this as

$$\mathsf{let}\ r = (\mathsf{ref}\ X)\ \mathsf{in}\ \mathsf{migrate\_to}\,\ell'(\mathsf{agent}\,\lambda a(\cdots r := Y\ ;(\mathsf{migrate\_to}\,\ell)a))\ ;\ \cdots\ ?r\ \cdots$$

(which is an example of both objective and subjective migration) for two reasons: after some steps, where r is given a value $\ell.u$, that is an address in the store at site ℓ containing the value X, and where a name $\ell.v$ is given for a, the agent runs at ℓ' the code

$$\cdots\ \ell.u := Y\ ;(\mathsf{migrate\_to}\,\ell)\ell.v$$

Since the address $\ell.u$ is created by an immobile thread, it will always remain in the store at ℓ, and will never move. Therefore, the agent is blocked in ℓ' waiting for the reference $\ell.u$ to be there. On the other hand, the "main thread" at ℓ may perform $?\ell.u$, but it will get the value X, which is certainly not what is intended. We have to use a signal to synchronize the operations, like with:

$$\begin{aligned}&\mathsf{let}\ r = (\mathsf{ref}\ X)\ \mathsf{and}\ s = \mathsf{sig}\\ &\mathsf{in}\ \mathsf{let}\ \mathit{write} \ = \ \lambda x.r := x\ ;\mathsf{emit}\ s\ \mathsf{and}\\ &\qquad\quad \mathit{read} \ = \ \mathsf{await}\ s\ ;?r\\ &\quad \mathsf{in}\ \cdots\end{aligned}$$

writing the body of the agent as:

$$\cdots\mathsf{let}\ y = Y\ \mathsf{in}\ (\mathsf{migrate\_to}\,\ell)a\ ;\mathit{write}\ y$$

One can see that the main thread cannot read a value from the reference r before the signal s has been set as present, which only occurs (provided that r and s are private to the functions *write* and *read*) when a *write* operation has occurred. This example shows that mobile computing should be "location aware", at least at some low level, as envisioned by Cardelli [9]. This example also shows that an object-oriented style of programming would be useful to complement mobile agent programming, to define synchronization and communication structures, such as the one we just introduced in this example, of a signal with a value, that we may call an *event*. We are currently investigating this.

4 Conclusion

In this paper we have introduced a computing model to deal with some new observables arising in a global computing context, and especially the unreliability of resource accesses resulting from the mobility of code. For this purpose, we have used some ideas of synchronous programming, and most notably the idea that the behaviour of a program can be seen as a succession of "instants", within which a reaction to the suspension of some operations can be elaborated. This is what we need to give a precise meaning to statements like "abort the computation

C if it gets suspended for too long, and run C' instead", that we would like to encode as an algorithmic behaviour.

During the last few years of the last century, a lot of proposals have been made to offer support for mobile code (see for instance the surveys [13,19], and the articles in [20]). As far as I can see none of these proposals addresses the unreliablity issue as we did (and most often they lack a clear and precise semantics). Most of these proposals are assuming, like Cardelli's *OBLIQ* [7], that a distributed scope abstraction holds, in the sense that the access to a remote resource is transparent, and does not differ, from the programmer's point of view, from a local access. The JoCaml language for instance [12] is based on this assumption. However, we think that this abstraction can only be maintained in a local network. Indeed, Cardelli later argued in [9] that global computing should be location aware, and should also take into account the fact that in a global context, failures become indistinguishable from long delays. The Sumatra proposal [1] acknowledges the need "to be able to react to changes in resource availability", a feature which is called "agility", and is implemented by means of exception handling mechanisms. However, as far as I can see, no precise semantics is given for what is meant by "react quickly to asynchronous events" for instance. That is, a precise notion of time is missing.

Softwares and languages that are based on Linda, such as JavaSpaces [18], Lime [16] or Klaim [11], or on the π-calculus, like the JoCaml language [12] or NomadicPict [17], all involve an implicit notion of suspension: waiting for a matching tuple to input in the case of Linda, waiting for a message on an input channel in the case of π. However, they all lack preemption mechanisms, and a notion of time (indeed, the semantics of these models is usually asynchronous). Summarizing, we can conclude that our proposal appears to be the first (apart from [10]) that addresses, at the programming language level, and with a formal semantics, the issue of reacting to an unreliable computing context. Clearly, a lot of work is to be done to develop this proposal. In the full version of this paper [4], we show how to predict, by a static analysis, that some uses of references may be considered as safe, that is, they do not need testing the presence of the reference. Then, we should extend ULM into a more realistic language, and provide a proof-of-concept implementation. We should also investigate the network communication aspect (network references, RPC for instance), and the dynamic linking of mobile agents, that we did not consider. Last but not least, we should investigate (some of) the (numerous) security issues raised by the mobility of code. (A formal semantics for the mobile code, as the one we designed, is clearly a prerequisite to tackling seriously these issues.) One may have noticed for instance that in our model, a thread may prevent the other components to compute, simply by running forever, without terminating or getting suspended. Clearly, this is not an acceptable behaviour for an incoming agent. We are currently studying means to restrict the agents to always have a cooperative behaviour, in the sense that they only perform, at each time slot, a finite, predictable number of transitions.

References

[1] A. Acharya, M. Ranganathan, J. Saltz, *Sumatra:* a language for resource-aware mobile programs, in [20] (1997) 111–130.

[2] A. Benveniste, P. Caspi, S.A. Edwards, N. Halbwachs, P. Le Guernic, R. de Simone, *The synchronous languages twelve years later*, Proc. of the IEEE, Special Issue on the Modeling and Design of Embedded Software, Vol. 91 No. 1 (2003) 64–83.

[3] G. Berry, G. Gonthier, *The ESTEREL synchronous programming language: design, semantics, implementation*, Sci. of Comput. Programming Vol. 19 (1992) 87–152.

[4] G. Boudol, ULM, *A core programming model for global computing*, available from the author's web page (2003).

[5] F. Boussinot, *La Programmation Réactive – Application aux Systèmes Communicants, Masson*, Coll. Technique et Scientifique des Télécommunications (1996).

[6] F. Boussinot, R. de Simone, *The SL synchronous language*, IEEE Trans. on Software Engineering Vol. 22, No. 4 (1996) 256–266.

[7] L. Cardelli, *A language with distributed scope*, Computing Systems Vol. 8, No. 1 (1995) 27–59.

[8] L. Cardelli, *Global computation*, ACM SIGPLAN Notices Vol. 32 No. 1 (1997) 66–68.

[9] L. Cardelli, *Wide area computation*, ICALP'99, Lecture Notes in Comput. Sci. 1644 (1999) 10–24.

[10] L. Cardelli, R. Dawies, *Service combinators for web computing*, IEEE Trans. on Software Engineering Vol. 25 No. 3 (1999) 303–316.

[11] R. De Nicola, G. Ferrari, R. Pugliese, KLAIM: *a kernel langage for agents interaction and mobility*, IEEE Trans. on Software Engineering Vol. 24, No. 5 (1998) 315–330.

[12] C. Fournet, F. Le Fessant, L. Maranget, A. Schmitt, JoCaml: *a language for concurrent, distributed and mobile programming*, Summer School on Advanced Functional Programming, Lecture Notes in Comput. Sci. 2638 (2003) 129–158.

[13] A. Fuggetta, G.P. Picco, G. Vigna, *Understanding code mobility*, IEEE Trans. on Software Engineering, Vol. 24, No. 5 (1998) 342–361.

[14] N. Halbwachs, *Synchronous Programming of Reactive Systems*, Kluwer (1993).

[15] The IST-FET Global Computing Initiative, `http://www.cordis.lu/ist/fet/gc.htm (2001)`.

[16] G.P. Picco, A.L. Murphy, G.-C. Roman, *LIME: Linda meets mobility*, ACM Intern. Conf. on Software Engineering (1999) 368–377.

[17] P. Sewell, P. Wojciechowski, *Nomadic Pict: language and infrastructure design for mobile agents*, IEEE Concurrency Vol. 8 No. 2 (2000) 42–52.

[18] Sun Microsystems, *JavaSpaces Service Specification* `http://www.sun.com/jini/specs` (2000).

[19] T. Thorn, *Programming languages for mobile code*, ACM Computing Surveys Vol. 29, No. 3 (1997) 213–239.

[20] J. Vitek, Ch. Tschudin, Eds, *Mobile Object Systems: Towards the Programmable Internet*, Lecture Notes in Comput. Sci. 1222 (1997).

A Semantic Framework for Designer Transactions

Jan Vitek, Suresh Jagannathan, Adam Welc, and Antony L. Hosking

Purdue University

Abstract. A transaction defines a locus of computation that satisfies important concurrency and failure properties; these so-called ACID properties provide strong serialization guarantees that allow us to reason about concurrent and distributed programs in terms of higher-level units of computation (*e.g.*, transactions) rather than lower-level data structures (*e.g.*, mutual-exclusion locks). This paper presents a framework for specifying the semantics of a transactional facility integrated within a host programming language. The TFJ calculus supports nested and multi-threaded transactions. We give a semantics to TFJ that is parameterized by the definition of the transactional mechanism that permits the study of different transaction models.

1 Introduction

The integration of transactional facilities into programming languages has been driven by applications ranging from middleware infrastructure for enterprise applications to runtime support for optimistic concurrency. The concept of transactions is well-known in database systems; the main challenge in associating transactions with programming control structures comes from the mismatch between the concurrency model of the programming language and the concurrency model of the transactional facility. Existing technologies enforce little or no relationship between these models, so that programmers can neither rely on transactions for complete isolation among concurrent threads, nor use concurrent threading to more conveniently program transaction logic.

As a first step towards addressing some of these concerns, we propose a semantic framework in which different transactional mechanisms can be studied and compared formally. Requirements for such a framework are that it be sufficiently expressive to allow the specification of core transactional features, that it provide a way to validate the correctness of the semantics, and that it support features found in realistic programs. We are interested in the impact of design choices on observable behavior (*e.g.*, aborts, deadlocks, livelocks) and on implementation performance (*e.g.*, space and time overhead). Our long-term goal is to leverage this framework to aid in the definition of program analyzes and optimization techniques for transactional languages.

D.A. Schmidt (Ed.): ESOP 2004, LNCS 2986, pp. 249–263, 2004.

This paper introduces TFJ, or *Transactional Featherweight Java*, an object calculus with syntactic support for transactions. The operational semantics of TFJ is given in terms of a stratified set of rewrite rules parameterized over the meaning of the transactional constructs. This allows us to define a variety of transactional semantics within the same core language. In this paper, we study *nested and multi-threaded* transactions with two different concurrency control models (two-phase locking and versioning). The primary contribution of this paper is a formal characterization and proof of correctness of different transactional models when incorporated into the core language. While there has been significant previous work on devising formal notation and specifications [16,5] to describe transactional properties, we are not aware of other efforts that use operational semantics to study the interplay of concurrency and serializability among different transactional models.

2 The Transactional Featherweight Java Calculus

Transactional Featherweight Java (TFJ) is a new object calculus inspired by the work of Igarashi *et al.* [14]. TFJ includes threads and the imperative constructs needed to model transactions. In this paper, we focus on a simplified variant of TFJ, that is dynamically typed and in which all classes directly inherit a distinguished `Object` class. We introduce the syntax and semantics of TFJ with an example. Consider the classes given in Fig. 1. Class `Updater` encapsulates an update to an object. Class `Runner` is designed to perform an action within a new thread. Class `Transactor` performs two operations within a transaction. In this example, class `Updater` has two fields, `n` and `v`, and an `update()` method which assigns `v` to `n`'s `val` field. `Runner` has a `run()` method which starts a new thread and invokes a method on its `r` field within that thread. `Transactor` has a `pick()` method which is used to evaluate two expressions in a non-deterministic order; non-determinism is achieved since the order in which arguments are evaluated

```
class Updater {
   n, v;
   init( n, v) { return (this.n := n; this.v := v; this); }
   update() { return this.n.val:= this.v; } }

class Runner {
   s;
   init( s) { return (this.s := s; this); }
   run() { return spawn this.s.run(); } }

class Transactor {
   u, r;
   init( r, u) { return (this.u := u; this.r := r; this); }
   pick( _, _, v) { return v; }
   run() { return (
         onacid;
         this.pick( this.u.update(), this.r.run(), this.u.n.val);
         commit); } }
```

Fig. 1. An example TFJ program.

in a method call is unspecified. It also has a `run()` method which starts a new transaction and invokes `update` on field `u` and `run()` on field `r`. The keyword **onacid** marks the beginning of a transaction and **commit** ends the current transaction (as determined by the last **onacid**). All objects have an `init()` method which assigns values to their fields and returns `this`. Fig. 2 gives a TFJ code fragment making use of the above class definitions. Variable `n` is bound to a new object of some class `Number` (whose only feature of interest is that it must have a `val` field; we further assume the existence of classes `One`, `Two`, and `Three` that define specific numbers). `Noop` is an initialized `Runner` object with an uninteresting `run` method. Objects `l1` and `l2` are transactors which will be used to initiate nested transaction (`l2` within `l1`). Two runner objects will be used to create threads t_1 and t_2.

```
n := new Number();
s1 := new Transactor.init()( Noop, new Updater().init( n, new One()));
r1 := new Runner().init( s1);
s2 := new Transactor.init()( r1, new Updater().init( n, new Two()));
new Runner().init( s2).run();
n.val := new Three()
```

Fig. 2. A TFJ code fragement using definition of Fig. 1.

Evaluating the program of Fig. 2 will result in the creation of two threads (t_1 and t_2) and two new transactions (l_1 and l_2). Thread t_1 executes solely within transaction l_1, while t_2 starts executing in l_1, before starting transaction l_2. We assume that there is a default top-level transaction, l_0 and primordial thread t_0. Fig. 3 shows the structure of this computation. The threads in a parent transaction can execute concurrently with threads in nested transactions. A design choice in TFJ is that all threads must join (via a commit) for the entire transaction to commit. Alternatives, such as interrupting threads that are not at a commit point when another thread in the same transaction is ready to commit, or silently committing changes while the thread is running are either programmer unfriendly or counter to the spirit of transactions.

The states in this program are defined completely by the instance of class `Number` that is threaded through transactions and handed down to `Updaters` for modi-

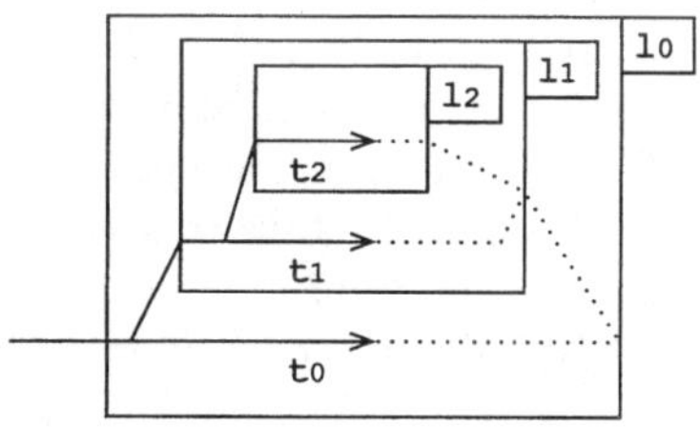

Fig. 3. Threads and transactions in Fig. 2.

fication. Each invocation of `update()` performs a read and a write of `val`. One valid interleaving of the operations is, for example:

$$[\mathtt{n} := \mathtt{One}()]_{\mathtt{l}_1} \rightarrow [\mathtt{n}]_{\mathtt{l}_1} \rightarrow [\mathtt{n} := \mathtt{Two}()]_{\mathtt{l}_2} \rightarrow [\mathtt{n}]_{\mathtt{l}_2} \rightarrow [\mathtt{n} := \mathtt{Three}()]_{\mathtt{l}_0}$$

This is correct because all of the changes performed by $\mathtt{l}_1$ occur before changes (reads and writes) performed by transactions $\mathtt{l}_2$ and $\mathtt{l}_0$. An invalid interleaving of these operations is:

$$[\mathtt{n} := \mathtt{One}()]_{\mathtt{l}_1} \rightarrow [\mathtt{n} := \mathtt{Two}()]_{\mathtt{l}_2} \rightarrow [\mathtt{n}]_{\mathtt{l}_1} \rightarrow [\mathtt{n}]_{\mathtt{l}_2} \rightarrow [\mathtt{n} := \mathtt{Three}()]_{\mathtt{l}_0}$$

In this schedule serializability is broken because $\mathtt{l}_1$ reads the value of `n.val` that was changed by $\mathtt{l}_2$. Thus from $\mathtt{l}_1$'s viewpoint the global state is $\mathtt{n.val} = \mathtt{Two}()$. Most concurrency control protocols will flag this as a conflict and abort $\mathtt{l}_1$. We note that in this particular case the conflict is benign as $\mathtt{l}_1$ discards the value it reads and thus the state of the system is not affected by it reading a stale value.

2.1 Syntax

The syntax of TFJ is given in Fig. 4. We take metavariables `L` to range over class declarations, `C`, `D` to range over classes, `M` to range over methods, and `f` and `x` to range over fields and parameters, respectively. We also use `P` for process terms, `e` for expressions and `v`, `u` for memory references. We use over-bar to represent a finite ordered sequence, for instance, $\overline{\mathtt{f}}$ represents $\mathtt{f}_1\,\mathtt{f}_2 \ldots \mathtt{f}_\mathtt{n}$. The term $\overline{\mathtt{l}}\mathtt{l}$ denotes the extension of the sequence $\overline{\mathtt{l}}$ with a single element `l`, and $\overline{\mathtt{l}}\,.\,\overline{\mathtt{l}'}$ for sequence concatenation. We write $\overline{\mathtt{l}} \lhd \overline{\mathtt{l}}'$ if $\overline{\mathtt{l}}$ is a prefix of $\overline{\mathtt{l}}'$.

The calculus has a call-by-value semantics. The expression $\mathtt{C}(\overline{\mathtt{v}}) \downarrow^{\mathtt{v}'}_{\mathtt{i}}$ yields an object identical to $\mathtt{C}(\overline{\mathtt{v}})$ except in the ith field which is set to $\mathtt{v}'$. The `null` metavariable is used to represent an unbound reference. By default all objects are null initialized (*i.e.* $\mathtt{C}(\overline{\mathtt{null}})$).

Since TFJ has by-value semantics for invocation, sequencing can be encoded as a sequence of method invocations. For readability, we sometimes write "$(\mathtt{e}_1;\mathtt{e}_2)$" in examples to indicate sequencing of expressions $\mathtt{e}_1$ and $\mathtt{e}_2$. The value of a sequence is always the value of the last expression.

An *expression* `e` can be either a variable `x`, the `this` pseudo variable, a reference `v`, a field access `e.f`, a method invocation $\mathtt{e.m}(\overline{\mathtt{e}})$, an object construction `newC()`, a thread creation `spawn e`, an `onacid` command or a `commit`. The latter three operations are unique to TFJ. The expression `spawn e` creates a new thread of control to evaluate `e`. The evaluation of `e` takes place in the same environment as the thread executing `spawn e`. A new transaction is started by executing `onacid`. The dynamic context of `onacid` is delimited by `commit`. Effects performed within the context of `onacid` are not visible outside the transaction until a `commit` occurs. Transactions may be nested. When the `commit` of an inner transaction occurs, its effects are propagated to its parent. Threads may be spawned within the context of a transaction. The local state of the transaction is visible to all threads which execute within it. Transactions may also execute concurrently. For example, in `spawn e`, `e` may be an expression that includes `onacid` and `commit`; the transaction created by `onacid` executes concurrently with the thread executing the `spawn` operation. A process term P can be either the empty process 0, the parallel composition of process $P \mid P$ or a thread t running expression e, denoted $\mathtt{t}[\,\mathtt{e}\,]$.

Note that the language does not provide an explicit `abort` operation. Transactions may abort *implicitly* because serialization invariants are violated. Our semantics expresses implicit aborts both in the definition of `commit` and in the treatment of read and write operations that would otherwise expose violations of necessary serializability invariants. Implicit aborts are tantamount to stuck states.

2.2 Reduction

The dynamic semantics of our language shown in Figs. 4 and 5 is given by a two-level set of rewrite rules. The computational core of the language is defined by a reduction relation of the from $\mathcal{E}\ \mathtt{e} \xrightarrow{\alpha} \mathcal{E}'\ \mathtt{e}'$. Here $\mathcal{E}$ is an environment containing bindings from references to objects ($\mathtt{v} \mapsto \mathtt{C}(\overline{\mathtt{v}})$), e is an expression and the action label α determines which reduction was picked. Action labels for the computational core are selected from the set $\{rd, wr, xt\}$, respectively read, write and extend. In addition to specifying the action on whose behalf a particular reduction is taken, we also specify the action's effects; for example, we write $wr\ vv'$to denote an action with label wr which has effect on locations v and v'. A read action effects the location being read, a write action has an effect on both the location being written and the location whose value it reads, and an extend operation has an effect on the newly created location.

A second reduction relation $\stackrel{\alpha}{\Longrightarrow}_{\mathtt{t}}$ defines operations over the entire program and has the form $\Gamma\ P \stackrel{\alpha}{\Longrightarrow}_{\mathtt{t}} \Gamma'\ P'$ where Γ is a program state composed of a sequence of thread environments $\overline{\mathtt{t}, \mathcal{E}}$ where each $\mathtt{t}, \mathcal{E}$ pair represents the association of a thread to its environment. The action label α can be one of the computational core labels or one of $\{sp, ac, co, ki\}$ for, respectively, spawn, onacid, commit, or kill.

The metavariable `l` ranges over transaction names, sequences of transaction names are used to represent the nesting structure. The transaction label $\overline{\mathtt{l}}$ identifies the transaction on whose behalf the reduction step was performed. As usual, $\stackrel{\alpha}{\Longrightarrow}_{\mathtt{t}} *$ denotes the reflexive and transitive closure of the global reduction relation. The congruence rules given in Figure 5 are straightforward.

We work up to congruence of processes ($\mathtt{P}|\mathtt{P}' \equiv \mathtt{P}'|\mathtt{P}$ and $\mathtt{P}|0 \equiv \mathtt{P}$). Congruence over expressions is defined in terms of evaluation contexts, $E[\,\bullet\,]$. The relations $\Downarrow_{\mathtt{spawn}}$, $\Downarrow_{\mathtt{onacid}}$ and $\Downarrow_{\mathtt{commit}}$ are used to extract nested expressions out of a context. The other definitions are similar to those used in the specification of FJ. *fields*

Syntax:

$$\begin{aligned}
\mathtt{P} &::= \mathtt{0} \mid \mathtt{P|P} \mid \mathtt{t[e]} \\
\mathtt{L} &::= \mathtt{class\ C\ \{\ \overline{f};\ \overline{M}\ \}} \\
\mathtt{M} &::= \mathtt{m(\overline{x})\ \{\ return\ e;\ \}} \\
\mathtt{e} &::= \mathtt{x} \mid \mathtt{this} \mid \mathtt{v} \mid \mathtt{e.f} \mid \mathtt{e.m(\overline{e})} \mid \mathtt{e.f := e} \mid \\
&\quad\ \mathtt{new\ C()} \mid \mathtt{spawn\ e} \mid \mathtt{onacid} \mid \mathtt{commit} \mid \mathtt{null}
\end{aligned}$$

Lookup:

$$\frac{CT(\mathtt{C}) = \mathtt{class\ C\ \{\ \overline{f};\ \overline{M}\ \}}}{\mathit{fields}(\mathtt{C}) = (\overline{\mathtt{f}})}$$

$$\frac{CT(\mathtt{C}) = \mathtt{class\ C\ \{\ \overline{f};\ \overline{M}\ \}} \qquad \mathtt{m(\overline{x})\ \{\ return\ e;\ \}} \in \overline{\mathtt{M}}}{\mathit{mbody}(\mathtt{m},\ \mathtt{C}) = (\overline{\mathtt{x}},\ \mathtt{e})}$$

Local Computation:

$$\frac{\mathcal{E}', \mathtt{C}(\overline{\mathtt{u}}) = \mathit{read}(\mathtt{v}, \mathcal{E}) \quad \mathit{fields}(\mathtt{C}) = (\overline{\mathtt{f}})}{\mathcal{E}\ \mathtt{v.f_i} \xrightarrow{rd\ \mathtt{v}} \mathcal{E}'\ \mathtt{u}_i} \quad \text{(R-Field)}$$

$$\frac{\mathcal{E}', \mathtt{C}(\overline{\mathtt{v}}) = \mathit{read}(\mathtt{v}, \mathcal{E}) \quad \mathcal{E}'' = \mathit{write}(\mathtt{v} \mapsto \mathtt{C}(\overline{\mathtt{v}})\downarrow_{\mathtt{i}}^{\mathtt{v}'}, \mathcal{E}')}{\mathcal{E}\ \mathtt{v.f_i} := \mathtt{v}' \xrightarrow{wr\ \mathtt{vv}'} \mathcal{E}''\ \mathtt{v}'} \quad \text{(R-Assign)}$$

$$\frac{\mathcal{E}', \mathtt{C}(\overline{\mathtt{u}}) = \mathit{read}(\mathtt{v}, \mathcal{E}) \quad \mathit{mbody}(\mathtt{m},\ \mathtt{C_0}) = (\overline{\mathtt{x}},\ \mathtt{e})}{\mathcal{E}\ \mathtt{v.m}(\overline{\mathtt{v}}) \xrightarrow{rd\ \mathtt{v}} \mathcal{E}'\ [\overline{\mathtt{v}}/\overline{\mathtt{x}}, \mathtt{v}/\mathtt{this}]\mathtt{e}} \quad \text{(R-Invk)}$$

$$\frac{\mathtt{v}\ \text{fresh} \quad \mathcal{E}' = \mathit{extend}(\mathtt{v} \mapsto \mathtt{C}(\overline{\mathtt{null}}), \mathcal{E})}{\mathcal{E}\ \mathtt{new\ C()} \xrightarrow{xt\ \mathtt{v}} \mathcal{E}'\ \mathtt{v}} \quad \text{(R-New)}$$

Global Computation:

$$\frac{\begin{array}{c} P = P'' \mid \mathtt{t[e]} \quad \mathcal{E}\ \mathtt{e} \xrightarrow{\alpha} \mathcal{E}'\ \mathtt{e}' \quad P' = P'' \mid \mathtt{t[e']} \\ \Gamma = \mathtt{t}, \mathcal{E}\ .\ \Gamma'' \quad \Gamma' = \mathit{reflect}(\mathtt{t},\ \mathcal{E}', \Gamma'') \quad \ell(\mathtt{t}, \Gamma) = \overline{\mathtt{l}} \end{array}}{\Gamma\ P \overset{\alpha}{\Longrightarrow}_{\mathtt{t}} \Gamma'\ P'} \quad \text{(G-Plain)}$$

$$\frac{\begin{array}{c} P = P'' \mid \mathtt{t[e]} \quad \mathtt{e} \Downarrow_{\mathtt{spawn}} \mathtt{e}', \mathtt{e}'' \quad P' = P'' \mid \mathtt{t[e']} \mid \mathtt{t'[e'']} \\ \mathtt{t}'\ \text{fresh} \quad \Gamma' = \mathit{spawn}(\mathtt{t}, \mathtt{t}', \Gamma) \quad \ell(\mathtt{t}, \Gamma) = \overline{\mathtt{l}} \end{array}}{\Gamma\ P \overset{sp\ \mathtt{t}'}{\Longrightarrow}_{\mathtt{t}} \Gamma'\ P'} \quad \text{(G-Spawn)}$$

$$\frac{\begin{array}{c} P = P'' \mid \mathtt{t[e]} \quad \mathtt{e} \Downarrow_{\mathtt{onacid}} \mathtt{e}' \quad P' = P'' \mid \mathtt{t[e']} \\ \mathtt{l}\ \text{fresh} \quad \Gamma' = \mathit{start}(\mathtt{l}, \mathtt{t}, \Gamma) \quad \ell(\mathtt{t}, \Gamma) = \overline{\mathtt{l}} \end{array}}{\Gamma\ P \overset{ac}{\Longrightarrow}_{\mathtt{t}} \Gamma'\ P'} \quad \text{(G-Trans)}$$

$$\frac{\begin{array}{c} P = P'' \mid \overline{\mathtt{t[e]}} \quad \overline{\mathtt{e}} \Downarrow_{\mathtt{commit}} \overline{\mathtt{e}'} \quad P' = P'' \mid \overline{\mathtt{t[e']}} \quad \overline{\mathtt{t}} = \mathit{intranse}(\mathtt{l}, \Gamma) \\ \Gamma = \mathtt{t_0}\ \mathcal{E}\ .\ \Gamma'' \quad \Gamma' = \mathit{commit}(\overline{\mathtt{t}}, \mathcal{E}, \Gamma) \quad \ell(\mathtt{t}', \Gamma) = \overline{\mathtt{l}} \end{array}}{\Gamma\ P \overset{co}{\Longrightarrow}_{\mathtt{t}'} \Gamma'\ P'} \quad \text{(G-Comm)}$$

$$\frac{P = P' \mid \mathtt{t[v]} \quad \Gamma = \mathtt{t}, \mathcal{E}\ .\ \Gamma' \quad \ell(\mathtt{t}, \Gamma) = \overline{\mathtt{l}}}{\Gamma\ P \overset{ki}{\Longrightarrow}_{\mathtt{t}} \Gamma'\ P'} \quad \text{(G-ThKill)}$$

Fig. 4. TFJ Syntax and Semantics.

returns the list of all fields of a class including inherited ones. *mbody* returns the body of the method in a given class.

Let $\mathcal{E}$ be an environment of the form $\mathtt{l}_0{:}\rho_0 \ldots \mathtt{l}_n{:}\rho_n$, then $\ell(\mathcal{E})$ extracts the order transaction label sequence, $\ell(\mathcal{E}) = \mathtt{l}_0 \ldots \mathtt{l}_n$ if $\Gamma = \mathtt{t}, \mathcal{E}\ .\ \Gamma'$ and $\ell(\mathtt{t}, (\mathtt{t}, \mathcal{E}\ .\ \Gamma)) = \ell(\mathcal{E})$. The auxiliary function $\mathit{last}(\mathtt{v}, \rho)$ is defined to return a one element sequence containing the last value referenced by v in the sequence of bindings ρ or the empty sequence if there is no binding for v. It is defined inductively to return $\langle\rangle$ if $\rho = \langle\rangle$, $\mathtt{C}(\overline{\mathtt{v}})$ if $\rho = \rho' \,.\, \mathtt{v} \mapsto \mathtt{C}(\overline{\mathtt{v}})$ and $last(\mathtt{v}, \rho')$ if $\rho = v\rho' \,.\, \mathtt{v}' \mapsto \mathtt{C}(\overline{\mathtt{v}})$ and $\mathtt{v} \neq \mathtt{v}'$. The function $first(\mathtt{v}, \rho)$ is similar but returns the first binding for v in the sequence. Finally, $findlast(\mathtt{v}, \mathcal{E})$ finds the last binding for v in environment $\mathcal{E}$.

There are four computational core reduction rules shown in in Fig. 4. (R-FIELD) evaluates a field access expression. (R-ASSIGN) evaluates an assignment expression, (R-INVK) evaluates a method invocation expression and (R-NEW) evaluates an object instantiation expression. Notice that TFJ has a by-value semantics which requires that arguments be fully evaluated before performing method invocations or field access. These rules are complemented by five global reduction rules. (G-PLAIN) corresponds to a step of computation, (G-SPAWN) corresponds to a thread creation, (G-TRANS) corresponds to the start of a new transaction, (G-COMM) corresponds to the commit of a transaction, and (G-THKILL) is a reclamation rule for threads in normal form. Most of the rules are straightforward. G-PLAIN makes use of a *reflect* operation that must propagate the action performed to other threads executing within this transaction; its specification is dependent on the particular transactional semantics adopted. Notice that (G-COMM) requires that, if some thread t running in transaction $\overline{\mathtt{l}}$ is ready to commit, all other threads executing in that transaction be ready to commit. The auxiliary predicate $intranse(\mathtt{l}, \Gamma)$ given in Fig. 5 returns the set of threads that currently have the transaction label $\overline{\mathtt{l}}$. Note that if there is any thread running in a nested transaction (*e.g.*, has label $\overline{\mathtt{l}}\mathtt{l}'$, for some l'), $intranse(\overline{\mathtt{l}}, \Gamma)$ will return the empty sequence as nested transactions must commit before their parent transaction. The (G-THKILL) rule takes care of removing threads that have terminated, to prevent blocking a transaction (terminated threads are not ready

Evaluation Contexts:

$$E[\bullet] \mid E[\bullet].\mathtt{f} := \mathtt{e} \mid \mathtt{e.f} := E[\bullet] \mid E[\bullet].\mathtt{m}(\overline{\mathtt{e}}) \mid \mathtt{e.m}(\ldots E[\bullet]\ldots)$$

$$\frac{\mathtt{e} = E[\,\mathtt{spawn}\ \mathtt{e}''\,] \quad \mathtt{e}' = E[\,\mathtt{null}\,]}{\mathtt{e} \Downarrow_{\mathtt{spawn}} \mathtt{e}', \mathtt{e}''} \qquad \frac{\mathtt{e} = E[\,\mathtt{onacid}\,] \quad \mathtt{e}' = E[\,\mathtt{null}\,]}{\mathtt{e} \Downarrow_{\mathtt{onacid}} \mathtt{e}'} \qquad \frac{\mathtt{e} = E[\,\mathtt{commit}\,] \quad \mathtt{e}' = E[\,\mathtt{null}\,]}{\mathtt{e} \Downarrow_{\mathtt{commit}} \mathtt{e}'}$$

Congruence:

$$\frac{\mathcal{E}\ \mathtt{e} \longrightarrow \mathcal{E}'\ \mathtt{e}'}{\mathcal{E}\ E[\,\mathtt{e}\,] \longrightarrow \mathcal{E}'\ E[\,\mathtt{e}'\,]}$$

Transaction membership:

$$\frac{}{nested(\mathtt{l}, \langle\rangle) = \langle\rangle} \qquad \frac{\Gamma = \mathtt{t}, \mathcal{E} \,.\, \Gamma' \quad nested(\mathtt{l}, \Gamma') = \overline{\mathtt{t}} \quad \overline{\mathtt{l}}\mathtt{l}\mathtt{l}'\overline{\mathtt{l}}' = \ell(\mathtt{t}, (\mathtt{t}, \mathcal{E}))}{nested(\mathtt{l}, \Gamma) = \mathtt{t}\overline{\mathtt{t}}} \qquad \frac{\Gamma = \mathtt{t}, \mathcal{E} \,.\, \Gamma' \quad nested(\mathtt{l}, \Gamma') = \overline{\mathtt{t}} \quad \mathtt{l} \notin \ell(\mathtt{t}, (\mathtt{t}, \mathcal{E})) \ \vee\ \overline{\mathtt{l}}\mathtt{l} = \ell(\mathtt{t}, (\mathtt{t}, \mathcal{E}))}{nested(\mathtt{l}, \Gamma) = \overline{\mathtt{t}}}$$

$$\frac{}{intranse(\mathtt{l}, \langle\rangle) = \langle\rangle} \qquad \frac{\Gamma = \mathtt{t}, \mathcal{E} \,.\, \Gamma' \quad intranse(\mathtt{l}, \Gamma') = \overline{\mathtt{t}} \quad \mathtt{l} \in \ell(\mathtt{t}, (\mathtt{t}, \mathcal{E})) \quad nested(\mathtt{l}, \Gamma) = \langle\rangle}{intranse(\mathtt{l}, \Gamma) = \mathtt{t}\overline{\mathtt{t}}} \qquad \frac{\Gamma = \mathtt{t}, \mathcal{E}\ \Gamma' \quad intranse(\mathtt{l}, \Gamma') = \overline{\mathtt{t}} \quad \mathtt{l} \notin \ell(\mathtt{t}, (\mathtt{t}, \mathcal{E}))}{intranse(\mathtt{l}, \Gamma) = \overline{\mathtt{t}}}$$

Fig. 5. Auxiliary definitions

to commit). Note also that $\Gamma = \mathtt{t}_0, \mathcal{E} \, . \, \Gamma''$ is used to extract the environment of *one* of the threads in $\overline{\mathtt{t}}$. Since all threads in $\overline{\mathtt{t}}$ execute in the same transaction all of their environments $\overline{\mathcal{E}}$ are identical.

The dynamic semantics leaves open the specification of a number of operations. In particular, the definitions of *read*, *write*, *spawn*, *extend*, *reflect*, *start*, and *join* are left unspecified. A particular incarnation of a transactional semantics must provide a specification for these operations.

3 Versioning Semantics

In Fig. 6 we define an instantiation of TFJ in which transactions implement sequences of object versions. The versioning semantics extends the notion of transaction environments to be an ordered sequence of pairs, each pair consisting of a transaction label and an environment. The intuition is that every transaction operates using a private *log*; these logs are treated as sequences of pairs, bindings a reference to its value. A log thus records effects that occur while executing within the transaction. A given reference may have different binding values in different logs. If $\mathcal{E} = \mathtt{l}_1{:}\rho_1 \, . \, \mathtt{l}_2{:}\rho_2$ then a thread $\mathtt{t}$ executing with respect to this transaction environment is evaluating expressions whose effects are recorded in log ρ_2 and which are part of the dynamic context of an `onacid` command with label $\mathtt{l}_2$. If $\mathtt{l}_2$ successfully commits, bindings in ρ_2 are merged with those in ρ_1. Once $\mathtt{l}_2$ commits, subsequent expressions evaluated by $\mathtt{t}$ occur within the dynamic context of an `onacid` command with label $\mathtt{l}_1$; effects performed by these expressions are recorded in environment ρ_1.

Thus, a transaction environment in a versioning semantics defines a chain of nested transactions: every $\mathtt{l}{:}\rho$ element in $\mathcal{E}$ is related to its predecessor in the sequence defined by $\mathcal{E}$ under an obvious static nesting relationship. A locus of computation can be therefore uniquely denoted by a thread $\mathtt{t}$ and the transaction label sequence $\overline{\mathtt{l}}$ in which $\mathtt{t}$ is executing.

When a new thread is created (cf. *spawn*), the global state is augmented to include the new thread; evaluation of this thread occurs in a transaction environment inherited from its parent. In other words, a spawned thread begins evaluation in the environment of its parent extant at the point where the thread was created.

When a thread enters a new transaction (cf. *start*), a new transaction environment is added to its state. This environment is represented as a pair consisting of a label denoting the transaction, and a log used to hold bindings for objects manipulated within the transaction. Initially, the newly created transaction is bound to an empty log.

The essence of the versioning semantics is captured by the *read*, *write*, and *commit* operations. If a *read* operation on reference $\mathtt{v}$ occurs within transaction $\mathtt{l}$, the last value for $\mathtt{v}$ in the log is returned via the auxiliary procedure *findlast*, and the log associated with $\mathtt{l}$ is augmented to include this binding. Thus, the first *read* operation for reference $\mathtt{v}$ within transaction $\mathtt{l}$ will bind a value for $\mathtt{v}$ computed by examining the logs of $\mathtt{l}$'s enclosing transactions, choosing the binding value found in the one closest to $\mathtt{l}$. Subsequent reads of $\mathtt{v}$ made within $\mathtt{l}$ will find a binding value within $\mathtt{l}$'s log. Thus, this semantics ensures an isolation property on reads: once an object is read within transaction $\mathtt{l}$, effects on that object performed within other transactions are not visible until $\mathtt{l}$ attempts to commit its changes.

The *write* operation is defined similarly. Note that *write* augments the log of the current transaction with two bindings, one binding the reference to its value

$$\frac{\begin{array}{c}\mathcal{E} = \mathcal{E}' \,.\, \mathtt{l}{:}\rho \quad \mathit{findlast}(\mathtt{v}, \mathcal{E}) = \mathtt{C}(\overline{\mathtt{v}}) \\ \mathcal{E}'' = \mathcal{E}' \,.\, \mathtt{l}{:}(\rho \,.\, \mathtt{v} \mapsto \mathtt{C}(\overline{\mathtt{v}}))\end{array}}{\mathit{read}(\mathtt{v}, \mathcal{E}) \;=\; \mathtt{C}(\overline{\mathtt{v}}), \mathcal{E}''} \qquad \frac{\begin{array}{c}\mathcal{E} = \mathcal{E}' \,.\, \mathtt{l}{:}\rho \quad \mathit{findlast}(\mathtt{v}, \mathcal{E}) = \mathtt{D}(\overline{\mathtt{u}}) \\ \mathcal{E}'' = \mathcal{E}' \,.\, \mathtt{l}{:}(\rho \,.\, \mathtt{v} \mapsto \mathtt{D}(\overline{\mathtt{u}}) \,.\, \mathtt{v} \mapsto \mathtt{C}(\overline{\mathtt{v}}))\end{array}}{\mathit{write}(\mathtt{v} \mapsto \mathtt{C}(\overline{\mathtt{v}}), \mathcal{E}) = \mathcal{E}''}$$

$$\frac{\begin{array}{c}\mathcal{E} = \mathcal{E}' \,.\, \mathtt{l}{:}\rho \\ \mathcal{E}'' = \mathcal{E}' \,.\, \mathtt{l}{:}(\rho \,.\, \mathtt{x} \mapsto \mathtt{C}(\overline{\mathtt{v}}))\end{array}}{\mathit{extend}(\mathtt{v} \mapsto \mathtt{C}(\overline{\mathtt{v}}), \mathcal{E}) = \mathcal{E}''}$$

$$\frac{\Gamma = \mathtt{t}, \mathcal{E} \,.\, \Gamma' \quad \Gamma'' = \mathtt{t}', \mathcal{E} \,.\, \Gamma}{\mathit{spawn}(\mathtt{t}, \mathtt{t}', \Gamma) = \Gamma''} \qquad \frac{\Gamma = \mathtt{t}, \mathcal{E} \,.\, \Gamma' \quad \Gamma'' = \mathtt{t}, (\mathcal{E} \,.\, \mathtt{l}{:}\langle\rangle) \,.\, \Gamma}{\mathit{start}(\mathtt{l}, \mathtt{t}, \Gamma) = \Gamma''}$$

$$\frac{}{\mathit{reflect}(\mathtt{t}, \mathcal{E}, \langle\rangle) = \langle\rangle} \qquad \frac{\begin{array}{c}\Gamma = \mathtt{t}', \mathcal{E}' \,.\, \Gamma' \quad \mathit{reflect}(\mathtt{t}, \mathcal{E}, \Gamma') = \Gamma'' \\ \mathit{copy}(\mathcal{E}, \mathcal{E}') = \mathcal{E}'' \quad \Gamma''' = \mathtt{t}', \mathcal{E}'' \,.\, \Gamma''\end{array}}{\mathit{reflect}(\mathtt{t}, \mathcal{E}, \Gamma) = \Gamma'''}$$

$$\frac{\begin{array}{c}\mathcal{E} = \mathcal{E}' \,.\, \mathtt{l}{:}\rho \quad \mathit{readset}(\rho, \langle\rangle) = \rho' \quad \mathit{writeset}(\rho, \langle\rangle) = \rho'' \mathit{check}(\rho', \mathcal{E}') \\ \mathcal{E}' = \mathcal{E}'' \,.\, \mathtt{l}'{:}\rho''' \quad \mathit{reflect}(\mathtt{t}, (\mathcal{E}'' \,.\, \mathtt{l}'{:}\rho'''.\rho''), \Gamma) = \Gamma'\end{array}}{\mathit{commit}(\mathtt{t}, \mathcal{E}, \Gamma) = \Gamma'}$$

$$\frac{\mathcal{E} = \overline{\mathtt{l}{:}\rho} \,.\, \overline{\mathtt{l}'{:}\rho'} \quad \mathcal{E}' = \overline{\mathtt{l}{:}\rho''} \,.\, \overline{\mathtt{l}''{:}\rho'''}}{\mathit{copy}(\mathcal{E}, \mathcal{E}') = \overline{\mathtt{l}{:}\rho} \,.\, \overline{\mathtt{l}''{:}\rho'''}} \qquad \frac{}{\mathit{check}(\langle\rangle, \mathcal{E})} \qquad \frac{\mathit{findlast}(\mathtt{v}, \mathcal{E}) = \mathtt{C}(\overline{\mathtt{v}}) \quad \mathit{check}(\rho, \mathcal{E})}{\mathit{check}(\rho \,.\, \mathtt{v} \mapsto \mathtt{C}(\overline{\mathtt{v}}), \mathcal{E})}$$

Mod sets:

$$\frac{}{\mathit{readset}(\langle\rangle, \_) = \langle\rangle} \qquad \frac{\rho = \mathtt{u} \mapsto \mathtt{C}(\overline{\mathtt{u}}) \,.\, \rho'' \quad \mathtt{u} \notin \overline{\mathtt{v}} \quad \mathit{readset}(\rho'', \overline{\mathtt{v}}\mathtt{u}) = \rho'}{\mathit{readset}(\rho, \overline{\mathtt{v}}) = \mathtt{u} \mapsto \mathtt{C}(\overline{\mathtt{u}}') \,.\, \rho'}$$

$$\frac{\rho = \mathtt{u} \mapsto \mathtt{C}(\overline{\mathtt{u}}) \,.\, \rho'' \quad \mathtt{u} \in \overline{\mathtt{v}} \quad \mathit{readset}(\rho'', \overline{\mathtt{v}}) = \rho'}{\mathit{readset}(\rho, \overline{\mathtt{v}}) = \rho'}$$

$$\frac{}{\mathit{writeset}(\langle\rangle, \_) = \langle\rangle} \qquad \frac{\begin{array}{c}\rho = \mathtt{v} \mapsto \mathtt{C}(\overline{\mathtt{v}}) \,.\, \rho'' \quad \mathit{writeset}(\rho'', \rho') = \rho''' \\ \mathtt{v} \mapsto \mathtt{C}(\overline{\mathtt{v}}) \neq \mathit{first}(\mathtt{v}, \rho')\end{array}}{\mathit{writeset}(\rho, \rho') = \mathtt{u} \mapsto \mathtt{D}(\overline{\mathtt{u}}) \,.\, \rho'''}$$

Fig. 6. Versioning semantics

prior to the assignment, and the other reflecting the effect of the assignment. The former binding is needed to guarantee transactional consistency. Consider a write to a reference `v` in transaction `l` which has not yet been read or written in `l`. The effects of this write can be made visible when `l` attempts to commit only if no other transaction has committed modifications to `v` in the interim between the time where the write occurred, and `l` attempts to commit. If this invariant were violated, the desired serialization semantics on transaction would fail to hold. The *extend* operation inserts a new binding in the current transaction's log; since the reference being bound is fresh, there is no existing binding in the parent transaction against which to check consistency upon commit.

The *commit* operation is responsible for committing a transaction. In our versioning semantics, a commit results in bindings for objects written within a transaction's log to be propagated to its parent. In order for a commit of transaction `l` to succeed, it must be the case that the binding value of every reference read or written in `l` must be the same as its current value in `l`'s parent transaction. Satisfaction of this condition implies the absence of a data race between `l` and its parent or siblings. The *reflect* operation defined in *commit* makes visible the effects of `l` in all threads executing in `l`'s parent transaction; when used in a transaction-local action, it propagates the effects of the action to other threads executing within this same transaction.

The versioning semantics defined here is akin to an optimistic concurrency protocol in which the validity of reads and writes of references performed within a transaction `l` is determined by the absence of modifications to those references in transactions which commit between the time the first read or write of the reference takes place in `l` and the time `l` commits. For example, consider transaction l_1 that commits v_1, transaction l_2 that commits v_2 and transaction `l` that accesses both v_1 and v_2; a valid serialization of these transactions would commit l_1 prior to the first access of v_1 in l_2, and would commit l_2 prior to the first access of v_2 in `l`. Provided l_2 does not modify v_1, no atomicity or consistency invariants on these transactions would be violated.

4 Strict Two-Phase Locking

With slight alteration, the versioning semantics can be modified to support a two-phase locking protocol. The semantics presented below is faithful to a two-phase locking protocol in which locks are first acquired on objects before the objects can be accessed, and released only when commit actions occur. The modifications necessary are shown in Fig. 7. The primary change is in the definition of *reflect*. In the versioning semantics, and in the global reduction rules, the *reflect* operator is used to propagate changes performed in one thread to all other threads executing within the same transaction; it is also used in the definition of commit to propagate updates to a parent transaction to all threads that execute within it.

To support two-phase locking, we exploit this functionality to allow transaction environments to reflect object ownership. We define a unique transaction environment $\mathcal{E}_L$ containing a unique log ρ_L; $\rho_L(\mathtt{v})$ maps v to the transaction label sequence which identifies the transaction that currently has exclusive access to v. If $\bar{\mathtt{l}} = \mathtt{l}_1.\mathtt{l}_2 \ldots \mathtt{l}_\mathtt{n}$ is such a sequence, and a thread t executing within $\mathtt{l}_\mathtt{n}$ attempts to read or write reference v, it must first acquire v's lock. A lock is acquired using *setlock*. A lock of an object can be acquired if (a) the transaction in which the action occurs is a child of the current owner, or (b) the lock is currently owned by the child, and needs to be propagated to the parent. The first condition arises for non-commit actions; in this case the transaction attempting to acquire the lock (l) is the same as the transaction in which the *setlock* is executed. The second condition arises on commit actions; in this case l is the transaction of the parent to whom ownership of all locks owned by the child $\mathtt{l}_\mathtt{t}$ must be transferred. Thus, locks are reset on a commit: when a commit occurs, lock ownership is changed from l to l's parent.

We distinguish between read and write operations and commit operations in the definition of *reflect* and *setlock* by observing that, in the former case, the transaction label sequence of the transaction performing the reflect is the same as the label sequence of the transaction in which the locks are to be acquired (i.e., $\ell(\mathcal{E}) = \ell(\mathcal{E}_t)$); in the latter case, the *reflect* operation is invoked by *commit*, and thus $\mathcal{E}$ is the parent transaction of $\mathcal{E}_t$, the transaction being committed. Recall that the definition of *commit* in Fig. 6 updates the transaction environment by propagating changes performed by the committing transaction to its parent.

5 Soundness

Proving the soundness of a particular transactional facility requires relating it to desired serialization characteristics that dictate a transaction's ACID properties. For any abort-free program trace there must be a corresponding trace in which the transactions executed serially, *i.e.* all concurrent transactions execute atomically wrt one another. The key idea is that we should be able to

$$\frac{\begin{array}{c}\mathcal{E}_L = \mathtt{l}{:}\rho_L \quad \rho = \mathtt{v} \mapsto \mathtt{C}(\bar{\mathtt{u}})\,.\,\rho' \quad \mathit{findlast}(\mathtt{v}, \mathcal{E}_L) = \mathtt{Lock}(\bar{\mathtt{l}}') \\ (\bar{\mathtt{l}}' \lhd \bar{\mathtt{l}} \wedge \bar{\mathtt{l}} = \bar{\mathtt{l}}_t) \vee (\bar{\mathtt{l}}_t = \bar{\mathtt{l}}\,.\,\mathtt{l}) \quad \mathcal{E}'_L = \mathit{setlock}(\rho', \bar{\mathtt{l}}, \mathcal{E}_L) \\ \mathcal{E}'_L = \mathtt{l}{:}\rho'_L \quad \rho''_L = \mathtt{v} \mapsto \mathtt{Lock}(\bar{\mathtt{l}})\,.\,\rho'_L \quad \mathcal{E}''_L = \mathtt{l}{:}\rho''_L\end{array}}{\mathit{setlock}(\rho, \bar{\mathtt{l}}, \bar{\mathtt{l}}_t, \mathcal{E}_L) = \mathcal{E}''_L}$$

$$\frac{\begin{array}{c}\Gamma/_{\mathtt{t}_\mathtt{L}, \mathcal{E}_\mathtt{L}} = \mathtt{t}, \mathcal{E}_t\,.\,\mathtt{t}', \mathcal{E}'\,.\,\Gamma' \quad \mathit{reflect}(\mathtt{t}, \mathcal{E}, \Gamma') = \Gamma'' \\ \Gamma''' = \mathtt{t}', \mathcal{E}''\,.\,\Gamma'' \quad \mathcal{E} = \mathcal{E}'''\,.\,\bar{\mathtt{l}}{:}\rho \quad \mathit{readset}(\rho, \langle\rangle) = \rho' \\ \mathit{setlock}(\rho', \ell(\mathcal{E}), \ell(\mathcal{E}_t), \mathcal{E}_L) = \mathcal{E}'_L \quad \mathit{copy}(\mathcal{E}, \mathcal{E}') = \mathcal{E}''\end{array}}{\mathit{reflect}(\mathtt{t}, \mathcal{E}, \Gamma) = \Gamma'''}$$

Fig. 7. Lock-based commitment semantics

reorder any abort-free sequence of reduction steps into a sequence that yields the same final state and in which reduction steps taken on behalf of different parallel transactions are not interleaved. We proceed to formalize this intuitive definition.

The height of an environment $\mathcal{E} = \mathtt{l}_0{:}\rho_0 \ldots \mathtt{l}_n{:}\rho_n$, written $|\mathcal{E}|$, is n. For a state Γ, $max(\Gamma)$ returns a thread environment $\mathtt{t}, \mathcal{E}$ such that $\mathcal{E}$ is the environment with the largest height $|\mathcal{E}|$ in Γ. Given a transition $P\,\Gamma \stackrel{\alpha}{\Longrightarrow}_{\mathtt{t}} P'\,\Gamma'$, we say that the corresponding action, written $\mathcal{A}$ is $(\alpha, \mathtt{t}, \ell(\mathtt{t}, \mathcal{E}))$.

Definition 1 (Well-defined). *Let $\Gamma = (t, \mathcal{E})\ .\ \Gamma'$. We say that environment Γ is well-defined if Γ' is also well-defined and for $\mathcal{E} = \mathtt{l}_1{:}\rho_1 \ldots \mathtt{l}_n{:}\rho_n$, we have* $\text{first}(\rho_j, \mathtt{v}) = \text{last}(\rho_{j-1}, \mathtt{v})$ *if $2 \le j \le n$, and $\mathtt{v} \in Dom(\rho_{j-1}) \cap Dom(\rho_j)$.*

To define soundness properties, we introduce the notion of control and data dependencies. A dependency defines a relation on actions which can be used to impose structure of transition sequences. In other words, a well-defined transition sequence will be one in which action dependencies are not violated, and thus define safe serial orderings.

Definition 2 (Control Dependency). *Define a preorder $\stackrel{c}{\leadsto}$ on actions such that $\mathcal{A}_1 \stackrel{c}{\leadsto} \mathcal{A}_2$ (read $\mathcal{A}_1$ is control-dependent on $\mathcal{A}_2$) if the following holds:*
1. $\mathcal{A}_1 = (\alpha, \mathtt{t}, \bar{\mathtt{l}})$ and $\mathcal{A}_2 = (sp\,\mathtt{t}, \mathtt{t}', \bar{\mathtt{l}})$.
2. $\mathcal{A}_1 = (co, \mathtt{t}, \bar{\mathtt{l}})$ and $\mathcal{A}_2 = (\alpha, \mathtt{t}', \bar{\mathtt{l}}')$ where $\alpha \in \{rd, wr, xt\}$ and $\bar{\mathtt{l}}' \lhd \bar{\mathtt{l}}$.
3. $\mathcal{A}_1 = (\alpha, \mathtt{t}, \bar{\mathtt{l}})$ and $\mathcal{A}_2 = (ac, \mathtt{t}', \bar{\mathtt{l}}')$ where $\bar{\mathtt{l}}' \lhd \bar{\mathtt{l}}$.

Definition 3 (Data Dependency). *Define a preorder $\stackrel{d}{\leadsto}$ on actions such that $\mathcal{A}_1 \stackrel{d}{\leadsto} \mathcal{A}_2$ (read $\mathcal{A}_1$ is data-dependent on $\mathcal{A}_2$) the if $\mathcal{A}_1$ is either $(rd\,\mathtt{v}, \mathtt{t}, \bar{\mathtt{l}})$, $(wr\,\mathtt{v}\mathtt{v}', \mathtt{t}, \bar{\mathtt{l}})$ or $(wr\,\mathtt{v}'\mathtt{v}, \mathtt{t}, \bar{\mathtt{l}})$, and $\mathcal{A}_2$ is either $(wr\,\mathtt{v}\mathtt{v}'', \mathtt{t}', \bar{\mathtt{l}}')$ or $(xt\,\mathtt{v}, \mathtt{t}', \bar{\mathtt{l}}')$, with $\bar{\mathtt{l}}' \lhd \bar{\mathtt{l}}$.*

The key property for our soundness result is the permutation lemma which describes the conditions under which two reduction steps can be permuted. Let $\mathcal{A}$ and $\mathcal{A}'$ be a pair of actions which are not related under a control or data dependency. We write $\mathcal{A} \stackrel{\bar{d}}{\leadsto} \mathcal{A}'$ and $\mathcal{A} \stackrel{\bar{c}}{\leadsto} \mathcal{A}'$ to mean action $\mathcal{A}$ has, respectively, no c-dependence or d-dependence on $\mathcal{A}'$.

Definition 4 (Independence). *Actions $\mathcal{A}$ and $\mathcal{A}'$ are independent if $\mathcal{A} \stackrel{\bar{c}}{\leadsto} \mathcal{A}'$ and $\mathcal{A} \stackrel{\bar{d}}{\leadsto} \mathcal{A}'$.*

Lemma 1 (Permute). *Assume that Γ and Γ'' are well-defined, and let R be the two-step sequence of reductions $P\,\Gamma \stackrel{\alpha}{\Longrightarrow}_{\mathtt{t}} P_0\,\Gamma_0 \stackrel{\alpha'}{\Longrightarrow}_{\mathtt{t}'} P'\,\Gamma'$. If $\mathcal{A}$ and $\mathcal{A}'$ are independent then there exists a two-step sequence R' such that R' is $P\,\Gamma \stackrel{\alpha'}{\Longrightarrow}_{\mathtt{t}'} P_1\,\Gamma_1 \stackrel{\alpha}{\Longrightarrow}_{\mathtt{t}} P'\,\Gamma'$.*

Definition 5 (Program Trace). *Let R be the sequence of reductions $P_0\, \Gamma_0 \overset{\alpha_0}{\Longrightarrow}_{t_0} \ldots P_n\, \Gamma_n \overset{\alpha_n}{\Longrightarrow}_{t_n} P_{n+1}\, \Gamma_{n+1}$. The trace of the reduction sequence R, written $tr(R)$, is $(\alpha_0, \mathtt{t}_0, \overline{\mathtt{l}}_0) \ldots (\alpha_n, \mathtt{t}_n, \overline{\mathtt{l}}_0)$ assuming that $\overline{\mathtt{l}}_i = \ell(\mathtt{t}_i, \Gamma_i)$ for $0 \leq i \leq n$.*

A program trace is *serial* if for all pairs of reduction steps with the same transaction label ($\overline{\mathtt{l}}$), all reductions occurring between the two steps are taken on behalf of that very transaction or nested transactions ($\overline{\mathtt{l}} \lhd \overline{\mathtt{l}}'$).

Definition 6 (Serial Trace). *A program trace, $tr(R) = (\alpha_0, \mathtt{t}_0, \overline{\mathtt{l}}_0) \ldots (\alpha_n, \mathtt{t}_n, \overline{\mathtt{l}}_n)$ is serial iff $\forall\, i, j, k$ such that $0 \leq i \leq j \leq k \leq n$ and $\overline{\mathtt{l}}_i = \overline{\mathtt{l}}_k$ we have $\overline{\mathtt{l}}_i \lhd \overline{\mathtt{l}}_j$.*

We can now formulate the soundness theorem which states that any sequence of reductions which ends in a good state can be reordered so that its program trace is serial.

Theorem 1 (Soundness). *Let R be a sequence of reductions $P_0\, \Gamma_0 \overset{\alpha_0}{\Longrightarrow}_{t_0} \ldots P_n\, \Gamma_n \overset{\alpha_n}{\Longrightarrow}_{t_n} P_{n+1}\, \Gamma_{n+1}$. If Γ_{n+1} is well-defined, then there exists a sequence R' such that R' is $P_0\, \Gamma_0 \overset{\alpha'_0}{\Longrightarrow}_{t'_0} \ldots P'_n\, \Gamma'_n \overset{\alpha'_n}{\Longrightarrow}_{t'_n} P_{n+1}\, \Gamma_{n+1}$ and $tr(R')$ is serial.*

6 Related Work

The association of transactions with programming control structures has provenance in systems such as Argus [17,15,18], Camelot [10] Avalon/C++ [9] and Venari/ML [13], and has also been studied for variants of Java, notably by Garthwaite [11] and Daynes [6,7,8]. There is a large body of work that explores the formal specification of various flavors of transactions [16,5,12]. However, these efforts do not explore the semantics of transactions when integrated into a high-level programming language. Most closely related to our goals is the work of Black *et. al.* [1] and Choithia and Duggan [4]. Choithia and Duggan present an extension of the pi-calculus that supports various abstractions for distributed transactions and optimistic concurrency. Their work is related to other efforts [3, 2] that encode transaction-style semantics into the pi-calculus and its variants. Our work is distinguished from these efforts in that it provides a simple operational characterization and proof of correctness of transactions that can be used to explore different trade-offs when designing a transaction facility for incorporation into a language.

7 Conclusions

This paper presented a semantic framework for specifying nested and mulithreaded transactions. The TFJ calculus is an object calculus which supports nested and multi-threaded transactions and enjoys a semantics parameterized by the definition of the transactional facility. We have proven a general soundness theorem that relates the semantics of TFJ to a serializability property, and have defined two instantiations: a versioning-based optimistic model, and a pessimistic two-phase locking protocol. In future work we plan to address typing issues as well as static analysis techniques for optimized implementations of transactional languages. Furthermore we plan to investigate higher-order transactions.

Acknowledgments. This work is supported by the National Science Foundation under grants Nos. IIS-9988637, CCR-0085792, 0093282, and 0209083, and by gifts from Sun Microsystems and IBM. The authors thank Krzysztof Palacz for his input.

References

1. Andrew Black, Vincent Cremet, Rachid Guerraoui, and Martin Odersky. An Equational Theory for Transactions. Technical Report CSE 03-007, Department of Computer Science, OGI School of Science and Engineering, 2003.
2. R. Bruni, C. Laneve, and U. Montanari. Orchestrating Transactions in the Join Calculus. In *13th International Conference on Concurrency Theory*, 2002.
3. N. Busi, R. Gorrieri, and G. Zavattaro. On the Serializability of Transactions in JavaSpaces. In *ConCoord 2001, International Workshop on Concurrency and Coordination*, 2001.
4. Tom Chothia and Dominic Duggan. Abstractions for Fault-Tolerant Computing. Technical Report 2003-3, Department of Computer Science, Stevens Institute of Technology, 2003.
5. Panos Chrysanthis and Krithi Ramamritham. Synthesis of Extended Transaction Models Using ACTA. *ACM Transactions on Database Systems*, 19(3):450–491, 1994.
6. Laurent Daynès. Implementation of automated fine-granularity locking in a persistent programming language. *Software—Practice and Experience*, 30(4):325–361, April 2000.
7. Laurent Daynès and Grzegorz Czajkowski. High-performance, space-efficient, automated object locking. In *Proceedings of the International Conference on Data Engineering*, pages 163–172. IEEE Computer Society, 2001.
8. Laurent Daynès and Grzegorz Czajkowski. Lightweight flexible isolation for language-based extensible systems. In *Proceedings of the International Conference on Very Large Data Bases*, 2002.
9. D. D. Detlefs, M. P. Herlihy, and J. M. Wing. Inheritance of synchronization and recovery in Avalon/C++. *IEEE Computer*, 21(12):57–69, December 1988.
10. Jeffrey L. Eppinger, Lily B. Mummert, and Alfred Z. Spector, editors. *Camelot and Avalon: A Distributed Transaction Facility*. Morgan Kaufmann, 1991.
11. Alex Garthwaite and Scott Nettles. Transactions for Java. In Malcolm P. Atkinson and Mick J. Jordan, editors, *Proceedings of the First International Workshop on Persistence and Java*, pages 6–14. Sun Microsystems Laboratories Technical Report 96-58, November 1996.
12. Jim Gray and Andreas Reuter. *Transaction Processing*. Morgan-Kaufmann, 1993.

13. Nicholas Haines, Darrell Kindred, J. Gregory Morrisett, Scott M. Nettles, and Jeannette M. Wing. Composing first-class transactions. *ACM Transactions on Programming Languages and Systems*, 16(6):1719–1736, November 1994.
14. Atsushi Igarashi, Benjamin C. Pierce, and Philip Wadler. Featherweight Java: a minimal core calculus for Java and GJ. *ACM Transactions on Programming Languages and Systems*, 23(3):396–450, May 2001.
15. B. Liskov and R. Scheifler. Guardians and actions: Linguistic support for robust distributed programs. *ACM Transactions on Programming Languages and Systems*, 5(3):381–404, July 1983.
16. Nancy Lynch, Michael Merritt, William Weihl, and Alan Fekete. *Atomic Transactions*. Morgan-Kaufmann, 1994.
17. J. Eliot B. Moss. Nested transactions: An approach to reliable distributed computing. In *Proceedings of the Second Symposium on Reliability in Distributed Software and Database Systems*, pages 33–39. IEEE Computer Society, 1982.
18. J. Eliot B. Moss. *Nested Transactions: An Approach to Reliable Distributed Computing*. MIT Press, Cambridge, Massachusetts, 1985.

Semantical Analysis of Specification Logic, 3
An Operational Approach

Dan R. Ghica*

Oxford University Computing Laboratory, Oxford, U.K. OX1 3QD
drg@comlab.ox.ac.uk

Abstract. We are presenting a semantic analysis of Reynolds's specification logic of Idealized Algol using the parametric operational techniques developed by Pitts. We hope that this more elementary account will make the insights of Tennent and O'Hearn, originally formulated in a functor-category denotational semantics, more accessible to a wider audience. The operational model makes clearer the special nature of term equivalence in the logical setting, identifies some problems in the previous interpretation of negation and also proves the soundness of two new axioms of specification logic. Using the model we show that even a very restricted fragment of specification logic is undecidable.

1 Introduction

The specification logic of Idealized Algol (IA) [1,2] is perhaps the best attempt to extend Hoare-style programming logic to a language with procedures. It is quite general and its usability has been clearly demonstrated. The semantics initially proposed by Reynolds is classical, with models of specifications consisting of environments of meanings for its free identifiers (universal specifications). Subsequently, Reynolds realized that making specifications stateful, i.e. including both environment and state in the model, would lead to more powerful and more useful programming axioms.

The soundness of specification logic with stateful specifications has been the object of important semantic research. Tennent [3] had the first insight that this logic is intuitionistic and requires a Kripke-style possible worlds model, with sets of states as worlds. The principal semantic innovation of his approach was the restriction of the behaviour of IA commands so that no states outside of the current world are visited in the course of the command's execution. The way this restriction is imposed mathematically in the denotational setting is quite striking, based on the functor-categorical construction initially developed by Reynolds and Oles as a denotational model for IA [4,5]. This mathematical construction is remarkable because the restriction it imposes is prima facie incompatible with denotational semantics, which is extensional rather than intensional; in addition, the semantic model of the specification logic connects seamlessly with that of the programming language. This semantic model was

* The author was partly funded by Canadian NSERC and UK EPSRC.

D.A. Schmidt (Ed.): ESOP 2004, LNCS 2986, pp. 264–278, 2004.

further refined by Tennent and O'Hearn, allowing the validation of several new axioms [6].

The semantic ideas of the research mentioned before carried over into further work on the semantics of IA, leading to several improved models. Much of this work is collected in [7]. One trait this line of research shares is the technical reliance on the functor-categorical construction of Reynolds and Oles. The presentation therefore demands a rather high level of mathematical sophistication from the reader. In addition, the denotational model of IA it leads to is not fully abstract, which is, to some extent, unsatisfactory. In an operational model, this issue would not arise.

A more elementary account of the semantic properties of IA, profoundly inspired by its denotational model, is given by Pitts, using parametric operational techniques [8]. The mathematical apparatus of this model is elementary, yet the model is powerful enough to prove many non-trivial properties of IA. In this paper we further develop Pitts's model to deal with specification logic. This should make the interesting ideas used to prove the soundness of specification logic more accessible in the same way as Pitts's work made accessible the semantic properties of the programming language. To illustrate the usefulness of the model we prove two additional new axioms of specification logic. One of the axioms has been proposed before by O'Hearn [9], but without a soundness proof. The other axiom is interesting because it relates Hoare triples and equivalence.

Although IA is not a programming language used in practice, it has been an influential prototypical language. In fact it is not far from Haskell with state monadic extensions [10]. A better understanding of IA's specification logic should help with the design of a similar logic for Haskell.

Finally, using the operational model of specification logic we show that even the very restricted fragment of specification logic consisting of first-order recursion-free boolean Algol with first-order quantifiers and without term equivalence is not decidable. This is despite the fact that observational equivalence of IA terms of first [11] and second [12] order IA is decidable.

Contributions. We present a new model for the specification logic of IA, based on the operational semantics of the language. Compared to the previous models, based on the denotational semantics of IA, ours is mathematically elementary and it does not suffer from a lack of full-abstraction. Two new axioms are added to the logic, and the special nature of equivalence and negation is better explained. We conclude by giving an undecidability result about a restricted fragment of specification logic.

2 Operational Semantics of IA

In this section we briefly present Pitts's parametric operational model of IA [8].

IA is simply-typed lambda calculus over booleans, integers, variables, expressions and commands. Variables, storing integers, form the state while commands can change the state. In addition to abstraction ($\lambda x : \sigma . M$) and application (FA), other terms of the language are conditionals, uniformly applied to any

$$w \vdash s; R \Downarrow_\sigma s; R, \quad \text{where } R ::= tt \mid ff \mid v \mid n \mid \mathbf{skip} \mid \lambda x:\sigma.M$$

$$\frac{w \vdash s; B \Downarrow_{\mathbf{bool}} s'; b \qquad w \vdash s'; M_b \Downarrow_\sigma s''; R}{w \vdash s; (\mathbf{if}\ B\ \mathbf{then}\ M_{tt}\ \mathbf{else}\ M_{ff}) \Downarrow_\sigma s''; R}$$

$$\frac{w \vdash s; N_1 \Downarrow_{\mathbf{int}} s'; n_1 \qquad w \vdash s'; N_2 \Downarrow_{\mathbf{int}} s''; n_2}{w \vdash s; (N_1 * N_2) \Downarrow_{\mathbf{int}} s''; n}\ n = n_1 * n_2$$

$$\frac{w \vdash s; F \Downarrow_{\sigma \to \sigma'} s'; \lambda x:\sigma.M \qquad w \vdash s'; M[A/x] \Downarrow_{\sigma'} s''; R}{w \vdash s; FA \Downarrow_{\sigma'} s''; R}$$

$$\frac{w \vdash s; M[\mathbf{fix}\, x:\sigma.M/x] \Downarrow_\sigma s'; R}{w \vdash s; \mathbf{fix}\, x:\sigma.M \Downarrow_\sigma s'; R} \qquad \frac{w \vdash s; V \Downarrow_{\mathbf{var}} s'; v}{w \vdash s; !V \Downarrow_{\mathbf{int}} s'; n}\ s'(v) = n$$

$$\frac{w \vdash s; V \Downarrow_{\mathbf{var}} s'; v \qquad w \vdash s'; N \Downarrow_{\mathbf{int}} s''; n}{w \vdash s; V := N \Downarrow_{\mathbf{comm}} (s'' \mid v \mapsto n); \mathbf{skip}}$$

$$\frac{w \vdash s; C \Downarrow_{\mathbf{comm}} s'; \mathbf{skip} \qquad w \vdash s'; C' \Downarrow_{\mathbf{comm}} s''; \mathbf{skip}}{w \vdash s; (C; C') \Downarrow_{\mathbf{comm}} s''; \mathbf{skip}}$$

$$\frac{w \vdash s; N \Downarrow_{\mathbf{int}} s'; n \qquad wv \vdash s' \otimes (v \mapsto n); C[v/x] \Downarrow_{\mathbf{comm}} s'' \otimes (v \mapsto n'); \mathbf{skip}}{w \vdash s; (\mathbf{new}\, x := N\, \mathbf{in}\, C) \Downarrow_{\mathbf{comm}} s''; \mathbf{skip}}$$

Fig. 1. IA evaluation relation

type, (**if** B **then** M **else** N), fix-point recursion ($\mathbf{fix}\, x:\sigma.M$), constants (integers, booleans) and arithmetic-logic operators ($M * N$); we also have command-type terms which are the standard imperative operators: dereferencing (explicit in the syntax, $!V$), assignment ($V := N$), sequencing ($C; C'$), no-op (**skip**) and local variable block ($\mathbf{new}\, x := N\, \mathbf{in}\, C$).

Let Γ be a function from identifiers to types. We write $\Gamma \vdash M : \sigma$ to indicate that term M has type σ and (typed) free identifiers in Γ.

The terms for abstraction, fix-point and local-variable block are identifier binders; IA terms are identified up to α-conversion. For any term M we denote the set of free identifiers and their type assignment $fi(M)$. By $IA_\sigma(w) = \{M : \sigma \mid fi(M) = \emptyset \text{ and } gv(M) \subseteq w\}$, we denote the set of closed IA terms of type σ with global variables in the set w.

The operational semantics of IA is defined inductively on the syntax of terms by an evaluation relation of the form $w \vdash s; M \Downarrow_\sigma s'; R$.. We call the set of global variables w *the world*, with terms $M, R \in IA_\sigma(w)$ and states $s, s' \in States(w) = \{f \mid f : w \to \mathbb{N}\}$. The interpretation of the rules is the following: term M executed in state s evaluates to term R (called a *canonical form*) and changes the state to s'. The evaluation relation is defined in Fig. 1.

The following notations are used: wv denotes the set w with a new element v added; $s \otimes (v \mapsto n) \in States(wv)$ denotes the state properly extending s by mapping v to n; $(s \mid v \mapsto n)$ denotes the state mapping v to n and otherwise acting like s. This notation is generalized to $s \otimes s' \in States(ww')$, $w \cap w' = \emptyset$, in the obvious way.

The evaluation rules are more general than really necessary. It is straightforward to show that the evaluation of non-command terms does not change the state. Conversely, command terms can only evaluate to **skip**. Therefore, the evaluation relation can be abbreviated to $w \vdash s; M \Downarrow_\sigma R$ if $\sigma \neq \mathbf{comm}$ and to $w \vdash s; C \Downarrow s'$, if $C : \mathbf{comm}$. If $w \vdash s; M \Downarrow_\sigma s'; R$ does not hold for any R and s' we write $w \vdash s; M \Uparrow_\sigma$.

A context $\mathcal{C}[-_\sigma]$ is an IA term in which a sub-term of type σ is replaced by a "hole" $-_\sigma$. The term resulting from filling the hole with term $M : \sigma$ is denoted by $\mathcal{C}[M]$. We write $traps(\mathcal{C}[-_\sigma])$ for the set of bound identifiers the scope of which includes the hole of $\mathcal{C}[-_\sigma]$, and their type assignments.

Terms or contexts without free identifiers are called *closed.* A key distinction is being made between *global variables* and *free identifiers of type* **var**. A closed term may have zero, one or more global variables. This distinction is also logically important because *contraction* of free identifier preserves equivalence whereas that of global variables does not.

Definition 1 (Contextual equivalence). *If $M_i : \sigma$, with $fi(M_i) \subseteq \Gamma$ and $gv(M_i) \subseteq w$ for $i = 1, 2$, we write $w, \Gamma \vdash M_1 \cong_\sigma M_2$ to indicated that the terms are* contextually equivalent. *By definition, this means that for all worlds $w' \supseteq w$, all closed contexts $\mathcal{C}[-_\sigma] : \mathbf{comm}$ with $gv(\mathcal{C}[-_\sigma]) \subseteq w'$ and $\Gamma \subseteq traps(\mathcal{C}[-_\sigma])$, and all states $s, s' \in States(w')$ we have $w' \vdash \mathcal{C}[M_1]; s \Downarrow s'$ iff $w' \vdash \mathcal{C}[M_2]; s \Downarrow s'$.*

Two terms are contextually equivalent if their occurrences can be interchanged in any closed command without affecting the meaning of the command, as a partial function from states to states.

The quantification over contexts in the definition of contextual equivalence makes the definition unwieldy for the proof of program properties. A more usable form of equivalence is *extensional equivalence.*

Definition 2 (Extensional equivalence). *If $M_i \in IA_\sigma(w)$, $i = 1, 2$, we write $w \vdash M_1 \equiv_\sigma M_2$ to indicate that the terms are* extensionally equivalent, *which is defined inductively on the structure of σ as follows:*

1. *If $\sigma = \mathbf{bool}, \mathbf{int}$ then $w \vdash M_1 \equiv_\sigma M_2$ if $\forall s \in States(w)$ and all constants c, $w \vdash M_1; s \Downarrow_\sigma c$ iff $w \vdash M_2; s \Downarrow_\sigma c$;*
2. *$w \vdash M_1 \equiv_{\mathbf{comm}} M_2$ if $\forall s, s' \in States(w)$, $w \vdash M_1; s \Downarrow s'$ iff $w \vdash M_2; s \Downarrow s'$;*
3. *$w \vdash M_1 \equiv_{\mathbf{var}} M_2$ if $w \vdash M_1 := n \equiv_{\mathbf{comm}} M_2 := n$ for all $n \in \mathbb{N}$;*
4. *$w \vdash M_1 \equiv_{\sigma_1 \to \sigma_2} M_2$ if $\forall w' \supseteq w$ and $A \in IA_{\sigma_1}(w')$, $w' \vdash M_1 A \equiv_{\sigma_2} M_2 A$.*

Extensional equivalence is extended to open terms via closed instantiations.

For all $M_i : \sigma_i$ with $fi(M_i) \subseteq \Gamma = \{x_1 : \sigma_1, \ldots, x_n : \sigma_n\}$, $gv(M_i) \subseteq w$, $i = 1, 2$, we define $w, \Gamma \vdash M_1 \equiv_\sigma M_2$ as $w' \vdash M_1[\vec{A}/\vec{x}] \equiv_\sigma M_2[\vec{A}/\vec{x}]$ for all $w' \supseteq w$ and all $A_j \in IA_{\sigma_j}(w')$, $j = 1, \ldots, n$.

The key result of [8] is the following (OE):

Theorem 1 (Operational Extensionality). *IA contextual equivalence coincides with extensional equivalence: $w, \Gamma \vdash M_1 \cong_\sigma M_2$ iff $w, \Gamma \vdash M_1 \equiv_\sigma M_2$.*

The proof technique used in [8] is perhaps as interesting as the result itself, involving an operational version of parametric logical relations for IA.

A useful ancillary property of IA proved in the same paper, and useful in proving the monotonicity of identity is Weakening and Strengthening (WS).

Lemma 1 (Weakening and Strengthening).
Suppose $w = w_1 w_2$, $s_i \in States(w_i)$, $i = 1, 2$. *Given* $M \in IA_\sigma(w_1)$, *then* $w \vdash s_1 \otimes s_2; M \Downarrow_\sigma s'; R$ *if and only if* $R \in IA_\sigma(w_1)$ *and* $s' = s_1' \otimes s_2$ *for some* $s_1' \in States(w_1)$ *with* $w \vdash s_1; M \Downarrow_\sigma s_1'; R$.

2.1 Identity Logic of IA

One important direct consequence of the OE Theorem, pointed out by Pitts, is that it allows one to establish familiar functional extensionality properties such as: $F \cong_{\sigma\to\sigma'} F'$ iff $\forall A\!:\!\sigma.\, FA \cong_{\sigma'} F'A$.

Extensionality is not an universal property of programming languages. In call-by-value languages with more complex computational features such as references or exceptions, such as Scheme or ML, this property fails. IA, which is a conservative extension of PCF [13], inherits extensionality as a generalised version of Milner's Context Lemma [14] for PCF.

We take this point further and we notice that the definitions of extensional equivalence for functions and open terms is strongly suggestive of the interpretation of the universal quantifier in an intuitionistic logic, with a Kripke structure of worlds w and domains $IA_\sigma(w)$, cf. [15, Chap. 5].

Let us define the (intuitionistic) identity logic of IA as its many-sorted predicate logic with identity.

Definition 3 (Identity logic). *The set of formulas* Φ *of the logic consists of:*

1. ***equality***: *if* $\Gamma \vdash M_i : \sigma$, $i = 1, 2$, *then* $\Gamma \vdash M_1 \doteq M_2 \in \Phi$;
2. ***connectives***: *if* $\Gamma \vdash \phi_i \in \Phi$, $i = 1, 2$, *then* $\Gamma \vdash \phi_1 \Box \phi_2 \in \Phi$, *where* $\Box \in \{\wedge, \vee, \rightarrow\}$;
3. ***quantifiers***: *if* $\Gamma, x\!:\!\sigma \vdash \phi \in \Phi$, *then* $\Gamma \vdash \forall x\!:\!\sigma.\phi \in \Phi$, $\Gamma \vdash \exists x\!:\!\sigma.\phi \in \Phi$.

We use the symbol $\doteq$ to signify equality *in the logic* (as opposed to in the meta-language or in IA). If no confusion is possible in context we may use just $=$ instead.

A formula with an empty environment is called *closed.*

The identity logic of IA has a standard Kripke-style semantics.

Definition 4 (Kripke model). *For any world* w *and closed formula* ϕ *we define* $w \Vdash \phi$, *read "*w *forces* ϕ,*" inductively on the structure of* ϕ:

1. $w \Vdash \phi_1 \vee \phi_2$ *if* $w \Vdash \phi_1$ *or* $w \Vdash \phi_2$;
2. $w \Vdash \phi_1 \wedge \phi_2$ *if* $w \Vdash \phi_1$ *and* $w \Vdash \phi_2$;
3. $w \Vdash \phi_1 \rightarrow \phi_2$ *if for all* $w' \supseteq w$, *if* $w' \Vdash \phi_1$ *then* $w' \Vdash \phi_2$;
4. $w \Vdash \forall x\!:\!\sigma.\,\phi$ *if for all* $w' \supseteq w$ *and for all* $A \in IA_\sigma(w')$, $w' \Vdash \phi[A/x]$;
5. $w \Vdash \exists x\!:\!\sigma.\,\phi$ *if there is* $A \in IA_\sigma(w)$ *such that* $w \Vdash \phi[A/x]$;
6. $w \Vdash M_1 \doteq M_2$ *if* $w \vdash M_1 \cong_\sigma M_2$.

Theorem 2 (Soundness). *If* ϕ *is a formula of the identity logic of IA derivable using the (standard) axioms of intuitionistic logic and identity then* $\Vdash \phi$.

3 Specification Logic

The logic of the previous section can be augmented with two more predicate symbols, Hoare triples and non-interference:

Definition 5 (Specification logic of IA). *The set of formulas Σ (specifications) of the logic consists of:*

1. ***equality:*** *if $\Gamma \vdash M_i : \sigma$, $i = 1, 2$, then $\Gamma \vdash M_1 \doteq M_2 \in \Sigma$;*
2. ***Hoare triple:*** *if $\Gamma \vdash P : \mathbf{assert}$, $\Gamma \vdash Q : \mathbf{assert}$ and $\Gamma \vdash C : \mathbf{comm}$, then $\Gamma \vdash \{P\}\ C\ \{Q\} \in \Sigma$;*
3. ***non-interference:*** *if $\Gamma \vdash P : \sigma$, $\Gamma \vdash Q : \sigma'$ then $\Gamma \vdash P \# Q \in \Sigma$;*
4. ***connectives:*** *if $\Gamma \vdash \phi_i \in \Sigma$, $i = 1, 2$, then $\Gamma \vdash \phi_1 \Box \phi_2 \in \Sigma$, where $\Box \in \{\wedge, \vee, \rightarrow\}$;*
5. ***quantifiers:*** *if $\Gamma, x : \sigma \vdash \phi \in \Sigma$, then $\Gamma \vdash \forall x : \sigma.\phi \in \Sigma$, $\Gamma \vdash \exists x : \sigma.\phi \in \Sigma$.*

The *pre-condition* P and *post-condition* Q of a Hoare triple belong to a special type, called *assertions.* The language of assertions is the language of boolean phrases augmented with universal and existential quantifiers. To keep the current presentation focused we only consider a reduced assertion language which consists of finitary boolean phrases (constructed without the fix-point operator). The introduction of assertion quantifiers or non-termination raises some technical complications, surveyed in [16]. It is common to use $\{R\}$ for $\{R\}$ **skip** $\{$**true**$\}$.

The axioms of specification logic are for the most part those of Hoare logic, with several new axioms to handle procedures and interfering side-effects [1].

A straightforward interpretation of the new predicate symbols is enough to show the soundness of much of Reynolds's original, universal, specification logic [1]:

1. $w \Vdash \{P\}\ C\ \{Q\}$ if $\forall s, s' \in \mathit{States}(w)$, $w \vdash s; P \Downarrow_{\mathbf{assert}} \mathit{tt}$ and $w \vdash s; C \Downarrow s'$ implies $w \vdash s'; Q \Downarrow_{\mathbf{assert}} \mathit{tt}$
2. $w \Vdash M \# N$ if $\forall s_0, s_1, s_2 \in \mathit{States}(w)$, and canonical forms R, R', if $w \vdash s_0; M \Downarrow_{\sigma'} s_1; R$ and $w \vdash s_0; N \Downarrow_\sigma s_2; R'$ then there is a state $s_3 \in \mathit{States}(w)$ such that $w \vdash s_1; N \Downarrow_\sigma s_3; R'$

To wit, if N evaluates to R' *before* the execution of M, then *after* its execution it also evaluates to R', although the state might have changed. For example, if i, j are distinct global variables then $i := 0 \# !j + 2$.

The stateful specification logic requires a more sophisticated approach. The reason we want to make specifications stateful is to "factor out" assumptions about the state in judgements of the form $\{R\} \rightarrow \{P\}\ C\ \{Q\}$, to be interpreted as "specification $\{P\}\ C\ \{Q\}$ is true in all states in which assertion R is true." Reynolds shows several examples where this is useful. The role of the world must be now played by a set of states, which we shall call W.

The new accessibility relation on worlds $\precsim$ reflects the fact that worlds, as sets of states, can change in two ways: they can expand through the introduction of new variables or they must "shrink" because of implication.

$$W \vdash s; R \Downarrow_\sigma s; R, \text{ where } R ::= tt \mid ff \mid v \mid n \mid \mathbf{skip} \mid \lambda x : \sigma . M$$

$$\frac{W \vdash s; B \Downarrow_{\mathbf{bool}} s'; b \qquad W \vdash s'; M_b \Downarrow_\sigma s''; R}{W \vdash s; \mathbf{if}\ B\ \mathbf{then}\ M_{tt}\ \mathbf{else}\ M_{ff} \Downarrow_\sigma s''; R}$$

$$\frac{W \vdash s; N_1 \Downarrow_{\mathbf{int}} s'; n_1 \qquad W \vdash s'; N_2 \Downarrow_{\mathbf{int}} s''; n_2}{W \vdash s; N_1 * N_2 \Downarrow_{\mathbf{int}} s''; n} \; n = n_1 * n_2$$

$$\frac{W \vdash s; F \Downarrow_{\sigma \to \sigma'} s'; \lambda x : \sigma . M \qquad W \vdash s'; M[A/x] \Downarrow_{\sigma'} s''; R}{W \vdash s; FA \Downarrow_{\sigma'} s''; R}$$

$$\frac{W \vdash s; M[\mathbf{fix}\, x : \sigma . M / x] \Downarrow_\sigma s'; R}{W \vdash s; \mathbf{fix}\, x : \sigma . M \Downarrow_\sigma s'; R} \qquad \frac{W \vdash s; V \Downarrow_{\mathbf{var}} s'; v}{W \vdash s; !V \Downarrow_{\mathbf{int}} s'; n} \; s'(v) = n$$

$$\frac{W \vdash s; V \Downarrow_{\mathbf{var}} s'; v \qquad W \vdash s'; N \Downarrow_{\mathbf{int}} s''; n}{W \vdash s; V := N \Downarrow_{\mathbf{comm}} (s'' \mid v \mapsto n); \mathbf{skip}} \; (s'' \mid v \mapsto n) \in W$$

$$\frac{W \vdash s; N \Downarrow_{\mathbf{int}} s'; n \qquad W \times States(v) \vdash s' \otimes (v \mapsto n); C[v/x] \Downarrow_{\mathbf{comm}} s'' \otimes (v \mapsto n'); \mathbf{skip}}{W \vdash s; (\mathbf{new}\, x := N\, \mathbf{in}\, C) \Downarrow_{\mathbf{comm}} s''; \mathbf{skip}}$$

Fig. 2. IA confined evaluation relation

Definition 6 (World accessibility). *We define the relation $W_1 \precsim W_2$, for $W_i \subseteq States(w_i)$, as the transitive and reflexive closure of $W_1 \precsim W_2$ if $W_2 = W_1 \times States(w_2 \setminus w_1)$ and $W_1 \precsim W_2$ if $W_2 \subseteq W_1$.*

It is straightforward to show that $\precsim$ is a partial order on sets of states.

The interpretation of the logical connectives is now given by:

Definition 7 (Stateful Kripke semantics).

1. *$W \Vdash \phi_1 \wedge \phi_2$ if $W \Vdash \phi_1$ and $W \Vdash \phi_2$*
2. *$W \Vdash \phi_1 \vee \phi_2$ if $W \Vdash \phi_1$ or $W \Vdash \phi_2$*
3. *$W \Vdash \phi_1 \to \phi_2$ if for all $W' \succsim W$, $W' \Vdash \phi_1$ implies $W' \Vdash \phi_2$*
4. *$W \Vdash \forall x : \sigma . \phi$ if for all $W' \succsim W$, $W' \in States(ww')$, for all $A \in IA_\sigma(ww')$, $W' \Vdash \phi[A/x]$,*
5. *$W \Vdash \exists x : \sigma . \phi$ if there is $A \in IA_\sigma(\mathrm{dom}\, W)$, such that $W \Vdash \phi[A/x]$.*

The straightforward interpretation of the Hoare triple is no longer satisfactory in this context, because the axiom of command composition is no longer sound. We need to apply Tennent's key idea that execution of commands must be restricted to the current world, not only in terms of its final state but also in terms of all the intermediary states that are visited [3].

We do this by introducing a more refined evaluation relation for IA, which we shall call *confined execution* and denote by $W \vdash s; M \Downarrow_\sigma s'; R$.

This relation is defined just like the normal evaluation (Fig. 1) with the exception of assignment and local variable definition. The relation is defined, inductively on the syntax of IA, in Fig. 2.

The only way a command can stray outside the current world is through assignment, but such an assignment is prevented by confined execution. If an illegal assignment is attempted the command cannot be executed. The world of a local variable block is expanded by all possible states involving the newly allocated variable.

Confined evaluation can be notationally simplified, similarly to standard evaluation, considering that only commands can change the state. We adapt the old notation in the straightforward way.

The interpretation of the Hoare-triple predicate is:

Definition 8 (Stateful Hoare-triple semantics). *$W \Vdash \{P\}\ C\ \{Q\}$ if and only if for all $s, s' \in W$, $W \vdash s; P \Downarrow_{\mathbf{assert}} tt$ and $W \vdash s; C \Downarrow s'$ implies $W \vdash s'; Q \Downarrow_{\mathbf{assert}} tt$.*

Using confined evaluation we can define stronger notions of contextual and extensional equivalence in the obvious way. Using exactly the same proof method as Pitts we can show that confined equivalence is also extensional.

Theorem 3 (Confined Oper. Extensionality). *IA confined contextual equivalence coincides with confined extensional equivalence: $W, \Gamma \vdash M_1 \cong_\sigma M_2$ iff $W, \Gamma \vdash M_1 \equiv_\sigma M_2$.*

It is easy to show, by induction on derivation of evaluation, that confined evaluation also satisfies a WS Lemma.

Lemma 2 (Conf. Weakening–Strengthening.). *Suppose that $w = w_1 w_2$, $W_i \subseteq States(w_i)$, and $s_i \in W_i$, $i = 1, 2$. Given $M \in IA_\sigma(w_1)$, then it follows that $W_1 \times W_2 \vdash s_1 \otimes s_2; M \Downarrow_\sigma s_1' \otimes s_2; R$ iff $R \in IA_\sigma(w_1)$ and $s_1' \in W_1$ with $W_1 \vdash s_1; M \Downarrow_\sigma s_1'; R$.*

Confined evaluation is a conservative extension of IA evaluation, and confined equivalence is strictly stronger than contextual equivalence, which corresponds to equivalence 'confined' to the set of all states.

We give the following interpretation for identity:

Definition 9 (Hyperfine identity semantics). *$W \Vdash M_1 \doteq M_2$ if and only if for all $W' \succsim W$, $W' \vdash M_1 \cong_\sigma M_2$.*

We call this new notion of equivalence *hyperfine* because, as we shall see, it is significantly stricter than observational equivalence.

3.1 Non-interference

Finally, we have come to the interpretation of the non-interference predicate, $M \# N$. As in the previous section, our approach is heavily influenced by concepts first introduced in the denotational setting.

Intuitively, non-interference is interpreted as follows. The term on the right-hand-side, typically an expression, is used to partition the world into smaller worlds in which the term evaluates to the same result. Then, we require any evaluation of the term on the left-hand-side to be confined to any set of equivalence classes. In other words, any execution of M must not change the possible values of N *even temporarily*.

Definition 10 (State equivalence). *We call* state-equivalence *any IA term-indexed family of equivalence relations* $[M]_W \subseteq W^2$, $W \subseteq States(w)$, *with the property that:*

1. *if* $\sigma = \mathbf{int}$ *(or* $\mathbf{bool}$*) then* $s_1\,[E]_W\,s_2$ *if and only if for all* $n \in \mathbb{N}$ *(or* $\{tt, ff\}$*)* $W \vdash s_1; E \Downarrow_\sigma n$ *iff* $W \vdash s_2; E \Downarrow_\sigma n$*;*
2. *if* $\sigma = \mathbf{var}$ *then* $s_1\,[V]_W\,s_2$ *if and only if* $s_1\,[!V]_W\,s_2$*;*
3. *if* $\sigma = \mathbf{comm}$ *then* $s_1\,[C]_W\,s_2$ *if and only if* $W \vdash s_1; C \Downarrow$ *iff* $W \vdash s_2; C \Downarrow$*;*
4. *if* $\sigma = \sigma_1 \to \sigma_2$ *then* $s_1\,[F]_W\,s_2$ *implies for all* w', $A \in IA_{\sigma_1}(ww')$ *and states* $s' \in States(w')$ *such that* $s_1 \otimes s'\,[A]_{W \times States(w')}\,s_2 \otimes s'$ *we have*

$$s_1 \otimes s'\,[FA]_{W \times States(w')}\,s_2 \otimes s'.$$

Proposition 1 (Existence & Admissibility).

1. *The family* $[M]_W \subseteq W^2$ *is non-empty.*
2. *State equivalence is preserved by confined equivalence: for all* $s_1, s_2 \in W$, $s_1\,[M]_W\,s_2$ *and* $W \vdash M \equiv M'$ *implies* $s_1\,[M']_W\,s_2$.
3. *There exists a state equivalence* $[M]^{\sim}_W \subseteq W^2$, *which we shall call an* admissible *state equivalence, such that whenever* $M_0 \in IA(\emptyset)$, $[M_0]^{\sim}_W = W^2$.

Proof. At ground types **exp** and **comm**, M_0 is a constant so the definition of state equivalence gives W^2. For **var** there is no constant in $IA(\emptyset)$ so the definition is vacuous. At function types we can construct an admissible relation $[-]^{\sim}$ from any state equivalence $[-]$ as follows: if $M \in IA(\emptyset)$ then for all $s_1, s_2 \in$, $s_1\,[M]^{\sim}_W\,s_2$; otherwise $s_1\,[M]^{\sim}_W\,s_2$ iff $s_1\,[M]_W\,s_2$. Using the fact that state equivalence is preserved by confined extensional equivalence we can show by induction on the type of M that $[-]^{\sim}$ does satisfy the definition of a state equivalence. □

In the following we will only be concerned with admissible state equivalences. Any such relation has the properties required to show the soundness of the non-interference logic. The definition above provides a sufficient framework for the operational model.

By $W/[N]$ we shall denote the set of equivalence classes of W under some admissible state equivalence $[N]_W$, which Prop. 1 established that exists. By $\mathbb{P}(W/[N])$ we shall denote the set of unions of equivalence classes under $[N]_W$.

The interpretation of the non-interference predicate $M \# N$ is also inductive, on the structure of M's type. The definition of higher-order non-interference is subtle. Reynolds initially defined it extensionally, but Tennent has shown that this definition is incompatible with a desirable axiom concerning non-interference decomposition [3]. A model proving the soundness of this axiom was given in [6].

An important technical role is played by the property of *confined termination*, which is a generalisation of the usual notion of termination to confined evaluation.

Definition 11 (Confined termination). $M \in IA(w)$ *is said to* confinedly terminate, *denoted by* $W \vdash M \Downarrow_\sigma$ *if*

1. $\sigma = \mathbf{comm}, \mathbf{int}, \mathbf{bool}$: *for all* $s \in W$, *there exists* $s' \in W$ *and canonical form* R *such that* $W \vdash s; M \Downarrow_\sigma s'; R$
2. $\sigma = \mathbf{var}$: *for all* $n \in \mathbb{N}$, $W \vdash M := n \Downarrow_{\mathbf{comm}}$
3. $\sigma = \sigma_1 \to \sigma_2$ *and for all* w' *and* $M' \in IA_{\sigma_1}(ww')$, *if* $W \times States(w') \vdash M' \Downarrow_{\sigma_1}$ *then* $W \times States(w') \vdash MM' \Downarrow_{\sigma_2}$.

We can now define higher-order non-interference.

Definition 12 (Non-interference). *If* $F \in IA_\sigma(w)$, *then* $W \Vdash F \# M$ *if and only if,* $W \vdash F \Downarrow_\sigma$ *implies that for all* $W_0 \in \mathbb{P}(W/[M])$, *we have that* $W_0 \vdash F \Downarrow_\sigma$.

Restricting the current world to any smaller world which is a union of equivalence classes $W/[M]$, should not change the confined termination status of F.

The knowing reader might notice that the operational definition of non-interference is not exactly an operational reproduction of the denotational interpretation. Whereas in the denotational model non-interference was interpreted as invariance under the application of an appropriately defined restriction (endo)morphism *at the same world*, in the operational model we allow a change of world but we interpret non-interference as the invariance of the confined termination property. The difference is purely of technical presentation: worlds W and W_0 are over the same set of locations w, and the meaning of F in the two worlds, if defined, is actually the same.

We can see how this definition works by examining the typical example of a non-interference specification which is validated by the Reynolds model but, correctly, invalidated by the Tennent-O'Hearn model:

$$\lambda c\!:\!\mathbf{comm}.\,\mathbf{if}\,!i = 1\,\mathbf{then}\,(c; \mathbf{if}\,!i > 1\,\mathbf{then}\, i := 0) \# i.$$

Let us call the λ-term above F. Consider $M \stackrel{\text{def}}{=} \mathbf{if}\,!i > 0\,\mathbf{then}\, i := !i + 1$. If we take $W_0 = \{(i \mapsto n) \mid n > 0\}$, which is indeed a union of equivalences classes of $W/[i]$: $\bigcup_{k>0}\{(i \mapsto k)\}$, it can be easily seen that $W_0 \vdash M \Downarrow_{\mathbf{comm}}$ but it is not the case that $W_0 \vdash FM \Downarrow_{\mathbf{comm}}$, since for $s = (i \mapsto 1)$, FM cannot be confinedly evaluated.

Theorem 4 (Soundness). *The specification logic of IA is sound.*

3.2 Proof of the Soundness Theorem

The key property that our modeling framework must satisfy is monotonicity.

Lemma 3 (Monotonicity of Non-interference). *If* $W \Vdash F \# M$ *then* $W' \Vdash F \# M$, *for all* $W' \succsim W$.

For the logical connectives and quantifiers we have a standard Kripke semantics. Using the Confined OE Theorem we can also show that the interpretation of identity satisfies the standard axioms.

For the identity, "hyperfine," semantics is truly required. Contextually equivalent IA phrases are not necessarily equivalent in non-interference contexts. Consider for example the simple case $x \vdash x := 0; x := 1 \equiv_{\mathbf{comm}} x := 1$. Although contextually equivalent, when confined to world $(x \mapsto 1)$ the LHS diverges but the

RHS does not, so they are not logically identical. The logical contexts in the presence of non-interference specification are highly intensional.

The Hoare-like axioms are proved in a standard way, and we have already showed the interesting bit regarding command composition for stateful specifications.

In the following we show the soundness of the most interesting axioms of Specification Logic.

Strong constancy. The proof for the constancy axiom:

$$\forall c\!:\!\mathbf{comm}.\forall pqr\!:\!\mathbf{assert}.\ c\,\#\,r\wedge(\{r\}\rightarrow\{p\}\ c\ \{q\})\rightarrow\{p\ \mathbf{and}\ r\}\ c\ \{q\ \mathbf{and}\ r\},$$

is straightforward. The non-interference condition ensures that command c does not satisfy $\{p\}\ c\ \{q\}$ trivially, by (even temporarily) breaking assertion $\{r\}$ and causing a (confined) divergence.

Left-side non-interference decomposition. We give a slightly different version of this axiom, which is equivalent with the traditional one but easier to deal with:

1. if $C\in IA_\sigma(\emptyset)$ then $\forall e\!:\!\sigma'.\,C\,\#\,e$;
2. $\forall f\!:\!\sigma\!\to\!\sigma'.\forall c\!:\!\sigma.\forall e\!:\!\sigma''.\,f\,\#\,e\wedge c\,\#\,e\rightarrow f(c)\,\#\,e$.

Closed terms without global variables cannot cause interference. Also, non-interference is compositional to the left.

For the first item, we need to prove that $W\Vdash C\,\#\,E$ for all $E\in IA_{\sigma'}(w)$. Using the WS Lemma we can show that for any $W_0\subseteq W$, $W_0\vdash C\Downarrow_\sigma$ if and only if $\mathit{States}(\emptyset)\vdash C\Downarrow_\sigma$, because C is a closed term.

The second item reduces, using the semantics of the universal quantifier at any arbitrary world W, to $W\Vdash F\,\#\,E$, $C\,\#\,E$ implies $W\Vdash FC\,\#\,E$, which follows directly from the definition of confined termination at function types.

Right-side non-interference decomposition. Again, we give a different but equivalent formulation for the axioms:

1. if $E\in IA_\sigma(\emptyset)$ then $\forall c\!:\!\sigma'.\,c\,\#\,E$;
2. $\forall f\!:\!\sigma\rightarrow\sigma'.\forall e\!:\!\sigma.\forall c\!:\!\sigma''.\,c\,\#\,f\wedge c\,\#\,e\rightarrow c\,\#\,f(e)$.

A closed term without global variables cannot be interfered with. Non-interference is also compositional to the right.

For the first item we can show using induction on the structure of σ and the WS Lemma that for any two states $s,s'\in W$, $s[E]_W s'$, i.e., the state-set is 'partitioned' in just one large partition. This follows from the admissibility property in Prop. 1.

For the second item first notice that $s[E]_W s'$, and $s[F]_W s'$ implies $s[F(E)]_W s'$, from the definition of state equivalence. To wit, the partitions generated by $F(E)$ include the partitions formed by F and E. It can be easily shown that $W/[F(E)] \in \mathbb{P}(W/[F\&E])$ where we define $s_1[F\&E]s_2$ as $s_1[F]s_2$ and $s_1[E]s_2$; therefore we can apply the hypothesis.

Note the technical importance that in the definition of non-interference the restricted world is a *collection* of equivalence classes rather than an equivalence class, since it is *not* the case in general that $W/[F(E)] \subseteq W/[F] \cap W/[E]$.

Local variable. Let M_i be arbitrary IA terms. The local variable axiom scheme is used to discard any good-variable and non-interference assumptions involving the local variable:

$$(\forall x : \mathbf{var}.\forall n : \mathbf{int}.\ \mathbf{good}(x) \wedge \cdots x \,\#\, M_i \cdots \wedge \cdots M_j \,\#\, x \cdots \\ \rightarrow \{P\}\ x := n; C\ \{Q\}) \rightarrow \{P\}\ \mathbf{new}\, x := n \,\mathbf{in}\, C\ \{Q\},$$

with $x \notin \mathit{fi}(E_i, C_j, P, Q)$, where the good variable predicate **good** is defined as:

$$\mathbf{good}(x) \stackrel{\text{def}}{=} \forall p : \mathbf{int} \rightarrow \mathbf{assert}.\forall e : \mathbf{int}.x \,\#\, p \rightarrow \{p(e)\}\ x := e\ \{p(!x)\}.$$

We first show that for any global variable v and world W, $W \Vdash \mathbf{good}(v)$. For any P, we can show that $v \notin gv(P)$ implies $W \vdash v \,\#\, P$. Then we apply the WS Lemma and the OE Theorem to show that $P(E)$ and $P(!v)$ evaluate the same value.

The second part is to show that local variable v cannot interfere or be interfered with. This also follows directly from the WS Lemma, since v does not occur in any other phrases other than the block of the command, $C[v/x]$.

3.3 Two New Axioms

In this section we show two new axioms of specification logic two be valid; they cannot be validated using the denotational model. The first one involves an existential quantifier and, therefore, one of the directions requires definability in the denotational model. The second involves equivalence and one of the directions would require the denotational model to be fully abstract. Since we work at an operational level, neither definability nor full abstraction are an issue for us.

Hoare-triple decomposition. If the programming language is finitary (only a finite set of integers can be stored in memory locations) then:

$$\forall pq : \mathbf{assert}.\forall c_1 c_2 : \mathbf{comm}.\ \{p\}\ c_1; c_2\ \{q\} \leftrightarrow \exists r : \mathbf{assert}.\ \{p\}\ c_1\ \{r\} \wedge \{r\}\ c_2\ \{q\},$$

It was suggested in [9], as a stronger tool necessary for the proof of IA equivalences.

Proof. (Soundness) The right-to-left direction is trivial and is simply the Hoare axiom for sequential composition.

The left-to-right direction requires us to prove that for all worlds $W \in States(w)$, if $W \Vdash \{P\}\ C_1; C_2\ \{Q\}$ holds, then $W \Vdash \exists r : \mathbf{assert}. \{P\}\ C_1\ \{r\} \wedge \{r\}\ C_2\ \{Q\}$ must hold, with $P, Q \in IA_{\mathbf{assert}}(w)$, $C_1, C_2 \in IA_{\mathbf{comm}}(w)$.

If the language is finitary, then W is finite. If $W \Vdash C_1; C_2, s \Downarrow s'$ then there must exist s'' such that $W \Vdash C_1, s \Downarrow s''$ and $W \Vdash C_2, s'' \Downarrow s'$. Let us denote the set of all such s'' by W'', which is also finite.

Let $R = \bigvee_{s \in W''} \bigwedge_{v \in w} !v = s(v)$. It follows that $R \in IA_{\mathbf{assert}}(w)$ and $W \Vdash \{P\}\ C_1; C_2\ \{Q\}$ implies $W \Vdash \{P\}\ C_1\ \{R\} \wedge \{R\}\ C_2\ \{Q\}$. □

Remark 1. Hoare-triple decomposition only holds for the finitary fragment of the language because the assertion language is finitary, i.e. it lacks recursion. If the assertion language is not finitary then we can prove this axiom using a weakest-precondition style argument, but a fix-point constructor is required in the assertion language. However, as we mentioned, the introduction of fix-point (and consequently divergence) into the assertion language complicates the properties of the logic.

Hoare-triple and equivalence

$$\forall c_1, c_2 : \mathbf{comm}. \big(\forall pq : \mathbf{assert}. \{p\}\ c\ \{q\} \leftrightarrow \{p\}\ c_2\ \{q\}\big) \leftrightarrow c_1 = c_2.$$

Proof. (Soundness) The right-to-left implication is trivial. The left-to-right is proved by contradiction. Assume that there is world W, and $C_1, C_2 \in IA_{\mathbf{comm}}(w)$ such that $W \not\Vdash C_1 = C_2$. We consider two cases:

1. There exists $s \in W$, $W \in States(w)$, such that $W \Vdash C_i, s \Downarrow$ and $W \Vdash C_{2-i}, s \Uparrow$, $i = 0, 1$. Then we take $P = \mathbf{true}$ and $Q = \mathbf{false}$.
2. There exists $s, s_1 \neq s_2 \in W$ such that $W \Vdash C_1, s \Downarrow s_1$ and $W \Vdash C_2, s \Downarrow s_2$. Then we take $P = \bigwedge_{v \in w} !v = s(v)$ and $Q = \bigwedge_{v \in w} !v = s_1(v)$. □

3.4 Computability Issues

The identity logic of full IA is undecidable, as the language is Turing-complete. What may come as a surprise is that even if we restrict IA to its boolean, first-order, recursion-free, subset, which is decidable [11], the congruence-free specification logic is still undecidable.

Theorem 5 (Undecidability of Spec. Logic). *The specification logic of recursion-free, first-order boolean IA without term equality is undecidable.*

Proof. We show that there exists a faithful encoding $\ulcorner - \urcorner : \mathbb{N}[X] \to IA$ of polynomials with integer coefficients into IA: $\ulcorner 0 \urcorner = \lambda c : \mathbf{comm}.\mathbf{skip}$, $\ulcorner n+1 \urcorner = \lambda c : \mathbf{comm}. \ulcorner n \urcorner(c); c, = \lambda c : \mathbf{comm}. c^{n+1}$, $\ulcorner X_i \urcorner = x_i : \mathbf{comm} \to \mathbf{comm}$, $\ulcorner P_1 + P_2 \urcorner = \lambda c : \mathbf{comm}. \ulcorner P_1 \urcorner(c); \ulcorner P_2 \urcorner(c)$, $\ulcorner P_1 \times P_2 \urcorner = \lambda c : \mathbf{comm}. \ulcorner P_1 \urcorner(\ulcorner P_2 \urcorner(c))$. Hilbert's tenth problem can be formulated in the intuitionistic identity logic of first-order, recursion-free, boolean IA as follows:

$$\exists x_1 : \mathbf{comm} \to \mathbf{comm} \cdots \exists x_n : \mathbf{comm} \to \mathbf{comm}. \ulcorner P_1 \urcorner = \ulcorner P_2 \urcorner, \tag{1}$$

$P_1, P_2 \in \mathbb{N}[X]$. Hilbert's Tenth Problem, is undecidable (see [17] for a comprehensive survey). Then, using the *Hoare triple and equivalence* axiom, validated earlier, we can formulate (1) using Hoare triples instead of term equality. □

4 Concluding Remarks

The remarkable achievement the Tennent-O'Hearn denotational model of specification logic was to give a compositional semantics for the highly intensional non-interference predicate. In an operational setting this task is substantially easier. The challenge, in the operational settings, is to provide a good semantics for the underlying Kripke structure of the logic. Properties, such as monotonicity, which come "for free" in the denotational setting need more elaborate proofs here. The semantics of quantifiers and the closely related properties of substitution are also more difficult to handle using operational methods.

At the heart of the successful operational treatment of specification logic is Pitts's result that contextual equivalence in IA coincides with extensional equivalence. In a language without this property, such as ML, this treatment cannot be reproduced. Consider for example the work of Honsell, Mason, Talcott and others [18,19], which represents the best attempt to create a specification logic for a call-by-value language with assignment. The logic is not technically a first-order logic; the logical properties of quantifiers, i.e. substitution, are not the expected ones. The logic requires sophisticated syntactic side-conditions in the quantifier axioms to ensure correctness, because contextual equivalence in that language holds only in certain circumstances, detailed in the so-called *ciu* ("closed instantiation of uses") Lemma.

The question of whether the definition of specification logic presented here is in some sense definitive remains open. The essential concept of non-interference has a definition which is deeply inspired by the denotational treatment. But, arguably, our semantics of the identity and existential quantifiers is better, since the issues of definability and full abstraction do not arise. The two new axioms of Sec. 3.3 illustrate this advantage. Perhaps a more profound question to ask is whether non-interference logic is the definitive specification logic for procedural languages.

Finally, another important point of this paper is that it shows a connection between the operational extensionality property of a programming language and the fact that it has an elegant and general specification logic. This confirms Reynolds's language design intuition that *call-by-name* and *local effects* are the quintessential features if a specification and verification-friendly programming language is desired.

Acknowledgements. Andrzej Murawski helped me simplify Section 3.4; Bob Tennent and Peter O'Hearn patiently answered my numerous (and often silly) questions about the functor-category model; Andy Pitts has pointed out several errors in an earlier draft of this work. I thank all of them for the help.

References

1. Reynolds, J.C.: The Craft of Programming. Prentice-Hall Intl., London (1981)
2. Reynolds, J.C.: IDEALIZED ALGOL and its specification logic. In Néel, D., ed.: Tools and Notions for Program Construction, Nice, France, Cambridge University Press, Cambridge, 1982 (1981) 121–161. Also [7, Chap. 6].
3. Tennent, R.D.: Semantical analysis of specification logic. Information and Computation **85** (1990) 135–162. Also [7, Chap. 13].
4. Reynolds, J.C.: The essence of ALGOL. In de Bakker, J.W., van Vliet, J.C., eds.: Algorithmic Languages, Proceedings of the International Symposium on Algorithmic Languages, Amsterdam (1981) 345–372. Also [7, Chap. 3].
5. Oles, F.J.: Functor categories and store shapes. [7, Chap. 11] 3–12
6. O'Hearn, P.W., Tennent, R.D.: Semantical analysis of specification logic, 2. Information and Computation **107** (1993) 25–57. Also [7, Chap. 19].
7. O'Hearn, P.W., Tennent, R.D., eds.: ALGOL-like Languages. Progress in Theoretical Computer Science. Birkhäuser, Boston (1997) Two volumes.
8. Pitts, A.M.: Reasoning about local variables with operationally-based logical relations. In: Proceedings of LICS 11, Washington (1996) 152–163. Also [7, Chap. 17].
9. O'Hearn, P.W.: The Semantics of Non-Interference: A Natural Approach. Ph.D. thesis, Queen's University, Kingston, Canada (1990)
10. Launchbury, J., Peyton Jones, S.: State in Haskell. Lisp and Symbolic Computation **8** (1995) 293–341
11. Ghica, D.R., McCusker, G.: Reasoning about Idealized ALGOL using regular languages. In: ICALP 27. Volume 1853 of LNCS., Springer-Verlag (2000) 103–116
12. Ong, C.H.L.: Observational equivalence of third-order Idealized Algol is decidable. In: Proceedings of LICS 17, Copenhagen (2002) 22–25
13. O'Hearn, P.W.: Note on ALGOL and conservatively extending functional programming. J. of Functional Programming **6** (1995) 171–180. Also [7, Chap. 4].
14. Milner, R.: Fully abstract models of typed λ-calculi. Theoretical Computer Science **4** (1977) 1–22
15. van Dalen, D.: Logic and Structure. Third edn. Springer, Berlin (1994)
16. Bencivenga, E.: Free logics. In Gabbay, D., Guenthner, F., eds.: Handbook of Philosophical Logic, vol. III: Alternatives in Classical Logic. Number 166 in Synthese Library. D. Reidel, Dordrecht, Holland (1986) 373–426
17. Matiyasevich, Y.V.: Hilbert's tenth Problem. Nauka Publishers, Fizmalit (1993) English translation: MIT Press, Cambridge, MA, 1993.
18. Mason, I.A., Talcott, C.L.: References, local variables, and operational reasoning. In: Proceedings of LICS 7, Santa Cruz, California, (1992) 186–197
19. Honsell, F., Mason, I., Smith, S., Talcott, C.: A variable typed logic of effects. Information and Computation **119** (1995) 55–90

Answer Type Polymorphism in Call-by-Name Continuation Passing

Hayo Thielecke

School of Computer Science
University of Birmingham
Birmingham B15 2TT
United Kingdom

Abstract. This paper studies continuations by means of a polymorphic type system. The traditional call-by-name continuation passing style transform admits a typing in which some answer types are polymorphic, even in the presence of first-class control operators. By building on this polymorphic typing, and using parametricity reasoning, we show that the call-by-name transform satisfies the eta-law, and is in fact isomorphic to the more recent CPS transform defined by Streicher.

1 Introduction

A continuation passing style (CPS) transform makes all control transfers, including function calls, explicit. For example, each call needs to pass not only the argument, but also a return continuation to the callee; returning a value from a function is achieved by passing it to the return continuation; and a jump works by replacing the current continuation with some other continuation.

The output of a CPS transform tends to be stylized in different ways. Depending on the source language and its control constructs, only certain uses of continuations are possible. Although CPS transforms can be defined on untyped terms independently of any typing, typing the source and target language can capture in a very concise way the stylized nature of a given CPS transform. Two advanced type systems have been used for this purpose: linearity and polymorphism.

A wide variety of control features, such as function calls, exceptions and some forms of jumps, admit linear typing [1]. On the other hand, first-class continuations in call-by-value, as given by Scheme's `call/cc` operator [10], defy linear typing of continuations in general: without restrictions, one cannot assume that any continuation is used linearly. In call-by-name, however, the situation regarding linearity is quite different. Laurent and Regnier [11] have observed that even in the presence of a first-class control operator, continuations in call-by-name are linear.

The polymorphic typing of answer types was studied in a recent paper [20] in call-by-value, where a close connection between control effects and answer type polymorphism was shown. In the present paper, the study of answer type polymorphism will be extended to call-by-name.

D.A. Schmidt (Ed.): ESOP 2004, LNCS 2986, pp. 279–293, 2004.

Following Plotkin's seminal paper [16], there have been two CPS transforms, one call-by-value and one call-by-name. Many variants of CPS transforms are possible, for instance by passing additional continuations [19], or introducing multiple levels of continuations [2]; but fundamentally, these tend to be variations on the call-by-value one. More recently, Streicher [8,18] has defined another call-by-name transform. The Streicher transform is very clearly call-by-name, in that it validates the η-law, while the Plotkin one in general does not. On the other hand, it seems different in character to the traditional transforms, since there are no continuations for function types, if continuations are taken to be functions to some answer type (rather, functions are passed a pair). The Plotkin call-by-name transform, by contrast, fits the same pattern as the call-by-value transform, with continuations for all types, just as in the call-by-value one. In fact, the Plotkin call-by-name transform factors over the call-by-value one via a so-called thunking transform [7].

Depending which of the two call-by-name transforms one considers, call-by-name continuation passing seems either a mild variation on call-by-value, or very different from it. This apparent contradiction is resolved by typing: it is the untyped[1] call-by-name CPS transform that factors over the call-by-value one, whereas polymorphically typing answer types in the Plotkin call-by-name transform, and thus capturing the stylized behaviour of continuations, yields a transform isomorphic to the Streicher call-by-name one.

1.1 Contribution

This paper makes the following contributions:

- We show answer type polymorphism in call-by-name, in close connection to some recent work [20,11].
- This typing then enables a more refined view of the call-by-name transform than in the usual untyped or simply-typed case.
- We apply parametricity reasoning to the call-by-name CPS transform.
- We establish an isomorphism between the two call-by-name transforms, tidying up the design space of CPS transforms.

1.2 Outline

After recalling the definition of CPS transforms in Section 2, we give a new typing with answer type polymorphism for the call-by-name transform in Section 3. To build on this, we need some background on parametricity and theorems for free in Section 4. We can then show that, if constrained by typing, the η-law holds (Section 5), and that the two call-by-name transforms are equivalent (Section 6).

[1] More accurately, single-typed regarding the answer type.

$$\frac{}{\Gamma, x : A \vdash x : A} \qquad \frac{}{\Gamma \vdash \mathsf{n} : \mathbb{N}}$$

$$\frac{\Gamma, x : A \vdash M : B}{\Gamma \vdash \lambda x : A.M : A \to B} \qquad \frac{\Gamma \vdash M : A \to B \qquad \Gamma \vdash N : A}{\Gamma \vdash MN : B}$$

$$\frac{\Gamma \vdash M : \forall\alpha.A}{\Gamma \vdash M[B] : A[\alpha \mapsto B]} \qquad \frac{\Gamma \vdash M : A}{\Gamma \vdash \Lambda\alpha.M : \forall\alpha.A}\ \alpha \text{ is not free in } \Gamma$$

$$\frac{\Gamma \vdash M : A \qquad \Gamma \vdash N : B}{\Gamma \vdash (M, N) : A \times B} \qquad \frac{\Gamma \vdash M : A_1 \times A_2}{\Gamma \vdash \pi_j\, M : A_j}$$

Fig. 1. Typing of the target language of the CPS transforms in Church style

$$\frac{\Gamma, x : A \vdash M : B}{\Gamma \vdash \lambda x.M : A \to B}$$

$$\frac{\Gamma \vdash M : \forall\alpha.A}{\Gamma \vdash M : A[\alpha \mapsto B]} \qquad \frac{\Gamma \vdash M : A}{\Gamma \vdash M : \forall\alpha.A}\ \alpha \text{ is not free in } \Gamma$$

Fig. 2. Curry-style typing

2 CPS Transforms

The source language consists of the simply-typed λ-calculus, together with constants and a control operator $\mathcal{K}$. Control operators for first-class continuations have classical types [5]. In particular, the type of $\mathcal{K}$ is Peirce's law:

$$\frac{\Gamma \vdash M : (A \to B) \to A}{\Gamma \vdash \mathcal{K} M : A}$$

This type can also be given to `call/cc` in Scheme and other call-by-value languages. We use the more neutral notation $\mathcal{K}$, since continuations in call-by-name are quite different from those in call-by-value. We assume that the natural numbers $\mathbb{N}$ are the only base type in the source language.

The target language of the CPS transforms consists of the polymorphic λ-calculus [17] together with pairs; see Fig. 1 for the typing rules. We usually omit type annotations in terms; the corresponding, Curry-style, rules are in Fig. 2. Greek letters range over type variables. A type variable not occurring in the context can be quantified to give a polymorphic type. For example, for the identity function we can infer

$$\vdash \lambda x.x : \forall\alpha.\alpha \to \alpha$$

As usual, pair patterns in λ-abstractions are syntactic sugar by way of $\lambda(x,y).M = \lambda z.M[x \mapsto \pi_1 z, y \mapsto \pi_2 z]$. A type of natural numbers is also assumed in the target language. To be parsimonious, we could assume this type to be syntactic sugar for the polymorphic natural numbers, $\forall\alpha.(\alpha \to \alpha) \to (\alpha \to \alpha)$ in the polymorphic target language. The important point is that the ground type is treated the same by both transforms. At the top level, we can then make ground type observations. The answer types of all continuations will either be a shared, global answer type α_1, or a local answer type given by a type variable α. We write $\neg A$ to abbreviate $A \to \alpha_1$.

Our first CPS transform is the traditional call-by-name transform first published by Plotkin [16], which we extend with a control operator $\mathcal{K}$.

Definition 1. *The Plotkin call-by-name CPS transform is defined as follows:*

$$\begin{aligned}
\underline{x} &= x \\
\underline{\lambda x.M} &= \lambda k.k(\lambda x.\underline{M}) \\
\underline{MN} &= \lambda k.\underline{M}(\lambda m.m\underline{N}k) \\
\underline{\mathsf{n}} &= \lambda k.k\mathsf{n} \\
\underline{\mathcal{K}\,M} &= \lambda k.\underline{M}(\lambda m.m(\lambda p.p(\lambda x k'.xk))k)
\end{aligned}$$

The traditional typing found in the literature [3] for this transform uses the double exponentiation monad [13] $T = \neg\neg(-)$ and the translation

$$\begin{aligned}
\underline{A \to B} &= T\underline{A} \to T\underline{B} \\
\underline{\mathbb{N}} &= \mathbb{N}
\end{aligned}$$

Then the transform preserves types in the following sense: if $x_1 : A_1, \ldots, x_n : A_n \vdash M : B$, we have

$$x_1 : T\underline{A_1}, \ldots, x_n : T\underline{A_n} \vdash \underline{M} : T\underline{B}$$

As Laurent and Regnier [11] have observed, the transform admits a more refined typing with $T = \neg\neg_\circ(-)$, where $\neg_\circ$ is a type of linear continuations: $\neg_\circ A = A \multimap \alpha_1$. This typing is relevant for the present paper inasmuch as it shows that some continuations are of a restricted form in the Plotkin call-by-name transform even in the presence of a first-class control operator. The second CPS transform which we will need has been studied by Streicher and others [8,18].

Definition 2. *The Streicher CPS transform $(\,)^*$ is defined as follows:*

$$\begin{aligned}
x^* &= x \\
(\lambda x.M)^* &= \lambda(x,q).M^*q \\
(MN)^* &= \lambda q.M^*(N^*,q) \\
\mathsf{n}^* &= \lambda q.q\mathsf{n} \\
(\mathcal{K}\,M)^* &= \lambda q.M^*((\lambda(x,q').xq),q)
\end{aligned}$$

The associated typing is this:

$$(A \to B)^* = \neg A^* \times B^*$$
$$\mathbb{N}^* = \neg \mathbb{N}$$

In the literature, one finds the control operators μ and $[a]$ associated with this transform, but we can define $\mathcal{K}$ by the standard encoding

$$\mathcal{K}\, M = \mu a.[a](M(\lambda x.\mu b.[a]x))$$

which amounts to the CPS transform as above.

This transform preserves types in the following sense: If $x_1 : A_1, \ldots, x_n : A_n \vdash M : B$, then

$$x_1 : \neg {A_n}^*, \ldots, x_n : \neg {A_n}^* \vdash M^* : \neg B^*$$

For understanding the Streicher transform, it is useful to bear in mind that in the translation of a whole judgement, another $\neg$ is applied to the type of each free variable and to the type of the whole expression. If M has type B, then its transform M^* has type $\neg B^*$. In particular for function types, we may think of $(A \to B)^*$ as the type of calling contexts for $(A \to B)$, which call a function by providing an argument of type $\neg A^*$ and and a calling context for the result with type B^*. A function of type $A \to B$ is then transformed into a thunk of type $\neg(A \to B)^*$, accepting a calling context and returning an answer. (There does not yet seem to be an agreed terminology for call-by-name continuation passing; the word *thunk* is standard in call-by-value [7], the term *calling context* perhaps less so.)

For the typing of the Streicher transform, it may also be useful to bear a logical view of types in mind: one may think of $(A \to B)^*$ as the *negation* of $A \to B$. It then becomes intuitively plausible that $(A \to B)^* = \neg A^* \times B^*$, since to negate an implication "A implies B", it is sufficient to have that A holds while B fails to hold.

3 Answer Type Polymorphism

So far, we have assumed that all answer types are global and equal. We gain a more refined view of CPS transforms if we observe that some answer types are more equal than others. In call-by-value with an effect system, a function without control effects [9] does not impose any constraints on the answer type, so it can have a locally quantified answer type. Whenever the function is called, its answer type is instantiated to that required by the call site [20].

In call-by-value, expressions in the operand position of an application are evaluated. In terms of continuation passing, that implies that we have continuations corresponding to evaluation contexts such as $(\lambda x.M)[\,]$, where the hole $[\,]$ indicates the position of the current expression. Such continuations can manipulate their argument in any way that a function in the language can. For example, continuations need not be linear: witness $(\lambda x.y)[\,]$. In call-by-name, by contrast, function application only generates evaluation contexts of the form $[\,]N_1 \dots N_j$ that apply the current expression to some arguments. Even if we have a first-class control operator to capture continuations, the continuations themselves are of a much more restricted kind than in call-by-value.

More technically, to see the restricted form of continuations in call-by-name, consider the clause for application:

$$\underline{MN} = \lambda k.\underline{M}(\lambda m.\underline{N}k)$$

The continuation $(\lambda m.\underline{N}k)$ passed to $\underline{M}$ is of a simple form, which we may regard as a calling context: m is called by being applied to $\underline{N}$ and k. In general, a calling context for the function type $A \to B$ takes a function that expects an argument of type A and a B-accepting continuation; the only thing the calling context is allowed to do with the function is to apply the function to the argument and continuation. This amounts to a tail call of the function, so that whatever the function returns will also be the result of the call. The expression $\underline{M}$ itself is then a thunk: if it is applied to a calling context, it yields an answer. Hence a calling context for the function type $A \to B$ has the following polymorphic type:

$$\forall\alpha.(A^+ \to B^\circ \to \alpha) \to \alpha$$

Here A^+ is the CPS-transformed type of the argument (a thunk), and B° is the type of calling contexts for the result type B. We have assumed that everything is call-by-name, so that the B-accepting continuation is again a calling context if B is a function type. The CPS transform of types is therefore defined in terms of thunks and calling contexts as follows.

Definition 3. *For any type A, we define types A^+ and A° by simultaneous induction as follows:*

$$\begin{aligned} A^+ &= A^\circ \to \alpha_1 \\ \mathbb{N}^\circ &= \mathbb{N} \to \alpha_1 \\ (A \to B)^\circ &= \forall\alpha.(A^+ \to B^\circ \to \alpha) \to \alpha \end{aligned}$$

For Curry-style typing, we can leave the transform on terms as it was in Definition 1. In Church style, the polymorphically typed Plotkin CPS transform reads as follows:

$$\begin{aligned} \underline{x} &= x \\ \underline{\lambda x : A.M} &= \lambda k : (A \to B)^\circ.k[\alpha_1](\lambda x : A^+.\underline{M}) \\ \underline{MN} &= \lambda k : B^\circ.\underline{M}(\Lambda\alpha.\lambda m : A^+ \to B^\circ \to \alpha.m\underline{N}k) \\ \underline{\mathsf{n}} &= \lambda k : \mathbb{N}^\circ.k\mathsf{n} \\ \underline{\mathcal{K}M} &= \lambda k : A^\circ.\underline{M}(\Lambda\alpha.\lambda m : ((A \to B)^+ \to A^\circ \to \alpha. \\ &\qquad m(\lambda p : (A \to B)^\circ.p[\alpha_1](\lambda x : A^+.\lambda k' : B^\circ.xk))k) \end{aligned}$$

Given this typing, it is a matter of straightforward typechecking to establish the following type preservation.

Proposition 1. *If* $x_1 : A_1, \ldots, x_n : A_n \vdash M : B$, *then*

$$x_1 : A_1{}^+, \ldots, x_n{:}\ A_n{}^+ \vdash \underline{M} : B^+$$

We can see this transform as an instance of data abstraction via polymorphism, in that a calling context satisfies the demand for an argument thunk and a calling context for the result in a similar way to an abstract data type satisfying the demand of possible users of the data type. Note that the answer type polymorphism is independent of any polymorphism in the source, since we have only considered a simply-typed source language. (This does not mean that there is no interaction between control effects and polymorphism in the source: as Harper and Lillibridge have pointed out, control effects render the naive ∀-introduction unsound [6].)

Furthermore, if we assume parametricity, then the type of calling contexts is isomorphic to the type of pairs consisting of an argument thunk and a calling context for the result:

$$\begin{aligned}(A \to B)^\circ &= \forall\alpha.(A^+ \to B^\circ \to \alpha) \to \alpha \\ &\cong A^+ \times B^\circ\end{aligned}$$

This is a standard encoding of a product in the polymorphic λ-calculus. We return to the isomorphism in Section 6 below. More specifically, the intuitive explanation of calling contexts in both the Plotkin and Streicher transforms will be justified, in that the two are in fact isomorphic.

The encoding of pairs in the polymorphic λ-calculus can itself be regarded as a form of continuation passing, in that a product type is first CPS-transformed by application of the double-negation monad $((-)\to\alpha)\to\alpha$ and then uncurried:

$$\begin{aligned}&((A \times B) \to \alpha) \to \alpha \\ \cong\ &(A \to (B \to \alpha)) \to \alpha\end{aligned}$$

An application of this is known as an idiom in the Scheme folklore: if one wants to avoid the overhead of constructing a `cons`-cell in the heap, one can transform the code into continuation-passing style and avoid the construction of pairs by using multi-argument procedures instead. Since multi-argument procedures are not curried in Lisp-like languages, the overhead of constructing a closure does not arise.

Although the transformation of terms has not been changed, the different transformation of types arguably makes a big difference at the conceptual level. If we read the Plotkin call-by-name transform in the untyped setting, then the notion of continuation appears similar to the one in call-by-value (a function from the transformed function type to the answer type), although all arguments are thunked. In fact, the Plotkin call-by-name transform can be derived from the call-by-value transform by composing with transform that thunks all arguments [7].

The polymorphic typing relies on everything being call-by-name. If we were to add strict constructs at function types, they could break the typing. Consider for example a strict sequencing operation $(M; N)$, which evaluates M, discards the result, and proceeds with N. We could define its CPS transform like this:

$$\underline{M; N} = \lambda k.\underline{M}(\lambda m.\underline{N}k) \qquad \text{where } m \text{ is not free in } N$$

The sequencing construct would break the typing, since the (non-linear) continuation of M, namely $(\lambda m.\underline{N}k)$, fails to have the required polymorphic type if M is a function. We will revisit this point in Section 5, after some prerequisites in the next section.

4 Parametricity Reasoning

We recall some of the basics of parametricity [17] to prove what Wadler calls "theorems for free" [21]: equational properties that follow from the type of an expression. We will use the informal style of parametricity reasoning from Section 3 of Wadler's paper. This should really be seen as only a shorthand for explicit proofs in a parametric model [21, Section 6]. A more rigorous account of parametricity is beyond the scope of this paper. Since the main result of the present paper (Theorem 1) depends only on one well-established isomorphism (polymorphic pairs), and equational reasoning about CPS terms, the naive use of parametricity does not seem overly hazardous.

The requirement that the polymorphic target language be interpreted in a parametric model is a strong one; since we are really only interested in reasoning about elements denoted by expressions, it may be possible to relax it. As an alternative to using a parametric model, it may also be possible to adapt the operational techniques developed by Pitts [15] for an operational semantics of the target language.

The following β and η-laws are assumed for the target language:

$$\begin{array}{rclrcll}
(\lambda x : A.M)N &=& M[x \mapsto N] & \lambda y.My &=& M & (y \text{ not free in } M) \\
\pi_j\,(M_1, M_2) &=& M_j & (\pi_1\,M, \pi_2\,M) &=& M & \\
(\Lambda\alpha.M)[B] &=& M[\alpha \mapsto B] & \Lambda\alpha.M[\alpha] &=& M & (\alpha \text{ not free in } M)
\end{array}$$

Informally, the assumption is that parametric functions work the same for all types. They cannot, for instance, dispatch on the type of their argument. A consequence of this requirement is that polymorphic functions are constrained in their behaviour: for instance, the only function polymorphic enough to have the type $\forall\alpha.\alpha \to \alpha$ is the identity, since the only value always guaranteed to be of the required result type α is the argument of the function.

To reason about parametricity, each operation on types is extended to an operation on relations. We write $R : A \leftrightarrow A'$ if R is a relation between A and A'.

- Let $R_1 : A \leftrightarrow A'$ and $R_2 : B \leftrightarrow B'$ be relations. Then we define a relation

  $$R_1 \to R_2 : (A \to B) \leftrightarrow (A' \to B')$$

  by $(F, F') \in R_1 \to R_2$ iff for all $(V, V') \in R_1$, $(FV, F'V') \in R_2$.

- We define $R_1 \times R_2 : A \times B \leftrightarrow A' \times B'$ by $((V, W), (V'W')) \in R_1 \times R_2$ iff $(V, V') \in R_1$ and $(W, W') \in R_2$.
- For each base type (in our case just $\mathbb{N}$), there is a corresponding relation given by the identity: $R_{\mathbb{N}} = \{(V, V) \mid V \in \mathbb{N}\}$.
- Let $\mathcal{R}$ be a function that maps relations to relations. We define a relation $\forall\mathcal{R}$ as follows: $(V, V') \in \forall\mathcal{R}$ iff for all types A, A', for all relations $R : A \leftrightarrow A'$, $(V, V') \in \mathcal{R}(R)$.

The parametricity theorem states that for each M of type A, M is related to itself by the relation corresponding to A. As Wadler has argued, a particularly useful instance is to take the (the graphs of) functions as relations. The simplest example is the following. For any K of type $\forall\alpha.(A \to \alpha) \to \alpha$, the identity

$$KP = P(K(\lambda x : A.x))$$

holds. Intuitively, all K can do is apply its argument to something, and return the result. Thus on the left-hand side, P is applied to some value. On the right-hand side, $(\lambda x.x)$ is applied to the same value, so that the expression $K(\lambda x.x)$ yields this value, to be fed to P. The parametricity argument is as follows: we have $((\lambda x : A.x), P) \in A \to P$. By specializing, K has type $(A \to A) \to A$. Furthermore, as $(K, K) \in (A \to P) \to P$, we have $(K(\lambda x : A.x), KP) \in P$, that is, $P(K(\lambda x : A.x)) = KP$.

A curried function can be pushed through a suitably polymorphic function G in a similar fashion. The identity looks a little more complicated due to the need for some currying and uncurrying. Let $G : \forall\alpha.(A \to B \to \alpha) \to \alpha$ and $P : A \to B \to C$. Then

$$GP = P(\pi_1\, (G(\lambda ab.(a, b))))(\pi_2\, (G(\lambda ab.(a, b))))$$

To prove this, we define a relation $R : A \times B \leftrightarrow C$ by $(V, W) \in R$ iff $P(\pi_1 V)(\pi_2 V) = W$. Then $((\lambda ab.(a, b)), P) \in (A \to B \to R)$. Since $G : (A \to B \to R) \to R$, this implies that $(G(\lambda ab.(a, b)), GP) \in R$. By definition of R, this means that

$$GP = P(\pi_1\, (G(\lambda ab.(a, b))))(\pi_2\, (G(\lambda ab.(a, b))))$$

as required.

Definition 4. *For types A and B, we define functions $i_{A,B}$ and $j_{A,B}$ as follows:*

$$\begin{aligned} i_{A,B} &= \lambda(a, b).\lambda f.fab \\ &: (A \times B) \to (\forall\alpha.(A \to B \to \alpha) \to \alpha) \end{aligned}$$

$$\begin{aligned} j_{A,B} &= \lambda g.g(\lambda ab.(a, b)) \\ &: (\forall\alpha.(A \to B \to \alpha) \to \alpha) \to (A \times B) \end{aligned}$$

We usually omit the type subscripts. We will need the following standard result:

Lemma 1. *The functions i and j defined in Definition 4 are inverses.*

Proof. (Sketch) That $i \circ j$ is the identity follows by straightforward calculation. For the other composition, $j \circ i$, we outline the following argument (which could be made more precise in a parametric model).

$$\begin{aligned}(j \circ i)g &= ((\lambda(a,b).\lambda p.pab) \circ (\lambda q.q(\lambda ab.(a,b))))\, g \\ &= (\lambda(a,b).\lambda p.pab)(g(\lambda ab.(a,b))) \\ &= (\lambda z.\lambda p.p(\pi_1\, z)(\pi_2\, z))(g(\lambda ab.(a,b))) \\ &= \lambda p.p(\pi_1\, (g(\lambda ab.(a,b))))(\pi_2\, (g(\lambda ab.(a,b)))) \\ &= \lambda p.gp \\ &= g\end{aligned}$$

Hence $(j \circ i)g = g$, that is, $j \circ i$ is the identity. □

We will need the isomorphism from Lemma 1 in Section 6, and use an argument similar to its proof in Section 5.

5 Control and the η-Law

In this section, we come to our first application of the polymorphic typing and parametricity reasoning. The Plotkin CPS transform $\underline{(-)}$ is considered a call-by-name transform, since it validates the full β-law:

$$\underline{(\lambda x.M)N} = \underline{M[x \mapsto N]}$$

for any term N, in contrast to the call-by-value transform. However, it does not a priori satisfy the η-law, in the sense that the CPS transforms of M and $\lambda x.Mx$ (where x is fresh) are not $\beta\eta$-equivalent. For this reason, some authors prefer to call the Plotkin CPS transform $\underline{(-)}$ a *lazy*, rather than a genuine call-by-name transform. To see the problem with the η-law, consider how $\lambda x.Mx$ is transformed into CPS:

$$\underline{\lambda x.Mx} = \lambda k_0.k_0(\lambda x k_1.\underline{M}(\lambda m.mxk_1))$$

Considered as untyped expressions, there is no reason why the above and $\underline{M}$ could be identified. For instance, k_0 could be a function that ignores its argument.

In fact, if we add strict sequencing to the source language, then we can find a source language context that invalidates the η-law. Recall that the sequencing operation was defined as

$$\underline{M;N} = \lambda k.\underline{M}(\lambda m.\underline{N}k) \qquad \text{where } m \text{ is not free in } N.$$

Proposition 2. *In the language extended with strict sequencing,* $\underline{y}$ *and* $\underline{\lambda x.yx}$ *can be separated: for any terms* P *and* Q*, there exists a context* C *such that*

$$\underline{C[y]} = \underline{P}$$
$$\underline{C[\lambda x.yx]} = \underline{Q}$$

Proof. Let $C = \mathcal{K}(\lambda k.((\lambda y.[\,])(k(\lambda q.P))); (\lambda b.b)))\,Q$. □

However, if CPS terms are restricted by polymorphic typing as given in Definition 3, then the η-law holds. Intuitively, one see this as follows. If M has type $A \to B$, then the CPS transformed term $\underline{M}$ expects a continuation with the type $\forall\alpha.(A^+ \to B^\circ \to \alpha) \to \alpha$. This continuation is restricted by its polymorphic typing in what it can do: it can only supply arguments of type A^+ and B° to its argument. But it cannot, for instance, just ignore its argument.

Proposition 3. *Suppose* $\vdash M : A \to B$ *and* x *is not free in* M*. Then*

$$\underline{M} = \underline{\lambda x.Mx}$$

Proof. (Sketch) Note that $\vdash \underline{M} : (\forall\alpha.(A^+ \to B^\circ \to \alpha) \to \alpha) \to \alpha_1$ and

$$\underline{\lambda x.Mx} = \lambda k.k(\lambda xy.\underline{M}(\lambda m.mxy)).$$

Assume $K : \forall\alpha.(A^+ \to B^\circ \to \alpha) \to \alpha$. Define a relation

$$R : (\forall\alpha.(A^+ \to B^\circ \to \alpha) \to \alpha) \leftrightarrow \alpha_1$$

by $(N(\lambda xy.\lambda m.mxy), L) \in R$ iff $\underline{M}N = L$. Then

$$((\lambda xy.\lambda m.mxy), (\lambda xy.\underline{M}(\lambda m.mxy)) \in (A^+ \to B^\circ \to R)$$

Hence, by applying K, with α instantiated to R, we have

$$((K(\lambda xy.\lambda m.mxy)), (K(\lambda xy.\underline{M}(\lambda m.mxy)))) \in R$$

By definition of R, this implies

$$\underline{M}K = K(\lambda xy.\underline{M}(\lambda m.mxy))$$

Hence

$$\underline{M} = \lambda k.\underline{M}k = \lambda k.k(\lambda xy.\underline{M}(\lambda m.mxy))$$

as required. □

6 Equivalence of the Call-by-Name Transforms

In this section, we use the polymorphic pair isomorphism to construct an isomorphism between the Plotkin and Streicher call-by-name transforms. We cannot expect the two call-by-name CPS transforms to produce terms that are equal in the sense of $\beta\eta$-equality in all cases. They employ, after all, different calling conventions. Rather, it is possible to translate back and forth between the results of the transforms. To do so, a function is mapped to a function which first translates its argument, then applies the original function, and then translates the result in the opposite direction. Hence the translation at a function type $A \to B$ is defined inductively in terms of the translation at the argument type A and the reverse translation at the result type B. This technique of inductively defined back-and-forth translation is very similar to the construction of a retraction between direct and continuation semantics by Meyer and Wand [12].

For making definitions that follow the structure of types, it is convenient to have operations on terms that parallel those on types.

Definition 5. *We define some combinators as follows:*

$$\begin{aligned} \circ &: (B \to C) \to (A \to B) \to (A \to C) \\ f \circ g &= \lambda x.f(gx) \end{aligned}$$

$$\begin{aligned} \mathsf{id}_A &: A \to A \\ \mathsf{id}_A &= \lambda x.x \end{aligned}$$

$$\begin{aligned} \neg &: (A \to B) \to (B \to \alpha_1) \to (A \to \alpha_1) \\ \neg &= \lambda f.\lambda p.p \circ f = \lambda fpa.p(fa) \end{aligned}$$

The functoriality of these operators makes calculations a little more structured. Concretely, we have equational laws like

$$\begin{aligned} \neg(f \circ g) &= \neg g \circ \neg f \\ (f_1 \times g_1) \circ (f_2 \times g_2) &= ((f_1 \circ f_2) \times (g_1 \circ g_2)) \end{aligned}$$

Definition 6. *For any type A, we define $I_A : A^* \to A^\circ$ and $J_A : A^\circ \to A^*$ by simultaneous induction over A as follows:*

$$\begin{aligned} I_{\mathbb{N}} &= \mathsf{id}_{\neg\mathbb{N}} \\ &: \neg\mathbb{N} \to \neg\mathbb{N} \\ I_{A\to B} &= i_{\neg A^\circ, B^\circ} \circ (\neg J_A \times I_B) \\ &: (\neg A^* \times B^*) \to (\forall\alpha.(\neg A^\circ \to B^\circ \to \alpha) \to \alpha) \\ J_{\mathbb{N}} &= \mathsf{id}_{\neg\mathbb{N}} \\ &: \neg\mathbb{N} \to \neg\mathbb{N} \\ J_{A\to B} &= (\neg I_A \times J_B) \circ j_{\neg A^\circ, B^\circ} \\ &: (\forall\alpha.(\neg A^\circ \to B^\circ \to \alpha) \to \alpha) \to (\neg A^* \times B^*) \end{aligned}$$

The type subscripts on I and J will occasionally be omitted to avoid clutter.

Lemma 2. *For all types A, we have $J_A \circ I_A = \mathsf{id}_{A^*}$ and $I_A \circ J_A = \mathsf{id}_{A^\circ}$.*

Proof. Induction on A, using the identities for i and j. □

Lemma 2 allows to convert back and forth between the types of the two call-by-name CPS transforms. We still need to show that these conversions fit together with the transformation on terms.

Lemma 3. *Let N be a term such that $\Gamma \vdash N : A$. Let σ and σ' be substitutions such that for all x free in N, $\sigma(x)$ is closed with $\sigma(x) = \neg I(\sigma'(x))$. Then*

$$N^*\sigma = \neg I_A \underline{N} \sigma'$$

Proof. Induction on N, using the definitions and functoriality of I and J. As an example, the case for $\mathcal{K}\,M$ is as follows. First, by the definitions of $\underline{\mathcal{K}\,M}$ as well as I and J, we calculate:

$$\begin{aligned}
&\neg I(\underline{\mathcal{K}\,M})\\
=&\ \underline{\mathcal{K}\,M} \circ I\\
=&\ (\lambda k.\underline{M}(\lambda m.m(\lambda p.p(\lambda x k'.xk))k) \circ I\\
=&\ \lambda q.\underline{M}(\lambda m.m(\lambda p.p(\lambda x k'.x(Iq)))(Iq))\\
=&\ \lambda q.\underline{M}(i(\lambda p.p(\lambda x k'.x(Iq))), (Iq))\\
=&\ \lambda q.\underline{M}(i((\neg J \times I)((\lambda(x,q').xq), q)))\\
=&\ \lambda q.(\underline{M} \circ i \circ (\neg J \times I))((\lambda(x,q').xq), q)\\
=&\ \lambda q.(\underline{M} \circ I)((\lambda(x,q').xq), q)\\
=&\ \lambda q.(\neg I\underline{M})((\lambda(x,q').xq), q)
\end{aligned}$$

Here we have used

$$\neg J(\lambda(x,q').xq) = \lambda p.p(\lambda x k'.x(Iq))$$

which follows from parametricity. Now suppose we have substitutions σ and σ' as above. Then

$$\begin{aligned}
&(\neg I(\underline{\mathcal{K}\,M}))\,\sigma'\\
=&\ (\lambda q.(\neg I\underline{M})((\lambda(x,q').xq), q))\,\sigma'\\
=&\ (\lambda q.(\neg I\underline{M}\sigma')((\lambda(x,q').xq), q)\\
=&\ \lambda q.(M^*\sigma)((\lambda(x,q').xq), q) \qquad \text{by the induction hypothesis}\\
=&\ ((\mathcal{K}\,M)^*)\sigma
\end{aligned}$$

Hence for $N = \mathcal{K}M$, we have shown that $N^*\sigma = \neg I\underline{N}\sigma'$, as required. □

We can now establish the main result. For closed terms of ground type, the transforms agree when both are given the identity as the top level continuation.

Theorem 1. *Let $\vdash M : \mathbb{N}$. Then*

$$\underline{M} = M^*$$

Proof. The statement follows from Lemma 3, since $\neg I_{\mathbb{N}} = \neg \mathsf{id}_{\neg\mathbb{N}} = \mathsf{id}_{\neg\neg\mathbb{N}}$ is the identity. □

7 Conclusions

We have used answer type polymorphism to analyze call-by-name continuation passing, building on and connecting earlier work on linear CPS [1,11] and answer type polymorphism [20]. The earlier paper on control effects in call-by-value [20], built on the isomorphism between any type and its polymorphic double negation:

$$\forall\alpha.(A \to \alpha) \to \alpha \cong A$$

In the present paper, we have used the very similar isomorphism giving the polymorphic encoding of pairs:

$$\forall\alpha.(A \to B \to \alpha) \to \alpha \cong A \times B$$

It is striking, however, that in the case of call-by-value, the CPS terms are parametrically polymorphic, whereas in call-by-name the *continuation* is polymorphic in the functional value passed to it. Similarly, in call-by-value, continuations tend to be linearly used, while in call-by-name they are themselves linear. At first sight, this reversal between term and continuation may seem reminiscent of a duality [4], but any such resemblance may well be accidental. After all, the polymorphism in the call-by-value setting holds only for some functions (without control effects), whereas in the call-by-name setting it holds for all functions, regardless of how the control operator is applied.

O'Hearn and Reynolds have used a translation to polymorphic λ-calculus to analyse state in programming languages [14]. The approach in this paper is similar in that the polymorphism does not arise from polymorphism in the (source) programming language itself, but from the stylized way in which effects operate.

In the light of the earlier paper [20] and Laurent's observation of linearity in call-by-name continuation passing [11], it may be useful to combine polymorphism and linearity, as in:

$$(A \to B)^\circ = \forall\alpha.(A^+ \to B^\circ \to \alpha) \multimap \alpha.$$

It has been shown, first for call-by-value [20] and now in this paper for call-by-name, that CPS transforms with their rich (and impredicative) polymorphic typing of answer types are a fruitful application of relational parametricity. A more semantic study, also incorporating recursion, could be interesting.

Acknowledgements. This work was begun during a visit to PPS (Preuves, Programmes et Systèmes) at the University of Paris. Thanks to Olivier Laurent and Paul-André Mellies for discussions, and the anonymous referees for comments.

References

1. Josh Berdine, Peter W. O'Hearn, Uday Reddy, and Hayo Thielecke. Linear continuation passing. *Higher-order and Symbolic Computation*, 15(2/3):181–208, 2002.

2. Olivier Danvy and Andrzej Filinski. Representing control, a study of the CPS transformation. *Mathematical Structures in Computer Science*, 2(4):361–391, December 1992.
3. Olivier Danvy and John Hatcliff. A generic account of continuation-passing styles. In *ACM Symposium on Principles of Programming Languages*, pages 458–471, 1994.
4. Andrzej Filinski. Declarative continuations: an investigation of duality in programming language semantics. In D. H. Pitt et al., editors, *Category Theory and Computer Science*, number 389 in Lecture Notes in Computer Science, pages 224–249. Springer-Verlag, 1989.
5. Timothy G. Griffin. A formulae-as-types notion of control. In *Principles of Programming Languages (POPL '90)*, pages 47–58. ACM, 1990.
6. Robert Harper and Mark Lillibridge. Explicit polymorphism and CPS conversion. In *Principles of Programming Languages (POPL '93)*, pages 206–219. ACM, 1993.
7. John Hatcliff and Olivier Danvy. Thunks and the λ-calculus. *Journal of Functional Programming*, 7(2):303–319, 1997.
8. Martin Hofmann and Thomas Streicher. Continuation models are universal for $\lambda\mu$-calculus. In *LICS: IEEE Symposium on Logic in Computer Science*, 1997.
9. Pierre Jouvelot and David K. Gifford. Reasoning about continuations with control effects. In *Prgramming Language Design and Implementation (PLDI)*, pages 218–226. ACM, 1988.
10. Richard Kelsey, William Clinger, and Jonathan Rees, editors. Revised^5 report on the algorithmic language Scheme. *Higher-Order and Symbolic Computation*, 11(1):7–105, 1998.
11. Olivier Laurent and Laurent Regnier. About translations of classical logic into polarized linear logic. In *Proceedings of the eighteenth annual IEEE symposium on Logic In Computer Science*, pages 11–20. IEEE Computer Society Press, June 2003.
12. Albert R. Meyer and Mitchell Wand. Continuation semantics in typed lambda-calculi (summary). In Rohit Parikh, editor, *Logics of Programs*, number 193 in Lecture Notes in Computer Science, pages 219–224. Springer-Verlag, 1985.
13. Eugenio Moggi. Computational lambda calculus and monads. In *Proceedings, Fourth Annual Symposium on Logic in Computer Science*, pages 14–23, 1989.
14. Peter W. O'Hearn and John C. Reynolds. From Algol to polymorphic linear lambda-calculus. *Journal of the ACM*, 47:167–223, 2000.
15. Andrew M. Pitts. Parametric polymorphism and operational equivalence. *Mathematical Structures in Computer Science*, 10:321–359, 2000.
16. Gordon D. Plotkin. Call-by-name, call-by-value, and the λ-calculus. *Theoretical Computer Science*, 1(2):125–159, 1975.
17. John C. Reynolds. Types, abstraction and parametric polymorphism. In R. E. A. Mason, editor, *Information Processing 83*, pages 513–523, Amsterdam, 1983. Elsevier Science Publishers B. V. (North-Holland).
18. Thomas Streicher and Bernhard Reus. Classical logic: Continuation semantics and abstract machines. *Journal of Functional Programming*, 8(6), 1998.
19. Hayo Thielecke. Comparing control constructs by double-barrelled CPS. *Higher-order and Symbolic Computation*, 15(2/3):141–160, 2002.
20. Hayo Thielecke. From control effects to typed continuation passing. In *30th SIGPLAN-SIGACT Symposium on Principles of Programming Languages (POPL'03)*, pages 139–149. ACM, 2003.
21. Philip Wadler. Theorems for free! In *4'th International Conference on Functional Programming and Computer Architecture (FPCA'89)*, pages 347–359. ACM, 1989.

System E: Expansion Variables for Flexible Typing with Linear and Non-linear Types and Intersection Types*

Sébastien Carlier[1], Jeff Polakow[1], J.B. Wells[1], and A.J. Kfoury[2]

[1] Heriot-Watt University, http://www.macs.hw.ac.uk/ultra/
[2] Boston University, http://www.cs.bu.edu/~kfoury/

Abstract. Types are often used to control and analyze computer programs. Intersection types give great flexibility, but have been difficult to implement. The ! operator, used to distinguish between linear and non-linear types, has good potential for better resource-usage tracking, but has not been as flexible as one might want and has been difficult to use in compositional analysis. We introduce System E, a type system with expansion variables, linear intersection types, and the ! type constructor for creating non-linear types. System E is designed for maximum flexibility in automatic type inference and for ease of automatic manipulation of type information. Expansion variables allow postponing the choice of which typing rules to use until later constraint solving gives enough information to allow making a good choice. System E removes many difficulties that expansion variables had in the earlier System I and extends expansion variables to work with ! in addition to the intersection type constructor. We present subject reduction for call-by-need evaluation and discuss program analysis in System E.

1 Discussion

1.1 Background and Motivation

Many current forms of program analysis, including many type-based analyses, work best when given the entire program to be analyzed [21,7]. However, by their very nature, large software systems are assembled from components that are designed separately and updated at different times. Hence, for large software systems, a program analysis methodology will benefit greatly from being *compositional*, and thereby usable in a *modular* and *incremental* fashion.

Type systems for programming languages that are flexible enough to allow safe code reuse and abstract datatypes must support some kind of polymorphic types. Theoretical models for type polymorphism in existing programming languages (starting in the 1980s through now) have generally obtained type polymorphism via ∀ ("for all") [15,6] and ∃ ("there exists") quantifiers [13] or closely related methods. Type systems with ∀ and ∃ quantifiers alone tend to

* Supported by grants: EC FP5 IST-2001-33477, EPSRC GR/L 41545/01, NATO CRG 971607, NSF 0113193 (ITR), Sun Microsystems EDUD-7826-990410-US.

D.A. Schmidt (Ed.): ESOP 2004, LNCS 2986, pp. 294–309, 2004.

be inadequate for representing modular program analysis results, because such systems fail to have *principal typings* [22,7] where each typable term has a best typing that logically implies all of its other typings. (Do not confuse this with the much weaker property often (mis)named "principal types" associated with the Hindley/Milner type system [12,5] used by Haskell, OCaml, Standard ML, etc.) In contrast, intersection type systems often have principal typings (see [8] for a discussion), leading to our interest in them.

Beyond basic type safety, type-based analyses can find information useful for other purposes such as optimization or security analysis. Linear type systems, with a ! operator for distinguishing between linear and non-linear types, are good for more accurate tracking of resource usage, but have not been as flexible as one might want [19,20,17,16,11]. Also, polymorphic linear type systems usually rely on quantifiers and thus are not suited for compositional analysis.

Several years ago, we developed a polymorphic type system for the λ-calculus called System I [8]. System I uses intersection types together with the new technology of *expansion variables* and has principal typings. Although the resulting program analysis can be done in a fully modular manner, there are many drawbacks to System I. The types are nearly linear (actually *affine*, i.e., used once or discarded) and multiple use of anything requires having intersection types with one branch for each use. An implication is that for any k there are simply-typable λ-terms that are not typable at rank k in System I. In contrast, rank 0 usually has the power of simple types and rank 2 usually contains the typing power of the Hindley/Milner system. System I does not have subject reduction, a basic property desired for any type system. And also, quite painfully, the substitutions used in type inference for System I do not support composition.

Some of System I's problems seemed solvable by allowing non-linear types. Also, we wanted analysis systems that can track resource usage. Toward these goals, we investigated combining the (nearly) linear intersection types of System I with the ! operator of linear type systems for controlled introduction of non-linear types. Because implementing intersection types has historically been hard, an additional goal was easier implementation. Our investigation led to System E.

1.2 Expansion and Expansion Variables

We solve the problems mentioned above with a new type system named System E that improves on previous work in the way it uses *expansion variables* (E-variables) to support *expansion*. This section gives a gentle, informal introduction to the need for expansion and how E-variables help.

Consider two typing derivations structured as follows, where λ and @ represent uses of the appropriate typing rules:

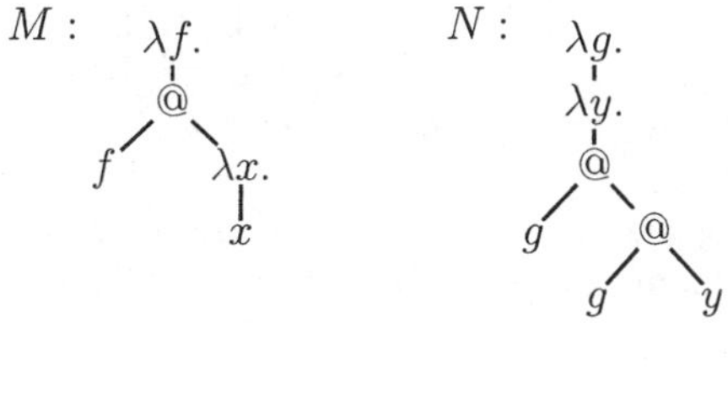

In a standard intersection type system, the derived result types could be these:

$$M : \underbrace{((\alpha \to \alpha) \to \beta)}_{\tau_1} \to \beta \qquad\qquad N : \underbrace{(\beta' \to \gamma') \sqcap (\alpha' \to \beta') \to \alpha' \to \gamma'}_{\tau_2}$$

In order to type the application $M @ N$, we must somehow "unify" τ_1 and τ_2. We could first unify the types $(\beta' \to \gamma')$ and $(\alpha' \to \beta')$ to collapse the intersection type $(\beta' \to \gamma') \sqcap (\alpha' \to \beta')$, but this would lose information and is not the approach we want to follow for full flexibility. Historically, in intersection type systems the solution has been to do *expansion* [4] on the result type of M:

$$M : ((\alpha_1 \to \alpha_1) \sqcap (\alpha_2 \to \alpha_2) \to \beta) \to \beta \tag{1}$$

Then, the substitution $(\alpha_1 := \alpha', \beta' := \alpha', \alpha_2 := \alpha', \gamma' := \alpha', \beta := \alpha' \to \alpha')$ makes the application $M @ N$ typable.

What justified the expansion we did to the result type of M? The expansion operation above effectively altered the typing derivation for M by inserting a use of intersection introduction at a nested position in the previous derivation, transforming it into the following new derivation, where $\sqcap$ marks a use of the intersection-introduction typing rule:

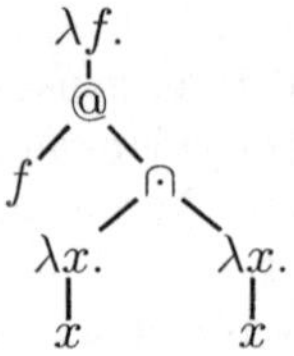

Expansion variables are a new technology for simplifying expansion and making it easier to implement and reason about. Expansion variables are *placeholders* for unknown uses of other typing rules, such as intersection introduction, which are propagated into the types and the type constraints used by type inference algorithms. The E-variable-introduction typing rule works like this (in traditional notation, not as stated later in the paper), where "$e\,A$" sticks the E-variable e on top of every type in the type environment A:

$$(\textsf{E-variable})\,\frac{A \vdash M : \tau}{e\,A \vdash M : e\,\tau}$$

Type-level substitutions in System E substitute types for type variables, and *expansions* for expansion variables. An expansion is a piece of syntax standing for some number of uses of typing rules that act uniformly on every type in a judgement. The most trivial expansion, $\boxdot$, is the identity. Intersection types can also be introduced by expansion; for example, given $M : (e\,(\alpha \to \alpha) \to \beta) \to \beta$, applying the substitution $e := \boxdot \sqcap \boxdot$ to this typing yields $M : ((\alpha \to \alpha) \sqcap (\alpha \to \alpha) \to \beta) \to \beta$. Substitutions are also a form of expansion; if we apply the substitution $e := (\alpha := \alpha_1) \sqcap (\alpha := \alpha_2)$ to M, we get the expanded typing given for M in (1) above.

Including substitutions as a form of expansion makes expansion variables effectively establish "namespaces" which can be manipulated separately. For example, applying the substitution $(e_1 := (\alpha := \alpha_1),\ e_2 := (\alpha := \alpha_2))$ to the type $(e_1\,\alpha) \sqcap (e_2\,\alpha)$ yields the type $\alpha_1 \sqcap \alpha_2$.

The syntactic expansion ω (introduced as expansion syntax in [3]) is also included, along with a typing rule that assigns the type ω (introduced in [4]) to any term. If we apply the substitution $e := \omega$ to the typing of M above, inside the typing derivation the result type for $\lambda x.x$ becomes ω. Operationally, a term which has type ω can only be passed around and must eventually be discarded.

The types in System E are by default *linear*. For example, $(\alpha_1 \to \alpha_1) \sqcap (\alpha_2 \to \alpha_2)$ is the type of a function to be used exactly twice, once at type $\alpha_1 \to \alpha_1$, and once at $\alpha_2 \to \alpha_2$. The ! operator creates a *non-linear* type allowing any number of uses, including 0. Subtyping rules for weakening (discarding), dereliction (using once), and contraction (duplicating) give this meaning to non-linear types. Introduction of ! is another possible case of expansion in System E.

The structure of expansions pervades every part of the design of System E. The main sorts of syntactic entities are types, typing constraints, skeletons (System E's proof terms), and expansions. Each of these sorts has cases for E-variable application, intersection, ω, and the ! operator. Other derived notions such as type environments also effectively support each of these operations. This common shared structure is the key to why System E works.

1.3 Summary of Contributions

We introduce System E and present its important properties. The proofs are in a separate long paper. System E improves on previous work as follows:

1. System E is the first type system to combine expansion variables, intersection types, the ! operator, and subtyping. Although not formally proved, we are confident that nearly every type system from the intersection type literature (without $\forall$ quantifiers) can be embedded in System E by putting enough !s in the types. System E has the polyvariant analysis power of intersection types together with the resource tracking power of linear types.
2. System E more cleanly integrates the notion of expansion from the intersection type literature (see [18] for an overview) with substitution. Unlike in System I, expansion is interleaved with substitution and, as a result, both expansions and substitutions are composable. Non-composable substitutions in System I made both proofs and implementations difficult.
3. System E cleanly supports associativity and commutativity of the intersection type constructor together with related laws that smoothly integrate intersection types with the ! type constructor.
4. System E generalizes previous notions of *expansion*. In System E's approach, expansion variables stand for any use of typing rules that operate uniformly on the result and environment types and do not change the untyped λ-term in the judgement. In System E, such rules include not only the intersection introduction rule but also rules for ! and type-level substitution. System E is the first to support such flexible expansion.
5. System E removes other difficulties of its predecessor System I. There are no restrictions on placement of expansion variables or intersection type constructors. System E has subject reduction for call-by-need evaluation. (It

does not have subject reduction for call-by-name evaluation because the type system can track resource usage precisely enough to distinguish.)

6. The uniform handling of expansion variables throughout System E makes implementation simple. Demonstrating this, we present output in this paper from our type inference implementation, which can be used at this URL: `http://www.macs.hw.ac.uk/ultra/compositional-analysis/system-E/`
7. System E is parameterized on its subtyping relation. We present 3 different subtyping relations relations with different amounts of typing power.
8. System E has additional features for flexible use. Its typing judgements have separate subtyping constraints to support either eager or lazy constraint solving together with its suspended expansion rule. To help both proofs and implementations, System E's judgements have two different kind of proof terms, one for the analyzed program and one for the proof structure.

2 Preliminary Definitions

This section defines generic mathematical notions. Let h, i, j, m, n, p, and q range over $\{0,1,2,\ldots\}$ (the natural numbers). Given a function f, let $f[a \mapsto b] = (f \setminus \{\,(a,c) \mid (a,c) \in f\,\}) \cup \{(a,b)\}$. Given a relation $\xrightarrow{r}$, let $\xrightarrow{r}\!\!\!\!\rightarrow$ be its transitive, reflexive closure, w.r.t. the right carrier set. Given a context C, let $C[U]$ stand for C with the single occurrence of $\square$ replaced by U. For example, $(\lambda x.\square)[x] = \lambda x.x$.

If S names a set and φ is defined as a metavariable ranging over S, let S^* be the set of *sequences* over S as per the following grammar, quotiented by the subsequent equalities, and let $\vec{\varphi}$ be a metavariable ranging over S^*:

$$\vec{\varphi} \in S^* ::= \epsilon \mid \varphi \mid \vec{\varphi}_1 \cdot \vec{\varphi}_2$$
$$\epsilon \cdot \vec{\varphi} = \vec{\varphi} \qquad \vec{\varphi} \cdot \epsilon = \vec{\varphi} \qquad (\vec{\varphi}_1 \cdot \vec{\varphi}_2) \cdot \vec{\varphi}_3 = \vec{\varphi}_1 \cdot (\vec{\varphi}_2 \cdot \vec{\varphi}_3)$$

For example, $\vec{n}$ ranges over $\{0,1,2,\ldots\}^*$ (sequences of natural numbers). Length 1 sequences are equal to their sole member.

3 Syntax

This section defines the syntactic entities by starting from the abstract syntax grammars and metavariable conventions in fig. 1 and then modifying those definitions by the equalities and well-formedness conditions that follow.

Operator precedence is defined here, including for ordinary function application ($f(a)$) and modification ($f[a \mapsto b]$), and for operations defined later such as expansion application ($[E]\,X$) and term-variable substitution ($M_1[x{:=}M_2]$). The precedence groups are as follows, from highest to lowest:

group 1: $Q^{:\tau}$, Q^{ν}, $f(a)$, $f[a \mapsto b]$, $M_1[x := M_2]$, $v := \Phi$
group 2: $e\,X$, $!\,X$, $[E]\,X$, $(\phi,\ S)$
group 3: $X_1 \cap X_2$, e/S
group 4: $\tau_1 \rightarrow \tau_2$, $M \mathbin{@} N$, $Q_1 \mathbin{@} Q_2$
group 5: $\tau_1 \leq \tau_2$, $\lambda x.M$, $\lambda x.Q$

The sorts and their abstract syntax grammars and metavariables:

$$
\begin{array}{rrl}
x, y, z \in & \textsf{Term-Variable} ::= & \mathsf{x}_i \\
V \in & \textsf{Value} ::= & x \mid \lambda x.M \\
M, N, P \in & \textsf{Term} ::= & V \mid M \mathbin{@} N \\
C^{\mathrm{t}} \in & \textsf{Term-Context} ::= & \square \mid \lambda x.C^{\mathrm{t}} \mid C^{\mathrm{t}} \mathbin{@} M \mid M \mathbin{@} C^{\mathrm{t}} \\
e, f, g \in & \textsf{E-Variable} ::= & \mathsf{e}_i \\
\alpha \in & \textsf{T-Variable} ::= & \mathsf{a}_i \\
\nu \in & \textsf{Env-Subtyping} ::= & x : \tau \\
\phi \in & \textsf{ET-Assignment} ::= & \alpha := \tau \mid e := E \\
S \in & \textsf{ET-Substitution} ::= & \boxdot \mid \phi,\ S \\
\tau \in & \textsf{Type} ::= & \tau_1 \sqcap \tau_2 \mid e\,\tau \mid !\,\tau \mid \omega \mid \alpha \mid \tau_1 \to \tau_2 \\
E \in & \textsf{Expansion} ::= & E_1 \sqcap E_2 \mid e\,E \mid !\,E \mid \omega \mid S \\
\Delta \in & \textsf{Constraint} ::= & \Delta_1 \sqcap \Delta_2 \mid e\,\Delta \mid !\,\Delta \mid \omega \mid \tau_1 \leq \tau_2 \\
Q \in & \textsf{Skeleton} ::= & Q_1 \sqcap Q_2 \mid e\,Q \mid !\,Q \mid \omega^M \mid \bar{Q} \\
\bar{Q} \in & \textsf{SimpleSkeleton} ::= & x^{:\tau} \mid \lambda x.\,Q \mid Q_1 \mathbin{@} Q_2 \mid Q^{:\tau} \mid Q^{\nu} \mid \langle Q, E \rangle
\end{array}
$$

Metavariables ranging over multiple sorts:

$$
\begin{array}{llll}
v ::= e \mid \alpha & T ::= \tau \mid \Delta & W ::= M \mid E \mid Q & U ::= M \mid \tau \mid E \mid \Delta \mid Q \\
\Phi ::= E \mid \tau & Y ::= \tau \mid E \mid \Delta & X ::= \tau \mid E \mid \Delta \mid Q &
\end{array}
$$

Fig. 1. Syntax grammars and metavariable conventions.

For example, $e\,\alpha_1 \sqcap \alpha_2 \to \alpha_3 = ((e\,\alpha_1) \sqcap \alpha_2) \to \alpha_3$, and $(e\,\alpha_1 \leq \alpha_2) = ((e\,\alpha_1) \leq \alpha_2)$, and $\lambda x.\,x^{:\alpha_1} \mathbin{@} y^{:\alpha_2} = \lambda x.\,(x^{:\alpha_1} \mathbin{@} y^{:\alpha_2})$. Application is left-associative so that $M_1 \mathbin{@} M_2 \mathbin{@} M_3 = (M_1 \mathbin{@} M_2) \mathbin{@} M_3$ (similarly for skeletons) and function types are right-associative so that $\tau_1 \to \tau_2 \to \tau_3 = \tau_1 \to (\tau_2 \to \tau_3)$.

3.1 Equalities

Terms and skeletons are quotiented by α-conversion as usual, where $\lambda x.M$ and $\lambda x.\,Q$ bind the variable x.

For types and constraints, the definition provided by fig. 1 is modified by imposing several equalities for E-variable application, the $\sqcap$ and ! operators, and the ω constant. The $\sqcap$ operator is associative and commutative with ω as its unit. E-variable application and ! both distribute over $\sqcap$ and ω. (The constant ω can be viewed as a 0-ary version of $\sqcap$.) The ! operator is idempotent and applications of E-variables and ! can be reordered. Formally, these rules hold:

$$
\begin{array}{llll}
T_1 \sqcap T_2 = T_2 \sqcap T_1 & e\,\omega = \omega & e\,(T_1 \sqcap T_2) = e\,T_1 \sqcap e\,T_2 \\
T_1 \sqcap (T_2 \sqcap T_3) = (T_1 \sqcap T_2) \sqcap T_3 & !\,\omega = \omega & !\,(T_1 \sqcap T_2) = !\,T_1 \sqcap !\,T_2 \\
\omega \sqcap T = T & !\,!\,T = !\,T & e\,!\,T = !\,e\,T
\end{array}
$$

Both α-conversion and the additional rules for types and constraints are imposed as *equalities*, where "=" is mathematical equality (as it should be). For example, $\omega \sqcap \alpha = \alpha$. After this modification, the syntactic sorts are not initial algebras. The underlying formalism to realize this could be, e.g., that types are equivalence classes closed under the rules. This level of detail is left unspecified.

Because we have imposed equalities (α-conversion and the rules for $\sqcap$, ω, !, and E-variable application in types and constraints), we can not use structural recursion and induction for definitions and proofs. To solve this, we define a size function and prove an induction principle. Details are in the long paper.

3.2 Additional Notions

Extending E-variable application to sequences, let $\epsilon X = X$ and $(\boldsymbol{e} \cdot e)\, X = \boldsymbol{e}\,(e\, X)$. Similarly, for environment subtyping, let $Q^{\epsilon} = Q$ and $Q^{\nu \cdot \boldsymbol{\nu}} = (Q^{\nu})^{\boldsymbol{\nu}}$.

Let $M[x := N]$ denote the usual notion of term-variable substitution in untyped terms. Let $\mathsf{FV}(M)$ denote the free term variables of M.

Let term be the least-defined function such that:

$$
\begin{array}{llll}
\mathsf{term}(x^{:\tau}) &= x & \mathsf{term}(Q^{:\tau}) &= \mathsf{term}(Q) \\
\mathsf{term}(\lambda x.\, Q) &= \lambda x.\mathsf{term}(Q) & \mathsf{term}(Q^{\nu}) &= \mathsf{term}(Q) \\
\mathsf{term}(Q_1 \mathbin{@} Q_2) &= \mathsf{term}(Q_1) \mathbin{@} \mathsf{term}(Q_2) & \mathsf{term}(!\,Q) &= \mathsf{term}(Q) \\
\mathsf{term}(\langle Q, E\rangle) &= \mathsf{term}(Q) & \mathsf{term}(\omega^{M}) &= M \\
\mathsf{term}(e\, Q) &= \mathsf{term}(Q) & & \\
\mathsf{term}(Q_1 \sqcap Q_2) &= \mathsf{term}(Q_1) \quad \text{if } \mathsf{term}(Q_1) = \mathsf{term}(Q_2) & &
\end{array}
$$

A skeleton Q is *well formed* iff $\mathsf{term}(Q)$ is defined. For example, $Q = x^{:\tau_1} \sqcap y^{:\tau_2}$ is not well formed if $x \neq y$, because $\mathsf{term}(Q)$ is not defined.

Convention 3.1 *Henceforth, only well formed skeletons are considered.* □

4 Expansion Application and Type-Level Substitution

This section defines the fundamental operation of *expansion application* which is the basis of the key features of System E. Expansion is defined, basic properties of expansion are presented, syntactic sugar for writing substitutions (a special case of expansions) is defined, and then examples are presented.

Definition 4.1 (Expansion Application). *Figure 2 defines the application of an expansion to E-variables, types, expansions, constraints, and skeletons.* □

Lemma 4.2 (Expansion Application Properties).

1. *X and $[E]\, X$ have the same sort (τ, E, Δ, or Q).*
2. *Expansion application preserves untyped terms, i.e.,* $\mathsf{term}([E]\, Q) = \mathsf{term}(Q)$.
3. *The substitution constant $\boxdot$ acts as the identity on types, expansions, constraints and skeletons, i.e., $[\boxdot]\, X = X$.* □

Lemma 4.3 (Expansion Application Composition). *Given any E_1, E_2, X, $[[E_1]\, E_2]\, X = [E_1]\, [E_2]\, X$.* □

$$
\begin{array}{llll}
[\boxdot]\,\alpha & = \alpha & [v := \Phi,\ S]\,v & = \Phi \\
[\boxdot]\,e & = e\,\boxdot & [v := \Phi,\ S]\,v' & = [S]\,v' \text{ if } v \neq v' \\
 & & & \\
[S]\,(X_1 \sqcap X_2) & = [S]\,X_1 \sqcap [S]\,X_2 & [E_1 \sqcap E_2]\,X & = [E_1]\,X \sqcap [E_2]\,X \\
[S]\,e\,X & = [[S]\,e]\,X & [e\,E]\,X & = e\,[E]\,X \\
[S]\,!\,X & = !\,[S]\,X & [!\,E]\,X & = !\,[E]\,X \\
[S]\,\omega & = \omega & [\omega]\,Y & = \omega \\
[S]\,\omega^{M} & = \omega^{M} & [\omega]\,Q & = \omega^{\mathsf{term}(Q)} \\
 & & & \\
[S]\,(\tau_1 \to \tau_2) & = [S]\,\tau_1 \to [S]\,\tau_2 & [S]\,(\tau_1 \leq \tau_2) & = [S]\,\tau_1 \leq [S]\,\tau_2 \\
[S]\,x^{:\tau} & = x^{:[S]\,\tau} & [S]\,\boxdot & = S \\
[S]\,\lambda x.\,Q & = \lambda x.\,[S]\,Q & [S]\,(v := \Phi,\ S') & = (v := [S]\,\Phi,\ [S]\,S') \\
[S]\,(Q_1 \mathbin{@} Q_2) & = [S]\,Q_1 \mathbin{@} [S]\,Q_2 & [S]\,Q^{:\tau} & = ([S]\,Q)^{:[S]\,\tau} \\
[S]\,\langle Q, E\rangle & = \langle Q, [S]\,E\rangle & [S]\,Q^{x:\tau} & = ([S]\,Q)^{x:[S]\,\tau}
\end{array}
$$

Fig. 2. Expansion application.

Let $E_1; E_2 = [E_2]\,E_1$ (composition of expansions). By lem. 4.3, the ";" operator is associative. Although $E_1; E_2$ is not much shorter than $[E_2]\,E_1$, it allows writing, e.g., $S_1; S_2; S_3; S_4; S_5$, which is easier to follow than $[S_5]\,[S_4]\,[S_3]\,[S_2]\,S_1$.

An assignment ϕ may stand for $S = (\phi,\ \boxdot)$ and is to be interpreted that way if at all possible. The higher precedence of $(v := \Phi)$ over $(\phi,\ S)$ applies here. For example, $e_1 := e_2 := S_2,\ e_3 := S_3$ stands for $(e_1 := (e_2 := S_2)),\ e_3 := S_3$ which stands for $(e_1 := ((e_2 := S_2),\ \boxdot)),\ (e_3 := S_3),\ \boxdot$.

Let e/S stand for $(e := e\,S)$. Thus, e/S stands for $((e := e\,S), \boxdot)$ when possible. The "/" notation builds a substitution that affects variables underneath an E-variable, because $[e/S]\,e\,X = e\,[S]\,X$ and $[e/S]\,X = X$ if $X \neq e\,X'$. For example, $S = (\mathsf{e}_0/(\mathsf{a}_1 := \tau_1),\ \mathsf{a}_0 := \tau_0)$ stands for $S = (\mathsf{e}_0 := \mathsf{e}_0\,(\mathsf{a}_1 := \tau_1,\ \boxdot),\ \mathsf{a}_0 := \tau_0,\ \boxdot)$ and in this case $[S]\,(\mathsf{e}_0\,\mathsf{a}_1 \to \mathsf{a}_0) = \mathsf{e}_0\,\tau_1 \to \tau_0$. We extend this notation to E-variable sequences so that $\boldsymbol{e} \cdot e/S$ stands for $\boldsymbol{e}/e/S$ and ϵ/S stands for S.

Example 4.4. E-variables effectively establish namespaces and substituting an expansion for an E-variable can merge namespaces. Define the following:

$$\tau_1 = \mathsf{e}_1\,\mathsf{a}_0 \to \mathsf{a}_0 \qquad S_1 = (\mathsf{e}_1 := \boxdot) \qquad S_2 = (\mathsf{a}_0 := \tau_2)$$

Then these facts hold:

$$
\begin{array}{ll}
[S_2]\,\tau_1 = \mathsf{e}_1\,\mathsf{a}_0 \to \tau_2 & [S_1]\,\tau_1 = \mathsf{a}_0 \to \mathsf{a}_0 \\
[S_2]\,[S_1]\,\tau_1 = \tau_2 \to \tau_2 & S_1; S_2 = (\mathsf{e}_1 := (\mathsf{a}_0 := \tau_2),\ \mathsf{a}_0 := \tau_2)
\end{array}
$$

In $[S_2]\,\tau_1$, the T-variable a_0 inside the E-variable e_1 is effectively distinct from the T-variable a_0 outside e_1, so the substitution only replaces the outer a_0. The operation $[S_1]\,\tau_1$ replaces e_1 by the empty expansion (which is actually the identity substitution), and this effectively lifts the inner a_0 into the root namespace, so that $[S_2]\,[S_1]\,\tau_1$ replaces both occurrences of a_0. □

Example 4.5. The composition $S; S'$ may take operations in one namespace in S and duplicate them to multiple namespaces in $S; S'$. Define the following:

$$\tau_1 = \mathsf{e}_1\, \mathsf{a}_0 \to \mathsf{a}_0 \qquad S_3 = (\mathsf{e}_1 := \mathsf{e}_2\, \boxdot) \qquad S_4 = (\mathsf{e}_2/(\mathsf{a}_0 := \tau_1))$$

Then these facts hold:

$$[S_4]\,[S_3]\,\tau_1 = \mathsf{e}_2\,\tau_1 \to \mathsf{a}_0 \qquad S_3; S_4 = (\mathsf{e}_1 := \mathsf{e}_2\,(\mathsf{a}_0 := \tau_1),\ \mathsf{e}_2/(\mathsf{a}_0 := \tau_1))$$

Both S_4 and its assignment $(\mathsf{a}_0{:=}\tau_1)$ appear in $S_3; S_4$. In general, arbitrary pieces of S' may appear in $S; S'$ copied to multiple places. Thus, an implementation should either compose lazily or share common substructures. □

Example 4.6. Substitutions can act differently on distinct namespaces and then merge the namespaces afterward. This is essential for composing substitutions. The key design choice making this work is making substitutions be the leaves of expansions. Define the following:

$$\tau = \mathsf{e}_1\, \mathsf{a}_0 \to \mathsf{a}_0 \qquad S_5 = \mathsf{e}_1/(\mathsf{a}_0 := \tau') \qquad S_6 = (\mathsf{e}_1 := \boxdot)$$

These facts hold:

$$\begin{array}{ll} [S_5]\,\tau\ = \mathsf{e}_1\,\tau' \to \mathsf{a}_0 & \\ [S_6]\,\tau\ = \mathsf{a}_0 \to \mathsf{a}_0 & [S_6]\,[S_5]\,\tau = \tau' \to \mathsf{a}_0 \\ S_5; S_6 = (\mathsf{e}_1 := (\mathsf{a}_0 := \tau'),\ \mathsf{e}_1 := \boxdot) & [S_5; S_6]\,\tau\ = \tau' \to \mathsf{a}_0 \end{array}$$

A "flat" substitution notion (as in System I [8]) which does not interleave expansions and substitutions can not express the composition $S_5; S_6$.

The substitution $S_5; S_6$ has an extra assignment $(\mathsf{e}_1{:=}\boxdot)$ at the end which has no effect (other than uglifying the example), because it follows the assignment $(\mathsf{e}_1 := (\mathsf{a}_0 := \tau'))$. The substitution $S_5; S_6$ is equivalent to the substitution $S_7 = (\mathsf{e}_1 := (\mathsf{a}_0 := \tau'))$, in the sense that $[S_5; S_6]\,X = [S_7]\,X$ for any X other than a skeleton with suspended expansions. Expansion application could have been defined to clean up redundant assignments, but at the cost of complexity. □

5 Type Environments and Typing Rules

This section presents the type environments and typing rules of System E. Also, the role of skeletons is explained.

A *type environment* is a total function from term variables to types which maps only a finite number of variables to types other than ω. Let A and B range over type environments. Make the following definitions:

$$\begin{aligned} [E]\,A &= \{\,(x, [E]\,A(x))\,|\,x \in \textsf{Term-Variable}\,\} \\ A \sqcap B &= \{\,(x, A(x) \sqcap B(x))\,|\,x \in \textsf{Term-Variable}\,\} \\ e\,A &= [e\,\boxdot]\,A = \{\,(x, e\,A(x))\,|\,x \in \textsf{Term-Variable}\,\} \\ !\,A &= [!\,\boxdot]\,A = \{\,(x, !\,A(x))\,|\,x \in \textsf{Term-Variable}\,\} \\ \mathsf{env}_\omega &= \{\,(x, \omega)\,|\,x \in \textsf{Term-Variable}\,\} \end{aligned}$$

$$\text{(abstraction)}\ \frac{(M \rhd Q) : \langle A \vdash \tau \rangle \;/\; \Delta}{(\lambda x. M \rhd \lambda x. Q) : \langle A[x \mapsto \omega] \vdash A(x) \to \tau \rangle \;/\; \Delta}$$

$$\text{(application)}\ \frac{(M_1 \rhd Q_1) : \langle A_1 \vdash \tau_2 \to \tau_1 \rangle \;/\; \Delta_1; \quad (M_2 \rhd Q_2) : \langle A_2 \vdash \tau_2 \rangle \;/\; \Delta_2}{(M_1 @ M_2 \rhd Q_1 @ Q_2) : \langle A_1 \sqcap A_2 \vdash \tau_1 \rangle \;/\; \Delta_1 \sqcap \Delta_2}$$

$$\text{(variable)}\ \frac{}{(x \rhd x^{:\tau}) : \langle (x : \tau) \vdash \tau \rangle \;/\; \omega} \qquad \text{(omega)}\ \frac{}{(M \rhd \omega^M) : \langle \mathsf{env}_\omega \vdash \omega \rangle \;/\; \omega}$$

$$\text{(intersection)}\ \frac{(M \rhd Q_1) : \langle A_1 \vdash \tau_1 \rangle \;/\; \Delta_1; \quad (M \rhd Q_2) : \langle A_2 \vdash \tau_2 \rangle \;/\; \Delta_2}{(M \rhd Q_1 \sqcap Q_2) : \langle A_1 \sqcap A_2 \vdash \tau_1 \sqcap \tau_2 \rangle \;/\; \Delta_1 \sqcap \Delta_2}$$

$$\text{(bang)}\ \frac{(M \rhd Q) : \langle A \vdash \tau \rangle \;/\; \Delta}{(M \rhd !\,Q) : \langle !\,A \vdash !\,\tau \rangle \;/\; !\,\Delta} \qquad \text{(E-variable)}\ \frac{(M \rhd Q) : \langle A \vdash \tau \rangle \;/\; \Delta}{(M \rhd e\,Q) : \langle e\,A \vdash e\,\tau \rangle \;/\; e\,\Delta}$$

$$\text{(suspended expansion)}\ \frac{(M \rhd Q) : \langle A \vdash \tau \rangle \;/\; \Delta}{(M \rhd \langle Q, E \rangle) : \langle [E]A \vdash [E]\tau \rangle \;/\; [E]\Delta}$$

$$\text{(result subtyping)}\ \frac{(M \rhd Q) : \langle A \vdash \tau_1 \rangle \;/\; \Delta}{(M \rhd Q^{:\tau_2}) : \langle A \vdash \tau_2 \rangle \;/\; \Delta \sqcap (\tau_1 \leq \tau_2)}$$

$$\text{(environment subtyping)}\ \frac{(M \rhd Q) : \langle A \vdash \tau_1 \rangle \;/\; \Delta}{(M \rhd Q^{x:\tau_2}) : \langle A[x \mapsto \tau_2] \vdash \tau_1 \rangle \;/\; \Delta \sqcap (\tau_2 \leq A(x))}$$

Fig. 3. Typing rules.

Let $(x_1 : \tau_1, \cdots, x_n : \tau_t)$ abbreviate $\mathsf{env}_\omega[x_1 \mapsto \tau_1] \cdots [x_n \mapsto \tau_n]$. Observe, for every E_1, E_2, A, and x, that $[E_1 \sqcap E_2]\, A = [E_1]\, A \sqcap [E_2]\, A$, that $(e\, A)(x) = e\, A(x)$, that $(!\, A)(x) = !\, A(x)$, that $\mathsf{env}_\omega = [\omega]\, A$, that $[E]\, A[x \mapsto \tau] = ([E]\, A)[x \mapsto [E]\, \tau]$, and that $[E]\,(A \sqcap B) = [E]\, A \sqcap [E]\, B$.

The typing rules of System E are given in fig. 3. The typing rules derive *judgements* of the form $(M \rhd Q) : \langle A \vdash \tau \rangle \;/\; \Delta$. The pair $\langle A \vdash \tau \rangle$ of a type environment A and a *result type* τ is called a *typing*. The intended meaning of $(M \rhd Q) : \langle A \vdash \tau \rangle \,/\, \Delta$ is that Q is a proof that M has the typing $\langle A \vdash \tau \rangle$, provided that the constraint Δ is *solved* w.r.t. some subtyping relation.

The precise semantic meaning of a typing $\langle A \vdash \tau \rangle$ depends on the subtyping relation that is used. The typing rules avoid specifying whether a constraint Δ is solved to allow the use of different subtyping relations, depending on the user's needs. Subtyping relations for System E are discussed in sec. 6.

A skeleton Q is a special kind of term that compactly represents a tree of typing rule uses that derives a judgement for the untyped term given by $\mathsf{term}(Q)$. Thus, a skeleton is basically a *typing derivation*.

Definition 5.1 (Valid Skeleton). *A skeleton Q is* valid *iff there exist M, A, τ, and Δ such that $(M \rhd Q) : \langle A \vdash \tau \rangle \;/\; \Delta$.* □

Lemma 5.2 (Valid Skeletons Isomorphic to Typing Derivations). *If $(M_1 \rhd Q) : \langle A_1 \vdash \tau_1 \rangle \,/\, \Delta_1$ and $(M_2 \rhd Q) : \langle A_2 \vdash \tau_2 \rangle \,/\, \Delta_2$, then $\mathsf{term}(Q) = M_1 = M_2$, $A_1 = A_2$, $\tau_1 = \tau_2$, and $\Delta_1 = \Delta_2$.* □

Subtyping rules for $\preceq_{\mathsf{refl}}, \preceq_{\mathsf{nlin}}, \preceq_{\mathsf{flex}}$:

$$\frac{}{\tau \preceq \tau}\ (\mathsf{refl}\text{-}\preceq) \qquad \frac{\tau_1 \preceq \tau_2 \quad \tau_2 \preceq \tau_3}{\tau_1 \preceq \tau_3}\ (\mathsf{trans}\text{-}\preceq) \qquad \frac{\tau_1 \preceq \tau_2}{e\,\tau_1 \preceq e\,\tau_2}\ (e\text{-}\preceq)$$

$$\frac{\tau_3 \preceq \tau_1 \quad \tau_2 \preceq \tau_4}{\tau_1 \to \tau_2 \preceq \tau_3 \to \tau_4}\ (\to\text{-}\preceq) \qquad \frac{\tau_1 \preceq \tau_3 \quad \tau_2 \preceq \tau_4}{\tau_1 \Cap \tau_2 \preceq \tau_3 \Cap \tau_4}\ (\Cap\text{-}\preceq) \qquad \frac{\tau_1 \preceq \tau_2}{!\,\tau_1 \preceq !\,\tau_2}\ (!\text{-}\preceq)$$

Subtyping rules for $\preceq_{\mathsf{nlin}}, \preceq_{\mathsf{flex}}$:

$$\frac{}{!\,\tau \preceq \omega}\ (\mathsf{weak}\text{-}\preceq) \qquad \frac{}{!\,\tau \preceq \tau}\ (\mathsf{derel}\text{-}\preceq) \qquad \frac{}{!\,\tau \preceq !\,\tau \Cap !\,\tau}\ (\mathsf{contr}\text{-}\preceq)$$

Subtyping rules for $\preceq_{\mathsf{flex}}$:

$$\frac{}{e\,(\tau_1 \to \tau_2) \preceq e\,\tau_1 \to e\,\tau_2}\ (e\text{-}\to\text{-}\preceq) \qquad \frac{}{!\,(\tau_1 \to \tau_2) \preceq !\,\tau_1 \to !\,\tau_2}\ (!\text{-}\to\text{-}\preceq)$$

$$\frac{}{\omega \preceq \omega \to \omega}\ (\omega\text{-}\to\text{-}\preceq) \qquad \frac{}{(\tau_1 \to \tau_3) \Cap (\tau_2 \to \tau_4) \preceq (\tau_1 \Cap \tau_2) \to (\tau_3 \Cap \tau_4)}\ (\Cap\text{-}\to\text{-}\preceq)$$

Fig. 4. Subtyping rules.

Convention 5.3 *Henceforth, only valid skeletons are considered.* □

Let typing, constraint, tenv, and rtype be functions s.t. $(M \rhd Q) : \langle A \vdash \tau \rangle \,/\, \Delta$ implies $\mathsf{typing}(Q) = \langle A \vdash \tau \rangle$, $\mathsf{constraint}(Q) = \Delta$, $\mathsf{tenv}(Q) = A$, and $\mathsf{rtype}(Q) = \tau$.

6 Subtyping and Solvedness

This section defines whether a constraint Δ is *solved* w.r.t. a subtyping relation $\preceq$, and presents three interesting subtyping relations. Sec. 7 will show that if Δ is solved w.r.t. one of these relations, then the judgement $(M \rhd Q) : \langle A \vdash \tau \rangle \,/\, \Delta$ is preserved by call-by-need evaluation of M (Δ may change to some solved Δ').

Let $\preceq$ be a metavariable ranging over subtyping relations on types. A constraint Δ is *solved* w.r.t. $\preceq$ iff $\mathsf{solved}(\preceq, \Delta)$ holds by this definition (where the double bar is meant as an equivalence):

$$\frac{\tau_1 \preceq \tau_2}{\mathsf{solved}(\preceq, \tau_1 \leq \tau_2)} \qquad \frac{\mathsf{solved}(\preceq, \Delta_1) \quad \mathsf{solved}(\preceq, \Delta_2)}{\mathsf{solved}(\preceq, \Delta_1 \Cap \Delta_2)}$$

$$\frac{\mathsf{solved}(\preceq, \Delta)}{\mathsf{solved}(\preceq, e\,\Delta)} \qquad \frac{\mathsf{solved}(\preceq, \Delta)}{\mathsf{solved}(\preceq, !\,\Delta)} \qquad \frac{}{\mathsf{solved}(\preceq, \omega)}$$

A skeleton Q is *solved* iff $\mathsf{constraint}(Q)$ is. Solved skeletons correspond to typing derivations in traditional presentations.

Fig. 4 presents subtyping relations $\preceq_{\mathsf{refl}}$ ("reflexive"), $\preceq_{\mathsf{nlin}}$ ("non-linear"), and $\preceq_{\mathsf{flex}}$ ("flexible") for use with System E.

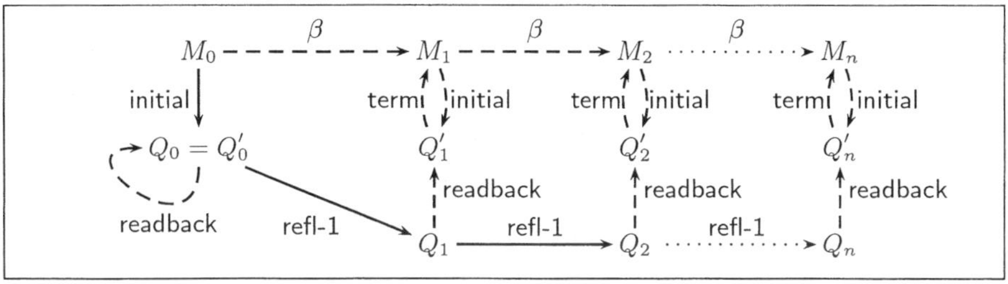

Fig. 5. Correspondence with β-reduction of a particular type inference process.

The $\preceq_{\mathsf{refl}}$ subtyping relation only allows using subtyping in trivial ways that do not add typing power. When using $\preceq_{\mathsf{refl}}$, System E is similar to System I [8], although it types more terms because it has ω. We have implemented type inference using $\preceq_{\mathsf{refl}}$ that always succeeds for any term M that has a β-normal form and that allows the β-normal form to be reconstructed from the typing.

Fig. 5 illustrates the type inference process. The full details will appear in a later paper. First, we build an initial skeleton Q_0 from the untyped term M_0 by giving every term variable the type a_0 and inserting E-variables under every abstraction (e_0) and application (e_1 for the function, e_2 for the argument). Then, the rule refl-1 is applied to $\mathsf{constraint}(Q_0)$ to generate a substitution S_0 which is used to calculate $Q_1 = [S_0]\, Q_0$. This is repeated as long as possible.

The dashed edges in the diagram in fig. 5 show a correspondence with untyped β-reduction. The function invocation $\mathsf{readback}(Q)$ looks only at $\mathsf{tenv}(Q)$, $\mathsf{rtype}(Q)$, and $\mathsf{constraint}(Q)$ to produce an initial skeleton. In addition to β-reduction following constraint solving, the converse also holds and constraint solving can follow any β-reduction sequence, e.g., the normalizing leftmost-outermost strategy. Thus, our algorithm types all β-normalizing terms. Once the β-normal form is reached, if it contains applications, an additional constraint solving rule refl-2 solves the remaining easy constraints.

Example 6.1. Consider $M_0 = (\lambda z.z \,@\, (\lambda x.\lambda y.x) \,@\, ((\lambda x.x \,@\, x) \,@\, z)) \,@\, (\lambda y.y \,@\, y)$. The normal form of M_0 is $M_5 = \lambda x.\lambda y.x$. Note that M_0 is not strongly normalizing. The initial and final skeletons for M_0 are

$$\begin{aligned} Q_0 = \;& \mathsf{e}_1\,(\lambda z.\,\mathsf{e}_0\,(\;\mathsf{e}_1\,(\mathsf{e}_1\,z^{:\mathsf{a}_0} \,@\, \mathsf{e}_2\,(\lambda x.\,\mathsf{e}_0\,\lambda y.\,\mathsf{e}_0\,x^{:\mathsf{a}_0}))\\ &\qquad\qquad @\;\mathsf{e}_2\,(\mathsf{e}_1\,(\lambda x.\,\mathsf{e}_0\,(\mathsf{e}_1\,x^{:\mathsf{a}_0} \,@\, \mathsf{e}_2\,x^{:\mathsf{a}_0})) \,@\, \mathsf{e}_2\,z^{:\mathsf{a}_0})))\\ @\;& \mathsf{e}_2\,(\lambda y.\,\mathsf{e}_0\,(\mathsf{e}_1\,y^{:\mathsf{a}_0} \,@\, \mathsf{e}_2\,y^{:\mathsf{a}_0}))\end{aligned}$$

$$\begin{aligned} Q_5 = \;& (\lambda z.\,(z^{:\tau_2}) \,@\, (\lambda x.\,\lambda y.\,x^{:\tau_1}) \Cap (\lambda x.\,\mathsf{e}_0\,(\lambda y.\,\mathsf{e}_0\,(x^{:\mathsf{a}_0}))) \,@\, \omega^{(\lambda x.x@x)@z})\\ @\;& (\lambda y.\,(y^{:\tau_1\to\omega\to\tau_1}) \,@\, (y^{:\tau_1}))\end{aligned}$$

where $\tau_1 = \mathsf{e}_0\,\mathsf{e}_0\,\mathsf{a}_0 \to \mathsf{e}_0\,(\omega \to \mathsf{e}_0\,\mathsf{a}_0)$ and $\tau_2 = (\tau_1 \to \omega \to \tau_1) \Cap \tau_1 \to \omega \to \tau_1$. The final judgement is that $(M_0 \rhd Q_5) : \langle \mathsf{env}_\omega \vdash \tau_1 \rangle \;/\; \Delta$ for some solved Δ. □

The $\preceq_{\mathsf{nlin}}$ subtyping relation adds the power of idempotent intersections:

$$!\,\tau \preceq_{\mathsf{nlin}} (!\,\tau \Cap !\,\tau) \preceq_{\mathsf{nlin}} !\,\tau$$

This allows many interesting terms to be typed at lower ranks. In particular, the system of simple types, the Hindley/Milner system, and the rank-k restrictions of traditional intersection type systems can all be embedded into System E when using $\preceq_{\mathsf{nlin}}$ by simply putting ! nearly everywhere in types.

Example 6.2. Using the $\preceq_{\mathsf{nlin}}$ subtyping relation, System E can encode arbitrarily imprecise usage information, unlike with $\preceq_{\mathsf{refl}}$ where it must be exact. For example, consider twice $= \lambda f.\lambda x.f \mathbin{@} (f \mathbin{@} x)$, and some of its typings:

$$\begin{array}{ll}(1) & \langle \mathsf{env}_\omega, !\,(\mathsf{a}_1 \to \mathsf{a}_1) \to \mathsf{a}_1 \to \mathsf{a}_1\rangle \\ (2) & \langle \mathsf{env}_\omega, (\mathsf{a}_2 \to \mathsf{a}_3) \sqcap (\mathsf{a}_1 \to \mathsf{a}_2) \to \mathsf{a}_1 \to \mathsf{a}_3\rangle \\ (3) & \langle \mathsf{env}_\omega, (\mathsf{a}_1 \to \mathsf{a}_1) \sqcap (\mathsf{a}_1 \to \mathsf{a}_1) \to \mathsf{a}_1 \to \mathsf{a}_1\rangle \\ (4) & \langle \mathsf{env}_\omega, (\mathsf{a}_1 \to \mathsf{a}_2) \sqcap !\,(\mathsf{a}_1 \to \mathsf{a}_1) \to \mathsf{a}_1 \to \mathsf{a}_2\rangle\end{array}$$

Typing (1) is like a typing with simple types; as in Linear Logic, the use of ! erases counting information, i.e., twice may use its first argument *any number of times.* Typing (2) looks like a typing in a traditional intersection type system. However, because System E types are linear by default, the typing gives more information, e.g., this typing states that the first argument is used *exactly twice.* Typing (3) is in a sense between typings (1) and (2): the first argument is used *exactly twice, at the same type.* In System E, even when intersection types are not used for additional flexibility, they can still encode precise usage information. (In an implementation, the linear part of types may of course be represented as a multiset.) Finally, typing (4) contains what we call a "must-use" type. The presence of ! on part of the argument's type erases some counting information. However, there is still one linear use: the first argument is used *at least once.* □

The $\preceq_{\mathsf{flex}}$ subtyping relation allows embedding all type derivations of the very flexible BCD type system [2], again by putting ! operators in nearly every position in types. The BCD system's subtyping rules are not satisfied by $\preceq_{\mathsf{flex}}$, but every BCD rule can be transformed into one satisfied by $\preceq_{\mathsf{flex}}$ by putting ! at all positions mentioned by the rule. The $\preceq_{\mathsf{flex}}$ relation also allows skeletons to hold the information present in Lévy-labeled λ-terms, such that constraint solving simulates labeled reduction. Our experimentation tool implements this.

Example 6.3. Consider the following variant Lévy-labeled reduction where each subterm is marked with an integer sequence. For an initial labeling, we use a distinct length-1 sequence for each subterm. The labeled reduction rule is this:

$$(\lambda x.M)^m \mathbin{@} N \xrightarrow{\beta\ell} M[x := N]^m$$

Lévy-labels (which we model with E-variables) track reduction history, and allow information flow for the original term to be extracted from the normal form (in System E, from the typing). Consider this labeled term and its normal form:

$$\begin{array}{l}M = ((\lambda x.(x^1 \mathbin{@} x^2)^3)^4 \mathbin{@} (\lambda z.(z^5 \mathbin{@} y^6)^7)^8)^9 \\ M \xrightarrow{\beta\ell}\!\!\!\!\rightarrow (y^{6\cdot 5} \mathbin{@} y^6)^{7\cdot 8\cdot 2\cdot 5\cdot 7\cdot 8\cdot 1\cdot 3\cdot 4\cdot 9}\end{array}$$

If we ask about the original term "what flows to z^5?", we can tell, by collecting labels immediately preceding label 5, that the subterms annotated 6 and 2 both flow to z^5. We can also tell which subterms influence the result. Similar to the way refl-1 corresponds to ordinary β-reduction, we have a rule flex-1 that solves constraints in a way corresponding to labeled reduction. Again, the full details will appear in a later paper. By using distinct E-variables throughout the initial skeleton, applying rule flex-1 until it no longer applies, and doing readback on the typing and constraint at that point, we get this skeleton from our implementation:

$$\mathsf{e}_9\,\mathsf{e}_4\,\mathsf{e}_3\,\mathsf{e}_1\,\mathsf{e}_8\,\mathsf{e}_7\,\mathsf{e}_5\,\mathsf{e}_2\,\mathsf{e}_8\,\mathsf{e}_7\,((\mathsf{e}_5\,\mathsf{e}_6\,(y^{:\mathsf{a}_0})^{:\mathsf{e}_6\,\mathsf{a}_0\to\mathsf{a}_0})\,@\,\mathsf{e}_6\,(y^{:\mathsf{a}_0}))$$

This skeleton has exactly the information in the reduced labeled term. □

7 Subject Reduction

This section presents subject reduction results for call-by-need reduction for the three subtyping relations presented in sec. 6.

Remark 7.1. In general, subject reduction does not hold for call-by-name reduction in System E. Consider the following example:

$$\begin{aligned}
&M = \mathsf{term}(Q) = (\lambda y.x_1 \,@\, y \,@\, y) \,@\, (x_2 \,@\, z)\\
&Q_1 = {x_1}^{:\mathsf{a}_1\to\mathsf{a}_1\to\mathsf{a}_3} \,@\, y^{:\mathsf{a}_1} \,@\, y^{:\mathsf{a}_1}\\
&Q_2 = {x_2}^{:\mathsf{a}_2\to(\mathsf{a}_1\sqcap\mathsf{a}_1)} \,@\, z^{:\mathsf{a}_2}\\
&Q = (\lambda y.\,Q_1) \,@\, Q_2\\
&\mathsf{typing}(Q_1) = \langle(x_1 : \mathsf{a}_1\to\mathsf{a}_1\to\mathsf{a}_3, y : \mathsf{a}_1\sqcap\mathsf{a}_1)\vdash\mathsf{a}_3\rangle\\
&\mathsf{typing}(Q_2) = \langle(x_2 : \mathsf{a}_2\to(\mathsf{a}_1\sqcap\mathsf{a}_1), z : \mathsf{a}_2)\vdash\mathsf{a}_1\sqcap\mathsf{a}_1\rangle\\
&\mathsf{typing}(Q) = \langle(x_1 : \mathsf{a}_1\to\mathsf{a}_1\to\mathsf{a}_3, x_2 : \mathsf{a}_2\to(\mathsf{a}_1\sqcap\mathsf{a}_1), z : \mathsf{a}_2)\vdash\mathsf{a}_3\rangle\\
&M \xrightarrow{\beta} N = \mathsf{term}(Q_1)[x := \mathsf{term}(Q_2)] = x_1 \,@\, (x_2 \,@\, z) \,@\, (x_2 \,@\, z)
\end{aligned}$$

The skeleton Q is valid since $\mathsf{rtype}(Q_2) = \mathsf{tenv}(Q_1)(y)$, and it is solved w.r.t. any subtyping relation since its constraint is ω. If subject reduction holds, we expect that there exists some Q' such that $\mathsf{term}(Q') = N$, and that has the same typing as Q. In particular, we expect that $\mathsf{tenv}(Q)(z) = \mathsf{tenv}(Q')(z) = \mathsf{a}_2$. However, the sub-skeletons of Q' corresponding to z must both have type a_2. This makes it impossible to construct Q' since, in general, $\tau \not\preceq \tau\sqcap\tau$ (i.e., $\mathsf{solved}(\preceq, \tau \leq \tau\sqcap\tau)$ does not hold for any $\preceq$ we use). Note that if we use $\preceq_{\mathsf{nlin}}$, or $\preceq_{\mathsf{flex}}$, and replace a_1 by $!\,\mathsf{a}_1$ and a_2 by $!\,\mathsf{a}_2$, then we could construct the needed skeleton Q'. □

Call-by-need reduction on untyped terms is performed by these rules:

$$\begin{array}{rcll}
(\lambda x.M) \,@\, V & \xrightarrow{\mathsf{cbn}} & M[x := V] & \\
((\lambda x.M) \,@\, (N_1 \,@\, N_2)) \,@\, P & \xrightarrow{\mathsf{cbn}} & (\lambda x.M \,@\, P) \,@\, (N_1 \,@\, N_2) & \text{if } x \notin \mathsf{FV}(P)\\
M \,@\, ((\lambda x.P) \,@\, (N_1 \,@\, N_2)) & \xrightarrow{\mathsf{cbn}} & (\lambda x.M \,@\, P) \,@\, (N_1 \,@\, N_2) & \text{if } x \notin \mathsf{FV}(M)
\end{array}$$

Let $\xrightarrow{[\mathsf{cbn}]}$ be the smallest relation such that $M \xrightarrow{\mathsf{cbn}} N$ implies $C^{\mathsf{t}}[M] \xrightarrow{[\mathsf{cbn}]} C^{\mathsf{t}}[N]$. Call-by-need evaluation is then a specific strategy of using these rules [1]. We do not include any rule for garbage collection, because it does not affect subject reduction.

Theorem 7.2 (Subject Reduction). *Given* $\preceq \in \{\preceq_{\mathsf{refl}}, \preceq_{\mathsf{nlin}}, \preceq_{\mathsf{flex}}\}$ *and a skeleton* Q_1 *such that* $(M_1 \triangleright Q_1) : \langle A \vdash \tau \rangle \;/\; \Delta_1$, $\mathsf{solved}(\preceq, \Delta_1)$, *and* $M_1 \xrightarrow{[\mathsf{cbn}]} M_2$, *there exists* Q_2 *s.t.* $(M_2 \triangleright Q_2) : \langle A \vdash \tau \rangle \;/\; \Delta_2$ *and* $\mathsf{solved}(\preceq, \Delta_2)$. □

Proof. The theorem is proved by induction on Q_1. The proof uses inversion properties for variant subtyping definitions without explicit transitivity. □

References

[1] Z. M. Ariola, M. Felleisen, J. Maraist, M. Odersky, P. Wadler. The call-by-need lambda calculus. In *Conf. Rec. 22nd Ann. ACM Symp. Princ. of Prog. Langs.*, 1995.

[2] H. Barendregt, M. Coppo, M. Dezani-Ciancaglini. A filter lambda model and the completeness of type assignment. *J. Symbolic Logic*, 48(4), 1983.

[3] S. Carlier. Polar type inference with intersection types and ω. In *Proceedings of the 2nd Workshop on Intersection Types and Related Systems*, 2002. The ITRS '02 proceedings appears as vol. 70, issue 1 of *Elec. Notes in Theoret. Comp. Sci.*

[4] M. Coppo, M. Dezani-Ciancaglini, B. Venneri. Principal type schemes and λ-calculus semantics. In J. R. Hindley, J. P. Seldin, eds., *To H. B. Curry: Essays on Combinatory Logic, Lambda Calculus, and Formalism.* Academic Press, 1980.

[5] L. Damas, R. Milner. Principal type schemes for functional programs. In *Conf. Rec. 9th Ann. ACM Symp. Princ. of Prog. Langs.*, 1982.

[6] J.-Y. Girard. *Interprétation Fonctionnelle et Elimination des Coupures de l'Arithmétique d'Ordre Supérieur.* Thèse d'Etat, Université de Paris VII, 1972.

[7] T. Jim. What are principal typings and what are they good for? In *Conf. Rec. POPL '96: 23rd ACM Symp. Princ. of Prog. Langs.*, 1996.

[8] A. J. Kfoury, J. B. Wells. Principality and decidable type inference for finite-rank intersection types. In POPL '99 [14]. Superseded by [10].

[9] A. J. Kfoury, J. B. Wells. Principality and type inference for intersection types using expansion variables. Supersedes [8], 2003.

[10] A. J. Kfoury, J. B. Wells. Principality and type inference for intersection types using expansion variables. *Theoret. Comput. Sci.*, 200X. To appear. Supersedes [8]. For omitted proofs, see the longer report [9].

[11] N. Kobayashi. Quasi-linear types. In POPL '99 [14].

[12] R. Milner. A theory of type polymorphism in programming. *J. Comput. System Sci.*, 17, 1978.

[13] J. C. Mitchell, G. D. Plotkin. Abstract types have existential type. *ACM Trans. on Prog. Langs. & Systs.*, 10(3), 1988.

[14] *Conf. Rec. POPL '99: 26th ACM Symp. Princ. of Prog. Langs.*, 1999.

[15] J. C. Reynolds. Towards a theory of type structure. In *Colloque sur la Programmation*, vol. 19 of *LNCS*, Paris, France, 1974. Springer-Verlag.

[16] D. N. Turner, P. Wadler. Operational interpretations of linear logic. *Theoret. Comput. Sci.*, 227(1–2), 1999.

[17] D. N. Turner, P. Wadler, C. Mossin. Once upon a type. In *7th International Conference on Functional Programming and Computer Architecture*, San Diego, California, 1995.

[18] S. J. van Bakel. Intersection type assignment systems. *Theoret. Comput. Sci.*, 151(2), 1995.

[19] P. Wadler. Linear types can change the world. In M. Broy, C. B. Jones, eds., *IFIP TC 2 Working Conference on Programming Concepts and Methods*, 1990.
[20] P. Wadler. Is there a use for linear logic? In *Partial Evaluation and Semantics-Based Program Manipulation (PEPM)*. ACM Press, 1991.
[21] K. Wansbrough, S. P. Jones. Once upon a polymorphic type. In POPL '99 [14].
[22] J. B. Wells. The essence of principal typings. In *Proc. 29th Int'l Coll. Automata, Languages, and Programming*, vol. 2380 of *LNCS*. Springer-Verlag, 2002.

A Hardest Attacker for Leaking References

René Rydhof Hansen

Informatics and Mathematical Modelling
Technical University of Denmark
DK-2800 Kongens Lyngby, Denmark
rrh@imm.dtu.dk

Abstract. Java Card is a variant of Java designed for use in smart cards and other systems with limited resources. Applets running on a smart card are protected from each other by the *applet firewall*, allowing communication only through *shared objects*. Security can be breached if a reference to a shared object is leaked to a hostile applet.
In this paper we develop a Control Flow Analysis for a small language based on Java Card, which will guarantee that sensitive object references can not be leaked to a particular (attack) applet. The analysis is used as a basis for formulating a *hardest attacker* that will expand the guarantee to cover *all possible* attackers.

1 Introduction

The Java Card platform is a multi-applet platform, meaning that a given Java Card may contain and execute several different applets from several different, possibly competing, vendors. In order for an applet to protect sensitive data from other, malicious, applets the Java Card platform implements an *applet firewall* to separate applets from each other by disallowing all communication, e.g., method invocation or field access, between applets. However, for certain applications, e.g., loyalty applets (applets implementing a customer loyalty scheme), it is desirable to allow (limited) communication between applets. Such communication is possible through the use of *shared objects* which allows an object with a reference to a shared object to invoke methods in the shared object. The problem with this approach is that it allows *any* object with such a reference to access the shared object. Thus it is necessary to ensure that certain objects references are not leaked to untrusted (attacker) applets. In [1] a static analysis is presented that for a given set of applets determines if a reference has been leaked. Such an approach works well provided the entire program is known *a priori*, which is not always possible because the Java Card framework allows dynamic loading of applets and therefore it is, in general, impossible to know the context in which an applet may run. This is a fundamental problem of any solution based on whole-program analysis. In this paper we solve the problem by developing a so-called *hardest attacker*, based on a control flow analysis [2] and inspired by the work on firewall validation in the ambient calculus [3]. By analysing a program in conjunction with the hardest attacker we can guarantee that object references are never leaked to *any* attacker, even if downloaded dynamically.

D.A. Schmidt (Ed.): ESOP 2004, LNCS 2986, pp. 310–324, 2004.

For presentation purposes we develop our solution for a small bytecode language based on the Java Card Virtual Machine Language (JCVML). We have chosen to work at the level of the virtual machine because it is at this level applets are actually loaded onto the card. It also has the added advantage that there is no need to trust a compiler to not insert malicious code. This helps reducing the size of the *trusted computing base.* The remainder of the paper is structured as follows. Section 2 introduces the target language, Section 3 formalises the notion of leaking references. Section 4 presents the underlying control flow analysis and discusses a number of theoretical properties of the analysis. Finally in Section 5 the hardest attacker is described and discussed. Section 6 concludes and discusses future work.

2 The Carmel$_0$ Language

Carmel$_0$ is an abstraction of the Java Card Virtual Machine Language (JCVML). It abstracts away some of the implementation details, e.g., the constant pool, and all the features that are not essential to our development, e.g., static fields and static methods. The language is a subset of Carmel which is itself a rational reconstruction of the JCVML that retains the full expressive power of JCVML. See [4] for a specification and discussion of the full Carmel language.

The instruction set for Carmel$_0$ includes instructions for stack manipulation, local variables, object generation, field access, a simple conditional, and method invocation and return:

$$\begin{aligned}\mathsf{Instr} ::= {} & \texttt{push}\ c \mid \texttt{pop}\ n \mid \texttt{numop}\ op \mid \texttt{load}\ x \mid \texttt{store}\ x \mid \texttt{new}\ \sigma \mid \texttt{return} \\ \mid {} & \texttt{getfield}\ f \mid \texttt{putfield}\ f \mid \texttt{if}\ cmpOp\ \texttt{goto}\ pc_0 \mid \texttt{invokevirtual}\ m\end{aligned}$$

A Carmel$_0$ program, $P \in \mathsf{Program}$, is then defined to be the set of classes it defines: $P.classes$. Each class, $\sigma \in \mathsf{Class}$, contains a set of methods, $\sigma.methods$, and each method, $m \in \mathsf{Method}$, comprises a number of instance fields, $m.fields \subseteq \mathcal{P}(\mathsf{Field})$, and an instruction for each program counter, $pc \in \mathbb{N}_0$ in the method, $m.instructionAt(pc) \in \mathsf{Instr}$. For two programs P and Q such that $P.classes \cap Q.classes = \emptyset$ we shall write $P \mid Q$ for the obvious composition (concatenation) of the two programs.

We shall use a JCVML-like syntax for our examples, as shown in Figure 1. The example is a simplified version of a typical situation in Java Card applications: two applets (classes) wish to communicate (in the form of a method invocation from `Alice` to `Bob`). The method invocation is set up in `Alice.m_Alice` by first loading a reference to the object of the method to be invoked (line 0) which has been passed as a parameter to `m_Alice` into local variable number 1, and then the actual parameters are loaded from local variable 1 (line 1), in this case it is a (self-)reference to `Alice`, which by convention can be found in local variable 0. Finally the method is invoked (line 2). Note that the method to be invoked is identified by its class name, method name, and type signature (hence the `Object` in line 2 of `Alice.m_Alice`). The semantics is formalised in Section 2.1.

In real JCVML applets method invocation is the only form of communication that is allowed to cross the firewall boundary and only if the right object reference is known (in the example `Alice` must have a reference to `Bob`). As mentioned earlier, this can lead to problems if references are leaked. In the example program `Alice` wishes to communicate with `Bob` but also wants to make sure that `Bob` does not leak the `Alice`-reference to anyone else. In Section 3 we formalise the notion of leaking references.

```
class Alice {
  void m_Alice(Bob) {
    0: load 1
    1: load 0
    2: invokevirtual Bob.update(Object)
    3: return
  }
  /* ... */
}
```

```
class Bob {
  Object cache;

  void m_Bob() {
    0: return
  }
  void update(Object) {
    0: load 0
    1: load 1
    2: putfield Bob.cache
    /* ... */
    3: return
  }
}
```

Fig. 1. Example Carmel$_0$ Program P_{AB}

2.1 Semantics for Carmel$_0$

The semantics for Carmel$_0$ is a straightforward small step semantics, based on the corresponding semantics for full Carmel [4]. We briefly discuss the semantic domains before specifying the reduction rules.

A value is either a number or an object reference (a location): $\mathsf{Val} = \mathsf{Num} + \mathsf{ObjRef}$. The (global) heap is then a map from object references to objects: $\mathsf{Heap} = \mathsf{ObjRef} \to \mathsf{Object}$, where objects are simply maps from field names to values: $\mathsf{Object} = \mathsf{Field} \to \mathsf{Val}$. The operand stack is modelled as a sequence of values: $\mathsf{Stack} = \mathsf{Val}^*$ and the local heap (for a methods local variables) is then modelled as a map from (local) variables to values: $\mathsf{LocHeap} = \mathsf{Var} \to \mathsf{Val}$. Stack frames record the current method and program counter along with a local heap and an operand stack: $\mathsf{Frames} = \mathsf{Method} \times \mathbb{N}_0 \times \mathsf{LocHeap} \times \mathsf{Stack}$

With the semantics domains we can now specify the semantic configurations and the reduction rules. The configurations are on the form: $\langle H, F :: SF \rangle$ where $H \in \mathsf{Heap}$, $SF \in \mathsf{Frames}^*$, and $F = \langle m, pc, L, S \rangle \in \mathsf{Frames}$, meaning that the program is currently executing the instruction at program counter pc in method m with local heap L and operand stack S. This leads to reduction rules of the following form for a given program, $P \in \mathsf{Program}$: $P \vdash \langle H, F :: SF \rangle \Longrightarrow \langle H', F' :: SF' \rangle$. In Figure 2 a few reduction rules are shown; for lack of space we only show the most interesting rules, the remaining rules are either trivial or obvious. In the reduction rule for `invokevirtual` (method invocation) we must take care to handle dynamic dispatch correctly. This is done as in JCVML by using a function, *methodLookup*, to represent the class hierarchy. It takes a method identifier, m', and a class, $o.class$, as parameters and returns the method, m_v, that implements the body of m', i.e., the latest definition of m' in the class hierarchy. In the same rule, note that a pointer to the object is passed to the object itself in local variable number 0.

$$\frac{m.instructionAt(pc) = \texttt{push}\ c}{P \vdash \langle H, \langle m, pc, L, S\rangle :: SF\rangle \Longrightarrow \langle H, \langle m, pc+1, L, c :: S\rangle :: SF\rangle}$$

$$\frac{m.instructionAt(pc) = \texttt{load}\ x}{P \vdash \langle H, \langle m, pc, L, S\rangle :: SF\rangle \Longrightarrow \langle H, \langle m, pc+1, L, L(x) :: S\rangle :: SF\rangle}$$

$$\frac{\begin{array}{c} m.instructionAt(pc) = \texttt{new}\ \sigma \wedge \\ loc \notin \mathrm{dom}(H) \wedge H' = H[loc \mapsto o] \wedge o = newObject(\sigma) \end{array}}{P \vdash \langle H, \langle m, pc, L, S\rangle :: SF\rangle \Longrightarrow \langle H', \langle m, pc+1, L, loc :: S\rangle :: SF\rangle}$$

$$\frac{\begin{array}{c} m.instructionAt(pc) = \texttt{putfield}\ f \wedge \\ H' = H[loc \mapsto o'] \wedge o' = H(loc)[f \mapsto v] \end{array}}{P \vdash \langle H, \langle m, pc, L, v :: loc :: S\rangle :: SF\rangle \Longrightarrow \langle H', \langle m, pc+1, L, S\rangle :: SF\rangle}$$

$$\frac{\begin{array}{c} m.instructionAt(pc) = \texttt{invokevirtual}\ m' \wedge \\ S = v_1 :: \cdots :: v_{|m'|} :: loc :: S_0 \wedge m_v = methodLookup(m', o.class) \wedge \\ o = H(loc) \wedge L' = L[0 \mapsto loc, 1 \mapsto v_1, \ldots, |m'| \mapsto v_{|m'|}] \end{array}}{P \vdash \langle H, \langle m, pc, L, S\rangle :: SF\rangle \Longrightarrow \langle H, \langle m_v, 0, L', \epsilon\rangle :: \langle m, pc, L, S\rangle :: SF\rangle}$$

Fig. 2. Semantic rules (excerpt)

In order to complete our discussion of the semantics, we need to define the initial configurations for a given program. In the JCVML applet execution is initiated by the run-time environment when the host sends the appropriate commands for installing and selecting an applet. The run-time environment then sets up an initial configuration with the appropriate method, applet instance, and parameters. We simplify this model by assuming that for a given program, $P \in \mathsf{Program}$, there exists an instance for each of the programs classes, $\sigma \in P.classes$, with a corresponding object reference, loc_σ, pointing to that instance, and a single entry point, m_σ.

In JCVML communication across the firewall boundary can only take place through so-called *shared objects*: When a JCVML applet wishes to communicate with another applet, it first has to obtain an object reference to such a shared object (if one exists) set up by the applet it wishes to communicate with. The shared objects can be thought of as an *access control* mechanism where holders of a reference to a shared object are allowed to communicate with that object. References to shared objects are obtained by executing a trivial, if tedious, protocol involving the run-time system to make the actual transfer across the firewall. While there are no real technical difficulties in modelling this, it does not add any particular insights and instead we choose a simpler model: Any allowed sharing is set up at initialisation time. Thus, when defining a program we must also define what sharing is allowed to take place in that program. Formally we must define a function, $\mathit{sharing} : \mathsf{Program} \times \mathsf{Class} \to \mathsf{Class}^*$, that for each class in a program returns a list of classes (applets) it is allowed to access. During initialisation the shared references of a class are then passed to the corresponding entry point as in a method invocation (including a self-reference to the class in question) to the local variables of the entry point. Taking all of the above into account we can now define initial configurations for Carmel_0 programs:

Definition 1 (Initial Configurations). *If* $P \in \mathsf{Program}$ *then* C *is an* initial configuration *if and only if* $\sigma \in P.\mathit{classes}$, $P.\mathit{sharing}(\sigma) = \sigma_1 :: \cdots :: \sigma_n$, $\sigma_i \in P.\mathit{classes}$, *and* $C = \langle H, \langle m_\sigma, 0, [0 \mapsto loc_\sigma, 1 \mapsto loc_{\sigma_1}, \ldots, n \mapsto loc_{\sigma_n}], \epsilon\rangle :: \epsilon\rangle$

3 Leaking References

Intuitively we say that a class, τ, has been "leaked" to another class, σ, if there is an object of class σ or a method invocation in an object of class σ that contains, either in an instance field or in the local heap or on the operand stack, a reference to τ. In order to formalise this intuition, we shall write $v \Subset S$ for operand stacks $S \in \mathsf{Stack}$ if $S = v_1 :: \cdots :: v_n$ and $\exists i : v = v_i$. A similar notation is adopted for local heaps, $L \in \mathsf{LocHeap}$: we write $v \Subset L$ if $\exists x \in \mathrm{dom}(L) : L(x) = v$. We are now ready to formally define when a class has been leaked:

Definition 2 (Leaked). *Given a configuration,* $\langle H, SF\rangle$ *a class* τ *is said to be* leaked to class σ in $\langle H, SF\rangle$, *written* $\langle H, SF\rangle \vdash \tau \rightsquigarrow \sigma$, *iff* $\exists loc_\tau \exists loc_\sigma \exists f$: $(H(loc_\tau).class = \tau \;\wedge\; H(loc_\sigma).class = \sigma \;\wedge\; H(loc_\sigma).f = loc_\tau)$ *or* $\exists loc_\tau$ $\exists \langle m, pc, L, S\rangle \in SF\colon H(loc_\tau).class = \tau \wedge m.class = \sigma \wedge (loc_\tau \Subset S \vee loc_\tau \Subset L)$.

In order to be really useful, it is not enough to consider only single configurations. We therefore extend the notion of "leaked" to cover entire programs:

Definition 3 (Leaked). *A class* τ *is* leaked to σ in program P, *written* $P \vdash \tau \rightsquigarrow \sigma$, *if and only if there exists* C_0 *and* C *such that* C_0 *is an initial configuration of* P *and* $P \vdash C_0 \Longrightarrow^* C$ *such that* $C \vdash \tau \rightsquigarrow \sigma$.

We shall write $P \vdash \tau \not\rightsquigarrow \sigma$ to mean that class τ is *not* leaked to class σ in P.

As an example, consider the program in Figure 1 extended with the program in Figure 3, i.e., $P_{AB} \mid P_M$, and let P_{ABM} denote the entire program. Let us further assume that both `Alice` and `Mallet` are allowed to communicate with `Bob`, i.e., $P_{ABM}.\mathit{sharing}(\texttt{Alice}) = P_{ABM}.\mathit{sharing}(\texttt{Mallet}) = \{\texttt{Bob}\}$ Then, by executing the program it is easy to see that $P_{ABM} \vdash \texttt{Alice} \rightsquigarrow \texttt{Mallet}$, and

```
class Mallet {
  void m_Mallet(Bob) {
    0: load 1
    1: getfield Bob.cache
    2: return
  }
}
```

Fig. 3. "Malicious" program P_M.

```
class Charlie {
  void m_Charlie(Bob) {
    0: load 1
    1: invokevirtual Bob.m_Bob()
    2: return
  }
}
```

Fig. 4. "Innocuous" program P_C.

therefore `Alice` can be attacked by `Mallet`, simply because `Bob` "caches" the reference from `Alice`. Consider on the other hand the program $P_{ABC} = P_{AB} \mid P_C$ obtained by extending program P_{AB} with the program in Figure 4. It should be intuitively clear that `Alice` is not leaked to `Charlie` in P_{ABC}, because `Charlie` does not access fields in `Bob` that it is not supposed to. However in order to prove that we must try *all possible* executions of the program. In the following section we develop a control flow analysis capable of computing a conservative estimate of all possible executions. This is then used to prove that $P_{ABC} \vdash$ `Alice` $\not\leadsto$ `Charlie`. In [1] a conceptually similar approach is taken, for a slightly different subset of JCVML, with a special focus on the initial sharing and the firewall; to simplify presentation and analysis a three-address representation/conversion of JCVML is used and relevant API calls, in particular those for exchanging references to shared objects, are modelled as instructions. The approach in [1] is essentially a whole-program approach and thus the problem of dynamically downloaded applets is not considered.

4 Control Flow Analysis for Carmel$_0$

In this section we describe a control flow analysis for Carmel$_0$. The analysis is quite similar, in spirit, to the analysis developed in [5]. However, in anticipation of our intended use of the analysis, we develop a somewhat simpler (less precise) analysis, although with the added feature that it is parameterised on two equivalence relations: one on (object) classes, $\equiv_C \subseteq \mathsf{Class} \times \mathsf{Class}$, and one on methods, $\equiv_M \subseteq \mathsf{Method} \times \mathsf{Method}$. We let $[\cdot]_C : \mathsf{Class} \to \mathsf{Class}_{/\equiv_C}$ and $[\cdot]_M : \mathsf{Method} \to \mathsf{Method}_{/\equiv_M}$ denote the corresponding characteristic maps, that map a class or method respectively to its equivalence class. The reason for introducing these equivalence relations into the analysis is mainly that they allow us to partition the infinite number of names (for classes and methods) into a finite number of partitions and thereby enabling us to generate a finite Hardest Attacker (cf. Section 5 for more details). Furthermore, the partitioning can be used to "fine tune" the precision of the analysis: by choosing fewer equivalence classes the less precise (and less costly) the analysis and vice versa. Next we define the abstract domains for the analysis.

4.1 Abstract Domains

The abstract domains are simplified versions of the concrete domains used in the semantics. The simplification consists of removing information that is not pertinent to the analysis. Our abstract domain for representing object references in the analysis is similar to the notion of *class object graphs* from [6], thus object references should be modelled as classes. However, we have to take the equivalence relation over classes into consideration and therefore define an abstract object reference to be an equivalence class: $\widehat{\mathsf{ObjRef}} = \mathsf{Class}_{/\equiv_C}$ In order to enhance readability we write $[\text{Ref } \sigma]_C$, rather than just $[\sigma]_C$, for abstract object references. Following the semantics values are taken to be either numerical values or object references: $\mathsf{AbsVal} = \{\mathsf{INT}\} + \widehat{\mathsf{ObjRef}}$ and abstract values to be sets of such values: $\widehat{\mathsf{Val}} = \mathcal{P}(\mathsf{AbsVal})$. Since we are only interested in control flow analysis we do not try to track actual values (data flow analysis). Objects are modelled simply as an abstract value representing the (union of the values of all the) fields of the object: $\widehat{\mathsf{Object}} = \widehat{\mathsf{Val}}$. Addresses consist of a (fully qualified) method and a program counter, making them unique in a program: $\mathsf{Addr} = \mathsf{Method} \times \mathbb{N}_0$. The local heap tracks the values contained in the local variables of a given method: $\widehat{\mathsf{LocHeap}} = \mathsf{Method}_{/\equiv_M} \to \widehat{\mathsf{Val}}$. The operand stack is represented in a similar manner: for each method we track the set of values possibly on the stack: $\widehat{\mathsf{Stack}} = \mathsf{Method}_{/\equiv_M} \to \widehat{\mathsf{Val}}$. Finally we model the global heap as a map from object references to objects: $\widehat{\mathsf{Heap}} = \widehat{\mathsf{ObjRef}} \to \widehat{\mathsf{Object}}$.

4.2 Flow Logic Specification

An analysis is specified in the Flow Logic framework [7] by defining what it means for a proposed analysis result to be correct with respect to the analysed program. Thereby separating the specification of the analysis from the implementation of the analysis, making it easy to construct new analyses.

The judgements of our Flow Logic specification will have the following general form: $(\hat{H}, \hat{L}, \hat{S}) \models \texttt{addr} : \texttt{instr}$ where $\hat{H} \in \widehat{\mathsf{Heap}}$, $\hat{L} \in \widehat{\mathsf{LocHeap}}$, $\hat{S} \in \widehat{\mathsf{Stack}}$, $\texttt{addr} \in \mathsf{Addr}$, and $\texttt{instr} \in \mathsf{Instr}$. Intuitively the above judgement can be read as: $(\hat{H}, \hat{L}, \hat{S})$ is a *correct* analysis of the instruction `instr` found at address `addr`.

The full Flow Logic specification is given in Figure 5. We shall only explain a few of the judgements in detail. First the judgement for the `new` instruction. In the semantics two things happen: a new location is allocated in the heap, and a reference to the newly created object is placed on top of the stack. In the analysis only the last step is modelled: $\{[\text{Ref } \sigma]_C\} \subseteq \hat{S}([m_0]_M)$. This is because in the analysis objects are abstracted into the union of values stored in the objects instance fields, and since a newly created object has no values stored in its fields (we do not model static initialisation) it is essentially empty. Modelling that in the analysis we would write: $\emptyset \subseteq \hat{H}([\text{Ref } \sigma]_C)$ which trivially holds and thus does not contribute to the analysis. Note that the specification for the pop-instruction is trivially true. This is because the operand stack is (over-)approximated simply as the set of values that could possibly be on the stack

$$
\begin{array}{lll}
(\hat{H},\hat{L},\hat{S}) \models (m_0,pc_0) : \texttt{new } \sigma & \text{iff} & \{[\text{Ref } \sigma]_C\} \subseteq \hat{S}([m_0]_M) \\
(\hat{H},\hat{L},\hat{S}) \models (m_0,pc_0) : \texttt{load } x & \text{iff} & \hat{L}([m_0]_M) \subseteq \hat{S}([m_0]_M) \\
(\hat{H},\hat{L},\hat{S}) \models (m_0,pc_0) : \texttt{store } x & \text{iff} & \hat{S}([m_0]_M) \subseteq \hat{L}([m_0]_M) \\
(\hat{H},\hat{L},\hat{S}) \models (m_0,pc_0) : \texttt{push } c & \text{iff} & \{\mathsf{INT}\} \subseteq \hat{S}([m_0]_M) \\
(\hat{H},\hat{L},\hat{S}) \models (m_0,pc_0) : \texttt{pop } n & \text{iff} & \mathit{true} \\
(\hat{H},\hat{L},\hat{S}) \models (m_0,pc_0) : \texttt{numop} & \text{iff} & \mathit{true} \\
(\hat{H},\hat{L},\hat{S}) \models (m_0,pc_0) : \texttt{if } \mathit{cmpOp} \texttt{ goto } pc & \text{iff} & \mathit{true} \\
(\hat{H},\hat{L},\hat{S}) \models (m_0,pc_0) : \texttt{getfield } f & \text{iff} & \forall [\text{Ref } \sigma]_C \in \hat{S}([m_0]_M) : \\
 & & \quad \hat{H}([\text{Ref } \sigma]_C) \subseteq \hat{S}([m_0]_M) \\
(\hat{H},\hat{L},\hat{S}) \models (m_0,pc_0) : \texttt{putfield } f & \text{iff} & \forall [\text{Ref } \sigma]_C \in \hat{S}([m_0]_M) : \\
 & & \quad \hat{S}([m_0]_M) \subseteq \hat{H}([\text{Ref } \sigma]_C) \\
(\hat{H},\hat{L},\hat{S}) \models (m_0,pc_0) : \texttt{return} & \text{iff} & \mathit{true} \\
\multicolumn{3}{l}{(\hat{H},\hat{L},\hat{S}) \models (m_0,pc_0) : \texttt{invokevirtual } m} \\
\multicolumn{3}{l}{\quad \text{iff } \forall [\text{Ref } \sigma]_C \in \hat{S}([m_0]_M) :} \\
\multicolumn{3}{l}{\qquad \forall [m_v]_M \in \mathit{methodLookup}_{/\equiv}(m, [\text{Ref } \sigma]_C)} \\
\multicolumn{3}{l}{\qquad\quad \hat{S}([m_0]_M) \subseteq \hat{L}([m_v]_M)} \\
\multicolumn{3}{l}{\qquad\quad [m_v]_M.\mathit{returnVal} \Rightarrow \hat{S}([m_v]_M) \subseteq \hat{S}([m_0]_M)}
\end{array}
$$

Fig. 5. Flow Logic specification

anytime during execution of the program and therefore pop has no effect in the analysis. Similarly for the `if`, `numop`, and `return` instructions. A prerequisite for analysing the `invokevirtual` instruction is a model of the dynamic dispatch, i.e., we need an abstract version of the *methodLookup* function, taking the equivalence classes on methods and classes into account: $\mathit{methodLookup}_{/\equiv}(m, [\text{Ref } \sigma]_C) = \{[m_v]_M | \, m_v = \mathit{methodLookup}(m, \text{Ref } \sigma'), \text{Ref } \sigma' \in [\text{Ref } \sigma]_C\}$. This is not the only possible choice, but fits the purpose well and is trivially sound. However, this definition introduces a minor problem with methods that return a value: In order to determine if a given method returns a value it is enough to check if the methods return type is different from `void` ($m.\mathit{returnType} \neq \texttt{void}$). Taking equivalence classes into account, we have to approximate this by saying that the equivalence class of a method returns a value if any one of the methods in the equivalence class returns a value, thus $[m]_M.\mathit{returnVal} = \mathit{true}$ if $\exists m' \in [m]_M : m.\mathit{returnType} \neq \texttt{void}$ and $[m]_M.\mathit{returnVal} = \mathit{false}$ otherwise. The predicate defines a sound approximation, since it will compute an over-approximation of the possible flows. With these auxiliary predicates in place, the Flow Logic judgement for the `invokevirtual` instruction is straightforward. We first locate any object references on top of the stack: $\forall [\text{Ref } \sigma]_C \in \hat{S}([m_0]_M)$. The object references found are used to lookup the method to execute, modelled by a set of method equivalence classes: $\forall [m_v]_M \in \mathit{methodLookup}_{/\equiv}(m, [\text{Ref } \sigma]_C)$. The next step is then to transfer any arguments from the operand stack of the invoking method to the local variables of the invoked method: $\hat{S}([m_0]_M) \subseteq \hat{L}([m_v]_M)$.

Finally, if the method returns a value we make sure to copy that back to the invoking method: $[m_v]_M.\mathit{returnVal} \Rightarrow \hat{S}([m_v]_M) \subseteq \hat{S}([m_0]_M)$. The remainder of the judgements are created by following similar reasoning. Having specified how to analyse individual instructions, we lift this to cover entire programs in a straightforward way based on initial configurations in the semantics:

$$\begin{array}{l}(\hat{H}, \hat{L}, \hat{S}) \models P \quad \text{iff} \\ \quad \forall (m, pc) \in P.\mathit{addresses} : \\ \quad\quad m.\mathit{instructionAt}(pc) = \texttt{instr} \Rightarrow (\hat{H}, \hat{L}, \hat{S}) \models (m, pc) : \texttt{instr} \\ \quad \forall \sigma \in P.\mathit{classes} : [\text{Ref } \sigma]_C \in \hat{L}([m_\sigma]_M) \\ \quad P.\mathit{sharing}(\sigma) = \sigma_1 :: \cdots :: \sigma_n \Rightarrow \{[\text{Ref } \sigma_1]_C, \ldots, [\text{Ref } \sigma_n]_C\} \subseteq \hat{L}([m_\sigma]_M)\end{array}$$

4.3 Theoretical Properties

In order to show the semantic soundness of the control flow analysis, we follow the approach of [8,5] and define *representation functions* for all the concrete domains. Intuitively a representation function maps a concrete semantics object, e.g., an integer, to its abstract representation in the corresponding abstract domain. In the case of integers this abstract representation is simply a token, INT, leading to the following representation function: $\beta_{\text{Num}}(n) = \{\mathsf{INT}\}$.

The notion of a location or an object reference only makes sense relative to a given heap, thus the representation function for locations is parameterised on the particular heap to use: $\beta^H_{\text{ObjRef}}(\mathit{loc}) = \{[\text{Ref } \sigma]_C\}$ if $H(\mathit{loc}).\mathit{class} = \sigma$. Combining the above two representation functions, that cover all of the basic values in a Carmel$_0$ program, we obtain a representation function for basic values: $\beta^H_{\text{Val}}(v) = \beta_{\text{Num}}(v)$ if $v \in \mathsf{Num}$ and $\beta^H_{\text{Val}}(v) = \beta_{\text{ObjRef}}(v)$ if $v \in \mathsf{ObjRef}$. Objects are represented simply as the "union" of all the values in all the objects fields, giving rise to the following representation function $\beta^H_{\text{Object}}(o) = \bigcup_{f \in \text{dom}(o)} \beta^H_{\text{Val}}(o.f)$. Finally we can define a representation function for heaps such that all objects of the same class are merged:

$$\beta_{\text{Heap}}(H)([\text{Ref } \sigma]_C) = \bigcup_{\substack{\mathit{loc} \in \text{dom}(H) \\ \beta^H_{\text{Val}}(\mathit{loc}) = [\text{Ref } \sigma]_C}} \beta^H_{\text{Object}}(H(\mathit{loc}))$$

The last step is to relate concrete semantic configurations to their abstract equivalents: $\langle H, SF \rangle\ \hat{\mathcal{R}}_{\text{Conf}}\ (\hat{H}, \hat{L}, \hat{S})$ iff $\beta_{\text{Heap}}(H) \sqsubseteq \hat{H} \wedge SF\ \hat{\mathcal{R}}^H_{\text{Frames}}\ (\hat{L}, \hat{S})$ where $(\langle m_1, pc_1, L_1, S_1 \rangle :: \cdots :: \langle m_n, pc_n, L_n, S_n \rangle)\ \hat{\mathcal{R}}^H_{\text{Frames}}\ (\hat{L}, \hat{S})$ iff $\forall i \in \{1, \ldots, n\}$: $\beta_{\text{LocHeap}}(L_i) \sqsubseteq \hat{L}([m_i]_M) \wedge \beta_{\text{Stack}}(S_i) \sqsubseteq \hat{S}([m_i]_M)$. We are now in a position to state and prove that the control flow analysis is semantically sound. Following the tradition of Flow Logic specifications this is done by establishing a *subject reduction* property for the analysis, i.e., that the analysis is invariant under semantic reduction; this is very similar to the approach taken for type and effect systems. Below we take $\Longrightarrow^*$ to mean the reflexive and transitive closure of $\Longrightarrow$:

Theorem 1 (Soundness). *If $P \in$ Program, C_0 is an initial configuration of P, $C_0 \Longrightarrow^* C$ and $(\hat{H}, \hat{L}, \hat{S}) \models P$, then $C \; \hat{\mathcal{R}}_{\text{Conf}} \; (\hat{H}, \hat{L}, \hat{S}) \wedge (C \Longrightarrow C') \Rightarrow C' \; \hat{\mathcal{R}}_{\text{Conf}} \; (\hat{H}, \hat{L}, \hat{S})$*

Proof. By case-inspection using a technical lemma establishing that the call-stack is well-formed. ■

While the above theorem establishes the semantic correctness for the analysis, it may not be entirely obvious how this is useful in the current setting. We therefore state a corollary below that follows as a trivial consequence of the above Theorem, showing that it is sufficient to check the analysis result in order to guarantee that no object references can be leaked:

Corollary 1. *Let $P \in$ Program, $(\hat{H}, \hat{L}, \hat{S}) \models P$. Assuming that $[\text{Ref } \tau]_C \notin \hat{H}([\text{Ref } \sigma]_C)$ and for all $[m_v]_M$ s.t. $[\text{Ref } \sigma]_C \in [m_v]_M.class$ implies $[\text{Ref } \tau]_C \notin (\hat{S}([m_v]_M) \cup \hat{L}([m_v]_M))$ then $P \vdash \tau \not\leadsto \sigma$.*

Note that the requirements above follow those of Definition 3 quite closely. This gives us a very convenient way to verify that there are no leaks in a given program by simply analysing the program and applying Corollary 1. The problem with this approach is of course that it requires access to the entire program which is not realistic in situations where users and third-party vendors are allowed to download applets onto a Java Card after it has been issued, as is the case for instance with newer mobile phones. In Section 5 we show how the analysis can be used to give strong security guarantees in precisely such situations.

Returning to the example programs P_{ABM} and P_{ABC} we wish to use the analysis to examine if `Alice` is leaked to `Mallet` and/or `Charlie` respectively. For simplicity we define the equivalence relations such that each class and method is in an equivalence class by itself. Analysing the programs, as described in Section 1, we find $(\hat{H}_{ABM}, \hat{L}_{ABM}, \hat{S}_{ABM})$ and $(\hat{H}_{ABC}, \hat{L}_{ABC}, \hat{S}_{ABC})$ such that $(\hat{H}_{ABM}, \hat{L}_{ABM}, \hat{S}_{ABM}) \models P_{ABM}$ and also $(\hat{H}_{ABC}, \hat{L}_{ABC}, \hat{S}_{ABC}) \models P_{ABC}$ respectively. Below the analysis results for the classes `Mallet` and `Charlie` are shown. We elide the corresponding results for `Alice` and `Bob` since they are of little consequence here.

$$\begin{aligned}
\hat{S}_{ABM}([\texttt{Mallet.m_Mallet}]_M) &= \{[\text{Ref } \texttt{Alice}]_C, [\text{Ref } \texttt{Bob}]_C, [\text{Ref } \texttt{Mallet}]_C\} \\
\hat{L}_{ABM}([\texttt{Mallet.m_Mallet}]_M) &= \{[\text{Ref } \texttt{Bob}]_C, [\text{Ref } \texttt{Mallet}]_C\} \\
\hat{H}_{ABM}([\text{Ref } \texttt{Mallet}]_C) &= \emptyset
\end{aligned}$$

$$\begin{aligned}
\hat{S}_{ABC}([\texttt{Charlie.m_Charlie}]_M) &= \{[\text{Ref } \texttt{Bob}]_C, [\text{Ref } \texttt{Charlie}]_C\} \\
\hat{L}_{ABC}([\texttt{Charlie.m_Charlie}]_M) &= \{[\text{Ref } \texttt{Bob}]_C, [\text{Ref } \texttt{Charlie}]_C\} \\
\hat{H}_{ABC}([\text{Ref } \texttt{Charlie}]_C) &= \emptyset
\end{aligned}$$

As can be seen from the results: $[\text{Ref } \texttt{Alice}]_C \in \hat{S}_{ABM}([\texttt{Mallet.m\_Mallet}]_M)$ thus we can deduce that *possibly* $P_{ABM} \vdash \texttt{Alice} \leadsto \texttt{Mallet}$ which is consistent with our earlier observations. On the other hand, using the results for P_{ABC} with Corollary 1, we conclude that $P_{ABC} \vdash \texttt{Alice} \not\leadsto \texttt{Charlie}$.

4.4 From Specification to Constraint Generator

While the high-level Flow Logic style, used above for the control flow logic, is very useful for specification of analyses and for proving correctness of analyses, it may be less obvious how to actually implement such a specification. Below we show how the Flow Logic specification can be turned into a *constraint generator*, generating constraints over the Alternation-free Least Fixed-Point (ALFP) logic, cf. [9]. This enables us to use the *Succinct Solver* to solve the generated constraints efficiently, cf. [9]. Furthermore, as we shall see in Section 5, the formulation of the analysis in terms of ALFP constraints is essential in achieving the goal of this paper: the development of a "Hardest Attacker" for verifying that programs do not leak object references.

It is actually trivial to convert the Flow Logic specification into a constraint generator, because the formulae in the specification are really just ALFP formulae, written in a slightly different notation for legibility (cf. [9]), over the universe formed by our semantic domains. Thus the translation amounts to a simple change of notation and below we therefore show only one example clause:

$$\begin{aligned}\mathcal{G}[\![(m_0, pc_0) : \texttt{putfield } f]\!] \;=\; & \forall [\text{Ref } \sigma]_C \in \hat{S}([m_0]_M) : \\ & \hat{S}([m_0]_M) \subseteq \hat{H}([\text{Ref } \sigma]_C)\end{aligned}$$

The following lifts the constraint generator to cover programs:

$$\begin{aligned}\mathcal{G}[\![P]\!] = & \bigwedge_{\substack{(m,pc) \in P.addresses,\\ m.instructionAt(pc) = \texttt{instr}}} \mathcal{G}[\![(m, pc) : \texttt{instr}]\!] \\ \wedge & \bigwedge_{\sigma \in P.classes} [\text{Ref } \sigma]_C \in \hat{L}([m_\sigma]_M) \\ \wedge & \bigwedge_{P.sharing(\sigma) = \sigma_1 :: \cdots :: \sigma_n} \{[\text{Ref } \sigma_1]_C, \ldots, [\text{Ref } \sigma_n]_C\} \subseteq \hat{L}([m_\sigma]_M)\end{aligned}$$

The next lemma establishes the correctness of the constraint generator

Lemma 1. *Let* $P \in \mathsf{Program}$, *then* $(\hat{H}, \hat{L}, \hat{S}) \models P$ *iff* $(\hat{H}, \hat{L}, \hat{S}) \models_{\text{ALFP}} \mathcal{G}[\![P]\!]$.

Finally, we can show that the solutions to the analysis constitute a *Moore family*, i.e., that the intersection of a set of acceptable analyses is also an acceptable analysis. This actually follows from Proposition 1 in [9] which establishes a general Moore family result for solutions to ALFP formulae[1]. Using that result in combination with the above we obtain the following

Corollary 2. *The set of acceptable analyses for a given program, P, is a* Moore family: $\forall X : X \subseteq \{(\hat{H}, \hat{L}, \hat{S}) \mid (\hat{H}, \hat{L}, \hat{S}) \models P\} \Rightarrow (\sqcap X) \models P$.

The implication of the Moore family result is that for every program there exists an acceptable analysis, $\sqcap\emptyset$, and there always exists a smallest, i.e., best, acceptable analysis, $\sqcap\{(\hat{H}, \hat{L}, \hat{S}) \mid (\hat{H}, \hat{L}, \hat{S}) \models P\}$. The Succinct Solver [9] will efficiently

[1] Since we do not use negation at all in our ALFP constraints, the stratification conditions on negation for Proposition 1 in [9] hold vacuously.

compute the smallest solution for a given set of ALFP constraints. A naïve and unoptimised implementation of the analysis and constraint generator presented in this paper gives rise to a worst case time complexity on the order of $\mathcal{O}(n^5)$, where n is the size of the program being analysed. This can be brought down to $\mathcal{O}(n^4)$ in a fairly straightforward manner and we conjecture that through careful analysis and optimisation this can even be lowered to $\mathcal{O}(n^3)$.

5 The Hardest Attacker

In this section we present a solution to the problem posed in the previous section: How to guarantee that a given applet does not leak object references, regardless of what other (malicious) applets run in the same environment. In the previous section, we showed that a simple control flow analysis can be used to guarantee that a specific program in a specific environment does not leak references. However, this is not enough to deal with the problem of applets loaded *after* the analysis is done. Therefore a different approach is needed. We follow the approach of [3,10] and identify a *hardest attacker* with respect to the control flow analysis specified earlier. A hardest attacker is an attacker with the property that it is no less "effective" than any other attacker and therefore, if the hardest attacker cannot execute a successful attack then *no other attacker* can. The key to making it work is that we only need to find a hardest attacker as seen from the perspective of the control flow analysis, rather than try and give a finite characterisation of all the infinitely many attackers, which may not be possible in general.

The idea behind our particular hardest attacker is that (modulo names) only finitely many "types" of constraints are generated, all specifically determined by the Flow Logic. Therefore it is possible to specify a finite set of constraints, in such a way that any constraints generated by another program will be contained within the constraints of the hardest attacker. Here we rely on the equivalence relations on classes and methods in order to deal with the (possibly infinitely many) names an attacker may use. Since the constraints generated depend only on the *equivalence classes* of names and not on the actual names used, we can simply select equivalence relations that partition the names into a *finite* number of equivalence classes.

Given a program, P, that we wish to protect, we shall call the classes and methods defined in P that should not be shared for *private* classes and methods; classes that are allowed to be shared with other programs are called *sharable* ($P.sharable$ denotes the set of sharable classes in P). Any other class or method is called *public*. We then define equivalence relations, called the *discrete* equivalence relations for P, on classes (methods) that map all private and sharable classes (methods) to an equivalence class of its own and all public classes (methods) to $\bullet_C$ ($\bullet_M$). A program that only defines and creates public classes, objects, and methods is called a *public* program. The set of public programs is denoted $\mathsf{Program}_\bullet$. For convenience we parameterise the set of public programs on the (sharable) classes a public program has initial knowledge of (through sharing): let $\mathcal{I} \subseteq \mathsf{Class}$, we then write $\mathsf{Program}_\bullet^{\mathcal{I}}$ to denote the set of public programs with access to the classes in $\mathcal{I}$, i.e., $\forall Q \in \mathsf{Program}_{\bullet}^{\mathcal{I}} : \forall \sigma \in Q.classes : Q.sharing(\sigma) \subseteq \mathcal{I}$.

Finally, we need to abstract the method names used in method invocation instructions. In general this can be done by using *static inheritance* instead of dynamic dispatch, i.e., syntactically duplicating inherited methods. For our use, however, it is sufficient to compute a conservative approximation of the abstract method lookup, denoted $\widehat{methodLookup}_{/\equiv}$, used in the control flow analysis:

$$\widehat{methodLookup}_{/\equiv}([\text{Ref } \sigma]_C) = \begin{cases} \bigcup_{m \in P.methods} methodLookup_{/\equiv}(m, [\text{Ref } \sigma]_C) & \text{if } [\text{Ref } \sigma]_C \neq \bullet_C \\ \{\bullet_M\} & \text{otherwise} \end{cases} \tag{1}$$

The above is sound and sufficient for the case where public programs are downloaded to run with our private program. Thus the public program can inherit from the private program, but not the other way around. Note that inheritance is not, as such, related to leaking references and is only mentioned here because we wish to model dynamic dispatch rather than use static inheritance.

We can now specify the hardest attacker (HA) as a constraint that contains all the constraints that the analysis can possibly give rise to:

Definition 4 (Hardest Attacker). *The* Hardest Attacker *with respect to the discrete equivalence relation for P, written $\mathcal{H}_P$, is defined as the following constraint*

$$\begin{aligned} \mathcal{H}_P = \{\bullet_C\} \subseteq \hat{S}(\bullet_M) \wedge \hat{L}(\bullet_M) \subseteq \hat{S}(\bullet_M) \wedge \hat{S}(\bullet_M) \subseteq \hat{L}(\bullet_M) \wedge \{\mathsf{INT}\} \subseteq \hat{S}(\bullet_M) \wedge \\ \forall [\text{Ref } \sigma]_C \in \hat{S}(\bullet_M) : \hat{H}([\text{Ref } \sigma]_C) \subseteq \hat{S}(\bullet_M) \wedge \\ \forall [\text{Ref } \sigma]_C \in \hat{S}(\bullet_M) : \hat{S}(\bullet_M) \subseteq \hat{H}([\text{Ref } \sigma]_C) \wedge \\ \forall \sigma \in P.sharable : \{[\text{Ref } \sigma]_C\} \subseteq \hat{L}(\bullet_M) \wedge \\ \forall [\text{Ref } \sigma]_C \in \hat{S}(\bullet_M) : \\ \forall [m_v]_M \in \widehat{methodLookup}_{/\equiv}([\text{Ref } \sigma]_C) \\ \hat{S}(\bullet_M) \subseteq \hat{L}([m_v]_M) \\ [m_v]_M.returnVal \Rightarrow \hat{S}([m_v]_M) \subseteq \hat{S}(\bullet_M) \end{aligned}$$

The Lemma below is the formal statement of the fact that the HA as defined actually generates (or contains) all the constraints that can possibly be generated from a program with initial knowledge of public classes and methods only:

Lemma 2. *Let $P \in \mathsf{Program}$ and $\mathcal{I} \subseteq P.sharable$ then $\forall Q \in \mathsf{Program}_{\bullet}^{\mathcal{I}}$: $(\hat{H}, \hat{L}, \hat{S}) \models_{\text{ALFP}} \mathcal{H}_P \Rightarrow (\hat{H}, \hat{L}, \hat{S}) \models_{\text{ALFP}} \mathcal{G}[\![Q]\!]$.*

This leads to the following observation:

Lemma 3. *Let $P \in \mathsf{Program}$, $\mathcal{I} \subseteq P.sharable$, and assume $(\hat{H}, \hat{L}, \hat{S}) \models_{\text{ALFP}} \mathcal{G}[\![P]\!] \wedge \mathcal{H}_P$, then $\forall Q \in \mathsf{Program}_{\bullet}^{\mathcal{I}}$: $(\hat{H}, \hat{L}, \hat{S}) \models_{\text{ALFP}} \mathcal{G}[\![P]\!] \wedge \mathcal{G}[\![Q]\!]$.*

We can now state and prove the main Theorem for hardest attackers:

Theorem 2. *For $P \in \mathsf{Program}$ and $\mathcal{I} \subseteq P.sharable$ assume $(\hat{H}, \hat{L}, \hat{S}) \models_{\text{ALFP}} \mathcal{G}[\![P]\!] \wedge \mathcal{H}_P$, then $\forall Q \in \mathsf{Program}_{\bullet}^{\mathcal{I}}$: $(\hat{H}, \hat{L}, \hat{S}) \models (P \,|\, Q)$.*

Proof. Follows from Lemmas 1 and 3, and a technical lemma regarding program composition. ■

Below we state a corollary showing explicitly how this can be used to validate that a program does not leak any private knowledge. However, the above theorem is of a more general nature since *any* property that can be validated using only an analysis result is amenable to the Hardest Attacker approach.

Corollary 3. *Let* $P \in \mathsf{Program}$, $\mathcal{I} \subseteq P.sharable$, *such that* $(\hat{H}, \hat{L}, \hat{S}) \models_{\text{ALFP}} \mathcal{G}[\![P]\!] \wedge \mathcal{H}_P$ *and assume that* $[\text{Ref } \tau]_C \notin \hat{H}([\text{Ref } \sigma]_C)$ *and for all* $[m_v]_M$ *s.t.* $[\text{Ref } \sigma]_C \in [m_v]_M.class$ *implies* $[\text{Ref } \tau]_C \notin (\hat{S}([m_v]_M) \cup \hat{L}([m_v]_M))$ *then* $\forall Q \in \mathsf{Program}_\bullet^{\mathcal{I}}\colon (P \,|\, Q) \vdash \tau \not\leadsto \sigma$

In other words: If no leaks can be detected in the result of analysing a program, P, in conjunction with the Hardest Attacker, then P will *never* leak to any public program Q.

In the following we apply the Hardest Attacker approach to the examples shown earlier. For program P_{AB} the discrete equivalence relations are easily computed: the classes `Alice` and `Bob` are in their own respective equivalence classes, denoted $[\text{Ref } \texttt{Alice}]_C$ and $[\text{Ref } \texttt{Bob}]_C$. Similarly for methods: every method defined in `Alice` of `Bob` is mapped to its own equivalence class.

The abstract method lookup is computed as specified by (1):

$$\widehat{methodLookup}_{/\equiv}(x) = \begin{cases} \{[\texttt{Alice.m\_Alice}]_M\} & \text{if } x = [\text{Ref } \texttt{Alice}]_C \\ \{[\texttt{Bob.m\_Bob}]_M, [\texttt{Bob.update}]_M\} & \text{if } x = [\text{Ref } \texttt{Bob}]_C \\ \{\bullet_M\} & \text{otherwise} \end{cases}$$

The next step is to generate constraints according to Theorem 2 and solving them: $\mathcal{G}[\![P_{AB}]\!] \wedge \mathcal{H}_{P_{AB}}$. From the small excerpt of the result, shown below, it follows that the requirements of Corollary 1 do not hold, since a reference to `Alice` potentially *can* be leaked, and thus the program is (potentially) not secure: $\{[\text{Ref } \texttt{Alice}]_C\} \subset \hat{S}(\bullet_M)$, $\{[\text{Ref } \texttt{Alice}]_C\} \subset \hat{L}(\bullet_M)$, $\{[\text{Ref } \texttt{Alice}]_C\} \subset \hat{H}(\bullet_C)$. Figure 6 shows a version of the program where the security flaw has been removed. Applying the same techniques as above, we obtain the following result: $(\hat{S}(\bullet_M) \cup \hat{L}(\bullet_M) \cup \hat{H}(\bullet_C)) \cap \{[\text{Ref } \texttt{Alice}]_C\} = \emptyset$. Thus, by Corollary 3, we conclude that for all $\mathcal{I} \subseteq P_{AB'}.sharable$: $\forall Q \in \mathsf{Program}_\bullet^{\mathcal{I}}$: $\forall \sigma \in$

```
class Alice {
  void m_Alice(Bob) {
    0: load 1
    1: load 0
    2: invokevirtual Bob.update(Object)
    3: return
  }
  /* ... */
}

class Bob {
  void m_Bob() {
    0: return
  }
  void update(Object) {
    /* ... */
    0: return
  }
}
```

Fig. 6. Program $P_{AB'}$: a corrected version of P_{AB}

Q.classes: $(P_{AB'} \,|\, Q) \vdash \texttt{Alice} \not\rightsquigarrow \sigma$ and therefore that program $P_{AB'}$ does not leak a reference to `Alice` to *any* public program.

6 Conclusions and Future Work

In this paper we have presented a method for verifying that applets do not leak sensitive object references to *any* attack-applet. The hardest attacker approach makes it possible to assure security of sensitive applets even when dynamic loading of applets is allowed. Our approach is not confined to checking for leaking references. Any property that can be verified by using the analysis result alone are amenable to the hardest attacker as described in Section 5. Investigating precisely what properties can be expressed this way is left for future work; as is extending the analysis to include more advanced features.

Acknowledgements. The author would like to thank Flemming Nielson, Mikael Buchholtz, and Andrei Sabelfeld for reading early drafts of this paper, and also the anonymous referees for helpful suggestions.

References

1. Élouard, M., Jensen, T.: Secure object flow analysis for Java Card. In: Proc. of Smart Card Research and Advanced Application Conference, Cardis'02. (2002)
2. Nielson, H.R., Nielson, F.: Hardest Attackers. In: Workshop on Issues in the Theory of Security, WITS'00. (2000)
3. Nielson, F., Nielson, H.R., Hansen, R.R., Jensen, J.G.: Validating Firewalls in Mobile Ambients. In: Proc. of conference on Concurrency Theory, CONCUR'99. Volume 1664 of Lecture Notes in Computer Science., Springer Verlag (1999) 463–477
4. Siveroni, I., Hankin, C.: A Proposal for the JCVMLe Operational Semantics. SECSAFE-ICSTM-001-2.2. Available from [11] (2001)
5. Hansen, R.R.: Flow Logic for Carmel. SECSAFE-IMM-001-1.5. Available from [11] (2002)
6. Vitek, J., Horspool, R.N., Uhl, J.S.: Compile-Time Analysis of Object-Oriented Programs. In: Proc. International Conference on Compiler Construction, CC'92. Volume 641 of Lecture Notes in Computer Science., Springer Verlag (1992)
7. Nielson, H.R., Nielson, F.: Flow Logic: a multi-paradigmatic approach to static analysis. In: The Essence of Computation: Complexity, Analysis, Transformation. Volume 2566 of Lecture Notes in Computer Science. Springer Verlag (2002) 223–244
8. Nielson, F., Nielson, H.R., Hankin, C.: Principles of Program Analysis. Springer Verlag (1999)
9. Nielson, F., Nielson, H.R., Seidl, H.: A Succinct Solver for ALFP. Nordic Journal of Computing **2002** (2002) 335–372
10. Nielson, F., Nielson, H.R., Hansen, R.R.: Validating Firewalls using Flow Logics. Theoretical Computer Science **283** (2002) 381–418
11. Siveroni, I.: SecSafe. Web page: `http://www.doc.ic.ac.uk/siveroni/secsafe/` (2003)

Trust Management in Strand Spaces: A Rely-Guarantee Method*

Joshua D. Guttman, F. Javier Thayer, Jay A. Carlson, Jonathan C. Herzog, John D. Ramsdell, and Brian T. Sniffen

The MITRE Corporation
{guttman,jt,nop,jherzog,ramsdell,bsniffen}@mitre.org

Abstract. We show how to combine trust management theories with nonce-based cryptographic protocols. The strand space framework for protocol analysis is extended by associating formulas from a trust management logic with the transmit and receive actions of the protocol principals. The formula on a transmission is a guarantee; the sender must ensure that this formula is true before sending the message. The formula on a receive event is an assumption that the recipient may rely on in deducing future guarantee formulas. The strand space framework allows us to prove that a protocol is sound, in the sense that when a principal relies on a formula, another principal has previously guaranteed it. We explain the ideas in reference to a simple new electronic commerce protocol, in which a customer obtains a money order from a bank to pay a merchant to ship some goods.

Cryptographic protocol analysis has aimed primarily to determine what messages another principal must have sent or received, when one principal is known to have sent or received certain messages. However, other questions are also important: what does a principal commit herself to when she executes a protocol? What assumptions must she accept, on the basis of her peers' assertions, to be willing to execute a protocol to the end? Answers to these questions spell out the *trust assumptions* of a protocol. We introduce here a method for reasoning about trust assumptions. The method clarifies the goals and consequences of engaging in a protocol, and the trust required to complete a protocol run.

Trust management allows principals to make access control decisions using a local policy to combine assertions made by their peers [18,5]. The same local access control policy also controls the action of making assertions (including requests) to other principals. Cryptographic methods such as digital signatures are used to determine which principal uttered each assertion. A central advantage of trust management is that it handles naturally different principals who trust each other for some kinds of assertions, but not all. A major subtrend is *logical trust management* [18,2,19]. Here the local policy is a logical theory held by the principal, so that access control is decided by logical derivation.

Despite sophisticated academic work, trust management has seen limited uptake. It imposes a substantial security management burden on organizations that

* Supported by the MITRE-Sponsored Research Program.

D.A. Schmidt (Ed.): ESOP 2004, LNCS 2986, pp. 325–339, 2004.

would use it. This burden is exacerbated by problems with key management and revocation. If the cryptographic secrets on which the method depends are poorly protected, then the likelihood of achieving benefits appears too low to offset the effort. From this point of view, Trusted Platform Modules (TPMs) [4], create an opportunity. These inexpensive cryptographic chips, now available in commercial personal computers, provide secure storage, on-chip cryptographic operations, and facilities to report securely on the system's software state. The TPM is organized around nonce-based protocols,[1] so remote principals receive freshness guarantees with the information they retrieve from TPM-equipped devices. Thus, the TPM is a promising platform for trust management [16], assuming trust management can effectively exploit nonce-based protocols.

Goal of this paper. Here we aim to resolve one underlying theoretical question needed to provide a rigorous basis for using the TPM as a platform for trust management. That is, what forms of reasoning can soundly combine information from nonce-based protocols and trust management theories?

Our answer uses the well-developed strand space theory. Strand spaces allow us to determine what security goals a cryptographic protocol achieves [12,24]; to decide when different cryptographic protocols may safely be combined [11]; to study interactions between protocols and the cryptography or message formatting used to implement them [13,15]; and to guide protocol design [10,23].

We now augment strand spaces with a rely-guarantee method [17]. The formulas are borrowed from a trust management logic, the choice of which is not tightly constrained by our method. The designer of a protocol annotates the behaviors of the principals with formulas. The formula associated with a message transmission must be *guaranteed* by the sender. Before sending the message, a principal obeying the protocol ensures the truth of the formula, presumably by combining reliable locally available data with guarantees offered earlier by other principals, using deduction in the local policy theory. The sender asserts the formula when sending the message. When another principal receives a message, that principal may *rely* on the fact that the sender has asserted the formula. The receiving principal can use the assertion in later deductions.

A protocol annotated with rely and guarantee formulas is *sound* if in every execution, whenever a principal receives a message and relies on a formula, there were corresponding message transmissions, guaranteeing assertions that are at least as strong. The existing methods of the strand space theory may be used to prove annotated protocols sound. They may also be used to prove that the guaranteeing message transmissions occurred *recently*, rather than involving time scales on which revocation or key compromise are realistic threats.

Section 1 introduces a simple illustrative protocol, based on money orders. Section 2 codifies the essential ingredients of logical trust management. The rely-guarantee method itself is in Section 3. Section 4 defines soundness and proves soundness for the example. Related work is in Section 5.

[1] A nonce is a randomly chosen bitstring, used in protocols to ensure freshness and avoid replay attacks.

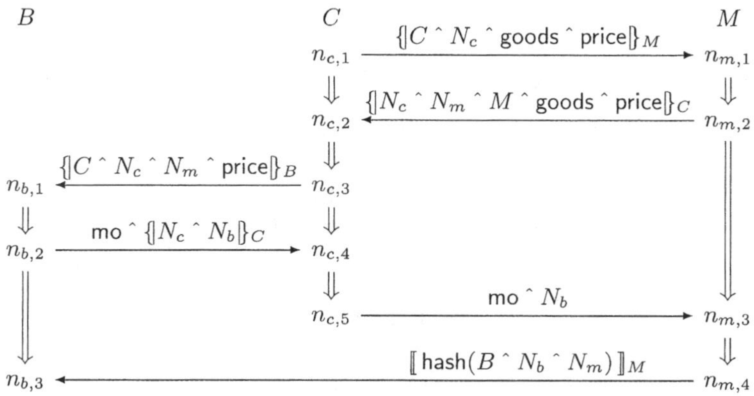

Fig. 1. EPMO with Money Order $\mathsf{mo} = [\![\, \mathsf{hash}(C \hat{}\ N_c \hat{}\ N_b \hat{}\ N_m \hat{}\ \mathsf{price}) \,]\!]_B$

1 Example: Electronic Purchase Using Money Orders

The new protocol EPMO (Figure 1) borrows ideas from [22,21], using the authentication tests as a design principle [10]. Variables N_p range over nonces; $[\![\, t \,]\!]_P$ is the message t signed by P; $\{\!|t|\!\}_P$ is t encrypted using P's public key; and $\mathsf{hash}(t)$ is a cryptographic hash of t.

A customer and a merchant want to agree on a purchase, transferring payment with the aid of a bank. Here goods is a description of the items requested; price is the proposed price. N_m serves as a transaction number. After obtaining a quote from the merchant, the customer obtains a "money order" containing N_b from the bank to cover the purchase, and delivers it to the merchant. The merchant "endorses" it by combining N_b with N_m, and delivers the endorsement to the bank. At the end of the protocol, the bank transfers the funds, and the merchant ships the goods; otherwise, the principals engage in a resolution protocol not specified here. B does not learn goods, and learns M only if the transaction completes. Although B does not transfer funds until M cashes the money order, B may put a "hold" on money in C's account. If the money order is not redeemed within an implementation-defined timeout period, then it expires and B releases the hold on C's account.

EPMO is designed not to disclose which principals are interacting, nor the goods or price. It does not protect against denial of service. An adversary can encrypt messages, using B's public key, to cause holds on all the money in C's account. Although a more complex protocol would prevent this attack, EPMO illustrates a more interesting interplay between protocols and trust.

2 Tenets of Logical Trust Management

A *trust management logic* consists of two ingredients, a language L and a consequence relation $\longrightarrow$. The language L is a set of formulas, some of which are assertions that we present in the form "P says ϕ," where $\phi \in L$. There may be other operators such as P authorizes ϕ. A formula is an *assertion* if it is of the form t says ϕ. Logical trust management is based on four underlying tenets.

1. Each principal P holds some set of statements as its theory Th_P. P derives conclusions within Th_P using other principals' utterances P' says ϕ as additional premises. P may utter P says ϕ after deriving ϕ.
2. Some assertions are self-certifying, namely P's statements about P's own utterances or desires. If P utters P says ϕ, then P has said something true. If P says P authorizes ϕ, then P has authorized it.
3. A principal P may have reliable knowledge of particular states of affairs. P draws only true conclusions about them, because P uses data available locally and sound inferences. For instance, a human resources department may reliably know the members of each department. It deduces that a person is an employee if there exists a department of which she is a member.
   Reliable knowledge is not a matter of logical form, however. Instead, a principal P_1 makes trust assumptions about other principals P_2. P_1 may believe that P_2 says ϕ implies ϕ. This implication expresses P_1's trust assumption that P_2 knows reliably about ϕ, and will speak truthfully.
   Th_P (from Tenet 1) includes both P's reliable knowledge and P's local policy for inferring conclusions.
4. A principal P_1 may control a resource r. P_1 takes an action $\phi(r, P_2)$ against r on behalf of another principal P_2, whenever P_1 derives a statement such as "P_2 requests $\phi(r, P_2)$ and P_2 should be permitted $\phi(r, P_2)$." Taking an action as a consequence of an inference is reminiscent of Aristotle's practical syllogism [3, Bekker 1144a31].

The derivations in Tenet 1 proceed according to the rules of inference of some underlying logic. In some recent work [19], these logics are simple, e.g. sublogics of Datalog. This has the advantage of a complete terminating deduction procedure, and some questions about trust between principals are efficiently decidable [20]. We adopt here the far stronger logic of [2], with syntactic sugar distinguishing "requests" and "authorizes" from "says".

3 A Rely-Guarantee Method for Strand Spaces

The rely-guarantee method was invented for reasoning about shared state parallel programs [17]. We adapt it here, with simplifications, for the case in which the "parallel program" or distributed system is a cryptographic protocol in which each regular (i.e. uncompromised) participant makes decisions according to a trust management theory. In this case, the shared state is the set of messages that have been sent and the set of formulas derived by each participant.

3.1 Annotated Protocols

A protocol designer must complete two successive steps, namely defining the protocol itself and then annotating the protocol.

Defining the Protocol. A protocol is a finite set of parameterized strands [13]; see Appendix A for definitions. Each strand contains a number of nodes. Each node transmits or receives a message $\pm t$, where the message t may depend on the parameters. The forms of the strands are given by a set $\{S_j[\boldsymbol{X}]\}_{j \in J}$; the indices j are called the *roles* of the protocol. The behavior of the role j is like a template, containing parameters $\boldsymbol{X} = X_1, \ldots, X_k$. We regard this template as determining, for each assignment of values to the parameters, a set of strands; any two strands in this set transmit and receive the same values. We use the notation $S_j[X_1, \ldots, X_k]$ both to refer to the template itself, and also, when values are assigned to the parameters $\boldsymbol{X}$, to refer to the set of concrete strands whose behavior is to send and receive messages with these parameters.

Each parameterized strand $S[\boldsymbol{X}]$ has a distinguished parameter X_p which is the principal executing this strand. We write $\mathsf{prin}(S[X_1, \ldots, X_k]) = X_p$ and $\mathsf{prin}(n) = X_p$ if n is a node lying on this strand.

In the case of EPMO, the roles are *Bank*, *Customer*, and *Merchant*, each containing the send and receive events shown in the corresponding column of Figure 1. Letting p, g stand for the price and goods, the parameters to the roles and their distinguished parameters are:

$$\begin{array}{ll} s_b \in \mathsf{Bank}[B, C, M, p, N_m, N_b] & \mathsf{prin}(s_b) = B \\ s_c \in \mathsf{Cust}[B, C, M, p, g, N_c, N_m, N_b] & \mathsf{prin}(s_c) = C \\ s_m \in \mathsf{Merch}[B, C, M, p, g, N_c, N_m, N_b] & \mathsf{prin}(s_m) = M \end{array}$$

Each of these is a set of strands, i.e. all strands s such that $tr(s)$ is the sequence of sends and receives shown in one column of Figure 1, for the given values of the parameters.

Annotating the protocol. Having defined a parametrized strand $S[\boldsymbol{X}]$ for each role, the protocol designer annotates them, attaching a formula to each node n.

If n is a positive (transmission) node, then the formula represents a guarantee that $\mathsf{prin}(n)$ asserts to its peers; we write these formulas as γ_n to emphasize their role as guarantees. If, for n positive, $\mathsf{prin}(n) = P$ and P holds theory Th_P, then the intended behavior of P at n is to attempt to derive γ_n within Th_P. Success means that P may continue the protocol and transmit term(n), in accord with Tenet 1; failure means that P must terminate executing this strand. Thus transmission of term(n) indicates that $\mathsf{prin}(n)$ says γ_n.

If n is a negative (reception) node, then $\mathsf{prin}(n)$ will rely on the formula associated with n, which we write ρ_n. Typically stating that other principals have made certain assertions, ρ_n is a premise that $\mathsf{prin}(n)$ can use in future deductions. In deriving γ_m for a later node m, P works from $\mathsf{Th}_P \cup \{\rho_n : n \Rightarrow^+ m\}$, i.e. the original theory augmented by rely statements ρ_n for earlier nodes on the strand.

The formulas γ_n and ρ_n may involve the parameters, so that the actual formula in a run involving values $\boldsymbol{v} = v_1, \ldots, v_j$ is $\gamma_i[\boldsymbol{v}/\boldsymbol{X}]$ or $\rho_i[\boldsymbol{v}/\boldsymbol{X}]$.

Definition 1. *An* annotated protocol Π *consists of a set of parameterized regular strands* $\{S_j[\boldsymbol{X}]\}_{j \in J}$ *together with a pair of functions* γ *and* ρ *from nodes of* *these strands to formulas of L, such that γ is defined on positive nodes and ρ is defined on negative nodes.*

The strand space Σ_Π over Π *consists of all instances of the parametric strands* $S_j[\boldsymbol{X}]$ *together with all penetrator strands from Definition 8. The* bundles over Σ_Π *are determined by Definition 7.*

Some earlier work [1,18] defines protocols whose messages contain formulas like the γ_n. However, protocols can work properly without embedded formulas, and can fail even with them. The approach does not allow sharing different information with different peers, as C shares goods with M but not with B. We thus associate the guarantee with the sending node, not with the message itself.

3.2 EPMO Annotated

In the example of EPMO, there are four non-trivial guarantees, and four non-trivial rely formulas (Table 1). We write them in terms of the predicates:

$\mathsf{transfer}(B, p, M, N)$	B transfers p to M in reference to N
$\mathsf{ship}(M, g, C)$	M ships g to C

The guarantee or rely formula associated with node $n_{p,i}$ is $\gamma_{p,i}$ or $\rho_{p,i}$ respectively. Any node not shown in Table 1 has the trivially true formula True.

Table 1. Guarantee and Rely formulas for EPMO

Bank:			
$\gamma_{b,2}$	$\forall P_M$	**if**	C authorizes $\mathsf{transfer}(B, \mathsf{price}, P_M, N_m)$, **and** P_M requests $\mathsf{transfer}(B, \mathsf{price}, P_M, N_m)$,
		then	$\mathsf{transfer}(B, \mathsf{price}, P_M, N_m)$.
$\rho_{b,3}$			C says $\gamma_{c,5}$, **and** M says M requests $\mathsf{transfer}(B, \mathsf{price}, M, N_m)$.
Customer:			
$\rho_{c,2}$			M says $\gamma_{m,2}$.
$\rho_{c,4}$			B says $\gamma_{b,2}$.
$\gamma_{c,5}$			C authorizes $\mathsf{transfer}(B, \mathsf{price}, M, N_m)$.
Merchant:			
$\gamma_{m,2}$	$\forall P_B$	**if**	$\mathsf{transfer}(P_B, \mathsf{price}, M, N_m)$, **then** $\mathsf{ship}(M, \mathsf{goods}, C)$.
$\rho_{m,3}$			B says $\gamma_{b,2}$, **and** C says $\gamma_{c,5}$.
$\gamma_{m,4}$			M requests $\mathsf{transfer}(B, \mathsf{price}, M, N_m)$, **and** $\mathsf{ship}(M, \mathsf{goods}, C)$.

Bank Behavior. The bank guarantees a quantified implication $\gamma_{b,2}$ on its second node $n_{b,2}$. The universally quantified payee makes the money order an instrument payable to the bearer. Its rely statement $\rho_{b,3}$ notes that C says C authorizes payment. Since "authorizes" is self-certifying (Tenet 2), this implies C does authorize payment. Formula $\rho_{b,3}$ also notes M's statement M says M requests price. B instantiates P_M with M, inferring that it should transfer price from C to M, as in Tenet 4. By Tenet 2, the bank does not need to trust either C or M.

Customer Behavior. The customer makes no guarantee on $n_{c,1}$. It relies on M's offer $\gamma_{m,2}$ on $n_{c,2}$, and B's assertion $\gamma_{b,2}$ on $n_{c,4}$.

The self-certifying guarantee $\gamma_{c,5}$ is crucial for the protocol, as it authorizes the transfer. C utters $\gamma_{c,5}$ only if the transfer is acceptable. There are two trust decisions here (Tenet 3), whether to accept the implications

$$(B \text{ says } \gamma_{b,2}) \supset \gamma_{b,2} \quad \text{and} \quad (M \text{ says } \gamma_{m,2}) \supset \gamma_{m,2}.$$

C presumably accepts the former, having already decided to establish an account with B. C's decision whether to trust M for $\gamma_{m,2}$, uses previous experience or data from the Better Business Bureau, as encoded in C's trust management theory Th_C. If C accepts the implication and derives $\gamma_{c,5}$, and if M requests price, then by $\gamma_{b,2}$ and $\gamma_{m,2}$, M will ship the goods.

Merchant Behavior. The merchant, upon receiving the first message, considers whether to sell goods for price to customer C. Deducing $\gamma_{m,2}$ from Th_M signals acceptance. In $\gamma_{m,2}$, the bank is universally quantified; the premise that the money will be transferred ensures M can reject an untrustworthy bank later.

On $n_{m,3}$, M relies on the self-certifying $\gamma_{c,5}$, as well as B says $\gamma_{b,2}$. M's criterion for trusting B for $\gamma_{b,2}$ is encoded in Th_M; possibly M checks a list of reputable banks. If M infers $\gamma_{b,2}$, it follows that B will transfer the funds upon request. If M makes the request, it must also ship the goods.

An affirmative decision is recorded in $\gamma_{m,4}$. The first conjunct is needed by B to justify the transfer. The second half, by Tenet 4, may have a side-effect, such as transmitting a shipping order to the shipping department.

4 Execution Semantics for Annotated Protocols

We now give a semantics for protocols by defining, given an assignment of theories to principals, what bundles can occur, namely the *permissible* bundles. We also define *soundness*, meaning that rely formulas always follow from previously asserted guarantees.

Definition 2. *Let Π be an annotated protocol, let $\mathcal{B}$ be a bundle over Σ_Π, and let each principal P hold theory Th_P. $\mathcal{B}$ is* permissible *if, for each positive regular $n \in \mathcal{B}$ with $\mathsf{prin}(n) = P$, γ_n is derivable from $\{\rho_m : m \Rightarrow^+ n\}$ in Th_P.*

Only permissible bundles can really occur, assuming that regular principals play by the rules and do not transmit a message without deducing the corresponding guarantee γ_n. There is no assumption that the penetrator deduces anything, as no formulas are associated with any penetrator node.

4.1 Sound Protocols

We next introduce a property of annotated protocols themselves, not concerned with individual bundles and principal theories. A protocol is sound if the formulas ρ_n on which principals rely are always true, in the sense that other principals have in fact made the assertions that ρ_n says they have made. A "soundness" attack on a protocol is a bundle $\mathcal{B}$ in which a regular principal relies on ρ_n, but without nodes $m \in \mathcal{B}$ whose guarantees γ_m would justify ρ_n. We give an example of unsoundness in Section 4.4.

Soundness is achievable only when certain nonces are unpredictable and certain keys are uncompromised. By a *security value* for a parameterized strand $S_j[\boldsymbol{X}]$, we mean a function $f(\boldsymbol{X})$. In practice f is always either a projection taking value X_i for some i or else an associated key such as $K_{X_i}^{-1}$. A *security value assignment* for a protocol Π is a pair of finite functions $\mathsf{unique}, \mathsf{non}$, each giving a set of security values for each role. An example appears in Table 2. If $s \in S_j[\boldsymbol{v}]$ is a strand and $\mathcal{B}$ is a bundle s intersects, then $\mathcal{B}$ *respects* $\mathsf{unique}, \mathsf{non}$ *for* s if $f \in \mathsf{unique}(S_j)$ implies $f(\boldsymbol{v})$ is uniquely originating in $\mathcal{B}$, and $f \in \mathsf{non}(S_j)$ implies $f(\boldsymbol{v})$ is non-originating in $\mathcal{B}$. $\mathcal{B}$ *respects* $\mathsf{unique}, \mathsf{non}$ if it respects it for every regular s such that $\mathcal{B}$ intersects s.

Definition 3. Soundness. *Bundle* $\mathcal{B}$ supports *a negative node* $n \in \mathcal{B}$ *iff* ρ_n *is a logical consequence of the set of formulas* $\{\mathsf{prin}(m) \text{ says } \gamma_m \colon m \prec_{\mathcal{B}} n\}$.

Let Π *be an annotated protocol, and let* $\mathsf{unique}, \mathsf{non}$ *be a security value assignment for* Π. Π is sound for $\mathsf{unique}, \mathsf{non}$ *if, whenever* $\mathcal{B}$ *is a bundle over* Π *that respects* $\mathsf{unique}, \mathsf{non}$, *for every negative* $n \in \mathcal{B}$, $\mathcal{B}$ *supports* n.

Typically, each rely formula ρ_n is a conjunction of assertions P says ϕ. Each conjunct is of the form $\mathsf{prin}(m)$ says γ_m, or, if γ_m is itself a conjunction $\phi_1 \wedge \ldots \wedge \phi_k$, alternatively $\mathsf{prin}(m)$ says ϕ_i.[2] Thus, one need only show there is such an $m \prec_{\mathcal{B}} n$. The rely formulas of Table 1 were chosen in this way. For instance, $\rho_{c,2}$ will be true as long as there is a merchant strand whose second node occurred previously and agrees with $n_{c,2}$ on the variables occurring in $\rho_{c,2}$, namely $C, M, \mathsf{goods}, \mathsf{price}, N_m$. Parameters not occurring in $\rho_{c,2}$ are unconstrained in the corresponding node. For instance, N_c is relevant to the working of the protocol, but does not occur in $\rho_{c,2}$.

Soundness is a *horizontal* condition: it concerns the message communication arrows that tie different strands together. By contrast, permissibility is a *vertical* condition: it concerns the local behaviors on the individual regular strands in a bundle. All the reasoning on our framework occurs locally on individual strands, while soundness ensures that the protocol coordinates assumptions with earlier conclusions on other strands.

4.2 Recent Soundness

Assertions do not last forever. A money order becomes stale, and the issuing bank will no longer redeem it. Goods are no longer worth the price, or are no

[2] Following [2], P says $(\phi \wedge \psi)$ implies P says $\phi \wedge P$ says ψ.

longer be available at a quoted price. Principals want to ensure that they rely only on recently made statements. We write $\mathsf{first}(s)$ to refer to the first node on a strand s and $\mathsf{last}(s)$ to refer to the last, and we define [10]:

Definition 4. Recency *A node m is* recent for n *in bundle $\mathcal{B}$ if there exists a strand s such that* $\mathsf{first}(s) \preceq_{\mathcal{B}} m$ *and* $n \preceq_{\mathcal{B}} \mathsf{last}(s)$.

When m is recent for n, strand s that "measures" the delay between them. Suppose there is a timeout value b, and all regular strands are implemented to time out before the total elapsed time between first node and last node reaches b. Then recency bounds the total elapsed time between m and n by b. The incoming and outgoing authentication tests establish recency (Appendix A, Propositions 4–5).

Definition 5. Recent Soundness. *Bundle $\mathcal{B}$* recently supports *a negative node $n \in \mathcal{B}$ iff ρ_n is a logical consequence of the set of formulas*

$$\{\mathsf{prin}(m) \text{ says } \gamma_m \colon m \prec_{\mathcal{B}} n \wedge m \textit{ is recent for } n\}.$$

Π is recent-sound for unique, non *if, whenever $\mathcal{B}$ is a bundle over Π that respects* unique, non, *for every negative $n \in \mathcal{B}$, $\mathcal{B}$ recently supports n.*

Organizations have various techniques to allow themselves to ensure assertions will remain true for the near future, the next b time units. In EPMO, B puts a hold on the amount price in C's account, so that when M redeems the money order, B will still be willing to transfer this amount of money.

4.3 Recent Soundness of EPMO

We now establish the soundness of EPMO, using the security value assignment in Table 2. We let K_P^{-1} be P's private decryption key, and let $K_{P,\mathsf{sig}}^{-1}$ be P's private signature key. The notation $S[v_1, *, v_3]$ means $\bigcup_{X_2} S[v_1, X_2, v_3]$. We assume tacitly that hashes are uninvertible, which could be formalized (Appendix A) as a non-origination assumption.

Table 2. Security Value Assignment for EPMO

Role	non	unique
Bank	$\{K_C^{-1}, K_{B,\mathsf{sig}}^{-1}, K_{M,\mathsf{sig}}^{-1}\}$	$\{N_m, N_b, N_c\}$
Cust	$\{K_C^{-1}, K_M^{-1}, K_B^{-1}\}$	$\{N_c\}$
Merch	$\{K_C^{-1}, K_{B,\mathsf{sig}}^{-1}\}$	$\{N_m, N_b, N_c\}$

Because the M's rely statement $\rho_{m,3}$ is a conjunction, M must be assured that there are matching bank and customer nodes $n_{b,2}$ and $n_{c,4}$. They must agree with $n_{m,3}$ at least for the variables B, C, p, N_m and B, C, M, p, N_m, respectively.

Proposition 1 *Suppose:* $m \in \mathsf{Merch}[B, C, M, p, g, N_c, N_m, N_b]$; $n_{m,3} \in \mathcal{B}$; $\mathcal{B}$ *respects* unique, non *for* m*; and* $N_c \neq N_m$. *Then* $n_{b,2}, n_{c,5} \in \mathcal{B}$ *for some* $b \in \mathsf{Bank}[B, C, *, p, N_c, N_m, N_b]$ *and* $c \in \mathsf{Cust}[B, C, M, p, g, N_c, N_m, N_b]$*; moreover* $n_{b,2}, n_{c,5}$ *are recent for* $n_{m,3}$.

Proof. Node $n_{b,2}$ follows by an incoming test on test value N_m. The message sent on $n_{b,2}$ takes the form $[\![\mathsf{hash}(C \mathbin{\hat{}} N_b \mathbin{\hat{}} N_m \mathbin{\hat{}} \mathsf{price})]\!]_B \mathbin{\hat{}} \{\!|N \mathbin{\hat{}} N_b|\!\}_C$ for some N. To establish $n_{c,5}$, observe that N_b is uniquely originating on $n_{b,2}$; $K_C^{-1} \in \mathsf{safe}$, and $\mathsf{hash}(\_)$ is uninvertible. Hence nodes $n_{b,2}$ and $n_{m,3}$ form an outgoing test. Thus there is a customer strand transforming $t \mathbin{\hat{}} \{\!|N' \mathbin{\hat{}} N_b|\!\}_{C'} \Rightarrow^+ t \mathbin{\hat{}} N_b$. By the protocol definition, t is a money order containing bank nonce N_b. Because N_b is uniquely originating, and a money order is always a point of origination for its bank nonce, $t = [\![\mathsf{hash}(C \mathbin{\hat{}} N_c \mathbin{\hat{}} N_b \mathbin{\hat{}} N_m \mathbin{\hat{}} \mathsf{price})]\!]_B$. Finally, to see that c agrees on p, observe that $n_{m,2} \Rightarrow n_{m,3}$ is also an outgoing test. Thus, there is a customer strand c' with parameters C, M, p, g, N_c, N_m; $c' = c$ because N_c originates uniquely, but originates on both customer strands.

For recency, observe that $N_m \sqsubset \mathrm{term}(n_{b,2})$ and $N_m \sqsubset \mathrm{term}(n_{c,3})$, while N_m originates uniquely at $n_{m,2}$; thus, m measures the delay since $n_{b,2}$ and $n_{c,3}$. ■

We show next that $\mathcal{B}$ gives guarantees for the rely formula $\rho_{b,3}$, i.e. it contains nodes $n_{c,5}$ and $n_{m,4}$. Nodes $n_{c,5}$ and $n_{m,4}$ must agree with $\rho_{b,3}$ on the parameters $B, C, M, \mathsf{price}, N_m$ occurring in $\gamma_{c,5}$ and in the first conjunct of $\gamma_{m,4}$.

Proposition 2 *Suppose that* $b \in \mathsf{Bank}[B, C, M, p, N_c, N_m, N_b]$*, where* $N_c \neq N_b \neq N_m$*; suppose* $\mathcal{B}$ *respects* unique, non *for* b*; and suppose* $n_{b,3} \in \mathcal{B}$. *Then* $n_{m,4}, n_{c,5} \in \mathcal{B}$ *for some*

$$m \in \mathsf{Merch}[B, C, M, p, *, N_m, N_b] \quad \textit{and} \quad c \in \mathsf{Cust}[B, C, M, p, *, *, N_m, N_b].$$

Nodes $n_{m,4}, n_{c,5}$ *are recent for* $n_{b,3}$.

Proof. By the incoming test principle (Proposition 5), there is a regular node between $n_{b,2}$ and $n_{b,3}$ emitting $[\![\mathsf{hash}(B \mathbin{\hat{}} N_b \mathbin{\hat{}} N_m)]\!]_M$. By pattern matching, this is node $n_{m,4}$ of a merchant strand with parameters B, M, N_b, N_m. Hence, it was preceded by a node receiving $\mathsf{mo}' = [\![\mathsf{hash}(C' \mathbin{\hat{}} N_b \mathbin{\hat{}} N_m \mathbin{\hat{}} p')]\!]_B$; by unique origination of N_b and because the protocol emits mo' only at a point of origination for N_b, $\mathsf{mo}' = \mathsf{mo}$. Thus, $C' = C$ and $p' = p$. Hence, by Proposition 1, the required customer strand exists. ■

Customer rely formulas may be justified similarly.

4.4 An Unsound Protocol

An unsound variant of EPMO, in the spirit of the original Needham-Schroeder protocol [22], replaces message 2 from M to C by $\{\!|N_c \mathbin{\hat{}} N_m \mathbin{\hat{}} \mathsf{price}|\!\}_C$. As M's name is absent, we can then mount a Lowe-like attack [21]. When, in $\rho_{m,3}$, M relies on C says C authorizes $\mathsf{transfer}(B, \mathsf{price}, M, N_m)$, there is no matching guarantee. Instead, C has authorized $\mathsf{transfer}(B, \mathsf{price}, M', N_m)$ for some different M'. Therefore, soundness is false.

M' can use the attack, e.g. to arbitrage for his own advantage some discount that C can obtain from M. Suppose that C contacts M', when the latter knows C could have got a discounted price from M. M' contacts M purporting to be C and requesting a larger amount of goods to make up the expected price. The remainder of the exchange occurs as expected, except that M' skims off the additional goods and delivers the expected shipment to C.

5 Conclusion

This paper appears to be the first offering a rigorous method for reasoning about trust management in the context of nonce-based cryptographic protocols, rather than using certificates with expiration dates, as in [18] and much other work. We have illustrated our method with an electronic commerce protocol. We are also using it to make TPMs a basis for access control via trust management [16].

Related Work. A large literature applies logics to reasoning about cryptographic protocols, stretching from [6] to [8]. However, the logics determine what authentication goals a protocol achieves. By contrast, we use the non-logical strand space framework to determine authentication. We cash in those authentication results using soundness (Definition 3), obtaining rely formulas that coordinate the local per-strand trust management reasoning of the distributed principals.

There is a well-entrenched tendency to regard protocol actions as assertions, reflecting the principal's beliefs and goals, and its appraisals of assertions by others. Generally, however, one has regarded the *messages* as statements, which may lead to confusion about who is drawing conclusions from the statements, and which masks whether the statement was made by the expected peer. Hence, we have attached the formulas to purely local transmission and reception events. The key notion of protocol soundness allows us to decide whether statements were uttered by the expected peer. A sound protocol is a reliable coordination mechanism for deduction carried out by separate principals.

Taking protocol actions as assertions animates Abadi and Needham's advice for protocol design [1]. Our interpretation of the assertions as associated with actions rather than with messages is compatible with much of what they say, and could lead to a more precise treatment. For instance, they write:

> Principle 1. Every message should say what it means: the interpretation of the message should depend only on its contents.

If the "interpretation" is the guarantee offered by the sender, then this principle recommends that for each message t, there should be a single guarantee γ asserted on every regular node on which t is sent. All parameters in γ should occur in t. Similarly:

> Principle 2. The conditions for a message to be acted upon should be clearly set out so that someone reviewing a design may see whether they are acceptable or not.

To act on a message means to continue the protocol and send the next message. Our trust management framework "clearly sets out" the condition for this in the guarantee and rely statements. To decide whether to act on a message received, P uses its rely statement, trying to deduce the next guarantee.

Future Work. An important question suggested by our work is how to determine the possible shapes that the bundles of a protocol may have. By a *shape*, we mean a set of parametric regular strands with a partial ordering $\preceq$, and a maximum node n_f that all other nodes precede. To be a shape, there must be a bundle, containing precisely the given regular strands, which is normal and efficient in the sense of [12]. In some protocols there is only one possible shape; a bundle for EPMO that contains $n_f = n_{b,3}$ has the shape shown in Figure 1. Other protocols (Otway-Rees, for instance) have more than one shape for a given n_f.

Shape analysis allows the protocol designer to explain, when P_1 draws some conclusion, exactly which other principals may have made guarantees contributing to P_1's conclusion. For instance, suppose that P_1 trusts P_2's local information, so P_1 would like to accept P_2 says $\phi \supset \phi$. However, P_1 may want to know that there is no execution in which P_2, when deducing ϕ, relied on another principal's assertions. A shape analysis tells us whether a strand of some P_3 may have preceded P_2's message transmission, in which case it may have contributed a guarantee on which P_2 relied. This is a novel protocol design criterion.

The ideas here also suggest an appealing implementation strategy, in which protocol principals are constructed using a trust management engine [19], together with tabular information describing the structure of the possible strands.

We would also like to know how this method relates to well-developed frameworks for reasoning about knowledge [9,14]. Can the elements of a *trust structure* [7] replace the formulas used here? Computational aspects of logic must also eventually be considered; our framework suggests new properties for which tractability would be desirable [19,20].

Conclusion. In this paper, we have developed a rely-guarantee method that can be used to combine trust management logics with nonce-based protocols. The key technical idea was *soundness*, which provides a criterion for whether the protocol is adequate to support the trust reasoning of the principals. We believe that the resulting theory can be useful as a mechanism for cross-organization access control, particularly when supported by hardware such as the TPM that provides reliable security services.

Acknowledgments. Boris Balacheff, Joe Pato, David Plaquin, and Martin Sadler of HP Labs helped orient this work in relation to the TPM environment. The informal Protocol Exchange seminar provided an excellent forum for discussion, at which Dusko Pavlovic and John Mitchell in particular planted seeds. Dale Johnson ironed out the Aristotle connection.

References

1. Martín Abadi and Roger Needham. Prudent engineering practice for cryptographic protocols. In *Proceedings, 1994 IEEE Symposium on Research in Security and Privacy*, pages 122–136. IEEE, IEEE Computer Society Press, 1994.
2. Andrew W. Appel and Edward W. Felten. Proof-carrying authentication. In *6th ACM Conference on Computer and Communications Security*, November 1999.
3. Aristotle. *Nicomachean Ethics.* Oxford University Press, 1953.
4. Boris Balacheff, Liqun Chen, Siani Pearson (ed.), David Plaquin, and Graeme Proudler. *Trusted Computing Platforms: TCPA Technology in Context.* Prentice Hall PTR, Upper Saddle River, NJ, 2003.
5. Matt Blaze, Joan Feigenbaum, and Jack Lacy. Distributed trust management. In *Proceedings, 1996 IEEE Symposium on Security and Privacy*, pages 164–173, 1997.
6. Michael Burrows, Martín Abadi, and Roger Needham. A logic of authentication. *Proceedings of the Royal Society*, Series A, 426(1871):233–271, December 1989. Also appeared as SRC Research Report 39 and, in a shortened form, in ACM Transactions on Computer Systems 8, 1 (February 1990), 18-36.
7. Marco Carbone, Mogens Nielsen, and Vladimiro Sassone. A formal model for trust in dynamic networks. In Antonio Cerone, editor, *International Conference on Software Engineering and Formal Methods.* IEEE CS Press, September 2003.
8. Nancy Durgin, John Mitchell, and Dusko Pavlovic. A compositional logic for proving security properties of protocols. *Journal of Computer Security*, 11(4):677–721, 2003.
9. Ronald Fagin, Joseph Y. Halpern, Yoram Moses, and Moshe Y. Vardi. *Reasoning about Knowledge.* MIT Press, Cambridge, MA, 1995.
10. Joshua D. Guttman. Authentication tests and disjoint encryption: a method for security protocol design. *Journal of Computer Security*, 2004. Forthcoming.
11. Joshua D. Guttman and F. Javier Thayer. Protocol independence through disjoint encryption. In *Proceedings, 13th Computer Security Foundations Workshop.* IEEE Computer Society Press, July 2000.
12. Joshua D. Guttman and F. Javier Thayer. Authentication tests and the structure of bundles. *Theoretical Computer Science*, 283(2):333–380, June 2002.
13. Joshua D. Guttman, F. Javier Thayer, and Lenore D. Zuck. The faithfulness of abstract protocol analysis: Message authentication. *Journal of Computer Security*, 2004. Forthcoming.
14. Joseph Y. Halpern and Riccardo Pucella. On the relationship between strand spaces and multi-agent systems. *ACM Transactions on Information and System Security*, 6(1):43–70, February 2003.
15. James Heather, Gavin Lowe, and Steve Schneider. How to prevent type flaw attacks on security protocols. In *Proceedings, 13th Computer Security Foundations Workshop.* IEEE Computer Society Press, July 2000.
16. Jonathan Herzog, Brian Sniffen, Jay Carlson, Joshua D. Guttman, and John D. Ramsdell. Trust management with cryptographic hardware assistance. MTR 03B0082, The MITRE Corp., Bedford, MA, September 2003.
17. Cliff B. Jones. Tentative steps toward a development method for interfering programs. *ACM Transactions on Programming Languages and Systems*, 1983.
18. Butler Lampson, Martín Abadi, Michael Burrows, and Edward Wobber. Authentication in distributed systems: Theory and practice. *ACM Transactions on Computer Systems*, 10(4):265–310, November 1992.

19. Ninghui Li, John C. Mitchell, and William H. Winsborough. Design of a role-based trust management framework. In *Proceedings, 2002 IEEE Symposium on Security and Privacy*, pages 114–130. May, IEEE CS Press, 2002.
20. Ninghui Li, William H. Winsborough, and John C. Mitchell. Beyond proof-of-compliance: Safety and availability analysis on trust management. In *Proceedings, 2003 IEEE Symposium on Security and Privacy*. May, IEEE CS Press, 2003.
21. Gavin Lowe. Breaking and fixing the Needham-Schroeder public-key protocol using FDR. In *Proceeedings of* TACAS, volume 1055 of *Lecture Notes in Computer Science*, pages 147–166. Springer Verlag, 1996.
22. Roger Needham and Michael Schroeder. Using encryption for authentication in large networks of computers. *Communications of the ACM*, 21(12), 1978.
23. Adrian Perrig and Dawn Xiaodong Song. Looking for diamonds in the desert: Extending automatic protocol generation to three-party authentication and key agreement protocols. In *Proceedings of the 13th IEEE Computer Security Foundations Workshop*. IEEE Computer Society Press, July 2000.
24. F. Javier THAYER Fábrega, Jonathan C. Herzog, and Joshua D. Guttman. Strand spaces: Proving security protocols correct. *Journal of Computer Security*, 7(2/3):191–230, 1999.

A Strand Spaces

A set A contains the messages ("terms") to be exchanged. They are freely generated from a set of atoms including texts and keys by concatenation and encryption, in which the second argument is a key. We formalize hashing as encryption with an asymmetric key of which no principal knows the inverse. Message transmission has positive sign, and reception has a negative sign.

Definition 6. *A* signed term *is a pair* $\langle \sigma, a \rangle$ *with* $a \in \mathsf{A}$ *and* σ *one of the symbols* $+, -$. *We will write a signed term as* $+t$ *or* $-t$. $(\pm\mathsf{A})^*$ *is the set of finite sequences of signed terms. A* strand space *over* A *is a set* Σ *with a trace mapping* $\mathrm{tr} : \Sigma \to (\pm\mathsf{A})^*$. *Fix a strand space* Σ*:*

1. *The subterm relation* $\sqsubset$ *is defined inductively, as the smallest relation such that* $a \sqsubset a$; $a \sqsubset \{\!|g|\!\}_K$ *if* $a \sqsubset g$; *and* $a \sqsubset g\,\hat{}\,h$ *if* $a \sqsubset g$ *or* $a \sqsubset h$.
   By this definition, for $K \in \mathsf{K}$, *we have* $K \sqsubset \{\!|g|\!\}_K$ *only if* $K \sqsubset g$ *already.*
2. *Suppose* I *is a set of terms. The node* $n \in \mathcal{N}$ *is an* entry point *for* I *iff* $term(n) = +t$ *for some* $t \in I$, *and whenever* $n' \Rightarrow^+ n$, $term(n') \notin I$.
3. *An term* t originates *on* $n \in \mathcal{N}$ *iff* n *is an entry point for* $I = \{t' : t \sqsubset t'\}$.
4. *An term* t *is* uniquely originating in $S \subset \mathcal{N}$ *iff there is a unique* $n \in S$ *such that* t *originates on* n, *and* non-originating *if there is no such* $n \in S$.

If a term t originates uniquely in a suitable set of nodes, then it can play the role of a nonce or session key. If it is non-originating, it can serve as a long-term secret, such as a shared symmetric key or a private asymmetric key. $\mathcal{N}$ together with both sets of edges $n_1 \to n_2$ (message transmission) and $n_1 \Rightarrow n_2$ (succession on the same strand) is a directed graph $\langle \mathcal{N}, (\to \cup \Rightarrow) \rangle$. A *bundle* is a subgraph of $\langle \mathcal{N}, (\to \cup \Rightarrow) \rangle$ for which the edges express causal dependencies of the nodes.

Definition 7. *Suppose $\to_{\mathcal{B}} \subset \to$; suppose $\Rightarrow_{\mathcal{B}} \subset \Rightarrow$; and let $\mathcal{B} = \langle \mathcal{N}_{\mathcal{B}}, (\to_{\mathcal{B}} \cup \Rightarrow_{\mathcal{B}}) \rangle$ be a finite acyclic subgraph of $\langle \mathcal{N}, (\to \cup \Rightarrow) \rangle$. $\mathcal{B}$ is a bundle if:*

1. *If $n_2 \in \mathcal{N}_{\mathcal{B}}$ and term(n_2) is negative, then there is a unique n_1 such that $n_1 \to_{\mathcal{B}} n_2$.*
2. *If $n_2 \in \mathcal{N}_{\mathcal{B}}$ and $n_1 \Rightarrow n_2$ then $n_1 \Rightarrow_{\mathcal{B}} n_2$.*

A node n is in a bundle $\mathcal{B} = \langle \mathcal{N}_{\mathcal{B}}, \to_{\mathcal{B}} \cup \Rightarrow_{\mathcal{B}} \rangle$, written $n \in \mathcal{B}$, if $n \in \mathcal{N}_{\mathcal{B}}$. The $\mathcal{B}$-height *of a strand s is the largest i such that $\langle s, i \rangle \in \mathcal{B}$. If $\mathcal{S}$ is a set of edges, i.e. $\mathcal{S} \subset \to \cup \Rightarrow$, then $\prec_{\mathcal{S}}$ is the transitive closure of $\mathcal{S}$, and $\preceq_{\mathcal{S}}$ is the reflexive, transitive closure of $\mathcal{S}$.*

Proposition 3 *If $\mathcal{B}$ is a bundle, $\preceq_{\mathcal{B}}$ is a partial order. Every non-empty subset of the nodes in $\mathcal{B}$ has $\preceq_{\mathcal{B}}$-minimal members.*

Definition 8. *A* penetrator trace *is one of the following:*

M_t: $\langle +t \rangle$ *where* $t \in$*text* $\quad$ K_K: $\langle +K \rangle$

$\mathsf{C}_{g,h}$: $\langle -g,\ -h,\ +g \,\hat{}\, h \rangle$ $\quad$ $\mathsf{S}_{g,h}$: $\langle -g \,\hat{}\, h,\ +g,\ +h \rangle$

$\mathsf{E}_{h,K}$: $\langle -K,\ -h,\ +\{\!|h|\!\}_K \rangle$ $\quad$ $\mathsf{D}_{h,K}$: $\langle -K^{-1},\ -\{\!|h|\!\}_K,\ +h \rangle$.

We write safe for *safe* keys, i.e. keys that the penetrator can never learn or use [12]. Since long term shared keys and private asymmetric keys are never transmitted in reasonable protocols, these keys are safe unless compromised before execution of the protocol. Session keys are safe if transmitted only protected by keys K with $K^{-1} \in \mathsf{safe}$.

When S is a set of terms, t_0 *occurs only within* S in t if, regarding t as an abstract syntax tree, every branch from the root to an occurrence of t_0 traverses some occurrence of a $t_1 \in S$ before reaching t_0. It *occurs outside* S in t if $t_0 \sqsubset t$ but t_0 does not occur only within S in t. A term t_0 *occurs safely* in t if it occurs only within $S = \{\{\!|h|\!\}_K : K^{-1} \in \mathsf{safe}\}$ in t.

Proposition 4 (Outgoing Authentication Test) *Suppose $\mathcal{B}$ is a bundle in which a originates uniquely at n_0; a occurs only within S in term(n_0) and a occurs safely in S; and $n_1 \in \mathcal{B}$ is negative and a occurs outside S in term(n_1).*

There are regular $m_0, m_1 \in \mathcal{B}$ such that $m_0 \Rightarrow^+ m_1$, where m_1 is positive, a occurs only within S in term(m_0), and a occurs outside S in term(m_1). Moreover, $n_0 \preceq m_0 \prec m_1 \prec n_1$.

Proposition 5 (Unsolicited, Incoming Test Principles) *Suppose $n_1 \in \mathcal{B}$ is negative, $\{\!|h|\!\}_K \sqsubset$ term(n_1), and $K \in \mathsf{safe}$. (Unsolicited test:) There exists a regular $m_1 \prec n_1$ such that $\{\!|h|\!\}_K$ originates at m_1. (Incoming test:) If in addition $a \sqsubset h$ originates uniquely on $n_0 \neq m_1$, then $n_0 \prec m_0 \Rightarrow^+ m_1 \prec n_1$.*

Just Fast Keying in the Pi Calculus

Martín Abadi[1], Bruno Blanchet[2], and Cédric Fournet[3]

[1] University of California, Santa Cruz
[2] CNRS, Département d'Informatique, École Normale Supérieure, Paris
and Max-Planck-Institut für Informatik, Saarbrücken
[3] Microsoft Research

Abstract. JFK is a recent, attractive protocol for fast key establishment as part of securing IP communication. In this paper, we analyze it formally in the applied pi calculus (partly in terms of observational equivalences, partly with the assistance of an automatic protocol verifier). We treat JFK's core security properties, and also other properties that are rarely articulated and studied rigorously, such as resistance to denial-of-service attacks. In the course of this analysis we found some ambiguities and minor problems, but we mostly obtain positive results about JFK. For this purpose, we develop ideas and techniques that should be useful more generally in the specification and verification of security protocols.

1 Introduction

The design of security mechanisms for the Internet has been the focus of much activity. In particular, IP security has received much attention; in this area, we have seen some progress but also some disappointment and some controversy. The Internet Key Exchange (IKE) protocol [12], an important method for establishing cryptographic keys for secure IP communication, has been the subject of considerable and reasonable criticisms. Those criticisms tend to concern not the core authenticity and secrecy properties that IKE offers but rather the complexity of IKE, some of its inefficiencies, and its poor resistance against denial-of-service (DOS) attacks. Several recent protocols aim to address IKE's shortcomings. These include the JFK protocol [5,6] (for "just fast keying") and the IKEv2 protocol [13], currently under development.

In some respects, IKE and its successors are fairly classical security protocols. They all employ common pieces in the standard arsenal of modern cryptography, and aim to guarantee the integrity and secrecy of IP communication. They are all subject to common efficiency considerations, which limit the use of expensive cryptographic operations and the number and size of messages. Beyond such basic aspects, however, these protocols—and JFK in particular—exhibit a number of interesting features because they address other security objectives. These other objectives are sometimes subtle; they are seldom articulated precisely. Moreover, they give rise to new tensions and delicate compromises. For instance, in the name of privacy, a protocol may attempt to hide the identities of the participants (that is, to provide identity protection) and to guarantee the plausible deniability of their actions, and may accordingly avoid or delay the authentication of the

D.A. Schmidt (Ed.): ESOP 2004, LNCS 2986, pp. 340–354, 2004.

participants. On the other hand, strong, early authentication can simplify DOS resistance. Of course, such tensions are not unique to JFK and its close relatives. Rather, they seem to be increasingly important in the design of modern security protocols. JFK exemplifies them well and resolves them nicely.

In this paper we analyze JFK, relying on the applied pi calculus, an extension of the standard pi calculus with functions. Specifically, we present a formalization of one of the two variants of JFK known as JFKr (the one closer to IKEv2). While fairly short and abstract, our formalization gives a fine level of detail in the modelling of contexts and parallel sessions. It also covers aspects of the protocol beyond the "messages on the wire", such as protocol interfaces, the checks performed by the participants, and other delicate features such as the treatment of duplicate requests.

We treat several properties of the protocol, such as plausible deniability and DOS resistance. (We consider all the properties with a single model of the protocol: we do not need to define special, partial models for particular properties.) We also provide proofs for those properties. Some of the proofs were done by hand, while others were done with an automated protocol verifier, ProVerif [7]. In some cases, there are overlaps between the two kinds of proofs; those overlaps provide extra assurance about the correctness of the formalization and the proofs. Moreover, while ProVerif can be used for establishing standard security properties such as correspondence assertions, it is still limited when it comes to subtler properties, which we therefore prove partly by hand.

In the course of this analysis, we identified some minor limitations and weaknesses of JFK. In particular, we discovered that JFK does not provide as much identity protection as one might have expected on the basis of informal descriptions of the protocol. However, we did not discover fatal mistakes. That is comforting but not surprising, since the authors of JFK have substantial experience in protocol design and since JFK benefited from careful review and prolonged discussion in the IETF context.

Beyond observations and results on JFK, this study contributes to the specification and verification of security protocols in several ways. Our basic approach and tools come from recent work; it is pleasing to confirm their effectiveness. On the other hand, the approach to formalizing several of the protocol's less mundane facets is largely new, and should be applicable elsewhere. Similarly, the proofs are non-trivial and motivate some new developments of our techniques. These novelties include a formulation of plausible deniability, a general lemma about state elimination, and extensions in ProVerif. The proofs also provide an opportunity for integrating manual and automatic methods in the applied pi calculus.

Contents. The next section is a review and informal discussion of JFK. Section 3 presents a model of JFKr in the applied pi calculus. Section 4 treats DOS resistance. Section 5 concerns core security properties (secrecy and authenticity). It also briefly addresses identity protection. Section 6 mentions some related work and concludes.

Because of space constraints, this version of the paper omits much material that appears in an extended version [3]: a discussion of the ambiguities and minor problems that we found, a description and partial analysis of the protocol variant JFKi, a review of the applied pi calculus, further material on identity protection and on DOS resistance, a study of plausible deniability, details on our use of ProVerif, and proofs.

2 The JFK Protocol

The JFK protocol has been discussed in a series of five Internet Drafts [5], starting in 2001, and it is also described in a conference paper [6]. While our work is based on all those documents, we tend to privilege the contents of the conference paper, since it should have some permanence. We refer to that paper for additional material on the protocol and its motivation. As indicated above, we focus on a variant called JFKr.

JFKr involves two principals that play the roles of an initiator and a responder. As in many other protocols, these two principals wish to open a secure communication channel, and they attempt to accomplish it by establishing a shared secret. This shared secret serves as the basis for computing session keys. The two principals should associate the shared secret with each other, verify each other's identities, and also agree on various communication parameters (for example, what sort of session keys to employ). Attackers may eavesdrop, delete, and insert messages; they may also attempt to impersonate principals [19]. Therefore, the communications between the initiator and the responder are cryptographically protected. Informally, JFKr consists of the following four messages:

Message 1	$I \rightarrow R:$	N_I, x_I
Message 2	$R \rightarrow I:$	$N_I, N_R, x_R, \mathsf{g}_R, t_R$
Message 3	$I \rightarrow R:$	$N_I, N_R, x_I, x_R, t_R, e_I, h_I$
Message 4	$R \rightarrow I:$	e_R, h_R

where:

$$x_I = \mathsf{g}\hat{\ }d_I \qquad\qquad x_R = \mathsf{g}\hat{\ }d_R$$

$$t_R = \mathsf{H}\{K_R\}(x_R, N_R, N_I, \mathsf{IP}_I)$$

$$K_u = \mathsf{H}\{x_R\hat{\ }d_I\}(N_I, N_R, \mathrm{u}) \quad \text{for } u = a, e, v$$

$$e_I = \mathsf{E}\{K_e\}(\mathsf{ID}_I, \mathsf{ID}'_R, \mathsf{sa}_I, s_I) \qquad e_R = \mathsf{E}\{K_e\}(\mathsf{ID}_R, \mathsf{sa}_R, s_R)$$

$$h_I = \mathsf{H}\{K_a\}(\mathrm{i}, e_I) \qquad h_R = \mathsf{H}\{K_a\}(\mathrm{r}, e_R)$$

$$s_I = \mathsf{S}\{K_I^-\}(N_I, N_R, x_I, x_R, \mathsf{g}_R) \qquad s_R = \mathsf{S}\{K_R^-\}(x_R, N_R, x_I, N_I)$$

Figure 1 summarizes the notations of this exchange.

The first pair of messages establishes a shared secret via a Diffie-Hellman exchange. Each principal generates and communicates a fresh nonce N_z. Each principal also selects or generates a secret exponent d_z, and communicates the corresponding exponential $x_z = \mathsf{g}\hat{\ }d_z$. Relying on the equation $x_R\hat{\ }d_I = x_I\hat{\ }d_R$, three independent shared keys are derived from nonces and exponentials: K_a and K_e are used in Messages 3 and 4, while K_v is returned to each principal as the newly-established session secret. The reuse of exponentials is allowed, with a trade-off between forward secrecy and efficiency; in any case, the freshness of nonces suffices to guarantee that the generated shared secrets differ for all sessions.

Message 2 includes an authenticator cookie t_R, keyed with a secret local to the responder, K_R. The responder expects to see this cookie in Message 3, and need not perform any expensive cryptography or allocate resources until such a successful round-trip with the initiator. Furthermore, after receiving Message 3, the responder can remember handling t_R, so as to avoid expense in the event that t_R is replayed.

$z = I, R$	one of the two roles in the protocol: initiator or responder.
N_z	random fresh nonce for the session.
d_z	Diffie-Hellman secret exponents.
$x_z = \mathrm{g}\hat{\ }d_z$	Diffie-Hellman exchange values (g^i and g^r in [6]).
g	Diffie-Hellman group (possibly obtained from a previously received g_R).
g_R	responder's choice of group g and cryptographic algorithms (*GRPINFO*$_R$ in [6]).
t_R	authenticator cookie used by the responder against DOS.
K_R	responder's secret hash key for authenticators t_R (HK_R in [6]).
$u = a, e, v$	one of the three usage for keys: authentication, encryption, and main session secret.
K_u	shared key obtained by a Diffie-Hellman computation, specialized for u.
E	shared-key encryption function.
H	keyed hash function for MACs (message authentication codes).
e_z, h_z	encrypted payload messages and their MACs (protecting z's identity and signature).
S	public-key signature function.
s_z	signed nonces and exponentials.
K_z^-	private signature key for the principal playing role z.
ID_z	identity for the principal playing role z, and its public signature-verification key.
ID'_R	"hint" of the responder identity, provided by the initiator.
IP_I	IP source address for the initiator (hashed in t_R).
sa_z	additional parameters for setting IP security associations (sa and sa$'$ in [6]).
A, B	principals, taking part in the protocol (in either or both roles).

Fig. 1. Main notations

The second pair of messages provides authentication. Specifically, Messages 3 and 4 include encrypted signatures of the nonces, exponentials, and other material. The encryptions protect identity information. The signatures can be interpreted as delegations from the principals that control the signature keys (possibly users) to the protocol endpoints that control the exponents. Only transient protocol data is signed—not identities or long-term keys associated with users. In this respect, the protocol is in tune with concerns about plausible deniability that have appeared from time to time in this context.

The protocol specification, although clear, focuses on the messages exchanged in a single successful protocol run. It does not say much on the local processing that the parties perform, on the deployment of the protocol, and other subjects relevant for security. For instance, it does not prescribe how principals should use the protocol (and especially what is the sharing of signing keys and exponentials); how messages should be checked; and how the responder should manage state in order to resist DOS attacks. We have reason to believe that implementations differ in some of these respects, sometimes with unfortunate consequences. The protocol specification does however state several security objectives. We discuss them and study them formally below.

3 A Model of JFK in the Applied Pi Calculus

In this section, we express JFKr in the applied pi calculus. This calculus is an extension of the pi calculus with function symbols, for instance for tupling and for encryption, that can be assumed to satisfy particular equations. (We refer to prior work [4] for its syntax and semantics.) So we first select function symbols and an equational theory for modelling the messages of JFKr, then we discuss our representations for the IP network, attackers, and principals, and assemble processes that represent configurations of principals. We also outline how we program these processes in ProVerif.

M, T, U, V ::=	Terms
N, K, k, x, y, z	variable
c, n, s	name
$\mathsf{g}, U\hat{}V$	Diffie-Hellman group and exponential
$\mathsf{E}\{U\}(T), \mathsf{D}\{U\}(T)$	shared-key encryption and decryption
$\mathsf{S}\{U\}(T), \mathsf{V}\{U, V\}(T), \mathsf{true}$	public-key signature and verification
$\mathsf{Pk}(U)$	public key (and identity) from private key
$\mathsf{H}\{U\}(T)$	keyed cryptographic hash function
e, a, v, i, r	constant tags for keyed-hash specialization
$\mathsf{cons}(V_1, V_2), 1(V_1, V_2), \ldots, 4(V_1, V_2)$	constructors for pairs and formatted messages
$\mathsf{F}_1^{\mathsf{cons}}(T), \mathsf{F}_2^{\mathsf{cons}}(T), \mathsf{F}_1^1(T), \ldots, \mathsf{F}_2^4(T)$	selectors for pairs and formatted messages
$\emptyset, U.V$	empty set and set extension
$\mathsf{RecoverKey}(V), \mathsf{RecoverText}(V)$	additional functions for the attacker

Equation	
$(\mathsf{g}\hat{}y)\hat{}z = (\mathsf{g}\hat{}z)\hat{}y$	Diffie-Hellman
$\mathsf{V}\{\mathsf{Pk}(k), \mathsf{S}\{k\}(x)\}(x) = \mathsf{true}$	public-key signature verification
$\mathsf{D}\{k\}(\mathsf{E}\{k\}(x)) = x$	shared-key decryption
$\mathsf{F}_i^{\mathsf{n}}(\mathsf{n}(x_1, \ldots, x_i, \ldots)) = x_i$	projections for tuples ($\mathsf{n} = \mathsf{cons}, 1, 2, 3, 4$)
$(\emptyset.x).x = \emptyset.x$	idempotence of set extension
$(x.y).z = (x.z).y$	commutativity of set extension
$\mathsf{RecoverKey}(\mathsf{S}\{k\}(x)) = \mathsf{Pk}(k)$	public key recovery from a signature (attacker)
$\mathsf{RecoverText}(\mathsf{S}\{k\}(x)) = x$	signed text recovery from a signature (attacker)

Fig. 2. Grammar and equational theory for JFK

An Equational Theory. We use the grammar for terms and the equations of Figure 2. These deal both with cryptographic operations and with auxiliary functions for constructing tags, pairs, formatted messages, and sets. (We have functions for constructing sets, but not a set membership relation; instead, we let $U \in V$ abbreviate $V.U = V$.)

The equations embody our (fairly standard) hypotheses on the primitives introduced in Section 2. For instance, the keyed hash function $\mathsf{H}\{\_\}(\_)$ does not appear in any equation, and in particular has no inverse; thus it represents a perfect one-way function. More interestingly, exponentiation $\_\hat{}\_$ has no inverse, but an equation accounts for the commutativity property used for establishing a shared secret. Some of the functions and equations are not needed in the protocol itself, but may (in principle) weaken the protocol for the benefit of an attacker: $\mathsf{RecoverKey}(\_)$ and $\mathsf{RecoverText}(\_)$ can be used to extract information from signatures. We could further refine our theory by reflecting known weaknesses of the underlying cryptographic algorithms or their interactions.

Syntax and Informal Semantics for Processes. We recall the main notations for processes in the applied pi calculus : **0** does nothing (and we typically omit it); $P \mid Q$ is the parallel composition of P and Q; $!P$ behaves as an infinite number of copies of P running in parallel; $\nu n.P$ makes a new name n then behaves as P; *if* $U = V$ *then* P *else* Q is standard, with $U = V$ depending on the equational theory. The input process $c(x).P$ is ready to input a message on channel c, then to run P with the actual message replaced for the formal parameter x, while the output process $\overline{c}\langle V\rangle.P$ is ready to output message V on channel c, then to run P. The process *let* $\{x_1 = V_1\} \mid \ldots \mid \{x_n = V_n\}$ *in* P is P with local variables $x_1, \ldots, x_n$ bound to $V_1, \ldots, V_n$, respectively. The active substitution $\{x_1 = V_1\} \mid \ldots \mid \{x_n = V_n\}$ similarly defines $x_1, \ldots, x_n$, but does not restrict their scope; hence, the environment can use $x_1, \ldots, x_n$ as aliases for $V_1, \ldots, V_n$ in its computations. A context $C[\_]$ is a process with a hole, and $C[P]$ is the result of filling $C[\_]$'s hole with P; when $\_$ is not under a guard, $C[\_]$ is an evaluation context.

Labelled transitions $P \xrightarrow{a(V)} Q$ and $P \xrightarrow{\nu\tilde{u}.\overline{a}\langle V\rangle} Q$ represent interactions with the environment—inputs and outputs, respectively. In both, a is a communication channel and V a message. Transitions $P \rightarrow Q$ represent internal computation steps.

Syntactic Sugar. We write *if* M *then* P instead of *if* $M = \mathsf{true}$ *then* P. We omit pair constructors and parentheses for nested pairs, writing for instance $\mathsf{H}\{K\}(x_R, N_R, N_I)$ for $\mathsf{H}\{K\}(\mathsf{cons}(x_R, \mathsf{cons}(N_R, N_I)))$. We use pattern matching on tuples as syntactic sugar for the corresponding selectors, writing for instance $c(1(=N_I, x_I)).P$ instead of $c(z).let\ \{x_I = \mathsf{F}_2^1(z)\}\ in\ if\ z = 1(N_I, x_I)\ then\ P$ for some fresh variable z; this process receives a message on channel c, matches it with $1(N_I, T)$ for some subterm T, then runs P with T substituted for x_I. We also define syntax for filtering duplicate messages: $!a(X)\backslash V.C[if\ T\ fresh\ then\ P]$ stands for

$$\nu f.(\overline{f}\langle V\rangle \mid !a(X).C[f(s).(\overline{f}\langle s.T\rangle \mid if\ T \notin s\ then\ P)])$$

where $C[\_]$ is a context, X is a pattern, f is a fresh channel name, and s is a fresh variable. We use the local channel f for maintaining a set V of previous values for the term T. The arrival of a message may cause the addition of a particular T (which may depend on variables bound in X) to this set, and the execution of P.

The Network and the Attacker. In our model, all IP messages are transmitted on a free pi calculus communication channel, c, which represents a public IP network in which message contents serve for differentiating traffic flows. An arbitrary environment (an arbitrary evaluation context) represents the attacker. This environment can interact with other principals by inputs and outputs on any free channel, including c.

As a special case, we sometimes model a weaker, passive attacker that only eavesdrops on messages but does not modify them. An attack step against a process P consists in eavesdropping on a message sent by P, and amounts to a message interception (formally, with an output label $\nu\tilde{u}.\overline{c}\langle V\rangle$) followed by a re-emission of the same message (with an input label $c(V)$). We write $P \xrightarrow{\nu\tilde{u}.c[V]} P'$ as a shorthand for the two transitions $P \xrightarrow{\nu\tilde{u}.\overline{c}\langle V\rangle}\xrightarrow{c(V)} P'$.

Configurations of Principals. Our model allows an arbitrary number of principals. Each principal may run any number of sessions, as initiator and as responder, and may perform other operations after session establishment or even independently of the protocol. Only some of these principals follow the protocol. We are interested in the security properties that hold for them.

For the present purposes, the essence of a principal lies in its ability to produce signatures verifiable with its public key. Accordingly, we refer to each principal by its public key, using variables $\mathsf{ID}_A, \mathsf{ID}_B, \ldots$ for both identities and public keys. We also associate the context $PK^A[\_]$ of Figure 3 with every principal A. This context restricts the use of the signing key K_A^- to the process in the context and it exports the corresponding verification key ID_A. Whenever we put a process R in this context, our intent is that R never communicates K_A^- to the environment.

We let $\mathcal{C}$ range over sets of compliant principals—that is, principals that entirely delegate the use of their signing keys to JFKr. While some properties will obviously hold only for compliant principals, the initiator and responder code do not assume knowledge of $\mathcal{C}$: indeed, compliant and non-compliant principals can attempt to establish sessions.

Our representation of a compliant principal A has two parts: an implementation of JFKr, written $\mathcal{S}$, and a "user process", written $\mathcal{P}^A$. The user process defines any additional behavior, such as when protocol runs are initiated and what happens to the shared secret K_v after each session establishment. While we define $\mathcal{S}$ below, we treat $\mathcal{P}^A$ as an abstract parameter, in the context that encloses $\mathcal{S}$, possibly under the control of the attacker. The user process interacts with $\mathcal{S}$ through the following control interface:

As initiator: $\mathcal{P}^A$ sends a message $\overline{init}^A\langle \mathsf{ID}'_R, \mathsf{sa}_I\rangle$ to initiate a new session, with responder hint ID'_R and security association sa_I. When the protocol completes successfully, $\mathcal{S}$ sends $\overline{connect}^A\langle \mathsf{ID}_B, \mathsf{ID}'_R, \mathsf{sa}_I, \mathsf{sa}_R, K_v\rangle$ to notify $\mathcal{P}^A$ that the session has been accepted, and that A now shares K_v with a principal with identifier ID_B.

As responder: $\mathcal{S}$ sends $\overline{accept}^A\langle \mathsf{ID}_B, \mathsf{ID}'_R, \mathsf{sa}_I, \mathsf{sa}_R, K_v\rangle$ to notify $\mathcal{P}^A$ that it has accepted a session initiated by a principal with identifier ID_B, parameters ID'_R, sa_I, sa_R and shared secret K_v. To control who can initiate a session with A, $\mathcal{S}$ is parameterized by a set S_I^A of acceptable initiator identities. (We do not need a set such as S_I^A at the initiator: after completion of the protocol, the initiator's user process can decide what to do with the new session depending on the responder identity in the *connect* message.) For simplicity, S_I^A and sa_R are fixed.

Thus, the interface between each principal A and JFKr consists of three communication channels $init_A$, $accept_A$, $connect_A$ plus a set of identities S_I^A. These channels can be restricted (with ν) in order to hide the interface from the environment. For instance, a principal A that does not play the role of an initiator can be modelled easily by restricting communication on $init^A$.

The Protocol. Figure 3 shows our implementation of JFKr in the applied pi calculus. It includes definitions of processes for each role: a single process (I_0^A) for the initiator, and two processes (R_1^A, R_3^A) that do not share session state for the responder. For each principal A, these replicated processes detail the tests performed on incoming messages, interleaved with the computations on outgoing messages. The figure also includes the definition of a configuration $\mathcal{S}$: an assembly of an arbitrary but fixed set of compliant principals $\mathcal{C}$ that potentially share an arbitrary but fixed pool of exponentials X.

The design of JFK allows reusing Diffie-Hellman exponents for several sessions, principals, and roles, and does not impose a particular policy for changing them. For each exponent, one can decide when to stop using that exponent in new sessions. For instance, an exponent may expire once the first session established using that exponent terminates, so that discarding session keys prevents their later compromise. In our model, all compliant principals may use any number of shared exponentials, in both roles, for any number of parallel sessions. Results for configurations with less sharing are immediate corollaries of ours.

The context $D_x[\_]$ represents a Diffie-Hellman party, d_x the corresponding secret exponent, x the derived exchange value (the exponential), and g the group (the same

$I_0^A = !init^A(\mathsf{ID}'_R, \mathsf{sa}_I).$	**Initiator for each message *init***
$\nu N_I.$	*create a fresh nonce*
$\overline{c}\langle 1(N_I, x_I)\rangle.$	*send Message 1*
$c(2(=N_I, N_R, x_R, g_R, t_R)).$	*wait for Message 2*
$let\ \kappa_I\ in$	*compute DH shared keys (see below)*
$let\ \{s_I = \mathsf{S}\{K_A^-\}(N_I, N_R, x_I, x_R, g_R)\}\ in$	*sign*
$let\ \{e_I = \mathsf{E}\{K_e\}(\mathsf{ID}_A, \mathsf{ID}'_R, \mathsf{sa}_I, s_I)\}\ in$	*encrypt*
$let\ \{h_I = \mathsf{H}\{K_a\}(\mathsf{i}, e_I)\}\ in$	*compute MAC*
$\overline{c}\langle 3(N_I, N_R, x_I, x_R, t_R, e_I, h_I)\rangle.$	*send Message 3*
$c(4(e_R, h_R)).$	*wait for Message 4*
$if\ \mathsf{H}\{K_a\}(\mathsf{r}, e_R) = h_R\ then$	*check MAC*
$let\ \{\mathsf{ID}_R, \mathsf{sa}_R, s_R = \mathsf{D}\{K_e\}(e_R)\}\ in$	*decrypt*
$if\ \mathsf{V}\{\mathsf{ID}_R, s_R\}(N_I, N_R, x_I, x_R)\ then$	*check signature*
$\overline{connect}^A\langle \mathsf{ID}_R, \mathsf{ID}'_R, \mathsf{sa}_I, \mathsf{sa}_R, K_v\rangle$	*complete keying*
$R_1^A = !c(1(N_I, x_I)).$	**Responder for each Message 1**
$\nu N_R.$	*create a fresh nonce*
$let\ \{t_R = \mathsf{H}\{K_R\}(x_R, N_R, N_I)\}\ in$	*compute anti-DOS token*
$\overline{c}\langle 2(N_I, N_R, x_R, g_R, t_R)\rangle$	*send Message 2*
$R_3^A = !c(3(N_I, N_R, x_I, x_R, t_R, e_I, h_I))\backslash\emptyset.$	**Responder for each Message 3**
$if\ t_R = \mathsf{H}\{K_R\}(x_R, N_R, N_I)\ then$	*check anti-DOS token*
$if\ t_R\ fresh\ then$	*accept token only once*
$let\ \kappa_R\ in$	*compute DH shared keys (see below)*
$if\ \mathsf{H}\{K_a\}(\mathsf{i}, e_I) = h_I\ then$	*check MAC*
$let\ \{\mathsf{ID}_I, \mathsf{ID}'_R, \mathsf{sa}_I, s_I = \mathsf{D}\{K_e\}(e_I)\}\ in$	*decrypt*
$if\ \mathsf{ID}_I \in S_I^A\ then$	*authorize*
$if\ \mathsf{V}\{\mathsf{ID}_I, s_I\}(N_I, N_R, x_I, x_R, g_R)\ then$	*check signature*
$\overline{accept}^A\langle \mathsf{ID}_I, \mathsf{ID}'_R, \mathsf{sa}_I, \mathsf{sa}_R, K_v\rangle.$	*accept the session*
$let\ \{s_R = \mathsf{S}\{K_A^-\}(N_I, N_R, x_I, x_R)\}\ in$	*sign*
$let\ \{e_R = \mathsf{E}\{K_e\}(\mathsf{ID}_A, \mathsf{sa}_R, s_R)\}\ in$	*encrypt*
$let\ \{h_R = \mathsf{H}\{K_a\}(\mathsf{r}, e_R)\}\ in$	*compute MAC*
$\overline{c}\langle 4(e_R, h_R)\rangle$	*send Message 4*
$\mathcal{S} = D_X\left[\prod_{A \in \mathcal{C}} PK^A\left[I^A \mid R^A\right]\right]$	**Compliant principal configuration**
$I^A = \prod_{x_I \in X} I_0^A$	*A as initiator*
$R^A = \nu K_R.\prod_{x_R \in X}(R_1^A \mid R_3^A)$	*A as responder*
$PK^A[\_] = \nu K_A^-.(\{\mathsf{ID}_A = \mathsf{Pk}(K_A^-)\} \mid [\_])$	*A's signing and verification keys*
$D_x[\_] = \nu d_x.(\{x = \mathsf{g}\hat{\ } d_x\} \mid [\_])$	*DH secret d and exchange value x*
$D_X[\_] = D_{x_1}[\ldots D_{x_n}[\_]]$ where $X = \{x_1, \ldots, x_n\}$	*shared exponentials*
$\kappa_I = \prod_{u=a,e,v}\{K_u = \mathsf{H}\{x_R\hat{\ } d_{x_I}\}(N_I, N_R, \mathsf{u})\}$	*key computations for I*
$\kappa_R = \prod_{u=a,e,v}\{K_u = \mathsf{H}\{x_I\hat{\ } d_{x_R}\}(N_I, N_R, \mathsf{u})\}$	*key computations for R*

Fig. 3. JFKr in the applied pi calculus

one for all compliant principals). The set X contains the exponentials shared by the compliant principals. The context $D_X[\_]$ consists of contexts $D_x[\_]$ for each $x \in X$. For simplicity, according to the code, compliant principals never disclose exponents.

In contrast with actual implementations of JFK, our model treats abstractly several aspects of the protocol. In particular, it uses an unambiguous format for all messages, thereby assuming, for instance, that the wire format for messages does not leak additional information, and that ill-formed messages are safely ignored. Furthermore, it does not cover IP addressing, routing, and fragmentation concerns, the contents of the security-association parameters sa_z, the handling of ID'_R, the potential usage of several groups g, aspects of caching, and error messages. We made such simplifications partly by choice, partly by necessity; the resulting model remains quite informative and rich.

Script for Proof Automation. We rely at least partially on ProVerif in most proofs. For that purpose, we code JFK configurations ($\mathcal{S}$ in Figure 3) in the input syntax of ProVerif (which is an ASCII syntax for the applied pi calculus), specify the properties to prove, and simply run ProVerif. The correctness of these proofs relies on the theory developed in prior work ([7,1] for secrecy, [8] for correspondence assertions, [2] for some extensions). Additional details on ProVerif and our script appear in the full paper [3]. The script differs superficially from $\mathcal{S}$ in that it gives an interface to the adversary that enables the creation of compliant principals (and provides their identities and control interfaces) and of shared exponents (and provides their exponentials). These unfoldings are best omitted in the statements of theorems. For a given configuration $\mathcal{S}$, one can apply an evaluation context to the process defined in the script so that the resulting process becomes observationally equivalent to $\mathcal{S}$ after exporting the exponentials, the principal identities, and the control channels $init^A$, $accept^A$, and $connect^A$.

4 Resistance to Denial-of-Service Attacks

We first consider the security mechanisms at the early stages of the protocol, before mutual authentication. These mechanisms aim at hardening JFK against certain DOS attacks relevant in IP security. Our formal analysis relies on an understanding of the costs incurred at these stages: we characterize the occurrences of operations deemed expensive, without a formal measure of their cost.

In JFK, protocol-based DOS is a concern mostly for the responder. By design, until the computation of κ_R, the processing of Messages 1 and 3 is fast and involves almost no state. From this point, the protocol performs CPU-intensive operations (including a Diffie-Hellman exponentiation and two public-key operations), and allocates some session state.

Since in general, in any protocol, the processing of a message depends on the contents of previously received messages, each principal may maintain some local state for each session of a protocol. This state can be problematic for servers that are willing to start a session whenever they receive a first message, before adequate authentication. Indeed, an attacker may send (or redirect) first-message traffic to the server, filling its buffers, and eventually causing valid session attempts to be dropped. This concern motivates a common protocol transformation: instead of keeping state for every session in progress, one or both parties MAC (or encrypt) the state, append the result to outgoing messages, and check (or decrypt) the corresponding values in later incoming messages before processing them. Next, we show that this transformation is correct (i.e., preserves equivalence) for a general class of protocols coded as processes.

We relate a sequential implementation of a protocol to a more complex but stateless implementation, using the observational-equivalence relation, $\approx$. This relation is closed by application of evaluation contexts, which can represent active attackers.

Lemma 1. *Let $C[\_]$ be a context that binds at most the variables $\widetilde{x}_2$, let K be a fresh name, let $P = !c(x_3)$, and*

$$R_2^\circ = \nu N.\nu t.\overline{c}\langle M_2\rangle.?c(3(=t,=N,=\widetilde{x}_2,\widetilde{x}_3)).R_4$$
$$R_2 = \nu N.let\ \{t = \mathsf{H}\{K\}(N,\widetilde{x}_2)\}\ in\ \overline{c}\langle M_2\rangle$$
$$R_3 = !c(3(t,N,\widetilde{x}_2,\widetilde{x}_3))\backslash\emptyset.if\ t = \mathsf{H}\{K\}(N,\widetilde{x}_2)\ then\ if\ t\ fresh\ then\ R_4$$

We have $C[R_2^\circ] \mid P \approx \nu K.(C[R_2] \mid R_3) \mid P$.

In R_2°, we rely on syntactic sugar for pattern-matching with a retry until a message that matches the pattern X is received, writing $?c(X).R$ for $\nu l.(\overline{l}\langle\rangle \mid !c(X).l().R)$. (In our automated proofs, we need to use an equivalent but more verbose encoding: $\nu l.(!c(X).\overline{l}\langle\widetilde{x}\rangle \mid l(\widetilde{x}).R)$, where $\widetilde{x}$ collects the variables bound in X.)

Informally, $N, \widetilde{x}_2$ represents the state of the protocol at the end of R_2 that is used later in R_4, M_2 represents a message carrying (at least) N and t, and $\widetilde{x}_3$ represents new data received in Message 3. The presence of the same state $N, \widetilde{x}_2$ in the message received in R_3 is checked using the authenticator t. The inclusion of a fresh nonce N guarantees that all generated authenticators are different. (In R_2°, the generation of a fresh t and the matching $=t$ do not serve any functional purpose; they are performed only so that the two implementations of the protocol behave similarly.) The additional process P is necessary to account for the possibility of receiving a message x_3 and discarding it after a failed test. The lemma is reminiscent of classical replication laws in process calculi, such as $!(Q_2 \mid !Q_3) \approx !Q_2 \mid !Q_3$, since R_2° and R_3 contain replications and $C[\_]$ typically will.

The next lemma applies this protocol transformation to JFKr. It relates our main model $\mathcal{S}$ (see Figure 3), which features a stateless responder till reception of a Message 3 with a valid token, to a simplified, linear model $\mathcal{S}^\circ$. The lemma enables us to prove properties of JFKr preserved by $\approx$ (such as trace properties) on $\mathcal{S}^\circ$ instead of $\mathcal{S}$.

Lemma 2. *We have $\mathcal{S}^\circ \approx \mathcal{S}$, where $\mathcal{S}^\circ$ is $\mathcal{S}$ after replacing $R_1^A \mid R_3^A$ in each R^A by*

$$\begin{aligned} R_1^{\circ A} = {} & !c(1(N_I, x_I)).\nu N_R, t_R.\overline{c}\langle 2(N_I, N_R, x_R, g_R, t_R)\rangle. \\ & ?c(3(=N_I, =N_R, x_I, =x_R, =t_R, e_I, h_I)). \\ & let\ \kappa_R\ in \ldots \qquad (as\ in\ R_3^A) \end{aligned}$$

Our next theorem expresses that the responder commits session-specific resources only once an initiator has established round-trip communication, that is, sent a Message 1, received a Message 2, and returned a Message 3 with matching nonces. This property helps because the responder controls the emission of tokens and can cheaply invalidate old ones by rekeying K_R, and because a "blind" attacker (weaker than a typical Needham-Schroeder attacker [19]) may send Messages 1 with fake IP addresses, but then may not be able to eavesdrop on the corresponding Messages 2.

Theorem 1 (Protection from DOS). *Let $A \in \mathcal{C}$, and let $\mathcal{S}_\$$ be $\mathcal{S}$ with an additional output $\overline{\$}\langle N_I, N_R\rangle$ before the Diffie-Hellman computation κ_R in R_3^A. For any trace $\mathcal{S}_\$ \xrightarrow{\eta} \mathcal{S}'$, for each output $\overline{\$}\langle N_I, N_R\rangle$, there are distinct, successive actions $c(1(N_I, \_))$, $\overline{c}\langle 2(N_I, N_R, \_, \_, \_)\rangle$, and $c(3(N_I, N_R, \_, \_, \_, \_, \_))$.*

The additional output on \$ serves as a marker for the start of expensive processing (public-key operations and session-state allocation). The theorem formulates "round-trip authentication" as an injective correspondence between actions. The correspondence depends on the authenticator; we prove it by applying a variant of Lemma 2 to obtain an equivalent, linear protocol, and invoking ProVerif on that protocol. In incorrect interpretations of JFKr, Theorem 1 is false, and many Messages 3 may be processed for the same authenticator [3].

5 Core Security: Secrecy and Authenticity

Next, we consider session-key secrecy and mutual authentication. Let $\mathcal{S}$ be a JFKr configuration with compliant principals $\mathcal{C}$ sharing exponentials X. We study arbitrary runs of the protocol by examining transitions $\mathcal{S} \xrightarrow{\eta} \mathcal{S}'$, where η is an arbitrary sequence of labels. In these labelled transitions, we omit internal steps $\rightarrow$. Informally, $\mathcal{S}'$ represents any reachable state of the configuration in the presence of an attacker that controls both the low-level IP network (c) and the control interfaces for the principals in $\mathcal{C}$.

The following theorem characterizes runs of the protocol that involve two compliant principals, A and B, in terms of what can be observed by an eavesdropper. We write $\xrightarrow{[1,2,3]}$ for the eavesdropped communications

$$\xrightarrow{\nu N_I.[1(N_I,x_I)]}\xrightarrow{\nu N_R\, t_R.[2(N_I,N_R,x_R,g_R,t_R)]}\xrightarrow{\nu e_I\, h_I.[3(N_I,N_R,x_I,x_R,t_R,e_I,h_I)]}$$

and $\xrightarrow{[4]}$ for $\xrightarrow{\nu e_R\, h_R.[4(e_R,h_R)]}$. We also write φ_3 and φ_4 for the frames that map the variables N_I, N_R, t_R, e_I, h_I and $N_I, N_R, t_R, e_I, h_I, e_R, h_R, K_v$, respectively, to distinct restricted names. (A frame is basically an active substitution with restricted names.) These frames represent the simplified "net effect" of the runs $\xrightarrow{[1,2,3]}$ and $\xrightarrow{[1,2,3]}\xrightarrow{[4]}$ (including the passing of K_v). Next we examine sessions between compliant principals starting from any reachable state $\mathcal{S}'$ of the protocol.

Theorem 2 (Secrecy for Complete Sessions). *Assume $\mathcal{S} \xrightarrow{\eta} \mathcal{S}'$. For any principals $A, B \in \mathcal{C}$, exponentials $x_I, x_R \in X$, and terms ID'_R, sa_I, there exists $\mathcal{S}_3$ such that*

$$\mathcal{S}' \xrightarrow{init^A(\mathsf{ID}'_R,\mathsf{sa}_I)}\xrightarrow{[1,2,3]} \mathcal{S}_3$$

and either (i) $\mathsf{ID}_A \in S_I^B$ and

$$\mathcal{S}_3 \xrightarrow{\nu K_v.\overline{accept}^B\langle \mathsf{ID}_A,\mathsf{ID}'_R,\mathsf{sa}_I,\mathsf{sa}_R,K_v\rangle}\xrightarrow{[4]}\xrightarrow{\overline{connect}^A\langle \mathsf{ID}_B,\mathsf{ID}'_R,\mathsf{sa}_I,\mathsf{sa}_R,K_v\rangle}\approx \mathcal{S}' \mid \varphi_4$$

or (ii) $\mathsf{ID}_A \notin S_I^B$ and $\mathcal{S}_3 \approx \mathcal{S}' \mid \varphi_3$.

This theorem first expresses the functioning of the protocol, with two normal outcomes depending on $\mathsf{ID}_A \in S_I^B$; the first disjunct is for acceptance, the second for rejection. It also uses observational equivalence to give a simple, abstract characterization of the protocol outcomes: we are (apparently) back to the state of the protocol just before the session began, $\mathcal{S}'$, except for φ_3 and φ_4 which export variables bound to plain names

($\nu N.\{x = N\}$), our representation of independent, fresh values in the pi calculus. From the viewpoint of an attacker that can eavesdrop on c and communicate on control interfaces, the intercepted message fields and the session key appear to be fresh, independent names, rather than computed values. In particular, the attacker can learn K_v only through the control interfaces, and e_I and e_R leak nothing about their encrypted contents. Furthermore, the equivalences ensure that the session does not depend on (or affect) any other session in $\mathcal{S}'$. Although the statement of the theorem deals only with a (temporarily) passive attacker, its combination with Theorem 4 (below) does cover all cases of complete sessions.

We also have complementary authentication properties, expressed as correspondence properties on control actions (that is, messages on the control interfaces), with an active attacker.

Theorem 3 (Authenticity for Control Actions). *Assume $\mathcal{S} \xrightarrow{\eta} \mathcal{S}'$. The actions in η have the following properties:*

1. *For each $\overline{accept}^B\langle \mathsf{ID}_A, \mathsf{ID}'_R, \mathsf{sa}_I, \mathsf{sa}_R, K_v\rangle$, we have $\mathsf{ID}_A \in S_I^B$ and, if $A \in \mathcal{C}$, there is a distinct $init^A(\mathsf{ID}'_R, \mathsf{sa}_I)$.*
2. *For each $\overline{connect}^A\langle \mathsf{ID}_B, \mathsf{ID}'_R, \mathsf{sa}_I, \mathsf{sa}_R, K_v\rangle$ there is a distinct $init^A(\mathsf{ID}'_R, \mathsf{sa}_I)$ and, if $B \in \mathcal{C}$, there is a distinct $\overline{accept}^B\langle \mathsf{ID}_A, \mathsf{ID}'_R, \mathsf{sa}_I, \mathsf{sa}_R, K_v\rangle$.*

The proof of these properties relies on ProVerif. For Property 1, we analyze the linear variant of JFKr, then extend the result to JFKr by Lemma 2; in contrast, the direct automated analysis of JFKr yields only a weaker, non-injective correspondence, because ProVerif does not keep track of the linearity enforced by the authenticator cache. ProVerif also yields proofs of these properties for variants of the protocol—with or without sharing of exponentials, for JFKr and for JFKi.

The next theorem also deals with an active attacker. It says that, whenever a trace includes a control message $\overline{connect}^A\langle \mathsf{ID}_B, \dots\rangle$ for some $A, B \in \mathcal{C}$, the trace essentially contains a normal successful run of the protocol with an eavesdropper, as described in Theorem 2. The hypotheses exclude internal communication on c; this assumption means that the attacker sees all messages on c, and is convenient but not essential.

Theorem 4 (Authenticity for Complete Sessions). *Let $A, B \in \mathcal{C}$ and assume*

$$\mathcal{S} \xrightarrow{\eta} \xrightarrow{\overline{connect}^A\langle \mathsf{ID}_B, \mathsf{ID}'_R, \mathsf{sa}_I, \mathsf{sa}_R, K_v\rangle} \mathcal{S}'$$

without internal communication steps on c, and with fresh, distinct exported variables.

1. *$\xrightarrow{\eta}$ contains a series of transitions that match*

$$\xrightarrow{init^A(\mathsf{ID}'_R, \mathsf{sa}_I)} \xrightarrow{[1,2,3]} \xrightarrow{\nu K_v.\overline{accept}^B\langle \mathsf{ID}_A, \mathsf{ID}'_R, \mathsf{sa}_I, \mathsf{sa}_R, K_v\rangle} \xrightarrow{[4]}$$

in the same order, except possibly for argument x_I in the first input on c and for argument t_R in the second input and third output on c.

2. *Let η' be η after erasure of these transitions. We have $\mathcal{S} \mid \varphi_4 \xrightarrow{\eta'}\approx \mathcal{S}'$.*

We use ProVerif to show the first point of this theorem, via Lemma 2.

Theorem 3 is simpler and more abstract than Theorem 4, as it deals with the interface of the protocol, through control actions. Theorem 4 is more complex, as it expresses properties on both control actions and lower-level IP messages exchanged by the protocol. These properties imply that certain protocol inputs match previous protocol outputs, so these inputs are authentic. In general, we would not expect an exact match of all message fields (even if such matches facilitate a formal analysis): some fields are not authenticated. Here, the absence of authentication of x_I in the first message weakens identity protection [3]. The absence of authentication of t_R by the initiator seems harmless, inasmuch as t_R is used only by R.

Perfect Forward Secrecy. As a corollary of Theorems 4 and 2, the session key K_v, exported in the control actions, is equivalent to a variable bound to a fresh, independent name, since φ_4 contains $\nu N.\{K_v = N\}$. Hence, up to observational equivalence, K_v is syntactically independent from S and the values intercepted by the attacker. As previously discussed [4], this provides a characterization of perfect forward secrecy for the session key. We obtain this property even with our liberal reuse of exponentials. We also derive a more specific (but still comforting) property that K_v is distinct from any key established in another session of the protocol.

Independently, ProVerif also shows that the key K_v exchanged between two compliant principals remains secret—that is, here, the adversary cannot compute it—even if we give the long-term secret keys K_A^- of all principals to the attacker after the end of the protocol run. (Similarly, ProVerif presupposes, then verifies, that the environment never obtains signing keys K_A^- for $A \in \mathcal{C}$ or Diffie-Hellman secrets d_x for $x \in X$.)

Identity Protection. We can rely on observational equivalence also for identity protection. The intercepted variables defined by φ_3 and φ_4 are independent from ID_A, ID'_R, and ID_B; this property is a strong privacy guarantee for sessions between compliant principals. Further guarantees can be obtained with particular hypotheses (see [11]). For instance, if all identities in S_I^B are of the form ID_A for some $A \in \mathcal{C}$ (that is, B does not accept sessions with the attacker) and there is no input on $init^B$ (that is, B is only a responder) then, using Theorems 4 and 2, we easily check that the identity ID_B occurs only in outputs on $connect^A$ and otherwise cannot be observed by an active attacker. We can prove additional identity-protection properties, in some cases with ProVerif; on the other hand, we have also found some limitations in identity protection [3].

6 Conclusion

Despite a substantial body of work on the formal analysis of security protocols, and despite much interest in IKE and related protocols, it seems that neither IKE nor its successors has been the subject of an exhaustive analysis until now. The paper that presents JFK argues informally about some of its core properties, and calls for a formal analysis. Recent work by Datta et al. explores how the STS protocol, two JFK variants, and the core of IKE can be derived by successive refinements [9,10]. In particular, it isolates the usage of authenticators and discusses the properties of JFKr (without however precise claims or proofs). Further afield, the literature contains partial but useful machine-assisted verifications of IKE and Skeme (a protocol that influenced IKE) [17, 7,8], and a framework for the study of DOS [18]. More broadly, the literature contains several formal techniques for protocol analysis and many examples (e.g., [14,16,20,21, 15]). While a number of those techniques could potentially yield at least partial results on JFK, we believe that the use of the applied pi calculus is particularly appropriate. It permits a rich formalization of the protocol, with a reasonable effort; the formulation of some of its properties via process equivalences and others in terms of behaviors; and proofs (sometimes automatic ones) that rely on language-based methods.

We regard the present analysis of JFK as an important case study that goes beyond what we have previously attempted, first because JFK is an attractive and intricate "state-of-the-art" protocol of possible practical impact (through its influence on IKEv2 and other protocols), because JFK tightly packages many ideas that appear elsewhere in the field, and also because our analysis explores properties that are central to JFK but that are not often, if ever, explained rigorously. Furthermore, as noted in the introduction, this case study contributes to the development of ideas and results for the specification and verification of security protocols that should be useful beyond the analysis of JFK.

An obvious next problem is the analysis of IKEv2. We have not undertaken it (instead or in addition to the analysis of JFK) because IKEv2 is relatively recent and, at the time of this writing, it continues to evolve, with influence from JFK and other sources. At present, JFK and its specification seem inherently more self-contained and interesting than IKEv2. On the other hand, there seems to be substantial awareness of the benefits of formal analysis in and around the IETF, so one may look forward to rigorous studies of IKEv2 and other significant protocols.

Acknowledgments. We are grateful to Ran Canetti and Angelos Keromytis for information on JFK, to John Mitchell for information on his research on refinement, to Véronique Cortier for comments on a draft of this paper, and to Michael Roe and Dieter Gollmann for early discussions on this work. Martín Abadi's work was partly done at Microsoft Research, Silicon Valley, and it was also partly supported by the National Science Foundation under Grants CCR-0204162 and CCR-0208800.

References

1. M. Abadi and B. Blanchet. Analyzing security protocols with secrecy types and logic programs. In *29th ACM SIGPLAN - SIGACT Symposium on Principles of Programming Languages (POPL'02)*, pages 33–44, Jan. 2002.
2. M. Abadi and B. Blanchet. Computer-assisted verification of a protocol for certified email. In *Static Analysis, 10th International Symposium (SAS'03)*, volume 2694 of *LNCS*, pages 316–335. Springer-Verlag, June 2003.
3. M. Abadi, B. Blanchet, and C. Fournet. Just fast keying in the pi calculus. Manuscript, available from `http://www.di.ens.fr/~blanchet/crypto/jfk.html`, Dec. 2003.
4. M. Abadi and C. Fournet. Mobile values, new names, and secure communication. In *28th ACM SIGPLAN-SIGACT Symposium on Principles of Programming Languages (POPL'01)*, pages 104–115, Jan. 2001.
5. W. Aiello, S. Bellovin, M. Blaze, R. Canetti, J. Ionnidis, A. Keromytis, and O. Reingold. Just fast keying (JFK). IETF Internet Draft `draft-ietf-ipsec-jfk-04.txt`, July 2002.

6. W. Aiello, S. Bellovin, M. Blaze, R. Canetti, J. Ionnidis, A. Keromytis, and O. Reingold. Efficient, DoS-resistant, secure key exchange for internet protocols. In *9th ACM Conference on Computer and Communications Security (CCS'02)*, pages 48–58, Nov. 2002.
7. B. Blanchet. An efficient cryptographic protocol verifier based on Prolog rules. In *14th IEEE Computer Security Foundations Workshop (CSFW-14)*, pages 82–96, June 2001.
8. B. Blanchet. From secrecy to authenticity in security protocols. In *Static Analysis, 9th International Symposium (SAS'02)*, volume 2477 of *LNCS*, pages 342–359. Springer-Verlag, Sept. 2002.
9. A. Datta, A. Derek, J. C. Mitchell, and D. Pavlovic. A derivation system for security protocols and its logical formalization. In *16th IEEE Computer Security Foundations Workshop (CSFW-16)*, pages 109–125, July 2003.
10. A. Datta, J. C. Mitchell, and D. Pavlovic. Derivation of the JFK protocol. `http://www.stanford.edu/~danupam/composition.ps`, 2002.
11. C. Fournet and M. Abadi. Hiding names: Private authentication in the applied pi calculus. In *Software Security – Theories and Systems. Mext-NSF-JSPS International Symposium (ISSS'02)*, volume 2609 of *LNCS*, pages 317–338. Springer-Verlag, Jan. 2003.
12. D. Harkins and D. Carrel. RFC 2409: The Internet Key Exchange (IKE). `http://www.ietf.org/rfc/rfc2409.txt`, Nov. 1998.
13. Internet Key Exchange (IKEv2) Protocol. IETF Internet Draft at `http://www.ietf.org/internet-drafts/draft-ietf-ipsec-ikev2-11.txt`, Oct. 2003.
14. R. Kemmerer, C. Meadows, and J. Millen. Three systems for cryptographic protocol analysis. *Journal of Cryptology*, 7(2):79–130, Spring 1994.
15. P. Lincoln, J. Mitchell, M. Mitchell, and A. Scedrov. A probabilistic poly-time framework for protocol analysis. In *Fifth ACM Conference on Computer and Communications Security (CCS'98)*, pages 112–121, 1998.
16. G. Lowe. Breaking and fixing the Needham-Schroeder public-key protocol using FDR. In *Tools and Algorithms for the Construction and Analysis of Systems*, volume 1055 of *LNCS*, pages 147–166. Springer-Verlag, 1996.
17. C. Meadows. Analysis of the Internet Key Exchange protocol using the NRL protocol analyzer. In *IEEE Symposium on Security and Privacy*, pages 216–231, May 1999.
18. C. Meadows. A cost-based framework for analysis of denial of service networks. *Journal of Computer Security*, 9(1/2):143–164, 2001.
19. R. M. Needham and M. D. Schroeder. Using encryption for authentication in large networks of computers. *Communications of the ACM*, 21(12):993–999, Dec. 1978.
20. L. C. Paulson. The inductive approach to verifying cryptographic protocols. *Journal of Computer Security*, 6(1–2):85–128, 1998.
21. F. J. Thayer Fábrega, J. C. Herzog, and J. D. Guttman. Strand spaces: Why is a security protocol correct? In *IEEE Symposium on Security and Privacy*, pages 160–171, May 1998.

Decidable Analysis of Cryptographic Protocols with Products and Modular Exponentiation

Vitaly Shmatikov*

SRI International
shmat@csl.sri.com

Abstract. We demonstrate that the symbolic trace reachability problem for cryptographic protocols is decidable in the presence of an Abelian group operator and modular exponentiation from arbitrary bases. We represent the problem as a sequence of symbolic inference constraints and reduce it to a system of linear Diophantine equations. For a finite number of protocol sessions, this result enables fully automated, sound and complete analysis of protocols that employ primitives such as Diffie-Hellman exponentiation and modular multiplication without imposing any bounds on the size of terms created by the attacker, but taking into account the relevant algebraic properties.

1 Introduction

Symbolic constraint solving for cryptographic protocols is a subject of very active research in the protocol analysis community [1,9,17,3,13,6,14,5]. While the analysis problem is undecidable in its most general form [8], it has been proved NP-complete [17] for a finite number of protocol sessions even without *a priori* bounds on the size of terms that may be created by the attacker. Therefore, symbolic constraint solving provides a *fully automated* technique for discovering attacks on trace-based security properties such as secrecy and authentication.

Attacker's capabilities are represented by a set of inference rules modeling how the attacker can learn new terms from the terms he already knows. Since protocol messages may include variables (representing data fields whose values are not known to the honest recipient in advance), an attack is modeled as a symbolic protocol trace or skeleton (*e.g.*, an interleaving of several protocol sessions, at the end of which the attacker learns the secret). The goal of symbolic constraint solving is to determine whether there exists a consistent instantiation of all variables such that every message sent by the attacker is derivable, using the chosen inference rules, from the set of terms available to him.

Initial research on symbolic protocol analysis [1,17,3,13] followed the so-called Dolev-Yao model in assuming that the attacker does not have access to the algebraic properties of the underlying cryptographic primitives. This assumption fails for primitives such as xor (exclusive or) and modular exponentiation, which are widely used in protocol constructions. The attacker may exploit associativity,

* Partially supported by ONR Grants N00014-01-1-0837 and N00014-03-1-0961.

D.A, Schmidt (Ed.): ESOP 2004, LNCS 2986, pp. 355–369, 2004.

commutativity, and cancellation of inverses. Bull's recursive authentication protocol [15,18] and group Diffie-Hellman protocol [19,16] had been proved correct in the free algebra model, but then attacks were discovered once algebraic properties of, respectively, `xor` and modular exponentiation were taken into account. In this paper, we demonstrate that the symbolic analysis problem is decidable even if the attacker term algebra is extended with an Abelian group operator and modular exponentiation from an arbitrary base. In particular, this result enables fully automated analysis of Diffie-Hellman-based protocols.

Overview. Section 2 introduces the term algebra that we use to model the attacker's capabilities, and the equational theory modeling algebraic properties of the relevant cryptographic primitives. In Section 3, we briefly describe how the protocol analysis problem is reduced to a sequence of symbolic inference constraints. In Section 4, we extend previous results on ground derivability [6] to modular exponentiation, and, following [14], demonstrate the existence of *conservative solutions.* Section 5 contains the main technical result: symbolic constraint solving problem in the presence of an Abelian group operator and modular exponentiation is reduced to the solvability in integers of a special *decidable* system of quadratic equations. Conclusions follow in Section 6.

Related work. The techniques of this paper follow closely those of [6,14]. In [6], the problem was only considered in the ground (as opposed to symbolic) case, and the term algebra did not include exponential terms. The reduction to a quadratic Diophantine system was first developed in [14], but only exponentiation from a constant base was supported and, most importantly, decidability remained an open question. Proving decidability is the main contribution of this paper.

Partial results for protocol analysis in the presence of Diffie-Hellman exponentiation were recently obtained by Boreale and Buscemi [4], and Chevalier *et al.* [5]. Neither addresses decidability for an Abelian group operator outside exponents. The decision procedure of [4] requires an *a priori* upper bound on the number of factors in each product. In general, computing upper bounds on the size of variable instantiations needed for a feasible attack is the most challenging task in establishing decidability. Therefore, [4] does not fully solve the problem.

Chevalier *et al.* [5] prove that the protocol analysis problem is NP-complete in the presence of Diffie-Hellman exponentiation, but only for a restricted class of protocols. No more than one new variable may be introduced in each protocol message, and the attacker is not permitted to instantiate variables with products. These restrictions rule out not only non-deterministic protocols, but also some well-defined, deterministic protocols.

Narendran *et al.* investigated decidability of unification modulo the equational theory of multiplication and exponentiation [11,10]. While equational unification is an important subproblem in symbolic protocol analysis, unification alone is insufficient to decide whether a particular symbolic term is derivable given a set of attacker's inference rules.

Pereira and Quisquater [16] analyzed the group Diffie-Hellman protocol [19] taking into account algebraic properties of Diffie-Hellman exponents. They did not attempt to address the general problem of deciding whether a particular symbolic attack trace has a feasible instantiation.

$\langle t_1, t_2 \rangle$	Pairing of terms t_1 and t_2
$\{t_1\}_{t_2}$	Term t_1 encrypted with term t_2 using a symmetric algorithm
$t_1 \cdot \ldots \cdot t_n$	Product of terms where $\forall i\ t_i \neq \mathsf{exp}(u, v)$
t^{-1}	Multiplicative inverse of term t where $t \neq \mathsf{exp}(u, v)$
$\mathsf{exp}(t_1, t_2)$	$t_1^{t_2}$ where t_1 is not headed with $\cdot$, $t_2 \neq \mathsf{exp}(u, v)$

Fig. 1. Message term constructors

2 Model

A protocol specification is a set of roles. Each role is a sequence of sent and received messages. Messages received by the role may contain variables, representing data fields whose value is unknown to the recipient (*e.g.*, the counterparty's nonce). Since the source of the received messages cannot be established on an insecure network, we assume that the attacker receives all messages sent by the honest roles, and sends all messages received by the honest roles.

An attack on any trace-based property of cryptographic protocols can be represented as a *symbolic attack trace* (see [13,3,9] for details). A symbolic trace is a particular interleaving of a finite number of protocol roles. For example, an attack on secrecy is modeled by an interleaving at the end of which the attacker outputs the value that was supposed to remain secret. An attack on authentication is modeled by an interleaving at the end of which the attacker has successfully authenticated himself to an honest party.

A trace is *feasible* if every message received by the honest roles can be derived by the attacker from his initial knowledge and intercepted messages. Therefore, for each message sent by the attacker, a symbolic inference problem must be decided: is there an instantiation of variables such that the sent term is derivable in the attacker's term algebra? To stage the attack, the attacker may need to send several messages in a particular order. Deciding whether the attack is feasible thus requires solving several symbolic inference problems simultaneously.

Term algebra. The attacker's capabilities are modeled by a term algebra with pairing, symmetric encryption, multiplication, and exponentiation. The notation is shown in fig. 1. For multiplication, there is a unit **1** and a multiplicative inverse. Like [5], do not allow products in the base of exponentials, nor permit exponential terms to be multiplied with other terms. This restriction is necessary, because introducing distributive laws for exponentials results in an undecidable equational unification problem [10]. In contrast to [5], we impose no restrictions on multiplication of terms other than exponentials, permit variables to be instantiated to products, and allow more than one new variable per message.

Our algebra is untyped, *e.g.*, we do not distinguish between keys and other messages. This enables us to discover a wider class of attacks than strongly typed techniques. Extensions of the algebra with primitives for public-key encryption, digital signatures, and one-way functions do not present any conceptual problems as far as decidability is concerned (*e.g.*, see [17,14]) and are left out for brevity.

Since our primary motivation is analysis of protocols based on Diffie-Hellman, we use the relations of fig. 2 to model the corresponding algebraic structure (see,

Rules for products:	Associative, commutative, and $t \cdot \mathbf{1} \rightarrow t$, $t \cdot t^{-1} \rightarrow \mathbf{1}$
Rules for inverses:	$(t^{-1})^{-1} \rightarrow t$, $(t_1 \cdot t_2)^{-1} \rightarrow {t_2}^{-1} \cdot {t_1}^{-1}$
Rules for exponentials:	$\mathsf{exp}(t, \mathbf{1}) \rightarrow t$, $\mathsf{exp}(\mathsf{exp}(t_1, t_2), t_3) \rightarrow \mathsf{exp}(t_1, t_2 \cdot t_3)$

Fig. 2. Normalization rules for products, inverses, and exponentials

Unpairing (UL, UR): $\dfrac{T \vdash \langle u, v\rangle}{T \vdash u} \quad \dfrac{T \vdash \langle u, v\rangle}{T \vdash v}$

Decryption (D): $\dfrac{T \vdash \{u\}_v \; T \vdash v}{T \vdash u}$

Pairing (P): $\dfrac{T \vdash u \; T \vdash v}{T \vdash \langle u, v\rangle}$

Encryption (E): $\dfrac{T \vdash u \; T \vdash v}{T \vdash \{u\}_v}$

Multiplication (M): $\dfrac{T \vdash u_1 \; \ldots \; T \vdash u_n}{T \vdash u_1 \cdot \ldots \cdot u_n}$ $\forall i \; u_i \neq \mathsf{exp}(u', v')$

Inversion (I): $\dfrac{T \vdash u}{T \vdash u^{-1}}$ $u \neq \mathsf{exp}(u', v')$

Exponentiation (X): $\dfrac{T \vdash u \; T \vdash v}{T \vdash \mathsf{exp}(u, v)}$ u is not headed with $\cdot$, $v \neq \mathsf{exp}(u', v')$

Fig. 3. Attacker's capabilities

e.g., [12]). In Diffie-Hellman, exponentiation is $\mod$ prime p, and the base α is chosen so as to generate a cyclic subgroup $\alpha, \alpha^2, \ldots, \alpha^q \equiv 1 \mod p$ of some prime order q that divides $p-1$. We implicitly assume that exponential terms are $\mod p$, and that multiplication is $\mod q$ (recall that exponential terms may not be multiplied in our term algebra). Because $\cdot$ forms a cyclic Abelian group, every member has a multiplicative inverse.

The rules of fig. 2 are convergent modulo associativity and commutativity of $\cdot$, thus every term t has a unique normal form $t\downarrow$ up to associativity and commutativity. We assume that terms are kept in normal form.

Attacker model. The attacker's ability to derive terms is characterized as a term set closure under the inference rules of fig. 3. These rules reflect common cryptographic assumptions about the difficulty of some number-theoretic problems. For example, the attacker cannot compute v when given $\mathsf{exp}(u, v)$ (the discrete logarithm problem). Given $\mathsf{exp}(u, v)$ and $\mathsf{exp}(u, v')$, there is no rule that enables the attacker to compute $\mathsf{exp}(u, v \cdot v')$ (the computational Diffie-Hellman problem).

3 Symbolic Inference Constraints

Any symbolic trace can be converted into a ordered sequence of symbolic inference constraints. Suppose u_i is the message received by some honest role, and let T_i be the set of all messages sent by the honest roles (and thus learned by the attacker) prior to sending u_i. The constraint sequence is simply $\mathbf{C} = \{u_i : T_i\}$.

Each constraint $u_i : T_i$ can be interpreted as "at step i, the attacker knows messages in T_i and must generate message u_i." We will refer to u_i as the *target term* of the constraint. Both u_i and messages in T_i may contain variables. We assume that T_1 contains terms that are initially known to the attacker, such as $\mathbf{1}$ and constants specific to the protocol. Observe that constraint sequences are *monotonic*: if $j < i$, then $T_j \subseteq T_i$. Also, since variables represent terms unknown to the recipient, every variable must occur for the first time in some target term u_i (this property is sometimes referred to as *origination*).

A ground substitution σ is a *solution* of $u : T$ (written $\sigma \Vdash u : T$) if $T\sigma \vdash u\sigma$ is derivable using the inference rules of fig. 3. Given a constraint sequence $\mathbf{C} = \{u_1 : T_1, \ldots, u_n : T_n\}$, σ is a solution of the constraint sequence ($\sigma \Vdash \mathbf{C}$) if $\forall i\ T_i\sigma \vdash u_i\sigma$ is derivable using the rules of fig. 3.

If T is a finite set of terms, let $\mathrm{St}(T)$ be the set of subterms defined in the standard way. Let $\mathrm{St}(\mathbf{C}) = \bigcup_{u_i:T_i \in \mathbf{C}} \mathrm{St}(T_i \cup u_i)$, and define $\mathcal{S}(\mathbf{C}) = \mathrm{St}(\mathbf{C}) \setminus \mathrm{Var}(\mathbf{C})$ to be the set of all non-variable subterms of $\mathbf{C}$. Let $\mathcal{S}^p(\mathbf{C})$ be the closure of this set under $\cdot$, inverse, and exponentiation, defined inductively: (i) if $t \in \mathcal{S}(\mathbf{C})$, then $t \in \mathcal{S}^p(\mathbf{C})$, (ii) if $t_{1,2} \in \mathcal{S}^p(\mathbf{C})$ and $t_{1,2} \neq \mathsf{exp}(u,v)$, then $t_1 \cdot t_2, {t_1}^{-1}, {t_2}^{-1} \in \mathcal{S}^p(\mathbf{C})$, (iii) if $t_{1,2} \in \mathcal{S}^p(\mathbf{C})$ and t_1 is not headed with $\cdot$ and $t_2 \neq \mathsf{exp}(u,v)$, then $\mathsf{exp}(t_1, t_2) \in \mathcal{S}^p(\mathbf{C})$.

Running example. We will use the following symbolic trace as an (artificial) running example to illustrate our constraint solving procedure. An event $A \longrightarrow t$ models honest role A sending message t, $B \longleftarrow t'$ models B receiving t', *etc.*

1. $A \longrightarrow a \cdot b$	3. $A \longrightarrow \{a\}_b$	5. $B \longrightarrow \langle b \cdot X, \mathsf{exp}(c, a)\rangle$
2. $B \longleftarrow a \cdot X \cdot Y$	4. $B \longleftarrow \{Y\}_b$	6. $A \longleftarrow \mathsf{exp}(c, a^7)$

The goal of symbolic protocol analysis is to determine whether there exists an instantiation of variables X and Y such that every term sent by the attacker and received by an honest participant (*i.e.*, every term t appearing as $P \longleftarrow t$) is derivable using the rules of fig. 3. This is equivalent to deciding whether the following constraint sequence has a solution:

$$a \cdot X \cdot Y : a \cdot b\ ; \quad \{Y\}_b : a \cdot b, \{a\}_b\ ; \quad \mathsf{exp}(c, a^7) : a \cdot b, \{a\}_b, \langle b \cdot X, \mathsf{exp}(c, a)\rangle$$

4 Normal Proofs and Conservative Solutions

We extend the results of [6,14] to the term algebra with exponentiation.

Definition 1 (Ground proof). *A* proof *of $T \vdash u$ is a tree labeled with sequents $T \vdash v$ and such that (a) every leaf is labeled with $T \vdash v$ such that $v \in T$; (b)* *every node has n parents $s_1, \ldots, s_n$ such that* $\dfrac{s_1 \quad \cdots \quad s_n}{T \vdash v}$ *is an instance of one of the inference rules of fig. 3; (c) the root is labeled with $T \vdash u$.*

Definition 2 (Normal ground proof). *A proof $\mathcal{P}$ of $T \vdash u$ is* normal *if either $u \in \mathrm{St}(T)$ and every node is labeled $T \vdash v$ with $v \in \mathrm{St}(T)$, or $\mathcal{P} = C[\mathcal{P}_1, \ldots, \mathcal{P}_n]$ where every proof $\mathcal{P}_i$ is a normal proof of some $T \vdash v_i$ with $v_i \in \mathrm{St}(T)$ and context C is built using the inference rules (P),(E),(X),(M),(I) only.*

Lemma 1 (Existence of normal ground proof). *If there is a ground proof of $T \vdash u$, then there is a normal ground proof of $T \vdash u$.*

Proposition 1. *If there is a ground proof of $T \vdash u$ that uses only rules (M), (I), and (X), then there exists a proof of $T \vdash u$ of the form* $\dfrac{T \vdash u_1 \quad T \vdash u_2}{T \vdash u}$ *where $u_1 \in T$, and either $u_2 \in T$, or the proof of $T \vdash u_2$ uses rules (M) and (I) only.*

If the constraint sequence $\mathbf{C}$ is solvable, then it has a *conservative* solution [14], in which every variable is instantiated to a product of subterms (and their inverses) that are already present in the original sequence, or to an exponential with a subterm as the base and a product of subterms as the exponent.

Definition 3 (Conservative substitution). *Substitution σ is* conservative *if $\forall x \in \mathrm{Var}(\mathbf{C}) \quad \mathrm{St}(x\sigma) \subseteq \mathcal{S}^p(\mathbf{C})\sigma$.*

Theorem 1 (Existence of conservative solution). *If there exists a solution $\sigma \Vdash \mathbf{C}$, then there exists a conservative solution $\sigma^* \Vdash \mathbf{C}$.*

Lemma 2 (Existence of conservative proof). *If $\sigma \Vdash \mathbf{C}$ is conservative, then $\forall u : T \in \mathbf{C}$ there exists a proof of $T\sigma \vdash u\sigma$ such that for every node labeled $T\sigma \vdash v$, either $v \in \mathrm{St}(\mathbf{C})\sigma$, or node $T\sigma \vdash v$ is obtained by an (M), (I), or (X) inference rule* and *is only used as a premise of an (M), (I), or (X) rule.*

5 Decision Procedure for Symbolic Inference Constraints

For any constraint sequence $\mathbf{C}$, we define a nondeterministic finite reduction $\leadsto$. For each step $\leadsto_i$, we show that there are finitely many $\mathbf{C}_i$ such that $\mathbf{C}_{i-1} \leadsto_i \mathbf{C}_i$, and that $\mathbf{C}_{i-1}$ has a solution if and only if some $\mathbf{C}_i$ has a solution. The final sequence has a solution if and only if a special system of quadratic Diophantine equations has a solution. Quadratic Diophantine equations are undecidable in general, but the system obtained in our case is solvable if and only if a particular linear subsystem is solvable. Since linear Diophantine equations are decidable, this establishes decidability of the symbolic protocol analysis problem.

Following Theorem 1, we will be interested only in conservative solutions. The reduction proceeds as follows (steps 1-3 are essentially the same as in [14]):

1. Guess subterm equalities.
2. For each constraint, guess all derivable subterms and add them to the set of terms available to the attacker.
3. Remove all constraints in which the derivation involves inference rules other than (M), (I), and (X).
4. Guess and instantiate bases of exponential terms.
5. Replace every constraint in which the derivation involves (X) with an equivalent constraint in which the derivation involves only (M) and (I).
6. Substitute all target terms that introduce new variables.
7. Solve a linear Diophantine system to determine whether the final sequence has a solution.

5.1 Determine Subterm Equalities

Suppose $\mathbf{C}$ has some solution σ. In the first reduction step $\rightsquigarrow_1$, we guess the equivalence relation on $\mathrm{St}(\mathbf{C})$ induced by σ, *i.e.*, $\forall s_i, s_j \in \mathrm{St}(\mathbf{C})$, we guess whether $s_i\sigma = s_j\sigma$ or not. Since $\mathrm{St}(\mathbf{C})$ is finite, there are finitely many equivalence relations to consider. Each relation represents a set of unification problems in an Abelian group, which are decidable [2]. There are finitely many most general unifiers consistent with any given equivalence relation. We nondeterministically guess the right unifier θ (in practice, θ would have to be found by by exhaustive enumeration), and let $\mathbf{C}_1 = \mathbf{C}\theta$.

Lemma 3. *$\exists\sigma \Vdash \mathbf{C}$ if and only if $\exists\sigma \Vdash \mathbf{C}_1$ for some $\mathbf{C}_1$ such that $\mathbf{C} \rightsquigarrow \mathbf{C}_1$.*

Proposition 2. *$\forall s, s' \in \mathrm{St}(\mathbf{C}_1)$ if $s \neq s'$, then $s\sigma \neq s'\sigma$.*

Running example. In our running example (Section 3), we guess that the only subterm equality is $\{Y\}_b = \{a\}_b$, giving us the unifier $[Y \to a]$ and this $\mathbf{C}_1$:

$$a^2 \cdot X : a \cdot b \;; \quad \{a\}_b : a \cdot b, \{a\}_b \;; \quad \mathsf{exp}(c, a^7) : a \cdot b, \{a\}_b, \langle b \cdot X, \mathsf{exp}(c, a)\rangle$$

5.2 Determine Order of Subterm Derivation

Following [14], the second reduction step $\rightsquigarrow_2$ guesses which subterms of $\mathbf{C}_1\sigma$ are derivable by the attacker using inference rules of fig. 3, and adds each derivable subterm s to every constraint $u_i : T_i$ such that s is derivable from $T_i\sigma$.

1. Guess $S_\vdash = \{s \in \mathrm{St}(\mathbf{C}_1) \mid \exists u_i : T_i \in \mathbf{C}_1 \text{ s.t. there exists a proof of } T_i\sigma \vdash s\sigma\}$.
2. $\forall s \in S_\vdash$ guess j_s s.t. there exists a proof of $T_{j_s}\sigma \vdash s\sigma$, but not of $T_{j_s - 1}\sigma \vdash s\sigma$.
3. Guess linear ordering $\prec$ on $S_\vdash$ such that
   - If $s \prec s'$, then the normal proof of $T\sigma \vdash s\sigma$ does not contain any node labeled with $T\sigma \vdash s'\sigma$.
   - If $j_s < j_{s'}$, then $s \prec s'$.

   Such an ordering always exists [14] and represents the order in which subterms of $\mathbf{C}_1$ are derived.
4. Arrange $s_1, \ldots, s_k \in S_\vdash$ according to the ordering $\prec$, and insert each s in the constraint sequence immediately before the $u_{j_s} : T_{j_s}$ constraint. Let $\mathbf{C}_2$ be the resulting constraint sequence.

Lemma 4. *$\exists\sigma \Vdash \mathbf{C}$ if and only if $\exists\sigma \Vdash \mathbf{C}_2$ for some $\mathbf{C}_2$ such that $\mathbf{C} \rightsquigarrow \mathbf{C}_2$.*

Running example. In our running example, we guess that subterms $b \cdot X$ and $\mathsf{exp}(c, a)$ are derivable from T_3. Therefore, we obtain the following $\mathbf{C}_2$:

$$a^2 \cdot X : a \cdot b; \quad \{a\}_b : a \cdot b, \{a\}_b;$$
$$b \cdot X : a \cdot b, \{a\}_b, \langle b \cdot X, \mathsf{exp}(c,a)\rangle; \quad \mathsf{exp}(c,a) : a \cdot b, \{a\}_b, \langle b \cdot X, \mathsf{exp}(c,a)\rangle, b \cdot X;$$
$$\mathsf{exp}(c, a^7) : a \cdot b, \{a\}_b, \langle b \cdot X, \mathsf{exp}(c,a)\rangle, b \cdot X, \mathsf{exp}(c,a)$$

5.3 Eliminate All Inferences Other than (M), (I), and (X)

Lemma 5. *Consider any $u : T \in \mathbf{C}_2$ and the last inference of the proof of $T\sigma \vdash u\sigma$.*

- *If $u\sigma \in T\sigma$, then $u \in T$.*
- *If $u\sigma$ is obtained by (UL), then $\langle u, t'\rangle \in T$ for some term t'.*
- *If $u\sigma$ is obtained by (UR), then $\langle t', u\rangle \in T$ for some term t'.*
- *If $u\sigma$ is obtained by (D), then $\{u\}_{t'} \in T$ for some term t'.*
- *If $u\sigma$ is obtained by (P), then $u = \langle u_1, u_2\rangle$ and $u_{1,2} \in T$ for some terms $u_{1,2}$.*
- *If $u\sigma$ is obtained by (E), then $u = \{u_1\}_{u_2}$ and $u_{1,2} \in T$ for some terms $u_{1,2}$.*

Lemma 5 implies that all constraints where derivation involves at least one instance of any rule other than (M), (I), or (X) can be discovered by syntactic inspection [14]. Let $\rightsquigarrow_3$ consist in eliminating all such constraints, and let $\mathbf{C}_3$ be the resulting constraint sequence.

Proposition 3. *$\forall u : T \in \mathbf{C}_3$, proof of $T\sigma \vdash u\sigma$ uses only inference rules (M), (I), and (X).*

Lemma 6. *$\exists\sigma \Vdash \mathbf{C}$ if and only if $\exists\sigma \Vdash \mathbf{C}_3$ for some $\mathbf{C}_3$ such that $\mathbf{C} \rightsquigarrow \mathbf{C}_3$.*

Running example. In our example, we guess the first and fifth constraints were obtained by application of rules (M), (I) and (X) only. We eliminate the middle three constraints, obtaining the following $\mathbf{C}_3$:

$$a^2 \cdot X : a \cdot b \ ; \quad \mathsf{exp}(c, a^7) : a \cdot b, \{a\}_b, \langle b \cdot X, \mathsf{exp}(c,a)\rangle, b \cdot X, \mathsf{exp}(c,a)$$

5.4 Instantiate Bases of Exponential Terms

For each subterm of $\mathbf{C}_3$, $\rightsquigarrow_4$ guesses whether the solution σ instantiates it to an exponential, and, if so, nondeterministically chooses the base of exponentiation. Let $\hat{S} = \{s \in \mathrm{St}(\mathbf{C}_3) \mid s\sigma = \mathsf{exp}(b, e)\}$. There are only finitely many subsets of $\mathrm{St}(\mathbf{C}_3)$, thus $\hat{S} = \{s_1, \ldots, s_r\}$ can be computed by exhaustive enumeration of all possibilities. By Definition 3 and because products may not appear in the base, $\forall s_i \in \hat{S}\ b_i \in \mathcal{S}(\mathbf{C}_3)\sigma$. Since $\mathcal{S}(\mathbf{C}_3)$ is finite, there are finitely many possible values for $t_{b_i} \in \mathcal{S}(\mathbf{C}_3)$ such that $t_{b_i}\sigma = b_i$. Let x_i be a fresh variable, and θ_i the (unique) most general unifier of s_i and $\mathsf{exp}(t_{b_i}, x_i)$. Define $\mathbf{C}_4 = \mathbf{C}_3\theta_1 \ldots \theta_r$.

Proposition 4 (Explicit exponentiation bases). *If $s\sigma = \mathsf{exp}(b, e)$ for some $s \in \mathrm{St}(\mathbf{C}_4)$, then $s = \mathsf{exp}(t_b, t_e)$ s.t. $t_b\sigma = b, t_e\sigma = e$.*

Lemma 7. *$\exists\sigma \Vdash \mathbf{C}$ if and only if $\exists\sigma \Vdash \mathbf{C}_4$ for some $\mathbf{C}_4$ such that $\mathbf{C} \rightsquigarrow \mathbf{C}_4$.*

Running example. Since exponentiation bases are already explicit, $\mathbf{C}_4 = \mathbf{C}_3$.

5.5 Replace Inferences Using (X) with Those Using (M) and (I)

This step is based on the following intuition. Suppose $u = \mathsf{exp}(b, v_1 \cdot \ldots \cdot v_p)$. Under the Diffie-Hellman assumption, the attacker cannot construct $\mathsf{exp}(b, x \cdot y)$ from $\mathsf{exp}(b, x)$ and $\mathsf{exp}(b, y)$, thus $u : T$ has a solution if and only if T contains some term $t = \mathsf{exp}(b, v'_1 \cdot \ldots \cdot v'_q)$ (if $q = 0$, then $t = b$), and $v_1 \cdot \ldots \cdot v_p = v'_1 \cdot \ldots \cdot v'_q \cdot x$ where x is derivable from T. Informally, x can be thought of as the "additional" exponent to which t must be raised in order to obtain u.

Consider all $u_i : T_i \in \mathbf{C}_4$ in order, and define $\rightsquigarrow_5$ as $\overset{(1)}{\rightsquigarrow}_5 \ldots \overset{(N)}{\rightsquigarrow}_5$ where N is the number of constraints in $\mathbf{C}_4$. By Propositions 1 and 3, the proof of $T_i\sigma \vdash u_i\sigma$ is of the form $\dfrac{T_i\sigma \vdash u_{i1} \quad T_i\sigma \vdash u_{i2}}{T_i\sigma \vdash u_i\sigma}$ where $u_{i1} \in T_i\sigma$, and either $u_{i2} \in T_i\sigma$, or the proof of $T_i\sigma \vdash u_{i2}\sigma$ is built up using rules (M) and (I) only.

If the last inference rule in the above proof is not (X), then the entire proof is built using inference rules (M) and (I) only. We set $\overset{(i)}{\rightsquigarrow}_5$ to be the identity.

Now suppose the last rule in the proof of $T_i\sigma \vdash u_i\sigma$ is (X). Then $u_i\sigma = \mathsf{exp}(u_{i1}, u_{i2}) \downarrow = \mathsf{exp}(b, e)$ for some ground b, e. Since u_{i1} must have the same base as $u_i\sigma$, $u_{i1} = \mathsf{exp}(b, e_1)$ for some ground e_1. By Proposition 1, $u_{i1} \in T_i\sigma$. Since $\mathrm{St}(\mathbf{C}_4) \subseteq \mathrm{St}(\mathbf{C}_1)$, by Proposition 2 $\exists t_1 \in T_i$ such that $t_1\sigma = u_{i1}$. There are finitely many candidates for t_1, and $\overset{(i)}{\rightsquigarrow}_5$ chooses one nondeterministically.

By Proposition 4, $u_i = \mathsf{exp}(t_b, t_e)$, $t_1 = \mathsf{exp}(t'_b, t_{e_1})$ where $t_b\sigma = t'_b\sigma = b$. Therefore, $t_b = t'_b$. We conclude that (i) $u_i = \mathsf{exp}(t_b, t_e)$; (ii) $t_1 = \mathsf{exp}(t_b, t_{e_1}) \in T_i$; (iii) $t_e\sigma = t_{e_1}\sigma \cdot u_{i2}$ (or, equivalently, $t_{e_1}\sigma^{-1} \cdot t_e\sigma = u_{i2}$); and (iv) proof of $T_i\sigma \vdash u_{i2}$ uses inference rules (M) and (I) only.

By Propositions 1 and 3, $u_i : T_i$ has a solution only if $x_{i2} : T_i$ has a solution where x_{i2} is a fresh variable such that $x_{i2}\sigma = u_{i2} = t_{e_1}\sigma^{-1} \cdot t_e\sigma$. Define $\overset{(i)}{\rightsquigarrow}_5$ to replace $u_i : T_i$ with $t_{e_1}{}^{-1} \cdot t_e : T_i$.

Proposition 5. *$\forall u : T \in \mathbf{C}_5$, proof of $T\sigma \vdash u\sigma$ uses only rules (M) and (I).*

Proposition 6. *$\forall x \in \mathrm{Var}(\mathbf{C}_5)$ let $u_{k_x} : T_{k_x} \in \mathbf{C}_5$ be the constraint in which x occurs for the first time. Then $u_{k_x} = x^{q_x} \cdot \prod_{j \geq 0} u_{k_x j}$ where q_x is an integer, $u_{k_x j}$ are not headed with $\cdot$, and $x \notin \mathrm{St}(T_{k_x} \cup \{u_{k_x j} \mid j \geq 0\})$.*

Lemma 8. *$\exists \sigma \Vdash \mathbf{C}$ if and only if $\exists \sigma \Vdash \mathbf{C}_5$ for some $\mathbf{C}_5$ such that $\mathbf{C} \rightsquigarrow \mathbf{C}_5$.*

Definition 4. *Define $\mathcal{Q}_{max} = \prod_{x \in \mathrm{Var}(\mathbf{C}_5)} q_x$ where q_x is the power of x in the constraint in which it occurs for the first time.*

Running example. Replace $\mathsf{exp}(c, a^7)$ with $a^{-1} \cdot a^7 = a^6$, obtaining this $\mathbf{C}_5$:

$$a^2 \cdot X : a \cdot b \;; \quad a^6 : a \cdot b, \{a\}_b, \langle b \cdot X, \mathsf{exp}(c, a)\rangle, b \cdot X, \mathsf{exp}(c, a)$$

5.6 Substitute Target Terms That Introduce New Variables

The $\rightsquigarrow_6$ step takes each target term in which some variable occurs for the first time, and replaces the entire term with a new variable. In the resulting sequence, every variable appears for the first time as the target term of some constraint. For example, if x occurs for the first time in $a \cdot x^2 : T_i$, let $\theta_i = [x \to \hat{x}^{\frac{1}{2}} \cdot a^{-\frac{1}{2}}]$ where $\hat{x}$ is a new variable, and apply θ_i to the entire constraint sequence.

Let k_x be the index of $u_i : T_i$ in which variable x first occurs. By Proposition 6, $u_i = x^{q_x} \cdot \prod_{j \geq 0} u_{ij}$ for some integer q_x.

Definition 5. *$\forall u_i : T_i \in \mathbf{C}_5$, define*

$$\theta_i = \begin{cases} [x \to \hat{x}^{\frac{1}{q_x}} \cdot \prod u_{ij}^{-\frac{1}{q_x}}] & \textit{if } i = k_x \textit{ for some } x\textit{; } \hat{x} \textit{ is a fresh variable} \\ \emptyset & \textit{otherwise} \end{cases}$$

If more than one variable appears for the first time in u_i, any one of them may be chosen.

Let $\mathbf{C}_6 = \mathbf{C}_5\theta_1 \ldots \theta_{N_5}$ where N_5 is the number of constraints in $\mathbf{C}_5$. Although only integer powers appear in $\mathbf{C}_5$, $\mathbf{C}_6$ may contain rational powers.

Proposition 7. *$\forall \hat{x} \in \mathrm{Var}(\mathbf{C}_6)$ $\hat{x}$ first occurs in $\hat{x} : T \in \mathbf{C}_6$ where $\hat{x} \notin \mathrm{St}(T)$.*

Informally, term sets T_i are well-ordered if terms appearing in multiple sets always appear in the same position. Due to monotonicity (Section 3), if $i < i'$, then $T_i \subseteq T_{i'}$. Without loss of generality, we can assume that $\mathbf{C}_6$ is well-ordered.

Definition 6. *$\mathbf{C}_6$ is* well-ordered *if, $\forall t_{ij} \in T_i$ $\forall t_{i'j} \in T_{i'}$ $t_{ij} = t_{i'j}$.*

Proposition 8. *For any rational r appearing as a power of some term in $\mathbf{C}_6$, $r \cdot \mathcal{Q}_{max}$ is an integer.*

Lemma 9. *$\exists \sigma \Vdash \mathbf{C}$ if and only if $\exists \sigma \Vdash \mathbf{C}_6$ for some $\mathbf{C}_6$ such that $\mathbf{C} \rightsquigarrow \mathbf{C}_6$.*

Running example. In our example, $\theta_1 = [X \to \hat{X} \cdot a^{-2}]$, $\theta_2 = \emptyset$. Therefore, $\mathbf{C}_6 = \mathbf{C}_5\theta_1\theta_2$ is:

$$\hat{X} : a \cdot b \; ; \quad a^6 : a \cdot b, \{a\}_b, \langle b \cdot \hat{X} \cdot a^{-2}, \mathsf{exp}(c,a)\rangle, b \cdot \hat{X} \cdot a^{-2}, \mathsf{exp}(c,a)$$

5.7 Solve System of Linear Diophantine Equations

We now convert the constraint sequence $\mathbf{C}_6$ into a system of quadratic Diophantine equations which is solvable if and only if $\exists\, \sigma \Vdash \mathbf{C}_6$. We then demonstrate that the quadratic part *always* has a solution as long as a particular *linear* subsystem is solvable. Since linear Diophantine equations are decidable [7], this establishes that the symbolic protocol analysis problem is also decidable.

The key to this result is Lemma 10. Intuitively, we prove that, for every constraint $u : T \in \mathbf{C}_6$, the target term $u\sigma$ must be equal to some product of integer powers of *non-variable* terms appearing in set T. We then represent each power as an integer variable, and convert the derivation problem for each constraint into a system of linear Diophantine equations.

Define $\Phi(t)$ to be the set of all top-level factors of t. If $t = t_1^{r_1} \cdot \ldots \cdot t_n^{r_n}$ where none of t_i are headed with $\cdot$, then $\Phi(t) = \{t_1^{r_1}, \ldots, t_n^{r_n}\}$. For example, $\Phi(a^{-2} \cdot b^{\frac{3}{2}}) = \{a^{-2}, b^{\frac{3}{2}}\}$. Define $\Psi(t) = \{t_i^{r_i} \in \Phi(t) \mid t_i \neq \hat{x} \in \mathrm{Var}(\mathbf{C}_6)\}$ to be the set of all non-variable factors of t. Let $\psi(t) = \prod_{f \in \Psi(t)} f$, *i.e.*, $\psi(t)$ is t with all factors of the form $\hat{x}^r$ removed. For example, $\psi(a \cdot (\{\hat{x}\}_k)^3 \cdot \hat{x}^{\frac{2}{5}}) = a \cdot (\{\hat{x}\}_k)^3$.

Lemma 10. *$\forall \hat{x} \in \mathrm{Var}(\mathbf{C}_6)$, let k_x be the index of the constraint in which variable x occurs for the first time. Then $\forall \sigma \Vdash \mathbf{C}_6, \forall u_i : T_i \in \mathbf{C}_6$*

$$u_i\sigma = \prod_{t_{ij} \in T_i} (\psi(t_{ij})\sigma)^{\hat{z}[i,j]} \tag{5.1}$$

such that

$$\hat{z}[i,j] = z[i,j] + \sum_{j'>j} (\sum_{\hat{x}^r \in \Phi(t_{ij'})} (\hat{z}[k_x, j] \cdot r \cdot z[i,j'])) \tag{5.2}$$

for some integers $\hat{z}[i,j], z[i,j]$, where $1 \leq i \leq |\mathbf{C}_6|$, $\forall i \; 1 \leq j, j' \leq |T_i|$, and $\forall j > |T_{k_x}| \; \hat{z}[k_x, j] = 0$.

Proof. By induction over the length of the constraint sequence. For the induction basis, consider $u_1 : T_1 \in \mathbf{C}_6$. By Proposition 5, the proof of $T_1\sigma \vdash u_1\sigma$ contains only rules (M) and (I). Therefore, $u_1\sigma = \prod_{t_{1j} \in T_1} (t_{1j}\sigma)^{z[1,j]}$ for some integers $z[1,j]$, where $1 \leq j \leq |T_1|$. By Proposition 7, no variables occur in T_1. Therefore, $\forall j \; t_{1j} = \psi(t_{1j})$ and $\forall \hat{x} \in \mathrm{Var}(\mathbf{C}_6), j', r \;\; \hat{x}^r \notin \Phi(t_{1j'})$. Then $\forall j \; \hat{z}[1,j] = z[1,j]$, and we obtain $u_1\sigma = \prod_{t_{1j} \in T_1} (\psi(t_{1j})\sigma)^{\hat{z}[1,j]}$.

Now suppose the lemma is true for all constraints up to and including $u_{i-1} : T_{i-1}$, $i \geq 2$. Applying Proposition 5 to $u_i : T_i$, we obtain that

$$u_i\sigma = \prod_{t_{ij'} \in T_i} (t_{ij'}\sigma)^{z[i,j']} \tag{5.3}$$

Consider any $t_{ij'}$ from the above product. By definition of $\psi(t_{ij'})$, $t_{ij'} = \psi(t_{ij'}) \cdot \hat{x}_1^{r_1} \cdot \ldots \cdot \hat{x}_m^{r_m}$ for some variables $\hat{x}_1, \ldots, \hat{x}_m$ and rational constants $r_1, \ldots, r_m$ where $m \geq 0$. Consider any variable $\hat{x} \in \{\hat{x}_1, \ldots, \hat{x}_m\}$, and let k_x be the index of the first constraint in which x occurs. By Proposition 7, the fact that $\hat{x}$ occurs in T_i implies that $u_i : T_i$ cannot be the first constraint in which $\hat{x}$ occurs. There must be a preceding constraint of the form $\hat{x} : T_{k_x} \in \mathbf{C}_6$ and $k_x < i$. By the induction hypothesis, $\hat{x}\sigma = \prod_{t_{k_x j} \in T_{k_x}} (\psi(t_{k_x j})\sigma)^{\hat{z}[k_x,j]}$. By monotonicity, $T_{k_x} \subseteq T_i$. By Definition 6, $\forall j \leq |T_{k_x}| \; t_{k_x j} = t_{ij}$. Moreover, since $\hat{x}$ occurs in $t_{ij'}$, $|T_{k_x}| < j'$ by Proposition 7. Set $\hat{z}[k_x, j] = 0 \; \forall j > |T_{k_x}|$, and replace each $t_{k_x j}$ with the corresponding t_{ij}, obtaining $\hat{x}\sigma = \prod_{j<j'} (\psi(t_{ij})\sigma)^{\hat{z}[k_x,j]}$.

Substituting values for $\hat{x}_1\sigma, \ldots, \hat{x}_m\sigma$ into equation 5.3, we obtain $u_i\sigma = \prod_{t_{ij'} \in T_i} (\; \psi(t_{ij'})\sigma \cdot \prod_{\hat{x}^r \in \Phi(t_{ij'})} (\prod_{j<j'} (\psi(t_{ij})\sigma)^{\hat{z}[k_x,j] \cdot r}) \;)^{z[i,j']}$.

Distributing the exponent $z[i,j']$, obtain that $u_i\sigma$ is equal to

$$\prod_{t_{ij} \in T_i} (\psi(t_{ij})\sigma)^{z[i,j]} \quad \cdot \prod_{t_{ij'} \in T_i} (\prod_{j<j'} (\; (\psi(t_{ij})\sigma)^{\sum_{\hat{x}^r \in \Phi(t_{ij'})} (\hat{z}[k_x,j] \cdot r \cdot z[i,j'])} \;))$$

Observing that $\prod_{t_{ij'} \in T_i}(\prod_{j<j'} \ldots t_{ij} \ldots) = \prod_{t_{ij} \in T_i}(\prod_{j'>j} \ldots t_{ij} \ldots)$, we conclude that $u_i\sigma = \prod_{t_{ij} \in T_i} (\psi(t_{ij})\sigma)^{z[i,j] + \sum_{j'>j}(\sum_{\hat{x}^r \in \Phi(t_{ij'})}(\hat{z}[k_x,j] \cdot r \cdot z[i,j']))}$, completing the induction.

We now convert each constraint into an equivalent system of linear Diophantine equations. If this system is unsolvable, the constraint cannot be satisfied. If, on the other hand, there exist some values of $\hat{z}[i,j]$ that solve the linear system, we will prove that quadratic equations 5.2 are guaranteed to have a solution.

Consider any $u_i : T_i \in \mathbf{C}_6$. By Lemma 10, $u_i\sigma = \prod_{t_{ij} \in T_i}(\psi(t_{ij})\sigma)^{\hat{z}[i,j]}$. By definition, $\psi(t_{ij})$ does not contain any variables as top-level factors. It is possible that $\hat{x}_k^{p_k} \in \Phi(u_i)$ for some variable $\hat{x}_k$ and rational p_k. Applying Proposition 7 and Lemma 10, we obtain that $\forall \hat{x}_k \in \mathrm{Var}(\mathbf{C}_6)\ \hat{x}_k\sigma = \prod_{t_{k_x j} \in T_{k_x}}(\psi(t_{k_x j})\sigma)^{\hat{z}[k_x,j]}$. Therefore, equation 5.1 can be rewritten as

$$\prod_{\hat{x}_k^{p_k} \in \Phi(u_i)}(\prod_{t_{k_x j} \in T_{k_x}}(\psi(t_{k_x j})\sigma)^{\hat{z}[k,j]})^{p_k} \cdot \prod_{u_{il} \in \Psi(u_i)} u_{il}\sigma = \prod_{t_{ij} \in T_i}(\psi(t_{ij})\sigma)^{\hat{z}[i,j]} \tag{5.4}$$

For any variable $\hat{x}_k$ occurring in u_i, it must be that $k_x \leq i$ since k_x is the index of the first constraint in which $\hat{x}_k$ occurs. According to Definition 6, $\forall \hat{x}_k, t_{k_x j} \in T_{k_x}\ t_{k_x j} = t_{ij}$. Dividing the right-hand side of equation 5.4 by $\prod_{\hat{x}_k^{p_k} \in \Phi(u_i)}(\prod_{t_{k_x j} \in T_{k_x}}(\psi(t_{k_x j})\sigma)^{\hat{z}[k_x,j]})^{p_k}$, we obtain

$$\prod_{u_{il} \in \Psi(u_i)} u_{il}\sigma = \prod_{t_{ij} \in T_i}(\psi(t_{ij})\sigma)^{y[i,j]} \tag{5.5}$$

where

$$y[i,j] = \hat{z}[i,j] - \sum_{\hat{x}_k^{p_k} \in \Phi(u_i)} p_k \cdot \hat{z}[k_x,j] \tag{5.6}$$

Recall that $\hat{z}[k_x,j] = 0$ if $j > |T_{k_x}|$.

Let $\mathbf{F}(\mathbf{C}_6) = \bigcup_{u_i:T_i \in \mathbf{C}_6}(\Psi(u_i) \cup \{\Psi(t_{ij}) \mid t_{ij} \in T_i\})$ be the set of all factors appearing in equations 5.5. Since $\mathbf{F}(\mathbf{C}_6) \subseteq \mathrm{St}(\mathbf{C}_6) \subseteq \mathrm{St}(\mathbf{C}_1)$, by Proposition 2 $\forall t, t' \in \mathbf{F}(\mathbf{C}_6)$ if $t \neq t'$, then $t\sigma \neq t'\sigma$. Therefore, $\forall \mathbf{t} \in \mathbf{F}(\mathbf{C}_6)\ \forall u_i : T_i \in \mathbf{C}_6$, the following system of linear equations must hold:

$$\underbrace{q}_{\substack{\text{if } \mathbf{t}^q \in \Psi(u_i), \\ 0 \text{ otherwise}}} = \sum_{t_{ij} \in T_i} \underbrace{q_j \cdot y[i,j]}_{\substack{\text{if } \mathbf{t}^{q_j} \in \Psi(t_{ij}), \\ 0 \text{ otherwise}}} \tag{5.7}$$

where $y[i,j]$ are integer variables (i ranges over the length of the constraint sequence, and, for each i, j ranges from 1 to $|T_i|$), and $q, q_1, \ldots, q_{|T_i|}$ are rational constants. Multiplying equation 5.7 by the lowest common multiplier of the denominators of $q, q_1, \ldots, q_{|T_i|}$, we obtain a linear system over $y[i,j]$.

Lemma 11. $\mathbf{C}$ *has a solution if and only if the system of equations 5.7 has a solution in integers for some* $\mathbf{C}_6$ *such that* $\mathbf{C} \rightsquigarrow \mathbf{C}_6$.

Proof. It follows immediately from the reduction in this section that if system 5.7 does not have a solution in integers, then $\mathbf{C}_6$ does not have a solution, either. It is necessary to show that if system 5.7 has a solution in integers, then system 5.6 and, especially, the quadratic system 5.2 also have a solution.

Let $\{y[i,j]\}$ be any solution of system 5.7. First, $\forall \hat{x} \in \mathbf{C}_6\ \forall j$ set $y[k_x, j] = 0$. Since $\forall \hat{x} \in \mathbf{C}_6\ \Psi(u_{k_x}) = \Psi(\hat{x}) = \emptyset$, equation 5.7 degenerates into $0 = \sum_{t_{k_x j} \in T_{k_x}} q_j \cdot y[k_x, j]$ and is still satisfied. By Proposition 7, $u_{k_x} = \hat{x}_k$. Therefore, $\sum_{\hat{x}_k^{p_k} \in \Phi(u_{k_x})} p_k \cdot \hat{z}[k_x, j] = \hat{z}[k_x, j]$, and $y[k_x, j] = \hat{z}[k_x, j] - \hat{z}[k_x, j] = 0$. System 5.6 is thus satisfied by $y[k_x, j] = 0$ as well.

Now, $\forall \hat{x} \in \mathbf{C}_6\ \forall j$ set $\hat{z}[k_x, j] = \mathcal{Q}_{max}$. Recall from Proposition 8 that $\mathcal{Q}_{max}$ is an integer such that $r \cdot \mathcal{Q}_{max}$ is an integer for any rational power r appearing in $\mathbf{C}_6$. We need to show that systems 5.6 and 5.2 are solvable in integers.

First, consider system 5.6. If $i = k_x$ for some x, it becomes $0 = \mathcal{Q}_{max} - \mathcal{Q}_{max}$. If $\forall x\ i \neq k_x$, it becomes $y[i,j] = \hat{z}[i,j] - \sum_{\hat{x}_k^{p_k} \in \Phi(u_i)} p_k \cdot \mathcal{Q}_{max}$, and is solved by setting $\hat{z}[i,j] = y[i,j] + \sum_{\hat{x}_k^{p_k} \in \Phi(u_i)} p_k \cdot \mathcal{Q}_{max}$ since $p_k \cdot \mathcal{Q}_{max}$ is an integer.

It remains to show that the quadratic system 5.2 has a solution in integers. Pick any $u_i : T_i \in \mathbf{C}_6$ and fix it. Proof is by induction over j from $|T_i|$ to 1. For the base case, consider $j = |T_i|$. Because there are no $j' > j$, set $z[i,j] = \hat{z}[i,j]$.

Now suppose the proposition is true for $z[i, j+1], \ldots, z[i, |T_i|]$. To complete the proof, it is sufficient to show that there exists an integer value for $z[i,j]$ that satisfies equation 5.2. Observe that $z[i,j']$ is an integer $\forall j' > j$ (by the induction hypothesis), and $\hat{z}[k_x, j] \cdot r = \mathcal{Q}_{max} \cdot r$ is an integer $\forall \hat{x}$ such that $\hat{x}^r \in \Phi(t_{ij'})$ (by Proposition 8). Therefore, $z[i,j] = \hat{z}[i,j] - \sum_{j'>j} (\sum_{\hat{x}^r \in \Phi(t_{ij'})} (\hat{z}[k_x, j] \cdot r \cdot z[i, j']))$ is an integer solution for equation 5.2. This completes the induction.

Running example. In our running example, we are solving the following $\mathbf{C}_6$:

$$\hat{X} : a \cdot b\ ; \quad a^6 : a \cdot b, \{a\}_b, \langle b \cdot \hat{X} \cdot a^{-2}, \mathsf{exp}(c,a) \rangle, b \cdot \hat{X} \cdot a^{-2}, \mathsf{exp}(c,a)$$

$\mathbf{C}_6$ has a solution *iff* the following system 5.5 is solvable in integers:

$$\begin{aligned} 1 &= (a \cdot b)^{y[1,1]} \\ a^6 &= (a \cdot b)^{y[2,1]} \cdot (\{a\}_b)^{y[2,2]} \cdot (\langle b \cdot \hat{X} \cdot a^{-2}, \mathsf{exp}(c,a) \rangle)^{y[2,3]} \cdot \\ &\quad (b \cdot a^{-2})^{y[2,4]} (\mathsf{exp}(c,a))^{y[2,5]} \end{aligned}$$

Since $\Psi(u_1) = \emptyset$, $\prod_{u_{1l} \in \Psi(u_1)} u_{1l}\sigma = 1$, and $\psi(b \cdot \hat{X} \cdot a^{-2}) = b \cdot a^{-2}$.

We set $y[1,1] = 0$ because $k_x = 1$, and convert the second equation into an equivalent linear Diophantine system 5.7, treating all non-atomic terms such as $\langle \ldots, \ldots \rangle$ and $\mathsf{exp}(c,a)$ as constants:

$$\begin{aligned} 6 &= y[2,1] - 2 \cdot y[2,4] & 0 &= y[2,2] \\ 0 &= y[2,1] + y[2,4] & 0 &= y[2,3] \\ & & 0 &= y[2,5] \end{aligned}$$

The solution of this system is $y[2,1] = 2, y[2,4] = -2$. Therefore, the constraint sequence has a solution, and the corresponding symbolic trace is feasible. In this example, $\mathcal{Q}_{max} = 1$, therefore, $\hat{z}[1,1] = 1$, and $\hat{X} = (a \cdot b)^{\hat{z}[1,1]} = a \cdot b$. Reconstructing the values of original variables, we obtain $X = \hat{X} \cdot a^{-2} = a^{-1} \cdot b$.

Theorem 2 (Soundness and completeness). *Symbolic constraint sequence* $\mathbf{C}$ *has a solution if and only if the system of linear equations 5.7 has a solution in integers for some* $\mathbf{C}_6$ *such that* $\mathbf{C} \rightsquigarrow \mathbf{C}_6$.

6 Conclusions

We have presented a decision procedure for symbolic analysis of cryptographic protocols employing Abelian group operators and modular exponentiation from arbitrary bases, assuming the number of protocol sessions is bounded. Decidability is proved by reducing the symbolic constraint satisfiability problem to the solvability of a particular system of linear Diophantine equations.

This result enables fully automated analysis of a wide class of cryptographic protocols, such as those based on group Diffie-Hellman, that cannot be analyzed in the standard Dolev-Yao model. The next step is development of practical protocol analysis techniques. Instead of nondeterministically guessing subterm equalities and the order of subterm derivation, the analysis tool would search for a solution by inductively analyzing the structure of target terms, similar to the techniques of [13]. We expect that this approach will result in better average-case complexity than the generic decision procedure presented here.

Acknowledgments. Thanks to the anonymous reviewers for insightful comments, and to Jon Millen whose collaboration was invaluable in developing the symbolic protocol analysis framework on which the results presented in this paper are based.

References

1. R. Amadio and D. Lugiez. On the reachability problem in cryptographic protocols. In *Proc. 11th International Conference on Concurrency Theory (CONCUR '00)*, volume 1877 of *LNCS*, pages 380–394, 2000.
2. F. Baader and W. Snyder. Unification theory. In A. Robinson and A. Voronkov, editors, *Handbook of Automated Reasoning*, volume 1, chapter 8, pages 445–532. Elsevier Science, 2001.
3. M. Boreale. Symbolic trace analysis of cryptographic protocols. In *Proc. 28th International Colloquium on Automata, Languages and Programming (ICALP '01)*, volume 2076 of *LNCS*, pages 667–681, 2001.
4. M. Boreale and M. Buscemi. On the symbolic analysis of low-level cryptographic primitives: modular exponentiation and the Diffie-Hellman protocol. In *Proc. Workshop on the Foundations of Computer Security (FCS)*, 2003.
5. Y. Chevalier, R. Küsters, M. Rusinowitch, and M. Turuani. Deciding the security of protocols with Diffie-Hellman exponentiation and products in exponents. Technical Report IFI-Report 0305, CAU Kiel, 2003.
6. H. Comon-Lundh and V. Shmatikov. Intruder deductions, constraint solving and insecurity decision in presence of exclusive or. In *Proc. 18th Annual IEEE Symposium on Logic in Computer Science (LICS '03)*, pages 271–280, 2003.
7. E. Contejean and H. Devie. An efficient algorithm for solving systems of Diophantine equations. *Information and Computation*, 113(1):143–172, 1994.

8. N. Durgin, P.D. Lincoln, J.C. Mitchell, and A. Scedrov. Undecidability of bounded security protocols. In *Proc. FLOC Workshop on Formal Methods in Security Protocols*, 1999.
9. M. Fiore and M. Abadi. Computing symbolic models for verifying cryptographic protocols. In *Proc. 14th IEEE Computer Security Foundations Workshop*, pages 160–173, 2001.
10. D. Kapur, P. Narendran, and L. Wang. An e-unification algorithm for analyzing protocols that use modular exponentiation. In *Proc. 14th International Conference on Rewriting Techniques and Applications (RTA '03)*, volume 2706 of *LNCS*, pages 165–179, 2003.
11. C. Meadows and P. Narendran. A unification algorithm for the group Diffie-Hellman protocol. In *Proc. Workshop of Issues in Theory of Security (WITS)*, 2002.
12. A. Menezes, P. van Oorschot, and S. Vanstone. *Handbook of Applied Cryptography.* CRC Press, 1997.
13. J. Millen and V. Shmatikov. Constraint solving for bounded process cryptographic protocol analysis. In *Proc. 8th ACM Conference on Computer and Communications Security (CCS '01)*, pages 166–175, 2001.
14. J. Millen and V. Shmatikov. Symbolic protocol analysis with products and Diffie-Hellman exponentiation. In *Proc. 16th IEEE Computer Security Foundations Workshop*, pages 47–61, 2003.
15. L. Paulson. Mechanized proofs for a recursive authentication protocol. In *Proc. 10th IEEE Computer Security Foundations Workshop*, pages 84–95, 1997.
16. O. Pereira and J.-J. Quisquater. A security analysis of the Cliques protocols suites. In *Proc. 14th IEEE Computer Security Foundations Workshop*, pages 73–81, 2001.
17. M. Rusinowitch and M. Turuani. Protocol insecurity with finite number of sessions is NP-complete. In *Proc. 14th IEEE Computer Security Foundations Workshop*, pages 174–190, 2001.
18. P. Ryan and S. Schneider. An attack on a recursive authentication protocol: A cautionary tale. *Information Processing Letters*, 65(1):7–10, 1998.
19. M. Steiner, G. Tsudik, and M. Waidner. Diffie-Hellman key distribution extended to group communication. In *Proc. 3rd ACM Conference on Computer and Communications Security (CCS '96)*, pages 31–37, 1996.

Functors for Proofs and Programs

Jean-Christophe Filliâtre and Pierre Letouzey

LRI – CNRS UMR 8623
Université Paris-Sud, France
{filliatr,letouzey}@lri.fr

Abstract. This paper presents the formal verification with the Coq proof assistant of several applicative data structures implementing finite sets. These implementations are parameterized by an ordered type for the elements, using functors from the ML module system. The verification follows closely this scheme, using the newly Coq module system. One of the verified implementation is the actual code for sets and maps from the Objective Caml standard library. The formalization refines the informal specifications of these libraries into formal ones. The process of verification exhibited two small errors in the balancing scheme, which have been fixed and then verified. Beyond these verification results, this article illustrates the use and benefits of modules and functors in a logical framework.

1 Introduction

Balanced trees are notoriously hard to implement without mistakes. Exact invariants are difficult to figure out, even for applicative implementations. Since most programming languages provide data structures for finite sets and dictionaries based on balanced trees, it is a real challenge for formal verification to actually verify one of these.

We choose to verify the `Set` module from the Objective Caml (OCAML) standard library [2]. This applicative implementation of finite sets uses AVL trees [4] and provides all expected operations, including union, difference and intersection. Above all, this is a very efficient and heavily used implementation, which motivates a correctness proof. In particular, a formalization requires to give precise specifications to this library, a non-trivial task. This article also presents the verification of two other implementations, using respectively sorted lists and red-black trees [8], both written in OCAML and using the same interface as `Set`.

Building balanced trees over values of a given type requires this type to be equipped with a total ordering function. Several techniques are available to build a parametric library: in ML, polymorphism gives genericity over the type and first-class functions give the genericity over the ordering function (e.g. it is passed when initially creating the tree); in object oriented languages, objects to be stored in the trees are given a suitable comparison function; etc. The most elegant technique is probably the one provided by the ML module system, as implemented in SML [9] and OCAML [11]. A *module* is a collection of definitions

D.A. Schmidt (Ed.): ESOP 2004, LNCS 2986, pp. 370–384, 2004.

of types, values and submodules. Its type is called a *signature* and contains declarations of (some of the) types, values and submodules. Modules can be parameterized by some signatures and later applied to actual modules. Such functions from modules to modules are called *functors*. The `Set` library is a nice illustration of the OCAML module system. It is naturally written as a functor taking the signature of an ordered type as argument and returning a signature for finite sets as a result.

The use of modules and functors introduces an extra challenge for formal proof. The recent introduction of an ML-like module system into the COQ proof assistant [1,5] makes it a perfect candidate for this verification. As a side effect, this article examplifies the use of modules and functors in a logical framework, which goes well beyond its use in programming languages.

Currently, COQ is not able to reason directly about OCAML code. To certify an OCAML applicative implementation, we first translate it into COQ's own programming language, GALLINA. Then the logic of COQ can be used to express properties of the GALLINA functions. Whereas the translation from OCAML to GALLINA is done manually and is thus error-prone, COQ provides an automated mechanism for the converse translation called *extraction*. The extraction takes a COQ function or proof, removes all its logical statements, and translates the remaining algorithmic content to OCAML. We end up with three versions of the code: the OCAML original handwritten one, its GALLINA translation certified in COQ, and the OCAML extracted version. Theoretical results about the extraction [12,13] ensure that the extracted code verifies the same properties as the GALLINA version.

Even if in this case the extracted code is not aimed at replacing the existing one, there are at least two reasons to perform this extraction. First, the extracted code often presents only syntactical differences with respect to the original code and thus ensures that no mistake was made during the hand-translation to COQ. Second, the extracted code behaves reasonably well in practice (see e.g. the final benchmarks) and thus shows that the extraction technique could be used directly without any original OCAML code.

Outline. This paper is organized as follows. Section 2 is devoted to the presentation of OCAML and COQ module systems. Section 3 introduces the signatures for ordered types and finite sets, and various utility functors over these signatures. Section 4 presents the verification of three finite sets implementations, using respectively sorted lists, AVL trees from the OCAML standard library and red-black trees. Section 5 concludes with a benchmark comparing performances of handwritten and extracted code.

Source code. This article only details the most important parts of the formal development. The whole source code would take too much space, even in appendix: the sole specification is 2472 lines long and the proof scripts amount to 5517 lines, not mentioning the original source code for AVL and red-black trees. All these files are available at `http://www.lri.fr/~filliatr/fsets/` for downloading and browsing. The COQ files need the development version of COQ to compile and a rather powerful machine: 10 minutes are indeed necessary to compile the whole development on a 1 Gigahertz Intel CPU. This web site also includes a slightly more detailed version of this paper.

The pieces of Coq and OCaml code given in this article are displayed in `verbatim` font, apart from the embellishment of a few symbols: $\rightarrow$ for `->`, $\leftrightarrow$ for `<->`, $\vee$ for `\/`, $\wedge$ for `/\`, $\neg$ for `~`, $\forall$ for universal quantifiers and $\exists$ for `EX`.

2 Modules and Functors

2.1 The OCaml Module System

The OCaml module system [11] is derived from the original one for SML [9]. The latter also evolved in return, both systems being now quite close and known as the Harper-Lillibridge-Leroy module system. This section briefly illustrates the OCaml module system with the `Set` library from its standard library, which signature is used throughout this paper and which code is verified in Section 4.2.

The `Set` library first defines a signature `S` for finite sets, given Figure 1. It contains the type `elt` of elements, the type `t` of sets, the value `empty` for the empty set, and 22 operations over sets. Most of them have an obvious meaning and the expected semantics. Other like `fold`, `elements` or `choose` have part of their specification left unspecified (this is detailed later in this paper).

The set implementation is parameterized by the type of its elements, which must be equipped with a total ordered function. The signature `OrderedType` is introduced for this purpose:

```
module type OrderedType =  sig
  type t
  val compare : t → t → int
end
```

The `compare` function is returning an integer such that `(compare x y)` is zero if `x` and `y` are equal, negative if `x` is smaller than `y` and positive if `x` is greater than `y`. For instance, a module `Int` realizing this signature for the type `int` of integers and the predefined comparison function `Pervasives.compare`[1] would be:

```
module Int : Set.OrderedType = struct
  type t = int
  let compare = Pervasives.compare
end
```

The implementation of the data structure for sets is provided as a functor `Make` taking a module `Ord` of signature `OrderedType` as argument and returning a module of signature `S`:

```
module Make (Ord : OrderedType) : S with type elt = Ord.t
```

[1] The subtraction can not be used as comparison function for integers because of overflows; consider for instance `min_int` − `max_int` = 1.

```
module type S = sig
  type elt
  type t
  val empty : t
  val is_empty : t → bool
  val mem : elt → t → bool
  val add : elt → t → t
  val singleton : elt → t
  val remove : elt → t → t
  val union : t → t → t
  val inter : t → t → t
  val diff : t → t → t
  val compare : t → t → int
  val equal : t → t → bool
  val subset : t → t → bool
  val iter : (elt → unit) → t → unit
  val fold : (elt → 'a → 'a) → t → 'a → 'a
  val for_all : (elt → bool) → t → bool
  val exists : (elt → bool) → t → bool
  val filter : (elt → bool) → t → t
  val partition : (elt → bool) → t → t * t
  val cardinal : t → int
  val elements : t → elt list
  val min_elt : t → elt
  val max_elt : t → elt
  val choose : t → elt
end
```

Fig. 1. OCAML signature `Set.S` for finite sets

The signature for the returned module needs to be more precise than `S`: we must identify the type `elt` in the returned signature with the type `Ord.t` given as argument. This is made explicit using the `with type` construct.

We would get sets of integers by applying this functor to the module `Int` above: `module IntSet = Set.Make(Int)`. It is important to notice that signature `S` contains a type `t` and a comparison function `compare` (with the expected behavior), allowing to build sets of sets by applying `Make` again on the resulting module. For instance, sets of sets of integers would be obtained with: `module IntSetSet = Set.Make(IntSet)`. The reader may refer to the OCAML manual [2] for further details on its module system.

2.2 The COQ Module System

A module system for the COQ proof assistant has been advocated for a long time, mainly in Courant's PhD thesis [7]. Clearly more ambitious than OCAML's, his module system appeared too complex to be implemented in the existing code of Coq. Instead, a module system *à la Caml* was recently implemented by Chrząszcz [5] following Leroy's modular module system [11].

One small difference with respect to OCAML is that Coq modules are *interactive*. While in OCAML a module is introduced as a single declaration, Coq allows to build it piece by piece. The declaration of a new module `M` starts with the command `Module M`. Then any subsequent Coq declaration (type, function, lemma, theorem, etc.) is placed in that module, until the closing of `M` with the command `End M`. This interactive process is plainly justified by the interactive building of (most) Coq theories. Developing a whole module with all its proofs one at a time would be intractable. Signatures and functors are also introduced interactively in a similar way.

A signature may contain a declaration such as `Parameter x : T`, claiming the existence of a value `x` of type `T` in any module implementing this signature. Depending on `T`, it corresponds either to an OCAML abstract type or to an OCAML value. A module or a functor body may contain logical properties and proofs. This is of course a novelty when compared to OCAML.

2.3 Extraction

The Coq extraction mechanism [12,13] handles naturally the module system: Coq modules are extracted to OCAML modules, Coq signatures to OCAML signatures and Coq functors to OCAML functors.

The first task of the extraction is to introduce a distinction between terms and types, since Coq has a unified notion of terms. For instance, a `Parameter` declaration may either be extracted to a type declaration or to a value declaration, depending on its type.

Then the extraction removes all the logical parts that "decorate" the computationally relevant terms: logical justifications, preconditions, postconditions, etc. These logical parts are not needed for the actual computation. The detection of these logical parts is done accordingly to the Coq sorts. A fundamental principle of Coq is that any Coq term belongs either to the logical sort `Prop`, or to the informative sorts `Set` and `Type`. The extraction follows this duality to decide which (sub-)terms must be erased.

3 Specifying a Finite Sets Library

3.1 Ordered Types

Similarly to OCAML code, our implementations are parameterized by the type of elements and its total ordering function. The OCAML ordering functions return integers for efficiency reasons. The Coq ordering functions could simply return into a three values enumeration type, such as

```
Inductive Compare: Set := Lt: Compare | Eq: Compare | Gt: Compare.
```

However, it is more idiomatic to introduce two predicates `lt` and `eq`—`lt` for the strict order relation and `eq` for the equality—and to have constructors for

```
Module Type OrderedType.
  Parameter t : Set.
  Parameter eq : t → t → Prop.
  Parameter lt : t → t → Prop.
  Parameter eq_refl : ∀x:t, (eq x x).
  Parameter eq_sym : ∀x,y:t, (eq x y) → (eq y x).
  Parameter eq_trans : ∀x,y,z:t, (eq x y) → (eq y z) → (eq x z).
  Parameter lt_trans : ∀x,y,z:t, (lt x y) → (lt y z) → (lt x z).
  Parameter lt_not_eq : ∀x,y:t, (lt x y) → ¬(eq x y).
  Parameter compare : ∀x,y:t, (Compare t lt eq x y).
End OrderedType.
```

Fig. 2. Coq signature for ordered types

the inductive type `Compare` carrying proofs of the corresponding relations. Since this type is going to be reused at several places, we make it polymorphic with respect to the type `X` of elements and to the relations `lt` and `eq`:

```
Inductive Compare [X:Set; lt,eq:X→X→Prop; x,y:X] : Set :=
  | Lt : (lt x y) → (Compare X lt eq x y)
  | Eq : (eq x y) → (Compare X lt eq x y)
  | Gt : (lt y x) → (Compare X lt eq x y).
```

Note that this type is in sort `Set` while `lt` and `eq` are in sort `Prop`. Thus the informative contents of `Compare` is a three constant values type, with the same meaning as integers in OCaml comparison functions.

Then we introduce a signature `OrderedType` for ordered types. First, it contains a type `t` for the elements, which is clearly informative and thus in sort `Set`. Then it equips the type `t` with an equality `eq` and a strict order relation `lt`, together with a decidability function `compare` such that `(compare x y)` has type `(Compare t lt eq x y)`.

Finally, it contains a minimal set of logical properties expressing that `eq` is an equivalence relation and that `lt` is a strict order relation compatible with `eq`. The final signature `OrderedType` is given Figure 2. Note that `compare` provides the totality of the order relation.

Many additional properties can be derived from this set of axioms, such as the antisymmetry of `lt`. Such properties are clearly useful for the forthcoming proof developments. Instead of polluting the `OrderedType` signature with all of them, we build a functor that derives these properties from `OrderedType`:

```
Module OrderedTypeFacts [O:OrderedType].
  Lemma lt_not_gt : ∀x,y:O.t, (O.lt x y) → ¬(O.lt y x).
  ...
End OrderedTypeFacts.
```

This way, the user only has to implement a minimal signature and all the remaining is automatically derived.

3.2 Finite Sets

Reproducing the OCAML Set.S signature in COQ is not immediate. First of all, four functions are not applicative. One is iter, which iterates a side-effects-only function over all elements of a set; we simply discard this function. The others are min_elt, max_elt and choose, which respectively return the minimum, the maximum and an arbitrary element of a given set, and raise an exception when the set is empty; we slightly change their type so that they now return into a sum type.

Then we face the problem of specifications: they are given as comments in the OCAML files, and are more or less precise. Sometimes the behavior is even left partly unspecified, as for fold. The remaining of this section explains how these informal specifications are translated into COQ.

Finally, we face a question of style. There are indeed several ways of defining, specifying and proving correct a function in COQ. Basically, this can be done in two steps—we first define a purely informative function and then we prove it correct—or in a single one—we use dependent types to have the function returning its result together with the proof that it is correct. Our formalization actually provides both styles, with bridge functors to go from one to the other, allowing the user to choose what he or she considers as the most convenient.

Non-dependent signature. We first introduce a signature S containing purely informative functions together with axioms. It is very close to the OCAML signature. It introduces an ordered type for the elements:

```
Module Type S.
  Declare Module E : OrderedType.
  Definition elt := E.t.
```

Then it introduces an abstract type t for sets:

```
  Parameter t : Set.
```

All operations have exactly the same types as in OCAML (see Figure 1), apart from min_elt, max_elt and choose:

```
  Parameter min_elt : t → (option elt).
  Parameter max_elt : t → (option elt).
  Parameter choose : t → (option elt).
```

and compare which uses the Compare type introduced in Section 3.1 and refers to two predicates eq and lt also declared in the interface:

```
  Parameter eq : t → t → Prop.
  Parameter lt : t → t → Prop.
  Parameter compare : ∀s,s':t, (Compare t lt eq s s').
```

The five properties of eq and lt are declared, making this interface a subtype of OrderedType and thus allowing a bootstrap to get sets of sets. To specify all the operations, a membership predicate is introduced:

```
Parameter In : elt → t → Prop.
```

We could have used the `mem` operation for this purpose, using `(mem x s)=true` instead of `(In x s)`, but it is more idiomatic in COQ to use propositions rather than boolean functions[2]. Moreover, it gives the implementor the opportunity to define a membership predicate without referring to `mem`, which may ease the correctness proof. An obvious property of `In` with respect to the equality `E.eq` is declared:

```
Parameter eq_In : ∀s:t, ∀x,y:elt, (E.eq x y)→(In x s)→(In y s).
```

Operations are then axiomatized using the membership predicate. The value `empty` and the operations `mem`, `is_empty`, `add`, `remove`, `singleton`, `union`, `inter`, `diff`, `equal`, `subset`, `elements`, `min_elt`, `max_elt` and `choose` have obvious specifications. The remaining six operations, namely `filter`, `cardinal`, `fold`, `for_all`, `exists` and `partition`, are not so simple to specify and deserve a bit of explanation.

Filtering and test functions. In the OCAML standard library, the `filter` operation is specified as follows:

```
val filter : (elt → bool) → t → t
(** filter p s returns the set of all elements in s that satisfy
    predicate p. *)
```

This is slightly incorrect, as the predicate p could return different values for elements identified by the equality `E.eq` over type `elt`. The predicate p has to be *compatible* with `E.eq` in the following way:

```
Definition compat_bool [p:elt→bool] :=
  ∀x,y:elt, (E.eq x y) → (p x)=(p y).
```

Then `filter` can be formally specified with the following three axioms:

```
Parameter filter_1 : ∀s:t, ∀x:elt, ∀p:elt→bool,
   (compat_bool p) → (In x (filter p s)) → (In x s).
Parameter filter_2 : ∀s:t, ∀x:elt, ∀p:elt→bool,
   (compat_bool p) → (In x (filter p s)) → (p x)=true.
Parameter filter_3 : ∀s:t, ∀x:elt, ∀p:elt→bool,
   (compat_bool p)→(In x s)→(p x)=true→(In x (filter p s)).
```

Note that it leaves the behavior of `filter` unspecified whenever p is not compatible with `E.eq`. Operations `for_all`, `exists` and `partition` are specified in a similar way.

Folding and cardinal. Specifying the `fold` operation poses another challenge. The OCAML specification reads:

```
val fold : (elt → 'a → 'a) → t → 'a → 'a
(** fold f s a computes (f xN ... (f x2 (f x1 a))...), where
    x1... xN are the elements of s. The order in which elements
    of s are presented to f is unspecified. *)
```

[2] Unlike most HOL-based systems, COQ does *not* identify propositions and booleans.

To resemble the OCAML specification as much as possible, we declare the existence of a list of elements without duplicate—the list x1,..., xN above—and we reuse the existing folding operation fold_right over lists:

```
Parameter fold_1 :
  ∀s:t, ∀A:Set, ∀i:A, ∀f:elt→A→A,
  (∃l:(list elt) |
     (Unique E.eq l) ∧
     (∀x:elt, (In x s) ↔ (InList E.eq x l)) ∧
     (fold f s i) = (fold_right f i l)).
```

Unique is a predicate expressing the uniqueness of elements within a list with respect to a given equality, here E.eq. The cardinal operation is specified in a similar way, using the operation length over lists. Note that cardinal could be defined with fold; this will be discussed later in Section 3.3.

Dependent signature. We introduce a second signature for finite sets, Sdep. It makes use of dependent types to mix computational and logical contents, in a COQ idiomatic way of doing. The part of the signature related to the type t and the relations eq, lt and In is exactly the same as for signature S. Then each operation is introduced and specified with a single declaration. For instance, the empty set is declared as follows:

```
Parameter empty : { s:t | ∀a:elt, ¬(In a s) }.
```

which must read "there exists a set s such that ...". Similarly, the operation add is declared as:

```
Parameter add : ∀x:elt, ∀s:t,
    { s':t | ∀y:elt, (In y s') ↔ ((E.eq y x) ∨ (In y s)) }.
```

and so on for all other operations.

Bridge functors. Signatures S and Sdep can be proved equivalent in a constructive way. Indeed, we can implement two *bridge* functors between the two signatures. The first one is implementing the signature Sdep given a module implementing the signature S:

```
Module DepOfNodep [M:S] <: Sdep with Module E := M.E.
...
End DepOfNodep.
```

and the second one is implementing the signature S given a module implementing the signature Sdep:

```
Module NodepOfDep [M:Sdep] <: S with Module E := M.E.
...
End NodepOfDep.
```

The practical interest is obvious: the user may prefer one style of programming/proving with COQ while a particular implementation of finite sets is available with the other style. Applying the appropriate functor provides the desired interface.

3.3 Additional Properties

Signatures `S` and `Sdep` intend to be minimal. Many additional properties can be derived. They may involve the set operations separetely or together, as in the following fact:

`cardinal (union a b)` + `cardinal (inter a b)` = `cardinal a` + `cardinal b`

Similarly to what we did for `OrderedType` in Section 3.1, we gather all such properties in a functor taking a module of signature `S` as argument:

```
Module Properties [M:S].
  Lemma union_inter_cardinal :
    ∀a,b:t, (cardinal (union a b)) + (cardinal (inter a b))
          = (cardinal a) + (cardinal b).
  ...
End Properties.
```

4 Verifying Finite Sets Implementations

Implementing and verifying a set library with all operations introduced so far is not necessarily difficult: indeed, all operations can be coded using the four *primitive* operations `empty`, `add`, `remove` and `fold`. However, most operations can be coded more efficiently in a direct way, at the extra cost of a more difficult formal proof.

In this section, we present the formal verification of three different implementations using respectively sorted lists, AVL trees and red-black trees. These three implementations are functors taking an ordered type `X` as argument.

4.1 Sorted Lists

Sets implemented as sorted lists offer poor performances. However, there are at least two reasons to start with such an implementation. First, this is a quick way to debug our signature `S` and, when done, to show its logical consistency—we indeed rephrased several specifications while doing this first verification. Second, some of the operations over lists are reused later in the code or verification of the other two implementations based on binary trees. The verification is (almost) straightforward.

4.2 AVL Trees

The next implementation to be verified is the `Set` module from OCAML standard library [2]. This is a heavily used library, including in OCAML's own code. It implements sets using AVL trees [4], that are binary search trees where the difference between the heights of any two sibling trees can not exceed a given value Δ. Although $\Delta = 1$ is an admissible choice [4], the OCAML implementation relaxes it to $\Delta = 2$, making a compromise between the overall balancing and the cost of rebalancing when inserting or deleting.

The Coq formalization implements signature Sdep, following OCaml code as close as possible. First a type for trees is introduced:

```
Inductive tree : Set :=
| Leaf : tree
| Node : tree → elt → tree → Z → tree.
```

The height is stored for greater efficiency, using the Coq type Z for arbitrary precision integers. Then we introduce two inductive predicates

```
Inductive bst : tree → Prop := ...
Inductive avl : tree → Prop := ...
```

where bst (resp. avl) is the property of being a binary search tree (resp. a balanced tree). Finally, the type t for sets is a record containing a tree and proofs that it is a balanced binary search tree:

```
Record t : Set := t_intro {
  the_tree : tree;
  is_bst : (bst the_tree);
  is_avl : (avl the_tree) }.
```

Properties bst and avl could have been defined simultaneously but separating them eases the proofs since most of the time one of the two is not relevant for the property to be proved.

Verification. Verifying the operations is mostly a matter of finding the precise specifications, where the OCaml code is only providing a few laconic comments. For instance, one of the internal function (bal l x r) is informally specified as

> "Same as create, but performs one step of rebalancing if necessary. Assumes l and r balanced."

but its precise specification is (among other things):

> "Assumes $|(\texttt{height l}) - (\texttt{height r})| \leq 3$. The size of the returned tree is either $\max(\texttt{height l}, \texttt{height r})$ or $\max(\texttt{height l}, \texttt{height r}) + 1$, and is always the latter when $|(\texttt{height l}) - (\texttt{height r})| \leq 2$.

Looking for these specifications, we actually discovered balancing bugs in OCaml code: two internal functions were building incorrectly balanced trees while they were supposed to. (The sets which were built were correct, though, i.e. were containing the right elements.) Patches have been quickly provided by the OCaml team and we could verify the new code without trouble.

A termination challenge. Only one operation poses a real verification challenge: the compare function providing a total ordering over sets. The idea is quite simple. Comparing two sets is just a matter of comparing the sorted lists of their elements in a lexicographic way. But the algorithm used is tricky. Instead of first building the two lists, the code is building them *lazily*, as soon as elements are needed for the comparison, using a technique of *deforestation* [15]. The problem is generalized to the comparison of two lists of trees, done as follows:

```
let rec compare_aux l1 l2 = match (l1, l2) with
  | ([], []) → 0
  | ([], _)  → -1
  | (_, []) → 1
  | (Empty :: t1, Empty :: t2) → compare_aux t1 t2
  | (Node(Empty,v1,r1,_) :: t1, Node(Empty,v2,r2,_) :: t2) →
      let c = Ord.compare v1 v2 in
      if c <> 0 then c else compare_aux (r1::t1) (r2::t2)
  | (Node(l1, v1, r1, _) :: t1, t2) →
      compare_aux (l1 :: Node(Empty, v1, r1, 0) :: t1) t2
  | (t1, Node(l2, v2, r2, _) :: t2) →
      compare_aux t1 (l2 :: Node(Empty, v2, r2, 0) :: t2)
```

Proving the termination of this function is hard. Indeed, the last two cases may recursively call `compare_aux` on "bigger" arguments when `l1` (resp. `l2`) is `Empty`. The reason why it terminates involves a global argument: the first elements of the lists will eventually become both `Empty` and will then fall into the fourth case of the pattern matching. Fortunately, the code can be slightly changed to recover a simpler termination argument, at the extra cost of two additional cases but without any loss of efficiency. This modified version is proved correct.

4.3 Red-Black Trees

Red-black trees [8] are another kind of balanced binary search trees. Nodes are colored either red or black and any red-black tree must satisfy the following two invariants:

- A red node has no red child;
- Every path from the root to a leaf contains the same number of black nodes.

Okasaki nicely introduces red-black trees in a functional setting [14] but only the membership and insertion operations are given. Xi specifies this code in DEPENDENT ML [16] but it is also restricted to the insertion operation. Even Adams general approach to balanced binary search trees [3] does not apply nicely to red-black trees. Generally speaking, we could not find a comprehensive implementation of finite sets using red-black trees and we wrote our own. This code is available from the web site of the formalization.

As for AVL trees, the COQ formalization implements signature `Sdep` following OCAML code as close as possible. First, colored trees are defined:

```
Inductive color : Set := red : color | black : color.
Inductive tree : Set :=
| Leaf : tree
| Node : color → tree → elt → tree → tree.
```

The binary search tree property `bst` is similar to the one for AVL trees. Then the red-black trees invariant is introduced as an inductive predicate `rbtree` parameterized by the height of black nodes. Finally, everything is collected into a record type:

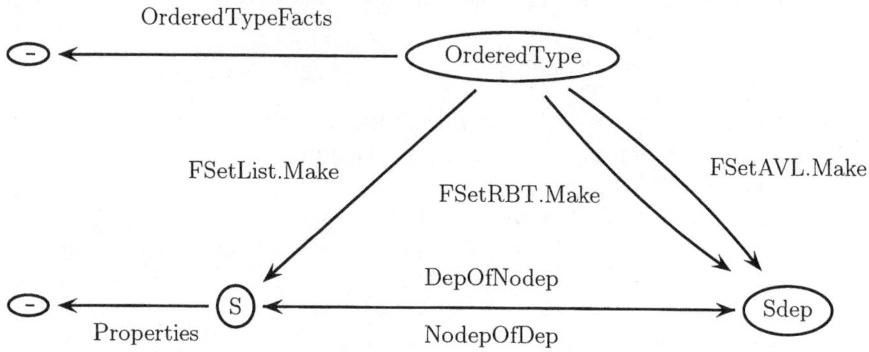

Fig. 3. The five signatures and the seven functors

```
Record t : Set := t_intro {
  the_tree :> tree;
  is_bst : (bst the_tree);
  is_rbtree : (∃n:nat | (rbtree n the_tree)) }.
```

Again, the formalization is roughly a matter of finding the right specification for each function, followed by a quite long process of Coq tactics scripting (figures are given in the conclusion). Some proofs from the AVL trees formalization could be reused with slight modifications (e.g. the `compare` operation).

5 Conclusion

In this article we presented the full formalization in Coq of three applicative implementations of finite sets libraries, including AVL and red-black trees. To our knowledge this is the first formal proof of a full set of operations over these two kinds of balanced binary search trees. This is also the first formal proof of a functorized piece of code.

This article also demonstrates the benefits of modules and functors in a logical framework, and their relevance for program proving. More precisely, the adequacy between the OCaml and Coq module systems allows the formalization of significant pieces of code. Correct-by-construction functorized code can be obtained using Coq extraction, which is a real improvement.

Overall picture. Figure 3 summarizes the dependencies between the five signatures and the seven functors used in this formalization. The following table details the size of the formalization, in terms of the size of code proved correct and size of the Coq development. The formalization roughly amounts to one man-month.

	specs	lists	AVL	RBT	**total**
lines of code		114	231	314	545
lines of Coq specs	1160	375	532	405	2472
lines of Coq proofs	1900	537	1800	1280	5517

Extraction and benchmark. Once the formalization done, OCAML code can be automatically extracted from the proofs [12,13]. Thus it can be compared to the original code. We run a little benchmark comparing OCAML's `Set` module (AVL), the extraction of its formalization (ε-AVL), a manual implementation of red-black trees (RBT) and the extraction of its formalization (ε-RBT). The benchmark consists in testing operations on randomly generated sets of various sizes[3]. Timings are shown below (in seconds).

	add-1	add-2	mem-1	mem-2	rem-1	rem-2	union	inter	diff	subset	cmp
AVL	3.01	15.50	9.52	11.10	4.67	4.20	11.40	4.76	4.68	11.50	11.50
ε-AVL	13.80	53.20	10.20	11.70	18.70	17.70	46.50	17.70	17.70	46.30	45.70
RBT	3.38	13.40	11.40	13.00	5.92	4.81	12.10	4.76	4.71	11.20	11.70
ε-RBT	4.02	16.70	12.10	13.60	6.85	5.58	17.30	6.19	5.76	14.00	13.90

The timings are very close, apart from ε-AVL when trees are built, that is for all operations except `mem`. The reason is that arithmetical computations over heights are done using COQ arbitrary precision arithmetic extracted to OCAML, which can not compete with the hardware arithmetic used in OCAML `Set`. We could parameterize the whole formalization of AVL trees with respect to the arithmetic used for computing heights, using yet another functor. But we would loose the benefits of the `Omega` tactic (the decision procedure for Presburger arithmetic) which is of heavy use in this development. A workaround would be an automatic substitution of a more realistic arithmetic for COQ arithmetic at extraction time, e.g. hardware or arbitrary precision provided it has been verified. But this is not yet a COQ feature.

Acknowledgements. We are grateful to Xavier Leroy for suggesting the verification of OCAML's AVL trees and for having provided patches almost immediately. We also thank Benjamin Monate for the very nice user-interface COQIDE and Diego Olivier Fernandez Pons for comments on implementing red-black trees.

References

1. The Coq Proof Assistant. `http://coq.inria.fr/`.
2. The Objective Caml language. `http://caml.inria.fr/`.
3. Stephen Adams. Functional pearls: Efficient sets – a balancing act. *Journal of Functional Programming*, 3(4):553–561, October 1993. Expanded version available as Technical Report CSTR 92-10, University of Southampton.

[3] The benchmark sources can be obtained from the authors.

4. G. M. Adel'son-Vel'skiĭ and E. M. Landis. An algorithm for the organization of information. *Soviet Mathematics–Doklady*, 3(5):1259–1263, September 1962.
5. Jacek Chrząszcz. Implementing modules in the system Coq. In *16th International Conference on Theorem Proving in Higher Order Logics*, University of Rome III, September 2003.
6. Jacek Chrząszcz. *Modules in Type Theory with generative definitions.* PhD thesis, Warsaw University and Université Paris-Sud, 2003. To be defended.
7. Judicaël Courant. A Module Calculus for Pure Type Systems. In *Typed Lambda Calculi and Applications 97*, Lecture Notes in Computer Science, pages 112 – 128. Springer-Verlag, 1997.
8. Leo J. Guibas and Robert Sedgewick. A dichromatic framework for balanced trees. In *19th Annual Symposium on Foundations of Computer Science*, pages 8–21, Ann Arbor, Michigan, 16-18 October 1978. IEEE.
9. Robert Harper and Mark Lillibridge. A type-theoretic approach to higher-order modules with sharing. In *Conference record of POPL '94: 21st ACM SIGPLAN-SIGACT Symposium on Principles of Programming Languages*, pages 123–137, Portland, OR, January 1994.
10. Ralf Hinze. Constructing red-black trees. In editor Chris Okasaki, editor, *Proceedings of the Workshop on Algorithmic Aspects of Advanced Programming Languages, WAAAPL'99*, pages 89–99, Paris, France, September 1999. Also technical report of Columbia University, CUCS-023-99.
11. Xavier Leroy. A modular module system. *Journal of Functional Programming*, 10(3):269–303, 2000.
12. Pierre Letouzey. A New Extraction for Coq. In Herman Geuvers and Freek Wiedijk, editors, *Types for Proofs and Programs, Second International Workshop, TYPES 2002, Berg en Dal, The Netherlands, April 24-28, 2002*, volume 2646 of *Lecture Notes in Computer Science*. Springer-Verlag, 2003.
13. Pierre Letouzey. *Programmation fonctionnelle certifiée en Coq.* PhD thesis, Université Paris Sud, 2003. To be defended.
14. Chris Okasaki. *Purely Functional Data Structures.* Cambridge University Press, 1998.
15. Philip Wadler. Deforestation: transforming programs to eliminate trees. *Theoretical Computer Science*, 73:231–248, 1990.
16. Hongwei Xi. Dependently Typed Data Structures. In *Proceedings of Workshop of Algorithmic Aspects of Advanced Programming Languages (WAAAPL '99)*, pages 17–32, Paris, September 1999.

Extracting a Data Flow Analyser in Constructive Logic

David Cachera[1], Thomas Jensen[2], David Pichardie[1], and Vlad Rusu[3]

[1] IRISA / ENS Cachan (Bretagne)
[2] IRISA / CNRS,
[3] IRISA / INRIA, Campus de Beaulieu, 35042 Rennes cedex, France

Abstract. We show how to formalise a constraint-based data flow analysis in the specification language of the Coq proof assistant. This involves defining a dependent type of lattices together with a library of lattice functors for modular construction of complex abstract domains. Constraints are expressed in an intermediate representation that allows for both efficient constraint resolution and correctness proof of the analysis with respect to an operational semantics. The proof of existence of a correct, minimal solution to the constraints is constructive which means that the extraction mechanism of Coq provides a provably correct data flow analyser in OCAML. The library of lattices together with the intermediate representation of constraints are defined in an analysis-independent fashion that provides a basis for a generic framework for proving and extracting static analysers in Coq.

1 Introduction

Static program analysis is a fully automatic technique for proving properties about the run-time behaviour of a program without actually executing it. The correctness of static analyses can be proved formally by following the theory of abstract interpretation [CC77] that provides a theory for relating two semantic interpretations of the same language. These strong semantic foundations constitute one of the arguments advanced in favor of static program analysis. The implementation of static analyses is usually based on well-understood constraint-solving techniques and iterative fixpoint algorithms. In spite of the nice mathematical theory of program analysis and the solid algorithmic techniques available one problematic issue persists, *viz.*, the *gap* between the analysis that is proved correct on paper and the analyser that actually runs on the machine. While this gap might be small for toy languages, it becomes important when it comes to real-life languages for which the implementation and maintenance of program analysis tools become a software engineering task. To eliminate this gap, we here propose a technique based on theorem proving in constructive logic and the program-as-proofs paradigm, which allows

– to specify static analyses in a way that ensures their *well-formedness* and facilitates their *correctness proof*,

D.A. Schmidt (Ed.): ESOP 2004, LNCS 2986, pp. 385–400, 2004.

– to extract a static analyser from the proof of existence of a correct program analysis result.

In this paper, we show how to specify a static analysis in the logical formalism underlying the proof assistant Coq. This formalism offers a strong type system for expressing correctness of specifications, together with a mechanism for compiling the specifications into the OCAML programming language. More precisely, we offer the following contributions:

– We show how to define a library of abstract domains of properties used in the analysis in a generic fashion (Section 3). The abstract domains are lattices satisfying a finite-ascending-chains condition which makes it possible to extract a provably correct, generic constraint solver based on fixpoint iteration.
– We show how to represent a constraint-based analysis in a constructive manner (Section 4) that allows at the same time to prove correctness of the analysis (Section 5) and to extract an analyser from the proof of the existence of a best solution to the constraints, using the program extraction mechanism available in Coq (Section 6).

We have chosen to develop this approach in the concrete setting of a flow analysis for Java Card byte code, presented in Section 2. The motivation for choosing this particular analysis is that it deals with a minimalistic, yet representative language with imperative, object-oriented and higher-order features, guaranteeing that the approach is transferable to a variety of other analyses. Section 7 compares with other work on formalizing the correctness of data flow analyses, and Section 8 concludes. The Coq sources of the development are available at `http://www.irisa.fr/lande/pichardie/CarmelCoq`.

Notation: Functions whose type depends on the program being analysed will have dependent type $F : (P : \text{Program}) \rightarrow T(P)$ with type T depending on P. We will write F_P for the application of F to a particular program P. The paper uses a mixture of logic and Coq notation for which we (due to space restrictions) cannot offer a full introduction.

2 A Static Analysis for Carmel

The analysis which serves as a basis for our work is a data flow analysis for the Carmel intermediate representation of Java Card byte code [Mar01] specified using the Flow Logic formalism [Han02] and proved correct on paper with respect to an operational semantics [Siv04]. The language is a byte code for a stack-oriented machine, much like the Java Card byte code. Instructions include stack operations, numeric operations, conditionals, object creation and modification, and method invocation and return. It is given a small-step operational semantics with a state of the form $\langle\langle h, \langle m, pc, l, s\rangle :: sf\rangle\rangle$, where h is the heap of objects, and $\langle m, pc, l, s\rangle :: sf$ is a call stack consisting of *frames* of the form $\langle m, pc, l, s\rangle$

where each frame contains a method name m and a program point pc within m, a set of local variables l and a local operand stack s (see [Siv04] for details). Here and everywhere in the paper, "::" denotes the "cons" operation on lists. The transition relation $\rightarrow_I$ describes how an instruction I affects the state. We give as example the rules defining the instructions `push` for pushing a value onto the operand stack, and `invokevirtual` for calling a virtual method.

The rule (1) reads as follows: the instruction `push` c at address (m, pc) of state $\sigma = \langle\langle h, \langle m, pc, l, s\rangle :: sf\rangle\rangle$ has the effect of pushing c on the operand stack s of σ and advancing to the instruction at $pc + 1$.

$$\frac{\text{instructionAt}_P(m, pc) = \texttt{push}\ c}{\langle\langle h, \langle m, pc, l, s\rangle :: sf\rangle\rangle \rightarrow_{\texttt{push}\ c} \langle\langle h, \langle m, pc+1, l, c :: s\rangle :: sf\rangle\rangle} \tag{1}$$

$$\frac{\begin{array}{c}\text{instructionAt}_P(m, pc) = (\texttt{invokevirtual}\ M)\\ m' = \text{methodLookup}(M, (h(loc))) \qquad f = \langle m, pc, l, loc :: V :: s\rangle\\ f' = \langle m', 1, V, \varepsilon\rangle \qquad f'' = \langle m, pc, l, s\rangle\end{array}}{\langle\langle h, f :: sf\rangle\rangle \rightarrow_{\texttt{invokevirtual}\ M} \langle\langle h, f' :: f'' :: sf\rangle\rangle} \tag{2}$$

The rule (2) is slightly more complicated. It reads: for M a method name, the instruction (`invokevirtual` M) at address (m, pc) of state $\sigma = \langle\langle h, f :: sf\rangle\rangle$ may only occur if the first frame f on the call stack of σ has an operand stack of the form $loc :: V :: s$, i.e., it starts with a *heap location* denoted by loc, followed by a vector of values V. The actual method that will be called is to be found in the object that resides in the heap h at the address $h(loc)$, and the actual parameters of that method are contained in the vector V. Then, the methodLookup function searches the class hierarchy for the method name M in that object, and returns the actual method to which the control will be transferred.

The new method, together with its starting point $pc = 1$, its vector V of actual parameters, and an empty operand stack ε, constitute a new frame f' pushed on top of the call stack of the resulting state $\sigma' = \langle\langle h, f' :: f'' :: sf\rangle\rangle$. Note, however, that the second frame in the call stack after the virtual method invocation is not f any more, but a new frame f'' with a different operand stack. This is because the `invokevirtual` instruction has a *side effect*: the location loc and the vector V of actual parameters are removed from f (cf. rule (2) above).

This rather intricate behavior is what actually happens in the Java Card language. It made for the most challenging part of the proof of correctness of the analysis with respect to the semantics (we return to this point in Section 5). The analysis is now briefly described.

2.1 Carmel Flow Logic

The Carmel Flow Logic defined by Hansen [Han02] specifies a constraint-based data flow analysis for Carmel. This analysis computes a safe approximation of the states that can occur at any program point during execution of the program.

The *abstract state* domain $\widehat{\text{State}}_P$, defined by

$$\widehat{\text{State}}_P = \widehat{\text{Heap}}_P \times \left(\text{methodName}_P \times \text{progCount}_P \to \widehat{\text{LocalVar}}_P\right)$$
$$\times \left(\text{methodName}_P \times \text{progCount}_P \to \widehat{\text{Stack}}_P\right)$$

contains an approximation of all possible heaps and, for each program point, an over-approximation of the value of each local variable and of the operand stack. The abstract domains are further described in Section 3.

The specification of the logic consists of a set of inference rules that for each Carmel instruction defines a constraint over an abstract state $\widehat{\Sigma} \in \widehat{\text{State}}$. In order for $\widehat{\Sigma} = \left(\hat{H}, \hat{L}, \hat{S}\right)$ to be a correct abstraction of program P, $\widehat{\Sigma}$ must satisfy the constraints imposed by all the instructions of P. For example, if a push instruction is present at address (m, pc), the following constraints should be satisfied:

$$\widehat{\text{push}}\left(c, \hat{S}\,(m, pc)\right) \sqsubseteq \hat{S}\,(m, pc+1) \tag{3}$$

$$\hat{L}\,(m, pc) \sqsubseteq \hat{L}\,(m, pc+1) \tag{4}$$

where $\widehat{\text{push}}$ is the abstract *push* operation from the abstract domain of stacks.

Correctness of the flow logic is proved by defining a relation $\sim$ between concrete domains of the operational semantics and the abstract domains. The definition of the relation $\sim$ is inductive over the structure of the domain. Due to lack of space we do not give here a formal definition of this relation (see [Han02] for details). The important property of the approximation relation $\sim$ is the *monotonicity with respect to the abstract order* $\sqsubseteq$. It says that, for each concrete value a (be it a heap, a stack, or a vector of local variables) and abstract values $\widehat{A}, \widehat{A'}$ in the corresponding abstract domain, if $a \sim \widehat{A}$ and $\widehat{A} \sqsubseteq \widehat{A'}$ then $a \sim \widehat{A'}$ holds as well. This property is proved in Coq once and for all for each concrete and corresponding abstract domain values. The relation $\sim$ is used extensively in Section 5 where we show how to prove correctness of the analysis in Coq.

3 Constructing Abstract Domains

In this section we define the type `(lattice A)` parameterised by the type of data manipulated in the lattice, and construct higher order functions which produce a lattice object from other lattice objects. This allows to construct the abstract domains (of local variables, stacks, *etc.*) in a compositional fashion starting from a collection of base abstract domains. This modular technique of combining and building lattices has the advantage that we do not have to prove properties (such as the finite ascending chain condition, see below) for one big, final lattice, but can do so in a modular fashion for every type of lattice used. Furthermore, local changes in the lattice structure do not invalidate the overall proof. A lattice object is a structure with two families of fields : the functional fields which are

5.2 Induction Step: The Case of the `return` Instruction

Formula (9) above has the general aspect of the induction step in a proof by *simple induction*. That is, **if** the abstract state $\widehat{\Sigma}$ approximates the concrete state σ **and** $\widehat{\Sigma}$ satisfies the constraints corresponding to σ, **then** $\widehat{\Sigma}$ also correctly approximates all *immediate* successors σ' of σ by an instruction.

However, this is not true for the `return` instruction. This is because every `return` is preceded somewhere along the execution by an `invokevirtual` instruction, and, as seen in Section 2, `invokevirtual` not only *pushes* a new frame f' on the call stack, but also makes a *side effect* on the operand stack of (the formerly first) frame f. Hence, the operand stack of frame f, as it was before the call, is not available any more when the `return` instruction occurs.

But, to prove correctness of the analysis, this information is essential. The information must be fetched from the state σ'' that *precedes* the `invokevirtual` call (responsible of the loss of the said information) that could have occurred arbitrarily far in the past. Hence, a *well-founded induction* argument is required.

Let $[\![P]\!]_{<n}$ (respectively, $[\![P]\!]_{=n}$) denote the set of states of program P that are reachable using less than n instructions (respectively, using exactly n) instructions. The induction step for the case of the instruction $I =$ `return` is:

$$\forall P : \text{Program}, \forall \widehat{\Sigma} : \widehat{\text{State}}_P, \forall n \in \mathbb{N}.[\forall \sigma'' \in [\![P]\!]_{<n}.\ \sigma'' \sim \widehat{\Sigma} \wedge \sigma'' \vdash_P \widehat{\Sigma}]$$
$$\Longrightarrow \forall \sigma \in [\![P]\!]_{=n}.[\ \sigma \sim \widehat{\Sigma} \wedge \sigma \vdash_P \widehat{\Sigma} \Rightarrow (\forall \sigma' : \text{State}.\sigma \rightarrow_I \sigma' \Rightarrow \sigma' \sim \widehat{\Sigma})] \quad (12)$$

Formula (12) reads: **if** the abstract state $\widehat{\Sigma}$ approximates, and satisfies all the constraints of all earlier states σ'' (well-founded induction hypothesis); **and** $\widehat{\Sigma}$ correctly approximates, and satisfies the constraints of state σ; **and** σ evolves, by performing a `return` instruction, into σ'; **then**, $\widehat{\Sigma}$ approximates σ' as well.

The proof of Theorem (12) is substantially more involved than the proofs of Theorems (9). It should be pointed out that this difficulty had been avoided by a previous pencil-and-paper proof [Han02], where the semantics of the `invokevirtual` instruction has been modified to avoid the side-effect on the call stack. This side-effect is the source of most difficulties in the correctness proof.

6 Resolution

Proofs in the Coq system are constructive. Via the Curry-Howard isomorphism, they thus may be seen as programs in a functional language benefiting from a rich type system. The program extraction mechanism provides a tool for automatic translation of these proofs into a functional language with a less rich type system, namely OCAML. The translation removes those parts of the proof that do not contribute to the actual construction of the result but are only concerned with proving that it satisfies its specification

The proof-as-programs paradigm is sometimes presented as developing programs as a by-product of building a constructive proof interactively and incrementally for an "existential" theorem with a proof assistant. While this approach is conceptually simple and appealing, the development of any non-trivial piece of software rather tends to be done by defining (most of) the function and then showing that it is indeed a witness to the theorem. In our case, this means that the type of the analyser function does not directly encode its correctness. Rather, correctness is proved after the definition of the function. This technique is favoured because it is simpler to control the efficiency of the resulting program.

6.1 Construction of the Analyser

The goal is to build an analyser that, given an input program, computes an abstract state that verifies all the constraints of the program. We construct a function `analyse` of dependent type $(P : \text{Program}) \to \widehat{\text{State}}_P$ which must verify

$$\forall P : \text{Program},\ \texttt{verifyAllConstraints}_P(\texttt{analyse}_P) \qquad (13)$$

In addition we want to obtain the least solution of the constraint system:

$$\forall P : \text{Program}, \widehat{\Sigma} : \widehat{\text{State}}_P\ \texttt{verifyAllConstraints}_P(\widehat{\Sigma}) \Rightarrow \texttt{analyse}_P \sqsubseteq \widehat{\Sigma} \quad (14)$$

The constraint resolution tool is based on the generic solver `lfp_list` (5) described in Section 3.2. The most difficult part of the work has already be done during the definition of the solver, i.e. proof of termination and correctness.

It is instantiated here with the particular abstract state lattice of the analysis (depicted in Figure 1); then,

- The constraints are collected from the lists defined by $\texttt{Flow}_P$ (cf. Section 4).
- Each constraint is translated into a *functional form*, using a mapping

  $$\mathcal{F}[\![\cdot]\!] : \texttt{Constraint}_P \to \left(\widehat{\text{State}}_P \to \widehat{\text{State}}_P\right)$$

  for which we prove that it preserves the monotonicity of constraints. *E.g.*,

  $$\mathcal{F}[\![(\texttt{S2S}\ ad_1\ ad_2\ F)]\!] := \lambda(H, L, S).\ (\bot, \bot, \bot[ad_2 \mapsto F(S(ad_1))])$$
  $$\mathcal{F}[\![(\texttt{L2L}\ ad_1\ ad_2\ F)]\!] := \lambda(H, L, S).\ (\bot, \bot[ad_2 \mapsto F(L(ad_1))], \bot)$$

  The resulting list of functional constraints is called $\texttt{collect\_func}_P$. Hence,

$$\forall f \in \texttt{collect\_func}_P\ f \text{ is monotone} \qquad (15)$$

We now have all the ingredients to define the constraint solver:

$$\texttt{analyse}_P := \texttt{lfp\_list}(\widehat{\text{State}}_P, \texttt{collect\_func}_P, \texttt{collect\_func\_monotone})$$

where `collect_func_monotone` is the name given to the proof of (15).
By the properties of `lfp_list` (defined by Formula (5)) we know that $\texttt{analyse}_P$ is the least abstract state $\widehat{\Sigma}$ in $\widehat{\text{State}}_P$ verifying

$$\forall f \in \texttt{collect\_func}_P \quad f(\widehat{\Sigma}) \sqsubseteq \widehat{\Sigma} \qquad (16)$$

3.2 The Constraint Solver

The basic fixpoint operator `lfp` takes a monotone function $f : A \to A$ on a lattice L (parameterised by a type A) and computes the least element x of L verifying $f(x) = x$, which, by a corollary of the Tarski's Fixed Point Theorem, can be iteratively calculated as the limit of the (stabilizing) sequence $(f^n(\bot))_{n\in\mathbb{N}}$.

Formally, we define the operator `lfp` of type

```
(A:Set) → (L:(Lattice A)) → (f:(A→A)) → (monotone L f) →
                  ∃x:A, (eq L x (f x)) ∧
                          ∀y:A (eq L y (f y)) ⇒ (order L x y)
```

That is, `lfp` takes four arguments : a data type A, a lattice L on A, a function f on A and a proof that f is monotone. It returns the least fixed point of f. We then prove in Coq that this type is non-empty, which here consists in instantiating the existentially quantified x in the type definition by $\lim_{n\to\infty} f^n(\bot)$.

Then, the extraction mechanism of programs from proofs generates for `lfp` the following OCAML code, in which the purely logical objects of the proof (i.e., the chosen witness verifies the fixpoint equation) have been removed:

```
let lfp L f =
  let rec aux x =
    if (L.eq_dec x (f x))  then x  else aux (f x)
  in aux L.bottom
```

This operator is then used to solve a list of constraints in the following way. Given a list $f_1, \dots, f_n$ of monotone functions of type $L \to L$, the operator `lfp_list` computes the least solution x of the system $f_i(x) \sqsubseteq x\ \forall i \in \{1, \dots, n\}$ by a round-robin iteration strategy in which the constraints are iterated in increasing order. This computation is implemented by applying the `lfp` operator on the monotone function $\tilde{f}_n \circ \dots \circ \tilde{f}_1$, where $\tilde{f}_i(x) = x \sqcup f_i(x)$ for every index i.

The type of `lfp_list` looks like

```
(l: (L → L) list) → (∀f ∈ l, (monotone L f)) →
      ∃x:A, (∀f ∈ l, (order L (f x) x)) ∧
              ∀ y:A (∀f ∈ l, (order L (f y) y)) ⇒ (order L x y)        (5)
```

This type means that any application of `lfp_list` to a list of functions f_i must be accompanied by a proof of the monotonicity of each f_i. Read on a proof-theoretic level, it states that from the proofs of monotonicity of the f_i, we can prove the existence of a least common pre-fixpoint for all of the f_i. This function will be used as a generic constraint solver in Section 6.

4 Constructive Constraints

We now turn to the problem of building an analyser that implements the flow analysis from Section 2. The development will be structured into three phases:

1. The definition of a set of constraints associated to each instruction.
2. The proof of correctness of these constraints wrt. the Carmel semantics.
3. The building of an analyser `analyse` that computes an abstract state verifying all the constraints generated for a given program.

Formally, we have to prove the two following theorems:

$$\forall P : \text{Program}, \widehat{\Sigma} : \widehat{\text{State}}_P.\ \texttt{verifyAllConstraints}_P(\widehat{\Sigma}) \Rightarrow [\![P]\!] \sim \widehat{\Sigma}$$
$$\forall P : \text{Program},\ \texttt{verifyAllConstraints}_P(\texttt{analyse}_P)$$

where $[\![P]\!]$ denotes the set of reachable states of program P. These two theorems imply the correctness of the analyser:

$$[\![P]\!] \sim \texttt{analyse}_P$$

When formalising the analysis, several representations of the constraints are possible. It turns out that for the correctness proof (Phase 2) it is more convenient to emphasize the *order relation* aspect of the constraints, whereas the construction of an effective analyser (Phase 3) requires to emphasize the explicit *computational content* of the constraints. This is why an intermediate representation of constraints is defined in Phase 1, which allows for both interpretations and leaves room for reuse in other analyses. Sections 4, 5 and 6 describe the three phases.

4.1 An Intermediate Representation for Constraints

To motivate the format chosen here for representing constraints, note that the constraints have three ingredients: a start adress ad_1 and an end address ad_2 of the data flow, the part of the state that is being affected, and the transformation F that is applied to the data that flows. For example, for the constraint (3) from Section 2.1 that corresponds to the instruction push c, we have $ad_1 = pc, ad_2 = pc + 1$, and $F = \lambda\hat{S}.\widehat{\text{push}}(c, \hat{S})$.

This naturally leads to an inductive data type of the form

$$\begin{array}{l}\texttt{type Constraint}_P = \\ \quad \texttt{| S2S of Address * Address * } (\widehat{\texttt{Stack}}_P \to \widehat{\texttt{Stack}}_P) \\ \quad \texttt{| L2L of Address * Address * } (\widehat{\texttt{LocalVar}}_P \to \widehat{\texttt{LocalVar}}_P)\ldots\end{array} \quad (6)$$

where each constructor represents a type of dependency between components of the abstract state. For example, S2S is a constructor to express a constraint on an abstract stack which depends on another abstract stack. For the particular analysis discussed here eleven constructors were employed. A constraint, *i.e.*, an object of type $\texttt{Constraint}_P$, is given the following *relational* interpretation:

$$\mathcal{R}[\![\cdot]\!] : \texttt{constraint}_P \to \left(\widehat{\text{State}}_P \to \text{Prop}\right)$$

For the constructors S2S and L2L the relational interpretation is

$$\mathcal{R}[\![(\texttt{S2S}\ ad_1\ ad_2\ F)]\!](\hat{H}, \hat{L}, \hat{S}) := F(\hat{S}(ad_1)) \sqsubseteq \hat{S}(ad_2)$$
$$\mathcal{R}[\![(\texttt{L2L}\ ad_1\ ad_2\ F)]\!](\hat{H}, \hat{L}, \hat{S}) := F(\hat{L}(ad_1)) \sqsubseteq \hat{L}(ad_2)$$

The alternative, *functional* view of constraints is given in Section 6.

4.2 Building the Intermediate Representation

As seen in Section 2.1 each instruction produces a set of constraints, *e.g.*, Formulas (3) and (4) for the `push` instruction. Thus, we define a function `Flow`, which for each instruction, returns the corresponding list of constraints in a syntax of the form (6).

However, defining this function is slightly complicated by the fact that the constraints make reference to actual program points of the form (m, pc) of the program P being analysed. In a paper-and-pencil proof, every instance of (m, pc) implicitly refers to a valid program point. In a formal proof however, this fact must be stated explicitly. In a dependently-typed framework, the constraint generation will thus be parameterised by the program being analysed, yielding a function $\texttt{Flow}_P$ which takes as argument an address (m, pc) in the program P and generates the constraints corresponding to the type of instruction at (m, pc). Continuing with the `push` instruction, the corresponding code part of $\texttt{Flow}_P$ is:

$$
\begin{array}{l}
\texttt{Flow}_P \;:=\; \lambda\texttt{(m,pc)} \\
\quad \texttt{Case instructionAt}_P\ \texttt{(m,pc) of} \\
\qquad \texttt{| (push } c\texttt{)} \rightarrow \texttt{(S2S (m,pc) (m,pc+1)}\ \lambda\hat{S}.\ \widehat{\texttt{push}}\left(\hat{c},\hat{S}\right)\texttt{) ::} \\
\qquad\qquad\qquad\qquad \texttt{(L2L (m,pc) (m,pc+1)}\ \lambda\hat{L}.\ \hat{L}\texttt{)} \\
\qquad \ldots
\end{array}
$$

We now define what it means for an abstract state $\widehat{\Sigma}$ to verify all the constraints of a program P. With Addr_P denoting the set of addresses appearing in P, and $\mathcal{R}[\![\cdot]\!]$ the relational interpretation of constraints defined in Section 4.1:

$$\texttt{verifyAllConstraints}_P(\widehat{\Sigma}):\quad \forall (m, pc) : \mathrm{Addr}_P . \forall c \in \texttt{Flow}_P(m, pc).\ \mathcal{R}[\![c]\!](\widehat{\Sigma})$$

Our constraint solver imposes two well-formedness properties on the constraints:

Monotonicity of the functional part of the constraints must be proved. This is easy once monotonicity of the basic operators of the lattices has been proved in the lattice library, and does not depend on the constraint solving technique.

Address validity of the constraints must also be proved to ensure that each address occurring in a constraint is in the range imposed by the different array lattices (*i.e.*, the `max` parameter, cf. Section 3.1). This is necessary to ensure that all operations made on array elements (reading, writing) are valid.

5 Correctness

The analysis is correct if every abstract state $\widehat{\Sigma}$ satisfying all the constraints of the analysis, is an approximation of the reachable states $[\![P]\!]$ of the program:

$$\forall P : \mathrm{Program}, \widehat{\Sigma} : \widehat{\mathrm{State}}_P .\ \texttt{verifyAllConstraints}_P(\widehat{\Sigma}) \Rightarrow [\![P]\!] \sim \widehat{\Sigma} \qquad (7)$$

The implication (7) has been proved in Coq by well-founded induction on the length of the program executions. The base step is trivial. The induction step depends on whether the last instruction is `return` or some other instruction.

5.1 Induction Step: The Non-return Instructions

Let $addr(\sigma)$ denote the address (m, pc) of a state σ (cf. Section 2), and

$$\sigma \vdash_P \widehat{\Sigma}: \quad \forall c \in \texttt{Flow}_P(addr(\sigma)).\ \mathcal{R}[\![c]\!](\widehat{\Sigma}) \tag{8}$$

the predicate expressing the fact that the abstract state $\widehat{\Sigma}$ satisfies all the constraints at address $addr(\sigma)$ of program P. Moreover, for I an instruction, let $\rightarrow_I$ denote the transition relation of I (examples of which have been given in Section 2). The general form of the induction step for an arbitrary Carmel instruction I, except **return**, is of the form (9) defined below.

$$\forall P : \text{Program}, \forall \sigma \in [\![P]\!], \forall \widehat{\Sigma} : \widehat{\text{State}}_P.\ \sigma \sim \widehat{\Sigma} \wedge \sigma \vdash_P \widehat{\Sigma} \Longrightarrow \\ \forall \sigma' : \text{State}. \sigma \rightarrow_I \sigma' \Rightarrow \sigma' \sim \widehat{\Sigma} \tag{9}$$

That is, if a state σ is approximated by an abstract state $\widehat{\Sigma}$ that satisfies all the constraints of σ, and if, by performing instruction I, the state σ evolves into σ', then σ' is approximated by $\widehat{\Sigma}$ as well. We now sketch the proof of (9).

1. A Coq tactic unfolds the definition of the transition rule for instruction I.
2. Then, another tactic unfolds the definitions of $\sigma \sim \widehat{\Sigma}$ and $\sigma \vdash_P \widehat{\Sigma}$ and automatically turns them into hypotheses of the current Coq goal[1]. For example, if $\sigma = \langle\langle h, \langle m, pc, l, s\rangle :: sf\rangle\rangle$, $\widehat{\Sigma} = (\widehat{H}, \widehat{L}, \widehat{S})$, and $I =$ **push** c then the following hypotheses are generated:

$$s \sim \widehat{S}(m, pc), \quad \widehat{\text{push}}\left(c, \widehat{S}\,(m, pc)\right) \sqsubseteq \widehat{S}\,(m, pc+1) \tag{10}$$

3. Next, the conclusion of the Coq goal: $\sigma' \sim \widehat{\Sigma}$ — *i.e.*, the new state σ' is approximated by the abstract state $\widehat{\Sigma} = (\widehat{H}, \widehat{L}, \widehat{S})$ — is split into three subgoals, one for each of the components $(\widehat{H}, \widehat{L}, \widehat{S})$ of $\widehat{\Sigma}$.
   In the case $I =$ **push** c, the subgoal corresponding to the abstract stack $\widehat{S}$ is

$$c :: s \sim \widehat{S}(m, pc+1) \tag{11}$$

4. Finally, the subgoals generated at Step 3 are proved using the hypotheses generated at Step 2 and monotonicity of $\sim$ with respect to $\sqsubseteq$ (cf. Section 2). In the case $I =$ **push** c, the only non-trivial subgoal is represented by Formula (11) above. It is proved using the fact that $\widehat{\text{push}}$ is a correct abstraction of the concrete *push* operator "::", *i.e.*, $c :: s \sim \widehat{\text{push}}\left(c, \widehat{S}\,(m, pc)\right)$. This, together with the hypothesis (10) and the monotonicity of the approximation relation for stacks, implies the subgoal (11), and the proof is done.

[1] This tactic simulates the standard Coq *inversion* tactic for inductive datatypes.

objects used in the extracted OCAML code, and the logical fields that contain properties about the lattice. *E.g.*, the field `join` is a functional field that contains the least upper bound operator of the lattice, whereas the field `acc_property` is a logical field stating that the lattice satisfies the ascending chain condition. Only the functional fields will appear in the OCAML code of the constructed analyser, but the properties in the logical fields are used to resolve proof obligations during the construction of the analyser.

The lattice type is conveniently defined as a record type in Coq, as shown in the following Coq declaration, where details for the `order` relation and the well-foundedness of the lattice are given.

```
Record Lattice [A: Set]:  Type := {
  eq   : A → A →  Prop;
  eq_prop : ...        ;;  eq is an equivalence relation
  order : A → A →  Prop;
  order_refl : ∀x,y:A (eq x y)  ⇒ (order x y);
  order_antisym : ∀x,y:A (order x y)  ⇒ (order y x)  ⇒  (eq x y);
  order_trans : ∀x,y,z:A  (order x y)⇒  (order y z)  ⇒  (order x z);
  join : A → A → A;
  join_prop :   ;;  join is a correct binary least upper-bound
  eq_dec : A → A → bool
  eq_dec_prop : ...    ;;  eq_dec is a correct test of equality
  bottom : A;
  bottom_prop : ....    ;;  bottom is the least element
  top : A;
  top_prop : ...    top is the greatest element
  acc_property :  (well_founded A (λx,y:A¬(eq y x)∧(order y x)))
}
```

Declaring a structure of `Lattice` type will result in a series of proof obligations, one for each of the logical fields. Of these, the last property `acc_property` is the most difficult to establish. It expresses that the strict dual order is well-founded, or, in other words, that there are no infinite, ascending chains. It is the key point to prove the termination of the final analyser.

Note that our definition of the `Lattice` type includes the ascending chain condition, thus, we are not defining a lattice in general. However, for convenience the term lattice is employed for such a structure in the rest of this document.

3.1 The Lattice Library

We present here the lattices that we have developed for our analysis. The lattices are built from two base lattices using four lattice constructors. These developments are largely analysis-independent and can be reused in other contexts.

Two base lattices are defined: the flat lattice of integer constants and the lattice of finite sets over a subset $\{0,\ldots,\mathtt{max}\}$ of integers. Additionally, there are four functions to combine lattices:

```
prodLattice : (Lattice A) → (Lattice B) → (Lattice A*B)
sumLattice : (Lattice A) → (Lattice B) → (Lattice (lift A+B))
```

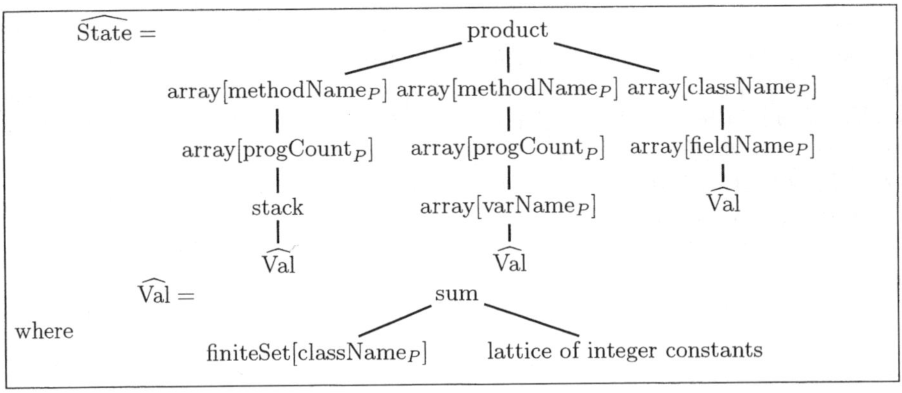

Fig. 1. The lattice of abstract states (each xX_P represents the number of distinct xX elements in program P).

```
arrayLattice : (max:nat) → (Lattice A) → (Lattice (array max A))
stackLattice : (Lattice A) → (Lattice (stack A))
```

The first two functions are the standard constructions of the cartesian product and the separate sum (disjoint union extended with a new top and bottom element) of two lattices. The `arrayLattice` function builds the type of arrays whose elements live in a lattice and whose size is bounded by a parameter `max`.

The array lattice frequently occurs in flow-sensitive analyses where the number of abstract variables depends on the program to analyse, and they are then conveniently collected in an array. An efficient implementation of arrays is therefore crucial for obtaining an efficient extracted code, and we have optimized it by using an efficient tree representation of integer maps [OG98]. Details are left out for space reasons.

The fourth constructor `stackLattice` builds the lattice of stacks of elements of type `A`. In this lattice, stacks with different sizes are incomparable. In addition to the standard lattice operations, this lattice also carries abstract versions of the usual stack operations *pop*, *push* and *top*.

The most difficult part of each lattice construction is the proof of preservation of `acc_property` (the ascending chain condition), which is essential for defining an analyser that terminates. This is essentially a termination proof, which is hard to conduct in a proof assistant because the standard techniques of structural orders or well-chosen measures do not apply in the case of lattice orders. The proof has to operate directly with the definition of a well-founded order.

However, once the preservation of the `acc_property` by the constructors (`prodLattice`, `sumLattice`, etc) is proved, the constructors can be used to combine lattices without having to prove `acc_property` for the resulting lattice.

The lattice employed in our particular analysis is shown in Figure 1. The modular construction saves a considerable amount of time and effort, *e.g.*, compared to proving `acc_property` for the lattice in Figure 1 as a whole.

To finish making the link between this result and the correctness of $\texttt{analyse}_P$ as defined by properties (13) and (14), we still have to prove the equivalence between relational and functional interpretation of constraints. Indeed, (16) deals with the functional interpretation, but the predicate `verifyAllConstraints` used in the specification of the analyser interprets constraints as relations. The following theorem establishes the equivalence of these two interpretations

$$\forall c : \texttt{Constraint}_P, \widehat{\Sigma} : \widehat{\text{State}}_P \ \mathcal{F}[\![c]\!](\widehat{\Sigma}) \sqsubseteq \widehat{\Sigma} \Leftrightarrow \mathcal{R}[\![c]\!]\widehat{\Sigma} \tag{17}$$

Note that the result depends on the validity of the addresses used in the constraints, a property that must be (and has been!) proved during the definition of $\texttt{Flow}_P$ (*cf.* Section 4).

By combining this result with (16), we finally can affirm that $\texttt{analyse}_P$ is the least solution of `verifyAllConstraints`. Thus, correctness of $\texttt{analyse}_P$ is proved.

We stress that this approach defines a methodology that remains valid for other analyses. Indeed, all proofs in this section are independent of the system of constraints defined by the user. They only depend on the different types of constraints introduced (`S2S`, `L2L`,...). As a consequence, modifications to the system of constraints only affect proofs made during Sections 4 and 5, rather than the construction and the correctness of the analyser.

7 Related Work

Proving correctness of program analyses is one of the main applications of the theory of abstract interpretation [CC77]. However, most of the existing proofs are pencil-and-paper proofs of analyses (formal specifications) and not mechanised proofs of analysers (implementations of analyses). The only attempt of formalising the theory of abstract intepretation with a proof assistant is, as far as we know, that of Monniaux [Mon98] who has built a Coq theory of Galois connections. Prost in his thesis [Pro99] conduces a theoretical study of the relation between type theory and program analysis, but this work did not lead to an implementation of a concrete analysis.

When it comes to program processing tools, mechanical verification has so far been focussed on the correctness of optimising compilers. Genet *et al.* [GJKP03] use the generic proof assistant PVS for proving the correctness of algorithms for transforming Java Card byte code into the more compact CAP format. Similar works was done by Denney [Den01], using the program extraction mechanism of Coq. These optimisations do not involve any sophisticated static analysis. Lerner *et al.* [LMC03] have developed Cobalt, a dedicated programming language for writing C program optimisers and automatically proving their soundness.

Several works on mechanical verification of program analyses have dealt with the Java byte code verifier. Barthe *et al.* [BDJ+01] have shown how to formalise the Java Card byte code verification in the proof assistant Coq by isolating the byte code verification in an executable semantics of the language. In [BDHdS01], they propose to automate the derivation of a certified verifier from a formalisation of the JCVM. Their approach does not rely on a general theory of static analysis, and is oriented towards type verification. Bertot [Ber01] used the Coq system to extract a certified bytecode analyser specialized for object initialization, but no attention has been paid to the efficiency of the analyser. In [CGQ98], Coglio *et al.* described their ongoing efforts to implement a bytecode verifier by refinement from the specification of a constraint-solving problem on lattices. Klein and Nipkow [KN02] have proved the correctness of a Java byte code verifier using the proof assistant Isabelle/HOL. In particular their work include a correctness proof of Kildall's iterative workset algorithm for solving data flow equations. They also provide a modular construction of lattices. The major difference with our approach is the use of abstract data types that are not implementable as such. Casset *et al.* [CBR02] have extracted a proof-carrying code-based on-card bytecode verifier for Java Card from a high-level specification by a succession of refinement steps using the B technique. The development required the proof of thousands of proof obligations, of which several hundreds could not be dealt with automatically by the B prover. The B tool could most probably be used for building an analyzer like ours but we doubt that using B would lead to a simpler proof effort. In addition, the program extraction mechanism in B does not enjoy the same solid foundations as that of Coq. Hence our decision to base our development on Coq.

All these byte code verifiers deal with **intra**-procedural type verification. In contrast, we have also shown how to handle **inter**-procedural data flow analysis in a natural manner. This is due to the fact that we have cast our development in the general setting of Flow Logic [NN98] and constraint-based analysis. The Carmel Flow Logic analysis specified by Hansen also covers exceptions which means it is straightforward to extend our analyser to determine data flow arising from exceptions. It is not evident how such an extension would be done in the formal byte code verifier frameworks cited above.

8 Conclusion

In this paper, we have shown that it is feasible to construct a non-trivial, provably correct data flow analyzer using the program extraction mechanism of constructive logic implemented in Coq. This eliminates the gap that often exists between a paper-specification of an analysis and the analyser that is actually implemented. Our approach applies to any analysis expressed in the constraint-based Flow Logic specification framework and is hence applicable to a large variety of program analyses for different language paradigms. We have instantiated it to a data flow analysis for Java Card. To the best of our knowledge, it is the first formal construction (with proof of correctness) of a data flow analysis other than the Java byte code verifier.

The approach presented here **helps in the development of the analyser**. Formalising a program analyser in a proof assistant imposes a strict discipline that catches a certain number of bugs, including typing errors in the specification. The present development revealed several (innocuous) inaccuracies in the pencil-and-paper specifications and proof of correctness. Moreover, it pinpointed the adjustment that had been made of the actual semantics of Java Card in the correctness proof on paper—an adjustment that (as argued in Section 5.2) made the proof far simpler than a proof done against a more accurate semantics.

The **ease of use** of the approach varies. The development of the lattice library required a Coq expert to structure the proofs of the properties associated with the lattice constructors. Once this library in place, it turned out to be a relatively *straightforward* task to prove correctness of the constraint generation and to extend the constraint generation to instructions others than those originally studied. It took a Coq neophyte less than two months to complete the correctness proof, including the time and effort needed to understand the general framework of the project. Only basic features of the tool, those available in any other general-purpose theorem prover, have been employed in this development.

Concerning **efficiency**, the extracted analyser performs well, taking only a few seconds to analyse 1000 lines of bytecode. The resulting extracted program is about 2000 lines of OCAML code. The extracted version of `analyse` have now a type Program $\rightarrow \widehat{\text{State}}$ because OCAML does not have dependent types. Future work will proceed in two directions. First, it would be desirable to be able to extract a variety of sophisticated constraint solvers from proofs using the general lattice theory. Whether such detailed programming is possible at the proof level remains to be seen. Second, further automation of the proof obligations in the above-described procedure for building analysers is necessary.

References

[BDHdS01] Gilles Barthe, Guillaume Dufay, Marieke Huisman, and Simão Melo de Sousa. Jakarta: A Toolset for Reasoning about JavaCard. *Lecture Notes in Computer Science*, 2140, 2001.

[BDJ$^+$01] Gilles Barthe, Guillaume Dufay, Line Jakubiec, Bernard Serpette, and Simão Melo de Sousa. A Formal Executable Semantics of the JavaCard Platform. *Lecture Notes in Computer Science*, 2028, 2001.

[Ber01] Yves Bertot. Formalizing a JVML Verifier for Initialization in a Theorem Prover. *Lecture Notes in Computer Science*, 2102, 2001.

[CBR02] Ludovic Casset, Lilian Burdy, and Antoine Requet. Formal Development of an embedded verifier for Java Card Byte Code. In *Proc. of IEEE Int. Conference on Dependable Systems & Networks (DSN)*, 2002.

[CC77] Patrick Cousot and Radhia Cousot. Abstract interpretation: A unified lattice model for static analysis of programs by construction of approximations of fixpoints. In *Proc. of 4th ACM Symposium on Principles of Programming Languages*, pages 238–252. ACM Press, New York, 1977.

[CGQ98] Alessandro Coglio, Allen Goldberg, and Zhenyu Qian. Towards a Provably-Correct Implementation of the JVM Bytecode Verifier. In *Proc. OOPSLA'98 Workshop on Formal Underpinnings of Java*, 1998.

[Den01] Ewen Denney. The synthesis of a Java Card tokenisation algorithm. In *Proc. of 16th Int. Conf. on Automated Software Engineering (ASE 2001)*, pages 43–50. IEEE Press, 2001.

[GJKP03] Thomas Genet, Thomas Jensen, Vikash Kodati, and David Pichardie. A Java Card CAP converter in PVS. In *Proc. of 2nd International Workshop on Compiler Optimization Meets Compiler Verification (COCV 2003)*, 2003.

[Han02] René Rydhof Hansen. Flow Logic for Carmel. Technical Report SECSAFE-IMM-001, Danish Technical University, 2002.

[KN02] Gerwin Klein and Tobias Nipkow. Verified Bytecode Verifiers. *Theoretical Computer Science*, 298(3):583–626, 2002.

[LMC03] Sorin Lerner, Todd Millstein, and Craig Chambers. Automatically proving the correctness of compiler optimizations. In *Proc. of the ACM SIGPLAN 2003 conference on Programming language design and implementation*, pages 220–231. ACM Press, 2003.

[Mar01] Renaud Marlet. Syntax of the JCVM language to be studied in the SecSafe project. Technical Report SECSAFE-TL-005, Trusted Logic SA, May 2001.

[Mon98] David Monniaux. Réalisation mécanisée d'interpréteurs abstraits. Rapport de DEA, Université Paris VII, 1998. In French.

[NN98] Hanne Riis Nielson and Flemming Nielson. Flow Logics for Constraint Based Analysis. In *Proc. CC'98*, number 1383 in Lecture Notes in Computer Science, pages 109–127. Springer-Verlag, 1998.

[OG98] Chris Okasaki and Andrew Gill. Fast mergeable integer maps. In *Workshop on ML*, pages 77–86, 1998.

[Pro99] Frédéric Prost. *Interprétation de l'analyse statique en théorie des types.* PhD thesis, École normale supérieure de Lyon, 1999. In French.

[Siv04] Igor Siveroni. Operational semantics of the Java Card Virtual Machine. *J. Logic and Automated Reasoning*, 2004. To appear.

Canonical Graph Shapes

Arend Rensink*

Department of Computer Science, University of Twente
P.O. Box 217, 7500 AE, The Netherlands
rensink@cs.utwente.nl

Abstract. Graphs are an intuitive model for states of a (software) system that include pointer structures — for instance, object-oriented programs. However, a naive encoding results in large individual states and large, or even unbounded, state spaces. As usual, some form of abstraction is necessary in order to arrive at a tractable model.
In this paper we propose a decidable fragment of first-order graph logic that we call *local shape logic* (LSL) as a possible abstraction mechanism, inspired by previous work of Sagiv, Reps and Wilhelm. An LSL formula constrains the multiplicities of nodes and edges in state graphs; abstraction is achieved by reasoning not about individual, concrete state graphs but about their characteristic shape properties. We go on to define the concept of the *canonical shape* of a state graph, which is expressed in a *monomorphic* sub-fragment of LSL, for which we define a graphical representation. We show that the canonical shapes give rise to an automatic finite abstraction of the state space of a software system, and we give an upper bound to the size of this abstract state space.

1 Introduction

This paper is part of an investigation into the use of graphs as models of system states, for the (eventual) purpose of system verification, especially of software. In this approach, an individual system state (state snapshot) is modeled as an *edge-labeled graph*, in which the nodes roughly stand for the entities (records, objects) present in the state and the edges for properties or fields (attributes, variables) of those resources. The dynamic behavior of a system is modeled as a *transition system* in which the states are graphs in the above sense.

As usual in the context of verification, the main problem is *state space explosion*; i.e., the effect that, even for small systems, the number of states to be analyzed exceeds all reasonable bounds. The most promising solution technique to cope with this is *abstraction*, meaning that information is discarded from the model, after which it can be represented more compactly — usually at the cost of either soundness or completeness of the verification. In the context of graphs, we have previously studied abstraction techniques in [6,7]. The idea there is to have one or more nodes whose cardinality is not *a priori* fixed but may grow

* The work in this paper took place in the GROOVE project (Graphs for Object-Oriented Verification), funded under the Dutch NWO grant 612.000.314

D.A. Schmidt (Ed.): ESOP 2004, LNCS 2986, pp. 401–415, 2004.

unboundedly in the course of system execution. This idea can be found also in *shape graphs*, as defined by Sagiv, Reps and Wilhelm in [18]. There, too, some graph nodes (called *summary nodes*) stand for multiple instances; furthermore, shape graphs contain additional information about whether an edge is necessarily there for every instance of a given node and whether outgoing edges may be pointing to (i.e., sharing) the same node instance.

The current paper is a consequence of our earlier efforts, inspired by the work on shape graphs. We define a theory of graph shapes by formulating additional information about the node and edge multiplicity as a constraint in what we call *local shape logic* (LSL). LSL is essentially a fragment of typed first-order logic, where the typing is controlled by a *type graph*. The definition of LSL is parameterized by a *multiplicity algebra*, which partially controls the expressiveness of the logic. We show LSL to be decidable.

The combination of a type graph and a shape constraint gives rise to a (generalized) shape graph. Thus, each shape graph defines a set of state graphs, viz. those instances of the type graph that satisfy the shape constraint. Unfortunately, LSL formulae in general lack the appealing pictorial representation of graphs. To alleviate this, we define a graphical representation of a so-called *monomorphic* fragment of LSL, and we show that any shape graph is equivalent to a set of monomorphic shape graphs. Finally, we define a restricted class of *canonical* monomorphic shapes, with the property that there is an automatic abstraction from state graphs to canonical shapes. We show that the set of distinct canonical shape graphs is finite, and we give an upper bound for its size.

The paper is structured as follows: Sect. 2 contains basic definitions, in Sect. 3 we introduce local shape logic and show its decidability; and in Sect. 4 we discuss (monomorphic) shape graphs. Sect. 5 concludes and discusses related work. A more extensive exposition of the material presented here, including proofs of the main theorems, can be found in the full report version: see [16].

2 Graphs and Type Graphs

We represent states as graphs. Nodes can be thought of as *locations* or *objects*, and edges are used to represent *variables*, in particular *references*. For the formal definition, we assume the existence of a global set $\mathbf{N}$ of *nodes*, ranged over by u, v, w; subsets of $\mathbf{N}$ are denoted N, V, W. We use the symbol $\perp$ ($\notin \mathbf{N}$) to denote an *undefined* node; for an arbitrary set $N \subseteq \mathbf{N}$ we write $N_\perp$ to denote $N \cup \{\perp\}$. We also assume a global set $\mathbf{L}$ of *labels*, ranged over by a, b, c.

Definition 1 (graph). *A* graph G *is a tuple* (N, E), *where* $N \subseteq \mathbf{N}$ *is a finite set of* nodes, *and* $E \subseteq N \times \mathbf{L} \times N_\perp$ *is a finite set of* edges.

It follows that a graph consists of binary edges (v, a, w) with $w \in \mathbf{N}$ but also *unary* edges $(v, a, \perp)$. We also refer to unary edges as *node properties* or *node predicates*. For most purposes unary and binary edges will be treated uniformly. We use $\mathbf{G}$ to denote the set of all graphs, ranged over by G, H. Given a graph G, we denote the node and edge sets of G by N_G, E_G, respectively. We drop the subscripts $_G$ when clear from the context.

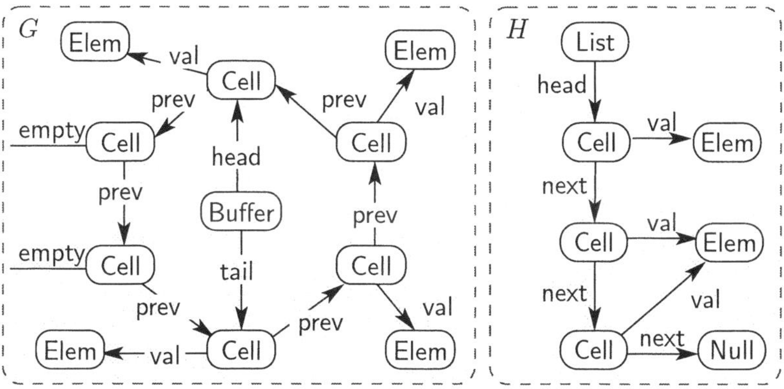

Fig. 1. State snapshots of a circular buffer and a linked list

As usual, we draw graphs by showing nodes as boxes and binary edges as arrows between them. Unary edges are represented by lines without arrow heads or target nodes, or by writing their labels inside the source nodes.

Example 1. Fig. 1 shows two state graphs. The graph G on the left hand side models a circular buffer, as a backwards-linked list of cells of which some have values (modeled by val-labeled edges to the nodes representing the respective values) and the others are empty (modeled by empty-labeled unary edges). One of the cells is designated head to indicate that this is the head of the buffer, whose value is to be retrieved next; in contrast, the tail cell contains the newest value. Buffer, Cell and Elem are node predicates used to reflect the types of the nodes. The right hand side graph H depicts a linked list, using a similar encoding.

The effects of execution steps are modeled by modifications to the state graphs, resulting in new graphs which differ (locally) from the original ones. This gives rise to a transition system in which the states are graphs and the transitions graph transformations. For instance, the primary operations upon a circular buffer are the insertion and retrieval of values: these result in changes in the neighborhood of the tail- and head-edges, which remove empty-predicates and add val-edges and Elem-nodes. See [16] for further details.

The particular choice of node identities in a given graph is regarded as incidental and not as part of the structure: they only serve to distinguish the nodes from one another. In figures we usually omit the node identities altogether; the nodes are then already distinguished by their position. The same principle can be found also in the notion of graph *morphism*: these preserve only the structurally important information.

Definition 2 (graph morphism). *Given two graphs G, H, a* graph morphism *f from G to H is a function $f : N_G \to N_H$, strictly extended to $\bot$, such that $(f(p), a, f(q)) \in E_H$ for all $(p, a, q) \in E_G$.*

$f : G \to H$ denotes that f is a morphism from G to H. A morphism f is called *injective* [*surjective, bijective*] if f is an injective [surjective, bijective] function both on nodes and edges.

In the following we also need the following (standard) notions of graph *partitioning*: for a given graph $G = (N, E)$, every node equivalence relation

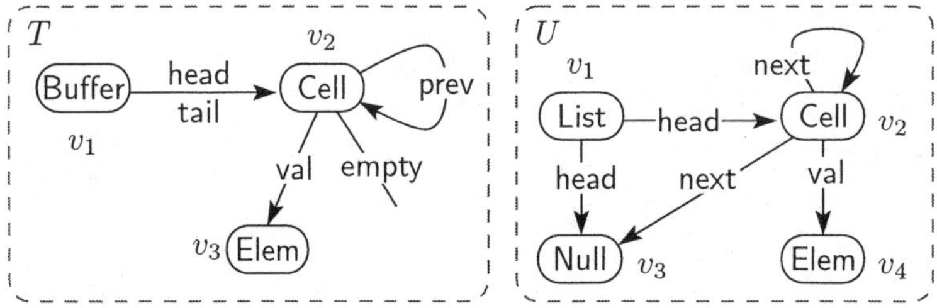

Fig. 2. Type graphs T for circular buffers and U for linked lists

$\sim \subseteq N \times N$ gives rise to a partitioned graph $G/\sim = (N/\sim, E/\sim)$ where

$$N/\sim = \{[v]_\sim \mid v \in N\}$$
$$E/\sim = \{[v]_\sim, a, [w]_\sim \mid (v, a, w) \in E\}$$

(in which, as usual, $[v]_\sim = \{w \in N \mid v \sim w\}$ for all $v \in N$; so $[\bot]_\sim = \bot$). Furthermore, we use $\pi_\sim : G \to G/\sim$ to denote the (surjective) morphism defined by $\pi_\sim(v) = [v]_\sim$ for all $v \in N$. Also, for an arbitrary partitioning Π of the set of nodes N and an arbitrary node $v \in N_\bot$, we use $[v]_\Pi$ to denote the unique $V \in \Pi$ such that $v \in V$; so $[\bot]_\Pi = \bot$.

The graphs used to model the states of a given software system are, of course, not arbitrary. For one thing, not all edges or combinations of edges are allowed. To take the circular buffer G of Fig. 1, there are only eight labels; Buffer, Cell and Elem only occur as node predicates of mutually exclusive nodes; prev-edges only occur between Cell-nodes; et cetera. Such information can be captured partially using *graph typings.*

Definition 3 (typing). *Let $G \in \mathbf{G}$ be arbitrary. A* typing *of G is a morphism $\tau : G \to T$, where $T \in \mathbf{G}$ is called a* type graph.

We call T a *type of* G and G an *instance of* T. We use $\mathbf{G}^T$ to denote the set of instances of a graph T. For instance, Fig. 2 shows types for the graphs in Fig. 1.

3 Shape Logic

The notion of graph typing is rather weak: the existence of a morphism from a would-be instance graph to a would-be type graph can only forbid but never enforce the presence of certain edges in the instance. To take the type graph U in Fig. 2, the *intention* is that any instance obeys the following structural properties (among others). Although H in Fig. 1 indeed satisfies these intended properties, U has many instances that do not.

1. Every List-labeled node has precisely one outgoing head-edge, to the first element of the corresponding list or to a Null-node;
2. There is precisely one Null-node;
3. Every Cell-node has precisely one outgoing next-edge, either to another Cell-node or to a Null-node;
4. Every Cell-node has either one incoming next-edge or one incoming head-edge (so Cell-nodes are not shared).

To strengthen the notion of typing we need to formulate additional constraints on instances. For this purpose we define a *shape logic*, SL^T, which is a first-order graph logic, defined relative to a type graph T. Later on (Sect. 3.2) we restrict this to a fragment of which we show decidability. We assume a countable set of variables $\mathbf{V}$. Formulae of SL^T are generated by the following grammar:

$$\phi \ ::= \ \mathbf{tt} \mid x = x \mid x \stackrel{a}{-} \mid x \xrightarrow{a} x \mid \neg\phi \mid \phi \vee \phi \mid \forall x{:}\, v.\, \phi \ .$$

In this grammar, $a \in \mathbf{L}$ denotes an arbitrary label, $x \in \mathbf{V}$ an arbitrary (node) variable and $v \in N_T$ a node of the type graph T. We employ the usual abbreviations $\phi \Rightarrow \psi$, $\phi \wedge \psi$, $\exists x{:}\, v.\, \phi$, $\exists! x{:}\, v.\, \phi$ and $\mathbf{tt}$.

The predicates $x \stackrel{a}{-}$ and $x \xrightarrow{a} y$ express that there exists a (unary resp. binary) a-labeled edge in a would-be instance of T, from the node denoted by x and leading (in the case of a binary edge) to the node denoted by y. It is sometimes convenient to write $x \xrightarrow{a} \bot$ rather than $x \stackrel{a}{-}$.

We consider only formulae that are *well-typed* according to T, in the sense that each free variable x in a formula has an associated type node $v_x \in N_T$ such that $(v_x, a, \bot) \in E_T$ for all propositions $x \stackrel{a}{-}$ and $(v_x, a, v_y) \in E_T$ for all propositions $x \xrightarrow{a} y$. We do not work this out formally here.

Example 2. Using SL we can give a much tighter characterization of lists than through type graphs. Given U in Fig. 2, consider the following SL^U-constraints:

$$\begin{aligned} &\forall x{:}\, v_1.\, x \stackrel{\mathsf{List}}{-} \wedge ((\exists! y{:}\, v_2.\, x \xrightarrow{\mathsf{head}} y \wedge \nexists y{:}\, v_3.\, x \xrightarrow{\mathsf{head}} y) \\ &\qquad \vee (\exists! y{:}\, v_3.\, x \xrightarrow{\mathsf{head}} y \wedge \nexists y{:}\, v_2.\, x \xrightarrow{\mathsf{head}} y)) \end{aligned} \tag{1}$$

$$(\exists! y{:}\, v_3.\, \mathbf{tt}) \wedge (\forall x{:}\, v_3.\, x \stackrel{\mathsf{Null}}{-}) \tag{2}$$

$$\forall x{:}\, v_2.\, (\exists! y{:}\, v_2.\, x \xrightarrow{\mathsf{next}} y \wedge \nexists y{:}\, v_3.\, x \xrightarrow{\mathsf{next}} y) \vee (\exists! y{:}\, v_3.\, x \xrightarrow{\mathsf{next}} y \wedge \nexists y{:}\, v_2.\, x \xrightarrow{\mathsf{next}} y) \tag{3}$$

$$\forall x{:}\, v_2.\, (\exists y{:}\, v_1.\, y \xrightarrow{\mathsf{head}} x \wedge \nexists y{:}\, v_2.\, y \xrightarrow{\mathsf{next}} x) \vee (\nexists y{:}\, v_1.\, y \xrightarrow{\mathsf{head}} x \wedge \exists! y{:}\, v_2.\, y \xrightarrow{\mathsf{next}} x) \tag{4}$$

$$\exists x{:}\, v_4.\, \nexists y{:}\, v_2.\, y \xrightarrow{\mathsf{val}} x \tag{5}$$

Constraints (1)–(4) precisely capture the list properties enumerated above. On the other hand, (5) expresses that there exists an Elem-node *not* reachable from a Cell-node; this is *not* satisfied by the U-typing of H.

Note that we can *not* express in SL that every v_2-instance should be connected by a sequence of next-edges to a v_3-instance. This is a consequence of the inability of first-order graph logic to express connectedness (see, e.g., Courcelle [5]).

Example 3. Assume an additional edge (v_4, leq, v_4) in U of Fig. 2, modeling a pre-order $<$ over Elem-nodes; that is, $(v, \mathsf{leq}, w) \in E$ implies $v < w$. The following constraints express that $<$ is transitive and Cell-values are in ascending order:

$$\forall x{:}\, v_4.\, \forall y{:}\, v_4.\, \forall z{:}\, v_4.\, x \xrightarrow{\mathsf{leq}} y \wedge y \xrightarrow{\mathsf{leq}} z \Rightarrow x \xrightarrow{\mathsf{leq}} z \tag{6}$$

$$\forall c_1{:}\, v_2.\, \forall c_2{:}\, v_2.\, \forall x_1{:}\, v_4.\, \forall x_1{:}\, v_4.\, c_1 \xrightarrow{\mathsf{next}} c_2 \wedge c_1 \xrightarrow{\mathsf{val}} x_1 \wedge c_2 \xrightarrow{\mathsf{val}} x_2 \Rightarrow x_1 \xrightarrow{\mathsf{leq}} x_2 \tag{7}$$

The meaning of a shape constraint is defined as the set of typings that satisfy it. Formally, satisfaction of a formula $\phi \in \mathsf{SL}^T$ is defined by a ternary predicate $\tau, \theta \models \phi$, where $\tau{:}\, G \to T$ is a typing and $\theta{:}\, \mathit{fv}(\phi) \to N_G$ a valuation of the free variables of ϕ (extended strictly to $\bot$) such that $\tau(\theta(x)) = v_x$ for all $x \in fv(\phi)$. The following rules, plus the obvious ones for **tt**, $\vee$ and $\neg$, define $\models$ ($\theta\{v/x\}$ denotes the valuation that maps x to v and equals θ elsewhere):

$$\tau, \theta \models x = y \quad \text{if } \theta(x) = \theta(y)$$
$$\tau, \theta \models x \xrightarrow{a} y \quad \text{if } (\theta(x), a, \theta(y)) \in E_G$$
$$\tau, \theta \models \forall x{:}\, v.\, \phi \text{ if } \tau, \theta\{w/x\} \models \phi \text{ for all } w \in \tau^{-1}(v).$$

Unfortunately, although shape logic clearly strengthens the notion of typing as intended, it does too much of that. Being a (non-monadic) first order logic, SL is not decidable, which is necessary if it is to be used for verification. Instead, we define a reduced fragment which only allows to express *local* shape properties: *multiplicities* of single node instances, and of their incoming and outgoing edges.

3.1 Multiplicities

A multiplicity is an abstract indication the cardinality of a given set; for instance, the set of instances of a given (type) node or the set of edges leaving a node.

Definition 4. *A* multiplicity algebra *is a tuple* $\langle \mathbf{M}, \_ : \_, \bigsqcap, \mathbf{0}, \mathbf{1} \rangle$ *where*

- $\mathbf{M}$ *is a set of* multiplicities*;*
- $\_ : \_ \subseteq \mathbb{N} \times \mathbf{M}$ *is* membership. *For* $\mu \in \mathbf{M}$ *we denote* $\mathbb{N}^\mu = \{m \in \mathbb{N} \mid m : \mu\}$*;*
- $\bigsqcap$: $2^\mathbf{M} \to \mathbf{M}$ *is* intersection, *such that* $\mathbb{N}^{\bigsqcap M} = \bigcap_{\mu \in M} \mathbb{N}^\mu$.
- $\mathbf{0} \in \mathbf{M}$ *is the* zero multiplicity, *such that* $\mathbb{N}^\mathbf{0} = \{0\}$*;*
- $\mathbf{1} \in \mathbf{M}$ *is the* singular multiplicity, *such that* $\mathbb{N}^\mathbf{1} = \{1\}$.

It can be deduced that $\mathbf{M}$ also contains the *inconsistent multiplicity* $\bot = \bigsqcap \mathbf{M}$ and a *universal multiplicity* $\top = \bigsqcap \emptyset$ (thus $\mathbb{N}^\bot = \emptyset$ and $\mathbb{N}^\top = \mathbb{N}$). Some derived concepts (where $\mu, \mu_1, \mu_2 \in \mathbf{M}$ are arbitrary and V is an arbitrary set):

- Lower bounds $\lfloor \mu \rfloor = \min \mathbb{N}^\mu$ (where $\min \emptyset = \omega$);
- Upper bounds $\lceil \mu \rceil = \max \mathbb{N}^\mu$ (where $\max \mathbb{N} = \omega$ and $\max \emptyset = 0$);
- Multiplicity addition $\mu_1 \oplus \mu_2 = \bigsqcap \{\mu \in \mathbf{M} \mid m_1{:}\mu_1 \wedge m_2{:}\mu_2 \Rightarrow m_1{+}m_2 : \mu\}$;
- A partial multiplicity ordering $\mu_1 \sqsubseteq \mu_2 \Leftrightarrow \mu_1 \sqcap \mu_2 = \mu_1$;
- Set multiplicity $\#_\mathbf{M} V = \bigsqcap \{\mu \in \mathbf{M} \mid \#V : \mu\}$ (where $\#V$ is V's cardinality).

It follows that $\mathbb{N}^{\mu_1 \oplus \mu_2} \supseteq \mathbb{N}^{\mu_1} + \mathbb{N}^{\mu_2}$ (where addition is extended pointwise to sets) and $\mu_1 \sqsubseteq \mu_2$ if and only if $\mathbb{N}^{\mu_1} \subseteq \mathbb{N}^{\mu_2}$.

- We call $\mathbf{M}$ *interval based* if $\mathbb{N}^\mu = \{i \in \mathbb{N} \mid \lfloor \mu \rfloor \le i \le \lceil \mu \rceil\}$ for all $\mu \in \mathbf{M}$.
- We say that $\mathbf{M}$ has *collective complements* if for all $\mu \in \mathbf{M}$, there is a set $\bar{\mu} \subseteq \mathbf{M}$ such that $\mu \sqcap \nu = \bot$ for all $\nu \in \bar{\mu}$, and $\mathbb{N}^\mu \cup \bigcup_{\nu \in \bar{\mu}} \mathbb{N}^\nu = \mathbb{N}$.

Henceforth, we only consider interval-based multiplicity algebras. In examples we will use, apart from the multiplicities enforced by the definition, $\uparrow$ for *at least one* and $\Uparrow$ for *more than one* (hence $\mathbb{N}^\uparrow = \{1, \ldots\}$ and $\mathbb{N}^\Uparrow = \{2, \ldots\}$). Note that $\{\bot, \mathbf{0}, \mathbf{1}, \uparrow, \Uparrow, \top\}$ has collective complements; in particular, $\bar{\mathbf{0}} = \uparrow$ and $\bar{\mathbf{1}} = \{\mathbf{0}, \Uparrow\}$. Membership, addition and intersection for this set are shown in Table 1.

Example 4. The multiplicities in the UML are ranges $i..j$ where $i \in \mathbb{N}$ and $j \in \mathbb{N} \cup \{*\}$ with $i \le j$ — where $*$ denotes "arbitrarily many" and satisfies $k < *$ and $*{+}k = k{+}* = *$ for all $k \in \mathbb{N}$. After adding $\bot$, this gives rise to the *largest* interval based multiplicity algebra.

Table 1. Multiplicity membership, addition and ordering

$m : \_$	condition
$\top$	**tt**
$\Uparrow$	$m > 1$
$\uparrow$	$m > 0$
$\mathbf{1}$	$m = 1$
$\mathbf{0}$	$m = 0$
$\bot$	**ff**

$\oplus$	$\top$	$\Uparrow$	$\uparrow$	$\mathbf{1}$	$\mathbf{0}$	$\bot$
$\top$	$\top$	$\Uparrow$	$\uparrow$	$\uparrow$	$\top$	$\bot$
$\Uparrow$	$\Uparrow$	$\Uparrow$	$\Uparrow$	$\Uparrow$	$\Uparrow$	$\bot$
$\uparrow$	$\uparrow$	$\Uparrow$	$\Uparrow$	$\Uparrow$	$\uparrow$	$\bot$
$\mathbf{1}$	$\uparrow$	$\Uparrow$	$\Uparrow$	$\Uparrow$	$\mathbf{1}$	$\bot$
$\mathbf{0}$	$\top$	$\Uparrow$	$\uparrow$	$\mathbf{1}$	$\mathbf{0}$	$\bot$
$\bot$	$\bot$	$\bot$	$\bot$	$\bot$	$\bot$	$\bot$

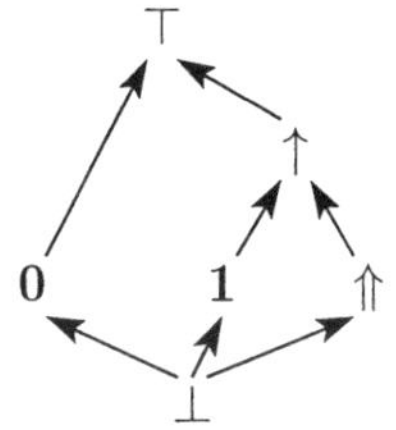

3.2 Local Shape Logic

On the basis of a multiplicity algebra we now define *local shape logic*, LSL^T, as the set of formulae ϕ generated by the following grammar:

$$\xi ::= v \mid \xrightarrow{a} v \mid \xleftarrow{a} v \mid \overset{a}{-} .$$
$$\phi ::= \mathbf{tt} \mid {}^{\mu}[\xi] \mid \neg\phi \mid \phi \vee \phi \mid \forall_v \phi .$$

ξ ranges over (node or edge set) *expressions*: v stands for the set of instances of the type node v ($\in N_T$); $\xrightarrow{a} v$ stands for the set of a-labeled edges from the current node to some instance of v; $\xleftarrow{a} v$ is the dual, expressing the set of a-labeled edges from some instance of v to the current node; and $\overset{a}{-}$ stands for the (empty or singleton) set of a-labeled unary edges from the current node.

The formula ${}^{\mu}[\xi]$ expresses that the set denoted by ξ has multiplicity μ ($\in \mathbf{M}$), and $\forall_v \phi$ expresses that ϕ holds for all *instances* of v. We write $\exists_v \phi$ for the dual of $\forall_v \phi$. The following example gives an impression of the scope of LSL^T.

Example 5. The constraints in Ex. 2 have equivalent counterparts in LSL^T:

(1′) $\forall_{v_1}({}^{\uparrow}[\overset{\mathsf{List}}{-}] \wedge (({}^{\mathbf{1}}[\xrightarrow{\mathsf{head}} v_2] \wedge {}^{\mathbf{0}}[\xrightarrow{\mathsf{head}} v_3]) \vee ({}^{\mathbf{0}}[\xrightarrow{\mathsf{head}} v_2] \wedge {}^{\mathbf{1}}[\xrightarrow{\mathsf{head}} v_3])))$
(2′) ${}^{\mathbf{1}}[v_3] \wedge \forall_{v_3} {}^{\uparrow}[\overset{\mathsf{Null}}{-}]$
(3′) $\forall_{v_2}(({}^{\mathbf{1}}[\xrightarrow{\mathsf{next}} v_2] \wedge {}^{\mathbf{0}}[\xrightarrow{\mathsf{next}} v_3]) \vee ({}^{\mathbf{0}}[\xrightarrow{\mathsf{next}} v_2] \wedge {}^{\mathbf{1}}[\xrightarrow{\mathsf{next}} v_3]))$
(4′) $\forall_{v_2}(({}^{\mathbf{1}}[\xleftarrow{\mathsf{head}} v_1] \wedge {}^{\mathbf{0}}[\xleftarrow{\mathsf{next}} v_2]) \vee ({}^{\mathbf{0}}[\xleftarrow{\mathsf{head}} v_1] \wedge {}^{\mathbf{1}}[\xleftarrow{\mathsf{next}} v_2]))$
(5′) $\exists_{v_4} {}^{\mathbf{0}}[\xleftarrow{\mathsf{val}} v_2]$

On the other hand, the constraints in Ex. 3 do *not* have an equivalent counterpart in LSL^T. Informally, the reason is that these constraints express structural properties involving more than two nodes at a time.

Clearly, LSL^T formulae can be regarded as sugared SL^T-formulae. We give a direct semantics for LSL^T, shown in [16] to coincide with the SL^T-semantics of the de-sugared formulae. The meaning of expressions ξ is given by the following function, where $\tau\colon G \to T$ is a typing and $u \in N_G$:

$$\begin{aligned}
[\![\xrightarrow{a} v]\!]_{\tau,u} &= \{(u, a, w) \in E_G \mid v = \tau(w)\} \\
[\![\xleftarrow{a} v]\!]_{\tau,u} &= \{(w, a, u) \in E_G \mid v = \tau(w)\} \\
[\![\overset{a}{-}]\!]_{\tau,u} &= \{(u, a, \bot) \in E_G\} \\
[\![v]\!]_{\tau,u} &= \{w \in N_G \mid v = \tau(w)\} .
\end{aligned}$$

We now define a satisfaction relation $\tau, u \models_{\mathsf{LSL}} \phi$ for $\phi \in \mathsf{LSL}^T$. The rules for negation and disjunction are as always; we just show the special constructors.

$$\begin{array}{ll} \tau, u \models_{\mathsf{LSL}} {}^{\mu}[\xi] & \text{if } \#[\![\xi]\!]_{\tau,u} : \mu \\ \tau, u \models_{\mathsf{LSL}} \forall_v \phi & \text{if } \tau, w \models \phi \text{ for all } w \in \tau^{-1}(v) \ . \end{array}$$

Henceforth, we will drop the suffix $_{\mathsf{LSL}}$. Some notational shorthand for LSL:

– ${}^{\mu}[\Xi]$ for a finite set of expressions Ξ will express that the *sum* of the multiplicities of the expressions in Ξ equals μ, i.e., $\mu = \bigoplus_{\xi \in \Xi} \mu_\xi$ where for all $\xi \in \Xi$, μ_ξ is the smallest multiplicity w.r.t. $\sqsubseteq$ such that ${}^{\mu_\xi}[\xi]$. More precisely:

$${}^{\mu}[\{\xi_i\}_i] \ \equiv \ \bigvee_{\mu = \bigoplus_i \mu_i} \bigwedge_i {}^{\mu_i}[\xi_i] \ .$$

– ${}^{\mu}[\xrightarrow{a} V]$ for a finite set of nodes V is equivalent to ${}^{\mu}[\{\xrightarrow{a} v \mid v \in V\}]$ and ${}^{\mu}[\xleftarrow{a} V]$ is equivalent to ${}^{\mu}[\{\xleftarrow{a} v \mid v \in V\}]$.

For instance, ${}^{\uparrow}[\{\xi_i\}_i]$ is shorthand for $\bigvee_i ({}^{\uparrow}[\xi_i] \wedge \bigwedge_{j \neq i} {}^{\top}[\xi_j])$ and ${}^{\mathbf{1}}[\{\xi_i\}_i]$ for $\bigvee_i ({}^{\mathbf{1}}[\xi_i] \wedge \bigwedge_{j \neq i} {}^{\mathbf{0}}[\xi_j])$. Concretely, we may abbreviate constraint (4′) of Ex. 5 to $\forall_{v_2} {}^{\mathbf{1}}[\xleftarrow{\mathsf{head}} v_1 \mid \xleftarrow{\mathsf{next}} v_2]$ and (3′) to $\forall_{v_2} {}^{\mathbf{1}}[\xrightarrow{\mathsf{next}} \{v_2, v_3\}]$. As another example, in the circular buffer type graph T in Fig. 2 we should have $\forall_{v_2} {}^{\mathbf{1}}[\overline{\mathsf{empty}} \mid \xrightarrow{\mathsf{val}} v_3]$.

Satisfiability, implication and equivalence of local shape logic are decidable. We prove this by defining a translation from LSL to sets of *integer programs* (IPs),[1] such that a given formula is satisfiable if and only if (at least) one integer program in the corresponding set has a solution.

Theorem 1. *Let $T \in \mathbf{G}$ be arbitrary and let $\mathbf{M}$ be an arbitrary multiplicity algebra with collective complements. For every formula $\phi \in \mathsf{LSL}^T$ there is a set $\mathbf{S}$ of IPs, such that ϕ is satisfiable if and only if some IP in $\mathbf{S}$ admits a solution.*

The proof (which can be found in [16]) proceeds by first defining a *disjunctive normal form* for LSL formulae; for each of the conjunctive sub-terms of the normal form there is a (more or less) direct translation to a characteristic IP. The inverse of the theorem also holds: for any IP there is an LSL-formula whose instances essentially correspond to solutions of the IP. See [16] for details. From the decidability of integer programming (see, e.g., [15]) follows:

Corollary 1 (decidability). *Satisfiability of LSL^T is decidable for any $T \in \mathbf{G}$.*

4 Shape Graphs

We now combine type graphs with shape constraints; the resulting models will take over the role of type graphs in capturing intended graph structure.

Definition 5. *A* shape graph *is a tuple $\Gamma = (T, \phi)$ where T is a type graph and $\phi \in \mathsf{LSL}^T$ a closed shape constraint. A Γ-*shaping *(or just* shaping*) is a typing $\tau : G \to T$ such that $\tau \models \phi$. We will call Γ a* shape of G *and G an* instance of Γ.

[1] An integer program is a set of linear equations for which an integer solution is sought. Such a program can be represented by a matrix $A \in \mathbb{Z}^{m \times n}$ together with a vector $b \in \mathbb{Z}^n$; a solution is then a vector $x \in \mathbb{Z}^m$ for which $A \cdot x = b$.

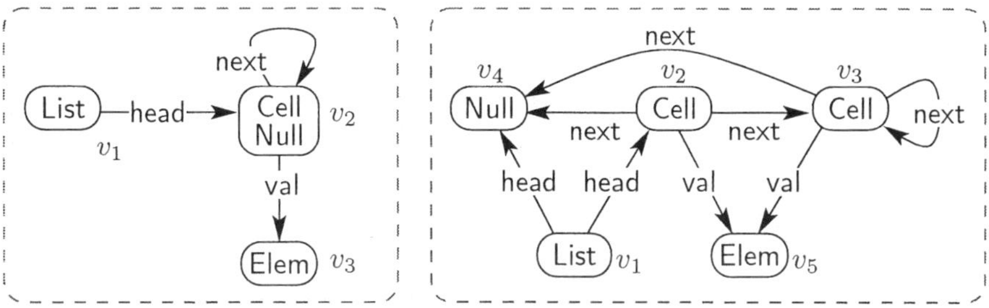

Fig. 3. Alternative list shapes (see Ex. 6)

We use N_Γ etc. to denote the components of Γ, and $\tau\colon G \to \Gamma$ to denote that τ is a shaping of G in Γ. Every state graph has many different shapes. We consider one shape to be more *abstract* than another if it allows more instances.

Example 6. An alternative shaping for lists is induced by the left hand graph in Fig. 3, with a shape constraint containing the following sub-formula for v_2:

$$\forall_{v_2} {}^{\mathbf{1}}[\xrightarrow{\mathsf{next}} v_2] \wedge (({}^{\mathbf{1}}[\underline{\mathsf{Cell}}] \wedge {}^{\mathbf{1}}[\xrightarrow{\mathsf{val}} v_3]) \vee {}^{\mathbf{1}}[\underline{\mathsf{Null}}]) \wedge {}^{\mathbf{1}}[\xleftarrow{\mathsf{head}} v_1 \mid \xleftarrow{\mathsf{next}} v_2] \ .$$

(The intended shape constraints for the other nodes are omitted here.) This is strictly more abstract than U in Fig. 2 with the constraints in Ex. 5, because it allows instances with arbitrarily many Null-nodes, whereas (2′) specifies that there should be precisely one such. In contrast, the right hand side of Fig. 3 shows a more *concrete* list shape: here the head Cell-node is explicitly distinguished.

To formalize this we have to relate shape constraints over different type graphs. The following converts a morphism $f\colon T \to U$ to a reverse mapping $f^{-1}\colon \mathsf{LSL}^U \to \mathsf{LSL}^T$. $\xi\langle N\rangle$ denotes the set obtained by replacing v in ξ by of the nodes in N.

$$\begin{aligned} f^{-1}({}^{\mu}[\xi]) &= {}^{\mu}[\xi\langle f^{-1}(v)\rangle] \\ f^{-1}(\neg\phi) &= \neg f^{-1}(\phi) \\ f^{-1}(\phi \vee \psi) &= f^{-1}(\phi) \vee f^{-1}(\psi) \\ f^{-1}(\forall_v \phi) &= \textstyle\bigwedge_{v=f(w)} \forall_w f^{-1}(\phi) \ . \end{aligned}$$

Definition 6. *Given two shape graphs Γ, Δ, an* abstraction *from Γ to Δ is a morphism $\alpha\colon T_\Gamma \to T_\Delta$ such that $\phi_\Gamma \Rightarrow \alpha^{-1}(\phi_\Delta)$.*

Example 7. Taking into account the shape constraints discussed in Examples 5 and 6, the following mapping α_1 defines an abstraction from the right hand side of Fig. 2 to the left hand side of Fig. 3, whereas α_2 defines an abstraction from the right hand side of Fig. 3 to the right hand side of Fig. 2.

$$\begin{aligned} \alpha_1 &= \{(v_1, v_1), (v_2, v_2), (v_3, v_2), (v_4, v_3)\} \\ \alpha_2 &= \{(v_1, v_1), (v_2, v_2), (v_3, v_2), (v_4, v_3), (v_5, v_4)\} \ . \end{aligned}$$

We write $\alpha\colon \Gamma \to \Delta$ to denote that α is an abstraction from Γ to Δ. Note that abstractions can be composed. The following is immediate.

Proposition 1. *If $\tau\colon G \to \Gamma$ is a shaping and $\alpha\colon \Gamma \to \Delta$ an abstraction, then $\alpha \circ \tau\colon G \to \Delta$ is a shaping.*

A shape graph can be seen as a *specification* of the set of state graphs of which it is a shape. Alternatively we may consider *sets* of shape graphs. We call two sets of shape graphs, $\mathbf{\Gamma}$ and $\mathbf{\Delta}$, *equivalent* if they specify the same sets of instances:

$$\mathbf{\Gamma} \equiv \mathbf{\Delta} \quad :\Leftrightarrow \quad \forall G \in \mathbf{G} : (\exists \Gamma \in \mathbf{\Gamma}, \tau : \tau : G \to \Gamma) \iff (\exists \Delta \in \mathbf{\Delta}, \tau : \tau : G \to \Delta) \ .$$

For instance, if $\phi_\Gamma = \bigvee_c \phi_c$ then $\{\Gamma\} \equiv \{T_\Gamma, \phi_c\}_c$.

4.1 Monomorphic Shapes

Due to the combination of conjunction and disjunction in shape constraints, shape graphs are not easy to visualize, or to reason about on an intuitive level. This may not be important from a formal point of view but makes shape graphs less useful when it comes to conveying ideas and principles. To alleviate this, we define a *monomorphic* fragment of local shape logic for which a concise visual representation can be given, and we show that every shape graph is equivalent to a set of monomorphic shape graphs.

Definition 7. *A shape graph Γ is* monomorphic *if there is a partitioning Π of N_Γ and consistent multiplicities μ^v for $v \in N_\Gamma$ and $\mu^{v,a,[w]_\Pi}, \mu^{[v]_\Pi,a,w}$ for $(v,a,w) \in E_\Gamma$, such that ϕ_Γ is equivalent to*

$$\bigwedge\nolimits_{v\in N} {}^{\mu^v}[v] \wedge \bigwedge\nolimits_{(v,a,w)\in E} \left(\forall_v {}^{\mu^{v,a,[w]_\Pi}}[\xrightarrow{a}[w]_\Pi] \wedge \forall_w {}^{\mu^{[v]_\Pi,a,w}}[\xleftarrow{a}[v]_\Pi]\right) \ .$$

Thus, the multiplicity of each edge $e = (v,a,w)$ in a monomorphic shape graph is constrained by precisely one (combined) incoming edge predicate $\xleftarrow{a}[v]_\Pi$ for w with multiplicity $\mu^{[v]_\Pi,a,w}$, and precisely one (combined) outgoing edge predicate $\xrightarrow{a}[w]_\Pi$ for v with multiplicity $\mu^{v,a,[w]_\Pi}$. Note that a monomorphic shape graph is completely characterized by the type graph T, the partitioning Π and the multiplicities μ^v for $v \in N$ and $\mu^{v,a,[w]_\Pi}, \mu^{[v]_\Pi,a,w}$ for $(v,a,w) \in E$.

We use the term *monomorphic* because, in a sense, these constraints specify a singular shape — as seen from their conjunctive form. To some degree, the nondeterminism in a monomorphic shape constraint is "pushed" into the syntactic sugar, i.e., the collective predicates of the form ${}^{\mu}[\Xi]$. Another degree of variability is obtained by taking *sets* of monomorphic shape graphs to represent states. Indeed, it can be proved that sets of monomorphic shape graphs are equally expressive to arbitrary shape graphs. Formally:

Theorem 2. *For any shape graph Γ there exists a set of monomorphic shape graphs $\mathbf{\Delta}$ such that $\{\Gamma\} \equiv \mathbf{\Delta}$.*

Example 8. The shape graph Γ consisting of U in Fig. 2 as a type graph and the conjunction of (1′)–(4′) in Ex. 5 as a shape constraint is *not* monomorphic: Constraint (4′) contains a disjunction $({}^{\mathbf{1}}[\xleftarrow{\mathsf{head}} v_1] \wedge {}^{\mathbf{0}}[\xleftarrow{\mathsf{next}} v_2]) \vee ({}^{\mathbf{0}}[\xleftarrow{\mathsf{head}} v_1] \wedge {}^{\mathbf{1}}[\xleftarrow{\mathsf{next}} v_2])$ that cannot be rewritten to the appropriate form. Indeed, this is a typical example where the local shape is not singular: the constraint expresses that a Cell-node *either* has an incoming head-edge *or* an incoming next-edge. For Γ to be monomorphic, these two cases should be embodied in distinct nodes of the type graph. The more concrete type graph on the right hand side of Fig. 3 does

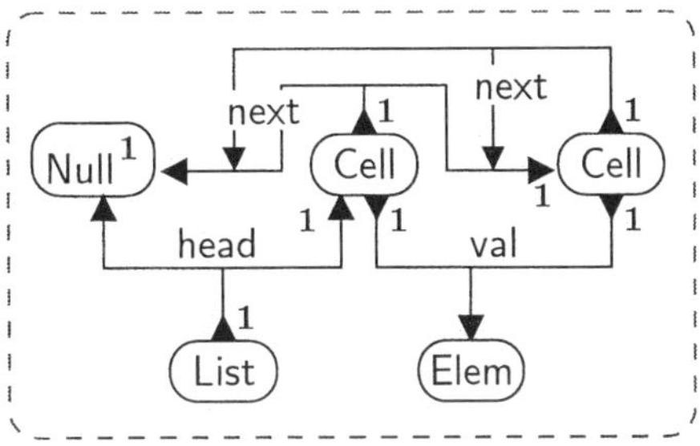

Fig. 4. A monomorphic list shape for the right hand side of Fig. 3

make this distinction and is, in fact, monomorphic. On the other hand, the similar formula $({}^{\mathbf{1}}[\xrightarrow{\text{head}} v_2] \wedge {}^{\mathbf{0}}[\xrightarrow{\text{head}} v_3]) \vee ({}^{\mathbf{0}}[\xrightarrow{\text{head}} v_2] \wedge {}^{\mathbf{1}}[\xrightarrow{\text{head}} v_3])$ in Constraint (1′) does *not* violate monomorphism: it is equivalent to ${}^{\mathbf{1}}[\xrightarrow{\text{head}} \{v_2, v_3\}]$.

As an example of the equivalence in Th. 2, note that the non-monomorphic Γ is equivalent to (the singleton set consisting of) the monomorphic shape graph in Fig. 4. The left hand shape in Fig. 3 gives rise to almost the same monomorphic shape graph, but without the **1**-multiplicity at the Null-node.

In the meanwhile, the single-shape property gives rise to the desired graphical representation. We can depict monomorphic shape graphs as follows:

- Nodes and edges with **0** multiplicity are omitted.
- Each node $v \in N$ receives an "outgoing edge port" for each a such that $\exists(v, a, w) \in E$; all outgoing a-edges are drawn as starting from this port, and the multiplicity $\mu^{v,a,[w]_\Pi}$, if unequal to $\top$, is written at the port.
- Likewise, v receives an "incoming edge port" for each a such that $\exists(w, a, v) \in E$; $\mu^{[w]_\Pi,a,v}$ is written there unless it equals $\top$.
- Node multiplicities unequal to $\top$ are written inside the nodes.

For instance, the monomorphic right hand shape graph of Fig. 3 is represented in this form in Fig. 4.

4.2 Canonical Shapes

Among the many different (monomorphic) shapes of a given state graph, it is useful to single out one that can be generated from the graph automatically, and whose size is bounded, not by the size of the state graph but by some global constant. For this purpose, we introduce the notion of a *canonical shape.* The idea of a canonical shape is that nodes are distinguished only if their local structure is sufficiently different in the first place.

To work this out, we just have to define "sufficiently different." In this paper we take a very straightforward notion: the multiplicities of the sets of incoming and outgoing edges should be the different for some edge label. For an arbitrary graph $G \in \mathbf{G}$, define *characteristic* functions $\gamma^G_\rightarrow, \gamma^G_\leftarrow : N \times \mathbf{L} \to \mathbf{M}$ as follows:

$$\gamma^G_\rightarrow : (v, a) \mapsto \#_\mathbf{M}\{u \mid (v, a, u) \in E\} \qquad \gamma^G_\leftarrow : (v, a) \mapsto \#_\mathbf{M}\{u \mid (u, a, v) \in E\} \quad .$$

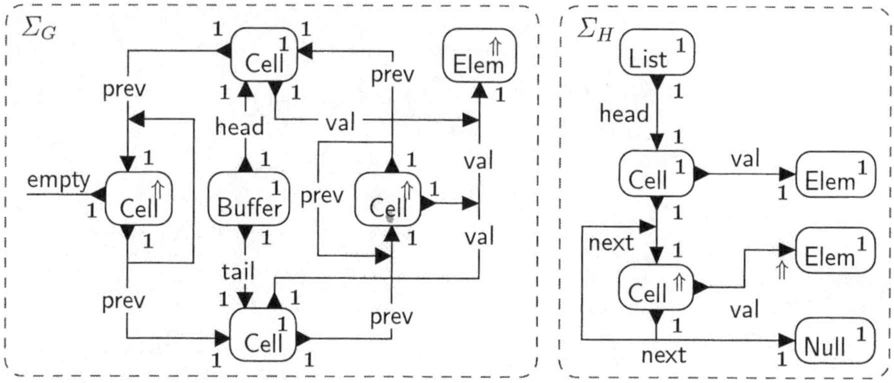

Fig. 5. Canonical shapings of the buffer and list graphs in Fig. 1

We consider $v, w \in N$ to be shape-indistinguishable if the characteristic functions yield the same result for all edge labels:

$$v \sim w \quad :\Leftrightarrow \quad \forall a \in \mathbf{L} : (\gamma^G_\leftarrow(v,a), \gamma^G_\rightarrow(v,a)) = (\gamma^G_\leftarrow(w,a), \gamma^G_\rightarrow(w,a)) \ .$$

The canonical shaping of a graph G will equate all $\sim$-equivalent nodes of G; the edge multiplicities are determined by the characteristic function.

Definition 8. *Let G be a graph and $i \in \mathbb{N}$. The* canonical shaping *of G is given by the projection morphism $\pi_\sim : G \to \Sigma$, where Σ is a monomorphic shape graph with $T_\Sigma = G/\sim$, $\Pi_\Sigma = \{N_G\}$ and for all $V \in N_\Sigma$ and $(V,a,W) \in E_\Sigma$*

$$\begin{aligned} \mu^V &= \#_\mathbf{M} V \\ \mu^{(V,a,N_G)} &= \gamma^G_\rightarrow(v,a) \ \ \textit{for any } v \in V \\ \mu^{(N_G,a,W)} &= \gamma^G_\leftarrow(w,a) \ \ \textit{for any } w \in W. \end{aligned}$$

By the definition of $\gamma^G_\leftarrow$ and $\gamma^G_\rightarrow$, the choice of $v \in V$ resp. $w \in W$ in the side conditions is irrelevant.

Example 9. Fig. 5 shows the canonical shapes Σ_G and Σ_H of the circular buffer instance G and the list instance H in Fig. 1. Note that the (only) Elem-node in Σ_G has multiplicity $\Uparrow$ but incoming edge multiplicity **1**. This indicates that there are multiple instances of this node, but they are not shared. In contrast, Σ_H has two distinct Elem-nodes, one of which is shared whereas the other is not.

By construction, canonical shapes are monomorphic; but we can actually characterize them more closely than that. For an arbitrary monomorphic shape graph Γ we again define characteristic functions $\gamma^\Gamma_\rightarrow, \gamma^\Gamma_\leftarrow : N \times \mathbf{L} \to \mathbf{M}$, as follows:

$$\begin{aligned} \gamma^\Gamma_\rightarrow &: (v,a) \mapsto \bigoplus \{\mu^{v,a,[w]_\Pi} \mid (v,a,w) \in E\} \\ \gamma^\Gamma_\leftarrow &: (v,a) \mapsto \bigoplus \{\mu^{[w]_\Pi,a,v} \mid (w,a,v) \in E\} \ . \end{aligned}$$

Definition 9. *A monomorphic shape graph Γ is called* canonical *if $\Pi = \{N_\Gamma\}$ and $\forall a \in \mathbf{L} : (\gamma^\Gamma_\leftarrow(v,a), \gamma^\Gamma_\rightarrow(v,a)) = (\gamma^\Gamma_\leftarrow(w,a), \gamma^\Gamma_\rightarrow(w,a))$ implies $v = w$.*

The following proposition states that this is a valid characterization of the canonical shapings obtained from Def. 8.

Proposition 2. *Σ_G is a canonical shape graph for any $G \in \mathbf{G}$.*

We propose canonical shape graphs as a workable state space abstraction. The following theorem states that the set of canonical shape graphs is finite, albeit still very large. As a corollary, it follows that, in contrast to monomorphic shapes, canonical shapes are not as expressive as general shape graphs: the number of inequivalent shape graphs is infinite.

Theorem 3. *Assume $\mathbf{L}$ to be a finite set.*

1. *The number of canonical shape graphs is $O\big(2^{n^2 \cdot \#\mathbf{L}} \cdot \#\mathbf{M}^n\big)$ with $n = \#\mathbf{M}^{2\#\mathbf{L}}$.*
2. *The number of canonical shape graphs over a type graph T is $O\big(\#\mathbf{M}^{n+2m}\big)$, where $n = \#N_T$ and $m = \min(\#E_T, \#N_T \cdot \#\{a \mid (p,a,q) \in E_G\}$.*

The upper bound can be improved somewhat (see [16]): $\#\mathbf{M}$ can be replaced by the number of *minimal consistent multiplicities*; for instance, in our chosen multiplicity algebra this is the set $\{\mathbf{0}, \mathbf{1}, \Uparrow\}$, hence $\#\mathbf{M} = 6$ can be improved to 3. Even so, however, the number of canonical shapes, even over a fixed type graph, is exponential. Still, canonical shape graphs do provide an automatic abstraction from possibly unbounded state graphs to a finite operational model. It will remain to be seen how well the abstraction performs in practice.

5 Conclusion

We discuss below some related work, which is in some cases quite close to that presented in the current paper. In this comparison we stress similarities not differences. Before doing so, however, we point out some aspects of our approach that, combined, distinguish our work from the papers cited below:

- The explicit use of a multiplicity algebra.
- The use of a decidable, but still quite expressive, logic over type graphs.
- The graphical representation of monomorphic shapes.
- The automatic abstraction to (bounded) canonical shapes.

Related work. The logic presented here is closely related to logics developed for *static analysis*, especially based on shape graphs, with Benedikt, Reps and Sagiv [3] as a prime example — but see also [9,12]. The main difference is that their approach is more language-oriented and models states as *stores*, in which pointer variables are distinguished from field selectors. For instance, the logic L_r defined in [3] can express the existence of paths between pointer variables, and node sharing along (forward) paths from pointer variables — where the pointer variables are fixed, i.e., no quantification is possible. We conjecture that LSL and L_r are independent.

In a setting more similar to ours, Baldan, König and König [2] have recently defined a graph abstraction logic for essentially the same purpose as LSL. The main difference is that their logic does not have nodes but edges as basic entities.

Another logic for graphs is studied by Cardelli, Gardner and Ghelli in [4]. This so-called *spatial* logic is intended for the purpose of *querying* graphs but looks to be suited also for *typing* them. It allows quantification over both nodes and edges and appears to be properly encompassing SL.

Also fairly recently, O'Hearn, Reynolds and Yang have proposed, in a series of papers [14,20,17], a branch of logic called *separation logic* for reasoning about dynamic storage allocation. A prime feature of the logic is the ability to express the partitioning of a graph into disjoint subgraphs — a feature also present in spatial logic. Apart from this commonality, however, separation logic is more similar in spirit to that by Sagiv et al., discussed above.

There is a close connection of LSL to *description logic*, a long-standing approach to knowledge representation; see [1] for an overview. One important feature of description logic that is missing altogether from LSL is the *intersection of concepts* — which in our setting would be represented best by an *inheritance* between nodes. In the theory of graph types, we have only seen this in a recent paper by Ferreira and Ribeiro [8]. Taking inspiration from description logic, node inheritance is an issue we intend to investigate in the future.

Expressiveness and decidability. One of our main results is the decidability of LSL (Cor. 1). This is actually a consequence of prior decidability results in first-order logic, though we became aware of the relevant facts only after finishing the work reported here. Briefly: any LSL formula containing just multiplicities $\uparrow$ is equivalent to a formula of $\mathcal{L}^2$, first order logic on two variables. This fragment was shown a long time ago to be decidable by Scott [19] and later to be NEXPTIME-complete [13,10]. Moreover, an *arbitrary* formula of LSL is equivalent to a formula in $\mathcal{C}^2$, two-variable first-order logic *with counting quantifiers*, which was shown decidable in [11]. In fact, LSL is strictly less expressive than $\mathcal{C}^2$. See [16] for a more extensive overview.

References

1. F. Baader, ed. *The Description Logic Handbook: Theory, Implementation and Applications.* Cambridge University Press, 2003.
2. P. Baldan, B. König, and B. König. A logic for analyzing abstractions of graph transformation systems. In R. Cousot, ed., *Static Analysis*, vol. 2694 of *LNCS*, pp. 255–272. Springer, 2003.
3. M. Benedikt, T. Reps, and M. Sagiv. A decidable logic for describing linked data structures. In S. D. Swierstra, ed., *European Symposium on Programming*, vol. 1576 of *LNCS*, pp. 2–19. Springer, 1999.
4. L. Cardelli, P. Gardner, and G. Ghelli. A spatial logic for querying graphs. In P. Widmayer et al., ed., *Automata, Languages and Programming*, vol. 2380 of *LNCS*, pp. 597–610. Springer, 2002.
5. B. Courcelle. Graph rewriting: An algebraic and logic approach. In J. van Leeuwen, ed., *Handbook of Theoretical Computer Science*, vol. A, pp. 193–239. Elsevier, 1990.
6. D. Distefano, A. Rensink, and J.-P. Katoen. Model checking birth and death. In R. Baeza-Yates, U. Montanari, and N. Santoro, eds., *Foundations of Information Technology in the Era of Network and Mobile Computing*, vol. 223 of *IFIP Conference Proceedings*, pp. 435–447. Kluwer Academic Publishers, 2002.

7. D. Distefano, A. Rensink, and J.-P. Katoen. Who is pointing when to whom: On model-checking pointer structures. CTIT Technical Report TR–CTIT–03–12, Department of Computer Science, University of Twente, Sept. 2003.
8. A. P. L. Ferreira and L. Ribeiro. Towards object-oriented graphs and grammars. In U. Nestmann and P. Stevens, eds., *Formal Methods for Open Object-Oriented Distributed Systems*, vol. 2884 of *LNCS*, pp. 16–31. Springer, 2003.
9. P. Fradet and D. Le Métayer. Shape types. In *Principles of Programming Languages*, pp. 27–39. ACM Press, 1997.
10. E. Grädel, P. G. Kolatis, and M. Y. Vardi. On the decision problem for two-variable first-order logic. *The Bulletin of Symbolic Logic*, 3(1):53–69, Mar. 1997.
11. E. Grädel, M. Otto, and E. Rosen. Two-variable logic with counting is decidable. In *Logic in Computer Science*, pp. 306–317. Computer Society Press, 1997.
12. N. Klarlund and M. I. Schwartzbach. Graph types. In *Principles of Programming Languages*, pp. 196–205. ACM Press, Jan. 1993.
13. M. Mortimer. On languages with two variables. *Zeitschrift für Mathematische Logik und Grundlagen der Mathematik*, 21:135–140, 1975.
14. P. O'Hearn, J. Reynolds, and H. Yang. Local reasoning about programs that alter data structures. In L. Fribourg, ed., *CSL 2001*, vol. 2142 of *LNCS*, pp. 1–19. Springer, 2001.
15. C. H. Papadimitriou. On the complexity of integer programming. *J. ACM*, 28(4):765–768, 1981.
16. A. Rensink. A logic of local graph shapes. CTIT Technical Report TR–CTIT–03–35, Faculty of Informatics, University of Twente, Aug. 2003.
17. J. Reynolds. Separation logic: A logic for shared mutable data structures. In *Logic in Computer Science*. Computer Society Press, 2002.
18. M. Sagiv, T. Reps, and R. Wilhelm. Solving shape-analysis problems in languages with destructive updating. *ACM Trans. Prog. Lang. Syst.*, 20(1):1–50, Jan. 1998.
19. D. Scott. A decision method for validity of sentences in two variables. *J. Symb. Log.*, 27:477, 1962.
20. H. Yang and P. O'Hearn. A semantic basis for local reasoning. In M. Nielsen and U. Engberg, eds., *Foundations of Software Science and Computation Structures*, vol. 2303 of *LNCS*, pp. 402–416. Springer, 2002.

Author Index

Lecture Notes in Computer Science

For information about Vols. 1–2876

please contact your bookseller or Springer-Verlag

Vol. 2996: V. Diekert, M. Habib (Eds.), STACS 2004. XVI, 658 pages. 2004.

Vol. 2995: C. Jensen, S. Poslad, T. Dimitrakos (Eds.), Trust Management. XIII, 377 pages. 2004.

Vol. 2993: R. Alur, G.J. Pappas (Eds.), Hybrid Systems: Computation and Control. XII, 674 pages. 2004.

Vol. 2992: E. Bertino, S. Christodoulakis, D. Plexousakis, V. Christophides, M. Koubarakis, K. Böhm, E. Ferrari (Eds.), Advances in Database Technology - EDBT 2004. XVIII, 877 pages. 2004.

Vol. 2991: R. Alt, A. Frommer, R.B. Kearfott, W. Luther (Eds.), Numerical Software with Result Verification. X, 315 pages. 2004.

Vol. 2989: S. Graf, L. Mounier (Eds.), Model Checking Software. X, 309 pages. 2004.

Vol. 2988: K. Jensen, A. Podelski (Eds.), Tools and Algorithms for the Construction and Analysis of Systems. XIV, 608 pages. 2004.

Vol. 2987: I. Walukiewicz (Ed.), Foundations of Software Science and Computation Structures. XIII, 529 pages. 2004.

Vol. 2986: D. Schmidt (Ed.), Programming Languages and Systems. XII, 417 pages. 2004.

Vol. 2985: E. Duesterwald (Ed.), Compiler Construction. X, 313 pages. 2004.

Vol. 2984: M. Wermelinger, T. Margaria-Steffen (Eds.), Fundamental Approaches to Software Engineering. XII, 389 pages. 2004.

Vol. 2983: S. Istrail, M.S. Waterman, A. Clark (Eds.), Computational Methods for SNPs and Haplotype Inference. IX, 153 pages. 2004. (Subseries LNBI).

Vol. 2982: N. Wakamiya, M. Solarski, J. Sterbenz (Eds.), Active Networks. XI, 308 pages. 2004.

Vol. 2981: C. Müller-Schloer, T. Ungerer, B. Bauer (Eds.), Organic and Pervasive Computing – ARCS 2004. XI, 339 pages. 2004.

Vol. 2980: A. Blackwell, K. Marriott, A. Shimojima (Eds.), Diagrammatic Representation and Inference. XV, 448 pages. 2004. (Subseries LNAI).

Vol. 2978: R. Groz, R.M. Hierons (Eds.), Testing of Communicating Systems. XII, 225 pages. 2004.

Vol. 2977: G. Di Marzo Serugendo, A. Karageorgos, O.F. Rana, F. Zambonelli (Eds.), Engineering Self-Organising Systems. X, 299 pages. 2004. (Subseries LNAI).

Vol. 2976: M. Farach-Colton (Ed.), LATIN 2004: Theoretical Informatics. XV, 626 pages. 2004.

Vol. 2973: Y. Lee, J. Li, K.-Y. Whang, D. Lee (Eds.), Database Systems for Advanced Applications. XXIV, 925 pages. 2004.

Vol. 2970: F. Fernández Rivera, M. Bubak, A. Gómez Tato, R. Doallo (Eds.), Grid Computing. XI, 328 pages. 2004.

Vol. 2964: T. Okamoto (Ed.), Topics in Cryptology – CT-RSA 2004. XI, 387 pages. 2004.

Vol. 2963: R. Sharp, Higher Level Hardware Synthesis. XVI, 195 pages. 2004.

Vol. 2962: S. Bistarelli, Semirings for Soft Constraint Solving and Programming. XII, 279 pages. 2004.

Vol. 2961: P. Eklund (Ed.), Concept Lattices. IX, 411 pages. 2004. (Subseries LNAI).

Vol. 2960: P.D. Mosses (Ed.), CASL Reference Manual. XVII, 528 pages. 2004.

Vol. 2958: L. Rauchwerger (Ed.), Languages and Compilers for Parallel Computing. XI, 556 pages. 2004.

Vol. 2957: P. Langendoerfer, M. Liu, I. Matta, V. Tsaoussidis (Eds.), Wired/Wireless Internet Communications. XI, 307 pages. 2004.

Vol. 2954: F. Crestani, M. Dunlop, S. Mizzaro (Eds.), Mobile and Ubiquitous Information Access. X, 299 pages. 2004.

Vol. 2953: K. Konrad, Model Generation for Natural Language Interpretation and Analysis. XIII, 166 pages. 2004. (Subseries LNAI).

Vol. 2952: N. Guelfi, E. Astesiano, G. Reggio (Eds.), Scientific Engineering of Distributed Java Applications. X, 157 pages. 2004.

Vol. 2951: M. Naor (Ed.), Theory of Cryptography. XI, 523 pages. 2004.

Vol. 2949: R. De Nicola, G. Ferrari, G. Meredith (Eds.), Coordination Models and Languages. X, 323 pages. 2004.

Vol. 2948: G.L. Mullen, A. Poli, H. Stichtenoth (Eds.), Finite Fields and Applications. VIII, 263 pages. 2004.

Vol. 2947: F. Bao, R. Deng, J. Zhou (Eds.), Public Key Cryptography – PKC 2004. XI, 455 pages. 2004.

Vol. 2946: R. Focardi, R. Gorrieri (Eds.), Foundations of Security Analysis and Design II. VII, 267 pages. 2004.

Vol. 2943: J. Chen, J. Reif (Eds.), DNA Computing. X, 225 pages. 2004.

Vol. 2941: M. Wirsing, A. Knapp, S. Balsamo (Eds.), Radical Innovations of Software and Systems Engineering in the Future. X, 359 pages. 2004.

Vol. 2940: C. Lucena, A. Garcia, A. Romanovsky, J. Castro, P.S. Alencar (Eds.), Software Engineering for Multi-Agent Systems II. XII, 279 pages. 2004.

Vol. 2939: T. Kalker, I.J. Cox, Y.M. Ro (Eds.), Digital Watermarking. XII, 602 pages. 2004.

Vol. 2937: B. Steffen, G. Levi (Eds.), Verification, Model Checking, and Abstract Interpretation. XI, 325 pages. 2004.

Vol. 2934: G. Lindemann, D. Moldt, M. Paolucci (Eds.), Regulated Agent-Based Social Systems. X, 301 pages. 2004. (Subseries LNAI).

Vol. 2930: F. Winkler (Ed.), Automated Deduction in Geometry. VII, 231 pages. 2004. (Subseries LNAI).

Vol. 2926: L. van Elst, V. Dignum, A. Abecker (Eds.), Agent-Mediated Knowledge Management. XI, 428 pages. 2004. (Subseries LNAI).

Vol. 2923: V. Lifschitz, I. Niemelä (Eds.), Logic Programming and Nonmonotonic Reasoning. IX, 365 pages. 2004. (Subseries LNAI).

Vol. 2919: E. Giunchiglia, A. Tacchella (Eds.), Theory and Applications of Satisfiability Testing. XI, 530 pages. 2004.

Vol. 2917: E. Quintarelli, Model-Checking Based Data Retrieval. XVI, 134 pages. 2004.

Vol. 2916: C. Palamidessi (Ed.), Logic Programming. XII, 520 pages. 2003.

Vol. 2915: A. Camurri, G. Volpe (Eds.), Gesture-Based Communication in Human-Computer Interaction. XIII, 558 pages. 2004. (Subseries LNAI).

Vol. 2914: P.K. Pandya, J. Radhakrishnan (Eds.), FST TCS 2003: Foundations of Software Technology and Theoretical Computer Science. XIII, 446 pages. 2003.

Vol. 2913: T.M. Pinkston, V.K. Prasanna (Eds.), High Performance Computing - HiPC 2003. XX, 512 pages. 2003. (Subseries LNAI).

Vol. 2911: T.M.T. Sembok, H.B. Zaman, H. Chen, S.R. Urs, S.H. Myaeng (Eds.), Digital Libraries: Technology and Management of Indigenous Knowledge for Global Access. XX, 703 pages. 2003.

Vol. 2910: M.E. Orlowska, S. Weerawarana, M.M.P. Papazoglou, J. Yang (Eds.), Service-Oriented Computing - ICSOC 2003. XIV, 576 pages. 2003.

Vol. 2909: R. Solis-Oba, K. Jansen (Eds.), Approximation and Online Algorithms. VIII, 269 pages. 2004.

Vol. 2908: K. Chae, M. Yung (Eds.), Information Security Applications. XII, 506 pages. 2004.

Vol. 2907: I. Lirkov, S. Margenov, J. Wasniewski, P. Yalamov (Eds.), Large-Scale Scientific Computing. XI, 490 pages. 2004.

Vol. 2906: T. Ibaraki, N. Katoh, H. Ono (Eds.), Algorithms and Computation. XVII, 748 pages. 2003.

Vol. 2905: A. Sanfeliu, J. Ruiz-Shulcloper (Eds.), Progress in Pattern Recognition, Speech and Image Analysis. XVII, 693 pages. 2003.

Vol. 2904: T. Johansson, S. Maitra (Eds.), Progress in Cryptology - INDOCRYPT 2003. XI, 431 pages. 2003.

Vol. 2903: T.D. Gedeon, L.C.C. Fung (Eds.), AI 2003: Advances in Artificial Intelligence. XVI, 1075 pages. 2003. (Subseries LNAI).

Vol. 2902: F.M. Pires, S.P. Abreu (Eds.), Progress in Artificial Intelligence. XV, 504 pages. 2003. (Subseries LNAI).

Vol. 2901: F. Bry, N. Henze, J. Ma luszyński (Eds.), Principles and Practice of Semantic Web Reasoning. X, 209 pages. 2003.

Vol. 2900: M. Bidoit, P.D. Mosses (Eds.), Casl User Manual. XIII, 240 pages. 2004.

Vol. 2899: G. Ventre, R. Canonico (Eds.), Interactive Multimedia on Next Generation Networks. XIV, 420 pages. 2003.

Vol. 2898: K.G. Paterson (Ed.), Cryptography and Coding. IX, 385 pages. 2003.

Vol. 2897: O. Balet, G. Subsol, P. Torguet (Eds.), Virtual Storytelling. XI, 240 pages. 2003.

Vol. 2896: V.A. Saraswat (Ed.), Advances in Computing Science – ASIAN 2003. VIII, 305 pages. 2003.

Vol. 2895: A. Ohori (Ed.), Programming Languages and Systems. XIII, 427 pages. 2003.

Vol. 2894: C.S. Laih (Ed.), Advances in Cryptology - ASIACRYPT 2003. XIII, 543 pages. 2003.

Vol. 2893: J.-B. Stefani, I. Demeure, D. Hagimont (Eds.), Distributed Applications and Interoperable Systems. XIII, 311 pages. 2003.

Vol. 2892: F. Dau, The Logic System of Concept Graphs with Negation. XI, 213 pages. 2003. (Subseries LNAI).

Vol. 2891: J. Lee, M. Barley (Eds.), Intelligent Agents and Multi-Agent Systems. X, 215 pages. 2003. (Subseries LNAI).

Vol. 2890: M. Broy, A.V. Zamulin (Eds.), Perspectives of System Informatics. XV, 572 pages. 2003.

Vol. 2889: R. Meersman, Z. Tari (Eds.), On The Move to Meaningful Internet Systems 2003: OTM 2003 Workshops. XIX, 1071 pages. 2003.

Vol. 2888: R. Meersman, Z. Tari, D.C. Schmidt (Eds.), On The Move to Meaningful Internet Systems 2003: CoopIS, DOA, and ODBASE. XXI, 1546 pages. 2003.

Vol. 2887: T. Johansson (Ed.), Fast Software Encryption. IX, 397 pages. 2003.

Vol. 2886: I. Nyström, G. Sanniti di Baja, S. Svensson (Eds.), Discrete Geometry for Computer Imagery. XII, 556 pages. 2003.

Vol. 2885: J.S. Dong, J. Woodcock (Eds.), Formal Methods and Software Engineering. XI, 683 pages. 2003.

Vol. 2884: E. Najm, U. Nestmann, P. Stevens (Eds.), Formal Methods for Open Object-Based Distributed Systems. X, 293 pages. 2003.

Vol. 2883: J. Schaeffer, M. Müller, Y. Björnsson (Eds.), Computers and Games. XI, 431 pages. 2003.

Vol. 2882: D. Veit, Matchmaking in Electronic Markets. XV, 180 pages. 2003. (Subseries LNAI).

Vol. 2881: E. Horlait, T. Magedanz, R.H. Glitho (Eds.), Mobile Agents for Telecommunication Applications. IX, 297 pages. 2003.

Vol. 2880: H.L. Bodlaender (Ed.), Graph-Theoretic Concepts in Computer Science. XI, 386 pages. 2003.

Vol. 2879: R.E. Ellis, T.M. Peters (Eds.), Medical Image Computing and Computer-Assisted Intervention - MICCAI 2003. XXXIV, 1003 pages. 2003.

Vol. 2878: R.E. Ellis, T.M. Peters (Eds.), Medical Image Computing and Computer-Assisted Intervention - MICCAI 2003. XXXIII, 819 pages. 2003.

Vol. 2877: T. Böhme, G. Heyer, H. Unger (Eds.), Innovative Internet Community Systems. VIII, 263 pages. 2003.